Running a Business

ALL-IN-ONE

FOR

DUMMIES®

**Starting &
Running a Business
ALL-IN-ONE
FOR
DUMMIES®**

By Liz Barclay, Colin Barrow, Paul Barrow, Gregory Brooks,
Ben Carter, Frank Catalano, Peter Economy, Lita Epstein,
Alexander Hiam, Greg Holden, Tony Levene, Bob Nelson,
Steven D. Peterson, Richard Pettinger, Bud E. Smith,
Craig Smith, Paul Tiffany, and John A. Tracy

Edited by Dan Matthews

BICENTENNIAL
1807
WILEY
2007
BICENTENNIAL

John Wiley & Sons, Ltd

Starting & Running a Business All-in-One For Dummies®

Published by

John Wiley & Sons, Ltd
The Atrium
Southern Gate
Chichester
West Sussex
PO19 8SQ
England

E-mail (for orders and customer service enquires): cs-books@wiley.co.uk

Visit our Home Page on www.wiley.com

Copyright © 2007 John Wiley & Sons, Ltd, Chichester, West Sussex, England

Published by John Wiley & Sons, Ltd, Chichester, West Sussex

For general information on our other products and services, please contact our Customer Care Department within the U.S. at 800-762-2974, outside the U.S. at 317-572-3993, or fax 317-572-4002.

For technical support, please visit www.wiley.com/techsupport.

Wiley also publishes its books in a variety of electronic formats. Some content that appears in print may not be available in electronic books.

British Library Cataloguing in Publication Data: A catalogue record for this book is available from the British Library

ISBN: 978-0-470-51648-5 (P/B)

Printed and bound in Great Britain by Bell & Bain Ltd, Glasgow

10 9 8 7 6

WILEY

About the Authors

Dan Matthews: Dan Matthews is Group Online Editor of Caspian Publishing, which produces magazines, Web sites, and events for an audience of UK entrepreneurs. Primarily working on `realbusiness.co.uk`, Dan writes about stellar business success stories as well as up-and-coming start-ups. He was previously Group Online Editor of Crimson Business Publishing, with responsibility for sites such as `startups.co.uk` and `growingbusiness.co.uk`. He has contributed to a range of business magazines, including being contributing editor of *Real Business Magazine* and *Growing Business Magazine*.

Liz Barclay is presenter of BBC Radio 4's daily consumer and social affairs programme *You and Yours*. Before joining the BBC she worked for Citizens Advice specialising in Employment and Family Law and Money Advice. She writes on business issues for *BBC Online* and has written on business and personal finance for various national newspapers, magazines, and Web sites over the past 10 years. Liz has also produced and presented 60 small business and 10 occupational health and safety programmes for BBC2 and written several booklets on work and personal finance to accompany BBC television and radio programmes. She chairs and speaks at conferences and seminars on work and business, is a trained counsellor, and lives in London.

Colin Barrow is Head of the Enterprise Group at Cranfield School of Management, where he teaches entrepreneurship on the MBA and other programmes. He is also a visiting professor at business schools in the US, Asia, France, and Austria. His books on entrepreneurship and small business have been translated into fifteen languages including Russian and Chinese. He worked with Microsoft to incorporate the business planning model used in his teaching programmes into the software programme, Microsoft Business Planner, now bundled with Office. He is a regular contributor to newspapers, periodicals, and academic journals such as the *Financial Times*, *The Guardian*, *Management Today*, and the *International Small Business Journal*. Thousands of students have passed through Colin's start-up and business growth programmes, raising millions in new capital and going on to run successful and thriving enterprises. He is a non-executive director of two venture capital funds, on the board of several small businesses, and serves on a number of Government Task Forces.

Paul Barrow trained and qualified as a Chartered Accountant with Deloitte & Touche before obtaining his MBA at Bradford University. As a senior consultant with Ernst & Young he was responsible for managing and delivering quality consulting assignments. During the mid-1980s, he was Investment Review

Director for a UK venture capital business. In 1998, as Group Finance Director of Adval Group plc, he was part of the team which took their software company on to the Alternative Investment Market. Adval specialises in providing multimedia training – both bespoke and generic. Paul has also been a director of several owner-managed businesses, and has started up and sold other businesses. He currently works with businesses as diverse as software, turkey farming, and food retailing. Paul is a Visiting Fellow at Cranfield University where he teaches on the Business Growth Programme. This programme is designed specifically for owner managers who want to grow and improve their businesses. He also teaches at Warwick University and Oxford Brookes on similar programmes. Paul has written several other business books: *The Business Plan Workbook* and *Raising Finance* (both Kogan Page/Sunday Times); *The Best Laid Business Plans* and *The Bottom Line* (both Virgin Books). All these books are aimed at owner managers trying to grow and improve their businesses.

Greg Brooks is a freelance journalist who has written for a number of broadcasters, newspapers, and magazines including Channel 4, *The Guardian*, *Marketing*, *New Media Age,* and *Marketing Direct*. He has also carried out corporate ghostwriting and consultancy duties for a number of blue-chip clients around the globe. As part of his role as an industry commentator, he has spoken to organisations such as the BBC about how to communicate with consumers and journalists using interactive channels.

Ben Carter runs his own digital agency helping famous and not so famous brands launch marketing initiatives to capitalise on the changing media landscape and ever-changing consumer behaviour. Current clients of Ben Carter & Associates include npower and AOL, and the company has also provided consultancy services for several major UK-based blue-chip companies. Before setting up BCA, Ben worked as a business journalist for eight years, covering the UK's media and marketing sectors and most recently was News Editor of *Marketing* magazine. He has also freelanced for a number of national newspapers including *The Times* and *The Guardian* and is used regularly as a commentator on the booming digital economy by different media, including the BBC, *The Independent*, and CNN.

Frank Catalano is a veteran marketing consultant and analyst. He's the principal of Catalano Consulting, a strategic marketing firm advising Internet and technology companies. His consulting assignments include stints as Managing Director for PC Data's Internet Monitoring Division, VP Marketing for McGraw-Hill Home Interactive, VP Marketing for iCopyright, and VP Marketing for Apex Computer. He also was a marketing manager for Egghead Software and for the Apple Programmers and Developers Association. When not consulting, Frank provides tech industry analysis and commentary for

KCPQ-TV Fox Seattle and is the author of the long-running Byte Me columns for *Seattle Weekly* and others. His essays and short fiction about technology have appeared in a wide variety of print and broadcast media, including ClickZ, Omni, Inside Multimedia, and Analog.

Peter Economy is associate editor of *Leader to Leader*, the award-winning magazine of the Peter F. Drucker Foundation for Nonprofit Leadership, and author of numerous books. Peter combines his writing expertise with more than 15 years of management experience to provide his readers with solid, hands-on information and advice. He received his bachelor's degree (with majors in economics and human biology) from Stanford University and his MBA at the Edinburgh Business School. Visit Peter at his Web site: www.petereconomy.com.

Lita Epstein, who earned her MBA from Emory University's Goizueta Business School, enjoys helping people develop good financial, investing, and tax planning skills. While getting her MBS, Lita worked as a teaching assistant for the financial accounting department and ran the accounting lab. After completing her MBA, she managed finances for a small nonprofit organization and for the facilities management section of a large medical clinic. She designs and teaches online courses on topics such as investing for retirement, getting ready for tax time, and finance and investing for women. She's written more than ten books, including *Streetwise Retirement Planning* and *Trading For Dummies*. Lita was the content director for a financial services Web site, MostChoice.com, and managed the Web site Investing for Women. As a Congressional press secretary, Lita gained firsthand knowledge about how to work within and around the Federal bureaucracy, which gives her great insight into how government programmes work. In the past, Lita has been a daily newspaper reporter, magazine editor, and fundraiser for the international activities of former US President Jimmy Carter through The Carter Center.

Alex Hiam is a consultant, corporate trainer, and public speaker with 20 years of experience in marketing, sales, and corporate communications. He is the director of Insights, which includes a division called Insights for Marketing that offers a wide range of services for supporting and training in sales, customer service, planning, and management. His firm is also active in developing the next generation of leaders in the workplace through its Insights for Training & Development. Alex has an MBA in marketing and strategic planning from the Haas School at U.C. Berkeley and an undergraduate degree from Harvard. He has worked as marketing manager for both smaller high-tech firms and a *Fortune* 100 company, and did a stint as a professor of marketing at the business school at U. Mass. Amherst. Alex is the co-author of the best-seller, *The Portable MBA in Marketing* (Wiley) as well as

The Vest-Pocket CEO and numerous other books and training programs. He has consulted to a wide range of companies and not-for-profit and government agencies, from General Motors and Volvo to HeathEast and the U.S. Army (a fuller list of clients is posted at www.insightsformarketing.com). Alex is also the author of a companion volume to this book, the *Marketing Kit For Dummies* (Wiley), which includes more detailed coverage of many of the hands-on topics involved in creating great advertising, direct mail letters, Web sites, publicity campaigns, and marketing plans. On the CD that comes with the *Marketing Kit For Dummies*, you'll find forms, checklists, and templates that may be of use to you. Also, Alex maintains an extensive Web site of resources that he organised to support each of the chapters in the book.

Greg Holden started a small business called Stylus Media, which is a group of editorial, design, and computer professionals who produce both print and electronic publications. The company gets its name from a recording stylus that reads the traces left on a disk by voices or instruments and translates those signals into electronic data that can be amplified and enjoyed by many. He has been self-employed for the past ten years. He is an avid user of eBay, both as a buyer and seller, and he recently started his own blog. One of the ways Greg enjoys communicating is through explaining technical subjects in nontechnical language. The first edition of *Starting an Online Business For Dummies* was the ninth of his more than 30 computer books. He also authored *eBay PowerUser's Bible* for Wiley Publishing. Over the years, Greg has been a contributing editor of *Computer Currents* magazine, where he writes a monthly column. He also contributes to *PC World* and the University of Illinois at Chicago alumni magazine. Other projects have included preparing documentation for an electronics catalog company in Chicago and creating online courses on Windows 2000 and Microsoft Word 2000. Greg balances his technical expertise and his entrepreneurial experience with his love of literature. He received an MA in English from the University of Illinois at Chicago and also writes general interest books, short stories, and poetry. Among his editing assignments is the monthly newsletter for his daughters' grade school. After graduating from college, Greg became a reporter for his hometown newspaper. Working at the publications office at the University of Chicago was his next job, and it was there that he started to use computers. He discovered, as the technology became available, that he loved desktop publishing (with the Macintosh and LaserWriter) and, later on, the World Wide Web. Greg loves to travel, but since his two daughters were born, he hasn't been able to get around much. He was able to translate his experiences into a book called *Karma Kids: Answering Everyday Parenting Questions with Buddhist Wisdom*. However, through the Web, he enjoys traveling vicariously and meeting people online. He lives with his family in an old house in Chicago that he has been rehabbing for – well, for many years now. He is a collector of objects such as pens, cameras, radios, and hats. He is always looking for things to take apart so that he can see how they work and fix them up. Many of the same skills prove useful in creating and maintaining Web pages. He is an active member of Jewel Heart, a Tibetan Buddhist meditation and study group based in Ann Arbor, Michigan.

Tony Levene is a member of *The Guardian* Jobs & Money team, writing on issues including investment and consumer rights as well as on taxation. He has been a financial journalist for nearly thirty years after a brief foray into teaching French to school children. Over his journalistic career, Tony has worked for newspapers including *The Sunday Times, Sunday Express, The Sun, Daily Star, Sunday Mirror,* and *Daily Express.* He has written eight previous books on money matters including *Investing For Dummies.* Tony lives in London with his wife Claudia, 'virtually grown up' children Zoe and Oliver, and cats Plato, Pandora, and Pascal.

Bob Nelson, PhD, is founder and president of Nelson Motivation, Inc., a management training and products firm headquartered in San Diego, California. As a practising manager, researcher, and best-selling author, Bob is an internationally recognised expert in the areas of employee motivation, recognition and rewards, productivity and performance improvement, and leadership. Bob has published 20 books and sold more than 2.5 million books on management, which have been translated into some 20 languages. He earned his BA in communications from Macalester College, his MBA in organisational behavior from UC Berkeley, and his PhD in management from the Peter F. Drucker Graduate Management Center of the Claremont Graduate University. Visit his Web site at www.nelson-motivation.com or contact Bob directly at BobRewards@aol.com.

Steven Peterson is a senior partner and founder of Home Planet Technologies, a management training company specializing in hands-on software tools designed to enhance business strategy, business planning, and general management skills. He is the creator and designer of The Protean Strategist, a state of the art computer-based business simulation. The simulation creates a dynamic business environment where participants run companies and compete against each other in a fast-changing marketplace. Each management team in the simulation is responsible for developing its own strategy, business plan, and program to make the plan work. Steven has used The Protean Strategist to add excitement, hands-on experience, teamwork, and a competitive challenge to corporate training programs around the world. He has worked with both large and small companies on products and services in industries ranging from telecommunications to financial services and from high technology to consumer goods and industrial equipment. He can be reached by e-mail at peterson@HomePlanetTech.com. When he's not planning his own business, Steven is planning to remodel his 80-year old house or to redesign the garden. And he confesses that of the three, the garden proves to be the most difficult. Steven holds advanced degrees in mathematics and physics, receiving his doctorate from Cornell University. He teaches part-time at the Haas School of Business, University of California at Berkeley, and lives in the Bay Area with his long-time companion, Peter, and their long-lived canine, Jake.

Richard Pettinger (BA, MBA, DipMktg) has taught at University College London since 1989, where he is senior lecturer in management. He teaches on the foundation courses, organisational change, and construction marketing courses. He has also taught strategic and operations management; the management of change; human resource management; and leadership to a wide range of undergraduate, postgraduate, professional, and international students. Richard is also enhancing and developing Management Studies Centre activities and courses, including the directorship of the new Information Management for Business course. Since 2005, Richard has been a visiting professor at the Jagiellonian Business School, Krakow, teaching strategic management and developing a common UCL/Jagiellonian syllabus in strategic management and organisational change. Richard is the author of over thirty business and management books and textbooks, and also writes journal, conference, and study papers.

Bud Smith's experience is split between the technical and marketing sides of the computer and Internet industries. Bud was a short-order cook before starting in the computer industry at age 21. He was a data entry supervisor, programmer, and technical writer before working as a competitive analyst and QuickTime marketing manager at Apple Computer. He has been a full-time writer and has joined Frank Catalano in several consulting projects. Bud is currently Director of Marketing at AllPublish, a venture-funded Silicon Valley startup. Bud's writing experience is all on the nonfiction side and includes computer and medical articles as well as a dozen computer books.

Craig Smith is the editor of *Marketing*, the UK's highest circulation weekly magazine, and PPA Weekly Business Magazine of the Year, serving the marketing and advertising industries. He has worked as a business journalist for 18 years and is a regular commentator on marketing issues to the national press and broadcast media. Craig works closely with industry trade bodies, the Association of Publishing Agencies, and Business in the Community to promote best practice in the areas of customer magazines and cause related marketing.

Paul Tiffany is the managing director of Paul Tiffany & Associates, a Santa Rosa, California-based firm that has offered management training and consulting services to organizations throughout the world for the past fifteen years. In addition, he has taught business planning courses at some of the top business schools in the USA, including Stanford, Wharton, and The Haas School of Business at the University of California, Berkeley, where he currently serves as adjunct professor. He holds an MBA from Harvard University and a PhD from Berkeley. He can be reached by e-mail at `tiffany@haas.berkeley.edu`.

John A. Tracy is Professor of Accounting, Emeritus, in the College of Business and Administration at the University of Colorado in Boulder. Before his 35-year tenure at Boulder he was on the business faculty for 4 years at the University of California in Berkeley. He has served as staff accountant at Ernst & Young and is the author of several books on accounting, including *The Fast Forward MBA in Finance* and *How To Read a Financial Report*. Dr Tracy received his MBA and PhD degrees from the University of Wisconsin and is a CPA in Colorado.

Publisher's Acknowledgements

We're proud of this book; please send us your comments through our Dummies online registration form located at www.dummies.com/register/.

Some of the people who helped bring this book to market include the following:

Acquisitions, Editorial, and Media Development

Project Editor: Daniel Mersey

Content Editor: Steve Edwards

Commissioning Editor: Samantha Clapp

Executive Editor: Jason Dunne

Executive Project Editor: Martin Tribe

Technical Reviewer: Faith Glasgow

Cover Photos: © Getty Images/Adam Gault

Cartoons: Ed McLachlan

Composition Services

Project Coordinator: Jennifer Theriot

Layout and Graphics: Claudia Bell, Carl Byers, Stephanie D. Jumper, Alicia B. South

Proofreaders: Laura Albert, John Greenough

Indexer: Valerie Haynes Perry

Publishing and Editorial for Consumer Dummies

Diane Graves Steele, Vice President and Publisher, Consumer Dummies

Joyce Pepple, Acquisitions Director, Consumer Dummies

Kristin A. Cocks, Product Development Director, Consumer Dummies

Michael Spring, Vice President and Publisher, Travel

Kelly Regan, Editorial Director, Travel

Publishing for Technology Dummies

Andy Cummings, Vice President and Publisher, Dummies Technology/General User

Composition Services

Gerry Fahey, Vice President of Production Services

Debbie Stailey, Director of Composition Service

Contents at a Glance

Table of Contents

Introduction

●●

*W*elcome to *Starting & Running A Business All-in-One For Dummies*, your launch pad to understanding the fundamentals of setting up, establishing, running, and growing a successful small business.

This book draws together information on the key areas of successful business – planning, funding, staying on the right side of the law, employing staff, bookkeeping, accounting and tax (grrrr!), marketing and promotion, and planning for growth – all in one bumper guide.

With help from this book, you can transform a simple idea into your very own business empire.

About This Book

This book is the ultimate business advisor providing expert guidance for businesses at every stage of the start-up process.

Starting & Running A Business All-in-One For Dummies draws on advice from several other For Dummies books, which you may wish to check out for more in-depth coverage of certain topics (all published by Wiley):

- ✔ *Bookkeeping For Dummies* (Paul Barrow and Lita Epstein)
- ✔ *Business Plans For Dummies* (Paul Tiffany and Steven D. Peterson, adapted by Colin Barrow)
- ✔ *Digital Marketing For Dummies* (Ben Carter, Gregory Brooks, Frank Catalano, Bud E. Smith)
- ✔ *Managing For Dummies* (Richard Pettinger, Bob Nelson, and Peter Economy)
- ✔ *Marketing For Dummies* (Craig Smith and Alexander Hiam)
- ✔ *Paying Less Tax 2006/2007 For Dummies* (Tony Levene)
- ✔ *Small Business Employment Law For Dummies* (Liz Barclay)
- ✔ *Starting A Business For Dummies* (Colin Barrow)
- ✔ *Starting and Running an Online Business For Dummies* (Dan Matthews and Greg Holden)

✔ *UK Law and Your Rights For Dummies* (Liz Barclay)

✔ *Understanding Business Accounting For Dummies* (John A. Tracy, adapted by Colin Barrow)

Conventions Used in This Book

To make your reading experience easier and to alert you to key words or points, we use certain conventions in this book:

✔ *Italics* introduces new terms, and explains what they mean.

✔ **Bold** text is used to show the action part of bulleted and numbered lists.

✔ `Monofont` is used to highlight Web addresses, showing you exactly what to type into your computer.

Foolish Assumptions

This book brings together the essential elements of knowledge that are essential for understanding the world of small business. As a consequence, to keep the book down to a reasonable number of pages, we've made a few assumptions about you (we hope you don't mind!). Maybe you're:

✔ A entrepreneur looking for a start-up bible

✔ A small business owner-manager seeking a comprehensive reference guide

✔ An aspiring business owner

How This Book Is Organised

We've divided *Starting & Running A Business All-in-One For Dummies* into six separate books. This section explains what you'll find out about in each one of these books. Each book is broken into chapters tackling key aspects of that part of the business world.

Book 1: Where to Start?

This book is the one to turn to first if you're thinking about starting up a new business. It runs through all of your main considerations during the initial planning phase, and offers all sorts of advice and information to get you off to a flying start.

Book II: Money in Mind

You might not be running your business to get rich (on the other hand, you actually might be running your business for exactly that reason!), but without mastering the basis of finance, you won't stay in business for long. This book walks you through the basic money matters you'll need to know and stay on top of.

Book III: Getting the Staff

Unless you're intending to run your business all by yourself, you need to master the essentials of recruiting and retaining staff, and employing them safely and legally. This book tackles the 'people management' section of business, regardless of whether you employ one or 100 members of staff.

Book IV: How Not to Cook the Books

Tax, financial records, profit and loss, and balance sheets. Unless your new or growing business is a firm of accountants, you need to know the facts and figures outlined in this book. And even if you are an accountant, this book tackles the business side of figures.

Book V: Bigging Up Your Business

One of the keys to successful business is bringing in customers. This book looks at the many and varied ways of doing just this, from humble beginnings for a new start-up to grander ideas for an expanding venture.

Book VI: Getting Bigger

If you've already made a success of your business – or if you've followed the advice in the other books to their most profitable conclusion – this is the book you need to read! Showing you how to expand your business into an even greater one, this book considers factors as diverse as being a great manager to undertaking a TV advertising campaign.

Icons Used in This Book

When you flick through this book, you'll notice some snazzy little icons in the margin. These pick out key aspects of starting and running a business, and present you with important nuggets of information:

Want to get ahead in business? Check out the text highlighted by this icon to pick up some sage advice.

They say elephants never forget, and nor should good business owners. This icon focuses on key information you should never be without.

Running a business isn't without it's dangers – be they financial or legal – and the text beside this icon points out common pitfalls to avoid like the plague.

Every once in a while, we all like to get a bit carried away. And that's where this icon comes in – sometimes we like to give you information that is interesting but not absolutely essential to starting or growing your own business. If you see this icon next to a paragraph, you have our permission to skip by if it's not of immediate interest to you – doing so won't harm your chances in business.

Where to Go from Here

Starting & Running a Business All-in-One For Dummies can help you succeed no matter what kind of business expertise you're looking for. If you have a great and proven business idea, you may want to plug straight into finding out how to raise finance (head over to Book II). If you need more than just yourself to get your great business idea off the ground, then you may want to find out how to find great employees (check out Book III). If you're planning to take care of your own bookkeeping and finances then you may want to find out how to successfully balance the books and take care of tax (flick through to Book IV). Or perhaps you've already started out and you're looking for advice on how to take you're business to the next level (Book VI gives some great advice). This book is set up so that you can dip in and out of it in a number of ways depending on your situation.

Book I
Where to Start?

'OK – Here's the business plan. Nigel takes charge
of marketing, Tristram sales, Keith accounts,
and Psycho makes sure clients pay on time.'

In this book . . .

If you're contemplating starting up a new business – or even if you just want to check that your current business is running smoothly – you've come to the right place! In this book we address the basic issues to consider when you're setting out on your career in business.

Here are the contents of Book I at a glance:

Chapter 1

Preparing for Business

- -

- -

*W*ould you go into the jungle without carrying out some pretty rigorous preparation? You'd need to know something about the terrain and how to navigate it, as well as the temperature, rainfall, and food supply. You would also be keen to know what predators you might meet on the way and how to defend yourself against them.

When you're starting a business, particularly your first business, you need to carry out the same level of preparation as you would for crossing the Gobi desert or exploring the jungles of South America. You are entering hostile territory.

Your business idea may be good, it may even be great, but such ideas are two a penny. The patent office is stuffed full of great inventions that have never returned tuppence to the inventors who spent much time and money filing them. It's how you plan, how you prepare and how you implement your plan that makes the difference between success and failure. And failure is pretty much a norm for business start-ups. Tens of thousands of small firms fail, some disastrously, each and every year.

In this chapter the scene is set to make sure you are well prepared for the journey ahead.

Getting in Shape to Start Up

You need to be in great shape to start a business. You don't have to diet or exercise, at least not in the conventional sense of those words, but you do have to be sure you have the skills and knowledge you need for the business you have in mind, or know how to tap into sources of such expertise.

The following sections help you through a pre-opening check-up so you can be absolutely certain that your abilities and interests are closely aligned to those needed by the business you have in mind. It will also help you to check that a profitable market exists for your products or services. You can use this section as a vehicle for sifting through your business ideas to see if they are worth devoting the time and energy that is needed to start up a business.

You may well not have all the expertise you need to do everything yourself. Zillions of agencies and advisers can fill in the gaps in your expertise.

Assessing your abilities

Business lore claims that for every ten people who want to start their own business only one finally does so. It follows that there are an awful lot of dreamers out there who, whilst liking the idea of starting their own business, never get around to taking action. Chapter 3 looks in detail at how you can assess whether you are a dreamer or a doer when it comes to entrepreneurship. For now, see whether you fit into one of the following entrepreneurial categories:

- **Nature**. If one of your parents or siblings runs their own business, successfully or otherwise, you are highly likely to start up your own business. No big surprise here as the rules and experiences of business are being discussed every day and some of it is bound to rub off. It also helps if you are a risk-taker who is comfortable with uncertainty.

- **Nurture**. For very entrepreneur whose parents or siblings have a business there are two who don't. If you can find a business idea that excites you, has the prospect of providing personal satisfaction and wealth, then you can assemble all the skills and resources needed to succeed in your own business. You need to acquire good planning and organisational skills and either develop a well-rounded knowledge of basic finance, people management, operational systems, business law, marketing and selling, or get help and advice from people who have that knowledge.

- **Risk-taker**. If you crave certainty in everything you do, then running your own business may be something of a culture shock. By the time the demand for a product or service is an absolutely sure-fired thing, there may already be too many others in the market to leave much room for you. Don't confuse risk taking with a pure gamble. You need to be able to weigh things up and take a calculated risk.

- **Jack-of-all-trades.** You need to be prepared to do any business task at anytime. The buck definitely stops with you when you run your own business. You can't tell a customer their delivery will be late, just because a driver fails to show up. You will just have to put in a few more hours and do the job yourself.

Discovering a real need

You might be a great potential entrepreneur but you still need to spell out exactly what it is you plan to do, who needs it, and how it will make money. A good starting point is to look around and see if anyone is dissatisfied with their present suppliers. Unhappy customers are fertile ground for new businesses to work in.

One dissatisfied customer is not enough to start a business for. Check out and make sure that unhappiness is reasonably widespread, as that will give you a feel for how many customers might be prepared to defect. Once you have an idea of the size of the potential market you can quickly see if your business idea is a money making proposition.

The easiest way to fill an endurable need is to tap into one or more of these triggers:

- ✔ **Cost reduction and economy.** Anything that saves customers money is always an attractive proposition. Lastminute.com's appeal is that it acts as a 'warehouse' for unsold hotel rooms and airline tickets that you can have at a heavy discount.

- ✔ **Fear and security.** Products that protect customers from any danger, however obscure, are enduringly appealing. In 1998, two months after Long-Term Capital Management (LTCM), one of America's largest hedge funds, was rescued by the Federal Reserve at a cost of $2 billion, Ian and Susan Jenkins launched the first issue of their magazine, *EuroHedge*. In the aftermath of the collapse of LTCM, which nearly brought down the US financial system single-handedly, there were 35 hedge funds in Europe, about which little was known, and investors were rightly fearful for their investments. *EuroHedge* provided information and protection to a nervous market and five years after it was launched the Jenkins's sold the magazine for £16.5 million.

- ✔ **Greed**. Anything that offers the prospect of making exceptional returns is always a winner. *Competitors' Companion*, a magazine aimed at helping anyone become a regular competition winner, was an immediate success. The proposition was simple. Subscribe and you get your money back if you don't win a competition prize worth at least your subscription. The magazine provided details of every competition being run that week, details of how to enter, the factual answers to all the questions and pointers on how to answer any tiebreakers. They also provided the inspiration to ensure success with this sentence: You have to enter competitions in order to have a chance of winning them.

- ✔ **Niche markets.** Big markets are usually the habitat of big business – encroach on their territory at your peril. New businesses thrive in markets that are too small to even be an appetite wetter to established firms. These market niches are often easy prey to new entrants as they have usually been neglected, ignored or ill-served in the past.

✔ **Differentiation.** Consumers can be a pretty fickle bunch. Just dangle something, faster, brighter or just plain newer and you can usually grab their attention. Your difference doesn't have to be profound or even high-tech to capture a slice of the market. Book buyers rushed in droves to Waterstones' for no more profound a reason than that their doors remained open in the evenings and on Sundays, when most other established bookshops were firmly closed.

Checking the fit of the business

Having a great business idea and having the attributes and skills needed to successfully start your own business are two of the three legs needed to make your business stool balance. Without the third leg, though, your stool isn't stable at all. You need to be sure that the business you plan to start is right for you.

Before you go too far, make an inventory of the key things that you are looking for in a business. These may include working hours that suit your lifestyle; the opportunity to meet new people; minimal paperwork; a chance to travel. Then match those up with the proposition you are considering. (Chapter 3 talks more about finding a good business fit.)

Checking Viability

An idea, however exciting, unique, revolutionary, and necessary is not a business. It's a great starting point, and an essential one, but there is a good deal more work to be done before you can sidle up to your boss and tell him or her exactly what you think of them.

The following sections explore the steps you need to take so that you won't have to go back to your boss in six months and plead for your old job back (and possibly eat a large piece of humble pie at the same time).

Researching the market

However passionate you are about your business idea, it is unlikely that you already have the answers to all the important questions concerning your market place. Before you can develop a successful business strategy, you have to understand as much as possible about your market and the competitors you are likely to face.

Inflated numbers on the Internet

If you plan to advertise on an Internet site it makes sense to check out the sites you're considering. Be aware that some sites publish a fair amount of gobbledygook about the high number of 'hits' (often millions) the site scores. Millions of hits doesn't mean the site has millions of visitors. Some Internet sites increase their hit rate by the simple expedient of adding the number of pages each viewer must download to view the page.

Another mildly meaningless measure of the advertising value of a site is the notion of a 'subscriber'. In Internet parlance anyone visiting a Web site and passing over their e-mail address becomes part of that company's share price! It is rather like suggesting that anyone passing a shop and glancing in the window will turn into hard cash tomorrow.

Any real analysis of Web site use starts with 'page impression', which is a measure of how many times an individual page has been viewed. The Audit Bureau of Circulations, which started its life measuring newspaper response, has now turned its attention to auditing Web sites (www.abce.org.uk).

The main way to get to understand new business areas, or areas that are new to you at any rate, is to conduct market research. The purpose of that research is to ensure that you have sufficient information on customers, competitors, and markets so that your market entry strategy or expansion strategy is at least on the target, if not on the bull's-eye itself. In other words, you need to explore whether enough people are attracted to buy what you want to sell at a price that will give you a viable business. If you miss the target altogether, which you could well do without research, you may not have the necessary resources for a second shot.

The areas to research include:

- ✔ **Your customers:** Who will buy more of your existing goods and services and who will buy your new goods and services? How many such customers are there? What particular customer needs will you meet?

- ✔ **Your competitors:** Who will you be competing with in your product/market areas? What are those firms' strengths and weaknesses?

- ✔ **Your product or service:** How should you tailor your product or service to meet customer needs and to give you an edge in the market?

- ✔ **The price:** What would be seen as giving value for money and so encourages both customer loyalty and referral?

- ✔ **The advertising and promotional material:** What newspapers, journals, and so forth do your potential customers read and what Web sites do they visit? Unglamorous as it is, analysing data on what messages actually influence people to buy, rather than just to click, holds the key to identifying where and how to promote your products and service.

- **Channels of distribution:** How will you get to your customers and who do you need to distribute your products or services? You may need to use retailers, wholesalers, mail order, or the Internet. They all have different costs and if you use one or more they all want a slice of the margin.

- **Your location:** Where do you need to be to reach your customers most easily at minimum cost? Sometimes you don't actually need to be anywhere near your market, particularly if you anticipate most of your sales will come from the Internet. If this is the case you need to have strategy to make sure potential customers can find your Web site.

Try to spend your advertising money wisely. Nationwide advertisements or blanketing the market with free disks may create huge short-term growth, but there is little evidence that the clients won by indiscriminate blunderbuss advertising works well. Certainly few people using such techniques made any money.

Doing the numbers

Your big idea looks as though it has a market. You have evaluated your skills and inclinations and you believe that you can run this business. The next crucial question is – will it make you money?

It's vital that you establish the financial viability of your idea before you invest money in it or approach outsiders for backing. You need to carry out a thorough appraisal of the business's financial requirements. If the numbers come out as unworkable you can then rethink your business proposition without having lost anything. If the figures look good, then you can go ahead and prepare cash flow projections, a profit and loss account and a balance sheet, and put together the all-important business plan.

You need to establish for your business:

- Day to day operating costs
- How long it will take to reach break-even
- How much start-up capital is needed
- The likely sales volume
- The profit level required for the business not just to survive, but also to thrive
- The retail price of your product or service

Many businesses have difficulty raising start-up capital. To compound this, one of the main reasons small businesses fail in the early stages is that too much start-up capital is used to buy fixed assets. While some equipment is clearly essential at the start, other purchases could be postponed. You may be better off borrowing or hiring 'desirable' and labour-saving devices for a specific period. This is obviously not as nice as having them to hand all the time but remember that you have to maintain every photocopier, electronic typewriter, word processor, micro-computer, and delivery van you buy and they become part of your fixed costs. The higher your fixed costs, the longer it usually takes to reach break-even point and profitability. And time is not usually on the side of the small, new business: it has to become profitable relatively quickly or it will simply run out of money and die.

Raising the money

Two fundamentally different types of money that a business can tap into are debt and equity:

- *Debt* is money borrowed, usually from a bank, and which you have to repay. While you are making use of borrowed money you also have to pay interest on the loan.

- *Equity* is the money put in by shareholders, including the proprietor, and money left in the business by way of retained profit. You do not have to give the shareholders their money back, but they do expect the directors to increase the value of their shares, and if you go public they will probably expect a stream of dividends too.

  If you do not meet the shareholders' expectations, they will not be there when you need more money – or, if they are powerful enough, they will take steps to change the board.

Alternative financing methods include raising money from family and friends, applying for grants and awards, and entering business competitions.

Check out Book II for a review of all these sources of financing.

Writing up the business plan

A *business plan* is a selling document that conveys the excitement and promise of your business to potential backers and stakeholders. These potential backers could include bankers, venture capital firms, family, friends, and others who could help you get your business launched if they only knew what you want to do.

Getting money is expensive, time-consuming, and hard work. Having said that, it is possible to get a quick decision. One recent start-up succeeded in raising £3 million in eight days, the founder having turned down an earlier offer of £1 million made just 40 minutes after his business plan was presented. Your business plan should cover what you expect to achieve over the next three years.

Most business plans are dull, badly written, and frequently read only by the most junior of people in the financing organisations they're presented to. One venture capital firm in the US went on record to say that in one year they received 25,000 business plans asking for finance and invested in only 40. Follow these tips to make your business plan stand out from the crowd:

- **Hit them with the benefits:** You need to spell out exactly what it is you do, for whom, and why that matters. One such statement that has the ring of practical authority about it is: 'Our Web site makes ordering gardening products simple. It saves the average customer two hours a week browsing catalogues and £250 a year through discounts, not otherwise available from garden centres. We have surveyed 200 home gardeners, who rate efficient purchasing as a key priority.'

- **Make your projections believable:** Sales projections always look like a hockey stick: a straight line curving rapidly upwards towards the end. You have to explain exactly what drives growth, how you capture sales, and what the link between activity and results is. The profit margins will be key numbers in your projections, alongside sales forecasts. These will be probed hard, so show the build-up in detail.

- **Say how big the market is:** Financiers feel safer backing people in big markets. Capturing a fraction of a percentage of a massive market may be hard to achieve – but if you get it at least it's worth it. Going for 10 per cent of a market measured in millions rather than billions may come to the same number, but it won't be as interesting.

- **Introduce you and your team:** You need to sound like winners with a track record of great accomplishments.

- **Include non-executive directors:** Sometimes a heavyweight outsider can lend extra credibility to a business proposition. If you know or have access to someone with a successful track record in your area of business who has time on their hands, you could invite them to help. If you plan to trade as a limited company you could ask them to be a director, without specific executive responsibilities beyond being on hand to offer their advice. But they need to have relevant experience or be able to open doors and do deals.

✔ **Provide financial forecasts:** You need projected cash flows, profit and loss accounts, and balance sheets for at least three years out. No-one believes them after Year One, but the thinking behind them is what's important.

✔ **Demonstrate the product or service:** Financiers need to see what the customer is going to get. A mock-up will do or, failing that, a picture or diagram. For a service, show how customers will gain from using it. That can help with improved production scheduling and so reduce stock holding.

✔ **Spell out the benefits to your potential investor:** Tell them that their money will be paid back within 'x' years, even on your most cautious projections. Or if you are speaking with an equity investor, tell them what return they will get on their investment when you sell the business on in three or five years time.

Going for Growth

Growth is as natural a feature of business life as it is of biological life. People, animals, and plants all grow to a set size range and then stop. A few very small and very large specimens come to fruition, but the vast majority fit within a fairly narrow size band.

Businesses follow a similar formula: most successful new businesses, those that survive that is, reach a plateau within five to seven years.

Gaining economies of scale

Once a business starts to grow, the overhead costs are spread over a wider base. You can buy materials and services in larger quantities, which usually means better terms and lower costs. The combination of these factors generally leads to a higher profit margin, which in turn provides funds to improve the business, which, in turn can lead to even lower costs. This *virtuous circle,* as it is known, can make a growing firm more cost competitive than one that is cautiously marking time.

Securing a competitive advantage

A new business can steal a march on its competitors by doing something vital that established businesses cannot easily imitate. For example a new hairdressing shop can locate where customers are, whilst an existing shop has to content itself with its current location, at least until its lease expires.

A growing firm can gain advantages over its slower competitors. For example, launching new products or services gives a firm more goods to sell to its existing customer base. This puts smaller competitors at a disadvantage because they are perceived as having less to offer than the existing supplier. This type of growth strategy can, if coupled with high quality standards, lead to improved customer retention and this too can lead to higher profits – a further push on the momentum of the virtuous circle.

Retaining key staff

The surest way to ensure a business fails is to have a constant churn of employees coming and going. Valuable time and money has to be invested in every new employee before they become productive, so the more staff you lose the more growth you sacrifice.

Most employers believe that their staff work for money and their key staff work for more money. The facts don't really support this hypothesis. All the evidence is that employees want to have an interesting job and be recognised and praised for their achievements. In Book VI you will see how to get the best out of your staff.

By growing the business you can let key managers realise their potential. In a bigger business your staff can be trained and promoted, moving up the ladder into more challenging jobs, with higher salaries earned on merit, whilst staying with you, rather than leaving for pastures new. And if employees are good at their jobs, the longer they stay with you the more valuable they become. You save time and money on the recruitment merry-go-round and you don't have to finance new managers' mistakes whilst they learn how to work in your business.

Gaining critical business mass

Bigger isn't always better, but a growing business will have a greater presence in its market, and that's rarely a bad strategy. Large businesses are also more stable, tending to survive better in turbulent times. Bigger businesses can and do sometimes go bust, but smaller 'doing nicely' small businesses are far more likely to go bump.

A small company often relies on a handful of customers and just one or two products or services for most or all of its profits. If its main product or service comes under competitive pressure, or if a principal customer goes bust, changes supplier, or simply spreads orders around more thinly, then that company is in trouble. Breaking out of the 80/20 cycle, in which 80 per cent of the business comes from just 20 per cent of customers, by expanding the number of customers is a sensible way to make your business safer and more predictable.

One-product businesses are the natural medium of the inventor, but they are extremely vulnerable to competition, changes in fashion, and technological obsolescence. Having only one product can limit the growth potential of the enterprise. A question mark must inevitably hang over such ventures until they can broaden out their product base. Adding successful new products or services helps a business to grow and become a safer and more secure venture. This process is much like buying a unit trust rather than investing in a couple of shares. The individual shares are inevitably more volatile, whilst the spread over dozens of shares smoothes the growth path, and reduces the chances of disaster significantly.

Chapter 2

Being Your Own Boss

A t some time or another, most people have thought about how good it would be to be your own boss – no more being at the beck and call of someone else or working hard just to put money into an employer's pocket! Every year, almost 300,000 people take the plunge. If you've got a big idea for your own business, this year may be the one to make it happen.

But running your own operation isn't always a bed of roses, and the more help and advice you get on the various aspects of it, the better prepared you'll be to deal with the problems as they arise – or, even better, to take steps to avoid them arising in the first place. Working for yourself can be very isolating, as well as extremely time-consuming. You and those around you need to be aware of just how much effort it takes to become successful and that your loved ones are willing to offer their support.

Going into Business

Around 500,000 new businesses are set up every year in the UK, and 300,000 of those go bust within the first three years. The ones that fall by the wayside usually do so because they've been set up on a wing and a prayer without all the necessary preparation.

Just because you've got a good idea doesn't mean that it will fly without a lot of research and planning. If you really want to work for yourself, talk to one of the organisations, such as the Government's small business advisory service Business Link, that can help you work out whether a sustainable market exists for your products or services or whether the competition has it sewn up already. You should also discuss how to set up your business, if you do decide it's worth a try.

The first step to setting up your business it to call *Business Link,* England's local business advice office. (If you're in Scotland, Wales, or Northern Ireland the equivalent services have slightly different names.) Business Link, the national business advice service, offers free advice and support and runs all sorts of useful courses for people starting up their own enterprises.

After you decide to take the plunge into entrepreneurship, you need to consider how you're going to trade. You can choose to go it alone as a *sole trader*, form a *partnership* with someone else, or set up a *limited company.* These entities differ in terms of the administration involved, whether you're prepared to risk your own personal assets, and how you want to be viewed for tax purposes. You can talk to a solicitor or an accountant about the legal form your business should take, but an adviser at Business Link is also able to help. The Law Society has a list of lawyers who offer small firms a free half-hour legal consultation; contact 020-7405-9075 or go to `www.lfyb.lawsociety.org.uk`. You can find a chartered accountant through the Institute of Chartered Accountants (`www.icaew.co.uk`).

Working as a sole trader

Are you going to go it alone? You can establish yourself as a sole trader very easily. You don't have to fill out a lot of forms, and you've got only yourself to answer to.

Most people who work on a freelance basis are sole traders, doing what they know best for a range of clients, as and when those clients need their services – say, a photographer who wants to work for himself rather than an employer. You can leave your job, make up a portfolio of your work or a brochure advertising your particular skills, and market your services to anyone you think might pay for them.

As a sole trader, you make your own business decisions; you answer only to clients, and the profits (and any losses) you make are yours. If you do make losses and run up debts, you're personally responsible for those debts. If things go badly wrong, you may ultimately have to sell some possessions, perhaps even your home, to pay off your debts. Basically, as a sole trader, you're running your business on your own. If you expand, you may decide to take on other people to work for you – as employees or as freelancers on short-term contracts – but the business is yours.

Most sole traders are self-employed and are taxed as such by Her Majesty's Revenue and Customs (HMRC). You need to register with HMRC within three months of starting up. You can find more information on the HMRC Web site at www.hmrc.gov.uk or from your local tax office, which is listed in the phone book.

You have to be careful because if you're a sole trader and you do most of your work for just one client, HMRC may not accept that you're self-employed. It may decide that you're an employee of that client. Talk your situation through with HMRC if you're in any doubt.

Someone who is genuinely self-employed works under a contract for service rather than a contract of employment. You're contracted to provide services. For more on how the tax office views self-employed people, see the section 'Minding the money matters,' later in this chapter.

Forming a partnership

If you're planning to set up your business with someone else or more than one other person, you can form a *partnership*. You run the business together and share all the management decisions, risks, costs, losses, and, hopefully, the profits. In any venture where you're working with other people, you need to be clear from the outset what your goals and priorities are. A partnership may be the answer if you don't have enough money to get up and running, and you know someone who has some money to invest.

You may think that you know your prospective partner or partners very well and will have no difficulty working together, but it's often said that you don't really know anyone until you live or work with them. Many a business falls apart because partners disagree on the basic aims of their venture and find that they can't work together.

Making it formal

If you simply form an informal partnership, nothing stops one partner from making decisions and going ahead without the consent of the others. One partner can take on binding contracts without the others having their say. As a result, it's a good idea to have a solicitor draw up a partnership agreement between you, setting out how the business will be run. (Another option is to use a Business Link adviser.)

You want to address issues such as how the profits are to be split, who puts in what in terms of finance, who is responsible for what aspects of the operation, and to what extent decisions can be made by individuals and which decisions must be made jointly. This partnership agreement helps everyone know where they stand from the beginning so that you can avoid disputes further down the line. If you do set out to draw up such an agreement, any differences of opinion are likely to surface before your commit yourself.

Partners are often taxed as self-employed, but as with sole traders, this setup isn't always the case, and you should talk it over with HM Revenue and Customs. Like a sole trader, you need to register with HMRC within three months of starting up.

Limiting the liability of the partnership

Members of a partnership are all liable for any debts their venture incurs. Partners are each personally liable so that means that they could end up selling personal possessions, perhaps even their homes, to clear their debts. If one partner can't pay their share of those debts or simply disappears owing money, the other partner or partners are left holding the bills.

You can, however, limit the personal responsibility of the partners for business debts by setting up a *limited liability partnership* (unless you're in Northern Ireland, where these partnerships don't exist). Basically, your liability as a partner in a limited liability partnership is limited to the amount of money you invested at the outset and to any personal guarantees you gave if you were borrowing money for the business. A limited liability partnership is a more complicated and expensive way to form a partnership, and you'll need the help of a solicitor or an agent who forms companies. The local Business Link can give you advice and information and help you decide whether this partnership is the right option for you.

Opting for a limited company

The other option when setting up a business is to become a *limited company*. A limited company is a private business set up in such a way that, legally, the liability of the owners for any debts it incurs is limited to their shares in the company. Their personal assets are safeguarded if the business gets into financial trouble. Limited companies have 'Limited' after their names and some people like the status that gives and feel that customers will be more impressed or confident in the organisation they're dealing with. But many limited companies are no more than a one-person organisation run from the spare room in the same way as sole traders operate.

Basically, if you set up a limited company, you and your business partners are directors of the company. You can buy a company that's already registered with Companies House 'off the shelf' with an existing name, but you may want to start from scratch and come up with your own name. Companies House is the official Government register of UK companies, and you can find more information on its Web site at www.companieshouse.gov.uk or call 0870-333-3636. Becoming a limited company is a fairly straightforward process and costs just a few hundred pounds.

The advantage for the directors is that you have a limited liability for any debts the company runs up so that you don't usually risk losing personal assets, such as your home. Your personal risk is limited to the amount of money you invest in the first place and to any financial guarantees you give to an organisation, such as the bank or individual investors when you're borrowing money to put into the business. You can raise money by allowing other people, businesses, or employees to buy shares in your business. If the company does well, your buyers make a return on their investment because they're entitled to a share of those profits – depending on how many shares they bought in the first place.

You don't usually risk losing personal assets if you form a limited company, but you do have duties as a company director. If the company goes down the pan because you haven't carried out those duties, you may become liable, personally, for company debts or be disqualified from being a director of another company.

What's in a name?

Many people opt for a limited company because they like having a business name that includes the word 'Limited'. They feel that clients will think they're better established and that it sounds more professional. It's all part of the image.

So, too, is the business name. As a sole trader or a partnership, you can operate under your own name – such as R. U. Reliable. If you decide to call yourself something else, such as Reliable Services, you have to put that name on all your letterheads, contracts, and invoices. You have to register the name of your Limited Liability Partnership or Limited company with Companies House. You can buy a company from the shelf of Companies House if one is already registered with a name that you want to use but isn't in use.

If you want to have a Web site for your company, it's a good idea to check out whether the name you're using is available as a domain name or already in use by someone else. You can check through Nominet UK at www.nic.uk or Netnames at www.netnames.co.uk. You can't register a company name that is already used by a company in operation and registered at Companies House. You can contact Companies House (0870-333-3636 or www.companieshouse.gov.uk) for more information on the do's and don'ts of company names.

You have to draw up a *Memorandum of Association* and *Articles of Association* to get started. These documents cover the details of how you run the business, where it will be based, and what it will do. You have to send this paperwork, along with registration forms, to Companies House before you start trading. Your solicitor or an agent who specialises in forming companies can help you through the process. An adviser at Business Link can also give you all the information you need and discuss the process with you before you make your decision about going down this path.

If you do become a limited company, you pay a *corporation tax* on your company profits and send yearly returns to Companies House with details of directors, shareholders, and finances. Your company account is audited if your turnover is big enough, but most small businesses don't make enough and are exempt.

Becoming a franchisee

A lot of the chains on the high street are franchises. The person who comes up with the original idea sets up the business – usually in the form of a limited company and then sells off licences to people who want to operate branches of that business. The franchisee buys the right to use the company name and logo, sell the company products or offer the company services. The franchisor – the originator of the business sets out in the contract various details of how the business is to be run; gives advice on running the operation and takes a share of the proceeds. You may find it easier to run a business this way because someone else has put all the effort into working out what will make it successful but you may eventually find it limiting because there won't be so much scope for using you own initiative or putting your own stamp on the business. You can get more information from Business Link or from the British Franchise Association at www.british-franchise.org or on 01491-578-050.

Taking on Employees

One of the most important decisions for any business owner – whether he's a sole trader, in a partnership, or operating as a limited company – is when to take on employees. One minute everything is ticking along nicely, and then suddenly you have too much work to cope with and you need help. If you take a look at *UK Law and Your Rights For Dummies* (Wiley), you can see what employees can expect from their employers and of their rights. You have to make sure that you don't do anything to contravene those rights, or you may find that your employees can make a claim against you at an employment tribunal. If the tribunal finds in favour of your employee, you can then face a bill for compensation.

Right from the moment you decide to take on a staff member, you have to stay on the right side of the law. *Small Business Employment Law For Dummies* (Wiley) covers the legalities in detail. If you need to talk things over with someone before taking the first steps, an adviser at Business Link is a good place to start.

Minding Money Matters

When it comes to money and your business, there are two sides to the coin. You may want to raise finance to get your business started or to help you run it and develop it. On the other hand, you must first consider the money you have to pay out, such as tax and national insurance.

Getting money to run the business

You may not need any capital to get going simply because the business you're starting up depends on little more than your own skills. You may simply turn your spare room into the place you work from, advertise your services, and wait for the jobs to roll in.

However, few businesses need no money to get off the ground. You'll probably need to pay for phone calls, Web site setup, advertising literature, and equipment. Many people start up by doing freelance work while keeping their day jobs, use their savings, or get help from family and friends.

When the venture is a bit bigger, though, finding the money you need can be harder. Banks are often not interested in dealing with a small venture. They're looking for something more profitable to invest in. Business people often say that borrowing ten million pounds is much easier than borrowing £100,000. That's not to say that approaching the banks isn't worth it. If you're looking to borrow money at the lower end of the scale, you may be able to arrange a small business loan. Other than that possibility, you can raise cash through other methods, including grants and loans. (Business Link can advise you about possible financial help from enterprise and development agencies.) Accountants are also an important source of business advice and support and many will give free advice on the phone. You can find a chartered accountant through the Institute of Chartered Accountants' Web site at www.icaew.co.uk.

In addition, venture capital companies and individual investors are looking for good business ideas to invest in. (Check with the Business Venture Capital Association at 020-7025-2950 or www.bvca.co.uk.) Business Angels are investors who have been in business themselves and have retired, but want to put something back in the form of financial backing and business expertise. National Business Angels attempts to match business ventures with angel investors – contact 0207-329-2929 or www.bestmatch.co.uk.

If you go to anyone to raise cash, whether it's a bank for a loan or an investor, they'll want to see detailed business plans. These documents set out your ideas and aims clearly and your projections for how the business will grow. You need to do your research to show that you know that a good, sustainable market exists for your goods or services and that the market has enough room for you. No matter how good a hairdresser you are, no one will be interested in investing in yet another hairdresser in a location that already has several hairdressers. The business plan should reflect your market research, your marketing plans, and your ideal location for your venture.

People need to be convinced that investing in your business is worth their while in terms of a fair return. Your business plan is your most important document, so get help to draft it. Business Link run courses and has advisers who can help with business planning or point you in the direction of funding sources.

Most people or organisations willing to give you business funding will want personal guarantees from you about how much money you're putting up yourself. Even if you're planning to trade as a limited company with limited liability for business debts, investors may expect you to give additional guarantees that you'll put in more that just your original investment in certain circumstances. You may have to adjust your ambitions to fit the amount of funding you're able to raise. Don't leave yourself in the position where you may lose your home and leave your partner and dependents without a roof over their heads. If you're going to take that kind of risk, everyone involved has to be convinced that the gamble is worth taking.

Paying out

After you're trading and getting paid for your work, you have to start paying out. How you're taxed depends on how you set up your business and how you run it. If you're set up as a sole trader or a partnership, whether you're taxed as self-employed or as an employee depends on how your work is organised. You're likely to be classed as self-employed if you:

✔ Can send someone else along in your place to do the work

✔ Can work for more than one business at the same time

✔ Can work as and when you're required

✔ Provide your own tools or equipment to do the job

✔ Pay your own support staff if you need any

✔ Are responsible for your own profits and loss

You may be classed as self-employed for one job that you do but as an employee for the next job, in which case the employer is expected to deduct the correct income tax from your wages before handing them to you. You must sort out your status with HMRC within three months of starting up (although it's best to sort it out before you start trading) to be sure that you're taxed properly. At the same time, you must sort out your National Insurance, either as a self-employed person or as an employee. You can con tact the local HMRC office – you can find details in the phone book, or you can find more information and contacts on the Web site at www.hmrc.gov.uk.

If you set up a limited company, you are considered a director of the company and are taxed as a company employee. The company also pays Corporation Tax on its profits. Again, HMRC, an accountant, or the local Business Link can help you put all the necessary processes in place to pay your tax.

If you take on employees, you or the company need to deduct the correct tax and national insurance from their wages and pay that amount to the HMRC.

You must also consider *Value Added Tax* (VAT). You don't pay VAT on profits, but on the sale of goods and services. Basically, as a business, you collect VAT on behalf of the Government. No matter how your business is set up, if you have a turnover in your business of £64,000 a year or more, you have to register for VAT with HMRC. Go to the HMRC Web site at www.hmrc.gov.uk to get information or get help from your local Business Link.

You also need to consider business rates and capital gains tax. All in all, a lot of financial issues are involved in setting up and running a business. While you can deal with these issues yourself, having an accountant or financial adviser on hand to give advice and support is helpful until you're completely confident.

Getting paid on time

If you're selling goods or services as a sole trader, in a partnership, or as a limited company, you can keep afloat only as long as you're getting paid for what you do. A large proportion of the businesses that go under cite cash flow problems as the main reason for their demise. For that reason, you need good processes in place to deal with preparing invoices and chasing money that's due.

Stipulate on your contracts the terms for payment. Even if your terms and conditions of invoices don't say it, you should receive your money within 30 days; if not, the law allows you to charge interest – of the Bank of England base rate plus 8 per cent – on the overdue amount. You can also claim compensation of £40 on debts of less than £1,000, £70 on debts of £1,000 up to £9,999, and £100 on debts of £10,000 or more.

If you pay late, other companies can take the same steps against you. Don't treat your creditors as a bank.

You don't want to be in the position where you have to charge interest or chase it up because you run the risk of losing your customers. You certainly don't want to go to the time and expense of chasing your debts through the courts. You may be throwing good money after bad. The best way is to have very clear payment terms from the minute you start up. If you do a good job, give your customers that little bit extra care and attention and form a good relationship with each of them, they're more likely to stick to those payment terms for fear that you won't be available next time they need your services.

Planning for your retirement

Many business owners forget about saving into a pension fund to provide an income for their own retirement. If your business is worth a lot of money when you retire, you may be able to sell it to provide you with a retirement income. However, if you sell your business, you may be liable for Capital Gains Tax. Seek advice from an accountant if you're planning to sell.

On the other hand, you may find that your business is worth very little without you in it. In that case, you need to plan ahead by paying into a pension or saving money in some other type of investment. If you have five or more employees, you can offer them access to some type of pension, even if it's just a stakeholder pension.

You don't have to make contributions to any pension you make available, but prospective employees may view pension contributions as a more important perk than a higher salary, enabling you to recruit the best people.

Talk to an accountant or financial adviser about pensions for yourself and your employees.

Safeguarding Your Business Assets

When you think of your business assets, you probably think first and foremost of your equipment or machinery, company cars, and so on. It's important to make sure that all those assets are looked after and insured, as well as protected by alarms and locks to cut down the risk of damage or loss. However, if you're in the business of inventing things or coming up with new ideas or you have logos or symbols that are a vital part of your business brand or image, those intangibles can be valuable assets. You can take care of most material assets, such as premises and computers, with insurance, but assets that fall under the heading of *intellectual property* are a lot harder to protect but even more damaging to lose.

Protecting your name

A rose by any other name may smell as sweet, but would your business be as successful if it was called something else? If you've worked hard to build a good reputation and your customers keep returning and sending referrals, your name is vitally important. For that reason, you don't want anyone else using it and perhaps tarnishing it by selling inferior goods or services to the ones you provide. If someone is in competition with you and tries to use the same or a similar name as yours, you can take them to court and claim that they're passing off their products as yours.

Of course, the last thing you want is to get involved in costly court proceedings, and you have to be sure that you have a good case. For example, the other company may not realise that another company with the same or similar name is doing a similar line of business. Try to negotiate before taking court action, but don't wait too long before taking action or your good reputation may be lost. Take legal advice as soon as you recognise a potential conflict with another firm.

Guarding your logos and trademarks

Often when you buy goods, you see a *registered trademark* – a symbol or logo that has been registered by that company as its own trademark. If you think about your favourite brands, you can conjure up in your mind their various logos and symbols. These items help customers recognise your products. People are searching for brands well known for quality, so logos and trademarks are important marketing tools.

If you register your trademarks, you can go to court to stop anyone else from using them, and you may even be able to claim damages as well. If you haven't registered your trademarks, you can still take legal action to stop another business from using them, but you have to prove the following:

✔ The trademark or symbol represents your good reputation.

✔ If someone else uses your trademark or symbol, customers will be confused.

✔ Your business has been damaged as a result of someone using your trademark or logo.

Register your trademarks at the Patent Office (www.patent.gov.uk or 08459-500-505). You can initially register them for ten years and then renew them every ten years for as long as you're trading.

Copyrighting your creations

You can't register *copyright* in the same way as you can trademarks. (See the preceding section for more information on trademarks.) Copyright is the exclusive legal right to print, publish, perform, film, or record literary, artistic, or musical material and to authorise other people to do the same. If you've created a piece of music or written a book, you are the owner of the copyright. The copyright exists automatically when the material becomes a physical entity – for example, when it's put onto paper. You can't copyright an idea, only the embodiment of the idea – the musical score as written on paper, for example but you have to prove that you own the copyright.

Copyright gives you say over how your material is used – for example, whether it can be copied, performed, or broadcast – and covers music, plays, books, stories, paintings, computer programs, sound recordings, films, videos, and so on.

You can sell or transfer ownership of your copyright to someone else, and you can give someone else license to use it – as composers of music or songs do. Each time someone else uses your copyrighted material, you receive *royalties* – an agreed sum of money that's paid each time a book sells or each time your music is performed in public. Copyright terms range from 50 years for broadcasts and sound recordings to 70 years after the death of the creator of books, plays, and music.

If you do come up with something that is eligible for copyright, keep records of when it was written or produced. You may even want to keep a dated, and sealed copy in a bank box or safe or lodged with your solicitor. That way, if copyright is ever an issue, you can prove that you were the original creator, and the copyright belongs to you.

If you employ someone to come up with this kind of material as part of his job, you are the owner of the copyright unless you've agreed otherwise. You may employ someone to design computer software, for example, and you will own the copyright of that software.

If you hire someone to do a particular job – on a contract specifically for that job – and it involves a piece of artistic work, such as taking photographs or designing a Web site, that person is likely to own the copyright unless you state otherwise in the contract. Make the situation clear when the contract is being drawn up.

Protecting your designs

If your creation is some type of design, you have protection similar to copyright. *Design right* is automatic after the design exists, and you can use it to stop other people from making, using, or selling your designs or similar ones. Design right applies to a product's outward shape.

If you want stronger protection, consider a *registered design,* which covers design features like the shape or patterns on a piece of pottery. You need to apply to the Patent Office for a registered design, which lasts for 5 years and can be extended for up to 25 years. You can get more information from the Patent Office (08459-500-505 or www.patent.gov.uk).

Patenting your inventions

When you buy certain goods, you may see a patent number on them or the words *patent pending,* which means that a patent has been applied for. Patents are meant to stop someone else from making, selling, or using something you've invented without your permission. If you invent a machine for making beds, for example, the patent covers the technical elements of the invention and how it works. You can patent the following items:

- Something that's completely new
- Something that's an improvement on something that already exists
- Something already existing that has a new use

People often worry that if they do apply for a patent at some point in the process, their idea will become known to other people and stolen. But without a patent, you can't stop someone else from using your product or process for their own good. Patents protect your invention for 20 years. You can go to court to enforce it and apply for compensation if someone else has damaged your business. In that time, you benefit because no one else can make and sell your product so you can charge whatever the market will pay without competition bringing down the price. You can also sell the patent or license it out to other people to use while paying you royalties.

You can get more information about Patents and how to apply for one from the Patent Office (08459-500-505 or www.patent.gov.uk) or from patent attorneys who are members of the Chartered Institute of Patent Agents (020-7405-9450 or www.cipa.org.uk).

Closing Down Your Business

Even if your business becomes very successful, you may decide that you've had enough and want to call it a day. If you have many willing buyers, you can sell to whomever you choose.

You should take advice because the rules over transferring your business, and in particular your staff and their contracts and rights, to a new owner are complicated. As with anything to do with your business, Business Link can help, but you need a solicitor to draw up all the necessary paperwork.

If the business is really all about you and won't continue without you, you may have no choice but to simply close it down. Even then, you're faced with the problem of having to make your employees redundant. (Refer to *UK Law and Your Rights For Dummies*, published by Wiley, for more details of the payments you must make if employees are made redundant.)

However, most businesses close down because they run into problems. You can be very successful for years and then go into a decline simply because the market has changed and you've failed to keep that necessary one step ahead of the game. Then the contracts dry up, and the customers move on to something new and more exciting elsewhere.

Laying off staff and cutting hours

If you're facing a shortage of orders but you haven't yet decided to make redundancies, you can consider laying off employees or putting them on short-time working – where they have less than half a normal week's work and pay. Be careful, though. If nothing in their contracts allows you to lay them off or put them on short-time, you'll be in breach of contract. If you cut their wages, they can claim for unauthorised deductions from wages.

If their contracts do allow you to lay them off or cut their hours, those employees who have worked for you for at least one month are entitled to a guaranteed payment for up to five days in the three-month period following the first day they were sent home because no work was available. If the staff contract, Written Statement of Employment Particulars, or the staff handbook says that employees will be paid their usual pay if they're laid off, then you must pay them that amount. If not, then you must pay the legal minimum.

Employees who have been laid off or put on short time may leave and may be entitled to claim redundancy payments if the lay off or short-time working lasts for:

✔ Four consecutive weeks or longer

✔ A series of six weeks or more – of which not more than three were consecutive – within a 13-week period.

Making people redundant

Redundancy means that jobs are going, and therefore the people who are doing those jobs are being dismissed by reason of redundancy. Redundancy isn't the same as sacking them for disciplinary reasons. It's fair to dismiss people because of redundancy, but, as with any dismissal, you have to go the right way about it.

You have to be fair in who you decide to make redundant and go through all the necessary procedures in the correct way; otherwise, your employees can claim that they were unfairly selected for redundancy and take a claim against you at an employment tribunal. Even if you're not selecting people for redundancy but closing down your whole operation and making everyone redundant, you have to do it properly. Talk to a business adviser as soon as you think redundancies may be in the pipeline so that you know how to tackle the process.

Before you issue a redundancy notice, you must consult with your employees, even if you believe you have nothing to discuss with them. If 20 to 100 jobs are to go, you have to have at least 30 days in which to consult with unions and staff. If more than 100 jobs are to go, the consultation period has to be at least 90 days. The purpose of consultation is to see whether you can find ways to save jobs. The staff may have ideas or perhaps even want to come up with some sort of proposal to buy the business and carry on.

If you're making 20 people or more redundant, you have to notify the Secretary of State through the Department of Trade and Industry. If you don't, you can be fined up to £5,000.

People are entitled to notice that their employment is ending. (Refer to *UK Law and Your Rights For Dummies* for more about notice periods and redundancy payment calculations.) Most employees are entitled to a redundancy payment. How much they're entitled to depends on how long they've worked for you, how much they earn, and what age they are. The Advisory, Conciliation and Arbitration Service (ACAS) produces a ready reckoner, which shows how many weeks payment your employees are entitled to. You can find it on the Web site at ACAS at www.acas.org.uk or by contacting the helpline on 08457-47-47-47.

If you don't give employees the right notice or money in lieu of notice or don't give them written details of the calculations of their redundancy payments, they can make claims against you at an employment tribunal.

Paying what you owe

Closing down your business can be an expensive process if you have quite a few employees, and you've been in operation for some time. Add up the final payments – redundancy payments, payments in lieu of notice, and wages owed (including any bonuses and overtime to be paid and any holiday pay due).

If you can't pay your employees what you owe them, they become creditors of your business and as such are entitled to what's owed to them if enough money is left in the pot after the business is sold. Your employees become preferred creditors and should receive their money after your secured creditors, who have security such as a mortgage. You need to keep employees informed of what's going on and make sure that they know how to claim from the state through the National Insurance Fund if you don't have enough money to go around. Your employees can contact the Redundancy Payments Helpline at 0845-1450-0034 for help. See the Department of Trade and Industry's Web site at www.dti.gov.uk.

Getting Help

If you want to work for yourself as a self-employed sole trader or are thinking much bigger and want to set up a company that grows and grows, take all the good advice you can get from the vast wealth of information out there.

Most big banks provide useful brochures, packs, and leaflets on all aspects of running a business. Your solicitor and accountant, if you have them, will be helpful, but don't take petty problems to them; you have to pay for their time, and you may have more cost-effective ways of getting help and support. If you do decide to turn to your solicitor or accountant, make sure that they are experienced in dealing with businesses the size of yours. Big businesses are quite different animals from small ones.

The government runs Business Link in England and the equivalent in Scotland, Wales, and Northern Ireland, with offices in most big towns and cities, as well as advisers with a whole range of business expertise. This free service provides advice, guidance, and support on everything to do with setting up and running a business. Business Link also has a very comprehensive Web site at www.businesslink.gov.uk, which gives you most of the information you need.

Of course, Web sites can't always give you the necessary support. You can get details about the nearest office to you on the Web site or in the local telephone directory or call 0845-600-9006. In Scotland, the organisation is Business Gateway (0845-609-6611 or `www.bgateway.com`). In Wales, contact Business Eye (0845-796-9798 or `www.businesseye.org.uk`). In Northern Ireland, contact Invest Northern Ireland (0289-023-9090 or `www.investni.com`).

ACAS (08457-47-47-47 or `www.acas.org.uk`) is an invaluable source of help for businesses.

The Federation of Small Businesses has 185,000 members with 1.25 million employees between them. For an annual subscription of between £100 and £750, depending on how many employees you have, you get various services, including access to the legal helpline where you can talk to an adviser about any legal problems you have. Call 01253-336-000 or check out the Web site at `www.fsb.org.uk`.

The Disability Rights Commission Helpline (08457622633 and `www.drc-gb.org`) can help on disability issues. The Women and Equality Unit Web site, located at `www.womenandequalityunit.gov.uk`, can help on equal pay; the Equal Opportunities Commission is at `www.eoc.org.uk`, and the Commission for Racial Equality (`www.cre.gov.uk`) may also be able to offer advice. These big three commissions are to become one around the end of 2006: The Commission for Equality and Human Rights.

Other organisations you may find useful include

- **British Chambers of Commerce** (`www.chamberonline.co.uk`) provides a range of business services locally.

- **Institute of Directors** (0207 839-1233 or `www.iod.com`) represents individual company directors.

- **The Prince's Trust** (0800-842-842 or `www.princes-trust.org.uk`) offers advice and financial support for young people starting up.

- **Shell LiveWIRE** (0845-757-3252 or `www.shell-livewire.org`) provides advice and support for people under 30 in business.

- **Inside UK Enterprise** (0870-458-4155 or `www.iuke.co.uk`) brings together established firms with startups for advice.

- **Disabled Entrepreneurs Network** (`www.disabled-entrepreneurs.net`) provides helps for business owners with disabilities.

- **Trade associations** (020-7395-8283 or `www.taforum.org`) can provide assistance.

Chapter 3

Can You Do the Business?

In This Chapter

▶ Understanding if being your own boss is right for you

▶ Taking a skills inventory to identify any gaps

*I*t's fairly clear why governments are so keen to foster entrepreneurship. New businesses create jobs for individuals and increased prosperity for nations, which are both primary goals for any government. If those new firms don't throw people out of work when recessions start to bite, supporting them becomes doubly attractive.

But people, you included, don't start businesses or grow existing ones simply to please politicians or to give their neighbours employment. There are many reasons for considering self-employment. Most people are attracted by the idea of escaping the daily grind of working for someone else and being in charge of their own destiny. But despite the many potential benefits there are real challenges and problems, and self-employment is not a realistic career option for everyone.

The questions you need to ask yourself are: Can I do it? Am I really the entrepreneurial type? What are my motivations and aims? How do I find the right business for me? This chapter can help you discover the answers to these questions.

Deciding What You Want From a Business

See whether you relate to any of the following most common reasons people give for starting up in business.

   ✔ Being able to make your own decisions

   ✔ Having a business to leave to your children

   ✔ Creating employment for the family

 ✔ Being able to capitalise on specialist skills

 ✔ Earning your own money when you want

 ✔ Having flexible working hours

 ✔ Wanting to take a calculated risk

 ✔ Reducing stress and worry

 ✔ Having satisfaction of creating something truly of your own

 ✔ Being your own boss

 ✔ Working without having to rely on others

The two central themes connecting all these reasons seem to revolve around gaining personal satisfaction, which can be seen as making work as much fun as any other aspect of life, and creating wealth, which is essential if an enterprise is going to last any length of time.

Even when your personality fits and your goals are realistic, you have to make sure that the business you're starting is a good fit for your abilities.

The following sections explore each of these reasons in more detail.

Gaining personal satisfaction (or, entrepreneurs just wanna have fun)

No one particularly enjoys being told what to do and where and when to do it. Working for someone else's organisation brings all those disadvantages.

The only person to blame if your job is boring, repetitive, or takes up time that should perhaps be spent with family and friends is yourself.

Another source of personal satisfaction comes from the ability to 'do things my way'. Employees are constantly puzzled and often irritated by the decisions their bosses impose on them. All too often managers in big firms say that they would never spend their own money in the manner they are encouraged or instructed to by the powers that be. Managers and subordinates alike feel constrained by company policy, which seems to set out arbitrary standards for dealing with customers and employees in the same way.

The high failure rate for new businesses would suggest that some people are seduced by the glamour of starting up on their own, when they might be more successful and more contented in some other line of endeavour.

Running your own firm allows you to do things in a way that you think the market, and your employees, believe to be right for the time. Until, of course, you become big and successful yourself!

Making money

Apart from winning the lottery, starting your own business is the only possible way to achieve full financial independence. That is not to say it is not without risks. In truth most people who work for themselves do not become mega rich. But many do and many more become far wealthier than they would probably have become working for someone else.

You can also earn money working at your own pace when you want to and even help your family to make some money too.

Running your own business means taking more risks than you do if you're working for someone else. If the business fails, you could stand to lose far more than your job. If, like most owner managers, you opt for *sole trader status*, that is someone working usually on their own without forming a limited company, you could end up personally liable for any business debts incurred. This could mean having to sell up your home and other assets to meet your obligations. In these circumstances, not only will all your hard work have been to no avail, you could end up worse off than when you started. Also winding up a business is far from fun or personally satisfying.

Running a business is never easy and on an hourly wage basis is often less well paid than working for someone else. So why do people set up their own business, and do your aims seem realistic in that context?

If you want to strike out on your own because you think you'll make millions, consider this: on an hourly wage basis, you'll probably make less than you do now. And, if you think, 'well, at least I'll be working for myself', consider for how long. The harsh reality is that most start-ups fail.

We don't want to discourage you, just to apply a reality check. The truth is that running your own business is hard work that often doesn't pay well at first. You have to be OK with those facts in order to have a chance of success.

Assessing Yourself

Business is not just about ideas or about market opportunities. Business is about people too, and at the outset it is mostly about you. You need to make really sure that you have the temperament to run your own business and the expertise and understanding required for the type of business you have in mind to start.

The test at the end of this section requires no revision or preparation. You will find out the truth about yourself and whether or not running a business is a great career option or a potential disaster.

Discovering your entrepreneurial attributes

The business founder is frequently seen as someone who is bursting with new ideas, highly enthusiastic, hyperactive, and insatiably curious. But the more you try to create a clear picture of the typical small business founder, the fuzzier that picture becomes. Many efforts have been made to define the characteristics of people who are best suited to becoming small business founders with limited success. In fact, the most reliable indicator that a person is likely to start a business is whether he or she has a parent or sibling who runs a business – such people are highly likely to start businesses themselves.

That being said, some fairly broad characteristics are generally accepted as being desirable, if not mandatory. Check whether you recognise yourself in the following list of entrepreneurial traits:

- **Totally committed:** You must have complete faith in your business idea. That's the only way that you can convince all the doubters that you are bound to meet on the way. But blind faith is not enough. That commitment has to be backed up with a sound business strategy.

- **Hard working:** Hard work should not be confused with long hours. There will be times when an owner-manager has to put in 18-hour days, but that should not be the norm. But even if you do work long hours and enjoy them, that's fine. Enthusiasts can be very productive. Workaholics, on the other hand, have a negative kind of black, addictive driven quality where outputs (results) become less important than inputs. This type of hard work is counterproductive. Hard work means sticking at a task however difficult until it is completed. It means hitting deadlines even when you are dead-beat. It means doing some things you don't enjoy much to work your way through to the activities that are really what you enjoy most.

- **Accepting of uncertainty:** An essential characteristic of someone starting a business is a willingness to make decisions and to take risks. This does not mean gambling on hunches. It means carefully calculating the odds and deciding which risks to take and when to take them.

Managers in big business tend to seek to minimise risk by delaying decisions until every possible fact is known. There is a feeling that to work without all the facts is not prudent or desirable. Entrepreneurs, on the other hand, know that by the time the fog of uncertainty has been completely lifted too many people will be able to spot the opportunity clearly. In point of fact an entrepreneur would usually only be interested in a decision that involved accepting a degree of uncertainty and would welcome, and on occasion even relish, that position.

✔ **Healthy:** Apart from being able to put in long days, the successful small business owner needs to be on-the-spot to manage the firm every day. Owners are the essential lubricant that keeps the wheels of the small business turning. They have to plug any gaps caused either by other people's sickness or because they just can't afford to employ anyone else for that particular job. They themselves cannot afford the luxury of sick leave. Even a week or so's holiday would be viewed as something of a luxury in the early years of a business life.

✔ **Self-disciplined:** The owner manager needs strong personal discipline to keep him or her and the business on the schedule the plan calls for. This is the drumbeat that sets the timing for everything in the firm. Get that wrong and wrong signals are sent to every part of the business, both inside and out.

One of the most common pitfalls for the novice business man or woman is failing to recognise the difference between cash and profit. Cash can make people feel wealthy and if it results in a relaxed attitude to corporate status symbols such as cars and luxury office fittings, then failure is just around the corner.

✔ **Innovative:** Most people recognise innovation as the most distinctive trait of business founders. They tend to tackle the unknown; they do things in new and difficult ways; they weave old ideas into new patterns. But they go beyond innovation itself and carry their concept to market rather than remain in an ivory tower.

✔ **Well-rounded:** Small business founders are rarely geniuses. There are nearly always people in their business who have more competence, in one field, than they could ever aspire to. But they have a wide range of ability and a willingness to turn their hands to anything that has to be done to make the venture succeed. They can usually make the product, market it, and count the money, but above all they have the self-confidence that lets them move comfortably through uncharted waters.

✔ **Driven to succeed:** Business founders need to be results-oriented. Successful people set themselves goals and get pleasure out of trying to achieve them as quickly as possible and then move on to the next goal. This restlessness is very characteristic.

Taking a skills and knowledge inventory

The self-evaluation questions in this section probe only those areas that you can control or affect. Do the evaluation and get one or two people who know you well to rate you too.

A high score is not a guarantee of success and a poor score does not necessarily bode failure. But the combination of answers should throw up some things to consider carefully before taking the plunge.

If the statement is rarely true, score 1; if usually true, score 2; and if nearly always true, score 3.

1. I know my personal and business objectives.
2. I get tasks accomplished quickly.
3. I can change direction quickly if market conditions alter.
4. I enjoy being responsible for getting things done.
5. I like working alone and making my own decisions.
6. Risky situations don't alarm me.
7. I can face uncertainty easily.
8. I can sell my business ideas and myself.
9. I haven't had a day off sick for years.
10. I can set my own goals and targets and then get on with achieving them.
11. My family is right behind me in this venture – and they know it will mean long hours and hard work.
12. I welcome criticism – there is always something useful to learn from others.
13. I can pick the right people to work for me.
14. I am energetic and enthusiastic.
15. I don't waste time.

A score of 30 plus is good; 20–30 is fair; below 20 is poor. A high score won't guarantee success but a low one should cause a major re-think.

Working out a business idea that's right for you

Take some time to do a simple exercise that can help you decide what type of business is a good match with your abilities. Take a sheet of paper and draw up two columns. In the left-hand column, list all your hobbies, interests, and skills. In the right-hand column, translate those interests into possible business ideas. Table 3-1 shows an example of such a list.

Table 3-1	Matching a business idea to your skills.
Interest/skills	*Business Ideas*
Cars	Car dealer/repair garage/home tuning service
Cooking	Restaurant/home catering service/bakery shop providing produce for freezer outlets
Gardening	Supplier of produce to flower or vegetable shop/running a nursery/running a garden centre/landscape design
Using a computer	Typing authors' manuscripts from home/typing back-up service for busy local companies/running a secretarial agency/web design/book-keeping service

Having done this exercise, balance the possibilities against the criteria important to you in starting a business.

Figuring out what you're willing to invest

I'm not just talking about money here. How much are you willing to invest of your time, your interest, and your education, as well as your (and your investors') money?

Spending time

How much time are you willing to devote to your business? That may sound a basic enough question, but different business done in different ways can have quite different time profiles. One business starter we know started a French bakery in London. He was determined to make his own croissants and did so for the first three months. But making his own bread meant starting work at 4 a.m. As he didn't close until city workers passed his door on their way home, by the time he cleaned up and took stock, he had worked a fifteen-hour day. But he still had the books to do, orders to place and plans to prepare. He eventually settled for a ten-hour day, which meant he had to buy in croissants already baked.

Furthering your education

You may have identified a market opportunity that requires skills over and above those that you currently have. There may, for example, be a gap in the market for Teaching English as a Foreign Language (TEFL), but to do so requires a month of intensive study plus a £1,000 course fee.

Doing the TEFL certificate may involve you in more skill upgrading than you want to commit to, at the outset at least. So either you need to find customers who don't require you to have that qualification, or you need to think about a less educationally challenging business.

Keeping things interesting

If you want to start a restaurant, and have never worked in one, get a job in one. That's the best way to find out if you would like a particular type of work. You may find that a restaurant looks very different from behind the chair as opposed to on it. Some businesses are inherently repetitive, with activities that follow a predictable pattern. If that suits you fine, but if not then perhaps you need to consider a business venture with a shifting range of tasks.

Weighting your preferences

After you have an idea of some of the businesses you may want to start, you can rank those businesses according to how closely they match what you want from starting a business.

Go through the standards you want your business to meet and assign a weight between 1 and 5 to each on a range from not important at all to absolutely must have. Next, list your possible business opportunities and measure them against the graded criteria.

Table 3-2 shows a sample ranking for Jane Clark, an imaginary ex-secretary with school-aged children, who needs work because her husband has been made redundant and is busy looking for another job. Jane isn't in a position to raise much capital, and she wants her hours to coincide with those of her children. She wants to run her own show and she wants to enjoy what she does. The criteria she selected were:

Table 3-2	Weighing up the Factors
Criteria	*Weighting factor*
Minimal capital required	5
Possibility to work hours that suit lifestyle	5
No need to learn new skills	4
Minimal paperwork	3
Work satisfaction	2
Opportunity to meet interesting people	1

Since minimal capital was a very important criterion for Jane she gave it a weight of five, whereas the opportunity to meet interesting people, being far less important to her, was only weighted one.

Jane then gave each of her three business ideas a rating, in points (out of five) against these criteria. A secretarial agency needed capital to start so was given only one point. Back-up typing needed hardly any money and was allocated five points.

Her worked-out chart is shown in Table 3-3.

Table 3-3			Scoring Alternatives					
			Secretarial agency		Back-up typing		Authors' manuscripts	
	Weighting factor	Points		Score	Points	Score	Points	Score
Criteria								
Minimal capital	5 x	1	=	5	5	25	4	20
Flexible hours	5 x	1	=	5	3	15	5	25
No new skills	4 x	2	=	8	5	20	5	20
Work satisfaction	3 x	4	=	12	1	3	3	9
Minimal paperwork	2 x	0	=	0	4	8	5	10
Meeting people	1 x	4	=	4	3	3	4	4
Total score				34		74		88

The weighting factor and the rating point multiplied together give a score for each business idea. The highest score indicates the business that best meets Jane's criteria. In this case, typing authors' manuscripts scored over back-up typing since Jane could do it exactly when it suited her.

Chapter 4

Starting Your Business Plan

. . . .

In This Chapter

▶ Getting the most out of your plan

▶ Using your plan as a record of the past and a guide to the future

▶ Making your plan function as your company description

▶ Figuring out who makes the plan

▶ Checking out what the written plan looks like

. . . .

Most of us go through life thinking ahead. We plan to paint the house, plan to go back to university, plan to take a holiday, and plan for retirement – we always have a plan or two in the works. Why do we plan so much? We certainly can't predict what's going to happen, so why bother? Certainly, none of us knows the future. But each of us knows that tomorrow will be different from today, and today isn't the same as yesterday. Planning for those differences is one way to move forward and face things that are unfamiliar and uncertain. Planning is a strategy for survival.

Companies make business plans for many of the same reasons. Planning is a strategy to improve the odds of success in a business world that's constantly changing. Business plans are not a guarantee, of course. Business planning isn't a science that offers you right and wrong answers about the future. But business planning is a process that gets you ready for what's to come. And making a plan increases the likelihood that down the road, your company will be in the right place at the right time.

In this chapter, we explore what planning is all about, how you can use your business plan, and why having a plan is so important.

Getting the Most Out of Your Plan

A *plan* originally meant only one thing: a flat view of a building, viewed from above. If you've ever had a house built or remodelled, you know that this kind of plan is still around (and still expensive). Over the centuries, however, the meaning of the word *plan* has expanded to include time as well as space. A *plan* in the modern sense also refers to a view of the future, seen from the present. You make plans for a birthday party next week or a business trip next month.

A *business plan* is a particular view of your company's future, describing the following things:

- ✔ What your industry will look like
- ✔ What markets you'll compete in
- ✔ What competition you'll be up against
- ✔ What products and services you'll offer
- ✔ What value you'll provide customers
- ✔ What long-term advantages you'll have
- ✔ How big and profitable your company will become

To create a detailed view of the future, you have to make a lot of predictions about what's going to happen down the road. If your company manufactures crystal balls, of course, you're in luck. If not, you have to find other ways to make some basic business assumptions about the future, which we share with you throughout this book.

In the end, your business plan is only as good as all the assumptions you put into it. To make sure that your assumptions make sense, much of your planning should involve trying to understand your surroundings today – what's going on right now in your own industry and marketplace. By making these assumptions, you can better predict your business and its future. Will your predictions actually come true? Only time will tell. Fortunately, the planning process makes you better prepared for whatever lies ahead.

Looking forward

A business plan provides a view of the future. Whether your company is large or small, whether you're just starting a business or are part of a seasoned company, you still need some sort of planning process to point you in the right direction and guide you along the way.

- ✔ A brand-new company makes a business plan to get its bearings and often uses the plan to get funding.
- ✔ An up-and-running company uses a plan to be better prepared.

✔ A large company needs a plan so that everybody sees the same view ahead.

✔ A small company makes a plan if it wants to make sure that it survives those crucial first two years.

In fact, a small company needs a business plan most of all. If you own or manage a small business, you already know that you're the jack-or-jill-of-all-trades. You hardly have enough time to get your daily business tasks done, much less plan for next week, next month, or next year. But because you run a small business, you simply can't afford *not* to plan.

When a giant company stumbles, it usually has the financial reserves to break the fall and get back on its feet. If your resources are limited, however, a single mistake – such as exaggerating the demand for your products or underestimating how long you have to wait to get paid – can spell the end of everything you've invested in and worked so hard to achieve. A business plan points out many dangers, alerting you to the hazards and obstacles that lie ahead, so that you can avoid such pitfalls. Remember: two-thirds of all new businesses cease trading within their first two or three years.

Looking back

A business plan paints a picture of where your company has been and how it has changed over the years. By reviewing past performance, you can use your plan to figure out what worked and what didn't. In effect, your business plan offers you an opportunity to keep score, allowing you to set goals for your company and then keep track of your achievements. For example

✔ Your plan creates a view of the future. In years to come, you can use old copies of your plan to look back and determine just how good you are at seeing what lies ahead.

✔ Your plan maps out a direction to go in and the route to take. You can use it to gauge how skilful you are at accomplishing what you set out to do.

✔ Your plan forecasts where you want to be. You can use it to check out how close you have come to your targets for the industry, your market, and your finances.

Your history, as described in your business plan, teaches you important lessons about the business you're in – so you aren't doomed to make the same mistakes over and over. If you can't remember exactly where your company has been, you probably won't see where it's headed.

Looking around

You can use your business plan to tell the world (or at least anyone out there who's interested) all about your company. No matter who you're dealing with or why, your plan has a ready-made description to back up the claims you make. Your plan comes in handy when you're dealing with the following people:

- Suppliers you are asking to extend you credit and offer you terms
- Distributors that want to add your product or service to their line-ups
- Big customers that hope to establish long-term business relationships with you
- The board of directors or other advisers who want to offer support
- Outside consultants you bring in to help out with specific issues
- Bankers who decide on whether or not to lend you money
- Investors who are interested in taking a stake in your company

All these people have their own special reasons for wanting more information about you, and each probably is interested in a different part of your plan. A well-written business plan satisfies all these groups and makes your company stronger in the process.

- A business plan improves your company's chances of success.
- A business plan shows you where your company has been and how it has changed.
- A business plan provides a blueprint for the future.
- Business planning is an ongoing process.

Naming Your Planners

Okay, a business plan is essential. Who's supposed to put the wretched thing together? In some sense, the answer depends on how big your company is.

- **Small businesses:** If your business is really just you – or maybe you and a couple of other people – you already know exactly who's responsible for making a plan for the company. That's not such a bad thing, when you think about it. Who better to create a view of the future and set business goals and objectives than the people who are also responsible for reaching the goals and making the future happen?

✔ **Medium-sized companies:** If your company is a bit bigger, you probably don't want to go it alone when it comes to putting together your business plan. First of all, putting together a plan is a big job. But more than that, involving all the key people in the planning process has a certain advantage: everyone involved in the plan has a stake in making sure that your company succeeds.

✔ **Large companies:** If you're part of a big company, you may need serious help to make a business plan that's complete and always up-to-date. To get all the work done, you may have to hire people who have nothing to do but tend to your company's business plan full time. Unfortunately, creating a planning staff involves a real danger: Your plan can take on a life of its own and get completely divorced from what's really happening with your business. Remember: You have to make sure that your planners don't create plans all by themselves. To be of any use in the long run, the planning staff must support the managers who actually have to carry out the business plan.

Putting Your Plan on Paper

When you put together a business plan, your efforts take you in many directions. You face all sorts of issues related to the business that you're in. Right off the bat, for example, you need to answer basic questions about your company and what you want it to be in the future. Then you have to decide what targets to aim for as you look ahead and set business goals and objectives.

A large part of creating a business plan requires only a dose of good common sense on your part. But if you want to make sure that your business plan succeeds, you also have to take the time to do the following:

✔ Look closely at your industry

✔ Get to know your customers

✔ Check out your competitors

✔ List all your company's resources

✔ Note what makes your company unique

✔ List your company's advantages

✔ Figure out your basic financial condition

✔ Put together a financial forecast and a budget

In addition, you have to be prepared for everything to change down the road. So you also need to think about other options and alternatives and be on the lookout for new ways to make your company prosper.

You don't want to scare people – yourself included – with a written plan that's too long. The longer your plan is, in fact, the less likely people are to read it. Ideally, for a small or medium-sized company, your written plan should be 15 or 20 pages maximum. Remember that you can always support the main text with all the exhibits, appendixes, and references that you think it needs. If you want to glance at a sample business plan, take a look at *Business Plans For Dummies* (Wiley).

To remind yourself (and other people) that your written plan is forever a work in progress, we suggest that you keep it in a three-ring binder, or its electronic equivalent. That way, you can add or delete pages, and swap entire sections in or out, as your business plan changes – and we're certain that it *will* change. Fortunately, however, the format you use – all the major sections of a business plan – will stay the same.

Executive summary

Your executive summary touches on everything that's important in your business plan. It's more than just a simple introduction; it's the whole plan, only shorter. In many cases, the people who read your plan won't need to go any further than the executive summary; if they do, the summary points them to the right place.

The executive summary isn't much longer than a page or two, and you should wait until the rest of the business plan is complete before you write it. That way, all you have to do is review the plan to identify the key ideas you want to convey.

If you want to make sure that people remember what you tell them, you have to say what you're going to say, say it, and then say what you've said. The executive summary is where you say what you're going to say.

Company overview

The company overview provides a place to make important observations about the nature of your business. In the overview, you discuss your industry, your customers, and the products and services you offer or plan to develop. Although you should try to touch on your company's business history and major activities in the overview, you can leave many of the details for the later sections.

To put together this kind of general company overview, you should draw on several key planning documents, including the following:

✓ **Mission statement:** A statement of your company's purpose, establishing what it is and what it does.

✓ **Goals and objectives:** A list of all the major goals that you set for your company, along with the objectives that you have to meet to achieve those goals.

✓ **Values statement:** The set of beliefs and principles that guide your company's actions and activities.

✓ **Vision statement:** A phrase or two that announces where your company wants to go or paints a broad picture of what you want your company to become.

Business environment

The section of your business plan that deals with your business environment should cover all the major aspects of your company's situation that are beyond your immediate control, including the nature of your industry, the direction of the marketplace, and the intensity of your competition. You should look at each of these areas in detail to come up with lists of both the opportunities that your business environment offers and the threats that your company faces. Based on your observations, you can then describe what it takes to be a successful company.

Pay special attention to how your industry operates. You should describe the primary business forces that you see out there, as well as the key industry relationships that really determine how business gets done. Next, you should talk about your marketplace and your customers in more detail, perhaps even dividing the market into segments that represent the kinds of customers you serve. Finally, spend some time on the competition, describing what those companies are, what they're like, how they work, and what they're likely to be up to in the future.

Company description

In the company description, you go into much more detail about what your company has to offer. The description should include some information about your management, the organisation, new technology, your products and services, company operations, your marketing potential – in short, anything special that you bring to your industry.

In particular, you should look carefully and objectively at the long list of your company's capabilities and resources. Sort out the capabilities that represent strengths from those that are weaknesses. In the process, try to point out where you have real advantages over your competitors.

Examining your company through your customers' eyes helps. With this viewpoint, you sometimes can discover customer value that you didn't know you were providing, and as a result, you can come up with additional long-term ways to compete in the market.

Company strategy

The section on company strategy brings together everything that you know about your business environment and your own company to come up with your projections of the future.

You want to take time in this section to map out your basic strategies for dealing with the major parts of your business, including the industry, your markets, and the competition. Talk about why the strategy is the right one, given your business situation. Describe how the strategy will play out in the future. Finally, point out specifically what your company needs to do to ensure that the strategy succeeds.

Everybody knows that the future is uncertain, so you should also talk about ways in which your business world may be different in the future than it is today. List alternative possibilities, and in each case, describe what your company is doing to anticipate the changes and take advantage of new opportunities.

Financial review

Your financial review covers both where you stand today and where you expect to be in the future.

You should describe your current financial situation by using several standard financial statements. True, these statements don't make for the liveliest reading, but the people who are interested in this part of your business plan expect to see them. The basic financial statements include:

- **Profit and loss account:** A list of numbers that adds up all the revenue that your company brings in over a month, a quarter, or a year and then subtracts the total costs involved in running your business. What's left is your *bottom line* – the profit that you make during the period.

✔ **Balance sheet:** A snapshot of your financial condition at a particular moment, showing exactly what things your company owns, what money it owes, and what your company is really worth.

✔ **Cash-flow statement:** A record that traces the flow of cash in and out of your company over a given period, tracking where the money comes from and where it ends up. The cash-flow statement only tracks money when you actually receive it or spend it.

Your projections about your future financial situation use exactly the same kind of financial statements. But for projections, you estimate all the numbers in the statements, based on your understanding of what's going to happen. Because nothing is certain, make sure to include all the assumptions you made to come up with your estimates in the first place.

Action plan

Your action plan lays out how you intend to carry out your business plan. This section should point out proposed changes in management or the organisation itself, for example, as well as new policies or procedures that you expect to put in place. You should also include any additional skills that you, your managers, and your employees may need to make the plan work. Finally, you want to talk a bit about how you're going to generate excitement for your business plan inside your company, so as to create a culture that supports what you're trying to accomplish. Only then can you have real confidence that your business plan is going to succeed.

✔ The executive summary touches on all the important parts of your plan.

✔ The company overview describes the nature of your business, using your mission, values, and vision statements.

✔ Your business plan should analyse your business environment.

✔ The company description identifies your company's specific capabilities and resources.

✔ The plan should discuss your current business strategy.

✔ A financial review includes a profit and loss account, balance sheet, and cash-flow statement.

Chapter 5

Establishing Your Starting Position

. . . .

In This Chapter

▶ Discovering your capabilities and resources

▶ Reviewing critical success factors

▶ Identifying company strengths and weaknesses

▶ Recognising opportunities and threats

▶ Analysing your situation by using a SWOT grid

. . . .

*W*hen you look into a mirror, you expect to see an image of yourself. When you listen to your voice on an answering machine, you expect to hear yourself. When you look at photos or home videos, you expect to recognise yourself. But how many times have you said

> *That doesn't look like me.*

or

> *Is that what I really sound like?*

An honest self-portrait – whether it's seeing and hearing yourself clearly or making objective statements about your own strengths and weaknesses – is tough to put together. Strengths and weaknesses have to be measured relative to the situations at hand, and a strength in one circumstance may prove to be a weakness in another. Leadership and snap decision making, for example, may serve you extremely well in an emergency. But the same temperament may be a liability when you're part of a team that's involved in delicate give-and-take negotiations.

You're going to face similar problems in seeing clearly and objectively when you take on the task of measuring your company's internal strengths and weaknesses. You may be surprised by how many businesses fail miserably at the job of objective self-analysis – companies that cling to a distorted image of the resources that they command and the capabilities that they bring to the marketplace.

In this chapter, we help you get a handle on your company's strengths and weaknesses in relation to the opportunities and threats that you face.

Situation Analysis

We examine your company's situation by using a tried-and-tested approach known as SWOT. Don't worry about guns or sharpshooters; *SWOT* is an acronym for *strengths, weaknesses, opportunities*, and *threats*.

Your company's strengths and weaknesses can't be measured in a vacuum, of course. Your situation depends not only on your own capabilities and resources, but also on the opportunities and threats that arise from things beyond your control. Depending on the situations that you face, opportunities and threats appear, disappear, and change all the time, and your company's strengths and weaknesses change with them.

A thorough SWOT analysis is something that you complete more than once. In fact, you probably should carry out a SWOT review on a regular basis, depending on how fast your business environment, the industry, and your own company change.

Identifying Strengths and Weaknesses

Your company's *strengths* are the capabilities, resources, and skills that you can draw upon to carry out strategies, implement plans, and achieve the goals that you've set for yourself. Your company's *weaknesses* are any lack of skills or a deficiency in your capabilities and resources relative to the competition that may stop you from acting on strategies and plans or accomplishing your goals.

To capture your own first impressions of your company, complete the Company Strengths and Weaknesses Questionnaire (see Figure 5-1). On the right side of the questionnaire, assess your capabilities and resources in each area. On the left side, rate the importance of these elements to your industry.

Frames of reference

Once you complete the questionnaire shown in Figure 5-1, you should have an initial list of your company's strengths and weaknesses. In order to be objective, however, you need to go beyond first impressions and look at your business assets from more than one point of view. Different frames of reference offer the advantage of smoothing out biases that are bound to creep into a single viewpoint. They also offer the best chance of making your list as complete as it can be.

Figure 5-1:
Company
Strengths
and
Weaknesses
Question-
naire.

Company Strengths and Weaknesses Questionnaire

Importance to Industry			Business Area	Your Capabilities and Resources			
Low	Moderate	High		Poor	Fair	Good	Excellent
❑	❑	❑	Management	❑	❑	❑	❑
❑	❑	❑	Organisation	❑	❑	❑	❑
❑	❑	❑	Customer base	❑	❑	❑	❑
❑	❑	❑	Research & development	❑	❑	❑	❑
❑	❑	❑	Operations	❑	❑	❑	❑
❑	❑	❑	Marketing & sales	❑	❑	❑	❑
❑	❑	❑	Distribution & delivery	❑	❑	❑	❑
❑	❑	❑	Financial condition	❑	❑	❑	❑

✔ **Internal view.** Draw on the management experience inside your company (use your own experience, or that of your friends and former co-workers if you're self-employed) to come up with a consensus on your business strengths and weaknesses. You may want to use the same people to get a sense of what's happened in the recent past as well. A little corporate history can show you how your company's strengths and weaknesses have changed over time – and how easily the organisation shifts gears.

✔ **External view.** Beware of becoming too self-absorbed in this analysis. It's important to step back and look around, using your competitors as yard-sticks, if you can. All of your competitors do business in the same industry and marketplace that you do, and they're strong or weak in all the key areas that you're interested in. If your list is going to mean anything when the time comes to apply it to your own business situation, your strengths and weaknesses have to be measured against those of your competitors.

✔ **Outside view.** Perhaps you identify company strengths that are assets only because your competitors haven't reacted yet, or maybe you ignore real weaknesses because everybody else has them, too. Every once in a while, you need an objective outside assessment of what's happening in your business. That's where consultants can actually be of some use. If you can't afford that kind of advice, make sure that you at least monitor the business press to get an outside view of what the experts are saying about your industry's key players. Business Link in England (and equivalents in Scotland and Wales) can generally help firms to set up an objective appraisal of the strengths and weaknesses of a business.

If you don't have a management team that can conduct a situation analysis, bring together one of the informal groups that you rely on for some of your other planning tasks. Ask the group members to spend a little time analysing strengths and weaknesses. Make sure that the group looks at your company's situation from various perspectives, using the different frames of reference in the preceding list.

Capabilities and resources

In putting together a list of your company's capabilities and resources, cast your net as widely as possible. Look at your capabilities and resources in a systematic way, reviewing all the business areas introduced in the Company Strengths and Weaknesses Questionnaire (refer to Figure 5-1 earlier in this chapter). In each area, try to identify as many capabilities and resources as possible by using different frames of reference. At the same time, assess how relevant each capability or resource is in helping you to carry out your plans and to achieve your business goals. You're going to use this master list as raw material when the time comes to identify your company's strengths and weaknesses.

Management: Setting direction from the top

Your company's management team brings together skills, talent, and commitment. You want team members to find their direction from your company's mission, vision, and values statements, as well as from the business goals and objectives that you plan to achieve. Top-notch managers and owners are particularly important in industries that face increasing competition or fast-changing technologies. It's hard to think of an industry that doesn't fit into one of these two categories.

Management is there to determine what your company's going to do. Senior managers are officially charged with setting the direction and strategy for your company, but all managers indirectly set a tone that encourages certain activities and discourages others. Office products leader 3M, for example, gives its managers the freedom to be entrepreneurs in their own right, allowing the company to recognise and invest in new business opportunities with the speed and flexibility of much smaller rivals. The Body Shop, on the other hand, is recognised for its environmentallly aware management. The company attracts highly qualified men and women who want to work in a business environment that values both personal and corporate social responsibility.

Following are some key questions to ask about the management and/or ownership of your company:

- How long have managers been around at various levels in your company? (Alternatively, what variety of experiences do you have as an owner?)
- Does your company plan to hire from the outside or promote from within?

- ✔ What's the general tone set by you or your company's management?

- ✔ Do you have a management development programme in place? (Alternatively, how do you plan to develop your own skills, if you're a sole proprietor?)

- ✔ What backgrounds do you or your managers have?

- ✔ How is management performance measured in your company?

- ✔ How would you rate the general quality of your own skills or those of your management team?

Organisation: Bringing people together

The people who make up your company and its work force represent a key resource, both in terms of who they are and how they are organised. Although human resources are important to all companies, they're especially critical to companies in service industries, in which people are a big part of the product. (We take a closer look at your organisation in *Business Plans For Dummies*.)

Your organisation starts with who your employees are, and that depends first on how well you select and train them. Beyond that, the work environment and your company's incentive systems determine who goes on to become a dedicated, hard-working employee and who gets frustrated and finally gives up. The setup of your organization (how it's structured and how it adapts) can be just as important as your employees are when it comes to creating a company team – even a small one – that performs at the highest levels, year in and year out.

Following are some key questions about your organisation to consider:

- ✔ What words best describe the overall structure of your organisation?

- ✔ How many reporting levels do you have between a front-line employee and your CEO?

- ✔ How often does your company reorganise?

- ✔ What are your employees' general attitudes to their jobs and responsibilities?

- ✔ How long does the average employee stay with your company?

- ✔ How does your absenteeism level compare with industry benchmarks?

- ✔ Does your company have ways to measure and track employees' attitudes and morale?

- ✔ What does your company do to maintain morale and positive job performance?

Customer base: Pleasing the crowds

Your company's business depends, to a great extent, on the satisfaction and loyalty of your customers.

Following are some key questions to consider when you study your own customer base:

- ✔ What does your company do to create loyal customers?
- ✔ How much effort do you put into tracking customers' attitudes, satisfaction, and loyalty?
- ✔ What do you offer customers that keeps them coming back?
- ✔ How easy and economical is it for your company to acquire new customers?
- ✔ How many years does a typical customer stay with you?
- ✔ How many markets does your company serve?
- ✔ Are you either number one or number two in the markets in which you compete?

Research and development: Inventing the future

Research and development (R&D) often plays an important role in the long-term success of a company, and R&D is particularly critical in industries in which new and better products are coming along. But research and product development must balance the other forces that are at work in your marketplace. R&D is one business area in which even an A-1 team effort doesn't automatically pay off.

The following key questions help you examine the role of R&D in your company:

- ✔ To what extent is your industry driven by technology?
- ✔ Can you get enough results for your money to bother with R&D?
- ✔ Does your company have a consistent, long-term commitment to R&D?
- ✔ How many pounds do you spend on basic research as opposed to applied research?
- ✔ How long have the key people on your research staff been with you?
- ✔ Does your company protect what it owns with copyrights and patents?
- ✔ Have you set up partnerships with universities or outside research labs?
- ✔ Do you have technology agreements with other companies in your industry?
- ✔ Are you aware of the favourable UK tax treatment of R&D expenditure?
- ✔ Are you aware of possible UK government grant aid for R&D projects?

Operations: Making things work

The operations side of your business is obviously critical if you happen to be a manufacturing company. The products that you make (and the way that they work, how long they last, and what they cost) depend entirely on the capabilities and resources of your production facilities and work force – so much so that you can easily forget that operations are equally important to companies in the service sector. Customers demand value in all markets today, and they're simply unwilling to pay for inefficiencies in any business. Whether you make cars or carpets, produce cereal boxes or serial ports, run a bank or manage a hotel, operations are at the heart of your enterprise.

Operations in your own company probably are driven, to some extent, by costs on one side and product or service quality on the other. The tension between controlling costs and improving quality has led many companies to explore ways to reduce costs and increase quality at the same time. One way for you to do that is to involve outside suppliers in certain aspects of your operations, if those suppliers have resources that you can't match. Another way to achieve both goals is to streamline parts of your operations (through automation, for example).

Automation can also be a source of growth and may even create new business opportunities for your company. The airline industry is as big as it is today because of the computer revolution; computers enable airlines to track millions of passenger reservations and itineraries at the same time. Imagine the queues at airports if airlines were still issuing tickets by hand and completing passenger flight lists by using carbon paper.

When American Airlines developed its computer-based SABRE reservation system, however, it couldn't predict that *yield management* – the capability to monitor demand for flights and continuously adjust prices to fill seats – would become as important as on-time arrivals. The company has increased its profit margins because yield-management software ensures that each American flight generates as much revenue as possible. The software is so sophisticated and successful that Robert Crandall, American Airlines' chairman, spun off SABRE as a separate company. SABRE's expertise can now be used to benefit industries such as the hotel business, in which yield-management software can automatically adjust room rates and make sure that as many beds as possible are filled each night.

Following are some questions on the operations side of your business to mull over:

- ✔ Does your company have programmes for controlling cost and improving quality?
- ✔ Has your company taken full advantage of new technologies?

✔ Are your production costs in line with those of the rest of the industry?

✔ How quickly can you boost production or expand services to meet new demand?

✔ Does your company use outside suppliers?

✔ Is your operations workforce flexible, well trained, and prepared for change?

✔ Can you apply your operations expertise to other parts of the business?

Sales and marketing: Telling a good story

The best product or service in the world isn't going to take your company far if it's not successfully marketed and sold to all those potential customers out there. Your sales and marketing people (or you, if you're operating your own small business) are your eyes and ears, giving you feedback on what customers think about and look for. Your sales and marketing people are also your voice. They tell your company's story and put your products in context, offering solutions, satisfying needs, and fulfilling wants in the marketplace.

Following are a few key questions to ask about the marketing of your product line:

✔ How broad is your company's product or service line?

✔ Do consumers identify with your company's brand names?

✔ Do you have special processes or technologies that your competitors can't take advantage of?

✔ Are you investing in market research and receiving continuous customer feedback?

✔ Are you using all the marketing resources that are at your disposal?

✔ Is your company's sales force knowledgeable, energetic, and persuasive?

Distribution and delivery: Completing the cycle

Distribution and delivery means that your products and services are actually getting to their final destinations and into your customers' hands. No matter how good you think your products are, your customers have to be able to get their hands on them when and where they want them. How customers shop is often just as important as what they buy, so it's not surprising that when a different way to deliver products and services comes along (over the Internet, for example), the new system revolutionises a marketplace or even an entire economy. The Internet promises a future in which companies can reach out to their customers more directly, increasing company clout and at the same time lowering distribution costs.

Right now, your company probably distributes its products and services through *traditional channels* – time-tested ways in which you and your competitors reach customers – and your distribution and delivery costs may represent a significant part of your total expenses. The standard costs often include warehouse operations, transportation, and product returns. If you're in a retail business, you can end up paying for expensive shelf space as well. Supermarkets now routinely ask for money up front before they stock a new item, and you pay more for the best locations. After all, supermarkets control what customers see – and buy – as harried shoppers troop down the aisles, children and trollies in tow.

Following are some questions about the distribution and delivery of your product or service:

- ✔ What are the costs associated with your company's inventory system?

- ✔ Can you reduce inventories by changing the way that orders are processed?

- ✔ How much time does it take for a customer order to get filled, and can the time be reduced?

- ✔ How many distribution channels does your company use?

- ✔ What are the relative costs in various channels, and which are most effective?

- ✔ How much control over your company do distributors have?

- ✔ Can you use any new channels to reach your customers more directly?

Financial condition: Keeping track of money

The long-term financial health of your company determines the health of your company, full stop. You simply can't survive in business for long without having your financial house in order. Come to think of it, the things that you have to track when it comes to company finances aren't all that different from the issues that you face in running your own household. If you're just starting in business, for example, how much money your company can get its hands on up-front (your *initial capital*) is a key to survival. (Does this sound like trying to buy and furnish your first house?) When your company's up and running, it's important to make sure that more money comes in than goes out (a *positive cash flow*), so that you can pay all your bills. (Remember those times when the mortgage and utility bills were due, and it wasn't payday yet?)

Figuring out how to keep your company financially fit is critical to planning your business. When you take the time to look over your important financial statements periodically, you give your company the benefit of a regular financial checkup. The checkup is usually routine, but every once in a while you uncover an early-warning symptom – profits that are too low, for example, or a promotional expense that's too large. That's when all your financial vigilance is worth it.

Following is a list of oh-so-painful questions to ask about your company's financial health:

✔ Are your revenue and profits growing?

✔ Are you carefully monitoring your company's cash flow?

✔ Does your company have ready access to cash reserves?

✔ Does your company – and every business unit or area – have a budget for the coming year?

✔ Do you consistently track key financial ratios for the company?

✔ How does your company's financial picture compare with that of the competition?

Critical success factors

It's important to decide whether your capabilities and resources represent company strengths that you can leverage or weaknesses that you must correct as you plan for the future. To do that, you have to be clear about exactly what's important to your industry and the marketplace. The *critical success factors* (CSFs) are those capabilities and resources that absolutely have to be in place if you want your company to succeed over the long haul.

You may have already prepared a list of CSFs. (If you haven't, take a look at *Business Plans For Dummies*, published by Wiley.) Along with a CSF list, you need a set of your company's capabilities and resources. You can use the two lists to construct a grid, which in turn allows you to compare your capabilities and resources with those that your industry thinks are important. In a perfect world, the lists would be identical, but that's seldom the case. The completed grid helps you identify your company's current strengths and weaknesses (see Figure 5-2).

To complete a grid similar to the one in Figure 5-2, remember the following:

✔ The capabilities and resources that you place up and down the left side of the grid are in your industry's 'must have' category. They represent critical success factors.

✔ The capabilities and resources that you place in the top-left corner of the grid are critical success factors in which your company is good or excellent. They represent your company's strengths.

✔ The capabilities and resources that you place in the bottom-left corner of the grid are critical success factors in which your company is only fair or even poor. They represent your company's weaknesses.

Figure 5-2:
Compare
your capa-
bilities and
resources
with those
that are
thought to
be critical
success
factors
in your
industry.

It's easy to find some value in the capabilities that your company already excels in, and it's just as easy to underestimate the importance of things that your company doesn't do as well. Try to be as objective as you can here. It's hard to admit that you're devoting valuable resources to things that don't really matter, and it's equally hard to admit that you may be neglecting key business areas.

✔ Different people have different ideas about what your company's strengths and weaknesses really are.

✔ By combining different viewpoints, both inside and outside your company, you get a more balanced picture.

✔ Be sure to assess your capabilities and resources in every area, from management to marketing to R&D to delivery.

✔ Strengths are strengths only if your capabilities and resources line up with the critical success factors in your industry.

Analysing Your Situation in 3-D

You must be prepared to take advantage of your company's strengths and minimise your weaknesses, which means that you have to know how to recognise opportunities when they arise and prepare for threats before they overtake you. Timing is everything here, and it represents a third major dimension that you have to think about.

A glance at competitors

It's a good idea to create strengths-and-weaknesses grids for two or three of your most intense competitors. You won't know as much about your competitors as you know about yourself, of course, so the grids aren't going to be as complete as they may be about your own company. But what you *do* know is going to tell you a great deal.

Comparing the strengths and weaknesses of competitors with your own can help you see where competitive opportunities and threats to your business may come from. Opportunities often arise when your company has a strength that you can exploit in a critical area in which your competition is weak. And you can sometimes anticipate a threat when the situation is reversed – when a competitor takes advantage of a key strength by making a move in an area where you're not as strong. Because the competitive landscape is always changing, plan to monitor these grids on a regular basis.

Completing your SWOT analysis

A SWOT analysis (an analysis of your strengths, weaknesses, opportunities, and threats) allows you to construct a strategic balance sheet for your company. In the analysis, you bring together all the internal factors, including your company's strengths and weaknesses. You then weigh these factors against the external forces that you've identified, such as the opportunities and threats that your company faces due to competitive forces or trends in your business environment. How these factors balance out determines what your company should do and when you should do it. Follow these steps to complete the SWOT analysis grid:

1. **Divide all the strengths that you've identified into two groups, based on whether they're associated with potential opportunities in your industry or with latent threats.**

2. **Divide all the weaknesses the same way– one group associated with opportunities, the other with threats.**

3. **Construct a grid with four quadrants.**

4. **Place your company's strengths and weaknesses, paired with industry opportunities or threats, in one of the four boxes (see Figure 5-3).**

The SWOT analysis provides a bit of useful strategic guidance. Most of it is common sense. First, fix what's broken. Next, make the most of the business opportunities that you see out there. Only then do you have the luxury of tending to other business issues and areas. Be sure to address each of the following steps in your business plan:

1. **Eliminate any company weaknesses that you identify in areas in which you face serious threats from your competitors or unfavourable trends in a changing business environment.**

2. **Capitalise on any business opportunities that you discover where your company has real strengths.**

3. **Work on improving any weaknesses that you identify in areas that may contain potential business opportunities.**

4. **Monitor business areas in which you're strong today so that you won't be surprised by any latent threats that may appear.**

Figure 5-3:
The SWOT grid balances your company's internal strengths and weaknesses against external opportunites and threats.

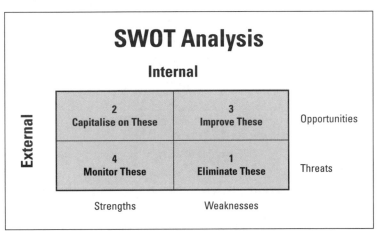

SWOT Analysis

Internal

	Strengths	Weaknesses	
External	**2** Capitalise on These	**3** Improve These	Opportunities
	4 Monitor These	**1** Eliminate These	Threats

Change is the only constant in your business, your industry, and your marketplace. Constant change means that you can't complete your SWOT analysis only one time; you have to revise the grid regularly as your company grows and as the environment around you changes. Think of your SWOT analysis as being a continuous process – something that you do repeatedly as an important part of your business-planning cycle.

✔ To identify potential opportunities and threats, take a close look at the strengths and weaknesses of your competitors.

✔ A SWOT grid places your strengths and weaknesses in the context of opportunities and threats, and thereby tells you what to do.

✔ The SWOT strategy is to eliminate weaknesses in areas where threats loom and also to capitalise on strengths in areas where you see opportunities.

Chapter 6

Researching Your Customers, Competitors, and Industry

*W*hat makes your product or service better or worse than that of your competitors? That question, and more like it, can help you tighten up your strategy, make more accurate sales projections, and decide what to emphasise (visually or verbally) in your marketing communications. A little research can go a long way toward improving the effectiveness of your marketing.

One per cent of companies do 90 per cent of all market research. Big businesses hire research firms to do extensive customer surveys and to run discussion groups with customers. The marketers then sit down to 50-page reports filled with tables and charts before making any decisions. We don't recommend this expensive approach, which can lead to analysis paralysis – where those that can afford to spend more time pouring over the mountains of data they have generated than they do on actually acting on it.

Instead, in this chapter, we help you adopt an inquisitive approach by sharing relatively simple and efficient ways of learning about customers, competitors and the environment. As a marketer, you need to challenge assumptions by asking the questions that lead to useful answers – something you can do on any budget. In the end, not only will you know what you need to know about your customers and competitors, but you'll also better understand your own business.

Why Research Matters – And What to Focus On

Many large companies do so much research, in part, to cover the marketer's you-know-what if the marketing campaign subsequently fails, and more than half of all market research expenditure really just builds the case for pursuing strategies the marketers planned to do anyway. These marketers use research in the same way a drunk uses a lamppost – for support rather than illumination. Other business people refuse to research anything at all because they know the answers already, or think they do. Gut instinct will only get them so far before the ideas, customers, or both run out.

Doing research to cover your derriere or to bolster your already-decided-upon plans is a waste of time and money spent doing endless surveys and focus groups. A *focus group* is a group of potential or actual customers who sit behind a one-way mirror discussing your product while a trained moderator guides their conversation and hidden video cameras immortalise their every gesture and phrase. Of course, you don't have to be so formal with your research techniques. You can always just ask your customers what they think of your product or service – it's not as impartial, but it may tell you everything you need to know without having to pay professional researchers.

So, what are good reasons to do research? Basically, if you can get a better idea or make a better decision after conducting market research, then research is worth your while. You should embrace research because it is the first step to making your company customer-orientated rather than product-orientated. In other words, asking what your customers want from your business is a better starting point than merely trying to sell them what you've already got – and makes for a more profitable business. If you can find out where your customers are, what they want, and how best to reach them, then you are on the right path to doing better business.

Research for better ideas

Information can stimulate the imagination, suggest fresh strategies, or help you recognise great business opportunities. So always keep one ear open for interesting, surprising, or inspiring facts. Don't spend much money on this kind of research. You don't need to buy in an expensive trendwatching service to keep a businesslike eye on new consumer developments that may affect your market. Instead, take subscriptions to a diverse range of publications and make a point of talking to people of all sorts, both in your industry and beyond it, to keep you in the flow of new ideas and facts. Also, ask other people for their ideas and interests.

Every marketer should carry an ideas notebook with them wherever they go and make a point of collecting a few contributions from people every day. This habit gets you asking salespeople, employees, customers, and complete strangers for their ideas and observations. You never know when a sugges-tion may prove valuable.

Research for better decisions

Do you have any situations that you want more information about before making a decision? Then take a moment to define the situation clearly and list the options you think are feasible. Choosing the most-effective advertis-ing medium, making a more accurate sales projection, or working out what new services your customers want – these situations provide examples of important decisions that research can help you make.

Suppose, for example, that you want to choose between print ads in industry magazines and e-mail advertisements to purchased lists. Figure 6-1 shows what your notes may look like.

Research for your strengths and weaknesses

Perception is everything. What customers think of your product or service is ultimately what determines the success of your business, which is why you should make a habit of asking them, on a regular basis, what they love and what they hate about it.

So how do you find out what customers think? By asking customers to rank you on a list of descriptors for your business/product/service. The scale ranges from 1 to 10 (to get a good spread), with the following labels:

1	2	3	4	5	6	7	8	9	10
Very bad		Bad		Average			Good		Very good

Decision	Information Needs	Possible Sources	Findings
Choose between print ads in industry magazines and e-mail advertisements to purchased lists	How many actual prospects can print ads reach?	Magazines' ad salespeople can tell us.	Three leading magazines in our industry reach 90 per cent of good customers, but half of these are not in our geographic region. May not be worth it?
	What are the comparable costs per prospect reached through these different methods?	Just need to get the budget numbers and number of people reached and divide available money by number of people.	E-mail is a third of the price in our market.
	Can we find out what the average response rates are for both magazine ads and e-mails?	Nobody is willing to tell us, or they don't know. May try calling a friend in a big ad agency; they may have done a study or something.	Friend says response rates vary wildly, and she thinks the most important thing is how relevant the customer finds the ad, not the medium used.
	Have any of our competitors switched from print to e-mail successfully?	Can probably get distributors to tell us this. Will call several and quiz them.	No, but some companies in similar industries have done this successfully.

Conclusions?

Seems like we'll spend less and be more targeted if we design special e-mails and send them only to prospects in our region. Don't buy magazine ad space for now; we can experiment with e-mail, instead. But we need to make sure the ads we send are relevant and seem important, or people just delete them without reading them.

Figure 6-1:
Analysing the information needs of a decision.

If you collect a rating of all the descriptive features of your product from customers, many of those ratings will prove quite ordinary. Consider the type of responses you'd get for a bank branch. The list of items to rate in a bank may include current accounts, savings accounts, speed of service, and friendliness of banking staff, along with many other things you'd need to put on the list in order to describe the bank, in detail. You're likely to discover that some items, like current accounts and saving accounts, get average ratings. The reason is that every bank offers those and, in general, handles such accounts in the same way. But a few of the features of a particular bank may be notably exceptional – for better or for worse.

Notable negatives, such as long queues at lunchtime when people rush out to do their banking, stand out in customers' minds. They remember those lines and tell others about them. Long queues at lunchtime may lead customers to switch banks and drive away other potential customers through bad word of mouth. Similarly, notable customer service sticks in customers' minds, too. If that same branch has very friendly staff and express queues for more simple transactions during busy periods, this notable warmth and efficiency can build loyalty and encourage current customers to recruit new customers through word of mouth.

With this information, you know what things your customers think you do brilliantly and what features you need to do some work on. You can now improve on the worst-on-the-list features to make them average, at least, and emphasise the high-rated items by talking them up in marketing and investing even more in them to maximise their attractiveness.

Here are a few tips to keep in mind as you gather customer ratings:

✔ Draw a graph of all the features of your product, rated from negative to neutral to positive. A graph will give you a visual image of how your customers perceive your business's strengths and weaknesses. You'll find that most features cluster in the middle of the resulting bell curve, failing to differentiate you from the competition. A few features stick out on the left as notably negative, other features, hopefully, stand out on the right as notably positive.

✔ Offer customers a reward for filling in a survey sheet (that's how important survey sheets are). You can offer a free prize draw from the returned survey sheets, a reduction on current fees, or a discount on future products. Whichever option you choose, let your customers know that their views matter to you – that in itself can improve your customer service scores.

✔ If you want to get fancy, you can also ask some customers to rate the importance of each item on the list to them, personally. If you're lucky, your brilliant areas are important to them and your bad areas aren't.

Planning Your Research

Start research with a careful analysis of the decisions you must make. For example, say you're in charge of a two-year-old software product that small businesses use to manage their invoicing. As the product manager, what key decisions should you be making? The following are the most likely:

- Should we launch an upgrade or keep selling the current version?
- Is our current marketing plan sufficiently effective, or should we redesign it?
- Is the product positioned properly, or do we need to change its image?

So before you do any research, you need to think hard about those decisions. Specifically, you need to

- Decide what realistic options you have for each decision.
- Assess your level of uncertainty and risk for each decision.

Then, for any uncertain or risky decisions, you need to pose questions whose answers can help you reduce the risk and uncertainty. And now, with these questions in hand, you're ready to begin your research!

When you work through this thinking process, you often find that you don't actually need research. For example, maybe your boss has already decided to invest in an upgrade of the software product you manage, so researching the decision has no point. Right or wrong, you can't realistically change that decision. But some questions make it through the screening process and turn out to be good candidates for research. For these research points, you need to pose a series of questions that have the potential to reduce your decision-making uncertainty or to reveal new and exciting options for you as a decision-maker.

Take the question, 'Is the product positioned properly, or do we need to change its image?' To find out whether repositioning your product makes sense, you may ask how people currently perceive the product's quality and performance, how they view the product compared with the leading competitor's, and what the product's personality is. If you know the answers to all these questions, you're far better able to make a good decision.

You must start by defining your marketing decisions very carefully. Until you know what decisions you must make, market research has little point. See Figure 6-2 for a flowchart of the research process.

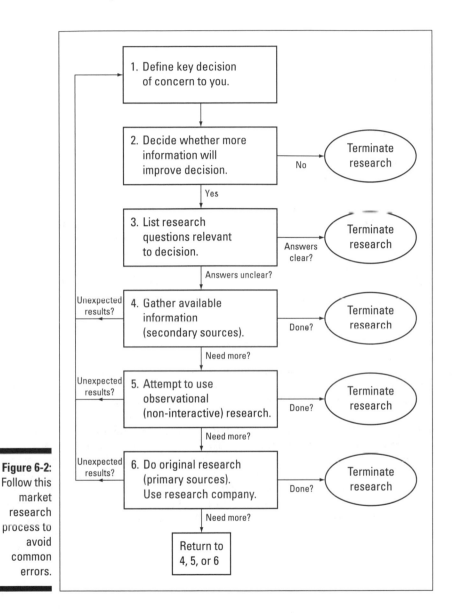

Figure 6-2: Follow this market research process to avoid common errors.

Carrying Out Primary Research

Primary research gathers data from people by observing them to see how they behave or by asking them for verbal or written answers to questions.

You can, and should, ask your customers all the time whether they are happy with the service they get from your company, but taking some time out to question your assumptions about how customers view your product or service can yield some of the most valuable insights.

Observing customers

Going 'back to the floor' has become something of a phenomenon of modern business. The experiences of a senior manager who is thrown back into the thick of things can make hilarious viewing – but how and why did they become so disengaged from the basics of their business in the first place? Getting and staying close to your customers, as well as the front-line staff who deal with them every day, is one of the most valuable ways to spend your time.

Consumers are all around you – shopping for, buying, and using products. Observing consumers, and finding something new and of value from doing so, is not hard. And even *business-to-business marketers* (who sell to other businesses instead of end-consumers) can find plenty of evidence about their customers at a glance. The number and direction of a company's lorries on various roads can tell you where their business is heaviest and lightest, for example. Despite all the opportunities to observe, most marketers are guilty of Sherlock Holmes's accusation that 'You have not observed, and yet you have seen.' Observation is the most underrated of all research methods.

Find a way to observe one of your customers as she uses one of your products. Professional research firms can provide a location for customers to come and use your products, or can even put their people into the homes of willing customers. We want you to observe, not just watch. Bring along a pad and pencil, and take care to notice the little things. What does the customer do, in what order, and how long does she spend doing it? What does she say, if anything? Does she look happy? Frustrated? Disinterested? Does anything go wrong? Does anything go right – is she surprised with how well the product performs? Take detailed notes and then think about them. We guarantee that you end up gaining at least one insight into how to improve your product.

Asking questions

Survey research methods are the bread and butter of the market research industry, and for a good reason. You can often gain something of value just by asking people what they think. If your product makes customers happy, those customers come back. If not, adios. And because recruiting new customers costs on average ten times as much as retaining existing ones, you can't afford to lose any. You need to measure and set goals for customer satisfaction.

The survey methods do have their shortcomings. Customers don't always know what they think or how they behave – and even when they do, getting them to tell you can be quite costly. Nonetheless, every marketer finds good uses for survey research on occasion.

Measuring customer satisfaction

Try to design a customer satisfaction measure that portrays your company or product in a realistic light. You can measure customer satisfaction with survey questionnaires or with the rate of customer complaints; the best measures combine multiple sources of data into an overall index.

Your customer satisfaction has to be high, relative to both customer expectations and competitors' ratings, before it has much of an effect on customer retention rates. So make sure that you ask tough questions to find out whether you're below or above customers' current standards. To gauge customer satisfaction, ask your customers revealing questions, similar to the following list:

1. **Which company (or product) is the best at present?**

   (Give a long list with instructions to circle one, and give a final choice, labelled Other, where respondents can write in their own answer.)

2. **Rate [your product] compared with its competitors:**

   Far worse   Same   Far better

   1   2   3   4   5   6   7

3. **Rate [your product] compared with your expectations for it:**

   Far worse   Same   Far better

   1   2   3   4   5   6   7

You can get helpful customer responses by breaking down customer satisfaction into its contributing elements. (Focus groups or informal chats with customers can help you come up with your list of contributing elements.) For example, you can ask the following questions about a courier company:

1. **Rate Flash Deliveries compared with its competitors on speed of delivery:**

   Far worse   Same   Far better

   1   2   3   4   5   6   7

2. Rate Flash Deliveries compared with its competitors on reliability:

Far worse   Same   Far better

1   2   3   4   5   6   7

3. Rate Flash Deliveries compared with its competitors on ease of use:

Far worse   Same   Far better

1   2   3   4   5   6   7

4. Rate Flash Deliveries compared with its competitors on friendliness:

Far worse   Same   Far better

1   2   3   4   5   6   7

You can find useful guidelines on how to design a questionnaire on the Web site of the Market Research Society (www.mrs.org.uk), under Frequently Asked Questions. The site also includes advice on how to select a research agency and lists sources of free statistical and demographic information.

Customer satisfaction changes with each new interaction between customer and product. Keeping up with customer opinion is a never-ending race, and you must make sure that you're measuring where you stand relative to those shifting customer expectations and competitor performances.

Traps to avoid

As you conduct a customer survey, avoid these all-too-common traps which can render your research practically useless:

- **Make sure your survey (or surveyor, for that matter) doesn't fluff up customer satisfaction to conceal problems.** In bigger companies, we sometimes see people pressurising customers to give them good ratings because it helps their own prospects. I (Craig) recently bought car insurance over the phone from an enthusiastic salesperson who unashamedly asked me to give her a high rating on a survey so that she could win the monthly customer service bonus – ten out of ten for effort, but probably not what the company had in mind when it set up the survey. Design your customer service measure to find areas of the business you can improve, which means asking questions that expose any weak spots. The more 'honest' your questions are, the more meaningful the responses will be.

- **Watch out for over-general questions or ratings.** Any measure based on a survey that asks customers to 'rate your overall satisfaction with our company on a 1-to-10 scale' isn't much use. What does an average score of 8.76 mean? This number seems high, but are customers satisfied? You didn't really ask customers this question – and even worse, you didn't ask them if they're more satisfied with you than they used to be or if they're less satisfied with competitors than with you. Ask a series of more specific questions, such as 'was it convenient and easy to do business with us?'

✔ **Don't lose sight of the end goal – customer satisfaction.** You may need to find out about a lot of other issues in order to design your marketing plan or diagnose a problem. None of what you find out matters, however, unless it boils down to increased customer satisfaction in the long run. Whatever else you decide to research, make sure you keep one eye on customer satisfaction: It's the ultimate test of whether your marketing is working!

Using the answers

When you have gathered the data, make sure that it gets put to good use, rather than becoming a pile of questionnaires gathering dust in the corner. So which parts of the information you have amassed should you include as an action point in your next marketing plan?

Even the most rudimentary piece of research can throw up a range of different, and sometimes contradictory, findings. One customer may think the most important thing is for you to lower your prices, another may be prepared to pay more for greater staff expertise. You probably can't achieve both of these goals at the same time. Here are a couple of strategies that can help you focus your response:

✔ **Your own instinct should allow you to sort the good research results from the bad.** This doesn't mean you should ignore what you don't want to hear, but it does mean you shouldn't unquestioningly react to everything the research tells you. When Sony asked people whether they would like a portable device so they could listen to music on the move, the company found there was no demand. They went ahead and launched the Walkman anyway, because they felt they had a great product innovation. You shouldn't believe the expression 'the customer is always right' but one that you can heed when doing any research is 'they don't know what they don't know'.

✔ **Concentrate on just one of the strengths and one of the weaknesses.** If you have a quality that's unique in your market in a meaningful way, then you need to exploit it to the full. If you have a real problem that may drive valuable customers away, it needs to be put right fast.

✔ **Pay attention to your most valuable customers.** You can't please all of the people all of the time, so don't try. One of the hidden benefits of observing and asking questions of customers is that it can help distinguish your most valuable customers from those you would be better off without (yes, they really do exist). By looking at survey responses, you will soon be able to spot ideas and customers that generate additional value, and those that simply want more for less. Surveys help you to establish priorities for your business that will keep profitable customers loyal.

The life cycle of any piece of research should last no longer than your next marketing plan – any longer and the market or competition will have moved anyway.

A Dozen Ideas for Low-Cost Research

You don't have to spend thousands of pounds researching ideas for a new ad campaign (or anything else). Instead, focus on ways of gaining insight or checking your assumptions using free and inexpensive research methods. But how can you do useful research without a lot of time, money, and staff to waste? This section shares a dozen ideas (plus an extra one for free) to get you off on the right foot.

Watching what your competitors do

When you compare your marketing approach to your competitors', you easily find out what customers like best. Make a list of the things that your competitors do differently to you. Does one of them price higher? Does another one give away free samples? Do some of them offer money-back guarantees? How and where do they advertise? Make a list of at least five points of difference. Now ask ten of your best customers to review this list and tell you what they prefer – your way or one of the alternatives. Keep a tally. And ask them why. You may find that all your customers vote in favour of doing something different to the way you do it now.

Creating a customer profile

Take photographs of people you think of as your typical customers. Post these pictures on a bulletin board and add any facts or information you can think of to create profiles of your 'virtual' customers. Whenever you aren't sure what to do about any marketing decision, you can sit down in front of the bulletin board and use it to help you tune into your customers and what they do and don't like. For example, make sure the art and wording you use in a letter or ad is appropriate to the customers on your board. Will these customers like it, or is the style wrong for them?

Entertaining customers to get their input

Invite good customers to a lunch or dinner, or hold a Customer Appreciation event. Entertaining your customers puts you in contact with them in a relaxed setting where they're happy to chat and share their views. Use these occasions to ask them for suggestions and reactions. Bounce a new product idea off of these customers or find out what features they'd most like to see improved. Your customers can provide an expert panel for your informal research, and you just have to provide the food!

Using e-mail for single-question surveys

If you market to businesses, you probably have e-mail addresses for many of your customers. Try e-mailing 20 or more of these customers for a quick opinion on a question. Result? Instant survey! If a clear majority of these customers say they prefer using a corporate credit card to being invoiced because the card is more convenient, well, you've just gained a useful research result that may help you revise your approach.

Watching people use your product

Be nosey. Find ways to observe people as they shop for and consume your product or service. What do they do? What do they like? What, if anything, goes wrong? What do they dislike? You can gain insight into what your consumers care about, how they feel, and what they like by observing them in action. Being a marketing voyeur provides you with a useful and interesting way to do research – at no charge. And if you're in a retail business, be (or ask someone else to be) a *secret shopper* by going in and acting like an ordinary customer to see how you're treated.

Establishing a trend report

E-mail salespeople, distributors, customer service staff, repair staff, or willing customers once a month, asking them for a quick list of any important trends they see in the market. You flatter people by letting them know that you value their opinion, and e-mail makes giving that opinion especially easy for them.

A trend report gives you a quick indication of a change in buying patterns, a new competitive move or threat, and any other changes that your marketing may need to respond to. Print out and file these reports from the field and go back over them every now and then for a long-term view of the effectiveness of your marketing strategies, too.

Researching your strengths

Perhaps the most important element of any marketing plan or strategy is clearly recognising what makes you especially good and appealing to customers. To research the strengths that set you apart from the competition, find the simplest way to ask ten good customers this simple but powerful question: 'What is the best thing about our [fill in the name of your product or service], from your perspective?' (Or you can do the more detailed survey we describe in the 'Research for your strengths and weaknesses' section earlier in this chapter.)

The answers to this question usually focus on one or, at most, a few features or aspects of your business. Finding out how your customers identify your strengths proves a great help to your marketing strategy. After you know what you do best, you can focus on telling the story about that best whenever you advertise, do publicity, or communicate with your market in any way. Investing in your strengths (versus your competitors' strengths or your weaknesses) tends to grow your sales and profits most quickly and efficiently.

Analysing customer records

Most marketers fail to mine their own databases for all the useful information those databases may contain. A good way to tap into this free data (because you already own it!) is to study your own customers with the goal of identifying three common traits that make them different or special.

A computer shop I'm (Craig) a customer of went through their records and realised that its customers are

- More likely to be self-employed or entrepreneurs than the average person
- More sophisticated users of computers than most people
- Big spenders who care more about quality and service than the absolute cheapest price

This store revised its marketing goal to find more people who share these three qualities. What qualities do your customers have that make them special, and that would make a good profile for you to use in pursuing more customers like them?

Surveying your own customers

You can gather input from your own customers in a variety of easy ways because your customers interact with your employees or firm. You can put a stamped postcard in shipments, statements, product packages, or other communications with your customers. Include three or fewer simple, non-biased survey questions, such as, 'Are you satisfied with this purchase? no = 1 2 3 4 5 – yes.' Also leave a few lines for comments, in case the customers have something they want to tell you. You generally get low response rates with any such effort, but that's okay. If someone has something to tell you, they let you hear about it, particularly when it's negative. And even a 5 per cent response gives you a steady stream of input you wouldn't otherwise have.

Testing your marketing materials

Whether you're looking at a letter, Web page, press release, or ad, you can improve that material's effectiveness by asking for reviews from a few customers, distributors, or others with knowledge of your business. Do they like the material? Do they like it a lot? If the responses are only lukewarm, then you know you need to edit or improve the material before spending the money to publish and distribute it. Customer reviewers can tell you quickly whether you have real attention-getting wow-power in any marketing communication.

Big companies do elaborate, expensive tests of ads' readability and pulling power, but you can get a pretty good idea for much less money. Just ask a handful of people to review a new marketing material while it's still in draft form.

Interviewing defectors

You can find out far more from an angry customer than you can from ten happy ones. If you have a customer on the phone who wants to complain, then look on it as an opportunity, not a call to be avoided. If you can find out what went wrong and fix it, that customer may well become one of your greatest advocates.

You can easily overlook another gold mine – company records of past customers. Work out what types of customer defect, when, and why. If you can't pinpoint why a customer abandoned ship, try to make contact and ask them directly.

Tracking these lost customers down and getting them on the phone or setting up an appointment may prove difficult. Don't give up! Your lost customers hold the key to a valuable piece of information: What you do wrong that can drive customers away. Talk to enough of these lost customers and you may see a pattern emerge. Probably three-quarters of them left you for the same reason (which can be pricing, poor service, inconvenient hours, and so on – that's for you to find out).

Plug that hole and you lose fewer customers down it. And keeping those customers means you don't have to waste valuable marketing resources replacing them. You can keep the old customers and grow every time you add a new one.

Asking your kids

Seriously! Your children, or any kids on hand that you can get to think about your market for a few minutes, probably have a unique and more contemporary view than you. Ask them simple questions like 'What will the next big thing be in [name your product or service here]?' 'What's cool and what's not this year?' Kids know, and you don't. In any consumer marketing, you need to make sure that you're cool and your competitors aren't. Because kids lead the trends in modern society, why not ask them what those trends are? Even in business-to-business and industrial markets, kids and their sense of what's happening in society can be helpful – often giving you early indicators of shifts in demand that may have an impact all the way up the line, from consumers to the businesses that ultimately serve them.

Finding Free Data

Whatever aspect of marketing you are looking at there is further information available to you – and it won't cost you a penny. Some of that data can give you just what you need to get started on your research project. So before you buy a report or hire a research firm, dig around for some free (or at least cheap) stuff.

There is a world of free data out there, if you know where to look. Also keep in mind that free data generally falls into a category known as *secondary data* – meaning already collected or published by someone else – so you get it second hand. This data is not specific to your company and your competitors can easily access it, too.

Getting info off the Web

Throughout this book, we include numerous Web sites, as these are the quickest and easiest places to find free information. For instance, the Interactive Advertising Bureau (IAB) has more data on how many customers are connected to the Internet and who shop online than we can include here. Look out for these Web site references, but more importantly remember that Internet search engines, such as Google, make finding free data simple – and the more you use them, the easier it is to filter out all the sites you're not interested in.

Hooking up with a librarian

If you don't want to do the search yourself, you can get a professional to search for you, and it will hardly cost you a penny (well, maybe a few pounds). Libraries are an undervalued national treasure, and librarians are trained to archive information as well as know how to access it. Your local library is a good starting place, but you can also get a wealth of market information from university libraries and specialist business libraries.

You can find a lot of what you might need, including industry guides, through the British Library (www.bl.uk/welcome/business.html). You can make enquiries by phone: 020 7412 7454, or by e-mail: business-information@bl.uk.

Tapping into government resources

Often, the best source of free information is national and local government. Many governments collect copious data on economic activity, population size, and trends within their borders. In the UK, the Office of National Statistics (ONS) is the best general source of data on a wide range of demographic and economic topics.

We're always amazed at the sheer range and quantity of information available on the ONS site, and we're sure you will be too. Of course, we don't know whether you need to know the state of North Sea fish stocks, but if you do, then this is the right place! Described as the 'home of official UK statistics', you can access National Statistics Online at www.statistics.gov.uk.

A lot of the data on the UK population is based on the Census. Although the Census only takes place every ten years, you'll find it's very detailed and, usefully, you can break the data down by neighbourhood. The statistics on inflation and prices, consumer spending, business investment – in fact, anything financial – is more up to date, usually to the last full quarter.

Getting media data

If you're doing any advertising, ask the magazine, newspaper, Web site, or radio station you buy advertising from to give you information about their customer base – snippets about the people exposed to your ads. This information can help you make sure you reach an appropriate audience. You can also use the exposure numbers to calculate the effectiveness of your advertising.

If you've yet to decide where to advertise, or even in which media, then there are some useful media sites you can visit that will give you the numbers on how many and what kind of consumers each title or station will deliver. You can trust these sources, because in most cases they were set up and are supported by the media owners operating in that area to provide an independent verification of sales and audience profiles so that advertisers can see what they're getting – and hopefully buy more. That's why most of the data, for occasional users like you, is free.

The Audit Bureau of Circulations, or ABC as it's more commonly known (www.abc.org), has data on magazines, national and local newspapers, exhibition visitors, and Web sites. You can find out how many people are reading the title, where they live, and what type of consumers they are; for business-to-business magazines, you can find out what sector they work in and what their job titles are. Most of the different media have organisations that provide data like this: For TV it's BARB (www.barb.co.uk), for radio it's RAJAR (www.rajar.co.uk), for outdoor media such as posters it's POSTAR (www.postar.co.uk).

Book II
Money in Mind

'It used to be called "The Economic Miracle" in the boom days.'

In this book . . .

Getting a solid financial footing is important to any business. Without this, you will never really be sure how well (or badly) you're doing. This book looks at the most straightforward ways of running the money side of your business – and don't worry, you won't need to be a mathematical wizard to make sense of the chapters included here.

Here are the contents of Book II at a glance:

Chapter 1: Finding the Money

Chapter 2: Figuring Out Financials

Chapter 3: Cash Flows and the Cash Flow Statement

Chapter 4: Forecasting and Budgeting

Chapter 1

Finding the Money

. . . .

. . . .

Setting up a business requires money – there is no getting away from that. You have bills such as rent to pay, materials and equipment to purchase, and all before any income is received. Starting a business on the road to success involves ensuring that you have sufficient money to survive until the point where income continually exceeds expenditure.

Raising this initial money and the subsequent financial management of the business is therefore vital, and great care should be taken over it. Unfortunately, more businesses fail due to lack of sufficient day-to-day cash and financial management than for any other reason. This chapter helps you avoid common pitfalls and helps you find the right type of money for your business.

Assessing How Much Money You Need

You should work out from the outset how much money you will need to get your business off the ground. If your proposed venture needs more cash than you feel comfortable either putting up yourself or raising from others, then the sooner you know the better. Then you can start to revise your plans. The steps that lead to an accurate estimate of your financial needs start with the sales forecast, which you do as part of feasibility testing, detailed in *Starting a Business For Dummies* (Wiley), along with advice on estimating costs for initial expenditures such as retail or production space, equipment, staff, and so on.

Forecasting cash flow is the most reliable way to estimate the amount of money a business needs on a day-to-day basis.

Do's and don'ts for making a cash flow forecast:

- ✔ Do ensure your projections are believable. This means you need to show how your sales will be achieved.

- ✔ Do base projections on facts not conjecture.

- ✔ Do describe the main assumptions that underpin your projections.

- ✔ Do explain what the effect of these assumptions not happening to plan could be. For example, if your projections are based on recruiting three sales people by month three, what would happen if you could only find two suitable people by that date?

- ✔ Don't use data to support projections without saying where it came from.

- ✔ Don't forget to allow for seasonal factors. At certain times of the year most business are influenced by regular events. Sales of ice-cream are lower in winter than in summer, sales of toys peak in the lead up to Christmas, and business-to-business sales dip in the summer and Christmas holiday periods. So rather than taking your projected annual sales figure and dividing by twelve to get a monthly figure, you need to consider what effect seasonal factors might have.

- ✔ Don't ignore economic factors such as an expanding (or shrinking) economy, rising (or falling) interest rates and an unemployment rate that is so low that it may influence your ability to recruit at the wage rate you would like to pay.

- ✔ Don't make projections without showing the specific actions that will get those results.

- ✔ Don't forget to get someone else to check your figures out – you may be blind to your own mistakes but someone else is more likely to spot the mistakes/flaws in your projections.

Projecting receipts

Receipts from sales come in different ways, depending on the range of products and services on offer. And aside from money coming in from paying customers, the business owner may, and in many cases almost certainly will, put in cash of their own. However not all the money will necessarily go in at the outset; you could budget so that £10,000 goes in at the start, followed by sums of £5,000 in months four, seven, and ten respectively.

There could be other sources of outside finance, say from a bank or investor, but these are best left out at this stage. In fact the point of the cash flow projection, as well as showing how much money the business needs, is to reveal the likely shortfall after the owner has put in what they can to the business and the customers have paid up.

You should total up the projected receipts for each month and for the year as a whole. You would be well advised to carry out this process using a spreadsheet program, which will save you the problems caused by faulty maths.

A sale made in one month may not result in any cash coming into the business bank account until the following month, if you are reasonably lucky, or much later if you are not.

Estimating expenses

Some expenses, such as rent, rates, and vehicle and equipment leases, you pay monthly. Others bills such as telephone, utilities, and bank charges come in quarterly.

If you haven't yet had to pay utilities, for example, you put in your best guesstimate of how much you'll spend and when. Marketing, promotion, travel, subsistence, and stationery are good examples of expenses you may have to estimate. You know you will have costs in these areas, but they may not be all that accurate as projections.

After you've been trading for a while, you can get a much better handle on the true costs likely to be incurred.

Total up the payments for each month and for the year as a whole.

Working out the closing cash balances

This is crunch time, when the real sums reveal the amount of money your great new business needs to get it off the ground. Working through the cash flow projections allows you to see exactly how much cash you have in hand, or in the bank, at the end of each month, or how much cash you need to raise. This is the closing cash balance for the month. It is also the opening cash balance for the following month as that is the position you are carrying forward.

The accounting convention is to show payments out and negative sums in brackets, rather than with minus signs in front.

Testing your assumptions

There is little that disturbs a financier more than a firm that has to go back cap-in-hand for more finance too soon after raising money, especially if the reason should have been seen and allowed for at the outset.

So in making projections you have to be ready for likely pitfalls and be prepared for the unexpected events that will knock your cash flow off target. Forecasts and projections rarely go to plan, but the most common pitfalls can be anticipated and to some extent allowed for.

You can't really protect yourself against freak disasters or unforeseen delays, which can hit large and small businesses alike. But some events are more likely than others to affect your cash flow, and it is against these that you need to guard by careful planning. Not all of the events listed here may be relevant to your business, but some, perhaps many, will at some stage be factors that could push you off course.

Getting the numbers wrong

It's called estimating for a reason. You can't know ahead of time how the future will pan out, so you have to guess, and sometimes you guess wrong. Some of the wrong guesses you can make about stock and costs are:

- **A flawed estimate:** There is no doubt that forecasting sales is difficult. The numbers of things that can and will go awry are many and varied. In the first place the entire premise on which the forecast is based may be flawed. Estimating the number of people who may come into a restaurant as passing trade, who will order from a catalogue mailing, or what proportion of Internet site hits will turn into paying customers, depends on performance ratios. For example a direct mail shot to a well-targeted list could produce anything from 0.5–3 per cent response. If you build your sales forecast using the higher figure and actually achieve the lower figure then your sales income could be barely a sixth of the figure in your cash flow projection. You can't avoid this problem, but you can allow for it by testing to destruction (see elsewhere in this checklist).

- **Carrying too much stock:** If your sales projections are too high, you will experience the double whammy of having less cash coming in and more going out than shown in your forecast. That is because in all probability you will have bought in supplies to meet anticipated demand. Your suppliers offering discounts for bulk purchases may have exacerbated the situation if you took up their offers.

- **Missed or wrong cost:** You may underestimate or completely leave out certain costs due to your inexperience. Business insurance and legal expenses are two often missed items. Even where a cost is not missed altogether it may be understated. So, for example, if you are including the cost of taking out a patent in your financing plan, it is safer to take it from the supplier's Web site rather than from a friend who took out a patent a few years ago.

- ✔ **Testing to destruction:** Even events that have not been anticipated can be allowed for when estimating financing needs. 'What if' analysis using a cash flow spreadsheet will allow you to identify worst-case scenarios that could knock you off-course. After this you will end up with a realistic estimate of the financing requirements of the business or project.

- ✔ **Late deliveries:** If your suppliers deliver late, you may in turn find you have nothing to sell. Apart from causing ill will with your customers, you may have to wait weeks or months for another opportunity to supply. This problem can be minimised using online order tracking systems, if your suppliers have them, but some late deliveries will occur. Increasing your stocks is one way to insure against deficiencies in the supply chain, but that strategy too has an adverse impact on cash flow.

Settling on sales

Sales may be slow, pricing may be high – just two of the ways sales can make your projections look silly. More ways follow:

- ✔ **Slower than expected sales:** Even if your forecasting premise is right, or nearly so, customers may take longer to make up their minds than you expect. A forecast may include an assumption that people will order within two weeks of receiving your mail-order catalogue. But until you start trading you will not know how accurate that assumption is likely to be. Even if you have been in business for years, buying patterns may change.

- ✔ **Not being able to sell at list price:** Selling price is an important factor in estimating the amount of cash coming into a business and hence the amount of finance needed.

  Often the only way a new or small business can win certain customers is by matching a competitor's price. This may not be the price in your list, but it is the one you have to sell at.

  Also the mix of products or services you actually sell may be very different from your projection and this can affect average prices. For example a restaurant owner has to forecast what wines his or her customers will buy. If the house wine is too good, then more customers might go for that rather than the more expensive and more profitable wines on the list.

- ✔ **Suppliers won't give credit:** Few suppliers are keen to give small and particularly new businesses any credit. So before you build in 30, 60, or even 90 days' credit into your financial projections, you need to confirm that normal terms of trade will apply to what a supplier may view as an abnormal customer.

  You need to remember that whilst taking extended credit may help your cash flow in the short term, it could sour relationships in the long term. So in circumstances where a product is in short supply poor payers will be last on the list to get deliveries and the problems identified above may be further exacerbated.

Miscounting customers

Customers can confound your most well-thought-out projections. They pay late, they may rip you off, and they may not buy your goods as quickly as you'd like. Some of the ways customers can be to blame for throwing your estimates off are:

- **Paying slowly:** Whilst you set the terms and conditions under which you plan to do business, customers are a law unto themselves. If they can take extra credit they will. Unless you are in a cash-only business, you can expect a proportion of your customers to be late payers. Whilst with good systems you will keep this to an acceptable figure, you will never get every bill paid on time. You need to allow for this lag in your cash flow projections.

- **Bad debts:** Unfortunately late payers are not the only problem. Some customers never pay. Businesses fail each year and individuals go bankrupt, each leaving behind a trail of unpaid bills. You can take some steps to minimise this risk, but you can't eliminate the risk. You can try to get a feel for the rate of non-payment in your sector and allow for it in your plans. For example, the building and restaurant industries have a relatively high incidence of bad debts, whilst business services have a lower rate.

- **Fraud and theft:** Retailers claim they could knock 5 per cent off everything they sell if they could eliminate theft. But despite their best endeavours with security guards and cameras, theft continues.

- **Repeat orders take longer to come in than expected:** It is hard to know exactly what a customer's demand for your product or service is. The initial order may last them months, weeks, or days. For strategic reasons they may want to divide up their business between a number of suppliers. If, for example, they have three suppliers and they order a month's worth at a time, it may be some time before they order from you again. If your customer sales are sluggish or seasonal, then that timeframe could extend further still. So even delighted customers may not come back for quite some time.

Reviewing Your Financing Options

Knowing how much money you need to get your business successfully started is an important first step, but it is only that: a first step. There are many sources of funds available to small firms. However not all are equally appropriate to all firms at all times. These different sources of finance carry very different obligations, responsibilities, and opportunities. The differences have to be understood to allow an informed choice.

Most small firms confine their financial strategy to long-term or short-term bank loans, viewing other financing methods as either too complex or too risky. In many respects the reverse is true. Almost every finance source other than banks shares some of the risks of doing business with you to a greater or lesser extent.

The great attraction of borrowing from a bank lies in the speed of the transaction. Most small businesses operate without a business plan so most events that require additional funds, such as sudden expansion or contraction, come as a surprise, either welcome or unwelcome, and with a sense of urgency. Basing financing choices on the fact that you need the money quickly may lead to more difficulties in the long run.

Deciding between debt capital and equity capital

At one end of the financing spectrum lie shareholders – either individual *business angels* who put their own money into a business, or corporate organisations such as *venture capital providers* – who provide equity capital which is used to buy a stake in a business. These investors share all the risks and vagaries of the business alongside you and expect a proportionate share in the rewards if things go well. They are less concerned with a stream of dividends, which is just as well as few small companies ever pay them, and instead hope for a radical increase in the value of their investment. They expect to realise this value from other investors who want to take their places for the next stage in the firm's growth cycle, rather than from any repayment by the founder. Investors in new or small businesses don't look for the security of buildings or other assets to underpin their investment. Rather they look to the founder's vision and the core management team's ability to deliver results.

At the other end of the financing spectrum are debt financiers – banks that try hard to take no risk and expect some return on their money irrespective of your business's performance. They want interest payments on money lent, usually from day one. Whilst they too hope the management is competent, they are more interested in making sure either you or the business has some type of asset such as a house that they can grab if things go wrong. At the end of the day, and that day can be sooner than the borrower expects, a bank wants all its money back, with interest. Think of bankers as people who help you turn part of an illiquid asset such as property into a more liquid asset such as cash – for a price.

Understanding the differences between lenders, who provide debt capital, and investors, who provide equity, or share, capital is central to a sound grasp of financial management.

In between the extremes of shareholders and the banks lie a myriad of other financing vehicles, which have a mixture of lending or investing criteria. You need to keep your business finances under constant review, choosing the most appropriate mix of funds for the risks you plan to take and the economic climate ahead. The more risky and volatile the road ahead, the more likely it is that taking a higher proportion of equity capital will be appropriate. In times of stability and low interest, higher borrowings may be more acceptable.

As a general rule, debt and equity should be used in equal amounts to finance a business. If the road ahead looks more risky than usual go for £2 of equity to every £1 of debt.

If your business sector is generally viewed as very risky, and perhaps the most reliable measure of that risk is the proportion of firms that go bust, then financing the business almost exclusively with borrowings is tantamount to gambling.

Debt has to be serviced whatever your business performance, so it follows that, in any risky, volatile marketplace, you stand a good chance of being caught out one day.

If your business risks are low, the chances are that profits are relatively low too. High profits and low risks always attract a flood of competitors, reducing your profits to levels that ultimately reflect the riskiness of your business sector. As venture capitalists and shareholders generally are looking for much better returns than they could get by lending the money, it follows they will be disappointed in their investment on low-risk, low-return business. So if they are wise they will not get involved in the first place, or if they do they will not put any more money in later.

Examining your own finances

Obviously the first place to start looking for money to finance your business is in your own pockets. Whilst you may not have much in ready cash you may have assets that can be turned into cash or used to support borrowing.

Start by totalling your assets and liabilities. The chances are that your most valuable assets are your house, your car, and any life assurance or pension policies you may have. Your liabilities are the debts you owe. The difference between your assets and liabilities, assuming you have more of the former than the latter, is your 'net worth'. That in effect is the maximum security you can offer anyone outside the business that you want to raise money from.

Now the big questions are: what is your appetite for risk and how certain are you your business will be successful? The more of your own money you can put into your business at the outset, the more you will be truly running your own business in your own way. The more outside money you have to raise, the more power and perhaps value you have to share with others.

Now you have a simple piece of arithmetic to do. How much money do you need to finance your business start-up, as shown in your worst-case scenario cash flow forecast? How much of your own money are you willing and able to put into your business? The difference is the sum you are looking to outside financiers to back you with.

If that sum is more than your net worth, then you will be looking for investors. If it is less then bankers may be the right people to approach.

If you do have free cash or assets that you could but won't put into your business, then you should ask yourself if the proposition is worth pursuing. You can be absolutely certain that any outsider you approach for money will ask you to put up or shut up.

Another factor to consider in reviewing your own finances is your ongoing expenses. You have to live whilst getting your business up and running. So food, heat, and a roof over your head are essential expenses. But perhaps a two-week long-haul summer holiday, the second car, and membership of a health club are not essentials. Great whilst you were a hired hand and had a pay cheque each month, but an expendable luxury once you are working for yourself.

Determining the Best Source of Finance for You

Choosing which external source of finance to use is to some extent a matter of personal preference. One of your tasks in managing your business's financial affairs is to keep good lines of communication open with as many sources as possible.

The other key task is to consider which is the most appropriate source for your particular requirement at any one time. The main issues you need to consider are explored in the following sections.

Considering the costs

Clearly if a large proportion of the funds you need to start your business are going to be consumed in actually raising the money itself, then your set-up costs are going to be very high. Raising capital, especially if the amounts are relatively small (under £500,000) is generally quite expensive. You have to pay your lawyers and accountants, and those of your investor or lender, to prepare the agreements and to conduct the due diligence examination (the business appraisal). It is not unusual to spend between 10 and 15 per cent of the first £500,000 you raise on set-up costs.

An overdraft or factoring agreement is relatively cheap to set up, usually a couple of per cent or so. However, long-term loans, leasing, and hire-purchase agreements could involve some legal costs.

Sharing ownership and control

The source of your money helps determine how much ownership and control you have to give up in return. Venture capitalists generally want a large share of stock and often a large say in how the business is run. At the other end of the spectrum are providers of long-term loans who generally leave you alone so long as you service the interest and repay the capital as agreed. You have to strike the balance that works best for you and your business.

If you do not want to share the ownership of your business with outsiders then clearly raising equity capital is not a good idea. Even if you recognise that owning 100 per cent of a small venture is not as attractive as owning 40 per cent of a business ten times as large it may not be the right moment to sell any of your shares. Particularly if, in common with many business founders, long-term capital gain is one of your principal goals. If you can hold onto your shares until profits are reasonably high you will realise more gain for every share sold than if you sell out in the early years or whilst profits are low.

Parting with shares inevitably involves some loss of control. Letting 5 per cent go may just be a mild irritation from time to time. However once 25 per cent has gone, outsiders could have a fair amount of say in how things are run. At that point, even relatively small groups of shareholders could find it easy to call an Extraordinary General Meeting and put it to a vote to remove you from the board. Nevertheless, whilst you have over 51 per cent you are in control, if only just. Once past the 51 per cent things could get a little dangerous. Theoretically you could be out voted at any stage. Some capital providers take a hands-on approach and will have a view on how you should run the business.

Beating the clock

Overdrafts can be arranged in days, raising venture capital can take months. Very different amounts of scarce management time are needed, dependent on the financing route taken. So if speed matters, your funding options may be limited.

Venture capital providers (also called Venture Capitalists or VCs) have been known to string out negotiations long enough to see if the bullish forecasts made in the business plan come to pass. After all, venture capital is there to help businesses to grow faster than they might otherwise do not just to keep them afloat. Don't expect a decision from a venture capital firm in under three months whatever their brochure says. Four to six months is a more realistic timescale and nine months is not too unusual.

Business Angels can usually make investment decisions much more quickly than VCs, after all it's their money they are risking. Weeks rather than months, is the timescale here.

Banks finance is usually a fairly speedy process. Even large loans of £100,000 and upwards can be arranged in a few weeks. But the speed depends more on how much collateral you have to give the bank manager comfort that his money is safe.

Staying flexible

As your plans change, the amount of money you actually need may alter during negotiations. Some sources of funds such as leasing, hire-purchase agreements, and long-term loans dictate the amount that has to be agreed at the outset. If you're selling shares in the company, you have some fluidity during negotiations, and if you're arranging overdrafts it is possible to draw down only what you need at any one time, with the upper limit negotiated usually each year.

Once you have investigated and used a source of funds you may want to be able to use that source again as your plans unfold. Loans and hire purchase/ leasing agreements are for a specific sum and it can be difficult and expensive going back to the same source for more. Many venture capitalists, for example, already have a full weighting of investments in your business sector and so may not be anxious to invest more, however successful your firm. So that might mean starting all over again with another venture capital firm.

It may pay to make sure that at least some of your financing comes from a source such as factoring, which gives you total flexibility to change the amount of money drawn down to mirror the amount needed at any one time – both upwards and downwards.

Adding value to the business

With some sources of finance you can get useful expertise as well as money. For example, with factoring you could get expertise in managing your home and overseas credit, which could result in better credit control, fewer bad debts, and less capital tied up in debtors. You could even close or reduce your credit control department. With new share capital you may get a director with relevant experience in the industry. While the director's principal task is to ensure the capital provides interest, you also get the benefit of his or her knowledge.

Gaining security and certainty

For most sources of money, if you comply with the agreed-upon terms, the future is reasonably predictable – in so far as that money is concerned. The exception to this rule is an overdraft. An overdraft is technically, and often actually, repayable on demand. Overdrafts are sometimes called in at the moment you need them most.

Limiting personal liability

As a general rule most providers of long-term loans and overdrafts look to you and other owners to provide additional security if the business assets are in any way inadequate. You may be asked to provide a personal guarantee – an asset such as your house. Only when you raise new share capital, by selling more stock in your company, do you escape increasing your personal liability. Even with the new share capital you may be asked to provide warranties to assure new investors that everything in the company's past history has been declared.

Going for Debt

You can explore borrowing from a number of possible sources in your search for outside finance. It is worth giving them all a once over, but it has to be said that most people start and stop at a bank. The other major first source of money is family and friends, but many business starters feel nervous about putting family money at risk and in any event would rather deal with professional financiers. *Credit Unions* and *mezzanine finance* are relatively unusual sources of finance for a start-up, but finding any money to start a business is a tough task, so no source should be completely overlooked. (These terms are explained later in this chapter.)

Borrowing from banks

Banks are the principal, and frequently the only, source of finance for nine out of every ten new and small businesses.

Banks are usually a good starting point for almost any type of debt financing. They are also able to provide many other cash flow and asset backed financing products, although they are often not the only or the most appropriate provider. As well as the main clearing banks, a number of the former building societies and smaller regional banks are competing hard for small firm lending.

Book II

Money in Mind

Seeing the five Cs

Bankers like to speak of the five Cs of credit analysis, factors they look at when they evaluate a loan request. When applying to a bank for a loan, be prepared to address the following points:

✔ **Character:** Bankers lend money to borrowers who appear honest and who have a good credit history. Before you apply for a loan, it makes sense to obtain a copy of your credit report and clean up any problems.

✔ **Capacity:** This is a prediction of the borrower's ability to repay the loan. For a new business, bankers look at the business plan. For an existing business, bankers consider financial statements and industry trends.

✔ **Collateral:** Bankers generally want a borrower to pledge an asset that can be sold to pay off the loan if the borrower lacks funds.

✔ **Capital:** Bankers scrutinise a borrower's net worth, the amount by which assets exceed debts.

✔ **Conditions**: Whether bankers give a loan can be influenced by the current economic climate as well as by the amount requested.

Banks also use CAMPARI, which stand for: Character, Ability, Means, Amount, Repayment, Interest and Insurance. You can find out more about this alternate system on the banking liaison group website: `www.bankexperts.co.uk/campari.htm`.

All the major clearing banks offer telephone banking and Internet services to their small business customers or are in the process of doing so. Branch location seems less likely to be a significant factor to bank customers in the future, so you no longer have to confine your search for a bank to those with a branch nearby.

Bankers, and indeed any other sources of debt capital, are looking for property, land, insurance policies, or any other investments you may have to back their loan and the near certainty of getting their money back. They also charge an interest rate that reflects current market conditions and their view of the risk level of the proposal.

If you import raw materials, the bank can provide you with Letters of Credit, which guarantees your suppliers payment from the bank when they present proof of satisfactory delivery. If you have a number of overseas suppliers who prefer settlement in their own currency for which you will need foreign currency, cheque facilities or buying forward, banks can make the necessary arrangements.

Running an overdraft

The principal form of short-term bank funding is an *overdraft*. An overdraft is permission for you to use some of the bank's money when you don't have enough of your own. The permission is usually agreed annually, but can be withdrawn at anytime. A little over a quarter of all bank finance for small firms is in the form of an overdraft. The overdraft was originally designed to cover the time between having to pay for raw materials to manufacture finished goods and selling those goods. The size of an overdraft will usually be limited to a modest proportion of the amount of money owed to you by your customers and the value of your finished goods stock. The bank will see those items as assets, which in the last resort can be used to get their money back.

Starting out in a cleaning business, for example, you need sufficient funds initially to buy the mop and bucket. Three months into the contract they will have been paid for and so there is no point in getting a five-year bank loan to cover this, as within a year you will have cash in the bank.

However if your overdraft does not get out of the red at any stage during the year then you need to re-examine your financing. All too often companies utilise an overdraft to acquire long-term assets, and that overdraft never seems to disappear, eventually constraining the business.

The attraction of overdrafts is that they are very easy to arrange and take little time to set up. That is also their inherent weakness. The keywords in the arrangement document are 'repayable on demand', which leaves the bank free to make and change the rules as they see fit. With other forms of borrowing, as long as you stick to the terms and conditions, the loan is yours for the duration. Not so with overdrafts.

Taking on a term loan

If you are starting up a manufacturing business, you will be buying machinery to last probably five years, designing your logo and buying stationery, paying the deposit on leasehold premises, buying a vehicle, and investing funds in winning a long-term contract. As the profits on this are expected to flow over a number of years, then they need to be financed over a similarly long period of time, either through a bank loan or inviting someone to invest in shares in the company – in other words a long-term commitment.

Term loans, as these long-term borrowings are generally known, are funds provided by a bank for a number of years. The interest can be either variable – changing with general interest rates – or it can be fixed for a number of years ahead. In some cases it may be possible to move between having a fixed interest rate and a variable one at certain intervals. It may even be possible to have a moratorium on interest payments for a short period, to give the business some breathing space. Provided the conditions of the loan are met in such matters as repayment, interest and security cover, the money is available for the period of the loan. Unlike having an overdraft, the bank cannot pull the rug from under you if their circumstances (or the local manager) change.

Going with a loan guarantee

These are operated by banks at the instigation of governments in the UK, and in Australia, the US, and elsewhere. These schemes guarantee loans from banks and other financial institutions for small businesses with viable business proposals, which have tried and failed to obtain a conventional loan because of a lack of security.

Loans are available for periods of up to ten years on sums up to £250,000. The government guarantees 75 per cent of the loan. In return for the guarantee the borrower pays a premium of 2 per cent per year on the outstanding amount of the loan. The commercial aspects of the loan are matters between the borrower and the lender.

Uniting with a credit union

If you don't like the terms on offer from the *high street banks,* as the major banks are often known, you may consider forming your own bank. It's not as crazy an idea as it sounds. Credit unions formed by groups of small business people, both in business and aspiring to start up, have been around for decades in the US, UK, and elsewhere. They have been an attractive option for people on low incomes, providing a cheap and convenient alternative to banks. Some self-employed people such as taxi drivers have also formed credit unions. They can then apply for loans to meet unexpected capital expenditure either for repairs, refurbishments, or technical upgrading.

Established credit unions will usually require you to be in a particular trade, have paid money in for a number of months or perhaps years and have a maximum loan amount limited to the types of assets people in their trade are most likely to need.

Certainly, few could argue about the attractiveness of an annual interest rate 30 per cent below that of the high-street lenders, which is what credit unions aim for. Members have to save regularly to qualify for a loan, though there is no minimum deposit and, after ten weeks, members with a good track record can borrow up to five times their savings, though they must continue to save while repaying the loan. There is no set interest rate, but dividends are distributed to members from any surplus, usually about 5 per cent a year. This too compares favourably with bank interest on deposit accounts.

Borrowing from family and friends

Those close to you are often willing to lend you money or invest in your business. This helps you avoid the problem of pleading your case to outsiders and enduring extra paperwork and bureaucratic delays. Help from friends, relatives, and business associates can be especially valuable if you've been through bankruptcy or had other credit problems that make borrowing from a commercial lender difficult or impossible.

Involving friends and family in your business brings a range of extra potential benefits, costs, and risks that are not a feature of most other types of finance. You need to decide if these are acceptable.

Some advantages of borrowing money from people you know well are that you may be charged a lower interest rate, may be able to delay paying back money until you're more established, and may be given more flexibility if you get into a jam. But once the loan terms are agreed to, you have the same legal obligations as you would with a bank or any other source of finance.

Borrowing money from relatives and friends can have a major disadvantage. If your business does poorly and those close to you end up losing money, you may well damage your personal relationships. So in dealing with friends, relatives, and business associates be extra careful not only to establish clearly the terms of the deal and put them in writing but also to make an extra effort to explain the risks. In short, it's your job to make sure your helpful friend or relative won't suffer true hardship if you're unable to meet your financial commitments.

When raising money from family and friends, follow these guidelines:

1. Do agree proper terms for the loan or investment.

2. Do put the agreement in writing and if it involves a limited partnership, share transaction, or guarantee have a legal agreement drawn up.

3. Do make an extra effort to explain the risks of the business and the possible downside implications to their money.

4. Do make sure when raising money from parents that other siblings are compensated in some way, perhaps via a will.

5. Do make sure you want to run a family business before raising money from them. It will not be the same as running your own business.

6. Don't borrow from people on fixed incomes.

7. Don't borrow from people who can't afford to lose their investment.

8. Don't make the possible rewards sound more attractive than you would say to a bank.

9. Don't offer jobs in your business to anyone providing money unless they are the best person for the job.

10. Don't change the normal pattern of social contact with family and friends after they have put up the money.

Book II

Money in Mind

Managing mezzanine money

Mezzanine finance (also known as subordinated debt) is a form of debt where the lender takes on more risk than a bank would normally be up for. Mezzanine finance providers accept the fact that they will only get their money back after bank overdraft and loans and the like have been paid back. But in return they expect a higher rate of interest and they may ask for an option to convert some of that debt into shares in the company at a certain point. By doing that they can get a slice of the upside if your business is a roaring success.

The benefit of mezzanine finance is that it often bridges the gap between the funds provided by a bank and the high-risk investment by you, a venture capitalist, and business angels.

Mezzanine finance can now also be considered a stand-alone funding solution, often as an alternative to more expensive equity finance. Mezzanine is now commonly used to provide acquisition finance, development capital, and replacement capital, as well as finance for the more traditional management buy-out, buy-in scenarios.

Sources of mezzanine finance include many of the clearing banks and insurance companies, as well as specialist finance boutiques. With larger transactions it is possible to access the capital markets using an investment bank to achieve public offerings of high yield or 'junk' bonds. These are typically sold to institutional investors such as insurance companies and pension funds.

The amount and cost of funds under a mezzanine arrangement will depend on many factors including industry sector, historic performance, credit ratings, seasonality, and predictability of revenues and forecasts for future cash flow and profitability, as well as the strength of management, the nature of a company's financial backers and the structure of the overall financing package.

It is usual for mezzanine finance to be provided on an interest-only basis until some or all of general bank debt has been repaid, typically after four to five years, with typical loan terms ranging up to ten years. Loans are usually secured with a second charge on a company's assets such as property, plant, and equipment.

Sharing Out the Spoils

If your business is particularly risky, requires a lot of up-front finance, or involves new technology, then you usually have to consider selling a portion of your business's shares to outside investors.

However, if your business plan does not show profit returns in excess of 30 per cent compound and you are not prepared to part with upwards of 15 per cent of your business, then equity finance is probably not for you.

A number of different types of investor could be prepared to put up the funds if the returns are mouth-watering enough. We talk about each type in the following sections.

Going for venture capital

Venture capital is a means of financing the start-up, development, expansion, or the purchase of a company. The venture capitalist acquires a share of the company in return for providing the requisite funding. Venture capital firms often work in conjunction with other providers of finance in putting together a total funding package for a business.

Venture capital providers (*VCs*) invest other people's money, often from pension funds. They are likely to be interested in investing a large sum of money for a large stake in the company.

Venture capital is a medium- to long-term investment, of not just money, but of time and effort. The venture capital firm's aim is to enable growth companies to develop into the major businesses of tomorrow. Before investing, a venture capital provider goes through *due diligence*, a process that involves a thorough examination of both the business and its owners. Accountants and lawyers subject you and your business plan to detailed scrutiny. You and your directors are required to warrant that you have provided *all* relevant information, under pain of financial penalties.

In general VCs expect their investment to pay off within seven years. But they are hardened realists. Two in every ten investments they make are total write offs, and six perform averagely well at best. So the one star in every ten investments they make has to cover a lot of duds. VCs have a target rate of return of 30 per cent plus, to cover this poor success rate.

Raising venture capital is not a cheap option. The arrangement costs will almost always run to six figures. The cost of the due diligence process is borne by the firm raising the money, but will be paid out of the money raised, if that's any consolation. Raising venture capital is not quick either. Six months is not unusual and over a year has been known. Every VC has a deal done in six weeks in their portfolio, but that truly is the exception.

Venture capital providers want to exit from their investment at some stage. Their preferred route is via a public offering, taking your company onto the stock market, but a trade sale to another, usually larger business in a related line of work, is more usual.

New venture capital funds are coming on stream all the time and they too are looking for a gap in the market.

The British Venture Capital Association (www.bvca.co.uk) and the European Venture Capital Association (www.evca.com) both have online directories giving details of hundreds of venture capital providers.

Benefiting by business angels

One source of equity or risk capital is a private individual, with their own funds, and perhaps some knowledge of your type of business, who is willing to invest in your company in return for a share in the business.

Such investors have been christened *business angels,* a term first coined to describe private wealthy individuals who backed theatrical productions, usually a play on Broadway or in London's West End.

By their very nature such investments are highly speculative in nature. The angel typically has a personal interest in the venture and may want to play some role in the company – often an angel is determined upon some involvement beyond merely signing a cheque.

Business angels are informal suppliers of risk capital to new and growing businesses, often taking a hand at the stage when no one else will take the chance; a sort of investor of last resort. But whilst they often lose their shirts, they sometimes make serious money. One angel who backed Sage with £10,000 in their first round of £250,000 financing, saw his stake rise to £40 million.

These angels often have their own agenda and frequently operate through managed networks. Angel networks operate throughout the world, in some cases on the Internet. In the UK and the US there are hundreds of networks with tens of thousands of business angels prepared to put up several billion pounds each year into new or small businesses.

One estimate is that the UK has approximately 18,000 business angels and that they annually invest in the region of £500 million.

Business Direct in Association with *Th e Daily Telegraph* (www.business-direct.uk.com), Business Link for London (www.bl4london.com), and National Business Angels Network (www.nationalbusangels.co.uk) all have online directories of business angels.

Research has unravelled these sketchy facts about business angels as a breed. Knowing them may help you find the right one for your business:

- Business angels are generally self-made, high net-worth individuals, with entrepreneurial backgrounds. Most are in the 45–65 year age group; 19 per cent are millionaires; and at least 95 per cent are men.

- Fifty per cent of angels conduct minimal or no research on the business in question, meet their entrepreneur an average of 5.4 times before investing (compared with venture capitalists who meet on average 9.5 times), and 54 per cent neglected to take up independent personal references compared to only 6 per cent of venture capitalists. Angels fundamentally back people rather than propositions and venture capitalists do the reverse.

- Typically business angels invest between £10,000 and £250,000 in start-up business ventures; most initial investments are less than £75,000. Their motivation is, first and foremost, financial gain through capital appreciation, with the fun and enjoyment of being involved with an entrepreneurial business an important secondary motive. A minority are motivated in part by altruistic considerations, such as helping the next generation of entrepreneurs to get started, and supporting their country or state.

✔ Business angels invest in only a very small proportion of investments that they see: typically at least seven out of eight opportunities are rejected. More than 90 per cent of investment opportunities are rejected at the initial screening stage.

✔ Around 30 per cent of investments by business angels are in technology-based businesses. Most will tell you that they vigorously avoid investing in industries they know nothing about.

✔ The majority of business angels invest in businesses located in close proximity to where they live – two-thirds of investments are made in businesses located within 100 miles of their home or office. They are, however, prepared to look further afield if they have specific sector-related investment preferences or if they are technology investors.

✔ Ninety-two per cent of angels had worked in a small firm compared, for example, with only 52 per cent of venture capitalists who had similar experience.

✔ On average, business angels sell their shareholding in the most successful investments after four years (and 75 per cent after seven years). Conversely, half of the investments in which business angels lost money had failed within two years of the investment being made.

✔ Business angels are up to five times more likely to invest in start-ups and early stage investments than venture capital providers in general.

Looking to corporate venturing

Alongside the venture capital firms are 200 or so other businesses who have a hand in the risk capital business, without it necessarily being their main line of business. For the most part these are firms with an interest in the Internet or high technology that want an inside track to new developments. Their own research and development operations have slowed down and become less and less entrepreneurial as they have gotten bigger. So they need to look outside for new inspiration.

Even successful firms invest hundreds of millions of dollars each year in scores of other small businesses. Sometimes, if the company looks a particularly good fit, they buy the whole business.

Finding Free Money

Sometimes, if you're very lucky or very smart – or both – you can get at least some of the money you need for free. The following sections tell you how to cash in on government grants and how winning a contest can earn you lots of lovely loot.

Getting help from the government

Unlike debt, which has to be repaid, or equity, which has to earn a return for the investors, grants and awards from the government or the European Union are often not refundable. So, although they are frequently hard to get, they can be particularly valuable.

In the UK, if you are involved in the development of a new technology then you may be eligible for a Government grant for Research and Development. Under this scheme, a grant of up to £20,000 is available on micro projects by businesses with fewer than 10 employees; up to £75,000 can be claimed on research projects by businesses with fewer than 50 employees; up to £200,000 on development projects by businesses with fewer than 250 employees; and up to £500,000 on exceptional development projects. Business Link can give full details.

Support for business comes in a very wide variety of forms. The most obvious is the direct (cash) grant but other forms of assistance are also numerous. The main types of grant also include *soft loans* – money lent on terms more advantageous than would usually be available from a bank – additional share capital, free or subsidised consultancy, which could help you with market research, staff development or identifying business opportunities, or with access to valuable resources such as research facilities.

Though several grant schemes operate across the whole of the UK and are available to all businesses that satisfy the outline criteria, there are a myriad of schemes that are administered locally. Thus the location of your business can be absolutely crucial, and funding may be strongly dependent on the area into which you intend to grow or develop. Additionally, there may well be additional grants available to a business investing in or into an area of social deprivation, particularly if it involves sustainable job creation.

The assistance provided for enterprise is limited so you will be competing for grants against other applicants. You can enhance your chances of success by following these seven rules:

1. **Keep yourself informed about which grants are available.**

   Grants are constantly being introduced (and withdrawn), but there is no system that lets you know automatically. You have to keep yourself informed.

   Business Link (`www.businesslink.org`), the Department of Trade and Industry (`www.dti.gov.uk`), Funders online (`www.fundersonline.org`), and Grants On-line (`www.co-financing.co.uk`) are all websites that can help you find out about grants.

2. **Do not start the project for which you want a grant before you make the application.**

   The awarding body will almost certainly take the view that if you can start the project without a grant you must have sufficient funds to complete it without assistance. Much better to show that your project is dependent on the grant being made.

3. **Talk to the awarding body before you apply.**

   Make contact with an individual responsible for administering the scheme. You will be given advice on whether it is worthwhile your applying before you start spending time and effort on making the application; you may get some help and advice on completing the application form; you may get an insight into how you should shape your application.

4. **Make sure your application is in respect of a project.**

   Usually, grants are given for specific projects, not for the normal organic growth of a business. If, for example, you need new equipment to launch a product, make sure your application emphasises the project, not the equipment. State the advantages of the project's success (for example, it will safeguard or create jobs) and explain that the purchase of the equipment is a prerequisite for that success.

5. **Get your application in early.**

   The chances of a successful application are always highest just after a scheme is launched. That is when there is the most money in the pot, and it's also the time when those administering the scheme are keenest to get applications in and grants awarded. Competition is likely to be less fierce.

6. **Make your application match the awarding body's objectives.**

   The benefits of your project should fit in with the objectives of the awarding body and the grant scheme itself. So if the grant is intended to help the country in the form of potential exports, for example, make sure your application details your exports.

Book II

Money in Mind

Most grant applications require the submission of a business plan, so make sure you have an up to date one.

7. **Make sure you have matching funds available.**

It is unusual for a grant to finance 100 per cent of the costs of any project. Typically nowadays a grant will contribute 15–50 per cent of the total finance required. Those making the decision about the grant are spending public money. They have a duty to ensure it is spent wisely and they will need to be absolutely convinced that you have, or can raise from other sources, the balance required.

Winning money

If you enjoy publicity and like a challenge then you could look out for a business competition to enter. Like government grants, business competitions are ubiquitous and, like national lotteries, they are something of a hit or miss affair. But one thing is certain. If you don't enter you can't win.

There are more than 100 annual awards in the UK alone, aimed at new or small businesses. For the most part, these are sponsored by banks, the major accountancy bodies, chambers of commerce, local or national newspapers, business magazines, and the trade press. Government departments may also have their own competitions as a means of promoting their initiatives for exporting, innovation, job creation, and so forth.

The nature and the amount of the awards change from year to year, as do the sponsors. But looking out in the national and local press, particularly the small business sections of *The Times*, *Daily Telegraph*, *Daily Mail*, and *The Guardian*, should put you in touch with a competition organiser quickly, as will an Internet search. Money awards constitute 40 per cent of the main competition prizes. For the most part, these cash sums are less than £5,000. However, a few do exceed £10,000 and at least one UK award is for £50,000. Other awards are for equally valuable goods and services, such as consultancy or accountancy advice, training, and computer hardware and software.

Chapter 2

Figuring Out Financials

· ·

· ·

*F*inancial statements tell the bank a great deal about you, and the bank learns even more by taking numbers from the statements and calculating a load of ratios. The bank totals your monthly loan payments and divides that number by your monthly income, for example, and then compares this ratio with the average for other borrowers. The result gives the bank a relatively good measure of your ability to repay the loan. Taken together, the statements and ratios create a financial portrait that the bank uses to get to know you better. And the better the bank knows you, the more reliable its decision is.

In this chapter, we introduce the basic financial statements and ratios that are widely used in business planning – which really are the same ones that paint a picture of your personal finances. First, we show you how a profit and loss account and a balance sheet are put together. Next, we explain cash-flow statements, which do pretty much what the name implies. Finally, we explore simple financial ratios that you can use to evaluate your business.

Understanding a Profit and Loss Account

A *profit and loss account* presents the proverbial bottom line. By adding all the revenue that you receive from selling goods or services and then subtracting the total cost of operating your company, the profit and loss account shows *net profit* – how much money the company has made or lost over a given period. Here's how to think of net profit:

Net profit = Revenue – Cost

The important thing to remember is the fact that the profit and loss account captures a simple idea. No matter what your accountants call it – a profit and loss account, earnings report, or statement of profit and loss – or how complicated accounting types make it look, it still uses the same basic principle of subtracting cost from revenue to come up with profit.

Your profit and loss account should cover a period that makes the most sense for your business planning: monthly, quarterly, or yearly. (The tax people, of course, are always interested in seeing your profit and loss account once a year.) You get a better financial picture of your company and where it's going if you look at profit and loss accounts over several periods and even over several years. In Chapter 4 you develop a pro-forma profit and loss account – a forecast of your profits based on projected revenue and costs.

Look at the various parts of a profit and loss account for Global Gizmos Company (see Figure 2-1). Notice that Global Gizmos includes a two-year comparison to show how revenue, costs, and profits have changed over time. Global Gizmos is a small company; if you want to make it a big company, add three zeros after all the numbers. In either case, the profit and loss account works exactly the same way.

Profit and Loss at a Glance

Global Gizmos Company

Figure 2-1: The profit and loss account starts with gross revenue and then subtracts the costs of various business activities to arrive at different kinds of profit.

PROFIT AND LOSS ACCOUNT AS OF DECEMBER 31

	This Year	Last Year
1 ▷ Gross Revenue on Sales	£ 810,000	£ 750,000
2 ▷ Cost of goods sold	-560,000	-520,000
Gross Profit	250,000	230,000
3 ▷ Sales, general, and administration	-140,000	-140,000
Depreciation expense	-30,000	- 25,000
Operating Profit	80,000	65,000
4 ▷ Dividend and interest income	+ 3,000	+ 2,000
Interest expense	- 13,000	- 14,000
Profit Before Taxes	70,000	53,000
5 ▷ Taxes	- 20,000	- 18,000
NET PROFIT FOR YEAR	**£ 50,000**	**£ 35,000**

Revenue

Revenue refers to all the money that a company receives as a result of being in business. The most important source of revenue (usually, the sale of goods or services) always appears as the first item in the income statement – in the case of Global Gizmos, gross revenue on sales. In this context, *gross* doesn't mean anything unpleasant; it indicates that the revenue is a total, without costs subtracted. Revenue from sources other than sales usually shows up a bit later in the profit and loss account.

Gross revenue on sales

Gross revenue on sales is based on the number of units actually sold during a particular period multiplied by the prices actually paid. Global Gizmos sold 32,400 widgets at a price of £25 each, for a gross revenue of £810,000. Things can be a little more complicated than this example, of course; your company may have several products or kinds of service, or your prices may change over time. Maybe you have to make an allowance for items that are returned. All these considerations contribute to your own calculation of gross revenue on sales.

Dividend and interest income

Your company may have sources of revenue besides sales – the income from savings accounts and other securities, for example. Because you must have money to operate the company anyway, you probably want that money to make money while it's sitting around. You should keep this investment income separate from your revenue on sales, however, so that you always know how much money the company itself is generating. In your profit and loss account your dividends and interest income should appear separately from your other revenue.

Costs

Unfortunately, you have to spend money to make money. The cost of doing business usually is divided into general categories that reflect the separate activities that a company is involved in and the different kinds of expenses that it incurs. Major cost categories include cost of goods sold, sales and administrative expenses, depreciation, interest expense – and don't forget taxes. Each item deserves its own entry in the profit and loss account.

Cost of goods sold

The *cost of goods sold* (COGS) combines all the direct costs of putting together your product or service. Raw materials, supplies, and the labour involved in assembling a product are all part of the COGS; so are the electricity, water, and gas used in manufacturing, as well as the costs of maintaining production facilities. If you offer dog-walking for pet owners, for example, the costs associated with delivering that service – leads and pooper scoopers – go into the COGS.

You may have to make a judgement call here and there about what is or isn't part of the COGS. Just remember to be consistent over time.

Sales, general, and administration

Sales, general, and administration expenses (SG&A) combine all the costs associated with supporting your product or service. If the company is just you, a telephone, and a tiny rented office above the hardware shop, the costs won't amount to much. But for larger companies, these costs seem to go on and on. SG&A includes salaries and overhead for the sales staff as well as the receptionist, secretary, and the boss. SG&A also includes advertising and promotion, travel, telephone calls, accounting fees, office supplies, dues and subscriptions, and everyone's favourite, miscellaneous expenses.

SG&A costs are tracked separately because they're not tied directly to revenue and can easily get out of hand. Make sure that you keep an eye on this particular entry.

Depreciation expense

Depreciation expense is a standard way to spread both the cost and the usefulness of expensive items out over time. Whether it's a building, a truck, or a computer, almost any durable item that your company buys slowly declines in value, because of simple wear and tear or because new technology makes the item obsolete. Bean-counters have come up with various ways to calculate that depreciation. All the methods allow you to allocate a portion of the purchase price as a business expense each year, to reflect a decrease in value. (Land, by the way, isn't included in depreciation expenses and can't be depreciated.)

Interest expense

Interest expense includes all the money that you pay out to the parties that loaned you funds to operate the company. You don't want to overlook this cost. You may have entered into agreements with banks or other investors, for example, and are obligated to pay back interest on a fixed schedule. An interest expense (often called a *fixed charge*) is isolated in the profit and loss account because it absolutely, positively has to be paid year after year.

Taxes

Even Albert Einstein stopped short of trying to figure his own taxes. But taxes are a fact of life and represent another cost of doing business. You can minimise your company's taxes by making sure that you keep careful track of all your other expenses.

Profit

Profit is the Holy Grail. When you do things right, the total costs flowing out of your business are less than all the revenue coming in. Your profit, of course, represents the difference. But it's useful to talk about different kinds of profit at various stages along the way. In particular, you can keep track of gross profit, operating profit, and profit before taxes, as well as your overall net profit. Comparing profit at different stages gives you a clearer picture of where your company is most efficient and where you could do better.

Gross profit

Gross profit measures how much money your company still has after you subtract all the direct costs of putting together your product or service (COGS) from the total revenue generated by sales. This profit doesn't include the many indirect expenses that you have in running the company or any revenue sources other than sales.

Operating profit

Operating profit accounts for all those additional sales, general, and administration (SG&A) costs that you incur as part of operating your business; it also subtracts the depreciation expense of your costly purchases. Operating profit reflects the money that you make from your overall business operations.

Profit before taxes

Profit before taxes takes everything else into account, including any financial transactions that you make. Your income from other sources (such as investment dividends and interest) is included here, as well as your interest payments to creditors.

Net profit

Net profit, of course, is the bottom line after the company's tax bite is subtracted. Global Gizmos made money in its most recent period.

> ✔ A profit and loss account begins with your revenue and subtracts all your costs to come up with net profit, usually for a year.
>
> ✔ Revenue includes all the money that you take in from sales, as well as income that you receive from dividends and interest.

✔ Your costs include the cost of goods sold; sales, general, and administrative expenses; depreciation; interest expense; and taxes.

✔ By calculating profit at various stages – gross profit, operating profit, and profit before taxes – you can see precisely where the money comes from and where it goes.

Interpreting the Balance Sheet

Whereas a profit and loss account captures the financial results of your operations for a given period, a *balance sheet* is more like a snapshot of your financial condition at a particular moment. The profit and loss account lists your revenue, your costs, and the profit that you make. The balance sheet, on the other hand, addresses what your company owns, what it owes, and what it's worth at a given moment. Ideally, the balance sheet tells you just how much money you'd have left over if you sold absolutely everything and then paid every last one of your debts.

The things that your company owns are called *assets* by the same people who look forward to audits and dream about accounting standards. The amounts that you owe make up your *liabilities*. The difference between the two represents the *equity* in your business. Think of equity in terms of the following equation:

Equity = assets – liabilities

You have to admit that the equation is simple. Unfortunately, our accounting friends have dreamed up another, less straightforward way of looking at this equation:

Assets = liabilities + equity

Go work that out. Anyway, the US balance sheet is based on this second equation.

A US balance sheet is always divided into two parts. One part deals with all the company's assets; the other part lists liabilities and equity. Because of the second equation, the two parts are always in balance, adding up to exactly the same amount. Although the two totals always match, the entries along the way say a great deal about the overall financial health of the company.

Just as the profit and loss account usually covers a full year, the balance sheet is often compiled for the last day of the year. Figure 2-2 shows Global Gizmos' balance sheet. In this case, figures are provided for two years, so that the reader (you or the accountant) can make a comparison between those years.

Balance Sheet at a Glance

Global Gizmos Company

BALANCE SHEET ON DECEMBER 31		
ASSETS	This Year	Last Year
Current Assets		
Cash	30,000	15,000
Investment portfolio	35,000	20,000
Debtors	135,000	150,000
Stock	115,000	120,000
Prepaid expenses	5,000	5,000
Total Current Assets	£ 320,000	£ 310,000
Fixed Assets		
Land	60,000	60,000
Buildings, equipment, machinery	355,000	315,000
Minus accumulated depreciation	-125,000	-95,000
Total Net Fixed Assets	£ 290,000	£ 280,000
Intangibles (goodwill, patents)	£ 5,000	£ 5,000
TOTAL ASSETS	**£ 615,000**	**£ 595,000**
LIABILITIES & OWNERS' EQUITY	This Year	Last Year
Current Liabilities		
Creditors	60,000	70,000
Accrued expenses payable	80,000	90,000
Total Current Liabilities	£ 140,000	£ 160,000
Long-term Liabilities	£ 90,000	£ 100,000
Owners' Equity		
Share capital	155,000	150,000
Reserves	230,000	185,000
Total Owners' Equity	£ 385,000	£ 335,000
TOTAL LIABILITIES & OWNERS' EQUITY	**£ 615,000**	**£ 595,000**

Markers on the left: 1, 2, 3, 4, 5, 6

Figure 2-2:
The US balance sheet.

Assets

Your company's *assets* include anything and everything you own that has any monetary value. When you think about your assets in terms of the balance sheet, all that you're concerned about is how much each asset is worth and how quickly it can be sold. So assets are separated into categories, depending on how *liquid* they are – how fast and easy it is to liquidate them, turning them into cold, hard cash. *Current assets* are those that you can dispose of within a year, if you have to, whereas *fixed assets* often take much longer to get rid of. *Intangibles* may never be converted to cash.

Current assets

Current assets represent your company's readily available reserves. As such, they're the assets that you draw on to fund your day-to-day business operations, as well as the assets that you may have to turn to in a financial emergency. Current assets include the following:

- **Cash.** You can't get any more liquid than cash, which is just what you expect it to be: notes and coins in the till, the petty-cash fund, and money on deposit in the bank.

- **Investment portfolio.** Investments are also usually liquid assets. Your investment portfolio includes savings accounts, short-term government bonds, and other safe securities that you invest in to watch your cash earn a bit of money while you wait to use it.

- **Debtors.** *Debtors* represent the money that customers owe you for goods and services that you've already delivered. Maybe you give customers 30, 60, or 90 days to pay. You want to keep tabs on this particular asset. You may end up reducing it by some percentage if you run into deadbeat customers who just won't pay up.

- **Stock.** The cash value of your stocks can be a bit tricky to calculate, but it should reflect the costs of the raw materials and supplies that you have on hand, as well as the value of partially finished products and products that are ready to be shipped.

- **Prepaid expenses.** If you pay any of your business expenses ahead of time, you should treat them as current assets. These expenses may include paid-up insurance premiums or retainers for unused accounting or advertising services.

Fixed assets

Fixed assets are fixed in the sense that they can't be readily converted to cash. These assets are the items that usually cost a great deal of money up front and are meant to last for several years – things like buildings, trucks, machines, and computers.

In the balance sheet, the value of a fixed asset is based on its original cost minus its accumulated depreciation over time, so the figure doesn't necessarily reflect the true market value of the asset or how much it may actually cost to replace it. Fixed assets can include the following:

- ✔ **Land.** The land that your company owns is listed separately in the balance sheet, because it doesn't depreciate over time; its value on the books remains the same from year to year.

- ✔ **Buildings, equipment, machinery.** This asset represents the original cost of all the expensive items that you've invested in to operate your company. The entry should include anything you purchase that's expected to last more than a year.

- ✔ **Minus accumulated depreciation.** Depreciation measures the decline in the useful value of an expensive item over time, so the original cost of all your fixed assets (excluding any land) is reduced by an amount equal to the total depreciation accumulated over the years. Notice that Global Gizmos shows accumulated depreciation increasing by £30,000 in its most recent year. Because its fixed assets are now worth £30,000 less on paper, Global Gizmos also takes a £30,000 depreciation expense in its profit and loss account (refer to number three in Figure 2-1).

Intangibles

Even though you can't polish any of these assets, intangibles can be extremely important to your company. *Intangibles* include such things as your rights to a manufacturing patent, a long-term contract, or an exclusive service franchise. Intangibles also cover something called goodwill. Although it's not at all obvious from the name, *goodwill* represents the extra money that you may spend for an asset above and beyond its fair market value – maybe because it's worth more to your company than to anybody else.

By definition, intangibles are hard to describe and difficult to put a real value on. Some companies don't even try. Instead, they place a nominal value of £1 on all their intangibles to indicate that although these assets exist, there's no way to measure what they're actually worth.

Liabilities and owners' equity

Your company's *liabilities* cover all the debts and obligations that you enter into while you run your company. In the same way that assets are divided up, your liabilities are separated into categories, based on how soon they are due. *Current liabilities* are those that have to be paid off within a year; *long-term liabilities* may stay on the books much longer. When these liabilities are subtracted from total assets, you're left with *owners' equity*, which is a measure of how much the company is actually worth.

Current liabilities

Current liabilities are the debts that your company has agreed to pay in the short term (say, within a year), so you have to be able to cover them from your current assets. What's left over (the difference between your current assets and current liabilities) is so important that it has a name: *working capital,* which is the chunk of money that you actually have to work with. Here are some standard liabilities:

- ✔ **Creditors.** *Creditors* represent the amounts that you owe your regular business creditors as part of your ongoing operations. At any given time, you may have accounts payable to all sorts of outside suppliers and service people, including the merchants, professionals, and even utility companies that you deal with every day.

- ✔ **Accrued expenses payable.** On any given day, your company also owes salaries and wages to its employees, interest on bank loans, and maybe insurance premiums – not to mention the taxes that you haven't sent in. To the extent that any of the obligations are unpaid on the date of the balance sheet, these liabilities are totalled as *accrued expenses payable*.

Long-term liabilities

Long-term liabilities usually represent large chunks of money that you're scheduled to pay back over several years. These liabilities are often at the centre of your company's financing. You may have issued bonds or a 'Director's Loan' to investors, for example, or you may have gone directly to the bank and secured a loan against your company's assets. In any case, you're probably using the money to invest in long-term growth of the company – acquiring new equipment, building a new manufacturing facility, developing additional products, or expanding into new markets.

Owners' equity

A company's owners come in various shapes and sizes. Their investments and equity in the company are arranged and distributed in all sorts of ways and can become incredibly complicated, especially if the company is a traded public limited company (plc). But don't be confused. All this complexity boils down to two major sources of equity: money and resources that flow in from outside the company, and profits that the owners keep and pump back into the company. Owners' equity can be any of the following:

- ✔ **Share capital.** The money that's invested in your company can take various forms, from the direct infusion of cash by inside owners who manage the business to the buying and selling of shares that represent small chunks of the company owned by outside investors. Share capital represents the total of all this money, no matter where it comes from or how it's described.

> ✔ **Retained earnings.** Your company makes a profit each year (at least, we hope it does), and you choose what to do with that excess cash. You can distribute it to the owners (that arrangement is where dividends come from) or keep part of it to reinvest in the company. If you put profits back into the company, it can grow. And if the company grows, you can increase the company's net worth and owners' equity (at least, we hope you do). *Retained earnings*, also known as reserves, represent the profits that you plough back into the company year after year.

Keep the following in mind when interpreting the balance sheet:

✔ A balance sheet is a snapshot of your financial condition at a particular moment usually, the end of the year.

✔ Your assets include everything that has monetary value, ranging from cash and investments to buildings and stocks.

✔ Liabilities include all the debts and financial obligations that you incur in running your company.

✔ Subtract liabilities from assets to calculate your equity in the business.

Book II

Money in Mind

Growing Up

Unless you are working in the United States, where the balance sheet is always set out in the straightforward and logical way we have used so far, you will have to enter the 'grown up' world of UK accountancy. Here, instead of keeping assets and liabilities apart, we jumble them up all over the place. Actually once you get used to the UK method its logic is appealing and it certainly makes analysing accounting data rather easier.

So far we have kept to this system as it is much simpler to explain, but we're afraid we always had to make that leap, so here goes.

Figure 2-3 sets out the same data as in Figure 2-2, for one year only, but follows the layout of the UK balance sheet. The conventions, concepts, rules, regulations, resulting ratios, in fact the whole thing, is exactly the same, its just that things are in a different order.

In this layout we start with the *fixed assets*, rather than liquid assets such as cash, and work our way down. After the fixed asset sum has been calculated we arrive at the residual unwritten down 'value' of those assets, tangible (land, buildings etc.), and intangible: in this case £295,000. We then work our way down the current assets in the reverse order of their ability to be turned into cash. Don't ask why it's done this way, it just is. Actually, it doesn't really matter a jot which order things come in as long as they are slotted into the right section of the balance sheet. The total of the current assets comes to £320,000.

Fixed assests	£s	£s	£s
Land	60,000		
Buildings, equipment, machinery	355,000		
Less accumulative depreciation	125,000		
Net book value		290,000	
Intangible (goodwill, patents)		5,000	
Total fixed assets			295,000
Current assets			
Pre-paid expenses	5,000		
Stock	115,000		
Debtors	135,000		
Investments	35,000		
Cash	30,000		
Total current assets		320,000	
Less current liabilities			
Creditors	60,000		
Accrued expenses payable	80,000		
Total current liabilities		140,000	
Net current assets			180,000
Total assets			475,000
Less creditors, amounts falling due in over one year			90,000
Net Total Assets			385,000
Financed by			
Share capital	155,000		
Reserves (retained earnings)	230,000		
Total owner's equity			385,000

Figure 2-3:
The UK balance sheet.

Next we get the *current liabilities*, which come to a total of £140,000, and take that away from the current asset total to come to a figure of £180,000. This is often referred to as the *working capital*, as it represents the money circulating through the business day to day.

By adding the *net current assets* (working capital) of £180,000 to the total fixed assets of £295,000 – bingo: we can see we have £475,000 tied up in net total assets. Deduct the money we owe long term, the creditors due over one year, a fancy way of describing bank and other debt other than overdraft, and we arrive at the net total assets. Net, by the way, is accountant-speak for deduction of one number from another, often adding a four-figure sum to the bill for doing so.

The net total assets figure of £385,000 bears an uncanny similarity to the total of the money put in by the owners of the business when they started out, £155,000, and the sum they have left in by way of profits undistributed over the years, £230,000. So the balance sheet balances, but at a very different total to that of the US balance sheet.

The UK balance figure is Shareholders Equity (= Assets – Liabilities)

The US balance figure is Assets (= Liabilities + Equity)

You will need to recognise both the UK and the US balance sheets, as chances are that some of the companies you compete with, buy from, won shares in, or perhaps plan to buy will be reporting using US balance sheets. Now you can see that the accounting processes, like the language, have much in common, but still have some pitfalls for the unwary.

Examining the Cash-flow Statement

If you know what your company is worth and how much it makes every year, can't you just relax and assume that your financial plan is in reasonably good order? After all, what else do you need to know?

As it turns out, you've got to keep close track of one other absolutely indispensable resource: cash. No matter how good things look on paper – no matter how bright the balance sheet and how rosy the income statement – you still need cash on hand to pay the bills. The fact that you've got assets and profits doesn't automatically mean that you have money in the bank. Cash can turn out to be much more important than income, profits, assets, and liabilities put together, especially in the early stages of your company.

The *cash-flow statement* monitors changes in your cash position over a set period. The top half of the statement tracks the flow of cash in and out of your company; the bottom half reports where the funds end up. Just like the balance sheet, the top and bottom halves of a cash-flow statement match. Given the importance of ready cash, you want to look at cash-flow statements on a regular basis – quarterly, monthly, or maybe even weekly.

Figure 2-4 shows a cash-flow statement for Global Gizmos Company. The cash-flow statement contains many of the same elements as a profit and loss account, but with a few critical adjustments.

Cash Flow at a Glance

Global Gizmos Company

CASH FLOW AS OF DECEMBER 31		
INFLOW AND OUTFLOW	This Year	Last Year
Funds Provided By:		
Gross receipts on sales	825,000	760,000
Dividend and interest income	3,000	2,000
Share capital	5,000	10,000
Total Funds In	£ 833,000	£ 772,000
Funds Used For:		
Cost of goods produced	555,000	515,000
Sales, general, and administration	160,000	150,000
Interest expense	13,000	14,000
Taxes	20,000	18,000
Buildings, equipment, machinery	40,000	50,000
Long-term debt reduction	10,000	5,000
Dividend distribution to owners	5,000	5,000
Total Funds Out	£ 803,000	£ 757,000
NET CHANGE IN CASH POSITION	£ 30,000	£ 15,000
CHANGES BY ACCOUNT	This Year	Last Year
Changes In Liquid Assets		
Cash	15,000	5,000
Investment portfolio	15,000	10,000
Total Changes	£ 30,000	£ 15,000
NET CHANGE IN CASH POSITION	£ 30,000	£ 15,000

Figure 2-4:
A cash-flow
statement
monitors
changes
in the
company's
cash
position
over time.

Cash in and cash out

The top half of the cash-flow statement deals with the inflow and outflow of
cash, tracking where your company gets funds and what you use those funds
for. Cash flow is a little more honest than a profit and loss account, because
the cash-flow statement shows money coming in only when you actually
deposit it and money going out only when you actually write a cheque.

Funds provided by

Where does all that money originate? Because the cash-flow statement reflects the actual receipt of cash, no matter where it comes from, the entries are a bit different from the revenue shown in a company's profit and loss account. These funds are usually made up of the following:

- **Gross receipts on sales.** This entry represents the total money that you take in on sales during the period. Gross receipts are based on your gross revenue, of course, but they also take into account when you actually receive payment. Global Gizmos, for example, received all of its £810,000 in gross revenue this year, plus £15,000 in debtors that the company was owed from last year, for a total of £825,000.

- **Dividend and interest income.** Your income from savings accounts and other securities is also reported in your profit and loss account. The amounts should be the same, as long as you actually receive the money during the period covered by the cash-flow statement.

- **Share capital.** The money invested in your company shows up as part of the owners' equity in your balance sheet. Invested capital doesn't represent revenue from your business operations, of course, so it never appears in the profit and loss account, but it can be a source of cash for the company. As Figure 2-4 shows, Global Gizmos received an additional £5,000 in invested capital this year.

Funds used for

Where does all the money go? The cash-flow statement keeps track of the costs and expenses that you incur for anything and everything. Some of the expenses appear in the profit and loss account; others don't, because they don't directly relate to your costs of doing business. These funds usually consist of the following:

- **Cost of goods produced.** This entry represents the total cost of producing your product or service during the period. The cost of goods produced often differs from the cost of goods sold shown in your profit and loss account, because the cost of goods sold also includes sales out of stock (items that your company has already produced and paid for) and doesn't include the cost of products that you add to stock. Global Gizmos, for example, reduced its overall inventory by £5,000 this period, so the company's cost of goods produced was £5,000 less than its cost of goods sold from the profit and loss account.

- **Sales, general, and administration (SG&A).** These expenses are the same SG&A expenses that appear in a profit and loss account, except that paying off bills that you owe or postponing payments may change the amount. Global Gizmos paid down £10,000 in both its accounts payable and expenses payable this year, increasing its SG&A cash outflow by £20,000, for a total of £160,000.

- **Interest expense.** Interest expense shows up in the profit and loss account as well. The number reflects the amount that you actually pay out during the period.

- **Taxes.** Taxes also appear in the profit and loss account. But in the cash-flow statement, taxes are the ones that you actually pay out during the period.

- **Buildings, equipment, machinery.** When your company buys an expensive item, it doesn't appear in your profit and loss account as an expense, because you're really just trading cash for another asset. Instead, you take a depreciation expense each year to reflect the spread of that cost over the asset's useful life. When you buy the building, lorry, or whatever, however, you've got to pay for it. The cash-flow statement reflects those costs. Global Gizmos, for example, shelled out £40,000 this year for new equipment.

- **Long-term debt reduction.** It costs you money to reduce any long-term debt that your company may have, and that expense doesn't appear in the profit and loss account. Global Gizmos reduced its long-term debt by £5,000 last year and £10,000 this year.

- **Dividend distribution to owners.** The portion of your company's profits that you decide to give back to the owners comes directly out of your cash box. Again, this entry isn't a business expense in the profit and loss account, but it costs you nonetheless. Global Gizmos distributed £5,000 to its owners this year.

What's left over

The flow of cash in and out of your business is like water flowing in and out of a reservoir. If more water comes in than goes out, the water level goes up, and vice versa. When your company's cash reserves rise, however, the money flows into one or more of your liquid-asset accounts. The bottom half of your cash-flow statement keeps track of what's happening to those accounts.

Changes in liquid assets

With cash flowing in and out of the company, your liquid assets are going to change during the period covered by the cash-flow statement. The items listed in this portion of the cash-flow statement are the same ones that appear in the balance sheet. This year, for example, Global Gizmos improved its cash reserves and investment portfolio by £15,000 each.

Net change in cash position

Raising the level of your liquid-asset accounts has the happy effect of strengthening your cash position. Global Gizmos increased its liquid assets and cash position by £30,000 this year. Not coincidentally, this £30,000 is also the difference between the £833,000 that Global Gizmos took in during the year (Total Funds In) and the £803,000 that it spent (Total Funds Out).

Evaluating Financial Ratios

Armed with a profit and loss account, a balance sheet, and a cash-flow statement, you have a relatively complete financial picture of your company in front of you. But when you look everything over, what does that financial picture actually tell you? Is it good news or bad news? What things should you plan to do differently as you go forward?

Book II

Money in Mind

Your financial picture may tell you that you pay your bills on time, keep a cash cushion, and make some money. But could your company do a better job down the road? It would be nice if you could look at the picture year after year and compare it against a competitor, several competitors, or even your entire industry. But companies come in all shapes and sizes, and it's hard to compare numbers from any two companies and make sense of them.

As a result, companies use *financial ratios*. When you divide one number by another, thereby creating a ratio, you eliminate many of the problems of comparing things on different scales.

Take your personal finances as an example. You're looking for help on investments. One friend boasts that they made £5,000 on the stock market last month; another made only £1,000. Who do you ask for advice? It depends. If the first friend has £500,000 invested and the second friend has only £20,000, who's the savvy investor?

A ratio gives you the answer. The first friend saw a return of only 1 per cent (5,000 ÷ 500,000), whereas the second friend realised a better return of 5 per cent (1,000 ÷ 20,000).

Comparing two companies of different sizes works just the same way. If you want to compare your company's financial ratios with those of major competitors or with an industry average, you need to get your hands on some outside data. You can always start by asking your banker, accountant, or investment adviser, because financial institutions keep close track of standard ratios across industries. But you should also check out financial-data services such as Standard and Poor's, Value-Line, and Moody's. Also, Dun & Bradstreet offers a publication called *Industry Norms and Key Business Ratios*.

With all these data in hand, you can see how your company measures up, because you can bet that your investors, creditors, and competitors are going to, even if you don't.

Financial ratios fall into three categories. The first two categories take your company's vital signs to see whether you're going to make it (remain solvent). One set of ratios measures the company's capability to meet its obligations in the short term; the other looks at the long term. The final set of ratios indicates just how strong and vigorous your company really is, measuring its relative profitability from several points of view.

Short-term obligations

The overriding importance of being able to pay your bills every month is the major reason why current assets and current liabilities are separated in the company's balance sheet. The difference between the two – your working capital – represents a safety net that protects you from almost certain financial catastrophe.

How much working capital do you need to ensure survival? Having the liquid assets available when you absolutely need them to meet short-term obligations is called *liquidity*. You can use several financial ratios to test your company's liquidity. You can monitor the following ratios year by year and measure them against your competitors' ratios and the industry averages.

Current ratio = current assets ÷ current liabilities

You determine your company's current ratio by looking at the balance sheet and dividing total current assets by total current liabilities. Global Gizmos Company, for example, has a current ratio of $320,000 ÷ $140,000, or 2.3 (refer to Figure 2-2). You can also express this ratio as 2.3 to 1 or 2.3:1.

Like most financial ratios, the current ratio isn't an especially precise measurement, so there's no point in calculating it to more than one or two decimal places.

What's the magic number to aim for? If your company falls below a current ratio of 1.0, you're in serious financial danger. In most cases, you want the number to stay above 2.0, meaning that you have more than twice the current assets that you need to cover current liabilities. But again, the answer depends on your industry. Companies that move stocks quickly can often operate with somewhat lower current ratios, because the stocks themselves are a little more liquid. You don't want your current ratio to get too high, either. Then you could be sitting on excess cash that should really be put to work and invested back in the company.

Quick ratio = (cash + investments + debtors) ÷ current liabilities

The quick ratio sometimes is called the *acid test,* because it's more stringent than the current ratio. The quick ratio doesn't allow you to count stock and prepaid expenses as part of your current assets, because it's sometimes hard to turn them back into cash quickly, especially in an emergency. This situation is particularly true in industries in which products go out of fashion rapidly or are quickly outdated by new technology.

Global Gizmos has a quick ratio of £200,000 ÷ £140,000, or 1.4, this year (refer to Figure 2-2). You want to keep your own company's quick ratio above 1.0 by a comfortable margin that is in line with your industry.

Book II

Money in Mind

Stock turnover = cost of goods sold ÷ stock

Stock turnover tells you something about how liquid your stocks really are. This ratio divides the cost of goods sold, as shown in your yearly profit and loss account, by the average value of your stock. If you don't know the average, you can estimate it by using the stock figure as listed in the balance sheet at the end of the year.

Global Gizmos has a stock turnover of £560,000 ÷ £115,000, or 4.9. (Refer to Figures 2-1 and 2-2 for the company's profit and loss account and balance sheet, respectively.) This ratio means that Global Gizmos turns over its stocks almost five times each year. Expressed in days, Global Gizmos carries a 75-day (365 ÷ 4.9) supply of stock.

Is a 75-day inventory good or bad? It depends on the industry and even on the time of year. A car dealer who has a 75-day supply of cars at the height of the season may be in a strong stock position, but the same stock position at the end of the season could be a real weakness. As automation, computers, and information systems make business operations more efficient across all industries, stock turnover is on the rise, and the average number of days that stock of any kind hangs around continues to shrink.

Debtor turnover = sales on credit ÷ debtors

Debtor turnover tells you something about liquidity by dividing the sales that you make on credit by the average debtors. If an average isn't available, you can use the debtors from a balance sheet.

If Global Gizmos makes 80 per cent of its sales on credit, its debtor turnover is ($810,000 × .8) ÷ £135,000, or 4.8. (Refer to Figures 2-1 and 2-2 for Global Gizmos' profit and loss account and balance sheet.) In other words, the company turns over its debtors 4.8 times per year, or once every 76 days, on average. That's not so good if Global Gizmos' payment terms are 30 or 60 days. Unlike fine wine, debtors don't improve with age.

Long-term responsibilities

Your company's liquidity keeps you solvent from day to day and month to month, but what about your ability to pay back long-term debt year after year? Two financial ratios indicate what kind of shape you're in over the long haul. The first ratio gauges how easy it is for your company to continue making interest payments on the debt; the second tries to determine whether the principal amount of your debt is in any danger.

If you've read this chapter from the beginning, you may be getting really bored with financial ratios by now, but your lenders – bankers and bondholders, if you have them – find these long-term ratios to be incredibly fascinating, for obvious reasons.

Times interest earned = earnings before interest and taxes ÷ interest expense

Don't get confused – earnings before any interest expense and taxes are paid (EBIT) really is just the profit that you have available to make those interest payments in the first place. Global Gizmos, for example, has an EBIT of £57,000 and an interest expense of £13,000 this year for a times-interest-earned ratio of 4.4. (Refer to Figure 2-1 for the company's income statement.) In other words, Global Gizmos can meet its interest expense 4.4 times over.

You may also hear the same number called an *interest coverage*. Lenders get mighty nervous if this ratio ever gets anywhere close to 1.0, because at that point, every last penny of profits goes for interest payments on the long-term debt.

Debt-to-equity ratio = long-term liabilities ÷ owners' equity

The debt-to-equity ratio says a great deal about the general financial structure of your company. After all, you can raise money to support your company in only two ways: borrow it and promise to pay it back with interest, or sell pieces of the company and promise to share all the rewards of ownership. The first method is debt; the second, equity.

Global Gizmos has a debt-to-equity ratio of £90,000 ÷ £385,000, or .23. (Refer to Figure 2-2 for Global Gizmos' balance sheet.) This ratio means that the company has more than four times as much equity financing as it does long-term debt.

Lenders love to see lots of equity supporting a company's debt, because they know that the money they loan out is safer. If something goes wrong with the company, they can go after the owners' money. Equity investors, on the other hand, actually want to take on some risk. They like to see relatively high debt-to-equity ratios, because that situation increases their leverage and (as the following section points out) can substantially boost their profits. So the debt-to-equity ratio that's just right for your company depends not only on your industry and how stable it is, but also on who you ask.

Relative profitability

If profit is the bottom line for your business, profitability is the finishing line. Profitability tells you how well you measure up when it comes to creating financial value out of your company. Profitability ratios allow you to keep track of your own performance year by year. They also allow you to compare that performance against that of other competitors, other industries, and even other ways of investing resources.

You could easily invest the money that flows into your company in other businesses, for example, or in bank accounts, property, or government bonds. Each of these investments involves a certain level of risk. By comparing profitability ratios, you begin to see whether your own company measures up, generating the kinds of financial rewards that justify the risks involved.

Profitability ratios come in three flavours. The first type of ratio examines profit relative to your company sales. The second type examines profit relative to total assets. The final type examines profit relative to owners' equity. Each of the ratios reflects how attractive your company is to an investor.

Net profit margin = net profit ÷ gross revenue on sales

The net profit margin is your net profit divided by your gross revenue. The ratio really says more about your costs in relation to the prices that you charge, however. If your net profit margin is low compared with that of other companies in your industry, your prices are generally lower or your costs are too high. Lower margins are quite acceptable if they lead to greater sales, larger market share, and bigger profits down the road, but you want to monitor the ratio carefully. On the other hand, no one's going to quibble with net profit margins that are on the high side, although they're an awfully good way to attract new competitors.

Global Gizmos Company has a net profit margin of $50,000 ÷ $810,000, or 6.2 per cent, this year. (To examine Global Gizmos' profit and loss account, refer to Figure 2-1.) That result is a substantial increase from the 4.6 per cent for the year before. The company didn't grow just in terms of revenue, but also became more profitable.

When you calculate your own net profit margin, you should also think about calculating margins based on your operating profit and gross profit. Together, these ratios give you a better idea of where your company's profitability really comes from.

Return on investment = net profit ÷ total assets

Net profit divided by total assets gives you the overall return that you're able to make on your company's assets – referred to as *return on assets* (ROA). Because these assets are equal to all your debt and equity combined, the ratio also measures an average return on the total investment in your company. What does the ratio mean? It's similar to the yield on Grandma's savings bonds or the return on that hot new mutual fund that you've discovered. *Return on investment* (ROI) is widely used as a test of company profitability, because you can compare it to other types of investments that an investor can put money into.

Watch out for one thing, though: The value of the total assets used in the calculation of ROI usually is taken from a company's balance sheet and can be misleading. If the assets have been around for a while, the numbers on the page may not reflect real replacement costs, and if the assets are undervalued, the ROI is bound to be a bit exaggerated.

Global Gizmos has an ROI of £50,000 ÷ £ 475,000, or 10.5 per cent, this year. (Refer to Figures 2-1 and 2-2 for the company's profit and loss account and balance sheet.) That figure is up from 7.1 per cent the year before, and the increase certainly is good news.

Whether your own company's ROI is where it should be depends to a large extent on your industry, as well as on what the economy is doing at the moment.

Return on equity = net profit ÷ owners' equity

Net profit divided by the owners' equity in your company gives you the return on just the equity portion of the investment (ROE). Keep in mind that you've already taken care of all your bankers and bondholders first by paying their return – the interest expense on your debt – out of your profits. Whatever is left over goes to the owners and represents their return on equity.

Your creditors always get paid first, and they get paid a fixed amount; everything else goes to the owners. That's where *leverage* comes in. The more you finance your company by using debt, the more leveraged you are, and the more leveraged you are, the more you're using other people's money to make money. Leverage works beautifully as long as you're good at putting that money to work – creating returns that are higher than your interest costs. Otherwise, those other people may end up owning your company.

Global Gizmos, for example, has an ROE of £50,000 ÷ £385,000, or 13.0 per cent. (The profit and loss account and balance sheet shown in Figures 2-1 and 2-2, earlier in this chapter, shed some light on where these figures come from.) Without any leverage, that ROE would be the same as the company's ROI, or only 10.5 per cent. More leverage probably would raise the ROE even higher, upping the risk at the same time. In short, leverage makes the good years better for the owners and the bad years much worse.

Chapter 3

Cash Flows and the Cash Flow Statement

*T*his chapter talks about *cash flows* – which in general refers to cash inflows and outflows over a period of time. Suppose you tell us that last year you had total cash inflows of £145,000 and total cash outflows of £140,000. We know that your cash balance increased by £5,000. But we don't know where your £145,000 cash inflows came from. Did you earn this much in salary? Did you receive an inheritance from your rich uncle? Likewise, we don't know what you used your £140,000 cash outflow for. Did you make large payments on your credit cards? Did you lose a lot of money at the races? In short, cash flows have to be sorted into different sources and uses to make much sense.

The Three Types of Cash Flow

Accountants categorise the cash flows of a business into three types:

✔ Cash inflows from making sales and cash outflows for expenses; sales and expense transactions are called the *operating activities* of a business (although they could be called profit activities just as well, because their purpose is to make profit).

✔ Cash outflows for making investments in new assets (buildings, machinery, tools, and so on), and cash inflows from liquidating old investments (assets no longer needed that are sold off); these transactions are called *investment activities.*

✔ Cash inflows from borrowing money and from the additional investment of money in the business by its owners, and cash outflows for paying off debt, returning capital that the business no longer needs to owners and making cash distributions of profit to its owners; these transactions are called *financing activities.*

The cash flow statement (or *statement of cash flows*) summarises the cash flows of a business for a period according to this three-way classification. Generally accepted accounting principles (GAAP) require that whenever a business reports its income statement, it must also report its cash flow statement for the same period – a business shouldn't report one without the other. A good reason exists for this dual financial statement requirement.

The income statement is based on the *accrual basis of accounting* that records sales when made, whether or not cash is received at that time, and records expenses when incurred, whether or not the expenses are paid at that time. Because accrual basis accounting is used to record profit, you can't equate bottom-line profit with an increase in cash. Suppose a business's annual income statement reports that it earned £1.6 million net income for the year. This does not mean that its cash balance increased £1.6 million during the period. You have to look in the cash flow statement to find out how much its cash balance increased (or, possibly, decreased!) from its operating activities (sales revenue and expenses) during the period.

In the chapter, we refer to the net increase (or decrease) in the business's cash balance that results from collecting sales revenue and paying expenses as *cash flow from profit*, as the alternative term for *cash flow from operating activities.* Cash flow from profit seems more user-friendly than cash flow from operating activities, and in fact the term is used widely. In any case, do not confuse cash flow from profit with the other two types of cash flow – from the business's investing activities and financing activities during the period.

Before moving on, here's a short problem for you to solve. Using the three-way classification of cash flows explained earlier, below is a summary of the business's net cash flows (in thousands) for the year just ended, with one amount missing:

(1) From profit (operating activities)	?
(2) From investing activities	– £1,275
(3) From financing activities	+ £160
Decrease in cash balance during year	– £15

Note that the business's cash balance from all sources and uses decreased £15,000 during the year. The amounts of net cash flows from the company's investing and financing activities are given. So you can determine that the net cash flow from profit was £1,100,000 for the year. Understanding cash flows from investing activities and financing activities is fairly straightforward. Understanding the net cash flow from profit, in contrast, is more challenging – but business managers and investors should have a good grip on this very important number.

Setting the Stage: Changes in Balance Sheet Accounts

The first step in understanding the amounts reported by a business in its cash flow statement is to focus on the *changes* in the business's assets, liabilities, and owners' equity accounts during the period – the increases or decreases of each account from the start of the period to the end of the period. These changes are found in the comparative two-year balance sheet reported by a business. Figure 3-1 presents the increases and decreases during the year in the assets, liabilities and owners' equity accounts for a business example. Figure 3-1 is not a balance sheet but only a summary of *changes* in account balances. We do not want to burden you with an entire balance sheet, which has much more detail than is needed here.

Take a moment to scan Figure 3-1. Note that the business's cash balance decreased £15,000 during the year. (An increase is not necessarily a good thing, and a decrease is not necessarily a bad thing; it depends on the overall financial situation of the business.) One purpose of reporting the cash flow statement is to summarise the main reasons for the change in cash – according to the three-way classification of cash flows explained earlier. One question on everyone's mind is this: How much cash did the profit for the year generate for the business? The cash flow statement begins by answering this question.

Assets	
Cash	(15)
Debtors	800
Stock	975
Prepaid Expenses	145
Fixed Assets	1,275
Accumulated Depreciation*	(1,200)
Total	1,980
Liabilities & Owners' Equity	
Creditors	80
Accrued Expenses Payable	120
Income Tax Payable	20
Overdraft	200
Long-term Loans	300
Owners' Invested Capital	60
Retained Earnings	1,200
Total	1,980

* Accumulated Depreciation is a negative asset account which is deducted from Fixed Assets. The negative £1,200 change increases the negative balance of the account.

Figure 3-1: Changes in balance sheet assets and operating liabilities that affect cash flow from profit.

Getting at the Cash Increase from Profit

Although all amounts reported on the cash flow statement are important, the one that usually gets the most attention is *cash flow from operating activities,* or *cash flow from profit* as we prefer to call it. This is the increase in cash generated by a business's profit-making operations during the year, exclusive of its other sources of cash during the year (such as borrowed money, sold-off fixed assets, and additional owners' investments in the business). *Cash flow from profit* indicates a business's ability to turn profit into available cash – cash in the bank that can be used for the needs of business. Cash flow from profit gets just as much attention as net income (the bottom-line profit number in the income statement).

Computing cash flow from profit

Here's how to compute cash flow from profit based on the changes in the company's balance sheet accounts presented in Figure 3-1:

Computation of Cash Flow from Profit (in Thousands of Pounds)		
Negative Cash Flow Effects		**Positive Cash Flow Effects**
Net income for the year		£1,600
Debtors increase	£800	
Stock increase	£975	
Prepaid expenses increase	£145	
Depreciation expense		£1,200
Creditors increase		£80
Accrued expenses payable increase		£120
Income tax payable increase		£20
Totals	£1,920	£3,020
Cash flow from profit (£3,020 positive increases minus £1,920 negative increases)	£1,100	

Note that net income (profit) for the year – which is the correct amount of profit based on the accrual basis of accounting – is listed in the positive cash flow column. This is only the starting point. Think of this the following way: If the business had collected all its sales revenue for the year in cash, and if it had made cash payments for its expenses exactly equal to the amounts recorded for the expenses, then the net income amount would equal the increase in cash. These two conditions are virtually never true, and they are not true in this example. So the net income figure is just the jumping-off point for determining the amount of cash generated by the business's profit activities during the year.

We'll let you in on a little secret here. The analysis of cash flow from profit asks what amount of profit would have been recorded if the business had been on the cash basis of accounting instead of the accrual basis. This can be confusing and exasperating, because it seems that two different profit measures are provided in a business's financial report – the true economic profit number, which is the bottom line in the income statement (usually called *net income*), and a second profit number called *cash flow from operating activities* in the cash flow statement.

When the cash flow statement was made mandatory many accountants worried about this problem, but the majority opinion was that the amount of cash increase (or decrease) generated from the profit activities of a business is very important to disclose in financial reports. In reading the income statement, you have to wear your accrual basis accounting lenses, and in the cash flow statement you have to put on your cash basis lenses. Who says accountants can't see two sides of something?

The following sections explain the effects on cash flow that each balance sheet account change causes (refer to Figure 3-1).

Getting specific about changes in assets and liabilities

As a business manager, you should keep a close watch on each of your assets and liabilities and understand the cash flow effects of increases (or decreases) caused by these changes. Investors should focus on the business's ability to generate a healthy cash flow from profit, so investors should be equally concerned about these changes.

Debtors increase

Remember that the debtors asset shows how much money customers who bought products on credit still owe the business; this asset is a promise of cash that the business will receive. Basically, debtors is the amount of uncollected sales revenue at the end of the period. Cash does not increase until the business collects money from its customers.

But the amount in debtors *is* included in the total sales revenue of the period – after all, you did make the sales, even if you haven't been paid yet. Obviously, then, you can't look at sales revenue as being equal to the amount of cash that the business received during the period.

To calculate the actual cash flow from sales, you need to subtract from sales revenue the amount of credit sales that you did not collect in cash over the period – but you add in the amount of cash that you collected during the period just ended for credit sales that you made in the *preceding* period. The key point is that you need to keep an eye on the increase or decrease in debtors from the beginning of the period to the end of the period:

 ✔ If the amount of credit sales you made during the period is greater than the amount collected from customers during the same period, your debtors *increased* over the period. Therefore you need to *subtract* from sales revenue that difference between start-of-period debtors and end-of-period debtors. In short, an increase in debtors hurts cash flow by the amount of the increase.

✔ If the amount you collected from customers during the period is greater than the credit sales you made during the period, your debtors _decreased_ over the period. In this case you need to _add_ to sales revenue that difference between start-of-period debtors and end-of-period debtors. In short, a decrease in debtors helps cash flow by the amount of the decrease.

An occasional hiccup in cash flow is the price of growth – managers and investors need to understand this point. Increasing sales without increasing debtors is a happy situation for cash flow, but in the real world you can't have one increase without the other (except in very unusual circumstances).

Stock increase

Stock is the next asset in Figure 3-1 – and usually the largest short-term, or _current,_ asset for businesses that sell products. If the stock account is greater at the end of the period than at the start of the period – because either unit costs increased or the quantity of products increased – what the business actually paid out in cash for stock purchases (or manufacturing products) is more than the business recorded as its cost-of-goods-sold expense in the period. Therefore, you need to deduct the stock increase from net income when determining cash flow from profit.

The cost that a business pays _this_ period for _next_ period's stock is reflected in this period's cash flow but isn't recorded until next period's income statement (when the products are actually sold). So if a business paid more _this_ period for _next_ period's stock than it paid _last_ period for _this_ period's stock, you can see how the additional expense would adversely affect cash flow but would not be reflected in the bottom-line net income figure. This cash flow analysis stuff gets a little complicated, we know, but hang in there. The cash flow statement, presented later in the chapter, makes a lot more sense after you go through this background briefing.

Prepaid expenses increase

The next asset, after stock, is prepaid expenses (refer to Figure 3-1). A change in this account works the same way as a change in stock and debtors, although changes in prepaid expenses are usually much smaller than changes in those other two asset accounts.

Again, the beginning balance of prepaid expenses is recorded as an expense this period but the cash was actually paid out last period, not this period. This period, a business pays cash for next period's prepaid expenses – which affects this period's cash flow but doesn't affect net income until next period. So the £145,000 increase in prepaid expenses from start-of-period to end-of-period in this business example has a negative cash flow effect.

As it grows, a business needs to increase its prepaid expenses for such things as fire insurance (premiums have to be paid in advance of the insurance coverage) and its stocks of office and data processing supplies. Increases in debtors, stock, and prepaid expenses are the price a business has to pay for growth. Rarely do you find a business that can increase its sales revenue without increasing these assets.

The simple but troublesome depreciation factor

Depreciation expense recorded in the period is both the simplest cash flow effect to understand and, at the same time, one of the most misunderstood elements in calculating cash flow from profit. To start with, depreciation is not a cash outlay during the period. The amount of depreciation expense recorded in the period is simply a fraction of the original cost of the business's fixed assets that were bought and paid for years ago. (Well, if you want to nit-pick here, some of the fixed assets may have been bought during this period, and their cost is reported in the investing activities section of the cash flow statement.) Because the depreciation expense is not a cash outlay this period, the amount is added back to net income in the calculation of cash flow from profit – so far so good.

When measuring profit on the accrual basis of accounting you count depreciation as an expense. The fixed assets of a business are on an irreversible journey to the junk heap. Fixed assets have a limited, finite life of usefulness to a business (except for land); depreciation is the accounting method that allocates the total cost of fixed assets to each year of their use in helping the business generate sales revenue. Part of the total sales revenue of a business constitutes *recovery of cost invested in its fixed assets*. In a real sense, a business 'sells' some of its fixed assets each period to its customers – it factors the cost of fixed assets into the sales prices that it charges its customers. For example, when you go to a supermarket a very small slice of the price you pay for that box of cereal goes toward the cost of the building, the shelves, the refrigeration equipment, and so on. (No wonder they charge so much for a box of cornflakes!)

Each period, a business recoups part of the cost invested in its fixed assets. In other words, £1.2 million of sales revenue (in the example) went toward reimbursing the business for the use of its fixed assets during the year. The problem regarding depreciation in cash flow analysis is that many people simply add back depreciation for the year to bottom-line profit and then stop, as if this is the proper number for cash flow from profit. It ain't so. The changes in other assets as well as the changes in liabilities also affect cash flow from profit. You should factor in *all* the changes that determine cash flow from profit, as explained the following section.

Net income + depreciation expense doesn't equal cash flow from profit!

The business in our example earned £1.6 million in net income for the year, plus it received £1.2 cash flow because of the depreciation expense built into in its sales revenue for the year. The sum of these is £2.8 million. Is £2.8 million the amount of cash flow from profit for the period? The knee-jerk answer of many investors and managers is 'yes'. But if net income + depreciation truly equals cash flow, then *both* factors in the brackets – both net income and depreciation – must be fully realised in cash. Depreciation is, but the net income amount is not fully realised in cash because the company's debtors, stock, and pre-paid expenses increased during the year, and these increases have negative impacts on cash flow.

Adding net income and depreciation to determine cash flow from profit is mixing apples and oranges. The business did not realise £1,600,000 cash increase from its £1,600,000 net income. The total of the increases of its debtors, stock, and prepaid expenses is £1,920,000 (refer to Figure 3-1), which wipes out the net income amount and leaves the business with a cash balance hole of £320,000. This cash deficit is offset by the £220,000 increase in liabilities (explained later) leaving a £100,000 net income *deficit* as far as cash flow is concerned. Depreciation recovery increased cash flow £1.2 million. So the final cash flow from profit equals £1.1 million. But you'd never know this if you simply added depreciation expense to net income for the period.

The managers did not have to go outside the business for the £1.1 million cash increase generated from its profit for the year. Cash flow from profit is an *internal* source of money generated by the business itself, in contrast to *external* money that the business raises from lenders and owners. A business does not have to 'go begging' for external money if its internal cash flow from profit is sufficient to provide for its growth.

In passing, we should mention that a business could have a negative cash flow from profit for a year – meaning that despite posting a net income for the period, the changes in the company's assets and liabilities caused its cash balance to decrease. In reverse, a business could report a bottom line *loss* in its income statement yet have a *positive* cash flow from its operating activities: The positive contribution from depreciation expense plus decreases in its debtors and stock could amount to more than the amount of loss. More realistically, a loss often leads to negative cash flow or very little positive cash flow.

Operating liabilities increases

The business in the example, like almost all businesses, has three basic liabilities that are inextricably intertwined with its expenses: creditors, accrued expenses payable and income tax payable. When the beginning balance of one of these liability accounts is the same as the ending balance of the same account (not too likely, of course), the business breaks even on cash flow for that account. When the end-of-period balance is higher than the start-of-period balance, the business did not pay out as much money as was actually recorded as an expense on the period's income statement.

Liability increases are favourable to cash flow – in a sense the business borrowed more than it paid off. Such an increase means that the business delayed paying cash for certain things until next year. So you need to add the increases in the three liabilities to net income to determine cash flow from profit, following the same logic as adding back depreciation to net income. The business did not have cash outlays to the extent of increases in these three liabilities.

The analysis of the changes in assets and liabilities of the business that affect cash flow from profit is complete for the business example. The bottom line (oops, we shouldn't use that term when referring to a cash flow amount) is that the company's cash balance increased £1.1 million from profit. You could argue that cash should have increased £2.8 million – £1.6 million net income plus £1.2 million depreciation that was recovered during the year – so the business is £1.7 million behind in turning its profit into cash flow (£2.8 million less the £1.1 million cash flow from profit). This £1.7 million lag in converting profit into cash flow is caused by the £1,920,000 increase in assets less the £220,000 increase in liabilities, as shown in Figure 3-1.

Presenting the Cash Flow Statement

The cash flow statement is one of the three primary financial statements that a business must report to the outside world, according to generally accepted accounting principles (GAAP). To be technical, the rule says that whenever a business reports a profit and loss account, it should also report a cash flow statement. The *profit and loss account* summarises sales revenue and expenses and ends with the bottom-line profit for the period. The *balance sheet* summarises a business's financial condition by reporting its assets, liabilities, and owners' equity.

You can probably guess what the *cash flow statement* does by its name alone: This statement tells you where a business got its cash and what the business did with its cash during the period. We prefer the name given in the old days in the US to the predecessor of the cash flow statement, the *Where Got, Where Gone* statement. This nickname goes straight to the purpose of the cash flow statement: asking where the business got its money and what it did with the money.

To give you a rough idea of what a cash flow statement reports, we repeat some of the questions we asked at the start of the chapter: How much money did you earn last year? Did you get all your income in cash (did some of your wages go straight into a pension plan or did you collect a couple of IOUs)? Where did you get other money (did you take out a loan, win the lottery, or receive a gift from a rich uncle)? What did you do with your money (did you buy a house, support your out-of-control Internet addiction, or lose it playing bingo)?

Getting a little too personal for you? That's exactly why the cash flow statement is so important: It bares a business's financial soul to its lenders and owners. Sometimes the cash flow statement reveals questionable judgment calls that the business's managers made. At the very least, the cash flow statement reveals how well a business handles the cash increase from its profit.

Book II

Money in
Mind

As explained at the start of the chapter, the cash flow statement is divided into three sections according to the three-fold classification of cash flows for a business:

- Cash flow from **operating activities** (which we also call *cash flow from profit* in the chapter): The activities by which a business makes profit and turns the profit into cash flow (includes depreciation and changes in operating assets and liabilities).

- Cash flow from **investing activities:** Investing in long-term assets needed for a business's operations; also includes money taken out of these assets from time to time (such as when a business disposes of some of its long-term assets).

- Cash flow from **financing activities:** Raising capital from debt and owners' equity, returning capital to these capital sources, and distributing profit to owners.

The cash flow statement reports a business's net cash increase or decrease based on these three groupings of the cash flow statement. Figure 3-2 shows what a cash flow statement typically looks like – in this example, for a *growing* business (which means that its assets, liabilities, and owners' equity increase during the period).

The trick to understanding cash flow from profit is to link the sales revenue and expenses of the business with the changes in the business's assets and liabilities that are directly connected with its profit-making activities. Using this approach earlier in the chapter, we determine that the cash flow from profit is £1.1 million for the year for the sample business. This is the number you see in Figure 3-2 for cash flow from operating activities. In our experience, many business managers, lenders, and investors don't fully understand these links, but the savvy ones know to keep a close eye on the relevant balance sheet changes.

Cash Flow Statement for Year (in Thousands of Pounds)		
Cash Flows from Operating Activities		
Net Income		£ 1,600
Debtors	£ (800)	
Stock Increase	£ (975)	
Prepaid Expenses Increase	£ (145)	
Depreciation Expense	£ 1,200	
Creditors Increase	£ 80	
Accrued Expense Increase	£ 120	
Income Tax Payable Increase	£ 20	£ (500)
Cash Flow from Operating Activities		£ 1,100
Cash Flows from Investing Activities		
Purchases of Property, Plant & Equipment		£ (1,275)
Cash Flows from Financing Activities		
Short-term Debt Borrowing Increase	£ 200	
Long-term Debt Borrowing Increase	£ 300	
Share Issue	£ 60	
Dividends Paid Stockholders	£ (400)	£ 160
Increase (Decrease) In Cash During Year		£ (15)
Beginning Cash Balance		£ 2,015
Ending Cash Balance		£ 2,000

Figure 3-2:
Cash flow statement for the business in the example.

What do the figures in the first section of the cash flow statement (refer to Figure 3-2) reveal about this business over the past period? Recall that the business experienced rapid sales growth over the last period. However, the downside of sales growth is that operating assets and liabilities also grow – the business needs more stock at the higher sales level and also has higher debtors.

The business's prepaid expenses and liabilities also increased, although not nearly as much as debtors and stock. The rapid growth of the business yielded higher profit but also caused quite a surge in its operating assets and liabilities – the result being that cash flow from profit is only £1.1 million compared with £1.6 million in net income – a £500,000 shortfall. Still, the business had £1.1 million at its disposal after allowing for the increases in assets and liabilities. What did the business do with this £1.1 million of available cash? You have to look to the remainder of the cash flow statement to answer this key question.

A very quick read through the rest of the cash flow statement (refer to Figure 3-2) goes something like this: The company used £1,275,000 to buy new fixed assets, borrowed £500,000, and distributed £400,000 of the profit to its owners. The bottom line is that cash decreased £15,000 during the year.

A better alternative for reporting cash flow from profit?

We call your attention, again, to the first section of the cash flow statement in Figure 3-2. You start with net income for the period. Next, changes in assets and liabilities are deducted or added to net income to arrive at cash flow from operating activities (the cash flow from profit) for the year. This format is called the *indirect method.* The alternative format for this section of the cash flow statement is called the *direct method* and is presented like this (using the same business example, with pound amounts in millions):

Cash inflow from sales	£24.2
Less cash outflow for expenses	23.1
Cash flow from operating activities	£1.1

You may remember from the earlier discussion that sales revenue for the year is £25 million, but that the company's debtors increased £800,000 during the year, so cash flow from sales is £24.2 million. Likewise, the expenses for the year can be put on a cash flow basis. But we 'cheated' here – we have already determined that cash flow from profit is £1.1 million for the year, so we plugged the figure for cash outflow for expenses. We would take more time to explain the direct approach, except for one major reason.

Although the Accounting Standards Board (ASB) expresses a definite preference for the direct method, this august rule-making body does permit the indirect method to be used in external financial reports – and, in fact, the overwhelming majority of businesses use the indirect method. Unless you're an accountant, we don't think you need to know much more about the direct method.

Sailing through the Rest of the Cash Flow Statement

After you get past the first section, the rest of the cash flow statement is a breeze. The last two sections of the statement explain what the business did with its cash and where cash that didn't come from profit came from.

Investing activities

The second section of the cash flow statement reports the investment actions that a business's managers took during the year. Investments are like tea leaves, which serve as indicators regarding what the future may hold for the company. Major new investments are the sure signs of expanding or mod-ernising the production and distribution facilities and capacity of the busi-ness. Major disposals of long-term assets and the shedding of a major part of the business could be good news or bad news for the business, depending on many factors. Different investors may interpret this information differently, but all would agree that the information in this section of the cash flow state-ment is very important.

Certain long-lived operating assets are required for doing business – for example, Federal Express wouldn't be terribly successful if it didn't have aeroplanes and vans for delivering packages and computers for tracking deliveries. When those assets wear out, the business needs to replace them. Also, to remain competitive, a business may need to upgrade its equipment to take advantage of the latest technology or provide for growth. These investments in long-lived, tangible, productive assets, which we call *fixed assets* in this book, are critical to the future of the business and are called *capital expenditures* to stress that capital is being invested for the long haul.

One of the first claims on cash flow from profit is capital expenditure. Notice in Figure 3-2 that the business spent £1,275,000 for new fixed assets, which are referred to as *property, plant, and equipment* in the cash flow statement (to keep the terminology consistent with account titles used in the balance sheet, because the term *fixed assets* is rather informal).

Cash flow statements generally don't go into much detail regarding exactly what specific types of fixed assets a business purchased – how many addi-tional square feet of space the business acquired, how many new drill presses it bought, and so on. (Some businesses do leave a clearer trail of their invest-ments, though. For example, airlines describe how many new aircraft of each kind were purchased to replace old equipment or expand their fleets.)

Financing activities

Note that in the annual cash flow statement (refer to Figure 3-2) of the busi-ness example we've been using, the positive cash flow from profit is £1,100,000 and the negative cash flow from investing activities is £1,275,000. The result to this point, therefore, is a net cash outflow of £175,000 – which would have decreased the company's cash balance this much if the business did not go to outside sources of capital for additional money during the year. In fact, the business increased its short-term and long-term debt during the year, and its owners invested additional money in the business. The third sec-tion of the cash flow statement summarises these financing activities of the business over the period.

The term *financing* generally refers to a business raising capital from debt and equity sources – from borrowing money from banks and other sources willing to loan money to the business and from its owners putting additional money in the business. The term also includes the flip side; that is, making payments on debt and returning capital to owners. The term *financing* also includes cash distributions (if any) from profit by the business to its owners.

Most businesses borrow money for a short term (generally defined as less than one year), as well as for longer terms (generally defined as more than one year). In other words, a typical business has both short-term and long-term debt. The business in our example has both short-term and long-term debt. Although not a hard-and-fast rule most cash flow statements report just the *net* increase or decrease in short-term debt, not the total amount borrowed and the total payments on short-term debt during the period. In contrast, both the total amount borrowed from and the total amount paid on long-term debt during the year are reported in the cash flow statement.

For the business we've been using as an example, no long-term debt was paid down during the year but short-term debt was paid off during the year and replaced with new short-term notes payable. However, only the net increase (£200,000) is reported in the cash flow statement. The business also increased its long-term debt by £300,000 (refer to Figure 3-2).

The financing section of the cash flow statement also reports on the flow of cash between the business and its owners (who are the stockholders of a corporation). Owners can be both a *source* of a business's cash (capital invested by owners) and a *use* of a business's cash (profit distributed to owners). This section of the cash flow statement reports capital raised from its owners, if any, as well as any capital returned to the owners. In the cash flow statement (Figure 3-2), note that the business did issue additional stock shares for £60,000 during the year, and it paid a total of £400,000 cash dividends (distributions) from profit to its owners.

Book II

Money in Mind

Free Cash Flow: What on Earth Does That Mean?

A new term has emerged in the lexicon of accounting and finance – *free cash flow*. This piece of language is not – we repeat, *not* – an officially defined term by any authoritative accounting rule-making body. Furthermore, the term does *not* appear in the cash flow statements reported by businesses. Rather, free cash flow is street language, or slang, even though the term appears often in *The Financial Times* and *The Economist*. Securities brokers and investment analysts use the term freely (pun intended). Like most new words being tossed around for the first time, this one hasn't settled down into one universal meaning although the most common usage of the term pivots on cash flow from profit.

The term *free cash flow* is used to mean any of the following:

- ✔ Net income plus depreciation (plus any other expense recorded during the period that does not involve the outlay of cash but rather the allocation of the cost of a long-term asset other than property, plant, and equipment – such as the intangible assets of a business)

- ✔ Cash flow from operating activities (as reported in the cash flow statement)

- ✔ Cash flow from operating activities minus some or all of the capital expenditures made during the year (such as purchases or construction of new, long-lived operating assets such as property, plant, and equipment)

- ✔ Cash flow from operating activities plus interest, and depreciation, and income tax expenses, or, in other words, cash flow before these expenses are deducted

In the strongest possible terms, we advise you to be very clear on which definition of *free cash flow* the speaker or writer is using. Unfortunately, you can't always determine what the term means in any given context. The reporter or investment professional should define the term.

One definition of free cash flow, in our view, is quite useful: cash flow from profit minus capital expenditures for the year. The idea is that a business needs to make capital expenditures in order to stay in business and thrive. And to make capital expenditures, the business needs cash. Only after paying for its capital expenditures does a business have 'free' cash flow that it can use as it likes. In our example, the free cash flow is, in fact, negative – £1,100,000 cash flow from profit minus £1,275,000 capital expenditures for new fixed assets equals a *negative* £175,000.

This is a key point. In many cases, cash flow from profit falls short of the money needed for capital expenditures. So the business has to borrow more money, persuade its owners to invest more money in the business, or dip into its cash reserve. Should a business in this situation distribute some of its profit to owners? After all, it has a cash *deficit* after paying for capital expenditures. But many companies like the business in our example do, in fact, make cash distributions from profit to their owners.

Scrutinising the Cash Flow Statement

Analysing a business's cash flow statement inevitably raises certain questions: What would I have done differently if I was running this business? Would I have borrowed more money? Would I have raised more money from the owners? Would I have distributed so much of the profit to the owners? Would I have let my cash balance drop by even such a small amount?

One purpose of the cash flow statement is to show readers what judgement calls and financial decisions the business's managers made during the period. Of course, management decisions are always subject to second-guessing and criticising, and passing judgment based on a financial statement isn't totally fair because it doesn't reveal the pressures the managers faced during the period. Maybe they made the best possible decisions given the circumstances. Maybe not.

The business in our example (refer to Figure 3-2) distributed £400,000 cash from profit to its owners – a 25% *pay-out ratio* (which is the £400,000 distribution divided by £1.6 million net income). In analysing whether the pay-out ratio is too high, too low, or just about right, you need to look at the broader context of the business's sources of, and needs for, cash.

First look at cash flow from profit: £1.1 million, which is not enough to cover the business's £1,275,000 capital expenditures during the year. The business increased its total debt £500,000. Given these circumstances, maybe the business should have hoarded its cash and not paid so much in cash distributions to its owners.

 So does this business have enough cash to operate with? You can't answer that question just by examining the cash flow statement – or any financial statement for that matter. Every business needs a buffer of cash to protect against unexpected developments and to take advantage of unexpected opportunities. This particular business has a £2 million cash balance compared with £25 million annual sales revenue for the period just ended which probably is enough. If you were the boss of this business how much working cash balance would you want? Not an easy question to answer! Don't forget that you need to look at all three primary financial statements – the profit and loss account and the balance sheet as well as the cash flow statement – to get the big picture of a business's financial health.

Book II

Money in Mind

You probably didn't count the number of lines of information in Figure 3-2, the cash flow statement for the business example. Anyway, the financial statement has 17 lines of information. Would you like to hazard a guess regarding the average number of lines in cash flow statements of publicly-owned companies? Typically, their cash flow statements have 30 to 40 lines of information by our reckoning. So it takes quite a while to read the cash flow statement – more time than the average investor probably has to read this financial statement. (Professional stock analysts and investment managers are paid to take the time to read this financial statement meticulously.) Quite frankly, we find that many cash flow statements are not only rather long but also difficult to understand – even for an accountant. We won't get on a soap-box here but we definitely think businesses could do a better job of reporting their cash flow statements by reducing the number of lines in their financial statements and making each line clearer.

Chapter 4

Forecasting and Budgeting

- -

In This Chapter

▶ Constructing your financial forecast

▶ Putting together a pro-forma profit and loss account

▶ Estimating a balance sheet

▶ Projecting your cash flow

▶ Exploring financial alternatives

▶ Preparing your company's budget

- -

For your company, its basic financial information resides in its financial statements. These financial statements – profit and loss accounts, balance sheets, cash flow – are fairly straightforward, because they're based on how your company performed last year or the year before. Unfortunately, financial information is not quite as easy to put together and use when you have to plan for next year, three years from now, or even five years from now.

Why go to all the trouble of putting financial information together in the first place? The answer is simple: Although the numbers and financials aren't your business plan by themselves, they help you to fulfil your business plan. Without them, you're in real danger of allowing your financial condition – money (or the lack of it) – to take control of, or even replace, your business plan.

Constructing a Financial Forecast

Assumptions about your own industry and marketplace – that you'll have no new competitors, that a new technology will catch on, or that customers will remain loyal, for example – provide a framework to plan a financial forecast around. Your expectations of what lies ahead influence your business objectives and the long-term goals that you set for the company.

Be clear about what your business assumptions are and where they come from, because your assumptions are as important as the numbers themselves when it comes to making a prediction. If you are convinced that no new competitors will enter the market, say why. If you see a period of rapid technological change ahead, explain your reasons. Don't try to hide your business assumptions in a footnote somewhere; place them in a prominent position. That way, you make your financial forecast as honest, adaptable, and useful as it can be. If all your assumptions are out in the open, nobody can possibly miss them.

- Everybody who looks at your forecast knows exactly what's behind it.

- You know exactly where to go when your assumptions need to be changed.

As you may have guessed, coming up with predictions that you really believe in isn't always easy. You may trust some of the numbers (next year's sales figures) more than you do others (the size of a brand-new market). Some of your financial predictions are based on your best estimate. You may arrive at others by using sophisticated number-crunching techniques. When you get the hang of it, though, you begin to see what a broad and powerful planning tool a financial forecast can be. You'll find yourself turning to it to help answer all sorts of important questions, such as the following:

- What cash demands does your company face in the coming year?

- Can your company cover its debt obligations over the next three years?

- Does your company plan to make a profit next year?

- Is your company meeting its overall financial objectives?

- Do investors find your company to be an attractive business proposition?

With so many important questions at stake, a financial forecast is worth all the time and effort that you can spend on it. Because if you're not careful, a forecast can turn out to be way off base. Did you ever hear the old computer programmer's expression 'Rubbish in, rubbish out'? The same is true of financial forecasts. Your financial forecast is only as good as the numbers that go into it. If the numbers are off the mark, it's usually for one of the following reasons:

- Expectations were unrealistic.

- Assumptions weren't objective.

- Predictions weren't checked and rechecked.

The following sections examine the financial statements that make up a financial forecast. After we explain how to put these statements together, we point out which of the numbers are most important and which are the most sensitive to changes in your assumptions and expectations about the future.

Pro-forma profit and loss account

Pro forma refers to something that you describe or estimate in advance. When you construct your financial forecast, you should try to include *pro-forma profit and loss accounts* – documents that show where you plan to get your money and how you'll spend it – for at least three years and for as long as five years in the future, depending on the nature of your business. You should subdivide the first two years into quarterly profit projections. After two years, when your profit projections are much less certain, annual projections are fine.

Your company's pro-forma profit and loss accounts predict what sort of profit you expect to make in the future by asking you to project your total business revenue and then to subtract all your anticipated costs. The following should help you get ready:

- ✔ If you're already in business and have a financial history to work with, get all your past financial statements out right away. You can use them to help you figure out what's likely to happen next.

- ✔ If you have a new company on your hands and don't have a history to fall back on, you have to find other ways to get the information that you need. Talk to people in similar businesses, sit down with your banker and your accountant, visit a trade association, and read industry magazines and newspapers.

The pro-forma profit and loss account has two parts – projected revenue and anticipated costs.

Projected revenue

Your company's projected revenue is based primarily on your sales forecast – exactly how much of your product or service you plan to sell. You have to think about two things: how much you expect to sell, naturally, and how much you're going to charge. Unfortunately, you can't completely separate the two things, because any change in price usually affects the level of your sales.

Your sales forecast is likely to be the single most important business prediction that you'll ever make. If you get it wrong, the error can lead to mountains of unsold stock or a sea of unhappy, dissatisfied customers – a financial disaster in the making. A souvenir-T-shirt company that *over*estimates how many Cup Final T-shirts customers will buy, for example, is going to be left with an awful lot of worthless merchandise. By the same token, the corner toy shop that *under*estimates how many kids will want the latest Bratz will have to answer to many frustrated parents and unhappy children – and will suffer lost sales.

How do you get the sales forecast right? Start by looking at its formula:

Sales forecast = market size × growth rate × market-share target

- ✔ Market size estimates the current number of potential customers.
- ✔ Growth rate estimates how fast the market will grow.
- ✔ Market-share target estimates the percentage of the market that you plan to capture.

Because your sales forecast has such a tremendous impact on the rest of your financial forecast – not to mention on the company itself – you should try to support the estimates that you make with as much hard data as you can get your hands on. Depending on your situation, you can also rely on the following guides:

Company experience. If you already have experience and a track record in the market, you can use your own sales history to make a sales prediction. But remember that your sales are a combination of the size of the market and your own share of the market. You may still need other sources of data (listed in the following paragraphs) to help you estimate how the market and your share of it are likely to change in the future. Using data from outside your company also ensures that you're taking full advantage of all the growth opportunities that are available. All too often, companies use last year's sales as a shortcut to estimating next year's sales, without taking the time to look at how their markets are changing. Because a sales forecast can be self-fulfilling, those companies may never know what they missed!

Industry data. Industry data on market size and estimates of future growth come from all quarters, including trade associations, investment companies, and market-research firms. You can also get practical and timely information from industry suppliers and distributors.

Outside trends. In certain markets, sales levels are closely tied to trends in other markets, social trends, or economic trends. Car sales, for example, tend to move with the general economy. So when car dealers track what's happening with the Gross Domestic Product (GDP), they get an estimate of where car sales are headed.

Next, multiply your sales forecast by the average price that you expect to charge. The result is your projected revenue and it looks like this:

Projected revenue = sales forecast × average price

Where does the average price come from? Your average price is based on what you think your customers are willing to pay and what your competitors are charging. Use the information that you pack away on your industry and the marketplace. The price should also take into account your own costs and your company's overall financial situation.

Now put all the numbers together and see how they work. We'll use a company called Global Gizmos as an example. Sally Smart, widgets product manager, is putting together a three-year revenue projection. Using industry and market data along with the company's own sales history, Sally estimates that the entire market for widgets will grow about 10 per cent a year and that Global Gizmos' market share will increase by roughly 2 per cent a year, with projected price increases of approximately £1 to £2. She puts the numbers together in a table so that she can easily refer to the underlying estimates and the assumptions that support them (see Table 4-1).

Table 4-1　Widget Revenue Projection for Global Gizmos Company

Revenue projection	Year 1	Year 2	Year 3
Projected market size (units)	210,000	231,000	254,100
Projected market share (%)	20	22	24
Sales forecast (units)	42,000	50,820	60,980
Average price	£26	£27	£29
Projected revenue	£1,092,000	£1,372,140	£1,768,420

Anticipated costs

When you complete your revenue projection, you're still not quite finished. You still have to look at anticipated costs – the price tag of doing business over the next several years. To make life a little easier, you can break anticipated costs down into the major categories that appear in a pro-forma profit and loss account: projected cost of goods sold, projected sales, general and administration expenses, projected interest expenses, and projected taxes and depreciation. The following list defines these categories.

Projected cost of goods sold (COGS). COGS, which combines all the direct costs associated with putting together your product or delivering your service, is likely to be your single largest expense. If you have a track record in the industry, you have a useful starting point for estimating your company's future COGS.

Even though the following formula may look ugly, it's actually a simple way to calculate your projected COGS. Based on the assumption that the ratio of your costs to your revenue will stay the same:

Projected COGS = (current COGS ÷ current revenue on sales) × projected revenue

If you haven't been in business long or if you're just starting a company, you won't have access to this kind of information. But you can still estimate your projected COGS by substituting industry averages or by using data that you find on other companies that have similar products or services.

Although this ratio approach has the advantage of being simple, you can get into trouble if you don't confirm the COGS that you come up with. At the very least, you should sum up the estimates of the major costs looming ahead (materials, labour, utilities, facilities, and so on) to make sure that the projected COGS makes sense. This method is tougher, but it gives you a chance to make separate assumptions and projections for each of the underlying costs. You may be pleasantly surprised; you may discover that as your company gets bigger and you're in business longer, your projected revenue goes up faster than your costs do. The effect is called the experience curve (explained thoroughly in Book VI), and it means that your COGS-to-revenue ratio will actually get smaller in the coming years.

Sales, general, and administration (SG&A). SG&A represents your company's overheads: sales expenses, advertising, travel, accounting, telephones, and all the other costs associated with supporting your business. If your company is brand-new, try to get a feel for what your support costs may be by asking people in similar businesses, cornering your accountant, or checking with a trade association for average support costs in your industry. Also come up with ballpark numbers of your own, including estimates for all the major overhead expenses that you can think of.

If you've been in business for a while, you can estimate a range for your SG&A expenses using two calculations. The first method projects a constant spending level, even if your company's sales are growing. In effect, you assume that your support activities will all get more efficient and will accommodate your additional growth without getting bigger themselves. The other method projects a constant SG&A-to-revenue ratio. In this case, you assume that support costs will grow as fast as your revenue and that you won't see any increase in efficiency. An accurate SG&A forecast probably lies somewhere in between. Given what you know about your company's operations, come up with your own estimate, and include the assumptions that you make.

Interest expense. Your interest expense is largely the result of decisions that you make about your company's long-term financing. Those decisions, in turn, are influenced by your ability to pay your interest costs out of profits. Think about what sort of financing you will need and what interest rates you may be able to lock in, then estimate your interest expense as best you can.

Taxes and depreciation. Taxes certainly affect your bottom line, and you want to include your projections and assumptions in your anticipated costs. It's usually pretty simple to estimate their general impact in the future by looking at their impact on your company now. If you're starting a new business, do a bit of research on tax rates.

Depreciation, on the other hand, is an accountant's way of accounting for the value that your asset purchases lose over the time in which you will be using them. As such, it's an expense that doesn't really come out of your pocket every year. You can estimate the numbers, but don't get too carried away. In the future, your depreciation expense will include a portion of those expensive items that you have to buy to keep the business healthy and growing (computers, cars, forklifts, and so on).

When you plug the numbers into your pro-forma profit and loss account and calculate your net profit, be prepared for a shock. You may discover that the profit you were expecting in the first year or two has turned into a projected loss. But don't panic. New business ventures often lose money for some time, until their products catch on and some of the startup costs begin to get paid off. Whatever you do, don't try to turn a projected loss into a profit by fiddling with the numbers. The point isn't to make money on paper; the point is to use the pro-forma profit and loss account as a tool that can tell you what sort of resources and reserves you need to survive until losses turn into predicted profits.

Even if your projection shows a healthy profit, ensure you also complete a Cash Flow Projection (see below) to make sure you can afford to trade at the projected level. Making a profit does not always mean that you will have *cash* on hand to buy raw materials, pay staff and pay taxes.

Estimated balance sheet

Another part of your financial forecast is the *estimated balance sheet,* which, like a regular balance sheet, is a snapshot of what your company looks like at a particular moment – what it owns, what it owes, and what it's worth. Over the years, these snapshots (estimated balance sheets) fill a photo album of sorts, recording how your company changes over time. Your estimated balance sheets describe what you want your company to become and how you plan to get it there. The estimated balance sheets that you put together as part of your financial forecast should start with the present and extend out three to five years in a series of year-end projections.

While the pro-forma profit and loss accounts in your financial forecast project future revenue, costs, and profits, your estimated balance sheets lay out exactly how your company will grow so that it can meet those projections. First, you want to look at what sorts of things (*assets*) you'll need to support the planned size and scale of your business. Then you have to make some decisions about how you're going to pay for those assets. You have to consider how you'll finance your company – how much debt you plan to take on (*liabilities*) and how much of the company's own money (*equity*) you plan to use.

Assets

Your company's projected assets at the end of each year include everything from the money that you expect to have in the petty-cash drawer to the buildings and machines that you plan to own. Some of these assets will be current assets, meaning that you can easily turn them into cash; others will be fixed assets. Don't be confused by the word *current;* we're still talking about the future.

Current assets. The cash on hand and your investment portfolio, as well as debtors and stocks, add up to your current assets. How much should you plan for? That depends on the list of current liabilities (debts) you expect to have, for one thing, because you'll have to pay short-term debts out of your current assets. What's left over is your working capital. The amount of working capital that you will need depends on your future cash-flow situation.

Your estimates of future debtors (money that customers will owe you) depend on the payment terms that you offer and on the sales that you expect to make on credit.

Projected stocks (the amount of stuff in your warehouse) depend on how fast your company can put together products or services and get them to customers. The longer it takes to build products, the bigger the stock cushion you may need.

Fixed assets. Land, buildings, equipment, machinery, and all the other things that aren't easy to dispose of make up your company's fixed assets. Your estimated balance sheets should account for the expensive items that you expect to purchase or get rid of. Your capital purchases (such as additional buildings, more equipment, and newer machines) can play a major role in company growth, increasing both your revenue and the scale of your business operations.

Keep an eye on how each machine or piece of equipment will help your bottom line. If you plan to buy something big, make a quick calculation of its *payback period* (how long it will take to pay back the initial cost of the equipment out of the extra profit that you'll make). Is the payback period going to be months, years, or decades? As you plan for the future, you also want to keep track of your overall expected *return on assets* (ROA), which is your net profits divided by your total assets. This figure monitors how well you expect all your assets to perform in the future. Compare your estimated ROA with industry averages and even with other types of investments.

Liabilities and owners' equity

Estimated balance sheets have to balance, of course, and your projected assets at the end of each future year have to be offset by all the liabilities that you intend to take on, plus your projected equity in the company. Think about how *leveraged* you intend to be (how much of your total assets you expect to pay for out of money that you borrow). Your use of leverage in the future says a great deal about your company. It shows how confident you are about future profits; it also says, loud and clear, how willing you are to take risks for future gain.

Current liabilities. This category consists of all the money that you expect to owe on a short-term basis. That's why these debts are called *current liabilities,* although we're still talking about the future. Current liabilities include the amounts that you expect to owe other companies as part of your planned business operations, as well as payments that you expect to send to the tax people. You have to plan your future current assets so that they not only cover these estimated liabilities, but also leave you some extra capital to work with.

Long-term liabilities. The long-term debt that you plan to take on represents the piece of your company that you intend to finance. Don't be surprised, however, if potential creditors put a strict limit on how much they will loan you, especially if you're just starting out. It's hard to buy a house without a down payment, and it's almost impossible to start a company without one. The down payment is your equity contribution. In general, bankers and other lenders alike want to see enough equity put into your business to make them feel that you're all in the same boat, risk-wise. Equity reassures them that you and other equity investors have a real financial stake in the company, as well as tangible reasons to make it succeed.

How much are lenders willing to loan you, and how much of a down payment do you need to come up with to satisfy them? The answer depends on several things. If you're already in business, the answer depends on how much debt your company already has, how long your company's been around, how you've done up to now, and what the prospects are in your industry. If your company is new, financing depends on your track record in other businesses or on how well you do your homework and put together a convincing business plan.

Before you take on a new loan, find out what kind of debt-to-equity ratios similar companies have. Make sure that yours will fall somewhere in the same range. As an additional test, run some numbers to make sure that you can afford the debt and the interest payments that come along with it.

Owners' equity. The pieces of your company that you, your friends, relatives, acquaintances, and often total strangers lay claim to are all lumped together as *owners' equity.* Although the details of ownership can become ridiculously complex, the result of the process is fairly straightforward. All owners own part of your company, and everybody sinks or swims, depending on how well the company does.

In general, you can estimate how well the company is likely to do for its owners by projecting the return that you expect to make on the owners' investment. Then you can compare that return with what investors in other companies, or even other industries, are earning.

In the initial stages of your company, equity capital is likely to come from the owners themselves, either as cash straight out of the wallet or from the sale of shares to other investors. The equity at this stage is crucial, because if you want to borrow money later, you're going to have to show your bankers that you have enough invested in your business to make your company a sound financial risk. When the company is up and running, of course, you can take some of your profits and (rather than buy the little sports car that you've always wanted) give them back to the company, creating additional equity.

Unfortunately, profit has another side, and the down side is definitely in the red. Although you probably don't want to think about it, your company may lose money some years (especially during the early years). Losses don't generate equity; on the contrary, they eat equity up. So you have to plan to have enough equity available to cover any anticipated losses that you project in your pro-forma profit and loss accounts (refer to the section 'Pro-forma profit and loss account' earlier in this chapter).

Projected cash flow

The flow of cash through a business is much like the flow of oil through an engine; it supports and sustains everything that you do and keeps the various parts of your company functioning smoothly. We all know what happens when a car's oil runs dry: the car belches blue smoke and dies. Running out of cash can be just as catastrophic for your company. If you survive the experience, it may take months or even years for your company to recover.

Cash-flow statements keep track of the cash that comes in and the cash that goes out of your company, as well as where the money ends up. These statements are crucial. Projected cash-flow statements ensure that you never find the cash drawer empty at the end of the month when you have a load of bills left to pay.

Cash-flow statements should project three to five years into the future, and for the first two years, they should include monthly cash-flow estimates. Monthly estimates are particularly important if your company is subject to seasonal cycles or to big swings in sales or expenses.

You get a bonus from all this work: The effort that you put into creating cash-flow statements for the company gives you a head start when the time comes to create a budget for your business (see 'Making a Budget' later in this chapter).

Exploring Alternatives

Wouldn't it be nice if you could lay out a financial forecast – create your pro-forma profit and loss accounts, estimated balance sheets, and projected cash-flow statements – and then just be done with it? Unfortunately the uncertain future that makes your financial forecast necessary in the first place is unpredictable enough to require constant attention. To keep up, you have to do the following things:

✔ Monitor your financial situation and revise the parts of your forecast that change when circumstances – and your own financial objectives – shift.

✔ Update the entire financial forecast regularly, keeping track of when past predictions were on target or off, and extending your projections another month, quarter, or year.

✔ Consider financial assumptions that are more optimistic and more pessimistic than your own best predictions, paying special attention to the estimates that you're the least certain about.

Why take the time to look at different financial assumptions? For one thing, they show you just how far off your forecast can be if things happen to turn out a bit differently than you expect. Also, the differences that you come up with are an important reminder that your forecasts are only that. You have to be prepared for alternatives.

The DuPont formula

If you really want to get a feel for what's going to happen when you change any of the estimates that make up your company's financial forecast, you have to understand a little bit about how the numbers relate to one other. The DuPont company came up with a formula that turned out to be so useful that other companies have been using a similar one ever since.

The idea behind the *DuPont formula* is simple. The recipe describes all the ingredients that play a role in determining your return on equity (ROE) – a number that captures the overall profitability of your company. ROE is your company's overall net profit divided by the owners' equity. But knowing that your ROE is 13 per cent, for example, is a lot like getting B+ on a test. You think that you did relatively well, but why did you get that particular mark? Why didn't you get an A? You want to know what's behind the mark so that you can do better next time.

By learning what's behind your company's ROE, you have a way to measure the impact of your financial predictions on your profitability. The DuPont chart shown in Figure 4-1 turns the formula into a pyramid, with the ROE at the top. Each level of the pyramid breaks the ratio into more basic financial ingredients.

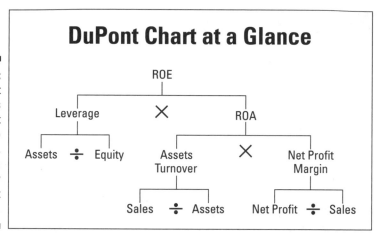

Figure 4-1:
The DuPont
chart turns
the DuPont
formula into
a pyramid,
with return
on equity
(ROE) at
the top.

First level

ROE = ROA × leverage

You can increase your company's return on equity by increasing the overall return on your company assets or by increasing your leverage (the ratio of your total company assets to equity).

Second level

Leverage = assets ÷ equity

As your debt increases relative to equity, so does your company's leverage.

ROA = asset turnover × net profit margin

You can increase your return on company assets by turning those assets into more sales or by increasing the amount of money that you make on each sale.

Third level

Asset turnover = sales ÷ assets

Asset turnover is the amount of money that you take in on sales relative to your company's assets. The bigger your asset turnover, the more efficient you are at turning assets into sales.

Net profit margin = net profit ÷ sales

Net profit margin is the profit that you make after subtracting expenses divided by the amount of money you take in on sales. The larger your profit margin, the lower your overall costs relative to the prices that you charge.

What-if analysis

After you see how the DuPont formula is put together, you can start exploring different assumptions and what happens when you change the financial forecast. With the DuPont formula, you can look at how those changes are likely to affect your projected profitability, measured by your return on equity. The DuPont formula makes answering questions like the following much easier:

- ✔ What if you cut prices by 3 per cent?
- ✔ What if you increase sales volume by 10 per cent?
- ✔ What if cost of goods sold goes up by 8 per cent?
- ✔ What if you reduce your leverage by 25 per cent?

Making a Budget

The pieces of your financial forecast – the pro-forma profit and loss accounts, estimated balance sheets, and projected cash-flow statements – are meant to create a moving picture of your financial situation tomorrow, next month, next year, and three or even five years out. Your financial picture is likely to be much clearer in the near term, of course, and much cloudier the farther out you try to look. Fortunately, you can use the best of your forecasts to make near-term decisions about where, when, and how much money to spend on your company in the future.

Making a budget for your company is one of the most important steps that you'll take as you prepare your business plan. Your budget, in effect, consists of a series of bets that you're willing to place, based on what you expect to happen in your industry and in the marketplace in general. Your budget spells out exactly where your company's resources will come from and where they're going to go, and helps ensure that you make the right financial decisions.

A budget is more than a collection of numbers, though. Your budget is also a business tool that helps you communicate, organise, monitor, and control what's going on in your business. Your company's budget does the following things:

- ✔ Requires managers to communicate with one another so that they can agree on specific financial objectives, including revenue levels and spending targets.
- ✔ Establishes roles and responsibilities for managers, based on how much money they're in charge of bringing in and how much they're allowed to spend.

✔ Creates a standard way of measuring and monitoring management performance by keeping track of how well the revenue targets and spending limits are met.

✔ Promotes the efficient and effective use of your financial resources by making sure that all your resources point toward a common set of business goals.

What's in the budget

The rough outlines of your company's budget look a lot like your projected cash-flow statement. In fact, the cash-flow statement is the perfect place to start. Projected cash flow is a forecast of where you think the company's money will come from and where it's going to go in the future. Your budget fills in all the details, turning your financial forecast into a specific plan for taking in money and doling it out.

The *master budget* that you create is meant to account for everything that your company plans to do over the next year or two. Although you spend your company's money in all sorts of ways, all those ways can be divided into short-term and long-term spending. In the short term, you use money to keep the business up and running every day, covering the costs and expenses of putting together and selling products and services. Over the longer term, you use money to invest in things that will make your company bigger, better, or more profitable.

If your company is small and you have only a few employees, a single master budget should be all that you need to keep your day-to-day finances on track as well as to make decisions in the future. When your company gets a little bigger, however, you may want to think about your company's finances in terms of more than one budget, each of which covers a different aspect of your business. You may want to create the following budgets:

✔ **Operating.** This budget deals with all the costs that are directly associated with putting your product or service together, such as materials, supplies, labour, utilities, services, and facilities.

✔ **Administrative.** This budget deals with the expenses that are involved in supporting your products and services, sales and advertising, administrative salaries, phone and fax lines, and travel expenses.

✔ **Financial.** This budget deals with the overhead expenses involved in managing your assets, including keeping your books, doing your taxes, controlling your product stock, and keeping track of your debtors (the money that customers owe you).

✔ **Capital.** This budget deals with funds that are earmarked for the purchase of expensive items, such as new equipment, computers, a company car, and additional office space.

✔ **Development.** This budget deals with money that is set aside for developing new products, opening branches in other cities, or marketing to brand-new groups of customers.

When you need several budgets, like those in the preceding list, you use a master budget to pull all the separate budgets together and make sure that they meet your company's larger goals and financial objectives.

Global Gizmos Company put together a budget for the next two years based on a financial forecast and its projected cash flow (see Figure 4-2). The company's master budget looks a great deal like one of its cash-flow statements. But the budget goes into more detail in dividing the broad financial objectives into actual revenue and expense targets for specific company activities. The cost of goods produced, for example, is broken down into the cost of raw materials and supplies, labour, and utilities and facilities.

How budgets are made

Somehow, it's never the right time to sit down and make a budget, there's always something much more important to do. This situation seems to hold true for household and company budgets alike. Why doesn't anybody like to do them? Often, there doesn't seem to be enough financial information around to make a budget that's of any real use. If you complete a financial forecast first, however, your company's budget is much easier to complete.

So when do you get started? If you're just starting your company, there's no time like the present. If you're already up and running, when you create a budget depends on the company's size. For really big companies, the yearly budget process may begin six to nine months in advance. No wonder that the job can feel a bit like never-ending drudgery! Most companies, however, can count on spending some serious time with their budgets three or four months before the next year gets under way.

Established companies can use their track records and financial histories as starting points for next year's budget. But be careful. When you're a veteran, it's all too easy to get a bad case of budgetary laziness, using last year's numbers as a shortcut to next year's numbers. Unfortunately, you can veer off financial course before you know it. A good compass for this situation is something called *zero-based budgeting*. When you insist on zero-based budgeting, you ask everybody – including yourself – to go back and start from the bottom in preparing a budget. Rather than use last year's budget numbers, you make full use of your financial forecast, building up a new set of numbers from scratch. The process takes a little longer but is almost always worthwhile.

Master Budget

Global Gizmos Company

REVENUE AND EXPENSES		
	Next Year	Year After
Budgeted Revenue:		
Gross receipts on sales	£895,000	£970,000
Dividend and interest income	4,000	5,000
Total Revenue Available	**£ 899,000**	**£ 975,000**
Budgeted Expenses:		
Cost of goods produced	£ 600,000	£ 650,000
Raw materials and supplies	250,000	275,000
Labor costs	300,000	325,000
Utilities and facilities	50,000	50,000
Sales, general, and administration	£ 165,000	£ 170,000
Sales and distribution	90,000	95,000
Advertising and promotion	30,000	30,000
Product service	15,000	20,000
Accounting and office support	30,000	30,000
Interest expense	12,500	12,000
Taxes	22,000	24,000
Buildings, equipment, machinery	40,000	£100,000
Equipment and computers	35,000	25,000
Expanded warehouse	5,000	75,000
Development projects	10,000	15,000
New product development	8,000	5,000
New market development	2,000	10,000
Long-term debt reduction	2,500	2,000
Dividend distribution to owners	6,000	7,000
Total Expenses Out	**£ 858,000**	**£ 980,000**
NET CHANGE IN CASH POSITION	**£ 41,000**	**£ -5,000**

Figure 4-2: The master budget looks a lot like the company's projected cash-flow statement.

The process of making a budget often gets a bad name in the business world. Rather than see budgeting as being a helpful business tool, business owners often rank budgeting among the greatest evils on earth, and managers often talk about it in unprintable ways. So what gives? When the budgeting process falls apart in a company, at least one of the following things probably happened:

✔ The budget was handed down from above and used to control the company's managers, taking away their ability to influence the business decisions that they were ultimately responsible for carrying out.

✔ The budget was based on short-term thinking, ignoring the company's longer-term plans and strategic goals.

✔ The budgeted revenue and expense targets had nothing to do with the company's larger financial objectives or its real financial situation.

To make sure that your own company's budget doesn't suffer these fatal flaws, take a close look at two ways to put together a budget.

Top-down budgeting approach

The top-down approach to making your budget is the simplest way to work through your company's financial plans. The process pretty much begins and ends with the people who are in charge. If your company is small, you may want to invite some outside people to join you – people whom you trust, such as your banker, accountant, or maybe a close business associate. The process goes something like this:

1. **Put the finishing touches on your company's financial forecast, including pro-forma profit and loss accounts, expected balance sheets, and projected cash-flow statements.**

   If certain pieces are missing or incomplete, try to get the information that you need, or make a note that the document you need is unavailable.

2. **Meet with the company's decision-makers (or your trusted group, if you're self-employed) to review the financial forecast.**

   Take time to discuss general expectations about the future. Talk about the business assumptions that go into the forecast and the key predictions and estimates that come out of it.

3. **Meet again to explore possible financial alternatives.**

   Look at different sets of business assumptions and weigh their potential effects on the forecast. Continue to meet until the group either agrees or agrees to disagree about the future.

4. **Come up with revenue and expense targets for each of your company's major business activities or functional areas (whichever is more appropriate to your company).**

5. **Meet one last time after the budget is in place to review the numbers and get it approved.**

   Put together a written summary to go along with the numbers so that everyone in the company knows what the budget is, where it comes from, and what it means.

Although top-down budgeting does a fairly good job when you know all the people in your company by their first names, the approach has some definite disadvantages when your company gets bigger. By including only the managers at the top, you run the risk of leaving out large chunks of the organisation and losing track of your real business situation when it comes time to plug in the numbers.

Bottom-up budgeting approach

The bottom-up approach to creating your budget really is just an expanded version of the top-down process, taking into account the demands of a bigger company and of more people who have something to say. You still want to begin putting together your budget by getting a group of senior managers together. That group should still spend time coming to a general understanding of, and agreement on, your company's financial forecast, along with the business assumptions and expectations for the future that go with it. But rather than forcing a budget from the top, this approach allows you to build the budget up from the bottom.

Don't ask the group of senior managers to go on and dictate the company's budget. At this point in the budget process, the bottom-up approach means that it's time to get managers and supervisors at all levels of the company involved. The process goes like this:

1. **Meet with senior managers and ask them to review the company's broad financial objectives for each of the major business areas.**

   Try to come up with guidelines that set the tone and direction for budget discussions and negotiations throughout the company.

2. **Ask managers to meet with their managers and supervisors at all levels in the organisation.**

   Meetings can start with a recap of the budget guidelines, but discussions should focus on setting revenue and expense targets. After all, these managers are the ones who actually have to achieve the numbers and stay within the spending limits.

3. **Summarise the results of the budget negotiations.**

   If necessary, get the senior group members together again to discuss revisions in the financial objectives, based on the insights, perceptions, and wisdom of the company's entire management team.

4. **Go through the process again, if you have to, so that everyone at every level of the organisation is on board (or at least understands the reasoning behind the budget and its numbers).**

5. **Approve the budget at the top.**

   Make sure that everybody in the company understands what the budget means, applying the budget not only to financial objectives but also to larger business goals

Book II

Money in Mind

Book III
Getting the Staff

'Being a pretty boy, being able to peel grapes, and being a good talker with flying experience would have made the perfect cabin steward but it would have saved us <u>both</u> a lot of time if you'd sent in a photograph, Mr Joseph.'

In this book . . .

Finding and keeping the best people is a challenge for any business, but this book gets you off to a flying start. As well as keeping your staff happy, you need to treat them fairly and abide by employment law, and this book navigates you through the basics. In addition to this vital information, we offer tips on developing your staff within their roles and inspiring them to greater achievements in the workplace.

Here are the contents of Book III at a glance:

Chapter 1: Staying on the Right Side of the Law

Chapter 2: Finding Person Friday – Advertising and Interviewing

Chapter 3: Employing People Successfully

Chapter 4: Disciplining and Dismissing Staff

Chapter 5: Paper Money, Money Paper – Payslips and Deductions

Chapter 6: Inspiring Employees to Better Performance

Chapter 7: Coaching and Development

Chapter 8: Tackling Performance Appraisals

Chapter 1

Staying on the Right Side of the Law

In This Chapter

▶ Understanding your employees' rights under the law

▶ Knowing who's an employee and who isn't

▶ Determining the kinds of workplace policies you need to draw up

▶ Managing without a whole lot of support systems

Small business owners are always worried about the amount of legislation that applies to them. There are a lot of laws, regulations, and codes of best practice out there, and staying on the right side of the law can be a tough job. Knowing what the law says before setting up a business or before employing your first member of staff is important, and if you start out with all the information you need, it's not as difficult or expensive to apply the law as you go along – and take it into consideration each time you make a business decision. Changing your habits later on can be much trickier.

Good employment practices encourage good employee–boss relationships. In turn that breeds loyalty and staff stay. People who are loyal work better. They have the interests of your business at heart because you have their interests at heart. Everyone's a winner.

Cutting through the Red Tape

'Red tape' is a term that conjures up images of bad regulations, strangling your business and making your life more difficult. Commentators sometimes blame the employment laws in the United Kingdom for putting too heavy a burden on business owners, but they're really intended to protect employees from bad employers, not from good ones. These laws also help employers protect themselves.

The law isn't a burden to good employers who want to do right by their employees; it's a source of clear guidance that helps you to keep employees instead of losing them to better employers. When hard workers with the skills you need seem hard to find, your business's success depends on your reputation as a desirable employer; rather than seeing the law as just so much red tape, think of it as a guide to becoming that kind of desirable employer.

Business people most often cite the National Minimum Wage and family friendly legislation about maternity, paternity and parental leave as causing them difficulties. Yet motivated employees who feel fairly paid and who know they can take the time needed to take care of family matters can increase your company's productivity so it's well worth your investment in sound policies.

Perhaps the biggest problem is that the legislation relating to small businesses is scattered around so many acts and regulations that keeping a grip on them can be difficult. Some acts, like the Data Protection Act or the Regulation of Investigatory Powers Act 2000, have such a wide scope that it's easy to forget that they can apply to small businesses and their employees. The headache isn't always so much the red tape as pulling it all together and knowing exactly what it means for your business.

Working Out What the Law Expects from You

Working out what the law expects from you can sometimes be quite demanding. Most employers wait until something has gone wrong or an employee has taken legal advice and made a claim against them before checking out where they stand legally. But forewarned is forearmed when it comes to small businesses and the law. If you're setting up a business or about to take on your first employee, this is the time to get advice on your legal position. If you already employ people and you haven't put a lot of thought into the legalities of your situation, take the time now to find out what your obligations and responsibilities are as an employer. It makes good business sense and will stop you making costly mistakes in the future.

Employees, whether full-time or part-time – apart from those who are exempt and as long as they've been employed by you for the relevant qualifying period – have employment rights including the following:

- ✔ National Minimum Wage

- ✔ Maximum weekly working hours (with breaks)

- ✔ Equal pay for equal work

- ✔ Four weeks' paid holiday (at least)

- ✔ Protection from discrimination

- ✔ A safe working environment

- ✔ Notice that their employment is ending (after one month)

- ✔ Written Statement of Employment Particulars (within the first eight weeks)

- ✔ Statutory sick pay and statutory maternity, paternity, and adoption pay

- ✔ Maternity, paternity, and adoption leave

- ✔ Parental leave and time off for family emergencies

- ✔ To request flexible working arrangements

- ✔ Protection from unfair dismissal (after one year)

- ✔ Redundancy pay (after two years)

If employees are unfairly treated and denied their employment rights, they can take a claim against you at an Employment Tribunal or in some cases in the civil courts. If you break the law, you can face prosecution in the criminal courts by an enforcing body such as the Health and Safety.

In most cases the legislation is reasonably clear, but some areas of employment law are governed by common law. *Common law* is the body of law that builds up as cases are heard in court and judges make their decisions, as opposed to *statutory law* which is passed by parliament.

Book III

Getting the Staff

Going the Extra Distance

Whatever the law says is just the start. You can go further and offer your workers better terms and conditions than the law demands. You can follow various codes of practice, which will help you to not merely to comply with the law but to go further. For example, the code on monitoring employees at work will not only help you comply with the Data Protection Act but following it will also help you to gain your employees' trust. ACAS – the Advisory, Conciliation and Arbitration Service – produces useful codes of practice on issues such as the new dismissal and disciplinary procedures which came into force in October 2004. You absolutely must comply with these if you are disciplining, dismissing or making someone redundant. Contact ACAS on

08457 474747 or through the Web site – www.acas.org.uk. Business Links will also point you in the right direction – their website www.businesslink. gov.uk has links to other organisations and departments which produce useful codes of practice.

Putting company policies in place dealing with workplace issues that don't come under the scope of legislation is a good idea. For example, you may decide to add a policy on the use of e-mail and the Internet. That's not a legal requirement but that way everyone knows up front whether employees can use company facilities for personal reasons.

None of this preparation costs much in terms of cash outlay, but planning, writing, and distributing policies does take time. However once you've brought yourself up to date with the law, implemented the codes of practice and drawn up your policies, all employees know where they stand, and staying on the right side of the law becomes second nature to your company's culture.

Deciding Who Has Rights

The people who work for you may not all have the same employment rights. Employees have different rights to people who work for you on a self-employed basis. Some rights are acquired by working for you for a particular length of time. Some are automatic no matter how long a person has worked for you and if you try to deny her those rights you will automatically be in the wrong. Some people who do particular types of work are excluded from rights that other people working in different jobs automatically have. Other rights apply to everyone who works in your workplace regardless of their status. Even people who don't work for you yet but have applied for jobs have some rights (see Chapter 2 on recruiting employees).

Potentially confusing? This section provides some definitions to help you navigate your way as your read through this chapter.

Employees

Employees work for you under a contract of employment. They include apprentices. It's all fairly clear-cut where a written document exists labelled 'contract of employment' or Written Statement of Employment Particulars. Problems arise when nothing is in writing and the worker argues that she's an employee and the employer argues that she's self-employed.

Employees start off from day one of your employment with some employment rights. Some of those rights are set out by law (known as *statutory rights*) and others are rights you give your employees through their contract terms and conditions (known as *contractual rights*). A contract exists as soon as you make an offer of employment and the employee accepts it, so anything in that contract stands and can't be changed without her agreement or you may be in breach of contract.

An employee has statutory rights from day one, such as the right to be paid at least the National Minimum Wage, the right not to be discriminated against, and the right to a healthy and safe environment to work in. The right to paid holidays starts to build up from day one and the regulations on working hours and breaks apply. Employees have to be given a Written Statement of Employment Particulars by the time they've been with you for eight weeks. If you try to deny an employee her statutory rights and sack her for asking for them, you have dismissed her unfairly in the eyes of the law.

You also give your employees rights through their contracts. You can give people better terms and conditions than the law allows – longer holidays, better rights to sickness pay, better redundancy payments – but you can't give them less than the law says. If you do offer better terms in the contract, you have to deliver or you're in breach of contact and the employee can take a claim against you.

If a contract is for a particular length of time – for example for three months – the employee has all the same rights as any other employee for those three months, but doesn't acquire the other rights that build up over time (such as maternity or paternity leave or redundancy payments).

Be careful if you go on extending someone's employment on short-term contracts: continuous employment for a year, or for two years, may allow an employee to argue at a tribunal that she has acquired rights, such as those to claim unfair dismissal (one year) and redundancy pay (two years) over that period of time.

Full time

A *full-time employee* is someone who works the normal working hours for your business. *Small Business Employment Law For Dummies* (Wiley) details the rules about the maximum number of hours someone can be expected to work in a week and the breaks you must give her, but all your full-time employees are entitled to all the statutory employment rights unless you work in certain employment sectors (see the section 'Exemptions', see later in this chapter).

Book III

Getting the Staff

Part-time

Anyone who works fewer than the normal number of full-time hours in your business is a *part-time employee*. Part-time employees have all the same statutory rights as full-timers and they can't be treated less favourably just because they don't work the same number of hours. Some employers try to give part-time employees less favourable conditions through their contracts – perhaps a lower hourly rate of pay – but you have to be careful not to discriminate.

You must pay part-time workers on a pro-rata basis. *Pro-rata pay* means that if they work half the hours of a full-time person you should pay them the same amount per hour for half the hours. You need to give them equal rates of pay, overtime pay, holiday pay, and the same rights in their contracts to training, career breaks, sick pay, maternity pay, and paternity pay. Similarly, if you offer full-time employees the right to join a company pension scheme and refuse your part time employees this scheme, you can be judged to be discriminating.

Self-Employed

Someone who works for you on a self-employed basis isn't an employee and doesn't enjoy the same rights as an employee. However, not everyone who works for you on what you might consider to be a self-employed basis is in reality self-employed. Some employers hire people on a self-employed basis in order to avoid giving them employment rights, but if a dispute arises and the worker takes a case to a tribunal, the tribunal may find that she has been an employee all along.

Someone who is genuinely self-employed works under a contract for service rather than a contract of employment. You are contracting that person to provide services. She is genuinely self-employed if some or all of the following apply; if she:

- ✔ Can send someone else along in her place to do the work
- ✔ Can work for more than one business at the same time
- ✔ Can work as and when she's required
- ✔ Provides her own tools or equipment to do the job
- ✔ Pays her own support staff if she needs any
- ✔ Is responsible for her own profits and loss

Employers sometimes see proof of self-employed status in the fact that workers pays their own tax, National Insurance, and VAT, don't get sickness pay, paid holiday, or regular wages, and don't come under the firm's disciplinary procedures. Those factors do count, but if those are the only factors that can be used to prove self-employment, a tribunal might decide that the relationship is really one of employer and employee and that you're just trying to avoid employment legislation.

People who are brought in as genuinely self-employed to do some work for you may not qualify for the same employment rights as your employees, but if they are working on your premises they have the right to a healthy and safe working environment (see *Small Business Employment Law For Dummies* for more details) and they have the right to have information about them treated properly and fairly under the Data Protection Act.

Consultants

Consultants working in your workplace are usually either self-employed or employees of other companies. If you take them on under a contract of employment on a temporary basis, they become employees. If their firms send them to deliver consultancy services under a contract for services, their employers should take steps to ensure that yours is a healthy and safe environment for them to work in, but you have the same obligations as for other self-employed workers.

Agency Workers

Companies often employ temporary workers through agencies. This saves you having to go through lengthy recruitment procedures to employ someone for a short time. These workers have a contract with the agency and the agency has a contract with you. In this case, the agency pays the worker direct and you pay the agency for delivering the service. The contract you have with the agency isn't an employment contract, so the worker isn't your employee.

However, it's not quite that straightforward. Over a period of time it's possible for a relationship to develop where something like a contract of employment exists between you and the agency temp, even if only in implied terms. If you insist that the agency can't send someone else along instead, if the person can't work for anyone else, if you supply all the tools and equipment, include the temp at your staff meetings, more or less treat her like one of your employees, and most importantly have control of the worker on the day-to-day supervision of her work a tribunal can decide that she is in reality an employee. A recent Court of Appeal case decided that once an agency worker has more than one year's service with a single 'end-user' employer they are almost bound to be the employer of the worker and other cases have followed suit. If you need to keep her on for longer than originally anticipated, offering her a job as an employee is a good idea.

A whole range of EU regulations giving workers protection have effectively given agency workers rights to paid holidays, rest breaks, minimum wages, maximum working hours, and protection from being treated less favourably if they are part time. The Secretary of State can extend individual employment rights to groups of people who aren't covered by current employment law, so it's likely that all workers, other than the ones who are genuinely self-employed, will eventually have the same protection as employees.

Home Workers

If people work in their own homes they will be employees unless they are genuinely self-employed. If you have an obligation to provide them with work, they can't pass that work on to someone else, you supply the tools and equipment, and they can't work under more than one contract for different employers at the same time, they are likely to be considered employees.

Exemptions

There are exceptions to every rule and some employees aren't entitled to all employment rights. Police, share fishermen, and merchant seamen employed wholly outside the UK and who are not ordinarily resident in the UK have no right to claim unfair dismissal or statutory redundancy pay. People who work for government departments can't claim statutory redundancy pay or minimum periods of notice. Members of the armed forces have no statutory employment rights other than the right not to be discriminated against. Temporary and casual workers won't usually be able to claim unfair dismissal or redundancy pay because they won't work for an employer long enough to acquire those rights.

The law does not protect people working under illegal contracts. If someone is, for example, paid cash in hand to avoid paying income tax and National Insurance, she has no employment rights. Anyone who is employed to do something illegal won't be protected either. The principle is that a wrong-doer mustn't benefit from her wrong-doing.

New age discrimination laws come into effect October 2006, so the best advice is to be very careful about treating your older workers less favourably than your younger ones. Of course you won't be able to discriminate against younger workers either.

Young People

From the age of 18, workers are entitled to the National Minimum Wage of £4.45 an hour (£4.60 from October 2007), which goes up to £5.35 an hour (£5.52 from October 2007) when they're 22. And you have to pay 16- and 17-year-olds a National Minimum Wage of £3.30 per hour, although apprentices under 19 are exempt, as are those over 19 and in the first 12 months of their apprenticeship. Anyone aged 16 and 17 may be entitled to time off with pay to study and you may be expected to help with those costs. You can take on someone under the age of 24 on an apprenticeship scheme. The Learning and Skills Council Web site has the details – www.lsc.gov.uk.

You can't employ a child under 13. The only exception is for child actors. Strict rules govern the hours that 13- to 16-year-olds are allowed to work: they can't work, paid or unpaid, before 7 a.m. and after 7 p.m, or during school hours. They can't work more than two hours on a school day or a Sunday and they can't work more than 12 hours a week during term time. In the school holidays 13- and 14-year-olds can work up to 25 hours a week and over-15s can do 35 hours. Rules also exist about breaks and time off. Some local authorities have other rules about school-age children working, so you should check with them before you take any young people onto your books.

After they are over school leaving age and up to the age of 18, the Children and Young Persons Act still protects young people and they can't work more than 8 hours a day or 40 hours a week. Their breaks are clearly set out too.

Book III

Getting the Staff

Deciding What to Put in the Contract

Employees have statutory rights and you can't do anything that takes away those rights. When it comes to the contract you can offer more generous terms and conditions of employment, but you can't write in clauses that take away the statutory rights.

Employees are entitled to a *Written Statement of Employment Particulars* within eight weeks of starting work. That should include all the main terms and conditions of their employment or refer employees to other relevant written documents.

Drawing Up Other Employment Policies

Your policies on pay, working hours, holidays, sickness absence, maternity, paternity and adoption leave should all be covered in the Written Statement of Employment Particulars. Apart from those and the terms that form part of the contract whether in writing or not, there are also policies for running your business that the law says you have to have and there may be others that would help everyone be clear about where they stand.

Some working parents have the legal right to request flexible working patterns and you might want to extend these to your whole work force.

You must have written policies on disciplinary procedures, grievance procedures, health and safety, discrimination including dealing with bullying, harassment and victimization (see *Small Business Employment Law For Dummies* for more details on all of these).

You might also want to consider drawing up policies on the use of alcohol and drugs, telephone, e-mail and the internet, smoking, even dress codes.

Your policies should all be in writing and you should make sure all your employees are aware of them and can have access to them at any time. They set the standards for everyone to aspire to and everyone knows exactly where they are from the start.

Managing Without an HR Department

Big firms usually have special departments employing human resources specialists to ensure they stay on the right side of the law, respond to all the government's latest demands on flexibility, and draw up policies that make everyone aware of how the workplace should operate. Most small businesses don't, but that doesn't prevent good small business bosses getting it right. Many of the small businesses that do get it right are no bigger than yours and have no more facilities, no bigger turnover, and no more profit. They have the systems in place right from the start to help them make sure they are complying with the law and good practice has become part of the culture. Each time a change in the law comes along that can pile on the pressure, little change is required because they're most of the way there already.

You don't need an HR or personnel department if everyone in the workplace knows exactly where they stand and everyone knows who is in charge of what. The person who pays the staff knows the legislation on pay and making deductions from pay and deals with sick and maternity or paternity pay. Someone else looks after the workplace, making sure that you don't break the health and safety regulations. It gets harder when it's just you who has to know everything about everything and make sure you don't break the law. However, it's still a question of putting the systems in place right from the start and building the business around them, instead of grafting on the means of complying with each piece of legislation as you find out about it.

Getting Help and Advice

You need good sources of information and some way of keeping up-to-date with changes as they come along the pipeline.

Most big banks provide very useful information on all aspects of running a business. Your solicitor and accountant, if you have them, will be helpful, but don't take petty problems to them as you have to pay for their time and there may be more cost-effective ways of getting help and support. Make sure any solicitor and accountant you use are experienced in dealing with small businesses. Big businesses are quite different animals and experience of working with big firms doesn't qualify people to work with small ones.

The government runs Business Links around the country, with offices in most big towns and cities and advisers with a whole range of business expertise. The service is free and can give you advice, guidance and support on everything to do with setting up and running a business, including how to deal with all aspects of employees' rights. Business Link also has a very comprehensive Web site where you can get most of the information you need (www.businesslink.gov.uk). Nevertheless, Web sites can't always give you the necessary support. You can get details of the nearest office to you on the Web site or in the local telephone directory or call 0845-6009006.

The Department of Trade and Industry (DTI) Web site also has lots of useful information for employers: www.dti.gov.uk.

ACAS (the Advisory, Conciliation and Arbitration Service) is an invaluable source of help to business. Its helpline number is 0845-7474747 and the Web site is www.acas.org.uk.

The Federation of Small Businesses is a group you may want to join. It has 205,000 members with 1.3 million employees between them. For an annual subscription of between £100 and £750 depending on how many employees you have, you get various services, including access to the legal helpline where you can talk to an adviser about any legal problems you have, including all aspects of employment law. The organisation lobbies government on issues of concern to small businesses, so as well as helping you stay on the right side of the law the Federation can give you a voice. Call 01253-336000 or check out the Web site at www.fsb.org.uk.

Book III

Getting the Staff

Chapter 2

Finding Person Friday – Advertising and Interviewing

• •

• •

As a small business manager, situations arise requiring you to find new members of staff. Whether you're looking to take on your first ever assistant, hoping to replace a worker who's left the business, or are expanding and need an extra pair of hands, you need to get the recruitment process correct. Good recruitment practice should bring in good candidates, and ultimately benefits your business.

But first things first! Do you really need to take on a new member of staff? It costs time and money to employ someone new, so take a careful look at how you staff your business at the moment. Be sure that you really need another person or to replace someone who's left before you start advertising.

Filling the Gap

Work out the skills that your new recruit should have and what his job will really involve. Think about whether you need someone permanent or someone to see you through a temporary period of increased workload. Maybe you don't really need another full-time person. Can a part-timer do the job? For many small businesses, part-timers are the answer when it comes to filling the gaps. They have all the same rights as full-time employees, but being part time allows many people to work and still fulfil their family or caring obligations when working full-time isn't an option. That gives you a wider pool of experienced and skilled people to recruit from.

If the job you have to offer is full-time, think about job sharing. As the name suggests, job sharing means that two (or more) people in effect share one job. They may split the week, work alternate weeks or alternate days, or some of their hours might overlap, but they do one job between them and share the pay and benefits of a full-time job. It can cost you a bit more in terms of training and admin, but job sharing can benefit you in a number of ways. Job sharing:

- ✔ Enables you to keep on experienced people who can't continue working full-time but who still want to be employed

- ✔ Gives you more flexibility if you have peaks and troughs in demand

- ✔ Means one job sharer is around when the other is on holiday or off sick, and because they have more control over their hours, job sharers usually have less time off sick and suffer less from stress

You need to choose people to job share who get on well together, which is never an exact science! They should have complementary skills and experience. Make sure that they divide the work fairly, that they have a way of communicating if they rarely see each other, and that each doesn't end up doing less or more than the hours you're paying them for.

Other methods of employment can be useful to know about. You can consider having people who work for you in term time and don't work during the school holidays. Or you can employ people on contracts where they're available as and when you need them and you pay them for the work they do (called *zero-hours contracts* because you don't specify any particular number of hours). Or you can recruit people temporarily as and when you need them to see you over periods of increased production.

You also have to think carefully about how much you can afford to pay any new employees. Pay has a bearing on whether or not you can afford to look for someone better qualified than a person who has left, or whether you can afford to entice someone from outside the area (which can be expensive in terms of relocation expenses).

 Don't forget the obvious factors like space and desks. If you're replacing someone and can use his old workspace that's fine, but adding an extra employee to the workforce means you'll need somewhere for him to work without leaving everyone else squashed and being in danger of breaching health and safety regulations.

Getting It Right from the Start

Getting your recruitment procedure right is crucial for the success of any business. If you hire the wrong person – someone with the wrong skills, someone who can't do the job, or someone who isn't competent and puts your other employees under stress or at risk – your whole operation is in danger of falling apart. At best working relationships become strained and at worst you start losing good employees or good customers or both. Don't waste time and money taking on the wrong person. And don't forget that certain aspects of employment law such as the laws on discrimination apply to people during the recruitment process, before they ever work for you.

Coming up with the job description

Having put a lot of thought into the kind of job or person you need, write a job description. No law says you have to have one, but it's a valuable exercise that helps you to define very clearly the job you want done. When you send the job description to potential applicants they can see exactly what they are applying for. A *job description* should:

- Give the job title
- Explain where the job fits into the overall structure – who the applicant will report to and who he will be responsible for
- Say where he will be expected to work
- Give all the duties he will be expected to carry out and the objectives of the job

Book III

Getting the Staff

As well as putting the details of the job on paper you can draw up a *person specification* of the kind of applicant you're looking for. You need to be careful when you're doing this: it's against the law even at this stage to discriminate against certain people (see *Small Business Employment Law For Dummies* for more details about discrimination). If specific skills, qualifications, and experience are required in order to do the job, you can list those. You might then list the qualities that you'd like the applicant to have that aren't essential for the job, but make it clear what's essential and what isn't.

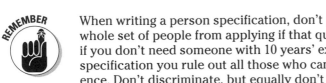

When writing a person specification, don't put down things that exclude a whole set of people from applying if that quality isn't essential. For example, if you don't need someone with 10 years' experience, by putting it in the specification you rule out all those who can do the job but have less experience. Don't discriminate, but equally don't reduce the pool of people you receive applications from or you may not get the best candidates.

Advertising – what you can and can't say

Writing a job description and a person specification makes writing an ad easier. You can say anything in your ad as long as it isn't discriminatory. If you say in a job ad that you want a man for the job, but in reality it's not absolutely essential, you're discriminating against women. But if you really do need a man (or woman) because it is a 'genuine occupational requirement', you're not discriminating. If, for instance, you run a shop selling women's clothes and you need someone who can help women in the changing-room, being female will be a requirement of the job.

Don't use words like waitress or manageress. Even if you will take on a man or a woman, it looks as if you intend to take just women and therefore discriminate against men. Use words that apply to both sexes or make it clear in the ad that the job is open to both sexes.

You can't discriminate against anyone on the grounds of race, sex, religion or other beliefs, sexual orientation, disability, or, since October 2006, age. You can find out more about the code at `www.agepositive.gov.uk`. You also can't refuse to appoint someone because they belong to a union or won't join a union.

In certain instances, you can advertise for someone solely from a particular sex or race. If in the last year, for example, few men or black people have been working in your particular field and you want to get a better representation in your workforce, you can encourage them to apply through your ads. But because the discrimination laws are a minefield, it's advisable to take advice from an organisation like the Equal Opportunities Commission at `www.eoc.org.uk` or 0845-6015901 or the Commission for Racial Equality at `www.cre.gov.uk` or 0207-9300000.

Placing your ads

Your ad needs to be to the point, but give enough information to allow people to decide whether or not to apply. Good job ads list:

- ✔ Essential skills required
- ✔ Relevant experience desired
- ✔ Necessary qualifications
- ✔ Application processes – where to send a CV or who to contact for an application form
- ✔ The job title and an outline of the tasks involved
- ✔ The closing date for applications

Where you decide to advertise depends on the audience you want to reach. If you're just looking for someone who lives locally, try the local papers (including any free ones that get put through letterboxes), local radio, schools or universities, and your local newsagent's notice-board. If you know that you're likely to have to go further afield to get the skills you need, think about the national papers.

Don't forget the trade press and magazines that people who work in your industry read. More employers are now using the Internet to reach a wider audience quickly. If you go into a search engine and type in 'job vacancies' you will see that there are many Web sites that carry job ads: www.jobsearch.co.uk; www.jobsin.co.uk or www.fish4jobs.co.uk to name just three. Some Web sites like www.reed.co.uk will carry job ads for free. If you want to attract people with disabilities, Jobcentre Plus offices are useful, but other options such as the Talking Newspaper Association are also available. You can contact them on 01435-866102 or at www.tnauk.org.uk. Think about making job descriptions available in large print or on tape for people with visual impairments or in different languages for applicants whose first language isn't English.

The wider you advertise the more applications, CVs, phone calls, and e-mails you're likely to get. Make sure that someone's available to deal with enquiries, send out forms, and collate all the applications.

Using an agency

Employment agencies can advertise on your behalf and can provide lists of possible candidates for you to look at. You have to pay a fee for an agency's services, so find out what they charge before you decide which agency to use.

Many agencies specialise in particular areas of work. These types of agencies can save you a lot of time, but they can also be very expensive.

You can recruit people through an agency on a temporary basis, meaning that the agency employs them rather than you – so the agency looks after their pay, tax, and National Insurance. This system enables you to try people out on a temporary basis before deciding whether to employ them yourself permanently. Using an agency also means that your business name doesn't have to be included in the advertising if you'd rather it didn't. Of course, if the agency can't find you anyone suitable you're back to square one and have lost valuable time, but you don't usually have to pay a fee in these circumstances. Just be aware that if you take on agency workers for more than a year, an Employment Tribunal may decide you have become their employer even if they're described as being self-employed by the agency or by themselves. For more on agency workers see Chapter 1.

Alternatively you can employ a firm of recruitment consultants to take you through the whole recruitment process from deciding on your person specification, to interviewing, to making a final choice. A recruitment consultancy differs from an employment agency in that the agency offer you the pick of people registered on its books and a recruitment consultancy charges a fee to do the job of recruiting for you. If the job is a very important one within your organisation you can use a firm of *headhunters* who actively look for the very best person on your behalf. They tend to be very specialised and because they know a lot about their industry they know where to look for people already working at the level you require.

Using the Jobcentre

You get a similar from Jobcentre Plus as from an employment agency (see the previous section 'Using an agency') but it doesn't cost you anything. You can advertise your job and get help from one of the vacancy managers. Advertising in the Jobcentre Plus can be a quick way to find new employees and you can arrange to take someone on, on a trial basis, before you offer them a permanent job. The people who use the Jobcentre are actively looking for work and often ready to start work straight away. If you employ someone through Jobcentre Plus you employ them and pay their salary direct to them, whereas if you recruit through an agency the person you take on may not be your employee, but paid by the agency.

Another advantage of using Jobcentre Plus is the advice the centre offers not only on recruitment but on just about every other aspect of employment, including help with employing people with disabilities.

The centres also run the *New Deal* scheme. Through New Deal you can get financial help if you take on a new employee and train them. Employers have been put off in the past because they felt that it was only people who were unemployed and therefore unemployable who went to Jobcentres to look for work, but as unemployment rates have fallen the people who use them are more often already employed and looking for better opportunities. You can find information on the New Deal and details of your local office at www.jobcentreplus. gov.uk or in the telephone directory.

Following up recommendations – and remembering to be fair!

Finding someone suitable to fill your vacancy can be as simple as asking around! Talk to your existing employees and colleagues, other people working in the area or industry, friends, family, or local business people and organisations.

How successful this method is usually depends on the level of expertise you're looking for. You may find someone if you're looking for a receptionist, but you may not if you're looking for a highly experienced financial director. It's certainly well worth thinking about as part of your recruitment plan, but you may be seen as trying to poach other people's employees. Also, if you rely on word of mouth alone you're limiting the pool of potential applicants to people who know people you know.

Considering Diversity

More and more businesses are realising the advantages of having members of staff of different racial and cultural backgrounds, ages, genders, sexual orientation, religious beliefs, and those with disabilities. Customers and suppliers appreciate being able to do business with a diverse workforce that reflects the community around it and it may improve your reputation. If you spread your net more widely when recruiting you're likely to have more applicants to choose from, with different experiences, knowledge, and skills, and your employees from varied backgrounds can help you understand your customers better. Some customers, for example, may prefer to deal with older people because they feel that older staff are more experienced and understand their needs better. If you only have young people on your staff those customers may well take their custom elsewhere.

Book III

Getting the Staff

Think carefully about having an equal opportunities policy. If you do face a claim for discrimination an Employment Tribunal will ask to see that policy. Use these guidelines to help prevent discrimination:

- ✔ Make sure that you don't exclude any one group when you write your job ad and job descriptions.

- ✔ Think about where you advertise. You may have to advertise in a wider range of publications than you have done in the past in order to get to all the people you'd like to reach.

- ✔ Make sure that people with disabilities who apply for jobs with you are able to get to interviews, and have access to your premises – otherwise you risk falling foul of the Disability Discrimination Act.

Grants (often up to 100 per cent of the costs) may be available to help you make reasonable adjustments around your workplace for disabled workers and to comply with the Disability Discrimination Act. Talk to your local Jobcentre Plus office for help and advice.

Sorting the Wheat from the Chaff – CVs and Application Forms

You need to decide how to extract the information from your candidates' applications in order to decide which ones to interview. Application forms and CVs both have their advantages and disadvantages, outlined in Table 2-1 for application forms and Table 2-2 for CVs.

Table 2-1	The Pros and Cons of Application Forms
Pros	**Cons**
You can decide exactly what you want to find out from your applicants, and can design the form yourself or buy ones from stationery suppliers.	You need to put a lot of thought into how the forms are designed and they need to be easy to fill in, or some people will be put off applying.
Every applicant fills in the same form so it's easy to compare skills, experience, and qualifications.	You have all the effort and cost of producing them and sending them out.
Some people feel happier about filling in a form as it gives them a guide as to what information is needed.	You have to be careful not to ask discriminatory questions.

Table 2-2	The Pros and Cons of CVs
Pros	**Cons**
The way a CV and covering letter are laid out will tell you something about the applicant's abilities.	You have no control over the information that's included on an individual's CV.
You don't have any of the costs of production, design, or sending them out.	All CVs have different information and layouts, so they're harder to compare.
People are more likely to apply if they don't have to fill in a form.	Applicants can easily hide work gaps.

Some employers prefer to use application forms that allow them to remove the personal information. This takes away the temptation not to see anyone over a certain age or who is of a particular sex or ethnic background. They then use just the parts of the forms that refer to skills, experience, and qualification when deciding who to interview, preventing bias or discrimination against a candidate when drawing up their short list. That's harder to do with CVs.

Whichever you decide to use, you're likely to get a better response in terms of the information people give you if you send them a copy of the job description and the person specification. Doing so gives applicants a much clearer idea than an ad can of what the job entails and of whether they've got a chance of getting it.

Under the Data Protection Act the personal information you collect about individuals has to be used for the recruitment process only. Only those people involved in the recruitment process should have access to it: You can't pass it on to anyone else without the applicant's consent and it should be kept confidential and in a secure place so it doesn't fall into the wrong hands.

Drawing up your short list

After you've got all the applications in you need to decide who to interview. Decide how many people you have time to interview (allowing 45 minutes to an hour is about right), and come up with a short list of that number. Five or six candidates is usually enough.

Book III

Getting
the Staff

Whittle the applications down to the number on your short list by using this process:

1. **List all the candidates and work out how well they fit your person specification and the job description.** Some applicants probably won't have the qualifications you need so you'll be able to reject them straight away.

2. **Give the rest a tick or a number of points for how well they meet each of the essential requirements to do the job.** If you do use a points system, make sure that you apply it equally fairly to all the applicants.

3. **From that you may have your short list.** If you still have too many people in the running look at how well each one of those who have the essentials match the other qualities you'd like your new employee to have.

If you take personal information into consideration, be very careful. Having more than one person involved in the short-listing process is a smart move because it helps avoid any personal bias on your part. For example, many employers still fall into the trap of thinking that men who have children won't want to ask for time off to look after them but that women will and make biased decisions on that basis. One employer was sued after a candidate submitted the same CV twice – once using an Indian name, the other time using an English name. The application with the English name was short-listed for interview and the one with the Indian name wasn't. Be fair.

Dealing with the ones that don't make the short list

Write to the applicants you don't want to interview so that they aren't kept hanging on, hoping. Thank them for their interest. If any of them do contact you to ask why they didn't get an interview, simply explain that other applicants were better suited to the job because they had more relevant qualifications, skills, or experience. Don't go down the route of saying that people were too old or too young or that they didn't have skills that you didn't specifically ask for in the job description or person specification.

Handling the Practicalities of Interviews

After deciding who's on your short list, invite them for an interview. However you contact the short-listed candidates, it's wise to confirm the details in writing.

Include the following information with your invite:

- Where the interview takes place
- When the interview takes place
- How long the interview will be
- Whether any tests or presentations are required and whether the person will complete them at the time of the interview or during a separate appointment
- Anything the candidates need to bring with them
- Details of who will be on the interview panel
- Who to ask for when they arrive
- How to get to the interview (with a map)
- Details of travel expenses

Also give the candidates a person to contact with any questions before the interview if they have problems getting there at the time you've given them or if they have any information they'd like you to know in advance (such as needing a car parking space close to the building because of a disability).

Making flexible appointments

The fun starts when everyone on your short list phones up to ask for a different date or time to the one you've allotted. Remember that you do need to hire someone suitable – these few candidates are your best chance so try to be as flexible as possible. Think before you allocate the times: If you're interviewing in Glasgow and someone is coming from Glossop, either allow time for him to get there and back in a day for an interview at a reasonable hour, or offer to put him up overnight in Glasgow. Similarly, there may be people on the list who have caring responsibilities first thing in the morning. In fact, some people may have applied and not told their current employer that they have an interview, so be prepared to start or finish later or earlier, to fit them in before or after work. Don't let a request for a later start immediately set alarm bells ringing about bad timekeeping. Keep an open mind.

Making sure everyone can get into the building

When you invite people for interview, ask them to let you know if they have any special needs. Someone may be a wheelchair-user, for example. You aren't expected to take out walls or build ramps, but you should be prepared to make reasonable adjustments so that the interview can take place without the candidate being in any way embarrassed or discriminated against. That can be something as simple as making sure someone gives up their car parking space for a few hours so that the candidate can park close to the main entrance. It may mean moving the interview from a room on the first floor to one on the ground floor, or making arrangements to use a room somewhere away from your work premises.

Book III

Getting the Staff

Paying for expenses

You don't have to pay for travel expenses. If your applicants are all from your local area, the issue probably won't arise. If they're coming from further afield and you don't cover expenses, you run the risk that your best applicants may not be able to afford the journey. After you've selected your short list, look at where people are in the country. If you decide that you probably do need to cover some people's costs, it's better to offer to pay everyone's expenses.

Planning the Interviews

Employers often give little thought to either the process building up to the interview or how to conduct the interview itself. You're spending time and money to recruit someone, so preparing for the interview is well worth doing so that you can be sure to get the best out of it.

You'll be making first impressions of the people you interview, but they'll also be making first impressions of you. If you don't seem very well organised they may decide there and then that they don't want to work for you.

Work out who, apart from yourself, should be on the interviewing panel. As a small business owner or manager you may decide to do the interviewing yourself, but it usually helps to have at least one other person's opinion. Two heads are normally better than one. Consider involving some of the following people on your interview panel:

- ✔ If you have business partners or management colleagues, see if one of them is available to help.

- ✔ If the new employee will report directly to someone other than you, consider involving that manager.

- ✔ If you have a human resources or personnel department, enlist their help.

- ✔ If you've used a recruitment agency to help find candidates, try to involve the agency in the interviews.

- ✔ If the job requires a particular skill, invite a relevant member of staff onto the panel, to assess the level of that skill for each candidate.

It really helps if everyone involved in the interview knows the candidates' application forms or CVs reasonably well and has them available at the interview. You can use this information to come up with the list of questions you want to ask. If there are any unexplained mysteries about gaps in employment, you may want to ask the candidate about those.

Decide how long you realistically need for each interview and leave some time afterwards to discuss each candidate with the other people on your interview panel. The length of the interview is important for the candidates as well as for you. You need time to extract the information you want and the interviewees need to feel they've had time to get their points across. So 45 minutes to an hour is usually enough, although you may want to set aside extra time for specific tests.

Working out what to ask

The essential skills, qualifications, and expertise to do the job are the most important issues to address at an interview. So those are the areas you should concentrate on! Asking good questions should get you good answers in return. Prepare the kinds of questions that don't invite a 'yes' or 'no' answer. Other questions will arise as the interview goes on, depending on what the candidate has to say.

Start by introducing everyone on the panel, explaining a little bit about your business and its structure and where the job fits into that. Outline how the interview will be conducted. That allows time for the interviewees to get settled. Give each interviewee a chance to ask you any questions they have at the end and explain what happens next.

Be very wary of asking personal questions. You can't ask women about their childcare arrangements and not ask men the same questions – unless you want to end up being sued for discrimination. Only ask questions that are relevant to the job: asking about whether someone is married or not or has children may be used against you later. Questions about disability have to be carefully worded too. You have to discuss how you can help someone with a disability to do the job you're offering rather than talk about why it would stop them doing the job. You can't use a disability as a reason not to employ someone unless it's justified. A person who is seriously visually impaired may not be able to drive your forklift truck, but if the job you are trying to fill is an office job his visual impairment may not rule him out. If he can do the job as long as you make reasonable adjustments around your workplace then you have to ignore the disability.

Don't make any rash promises during an interview – if you offer an interviewee the job there and then with a package that includes all sorts of benefits (such as a company car) and he accepts your offer, you can't then change the offer later if you realise you can't afford it.

Setting tests

If a job requires a very particular skill you may want to conduct some kind of test of that skill as part of the interview process – for example a typing or shorthand test or a forklift driving test. *Psychometric tests* (measuring intelligence, decision-making and problem-solving skills, aptitude, and personality) are popular, especially when it's difficult to compare every candidate's skills

Book III

Getting the Staff

and experience. If you do decide to include any tests, they must be relevant to the job and not discriminatory.

Tests can be done during, after, or before the interview, but you need to use them as part of the selection process rather than as the one and only method of choosing the best person for the job.

Taking notes

After each interview, write notes of key information, otherwise you may mix up important points. Only record what was said in the interview. Stick to the facts.

To make accurate notes as soon as possible, build into the interviewing time breaks where you can discuss the candidates and compare notes with fellow interviewers. Otherwise, by the end of a day remembering which candidate said what can become tricky!

After all the interviews are finished, you may want to add some notes that explain the criteria you used to select the eventual winner. The candidates have the right to see interview notes and may ask to see those notes if you don't offer them the job and they plan to bring a case against you at a tribunal for discrimination.

After the interviewing is over, only keep personal information if it's relevant to the selection process, and make sure that the notes and personal information are kept somewhere safe where they can't fall into other people's hands.

Checking Up on Your Chosen One

After going through the selection process and picking your best candidate, you can carry out a few checks before making the job offer, or you can make the job offer conditional on all your checks being satisfactory. Some checks are essential, others are your choice, as explained in this section.

When making your checks on the candidate:

- ✔ Only do checks that are necessary and for specific purposes
- ✔ Do checks only for the candidates you want to appoint
- ✔ Let people know you're going to do checks beforehand and whom you're checking with
- ✔ Don't use information that doesn't come from reliable sources

✔ If the checks throw up something negative, give the person the chance to explain

✔ Make sure that the information you get is kept confidential and secure

Following up references

You can take up references at any point during the recruitment process, but don't forget that most candidates will probably prefer you not to contact their current employers unless you are making them a firm job offer. You can't contact referees without a candidate's agreement, and previous employers don't have to give references unless they work in the financial services sector.

Despite the fact that many employers complain that they've had good references for employees who later turned out to be a disaster, most bosses do still use referees to check out a candidate's details.

You can insist on referees' details being given and make a job offer conditional on getting satisfactory references but an outside chance remains that if the references aren't satisfactory, or someone refuses to give one, and you do withdraw the job offer, you can still be sued for breach of contract.

When asking for references, you're using personal information supplied to you on application forms and CVs. Under the Data Protection Act you have to keep that information confidential. Get the applicant's permission before you follow up references. You can have a section on the application form that you ask applicants to sign to give their consent and that makes it clear you will be using the information they've given you.

Employers have to tell it as it is. If they do agree to give a reference it has to be truthful. If you later find that someone exaggerated an applicant's skills and you lose out because of that, you can sue the referee. Similarly, employees can take claims against employers who give them references that they feel unfairly damage their careers. The upshot is that many big organisations will now only give references confirming the very basic facts such as length of employment and job title. If you don't get the references you want, think about offering the job on a trial basis.

Proving that potential staff are entitled to work in the UK

All your employees have to be entitled to work in the UK and you have to check that they are. It's a criminal offence to employ anyone 16 or over who doesn't have permission to work in the UK or to do the type of work you're employing them for. There is now an unlimited fine for employers who break the rules.

The rules are very complicated, so check up with the Home Office Employers Helpline on 0845-0106677 or its Web site `www.employingmigrantworkers.org.uk`.

British citizens, Commonwealth citizens who have the right to live in the UK, and European Economic Area (EEA) nationals and their family members can work in the UK without restrictions on the length of time or the work they do. People who come into the UK under the Highly Skilled Migrant Programme or under the Working Holidaymaker Scheme – which allows Commonwealth citizens aged 17–30 to stay in the UK for 2 years – can work without work permits. Some students from outside the EEA over the age of 16 can work in the UK for up to 20 hours a week during term-time and full-time outside term-time. The dependents of existing UK permit holders are generally allowed to work without a permit themselves.

Checking convictions

If the job you're offering involves working with children or adults who are vulnerable – disabled or elderly – you must check convictions with the Criminal Records Bureau Disclosure Service (`www.disclosure.gov.uk`). Only make these checks if you've decided to offer someone the job, and make the offer conditional on getting a satisfactory result. Some legal and financial jobs require these checks too. If the job involves child care you can also ask on the Criminal Records Bureau application form whether someone is on the government's lists of people considered unsuitable for that kind of work.

Convictions are *spent* if someone was convicted of a crime and had no further convictions during his rehabilitation period. Treat someone with spent convictions as if those convictions had never happened. If the person was in prison for more than 30 months because of a conviction, it can never be spent.

Checking health

Some employers insist on a potential employee having a medical examination before starting the job. If that's the case, make it clear when you make the job offer that you want a satisfactory medical report to show that the candidate is fit to do the job and that if he refuses or the results aren't satisfactory the job offer won't stand. Other employers ask for a health questionnaire to be filled in, which, if it does throw up problems, can be followed up with a medical.

Only insist on health checks if you are sure that you want to take someone on. Don't insist that someone with a disability has a medical if you wouldn't insist on someone else having the same checks or you will be guilty of discriminating. Checks should really only be necessary if there's a legal requirement, such as an eye test for someone doing a driving job.

Some employers worry that candidates may be drug users and insist on health checks for that reason. If the employee may be at risk if his judgement is impaired due to drug use or he may put other employees at risk, tests can be justified. Make it clear when you make the job offer that drug use would rule the candidate out as being unfit to do the job and that relevant tests would be part of the medical.

Candidates have the right to refuse a health check; you have to have their written consent before you ask a doctor to do a medical report. If his own doctor does the examination a potential employee has a right to see the report and can refuse to let you see it even though you'll have to pay the doctor's fee. But of course, you have the ultimate sanction in that if you insist on a satisfactory medical report and don't get it, you can decide not to take the person on.

Checking qualifications

If a qualification is essential for the job, check it! You can make a job offer that's conditional on that check being positive. You can ask for certificates, or check with colleges, universities, or any other professional organisations or examining boards.

Experian offers a service for checking out degrees (www.uk.experian.com), the Qualifications and Curriculum Authority has a database of vocational qualifications (www.qca.org.uk), the Learning and Skills Council can help you check on National Vocational Qualifications (www.lsc.gov.uk), and the National Academic Recognition Information Centre can check overseas qualifications (www.naric.org.uk).

Book III

Getting the Staff

Offering the Job to Your Dream Candidate

As soon as you make an offer – whether it's over the phone, by e-mail, or by letter – and the candidate has accepted it, a contract exists between you and your new employee.

In theory you don't have to put anything in writing at this stage. The law says that an employee has to be given a Written Statement of Particulars of Employment not later than eight weeks after he starts his employment with you.

If you don't really want to appoint any of the candidates or you don't feel any are right, don't appoint anyone. Get a temp in to tide you over and start looking again. Better this than giving the job to the wrong person.

Making an offer that can't be refused

After you find the right candidate, you have to discuss money. You may have mentioned ball-park figures during the interview, but now it's time to make an offer and negotiate a deal that suits both you and the employee.

Think about the whole package you are prepared to offer. You may have already thought this through when you were considering employing someone in the first place. You can attract good employees with contributions to an occupational pension scheme, use of a company car, or better holiday and sick pay than most employers.

Sometimes it's not just money that matters to employees. The other terms and conditions on offer can be what makes or breaks the negotiations. Your chosen candidate may be happy to settle for the money you're offering as long as he has a few extra days of holiday or flexible hours of work. Discuss and negotiate and come up with a package he can't refuse. Don't forget that if he's moving from a job outside your local area he may have the costs of selling a home and buying another, plus the costs of moving and getting his family settled.

After an agreement has been reached, put the whole deal in a follow-up letter with the main terms and conditions of employment. It makes things easier for everybody and allows no cause for dispute.

Setting the start date

You may want your new employee to start straight away, but unless he's already out of work that's not likely to be possible. Most people have to give their bosses at least a week's notice and many have contracts that stipulate much longer notice periods. He isn't likely to be willing to hand in his notice while there are conditions to the offer and he may well want an unconditional offer, with all the main terms and conditions, in writing, before he takes that final step. He may be able to negotiate that his current boss lets him go sooner than the contract allows, but think about how you'd feel if one of your employees wanted to go without working out his notice.

Withdrawing a job offer

After the job offer has been made and accepted, a contract exists. If you made it conditional on getting satisfactory checks and the results weren't what you'd hoped for, you can withdraw your offer. However, if you made the offer conditional on satisfactory references and you don't get them and withdraw the offer, you can be sued for breach of contract.

If you just change your mind after making an offer or you made promises of terms and conditions that you later find you can't deliver, the employee can sue you for breach of contract and damages. Someone who has been unemployed would find it difficult to claim damages, but someone who gives up a good job and starts to make arrangements to move homes can run up quite a lot of expenses and have quite a sizable claim.

You can offer the job on a trial basis for a particular period of time – long enough to find out if the chosen candidate is really up to the job. If you then decide to withdraw the job offer at the end of that time, you have to give the employee the correct period of notice, or extend the trial period and provide some training. If you withdraw the job offer after a trial period but you don't come up with the training you promised at the outset, the employee can sue for breach of contract.

Book III

Getting the Staff

Chapter 3

Employing People Successfully

In This Chapter

▶ Finding motivations and rewards

▶ Keeping on the right side of employment law

*U*nless you intend working on your own, you will be involved in employing and motivating others to do what you want them to do. Even if you don't employ people full-time, or if you outsource some portion of your work to others, you will have to choose how to get the best out of them and how to reward their achievements.

Motivating and Rewarding Employees

Management is the art and science of getting people to do what you want them to do, because *they* want to do it. This is easier said than done.

Most entrepreneurs believe that their employees work for money and their key staff work for more money. Pay them enough and they'll jump through any hoop. This view is not borne out by most of the research, which ranks pay as third or even fourth in the reasons why people come to work.

If it isn't necessarily money, why do people work where they do? We help provide some of the answers in the following sections.

The practice of management

In this section, I give you some practical tools you can use to get the very best out of your employees.

The starting point in getting people to give of their best is to assess them as individuals and to recognise their specific needs and motivations. These differences are in part influenced by age, gender, or job. They are also affected by an individual's personality. You need to tailor your actions to each person to get the best results.

Our best advice is: Get to know everyone. This may sound insane in a small firm and after all you almost certainly recruited them all in the first place. By observing and listening to your employees you can build a picture of them that will help you motivate them by making them feel special:

✔ **Show an interest in people's work.** This is nothing to do with monitoring performance and more to do with managing by walking about, and seeing everyone, and talking with them as often as possible.

If you employ less than five people you need to spend some time with each of them every day, up to ten people every week. After that, you should have managers doing much the same thing, but you still need to get around as often as possible.

✔ **Promote from within when you can.** Too often people look outside for every new appointment. That is more or less saying that people you currently employ are not up to the task. There will be occasions where you have to bring someone in with new skills and special abilities. But if you can promote from within everyone can be a winner. When one employee gets a promotion others see career prospects perhaps they hadn't seen before, and you have someone you know and trust in a key job. Your newly promoted employee can help train someone up to take his or her former job, thereby saving you training time, also.

✔ **Give title promotions in lieu of job promotions.** A worker you don't want to lose may crave a certain position that you know he or she would fail in. Make the employee's benefits and status the same as for the desired position and add a new title to show that you value the employee and his or her work.

A likely situation is with a great salesperson. If they are ambitious as well as a brilliant salesperson they will want to become sales manager, which is an important step on their career ladder and demonstrates to their spouse, partner, and peers, as well as to themselves that they are doing a good job. Unfortunately most great salespeople make lousy managers. If you promote them the chances are you'll lose a good salesperson and have to fire them for being a useless manager in a few months' time. So keep them motivated by giving them the same package you would a sales manager, the same level of car, salary and other employment conditions, and promote them to a new title, sales executive or key account manager, for example. After all if they are selling so much they must be making good money for the business. They have the status and the cash and you keep a great salesperson doing what they do best, selling.

This can be a strategy in a small firm to create career progression for more people than might otherwise be possible.

✔ **Give praise as often as you can.** The rule is simple: Minimise your reaction to bad results and maximise your appreciation of good results. Autocratic employers continually criticise and complain, finding only poor performance wherever they look. Criticism reinforces poor behaviour.

Everyone wants to be recognised and strangely enough people often prefer to be shouted at than ignored. So if doing things wrong is the only way to get noticed that's what may well happen.

You can always leaven out criticism with some favourable comment. For example if an employee is making some progress, but is short of being satisfactory, saying something like, 'This is certainly an improvement, but we still have a way to go. Let's spend a little time together and I'll see if we can't get to the bottom of what is holding you back', might produce a better level of motivation than just shouting out your criticism.

✔ Create a no-blame culture. Everything in business is a risk. If it were not there would be no chance of making a profit. It's the uncertainty around all business processes that creates that opportunity to make money. Not many bookmakers would be prepared to take a bet on a horse race after it had happened and the winner had been announced.

To a greater or lesser extent, you delegate some of the responsibility for taking risks on to your employees. But how should you react when the inevitable happens and things go wrong, as they will in some cases. If you jump up and down with rage, then no one will ever take a risk again. They'll leave all the decisions to you and you'll become even more overworked. Good people will get highly de-motivated and leave. If you take a sympathetic and constructive attitude to failure you will motivate and encourage employees to try again.

You need to make clear that tolerance of mistakes has its limits and repetition of the same mistake will not receive an equally tolerant reaction.

✔ Reduce de-motivation. In fact, very often the problem is not so much that of motivating people, but of avoiding de-motivating them! If you can keep off the backs of employees, it is quite possible that they will motivate themselves. After all, most of us want the same things: a sense of achievement or challenge, recognition of our efforts, an interesting and varied job, opportunities for responsibility, advancement, and job growth. But in a small firm the potential for de-motivation is high. Workloads invariably peak and there is never any slack in the systems of a small firm. Inevitably some employees will feel overloaded, neglected, or just plain hard done by. It may not reach the stage where people will complain, or start taking time off sick, but having de-motivated people around can create an unhealthy climate for everyone else.

So you need to look out for any negative behaviour and find out the cause. A 'couldn't care less attitude', lack of enthusiasm, or any signs of aggression can be useful indicators that all is not well. You need to counter de-motivators with a burst of motivators such as recognition and advancement, which cause satisfaction.

✔ Motivate off-site employees. Part-time workers, telecommuters, and key subcontractors, who either do much of their work off-site or who are not around all of the time, have to be built into your motivational plans too.

Book III

Getting the Staff

Dealing with difficult or de-motivated employees

Difficult or de-motivated people need prompt and effective managing. Dissatisfaction can spread quickly and lower motivation levels in others. The first step is to identify the causes of the problem. The causes may be to do with the employee or with the job itself. The problem may be brought about by illness, stress, or a personality clash between people working together.

Whatever the cause, the initiative for re-motivating them has to come from you. However the only reason for going through this effort is because either that employee has delivered satisfactory results in the past or you believe they have the potential to do so, if you can just find the key.

A good starting point is to recognise some basic truths about difficult or de-motivated people.

- ✔ Difficult people are not always out to take advantage of you or others. It is possible to pull them into a partnership if you can find the right shared goals. These have to be exciting, realistic, attainable, and important to them as well as the business.

- ✔ Difficult people can change. Dramatic changes in behaviour are possible and even the most intransigent employee can be won over. Very often it's just the approach taken to the problem that limits a difficult person's desire to change. If, for example, an employee consistently comes in late, you could start by warning them, then shouting at them, and finally you could threaten them with disciplinary action. It may even have to come to that. But how would events turn out if you started by giving the business reasons why turning up on time is important, with some examples of how being late affects their performance and ultimately limits their options for advancement.

- ✔ Difficult people can't be ignored. Unfortunately employees who set their own standards of behaviour well below the standard you expect of others do have a bad influence, especially on new employees. You can hardly demand punctuality of some people and not of others. Nor can you adopt the philosophy that if you leave them long enough they will really step out of line and then you can fire them. As the boss you have to manage all those who you employ and motivate them to perform.

Keeping motivation all in the family

Over 80 per cent of small businesses are family businesses in which one or more family members work in the organisation. Family businesses have both strengths and weaknesses when it comes to motivation. By being aware of them you can exploit the former to do your best to overcome the latter to give your business a better chance of prospering.

The factors that motivate or de-motivate family members can be different than those affecting non-family members.

The overwhelming strength of the family business is the different atmosphere and feel that a family concern has. A sense of belonging and common purpose more often than not leads to good motivation and performance. Another advantage is that the family firm has greater flexibility, since the unity of management and shareholders provides the opportunity to make quick decisions and to implement rapid change if necessary. On the downside, there are several weaknesses. Although these are not unique to family businesses, family firms are particularly prone to them. These are the main ones:

- ✔ Unwillingness to change has been identified as the single most common cause of low motivation in family firms. Family firms often do things the way they've always done them just because that's the way they've always done them. This can lead to stagnation in the marketplace and failing confidence in investors. Resistance to change is exacerbated by diminishing vitality, as founders grow old.

- ✔ Family goals and commercial goals come into conflict. Unlike other businesses, family firms have additional objectives to their financial performance targets, for example: building family reputation and status in the community; providing employment for the family; protecting family wealth; ensuring independence; a dynastic wish to pass on a position, in addition to wealth, to the next generation. However, superimposing these family values on the business can lead to difficulties. For example nepotism may lead to employment of family members beyond their competence, or a salary above their worth. This can lead to discontent and be de-motivational for non-family members.

- ✔ Facing conflict between growth and ownership. Families prefer majority ownership of a small company to minority holdings in a big company where they are answerable to outside shareholders. Basically a dilemma that all family managers face is one of either growing the company, keeping purely commercial goals in mind at whatever risk to family control, or to subordinating the firm's welfare to family constraints. This affects all areas of the business, from recruitment through to management.

- ✔ Impact of and career prospects of non-family employees may be limited. At management level family pride will sometimes not allow a situation where its members are subordinate to an outsider – even if the outsider is a better person for the job. Also, reliance on family management to the exclusion of input from outsiders may starve a growing firm of new ideas. A family firm may become inward looking, insensitive to the message of the marketplace, unreceptive to outside ideas, and unwilling to recruit competent outside managers. None of these are factors likely to be motivational to others in the business.

Book III

Getting the Staff

These are problems a family firm must address if all the effort put into motivating employees is not to be seen as a cynical deception. It would certainly be helpful to have a clear statement of family policy on the employment of family members, succession, and on ownership. Then non- family members can either buy in or not join in the first place.

Rewarding achievements

Whilst people often come to work for a set number of hours each week, it is what they do during that time that matters most to the organisation. Different types of work have different measurable outcomes. Those outcomes have to be identified and a scale arrived at showing the base rate of pay and payment above that base for achieving objectives. Different types of 'payment by results' schemes are in common use in different types of firm and the conditions that most favour these types of pay need to be carefully examined to make sure you pick the right mix of goals and rewards.

Ground rules in matching pay to performance:

- Make the rules clear so everyone knows how the reward system will work.
- Make the goals specific and if possible quantifiable.
- Make the reward visible so everyone knows what each person or team gets.
- Make it matter. The reward has to be worthwhile and commensurate with the effort involved.
- Make it fair, so people believe their reward is correctly calculated.
- Make it realistic because if the target is set too high no one will try to achieve it.
- Make it happen quickly.

The following sections address specific reward systems.

Paying a commission

This is perhaps the easiest reward system, but it really only works for those directly involved in selling. A *commission* is a payment based in some way on the value of sales secured by the individual or team concerned.

You have to make sure that the order is actually delivered or executed before any commission is paid and you may even want to make sure the customer has paid up. However, as with all rewards, you must keep the time-scale between doing the work and getting the reward as short as practicably possible, otherwise people will have forgotten what the money is for.

It makes sense to base the commission on your gross profit rather than sales turnover; otherwise you could end up rewarding salespeople for generating unprofitable business.

Awarding bonuses

A *bonus* is a reward for successful performance, usually paid in a lump sum related as closely as possible to the results obtained by an individual, team, or the business as a whole. In general, bonuses are tied to results so that it's less obvious how an individual contributed directly to the result achieved. For example a company bonus may be paid out if the firm achieves a certain level of output. Keeping everyone informed as to how the firm is performing towards achieving that goal may well be motivational, but the exact role say a cleaner or office-worker has in helping attain that goal is not easy to assess – not as easy as it is to calculate a salesperson's commission, say.

Bonuses can be paid out periodically or as a one-off payment for a specific achievement.

Sharing profits

Profit sharing involves giving a specific share of the company's profit to the firm's employees. The share of the profits can be different for different jobs, length of service, or seniority.

This type of reward has the great merit of focusing everyone's attention on the firm's primary economic goal – to make money. It is quite possible that one or more employees can be performing well, but others drag down the overall performance. The theory is that the performing staff puts pressure on the others to come up to the mark.

If profits go up, people get more; but it can go the other way too, which can be less attractive. Also, profit targets can be missed for reasons outside of the employees' direct control. If you are dependent on customers or supplies from overseas, for example, and the exchange rate moves against you, profits, and hence profit-related pay, can dip sharply. However unfair this may seem to a receptionist who has been hoping for extra cash to pay for a holiday, this is the hard reality of business. If you think your employees are adult enough to take that fact on board, then this can be a useful way to reward staff.

Sharing ownership

Share option schemes give employees the chance to share in the increase in value of a company's shares as it grows and prospers.

Book III

Getting the Staff

The attraction of turning employees into shareholders is that it gives them a long-term stake in the business and hopefully will make them look beyond short-term issues and ensure their long-term loyalty. Of course, there can be unwelcome side effects if the value of the business goes down rather than up.

Giving skill and competence awards

You can give a skill or competence award when an employee reaches a certain level of ability. These awards are not directly tied to an output such as improved performance, but you must believe that raising the skill or competence in question will ultimately lead to better business results.

The award itself could be cash, gift certificates, extra days of holiday, a trip to a show or sports event, or whatever else your employees might appreciate. Bottles of wine always seem to be well received!

Compensating Your Employees

Finding and motivating employees is one part of the employment equation. The other is recompensing them for their efforts and achievements either by way of pay, or by some other benefit that is at least as appealing to each individual employee.

Setting payment levels

It's certainly true that people don't come to work just for money. But they certainly won't come if you don't pay them and they won't stay and be motivated to give of their best if you don't give them the right pay. But how much is the right amount? Get it too low and your ability to attract and retain productive and reliable people capable of growing as your business grows is impaired. But pay too much and your overheads rise so much you become uncompetitive. That is a real danger for small firms where the wages bill often represents the largest single business expense.

These ground rules are not very complicated but they are important:

- Only pay what you can afford. There is no point in sinking the company with a wage bill that it can't meet.
- Make sure pay is fair and equitable and is seen as such by everyone.
- Make sure people know how pay scales are arrived at.
- See that pay scales for different jobs reflect the relative importance of the job and the skills required.

✔ Ensure your pay scales are in line with the law on minimum wage requirements. Since April 1999 a *statutory minimum wage* is in effect in the UK.
The amount is governed by the age of the employee and whether an
employee is undergoing training. The hourly rate changes over time, so
you need to keep abreast of the latest rates (www.jobcentreplus.gov.uk
has information on current rules in this area).

✔ Ensure your pay scales are competitive with those of other employers in
your region or industry.

Big companies go in for a process known as *job evaluation*. This involves
looking at each job and evaluating it against a range of factors such as complexity, qualifications, skills, experience required, any dangers or hazards
involved, and the value of the contribution to your business. Creating and
maintaining a structure like this is a full-time job in itself. It is certainly not
something a small business should undertake lightly.

You can get most of the advantages of having a job evaluation system by finding out the going rate for key jobs in other people's businesses. The going rate
is the pay rate that normally applies to a particular job in a particular geographic area. Inevitably not all jobs are identical and certain aspects involve
differences in employment conditions that inevitably affect the going rate. For
example, working hours, employment conditions, security of tenure, pension
rights, and so forth vary from firm to firm. You need to have a procedure in
place to routinely monitor local going rates and a system to correct for variations in employment conditions between your firm and other similar firms.

The consequence of being too far out of line with the going rate is that staff
turnover will rise. As long as the businesses you look at are reasonably similar and the jobs much the same you will end up with a defendable, credible,
and acceptable pay structure, which should only take you a couple of hours'
work twice or at most three times a year.

Ways to find out the going rate for a job include:

✔ Read articles on pay, job advertisements on the Internet, in the local
papers and the relevant trade journals. You may have to correct some pay
rates to allow for variations. For example, pay rates for similar jobs are
often much higher in or near major cities than they are in rural areas.

✔ Talk to your Chamber of Commerce or Trade Association, some of whom
publish salary surveys, and to other local employers and business
owners in your network.

✔ Contact employment agencies including those run by government agencies. They are usually a bit ahead of the rest of the market in terms of
pay information. Other employers only know what they are paying their
present staff. Recruitment agencies know what you will have to pay to
get your next employee.

Book III

**Getting
the Staff**

Deciding arbitrarily the pay rates of people who work for you may appear to be one of the perks of working for yourself. But inconsistent pay rates will quickly upset people and staff will jump ship at the first opportunity.

Creating a menu of benefits

A *benefit* is defined as any form of compensation that is not part of an employee's basic pay and that isn't tied directly to their performance in those jobs. These non-salary benefits such as pension, working conditions, and company policy can also play a part in keeping people on side.

A wide range of other perks ranging from being allowed to wear casual dress (almost essential) to onsite childcare is on offer to employees in organisations. Personal development training, company product discounts, flexible hours, telecommuting, and fitness facilities are all benefits that people can expect in certain jobs today.

Staying on the Right Side of the Law

A business operates within a legal framework, the elements of which the owner-manager must be aware. The areas I cover in the following sections summarise only a few of the key legal issues. Different types of business may have to pay regard to different legal issues and employment law itself is dynamic and subject to revision and change.

The Advisory, Conciliation and Arbitration Service (ACAS) (www.acas.org.uk) and The British Safety Council (www.britishsafetycouncil.org) are useful organisations who can help with aspects of employment issues, and Emplaw (www.emplaw.co.uk) is a Web site covering basic British employment law information and will direct you to a lawyer in your area who specialises in the aspect of employment law you are concerned with.

Keeping employment records

You need to keep records about employees both individually and collectively. When you only employ one or two people this may seem like a bureaucratic chore. You may even feel that you can remember all the important details about your employees without keeping copious records. However the particulars on even a few employees are too much data to carry in your head, especially alongside all the other things you have to remember. The record system can be a manual one, it can be computerised or, as is the case in most small firms, a mix of the two. The great strength of computerised records lies in the ease with which collective data on employees past and present can be produced.

This can throw up trends, which may help in recognising problems and setting them in proper context. For example the collective employee data will show average absenteeism and lateness statistics, which you can then use as a comparison during an individual's appraisal.

Some of the data you need to keep is a legal requirement, such as information on accidents. Some of the information will be invaluable in any dispute with an employee, for example in a case of unfair dismissal. All of the information makes the process of employing people run more smoothly.

Individual employee information should include:

- The application form
- Interview record and the results of any selection tests used
- Job history, including details of promotions and assignments
- Current and past job descriptions
- Current pay and bonus details and a record of the amount and date of any changes
- Details of skills and competences
- Education and training records with details of courses attended
- Details of performance assessments and appraisals
- Absence, lateness, accident, medical and disciplinary records, together with details of any formal warnings and suspensions
- Holiday entitlement
- Pension contribution data
- Termination record giving date, details of exit interview, and suitability for re-engagement
- Copies of any correspondence between you and the employee

Collective information should include:

- Numbers, grades, and job titles
- Absenteeism, staff turnover, and lateness statistics
- Accident rates
- Age and length of service records
- Wage and salary structures
- Employee costs
- Overtime statistics showing hours worked and costs
- Records of grievances and disputes

✔ Training records showing how many person days have been devoted to training and how much that has cost

✔ Gender, ethnic, and disability profiles

Employees have three basic rights over the information an employer keeps in their employment records:

✔ To be able to obtain access to their own personal data

✔ To be able to claim damages for losses caused by the use of inaccurate data or the unauthorised use of data, or by the loss or destruction of data

✔ To apply to the courts if necessary for rectification or erasure of inaccurate data

This means that an employee is entitled to gain access to his or her personal data at reasonable intervals and without undue delay or expense. It is a legal requirement that this request be put in writing, although you may choose not to insist on this; you may charge a fee of no more than £10 and you must provide the information within 40 days of the request.

Preparing contracts of employment

Employees have to be given a written statement of a defined list of terms and conditions of their employment within two months of starting working for you.

The list of terms which go into a job description include the following:

✔ The employee's full name

✔ When the employee started working for you

✔ How and how much your employee is paid

✔ Whether pay is weekly or monthly

✔ The hours you expect them to work

✔ The number of days holiday they are allowed, including public holidays and how that holiday is accumulated

✔ The employee's job title or a brief description of his or her work

✔ Where you expect the employee to work and what conditions will apply if you expect them to work elsewhere

✔ You need to state if you intend the employment to be permanent or, if it is for a fixed term, when it will start and finish

- Details of who the employee will be managed by and who they can talk to if they have any dispute with that person

- Any terms and conditions relating to sickness or injury, including any provision for sick pay

- Any terms and conditions relating to pensions and pension schemes

- Any disciplinary rules applicable to the employee

- The period of notice required, which increases with length of service; a legal minimum of one week's notice per year of service is required up to a maximum of 12 weeks (this may be overridden by express terms in the contract)

The job description forms the cornerstone of the contract of employment that exists between employer and employee. However the contract is rarely a single document and may not even be completely documented. A contract comes into existence as soon as someone accepts an offer of paid employment, even if both offer and acceptance are only oral. In practice the most important contractual document may be the letter offering a person the job, together with the salary and other basic employment conditions.

The contract consists of four types of condition:

- **Express terms:** Terms specifically agreed to between employer and employee, whether in writing or not.

- **Implied terms:** Terms considered to be so obvious that they don't need spelling out. These include such matters as the employee complying with reasonable instructions and taking care of business property and equipment. For the employer these can include taking reasonable care of the employee and paying them for work done.

- **Incorporated terms:** Terms from outside sources, most commonly from trade union agreements, that are included in the contract.

- **Statutory terms:** These include any work requirements laid down by law – safety regulations, for example.

Working legal hours

Whilst the owner of a business may be content to work all hours, since 1999 the law has strictly governed the amount of time employees can be asked to put in. The Working Time Regulations, as they are known, apply to any staff over 18. This includes temporary workers, home workers, and people working for you overseas. The regulations are summarised in the following points:

- ✔ Staff cannot be forced to work more than 48 hours a week. However, an employee may work over those hours if he or she agrees to it by signing an opt-out agreement.

- ✔ You cannot force an employee to sign an opt-out agreement from any aspect of the regulations.

- ✔ Working time includes travelling when it is part of the job, working lunches and job-related training.

- ✔ For night workers, there is a limit of an average of eight hours' work in 24. They are also entitled to receive a free health assessment.

- ✔ All workers are entitled to 11 hours rest a day, a day off each week, and an in-work rest break of at least 20 minutes if the working day is longer than six hours.

- ✔ Full-time staff are entitled to four weeks' paid holiday a year after a 13-week qualification period. However, they do not have the right to choose when to take leave. It must be agreed with the employer.

Young workers (under the age of 18) may not work more than eight hours a day or 40 hours a week; these hours cannot be averaged out, nor is any opt-out available. Special rules also apply to the rest breaks they are entitled to.

As an employer, you must keep records that show you comply with the working-time limits and that you have given night workers the opportunity for a health assessment.

Granting leaves

As an employer, occasions are bound to arise when you will be obliged, to give your staff time off work other than their usual holidays or when they are unwell. You may not have to pay them when these occasions occur, but you do have to respect their right to be absent.

Protecting maternity and paternity rights

All pregnant employees have rights in four main areas. These include the right to reasonable time off to have antenatal care; the right not to be unfairly dismissed; the right to maternity leave; and the right to return to work. There are many conditions and exceptions so you need to examine each case carefully to see how to proceed.

Parental leave applies to men and women alike who have been employed for more than one year and have responsibility for a child as a biological, foster, adoptive, or step parent. Each parent is entitled to up to 13 weeks' leave for each child, up to their child's fifth birthday. The minimum period of parental leave that can be taken in one go is one week (unless the child is entitled to disability living allowance) and the maximum is four weeks.

Recognising emergency leave

Employees have the right to reasonable unpaid leave where their *dependants* – spouses, children, parents, and other people living in an employee's house (except lodgers), and others who might rely on an employee in emergencies, such as elderly neighbours – are affected by:

- Illness, injury, assault, or childbirth
- Breakdown in childcare/other care arrangements
- The consequences of a death
- A serious incident at school or during school hours

To take this leave, your employee should give notice as soon as reasonably practicable giving the reason for, and likely duration of, absence. 'Reasonable' time off is not defined but, usually, one or two days should suffice.

Avoiding discrimination

By and large business owners can employ whomever they want to employ. However when setting the criteria for a particular job or promotion it is usually illegal to discriminate on the grounds of sex, race, marital status, or union membership. If you employ more than 15 people, then disabled employees have the right not to be discriminated against in either the recruitment process or when they are employed.

Whether you can impose age limits on job applicants or on your employees is debatable. You may find that by imposing an age limit you are indirectly discriminating against women, for example, who have had time off work to have children.

New regulations designed to prevent part-time employees from being treated less favourably than comparable full-time employees – that is someone doing broadly similar work and with a similar level of skills and qualifications – are coming into force in the UK. Business owners will have to ensure part-time employees receive equal sick pay and maternity pay (on a pro rata basis), equal hourly rates of pay, and equal access to pension schemes. Employers will also be obliged to ensure that part-time employees have equal access to training opportunities and that part-time employees are not treated less favourably than full-timers in a redundancy situation. The Emplaw website (www.emplaw.co.uk) has a free area covering the current regulations on UK

Employment Law and also details on how you can find a lawyer in your area who specialises in the aspect of employment law you are concerned with.

It is also illegal to victimise by treating unfairly someone who has complained about being discriminated against. Sexual harassment is also a form of discrimination defined as the 'unwanted conduct of a sexual nature or other conduct based on sex affecting the dignity of men and women at work'. This can include unwelcome physical, verbal, or non-verbal conduct. Finally it is unfair to include in your reason for dismissing an employee that they are a member of a particular minority group protected by law.

To avoid discriminating in your employment you need to ensure that all your policies and procedures meet the following criteria:

- ✓ They are applied equally to all who work for you irrespective of sex, race, and so forth
- ✓ They don't limit the proportion of one group who comply compared with another
- ✓ They don't disadvantage an individual
- ✓ They can be objectively justified. For example there is no case to argue when being a man or woman is a genuine occupational qualification – for example, for the purpose of a particular photographic modelling assignment or an acting role. The same is true when you have a part-time vacancy so have no need of a full-time employee.

To make sure you are not discriminating at work follow this six-point checklist:

- ✓ Ensure your business has an equal opportunities policy
- ✓ Train staff in equal opportunities
- ✓ Keep records of interviews showing why candidates were rejected
- ✓ Ensure complaints are taken seriously, fully investigated, and addressed if needed
- ✓ Conduct staff surveys to help determine where discrimination may exist within your business
- ✓ Examine the payroll – pay should reflect an employee's job title, not their gender

Keeping the work environment safe

You have to provide a reasonably safe and healthy environment for your employees, visitors, and members of the general public who may be affected by what you do. This applies to both the premises you work from and the work itself. An inspector has the right to enter your premises to examine it and enforce legal requirements if your standards fall short in any way.

Once you have employees you must take some or all of the following measures dependent on the number of people you employ. However a prudent employer should take all these measures whether or not required by law. Doing so sets the standard of behaviour that is common in the very best firms.

- ✔ Inform the organisation responsible for health and safety at work for your business of where you are and what you do. For most small businesses this is the Environmental Health Department of your local authority (contact details may be found in your local telephone directory). The Health and Safety Executive Web site has a section devoted to Small Firms, covering both regulations and advice on making your work environment safer (their Web site is www.hse.gov.uk).

- ✔ Get employer's liability insurance to cover you for any physical injury or disease your employees may gct as a result of their work. The amount of coverage must be at least £2 million and the insurance certificate must be displayed at all your places of work.

You, as an employer, can in turn expect your employees:

- ✔ To take reasonable care of their own health, safety at work, and of other persons who may be affected by their acts or omissions.

- ✔ To co-operate with the employer in ensuring that the requirements imposed by the relevant statutory provisions are complied with.

Book III

Getting the Staff

Chapter 4

Disciplining and Dismissing Staff

. . . .

In This Chapter

▶ Implementing a disciplinary procedure

▶ Getting rid of employees – the correct way

▶ Avoiding wrongful or constructive dismissal

▶ Understanding what happens if you do get dismissals wrong

. . . .

Sacking people isn't a nice job, but sometimes you're left with no other choice. If the job an employee has been doing no longer needs to be done and you have no other job that's suitable, you can make that member of staff redundant; but if you want to dismiss an employee for another reason and their job still exists, you have to be sure of your standing and tread very carefully through the legal minefield of dismissal.

New Dispute Resolution Regulations came into force in October 2004 which substantially changed the way employers have to deal with disputes and disciplinary and grievance procedures. An employer who dismisses someone and gets those procedures wrong can have a case brought against them at an Employment Tribunal. They may be found to have unfairly dismissed the employee, and as a result they can be ordered to pay greatly increased compensation. Don't think you can ignore the new rules and procedures. More and more cases are being brought against employers who simply don't know the law has changed.

Most importantly, the reason for the dismissal has to be fair; the way you dismiss also has to be fair and you have to follow all the right procedures. This chapter helps you to work out what's fair and what's not, and begins by taking a look at your disciplinary options *before* deciding to sack a member of staff.

Resolving Disputes

Firing an employee really should be the very last option you consider. If a member of staff's performance is causing you or other employees concern, your first step is to follow your company's disciplinary procedure (see the section 'Following a disciplinary procedure'). New statutory dismissal and disciplinary procedures came into force in October 2004, and your company procedures must at least comply with those minimum standards.

Pretty much every story has two sides to it, so if you go into a meeting or begin an investigation with the idea of resolving the problem, rather than being determined to get rid of the thorn in your side, it's better all round. A disciplinary meeting is an opportunity to find a solution to a problem rather than just to mete out discipline and punishment.

Morale around the workplace can plummet when an employee is sacked. Unless the person has been a complete pain, colleagues may feel you've just been looking for an excuse and weren't listening to the employee's views. Resolving a dispute and making things work can have a very positive effect on the rest of the workers and ultimately your business will benefit.

Following a disciplinary procedure . . . right through to dismissal

All employers are legally required to have a disciplinary procedure. We just outline the procedure here – *Small Business Employment Law For Dummies* (Wiley) deals with it in a lot more detail. Some bosses have separate procedures dealing with conduct and underperformance; some use the same procedure for both. When employees join your firm you have to let them know how the disciplinary procedure operates and the kind of behaviour that gets employees fired. If this information isn't spelled out in detail in the Written Statement of Employment Particulars it has to be in a company handbook or in some other written document that your employees have easy access to.

ACAS (the Advisory, Conciliation and Arbitration Service) produces a code of practice on disciplinary procedures with details on how to draw up and operate a disciplinary procedure. The code is used as the yardstick to judge how reasonable an employer has been if an employee brings a claim for unfair dismissal to an Employment Tribunal so get a copy and incorporate it into your own procedures. You can contact ACAS at 0845-7474747 or through the website at www.acas.org.uk.

The minimum the law says you have to implement in your disciplinary procedure is the following:

1. **Get all the facts straight, and decide whether or not any further action must be taken.** Investigate the situation fully by talking to the employee concerned and any other employees who might be able to throw some

light on events. Gather any evidence you can find – e-mails, letters and so on. Interview any witnesses and take signed written statements from them.

2. **Start informal discussions, coaching, or counselling for the employee involved.** Make it clear to them that this isn't part of a formal disciplinary procedure – you're trying to help them and to avert more problems.

3. **If the problematic situation doesn't change let the employee know in writing what they're doing wrong.** Be sure to include any evidence you have, and explain to them why the situation cannot continue, what you expect them to do to remedy the situation and by when.

4. **Hold a disciplinary hearing to discuss the situation.** The employee can bring along a work companion or a union representative. Before the hearing you must set out in writing the concerns which have led you to hold the meeting and the employee must have a copy of that statement. At the hearing explain your complaint and your evidence and give the employee the chance to state their case, ask questions, give evidence, and call their own witnesses.

5. **Let the employee know what you've decided in light of the hearing.** If you decide on disciplinary action rather than the sack, give them a written warning spelling out what the misconduct is, what has to be done about it, and by when. And explain the consequences if things don't change – perhaps a final written warning and then the sack.

6. **Allow the employee the right to appeal.** If they do, hold an appeal meeting. If your business is big enough try to have a different manager hear the appeal to the one who made the decision to dismiss. Once the appeal is over you have to let the employee know your final decision.

The list shows the basic statutory requirements – your own disciplinary procedure may allow for more warnings and more meetings and other courses of action such as demotion or suspension.

If you don't follow this basic procedure and you have employed the member of staff for more than a year, they can claim automatic unfair dismissal and the resulting tribunal can increase the compensation it orders you to pay.

Calling in the arbitrators

If you can't resolve a disciplinary problem inside your organisation, think about calling in an outsider as an arbitrator. If your organisation recognises a union (see Chapter 7), that union may be able to send someone in to arbitrate. ACAS may also be able to help – the contact details are earlier in this chapter.

Dismissing of Staff – the Right Way

Most things in life can be done in a right way and a wrong way, and dismissing staff is definitely one of those areas where you have to get it right. The law protects most employees from being unfairly dismissed or from being forced to quit because of their boss's unreasonable behaviour. And that means that if an employee thinks they have been unfairly dismissed, they can take a case against you at an Employment Tribunal.

If you need any incentive to stop and reflect before you wield the axe, just remember that a tribunal can order you pay compensation if it decides you've got it wrong. That comprises a basic award, currently between £135 and £435 (depending on your age) for each whole year of employment with you (up to 20 years), plus a compensatory award set by the tribunal, with a current maximum of £58,400. The award limits increase annually. It wouldn't take too many payments like that to bring many small businesses to their knees. If the tribunal also decides that the dismissal was discriminatory the compensation is uncapped!

Having fair grounds to sack an employee

For a dismissal to be fair you have to have an acceptable reason for getting rid of your employee.

It's fair to dismiss a member of staff when:

- ✔ Their job no longer exists. But remember it's the job that's redundant, never the person.

- ✔ They turn out not to be capable of doing the job or are not qualified (including lying about qualifications in a job application).

- ✔ They're guilty of some misdemeanour (constantly being late, absent, careless, or having a bad attitude, for example).

- ✔ They do something so bad that it amounts to gross misconduct (such as stealing something, hitting someone, committing fraud, or sexually harassing other staff). See the later section 'Dismissing for gross misconduct'.

- ✔ You can't let the employee go on doing their job because to do so would be breaking the law (such as a job that involves driving when the employee has been banned from driving).

If none of those reasons apply to the employee you want to sack, one more category may give you a get-out clause. You may be able to fire someone for 'some other substantial reason'. Isn't the law wonderfully clear? Basically, this other reason has to be one that you can defend in a tribunal hearing. One of the most common reasons is that you have to restructure your business for financial reasons and that means jobs aren't redundant but are changing and so your contract with your employee has to change too. If an employee refuses to accept these contractual changes it can then be fair to dismiss him.

Although employees past retirement age haven't been protected against unfair dismissal in the past, some recent legal cases cast doubt on this. If you haven't set a normal retirement age for your workplace, employees over 65 generally count as being of an age to retire. Age discrimination legislation introduced in 2006 makes it illegal for employers to retire an employee before the employer's usual retirement age (if there is one), or before the default retirement age of 65, without an objective justification.

Applying your decision

If you've got good grounds for dismissing an employee, the next step is to go about the dismissal fairly. That means first giving the employee a fair hearing by going through all the necessary disciplinary procedures explained in the section 'Following a disciplinary procedure . . . right through to dismissal' earlier in this chapter.

Even if you have no choice but to sack someone because it would be breaking the law for them to carry on in their job, you still have to be fair in how you go about it. You have to discuss, investigate, and consider the possibility of keeping the person on in another capacity if other jobs are available. If you end up having to explain yourself to a tribunal panel they will want to know that you gave the employee a fair hearing; that you investigated the whole situation fully; and that you were being reasonable when you decided that the reason was substantial enough to merit the sack. A dismissal has to be fair all round.

Keep detailed records of all the procedures you go through – copies of letters, warnings, records of meetings, and the evidence you gather. If the case does come to a tribunal, you'll need to be able to prove that you did everything fairly and squarely.

Giving written reasons for dismissal

If you've investigated, warned, followed the procedure, and finally decided you have good reason to dismiss someone, you've got to let the employee know what your reasons are. If you've followed the correct disciplinary procedure

Book III

Getting the Staff

outlined in the section 'Following a disciplinary procedure . . . right through to dismissal', this shouldn't come as a surprise to the employee and they should be fully aware of all the reasons already – but you still have to put the reasons for dismissal in writing.

Giving notice of dismissal

Except in cases of gross misconduct, you have to give the appropriate period of notice for any dismissal. Details of an employee's notice entitlement should be outlined in their contract.

The law says that someone who has worked for at least a month but less than a year is entitled to one week's notice. Someone who has worked for two full years is entitled to two weeks' notice; three full years means three weeks' notice, and so on up to a maximum of 12 weeks' notice. You may offer more generous terms in your employees' contracts. You can increase the amount of notice employees are entitled to depending on how long they've worked for you, and your more senior employees – such as managers – may have longer notice periods.

Don't forget that an employee who is retiring is in reality being dismissed (because of retirement) and so is entitled to be given notice of dismissal in the same way as anyone else or to be paid money in lieu of notice.

If you don't want the employee around the workplace after you've given them notice, you can let them go immediately but you have to pay them in place of the notice period anyway. So if they're entitled to six weeks' notice, you have to give them six weeks' pay. They also have to be paid for any other fringe benefits they may be entitled to under the contract such as the use of a company car.

Dismissing for gross misconduct

Examples of misconduct can be constantly being late or not turning up at all, making careless mistakes, or not really caring how their work goes! Misconduct is irritating in the extreme and possibly a reason to sack someone. While ordinary misconduct may be annoying, beyond that it becomes gross misconduct.

Gross misconduct is something so serious that it brings the contract between you and the guilty party to an end immediately. Examples of acts at work that may constitute gross misconduct include:

- Theft
- Dishonesty

✔ Fraud

✔ Violence

✔ Deliberately damaging company property

✔ Sexual harassment

✔ Bullying

✔ Downloading pornographic material from the Internet

✔ Inciting racial hatred

✔ Gross insubordination

If you sack someone for gross misconduct, without notice, you have to be able to justify that action. What you are actually saying is that the employee has done something that has damaged the relationship of trust and confidence between you, destroyed their working contract, and made it impossible to carry on as boss and employee. If you can't prove that, the employee may make a claim for wrongful dismissal at a tribunal.

In such cases, the tribunal will want to know:

✔ Whether any of your other staff ever acted in the same way and whether you took that case seriously enough to fire them without notice.

✔ If whatever has happened really has broken down the trust and confidence between you and your employee.

This means that you have to have fully investigated the incident and given the employee a fair hearing before you come to your decision. The principles of fairness apply just the same to cases of gross misconduct as they do to ordinary cases of misconduct or poor performance (read the section on 'Avoiding wrongful dismissal', later in this chapter). Employees should already know what kind of gross misconduct will get them fired on the spot – this should be in your staff handbook.

Be very careful about summarily dismissing someone for what you see as gross misconduct. If they bring a case against you at an Employment Tribunal and the tribunal decides the conduct didn't amount to gross misconduct, you can end up having to pay greatly increased compensation. You must follow all the basic dismissal and disciplinary procedures outlined earlier in this chapter.

If employees are guilty of actions outside the workplace that would constitute gross misconduct at work you may be able to fairly dismiss them. If that happens take your solicitor's advice.

Plain old ordinary misconduct is handled differently. Ordinary misconduct doesn't bring the contract to an immediate end, and you must follow a fair disciplinary procedure with all the necessary warnings.

Dismissing for underperformance

We all have days when we go home without having done much (although my development editor insists he doesn't). But you can't sack an employee for the occasional lazy day unless it happens week in, week out.

If an employee is seriously underperforming – their work isn't up to scratch, they just aren't capable of doing the job, or they're always off, sick, or late so that the job isn't getting done properly, or they haven't got the qualifications they need – you can have a reason for firing them fairly on the grounds of lack of capability or qualifications.

The minimum procedures you have to go through are the same as for other disciplinary procedures (see the section 'Following a disciplinary procedure . . . right through to dismissal' earlier in this chapter) or follow your company's own disciplinary procedure.

Give people the chance to improve before dismissing them, and be reasonable about the timescale you set for seeing their work improve. You can allow any amount of time between a few weeks and several months. A tribunal considers how long the employee has been with you, how bad the performance was, what warnings you had given that things had to improve, the effect on your business, and the size of the workforce. If you have other people who can 'carry' underperforming employees while they are trying to improve, you can afford to give them a bit longer than if you are dependent on that one person.

Be objective about deciding whether or not an employee has made an improvement. Getting exasperated and being determined not to see any improvement isn't your best way forward. Taking a second opinion from another manager or a colleague is a good idea.

Annual appraisals are a good way of assessing how people are performing and they give you a legitimate reason to discuss any problems. It's good to talk.

Dismissing Staff – the Wrong Way

If you just snap and fire a member of staff without a full investigation, without giving her the chance to put her case across or to improve, and without going through all the correct procedures, your sacked employee will likely feel very aggrieved and seek legal advice. And a solicitor is likely to tell her that she has a case for unfair dismissal, if she has at least one years' service. The next thing you know, your former employee has filed a claim, and you have to prepare your case for the defence.

Avoiding wrongful dismissal

Wrongful dismissal is when you decide to end a member of staff's contract by dismissing them without notice or by giving them a period of notice less than what they're entitled to. Doing so means you're in breach of contract and the aggrieved party can file a claim against you at a tribunal within three months of the event or within 6 years in the courts.

You must give the notice period set out in the employee's contract unless you are firing them for gross misconduct (refer to the section 'Dismissing for gross misconduct' earlier in this chapter). If you haven't put a notice period into the employee's contract, the statutory minimum applies. See 'Giving Notice of Dismissal'.

You have to give notice or pay in lieu of notice. If the employee can show that they didn't get the right notice and that they have suffered financially as a result, they can claim at an Employment Tribunal, the County Court, or the High Court (depending on the sum involved).

If you haven't made clear in the contract how much notice an employee gets and you fire them using the statutory minimum, in some cases they can also ask a court or tribunal to rule that the period of notice, although perfectly legal, was unreasonably short. The more skilled, well-paid, and senior an employee is, the more likely the tribunal is to agree.

Steering clear of constructive dismissal

If you behave in such a way that employees feel they have no choice but to quit, that's *constructive dismissal* (to use the full title, constructive unfair dismissal). Once the employee has gone, providing they have one years' service, they can take a claim against you for unfair dismissal and possibly wrongful dismissal too if you haven't got the notice period or pay right.

If as an employer you just keep forgetting to buy the teabags and coffee or are merely an irritable pain, no-one can quit and claim constructive dismissal. You have to have done something seriously wrong – such as changing the job they do without any discussion. The trust and confidence that exist in the employee's contract, whether in writing or not, have to be broken.

If you do something serious, such as reduce an employee's pay without his agreement, the longer he stays on after the event, the more he would be seen to have accepted the change and the less likely he would be to win a constructive dismissal claim. If, however, the employee works 'under protest', making it clear that she does not accept the changes, it's possible for her to

Book III

Getting
the Staff

resign some time after the breach of contract and successfully sue you. If she left because she had a better job offer, she would have a hard time proving that your behaviour was the catalyst pushing her into going.

Automatic unfair dismissal

You can't dismiss an employee for being pregnant or because she has dared to ask for something that she's entitled to by law (such as written terms and conditions of employment or parental leave). A situation where you sack an employee for asking for something she had the right to ask for is known as *automatic unfair dismissal*. In cases of automatic unfair dismissal, the tribunal will automatically come down on the side of the employee. The tribunal has no choice – because you have broken the law – and this is costly for the employer.

As I've said earlier in this chapter if you dismiss someone without following all the right procedures that will also be automatic unfair dismissal and you can be penalised by being ordered to pay increased compensation.

Tying up the Loose Ends

Even when all the procedures have been gone through and a leaving date is settled, that's not the end of the matter. You aren't under any obligation to offer an exit interview to an employee who is leaving, but it can be useful for you as well as the employee. They may have comments to make about the way your business operates that would be useful to consider – as well as letting them get it off their chest! It can help to clear the air.

Don't forget the paperwork. Just as you have to do when an employee hands in their notice and chooses to leave, there are loose ends that need to be tidied up.

Handing over paperwork to a new employer

Paperwork is always involved when an employee leaves. Tax forms need to go to HMRC (HM Revenue and Customs – formerly the Inland Revenue) as well as to a new employer. Here's a summary of the paperwork that you need to sort out before your dismissed employee leaves:

✓ **A P45.** This form is the most important piece of paperwork, because it details where you're up to with deducting tax and national insurance for the year so far. The P45 can be passed on directly to a new employer, but if the employee doesn't have a job to go to you should give it to them. They will need it to claim Job Seeker's allowance until they get back into work.

✓ **A P60.** If the redundancy happens near the end of the tax year, the employee should get a P60, detailing all of their tax deductions for the year.

✓ **A P11D.** This form shows all the benefits in kind that the employee has received so far during the year. The HMRC's Web site (www.hmrc.gov.uk) has details of all the forms you need and provides downloadable forms too.

You must also give new employers details of all the entitlements employees have taken so far in the current year of employment – maternity leave, paternity leave, or parental leave, for example.

Give the dismissed employee a copy of all their tax and benefits details plus any certificates they may have gained while they've been employed by you (such as qualifications or safety certificates or courses related to their job).

Sorting out outstanding payments

Check that the dismissed employee has been paid everything they're owed. They may not have taken their full holiday entitlement up to and including their last day.

If this is the case they may be entitled to be paid for that accrued holiday under the terms of their contract or under the working time regulations. You can agree that they take their remaining holiday during their notice period, but if you want them to do that, make sure that you give them enough notice to do so.

You also need to check that a dismissed employee has been fully paid for any overtime, extra hours they've put in, expenses they're due, or for anything else that they would normally expect to have been paid for while in your employment, such as bonuses and commissions.

If you decide to take a company car away from an employee during their notice period, you have to work out how much they should be paid to compensate for that loss.

You need to check if the employee is entitled to any tax rebates through the PAYE (Pay As You Earn) scheme. The member of staff who works out wages should be able to sort this out with the help of HMRC.

Paying instead of allowing staff to work their notice

If you want your employee to go this minute and never darken your door again, you have to pay them money for the period they would otherwise have had to work – money in place of the notice that their contract or the law says they're entitled to. Not only that, but they have to be in the same financial position as they would have been in if you had let them work through the notice period. That might mean paying out more than just a few weeks' pay. For example, if the employee had the use of a company car, they can have expected to use that during the notice period so you will have to compensate them for the loss of that too.

The right to pay in lieu of notice is always an option open to an employer, whether or not it says so in the employee's contract, and the employee doesn't have the right to demand to work out their notice.

The other thing you might do is to send the employee on garden leave. *Gardening leave* means that your dismissed employee spends the period of their notice still employed by you but at home and with no work to do while still being paid. You might decide to do that if you're worried about what damage they can do to your business if they worked out their notice in the office – maybe by stealing all your best customers or contacts.

Dealing with pensions

When employees leave a job and start a new one, they have to decide what to do about the money they've paid into your company pension, if you provided one. The same goes for employees you dismiss.

Restricting what employees can do after leaving

In certain cases, the new business activities of a recently dismissed employee can harm your company. For example, if you are a hairdresser and a former employee sets up her own salon in close proximity and takes her customers away, you will lose out.

You have the option of taking steps to protect your business by putting into your employees' contracts terms that limit what they can do when they leave you. These are known as *restrictive covenants*. You can say that former employees are not to set up in competition with you for a period of three months after leaving your firm or restrict them to setting up their business outside a particular geographical area.

You have to be reasonable about any restrictive covenants you put in a contract if you're not likely to be able to enforce them if the employee ignores them. If you try to sue for breach of contract the courts can find your restrictive covenants too restrictive and you will lose – and be out of pocket for the legal fees. Take advice from a good lawyer before you draw up contracts with these kinds of restrictions.

Giving references

You don't have to give any employee a reference, whether they've resigned or been dismissed, but if you do agree to, the reference has to say what you believe to be accurate and fair and you have to give it without malice.

If you give an unfair, malicious, or negligent reference and the employee loses out as a result, they can sue you. On the other hand, you have to be truthful for the sake of any prospective employers as well. If they lose out as a result of a negligent reference, they can sue you too!

Book III

Getting the Staff

If you've dismissed an employee you may not be too bothered about how quickly they get back to work, but be objective about this. They may have been in the wrong job and may be rather good in a different company with a job that suits them better.

Be truthful in your reference, but don't be tempted to exaggerate an employee's negative points. Employees will have the right to see what you have written about them in references once they've started work with their new employer, so make sure that what's in the reference is what has already been discussed in the course of the fair dismissal procedure and can be proved to be true. Don't add little extras out of spite.

Make sure you don't give a discriminatory reference to someone because of their sex, race, disability, religion or religious beliefs, or sexual orientation, and be careful too about age!

Don't be tempted to try to smooth things over with an employee you're dismissing over a dispute by offering a glowing reference. This can backfire on you. The employee can use your reference to prove that they weren't guilty of misconduct or incompetence after all.

Facing Tribunals – Something to Be Avoided

Tabloid writers love a good story about an unfairly dismissed employee managing to win thousands of pounds from their employer. Some very high-profile cases take place, for example where employees of big financial firms win huge sums at Employment Tribunals for discrimination or in court for breaches of contract. They should act as a warning that you can't afford to be unfair.

If you do unfairly dismiss, wrongfully dismiss, or constructively unfairly dismiss an employee, they can take a claim against you at an Employment Tribunal (find out more about Employment Tribunals by reading *Small Business Employment Law For Dummies*).

Sometimes, even when you are in the right, vexed employees feel you've acted unfairly and want their day in court. If you really do have good reason to dismiss and scrupulously follow the correct dismissal procedures (explained in the earlier section 'Following a disciplinary procedure . . . right through to dismissal') you'll be able to convince a tribunal should it come to that. But avoid this scenario if at all possible!

If an ex-employee brings a claim of unfair dismissal against you and wins, the tribunal can instruct you to:

- Pay compensation comprising a basic award plus a compensatory award of up to £58,400 depending on the details of the case (the maximum amount is index-linked and increases each year).
- Reinstate the employee in their former job.
- Re-engage the employee in a different job.

The employee is less likely to want reinstatement or re-engagement because it isn't likely that the two of you will be able to work together again comfortably. For a small business, even sums of far less than the maximum compensation figure can be crippling. So you really do want to make sure that you are on a very solid footing before you decide to sack someone. It pays to be fair.

Chapter 5

Paper Money, Money Paper –
Payslips and Deductions

In This Chapter

▶ Wading through wage slips

▶ Understanding tax and National Insurance wage deductions

▶ Being aware of other possible wage deductions

*W*hatever, however, and whenever you decide to pay your employees, a lot of calculations and paperwork are involved. Not only giving with one hand, you have to take back quite a bit with the other and hand it over to the taxman. People working for you on a freelance or self-employed basis usually send you an invoice at the end of the job or at intervals you've agreed and you pay them in full, leaving them to work out and hand over their own income tax and National Insurance payments to HM Revenue & Customs, but you have a responsibility to collect tax and insurance from your own employees. On top of that you have to comply with the law on the National Minimum Wage, Statutory Sick Pay, maternity, paternity, and adoption pay, and holiday pay. Phew – is it any wonder that one of the first jobs many bosses farm out is the payroll?

Setting Everything Out on the Payslip

Employees have a legal right to a written pay statement – a *payslip* or *wage slip* – that itemises their pay and anything deducted from their pay. One of the main reasons for these written statements is that they notify employees of the deductions made from their pay. You have to give out these itemised statements each time (or just before) you pay your employees.

An employee's payslip must include:

- ✔ The *gross amount* of her wages (her salary before any deductions).

- ✔ The *net amount* she earns (what's left after you have made any deductions).

- ✔ Any amounts that you have deducted and why (some of these are fixed deductions made every pay-day and some are variable from pay period to pay period).

- ✔ The breakdown of different payment methods, if you pay your employees in this way (for example, what amounts are paid by cheque and what are paid in cash).

If you don't provide wage slips or don't include the correct details on them, your employees can complain to an Employment Tribunal. The Tribunal can make you pay back any unnotified deductions you made in the 13-week period before the employee complained – even if you were entitled to make them.

Gross pay

Gross pay is the amount of pay your employee earns before you make any deductions. Gross pay comprises the basic wage and any other elements of pay due in the pay period, and may include elements such as:

- ✔ Bonuses
- ✔ Commission
- ✔ Holiday pay
- ✔ Statutory Sick Pay
- ✔ Maternity pay
- ✔ Overtime

The gross pay is the top line – earnings go downhill from there. Gross pay doesn't include items such as loans or advances in wages, expenses, or redundancy payments.

Deductions

Employees are entitled to know in advance what deductions you will be making from their gross pay and why.

Most deductions are regulated by the Employment Rights Act 1996 and are legal only when your employees' contracts clearly explain in what circumstances you will make such deductions, or when your employees give you written consent to make them. But some deductions are exempt from regulation by the Employment Rights Act (more details are given later in this chapter):

- Deductions for previous overpayment of wages.

- Deductions under statutory provisions such as tax and National Insurance.

- Deductions that you make by law and hand over to a third party, such as an attachment of earnings order.

- Deductions that you pay to a third party where the employee consents in writing, such as payments to a pension company.

- Deductions relating to strike action.

- Deductions to satisfy a ruling by a court or tribunal that an employee has to pay you a certain amount.

If you're intending to make any deductions not shown on this list, you need prior written consent from your employee (you must have the consent in writing before the event that gives rise to the deduction). If you get consent _after_ you've deducted the money, that deduction is considered unlawful. That's because you have changed an employee's pay without her consent and were in breach of contract. In other words, the contract needs to include a provision (agreed to by the employee) that in the particular circumstances you can take money out of her wages.

If you're making exactly the same fixed deductions each pay period, you can give out _standing statements_ notifying employees of these deductions in advance; standing statements may be valid for up to a year (so you'll have to issue them annually at the least). Any variable or additional deductions still have to appear on the monthly or weekly payslips, and any changes to the fixed deductions must be notified in writing or through an amended standing statement of fixed deductions.

Book III

Getting the Staff

Net pay

Net pay is what your employee's left with after the taxman and anyone else entitled to a cut has had their share; net pay amounts to gross pay minus any deductions. Net pay is the bottom line, and it's what your employee is left to play with to reward her for all her hard work!

Carrying Out Your Duties as a Tax Collector

Small business owners often complain that life would be a lot simpler if – on top of running the business – they didn't have to act as unpaid collectors of taxes. But unfortunately, you do have to fulfil certain duties on behalf of HMRC. You must:

✔ Work out how much tax and national insurance your employees should be paying (along with any contributions you, as boss of the outfit, have to make to the Exchequer yourself).

✔ Collect these payments and get them to the right government department by the correct date.

Rather than doing this complicated task yourself and tackling the payroll on your own, you may wish to call in expert accountants. Not all employers can afford to do this, of course, and even if you can, it's still a good idea to read the following sections to understand what deductions you must make from your employees' payslips.

Deducting income tax

PAYE (or Pay As You Earn) is HM Revenue & Customs' system for collecting income tax from employees. As an employer, you're responsible for the administration of your employees' PAYE deductions.

All the help you need in calculating income tax is available from HM Revenue & Customs in the form of tables, forms, advice, and software. HM Revenue & Customs used to have a reputation for being less than helpful, but that really isn't true any more. It runs helplines for just about every aspect of tax that you'll ever have to deal with. Two phone helplines are specifically for employers:

✔ 0845-6070143 for new employers.

✔ 0845-7143143 for established employers

✔ The HM Revenue and Customs Web site holds lots more information covering all aspects of tax in the UK: www.hmrc.gov.uk.

Employees normally have to pay income tax on just about every payment you give them:

✔ Wages

✔ Overtime and shift pay

✔ Tips

✔ Bonuses and commissions

✔ Statutory sick, maternity pay, paternity pay, and adoption pay

✔ Lump sums (such as redundancy payments) over and above any tax-free amount

✔ Some cash expense allowances

Not all of the money an employee earns is taxable. Certain sums must be earned before a person starts to pay tax; this amount is known as a *personal allowance*. The personal allowance for a person under 65 is currently £5,225 (2007/08), which means that the first £5,225 an employee earns in any tax year isn't taxable.

When an employee earns more than her tax-free amount the employer deducts tax from her pay at different rates. Table 5-1 shows the correct breakdown. And rather than paying an employee her full tax-free earnings in the first part of the tax year, you give her a proportion of these earnings in every wage packet throughout the tax year, adding up to her full tax-free earnings by the end of the year, but taxing her that little increment less throughout the year.

Table 5-1	Taxable Pay Breakdown
Taxable pay	*Rate taxed at*
The first £2,020	10%
£2,020 to £31,400	22%
Beyond £31,400	40%

Book III

Getting the Staff

Each employee's own circumstances dictate how much income tax she has to pay. HM Revenue and Customs gives each of your employees a tax code each year showing how much tax-free earnings they're entitled to before you need to start deducting their tax contributions. When a new employee joins your staff her P45 shows you her current tax code.

Special PAYE situations

All sorts of reasons may occur allowing an employee to earn more than her personal allowance before starting to pay tax, or requiring her to pay tax on some of the first £5,225 she earns. She may be entitled to some tax relief or have paid too much tax last year and so the figure will be higher. She may have paid too little tax last year and the figure will be lower. Any benefits that she gets on which she has to pay tax will affect that tax-free amount. Benefits in kind, such as company cars and medical insurance, are subject to tax – but only at the end of your tax year, rather than through the PAYE system. If you pay your employees with shares or vouchers, HMRC taxes these on their cash value under the PAYE system.

Help with childcare costs is an exception. If you give an employee childcare or childcare vouchers up to the value of £55 a week, this won't be taxed as long as:

- ✔ The childcare scheme is registered childcare or approved home childcare.
- ✔ The childcare scheme is available to all your employees.

If a new employee turns up without a P45 (which sometimes happens – usually because her previous employer hasn't handed over all the necessary paperwork), you won't immediately have the correct tax code for her. She needs to fill in a form P46, available from the HMRC Web site or your local office, which you must send off to HMRC; doing so eventually results in a new P45 and tax code being issued. In the meantime you have to deduct tax from any wages she gets using an emergency code, meaning that you may deduct more tax than necessary (but that can be refunded in future wage packets when you have received your employee's correct tax code).

Keeping PAYE records

Because PAYE is such a complicated system covering all sorts of individual situations, you should maintain your tax deduction records in good order. Using HMRC forms is the easiest way to do this – you can get your local tax office to send them to you or download them from the HMRC Web site www.hmrc.gov.uk.

You need to keep the following for your own records:

- ✔ Records showing all wage and salary payments you've made in whatever form, including benefits in kind.
- ✔ Wage slips showing how you have calculated each employee's wages along with her tax deductions.
- ✔ P45s for each employee, showing her tax codes. (And when an employee leaves, you give her a P45 to pass on to her new employer.)
- ✔ P60s for each employee, showing the total amount of tax that you've deducted for the whole tax year.

At the end of the tax year, send HMRC the following:

- ✔ Details of each employee's pay and deductions.
- ✔ Details of all employee expenses and benefits.
- ✔ Details of National Insurance contributions (see 'Deducting National Insurance' for more details about this).

At the end of the tax year, you must also give each employee:

- Her P60.
- A copy of the information you've sent the Inland Revenue about her expenses and benefits.

Deducting National Insurance

National Insurance Contributions (NICs) fund future benefits for the contributor, such as state pensions and Job Seeker's Allowance. NICs fall into different classes, and the class of contributions paid affects the benefits the contributor's entitlements in future.

Most people who work have to pay NICs and as an employer you also have to pay NICs on most of your workers. HM Revenue and Customs collects National Insurance and again you get to play the role of unpaid collector. You don't have to pay NICs for people who are self-employed – they take care of their own NICs.

As with the PAYE scheme, it's up to you to calculate, deduct, and pay HM Revenue and Customs. Once you have registered as an employer with the HMRC you will get payment slips to fill in and return with your NICs.

NICs for employees

Different classes of NICs exist. Some classes are paid at a flat rate and some depend on earnings. Self-employed people pay their own contributions, so you don't have to deduct them from any money you pay out to people working for you on a self-employed basis. All other employees pay Class 1 contributions, and some employees may also pay Class 3 contributions. Here's how you know who pays what:

- **Employees pay Class 1 contributions on earnings over the *Earnings Threshold* (ET).** The ET usually changes at the beginning of each tax year. The 2007 rate was £100 a week. An employee pays 11 per cent of her gross earnings over the ET into National Insurance up to the *Upper Earnings Limit* (£670 per week in 2007). If she earns more than the Upper Earnings Limit, she just pays 1 per cent on any earnings above that rate.

- **People who haven't paid enough National Insurance in the past to qualify for certain benefits like a full state pension pay Class 3 contributions at a flat rate.** Usually that's because the person's been taking time out of work or she's been abroad. You usually pay Class 3 contributions direct to HM Revenue and Customs.

Reduced NICs

You may come across the occasional female employee who's paying Reduced NICs (sometimes known as the married woman's stamp). The government allowed these employees to choose to pay reduced contributions on the grounds that they were married and would be entitled to a full state pensions based on their husbands' National Insurance payments. Women paying reduced NICs pay 4.85 per cent on earnings between the Earnings Threshold and the Upper Earnings Limit and 1 per cent on anything over that. Women can no longer choose this option, so it's something of a rarity these days.

NICs for employers

As well as organising the payment of your employees' NICs, and paying your own personal NICs, you must make two other National Insurance payments from your business:

- ✔ **Secondary Class 1 contributions.** You pay these at 12.8 per cent on all your employees' gross earnings over the Earning Threshold (refer to 'NICs for employees' for an explanation of that). Unlike your employees' own contributions, there's no Upper Earnings Limit on how much you pay.

- ✔ **Class 1A contributions.** You pay these on your employees' benefits in kind, such as the company car or medical insurance.

You have to pay Class 1 NICs to HM Revenue & Customs monthly and you calculate and pay the Class 1A contributions annually.

Keeping NIC records

All sorts of records need to be kept showing how you arrived at the calculations and what payments you have made. You need to keep the following records relating to NICs:

- ✔ Payroll records for all staff including payslips, deductions, salary details, and NICs deducted.
- ✔ Evidence of how you calculated the NICs.
- ✔ Records of NIC payment to HMRC.
- ✔ Copies of P60s given to employees each year showing NICs for the year.
- ✔ Copies of P11D forms for each employee showing the benefits in kind and the NICs due on them.
- ✔ Evidence of calculations and payments of any additional NICs over the year.

You need to keep these records for the current year and for at least the previous three tax years.

Counting Up Any Other Deductions

Your employees' wage deductions don't necessarily stop with tax and National Insurance. Depending on your employees' circumstances, you may need to deduct other amounts too.

Most students won't get through university without taking on a student loan and they have to pay this money back as soon as they are earning enough. HM Revenue and Customs is responsible for collecting repayments on loans taken out after August 1998, meaning that you end up with the job of collecting them on HMRC's behalf. When you take on a new employee look on her P45 form for a box marked 'Continue Student Loans Deduction'. If there's a 'Y' for yes in that box you need to make deductions. Alternatively the Inland Revenue may send you a *Start Notice* (form SL1) relating to one of your employees; in this case you must start making deductions. Special student loan deduction tables are available to help you work out what to deduct and pay to HM Revenue & Customs.

Include details of student loan deductions on the employee's payslips; if she leaves you have to put details of the deductions on her P45 so that the next employer knows the score.

You can get help administering student loan repayments from HM Revenue and Customs' telephone helpline: 0845-7646646 or by looking at their Web site: www.hmrc.gov.uk.

Deducting pension contributions

If you have five or more employees, you must offer them the chance to belong to a pension scheme. This can be an occupational scheme, a group personal pension, or at the very least a stakeholder scheme. If an employee is a member of a scheme you need her permission in writing to take her pension contributions out of her wages. It's your job to:

- ✔ Pass contributions to the pension scheme.
- ✔ Keep records of these payments.
- ✔ Pay the contributions by the date they're due or by the 19th of the following month.

Making child support payments

You can find yourself having to make deductions from an employee's pay to cover child support payments. The Child Support Agency sometimes has difficulties getting non-resident parents to pay towards their child's upbringing and has the right to ask the court to order that the employer takes the payments directly from an employee's wages. If that happens you are the one who will have to deduct the money and hand it over to the agency. This is known as a *Deductions from Earning Order*. The section on 'Handling Attachment of Earnings Orders' later in this chapter deals with these sorts of deductions.

Child support payments must be handed over to the Child Support Agency by the 19th of the month following the deduction from pay and it's an offence not to comply with one of these orders.

The Child Support Enquiry Line can provide assistance to you; the telephone number is 0845-7133133 and the website address is www.csa.gov.uk.

Giving to charity

Enabling staff to make regular charitable donations directly from their wages (known as a *payroll-giving scheme*) is an extra option you may want to provide. It's very little effort for many good causes; it makes it easier and more worthwhile for employees who want to give to charity; and it boosts your image as a caring, socially responsible employer. Employees don't pay tax on the amounts they give to charity and most of the paperwork is done by Payroll-Giving Agencies approved by HM Revenue and Customs. If you set up a contract with one of these agencies, you need to keep the following records:

- A copy of your contract with the payroll-giving agency.
- Forms filled in by your employees authorising you to take their contributions.
- Details of the deductions from pay.
- Receipts from the agency.

If you don't already have such a scheme in place, you can set one up. The HMRC Charities Helpline can provide more advice; call them on 0845-3020203.

Dishing out union dues

Members of a union have to pay their regular union subscriptions, and if you have a recognised union in your workplace these subs will usually come directly out of pay – which you deduct and hand over to the union. You will need written consent from employees to make the deductions and should either show the deduction on each payslip or (as the deduction's likely to be a fixed deduction each month) give employees a standing statement of what the deductions will be for the next year.

Handling Attachment of Earnings Orders

You may sometimes have to take deductions from an employee's wages due to a court order. That is, a court may order that a certain amount of money must be taken directly from your employee's wages in order to pay someone she owes money to. This is called an *Attachment of Earnings Order* (or in some cases a *Deduction from Earnings Order*).

The order instructs you (the employer) to pay a certain sum of money at a regular interval – probably monthly – directly to the court office. You must take that sum of money directly from the employee's wages before you pay her. The main reasons a court will issue an attachment of earnings order are when someone:

- Owes child support.
- Owes maintenance to an ex-partner.
- Has a court judgment against them for debts of more than £50.
- Has to make payments under an *administration order* (an order for a single regular payment to cover a series of debts owed to various creditors).
- Has to pay fines having been convicted in a criminal court.
- Has to make contributions towards the repayment of legal aid.

Under an Attachment of Earnings Order you have a legal obligation to make the deduction and send it on to the court. For the purposes of an order, 'earnings' means:

- Wages
- Bonuses
- Commission
- Overtime
- Pension payments

These are called *attachable earnings*. But limits as to what can be deducted are in place – your employee can't be left with nothing to live on. The court has to assess what the employee needs to live on for her basic needs, and that amount is known as *protected earnings*. The court can't order deductions that will leave your employee with less than the protected earnings amount.

The courts can make more than one attachment of earnings order against an employee at any one time and these take priority in chronological order.

You're within your rights to charge your employee a small amount to cover any extra administration costs that you run up as a result of an Attachment of Earnings Order. You can deduct that amount from her wages too, but you have to give her notice in writing.

Be fair. If you can absorb the costs and forget about them it will be better for your working relationship. If you do charge her, don't charge more than your actual costs – such as postage and stationery. She can already be struggling to survive on what the court has left her to live on.

If you're faced with an Attachment of Earnings Order you have no choice but to do the court's bidding or you'll be in the dock yourself. If you don't make the deductions and pass the money on to the court office, you can be convicted and fined.

Overpayments

If you have overpaid an employee you are usually legally entitled to have that money paid back to you. You can deduct it from future wages. In this situation, you don't have to have an employee's written consent to make the 'pay-back' deductions but you need her agreement in writing before you begin to make the deductions.

The employee may plead that she's already spent the money but that doesn't mean that she doesn't have to pay up. Take into consideration that she may have genuinely been unaware that she'd been overpaid – maybe through a clerical error. If the error has been made for a few months in a row it's possible she owes you quite a lot of money. It will be unreasonable to ask her to pay it back all in one lump sum. Be prepared to negotiate a deal whereby she pays back – or you deduct out of her wages – a certain manageable amount each pay-day. This is the kind of scenario where you'd certainly want her consent to the deal in writing.

The odd occasion may arise when an employee argues that (in good faith) as a result of the extra money she changed her financial standing and ran up bills that she wouldn't otherwise have run up. If you take her to court to get the money back or she takes you to an Employment Tribunal because she feels you were unlawfully deducting money from her wages to recover the overpayment and she can convince the court she spent the money in good faith, you won't get it back. The *good faith* element of this defence is crucial, implying that she didn't know and can't reasonably have known that she was being overpaid.

Make sure that your pay system is very transparent so that your employees know what to expect in their pay packets and there's no chance of a member of staff getting extra pay without realising that it's a mistake.

Money to Make Up for Shortfalls

If you work in the retail industry the till may sometimes be short, or unexplained gaps in your stock may occur; if so, you can make deductions from wages to recover those. But you can only do so as long as this is covered in the employee's contract and:

- ✔ You tell the employee in writing what the total shortfall amounts to.
- ✔ You make a written demand for payment on the pay-day you're making the deduction from.

You have to make the deduction within 12 months of discovering that there was a shortfall and you can't take any more than one tenth of an employee's gross wages out of any wage packet (unless it's a final wage). Investigate fully and make sure the employee is the one responsible for the shortfall – otherwise the employee may make a claim against you for an unlawful deduction of wages. She may even feel that your actions had left her unable to go on working for you; that she had no choice but to quit and claim constructive unfair dismissal.

Book III

Getting the Staff

Chapter 6

Inspiring Employees to Better Performance

The question of how to motivate employees has loomed large over managers ever since management was first invented. Most of management comes down to mastering skills and techniques for motivating people – to make them better, more productive employees who love their jobs more than anything else in the world. Well, perhaps not quite that much; but you do want them to turn up and be as happy, effective, and productive as possible.

By leading with positive reinforcements, not only can you inspire your employees to do what you want, but you can also develop happier, more productive employees in the process – and that combination is tough to beat.

The Greatest Management Principle in the World

We're about to let you in on the Greatest Management Principle in the World. This simple rule can save you countless hours of frustration and extra work, and it can save your company many thousands or perhaps even millions of pounds. Sounds pretty awe inspiring, doesn't it? Are you ready? Okay, the statement is:

> You get what you reward.

Don't let the seeming simplicity of the statement fool you – read on to explore it.

Recognition isn't as simple as it looks

You may think that you're rewarding your employees to do what you want them to do, but are you really?

Consider the following example. You have two employees: Employee A is incredibly talented and Employee B is a marginal performer. You give similar assignments to both employees. Employee A completes the assignment before the due date and hands it in with no errors. Because Employee A is already done, you give her two additional assignments. Meanwhile, Employee B is not only late, but when she finally hands in the report you requested, it is full of errors. Because you're now under a time crunch, you accept Employee B's report and then correct it yourself.

What's wrong with this picture? Who's actually being rewarded: Employee A or Employee B?

If you answered Employee B, you're right. This employee has discovered that submitting work that is substandard and late is okay. Furthermore, she also sees that you personally fix it. That's quite a nice reward for an employee who clearly doesn't deserve one. (Another way to put it is that Employee B certainly has you well trained!)

On the other hand, by giving Employee A more work for being a diligent, outstanding worker, you're actually punishing her. Even though you may think nothing of assigning more work to Employee A, she knows the score. When Employee A sees that all she gets for being an outstanding performer is more work (while you let Employee B get away with doing less work), she's not going to like it one little bit. And if you end up giving both employees basically the same pay rise (and don't think that they won't find out), you make the problem even worse. You lose Employee A, either literally, as she takes another job, or in spirit, as she stops working so hard.

If you let the situation continue, all your top performers eventually realise that doing their best work is not in their best interest. As a result, they leave their position to find an organisation that values their contribution, or they simply sit back and forget about doing their best work. Why bother? No one (that means you, the manager) seems to care anyway.

Biscuit motivation

Giving everyone the same incentive – the same salary increase, equal recognition, or even equal amounts of your time – we call *biscuit motivation*. Although this treatment may initially sound fair, it isn't.

Nothing is as unfair at work as the equal treatment of unequal performers. You need to assess the performance of everyone. You then make clear to each person why they have received rewards and bonuses, or why they have not. These rewards must be evenly and honestly distributed. And if everyone meets the standards demanded, then reward them all as you have promised.

If people are not performing up to standard, then take the particular individuals aside and tell them why. Tell them what they need to do to make the grade, and how they can go about it. This is a much better way of going about things than letting people go about things without your active involvement and interest. You want everyone working as well as possible, and your job is to sort out those who aren't up to scratch.

Don't forget the Greatest Management Principle in the World – you get what you reward.

Before you set up a system to reward your employees, make sure that you know exactly what behaviours you want to reward and then align the rewards with those behaviours.

After you put your employee reward system in place, check periodically to see that the system is getting the results that you want. Check with those you're trying to motivate and see if the programme is still working. If it isn't, change it!

Discovering What Employees Want

In today's tight, stressful, changing times, what things are most important to employees? Bob conducted a survey of about 1,500 employees from across

Book III

Getting the Staff

seven industries to answer that question. We list the top ten items that employees said were most important, along with some thoughts on how you can better provide each of these elements to your own employees:

- **A learning activity (No. 1) and choice of assignment (No. 9):** Today's employees most value opportunities in which they gain skills that can enhance their worth and marketability in their current job as well as future positions. Discover what your employees want to find out, how they want to grow and develop, and where they want to be in five years. Give them opportunities as they arise and the ability to choose work assignments whenever possible. When you give employees the choice, more often than not they rise to meet or exceed your expectations.

- **Flexible working hours (No. 2) and time off from work (No. 7):** Today's employees value their time – and their time off. Be sensitive to their needs outside work, whether these needs involve family or friends, charity or church, education or hobbies. Provide flexibility whenever you can so that employees can meet their obligations. Time off may range from an occasional afternoon to attend a child's play at school or the ability to start the workday an hour early so the employee can leave an hour early. By allowing work to fit best with an employee's life schedule, you increase the chances that they're motivated to work harder while they are at work, and do their best to make their schedule work. And from a managerial standpoint, as long as the job gets done, what difference does it matter what hours someone works? And in any case, employees now have a legal right to request flexible working hours, and you have a legal obligation to consider their request.

- **Personal praise – verbal (No. 3), public (No. 8), or written (No. 10):** Although you can thank someone in 10 to 15 seconds, most employees report that they're never thanked for the job they do – especially not by their manager. Systematically start to thank your employees when they do good work, in person, in the hallway, in a group meeting, on voice-mail, in a written thank-you note, on e-mail, or at the end of each day at work. Better yet, go out of your way to act on and share and amplify good news when it occurs – even if it means interrupting someone to thank her for a great job she's done. By taking the time to say you noticed and appreciate her efforts, you help those efforts – and results – to continue. And bring her efforts to your manager's attention – this reinforces your own integrity, as well as making sure that full credit goes where it's due.

- **Increased autonomy (No. 5) and authority (No. 4) in their job:** The ultimate form of recognition for many employees is to have increased autonomy and authority to get their job done, including the ability to spend or allocate resources, make decisions, or manage others. Greater autonomy and authority says, 'I trust you to act in the best interests of the company, to do so independently and without approval of myself or others.' Increased autonomy and authority should be awarded to employees as a form of recognition itself for the past results they achieved. Autonomy and authority are privileges, not rights, which should be granted to those employees who have most earned them, based on past performance, and not based on tenure or seniority.

✓ **Time with their manager (No. 6):** In today's fast-paced world of work in which everyone is expected to get more done faster, personal time with your manager is in itself also a form of recognition. As managers are busier, taking time with employees is even more important. The action says, 'Of all the things I have to do, one of the most important is to take time to be with you, the person or people I most depend on for us to be successful.' Especially for younger employees, time spent with a manager is a valued form of validation and inspiration, as well as serving a practical purpose of learning and communication, answering questions, discussing possibilities, or just listening to an employee's ideas, concerns, and opinions.

By the way, you may wonder where money ranked in importance in this survey. A 'cash reward' ranked thirteenth in importance to employees. (We say more about the topic of money as a motivator later in this chapter.) Everyone needs money to live, but work today involves more than what anyone gets paid.

Employees report that the most important aspects at work today are primarily the intangible aspects of the job that any manager can easily provide – if she makes it a priority to do so. Now we're going to tell you a big secret. This secret is the key to motivating your employees. You don't need to attend an all-day seminar or join the management-video-of-the-week club to discover this secret: We are letting you in on it right here and right now at no extra charge:

Ask your employees what they want. This statement may sound silly, but you can take a lot of the guesswork out of your job by simply being clear about what your employees most value in their jobs. It may be one or more of the items mentioned earlier in this section, or it may be something entirely different. The simplest way to find out how to motivate your employees is to ask them. Often managers assume that their employees want only money. These same managers are surprised when their employees tell them that other things – such as being recognised for doing a good job, being allowed greater autonomy in decision making, or having a more flexible work schedule – may be much more motivating than cash. Regardless of what preferences your employees have, you're much better off knowing those preferences explicitly rather than guessing or ignoring them. So:

> ✔ **Plan to provide employees with more of what they value.** Look for opportunities to recognise employees for having done good work and act on those opportunities as they arise, realising that what motivates some employees doesn't motivate others.
>
> ✔ **Stick with it over time.** Motivation is a moving target and you need to constantly be looking to meet your employees' needs in order to keep them motivated to help you meet your needs.

Consider the following as you begin setting the stage for your efforts:

1. **Create a supportive environment for your employees by first finding out what they most value.**

2. **Design ways to implement recognition to thank and acknowledge employees when they do good work.**

3. **Be prepared to make changes to your plan, based on what works and what doesn't.**

Creating a supportive environment

The new business realities of the present day bring a need to find different ways to motivate employees. Motivation is no longer an absolute, my-way-or-the-highway proposition. The incredible acceleration of change in business and technology today is coupled with greatly expanded global competitive forces. With these forces pressing in from all sides, managers can have difficulty keeping up with what employees need to do, much less figure out what to tell them to do. In fact, a growing trend is for managers to manage individuals who are doing work that the managers themselves have never done. (Fortunately, given a little time and a little trust, most employees can work out what needs to be done by themselves.)

Inspiring managers must embrace these changing business forces and management trends. Instead of using the power of their position to motivate workers, managers must use the power of their ideas. Instead of using threats and intimidation to get things done, managers must create environments that support their employees and allow creativity to flourish.

You, as a manager, can create a supportive workplace in the following ways:

> ✔ **Build and maintain trust and respect.** Employees whose managers trust and respect them are motivated to perform at their best. By including employees in the decision-making process, today's managers get better ideas (that are easier to implement) and, at the same time, they improve employees' morale, loyalty, and commitment.

✔ **Removing the barriers of getting to work.** If you ask your employees what are the biggest hurdles they face in coming to work, you get a huge range of answers – rush-hour traffic, getting the kids to school, having to use public transport, and so on. By allowing them to choose their hours of work, you give them the opportunity to work around these barriers. You are also entitled to expect that, having chosen their hours of work, they then show up and do a good job. You cannot do this for every eventuality, and crises always happen. However, as long as the employee is prepared to give you a reasonable and regular pattern of hours, you should at least consider being flexible.

✔ **Open the channels of communication.** The ability of all your employees to communicate openly and honestly with one another is critical to the ultimate success of your organisation and plays a major role in employee motivation. Today, quick and efficient communication of information throughout your organisation can be what differentiates you from your competition. Encourage your employees to speak up, to make suggestions, and to break down the organisational barriers – the rampant departmentalisation, turf protection, and similar roadblocks – that separate them from one another, where and whenever they find them.

✔ **Make your employees feel safe.** Are your employees as comfortable telling you the bad news as they are telling you the good news? If the answer is no, you haven't created a safe environment for your employees. Everyone makes mistakes; people discover valuable lessons from their mistakes. If you want employees who are motivated, make it safe for them to take chances and to let you know the bad along with the good. And use mistakes and errors as opportunities for growth and development; never ever punish mistakes and errors except those generated as the result of negligence or incompetence.

✔ **Develop your greatest asset – your employees.** By meeting your employees' needs, you also achieve your organisation's needs. Challenge your employees to improve their skills and knowledge and provide them with the support and training that they need to do so. Concentrate on the positive progress they make and recognise and reward such success whenever possible.

Having a good game plan

Motivated employees don't happen by accident. You must have a plan to reinforce the behaviour you want. In general, employees are more strongly motivated by the potential to earn rewards than they are by the fear of punishment. Clearly, a well thought out and planned motivation, incentive, and rewards system is important to creating a committed, effective workforce.

Here are some simple guidelines for setting up a system of low-cost rewards in your organisation:

- **Link rewards to organisational goals.** To be effective, rewards need to reinforce the behaviour that leads to achieving an organisation's goals. Use rewards to increase the frequency of desired behaviour and decrease the frequency of undesired behaviour.

- **Define parameters and mechanics.** After you identify the behaviours you want to reinforce, develop the specifics of your reward system. Create rules that are clear and easily understood by all employees. Make sure that goals are attainable and that all employees have a chance to obtain rewards, whatever their job and occupation.

- **Obtain commitment and support.** Of course, communicate your new rewards programme to your employees. Many organisations publicise their programmes at group meetings. They present the programmes as positive and fun activities that benefit both the employees and the company. To get the best results, plan and implement your rewards programme with your employees' direct involvement.

- **Monitor effectiveness.** Is your rewards system getting the results you want? If not, take another look at the behaviours you want to reinforce and make sure that your rewards are closely linked to the behaviours. Even the most successful reward programmes tend to lose their effectiveness over time as employees begin to take them for granted. Keep your programme fresh by discontinuing rewards that have lost their lustre and bringing in new ones from time to time.

Deciding What to Reward

Most organisations and managers reward the wrong things, if they reward their employees at all. This tendency has led to a crisis of epic proportions in the traditional system of incentives and motivation in business. For example:

- A major London commodity market gave bonuses of 6 per cent of salary to outstanding employees; and it gave bonuses of 3 per cent of salary to everyone else. Average and adequate performers were therefore receiving exactly the same reward except for the extra three per cent of salary delivered to top performers.

- A top professional footballer on many thousands of pounds a week joined one of the very top football clubs, only to find himself playing in the reserve team at exactly the time when he was trying to develop his career and reputation through playing regularly. He was therefore receiving a very good reward, but not the one that he wanted.

✔ A council employee rated 'exceptional' was told by her manager that she had to be downgraded to 'average' because the County Council Social Services Department had no money to pay her bonus.

If workers aren't being rewarded for doing outstanding work, what are they being rewarded for? As we point out in the 'Biscuit motivation' section earlier in the chapter, organisations often reward employees just for showing up for work.

For an incentive programme to have meaningful and lasting effects, it must be contingent; that is, it must focus on performance – nothing less and nothing more.

'But wait a second,' you may say, 'that isn't fair to the employees who aren't as talented as my top performers.' If that's what you think, we can straighten out that particular misunderstanding right now. Everyone, regardless of how smart, talented, or productive they are, has the potential to be a top performer.

Suppose that Employee A produces 100 widgets an hour and stays at that level of performance day in and day out. On the other hand, Employee B produces 75 widgets an hour but improves output to 85 widgets an hour. Who should you reward? Employee B! This example embodies what you want to reward: The efforts that your employees make to improve their performance, not just to maintain a certain level (no matter how good that level is).

The following are examples of _performance-based measures_ that any manager must recognise and reward. Consider what measures you should be monitoring, measuring, and rewarding in your organisation. Don't forget, just showing up for work doesn't count.

✔ Defects decrease from 25 per 1,000 to 10 per 1,000.

✔ Annual sales increase by 20 per cent.

✔ The department records system is reorganised and colour-coded to make filing and retrieval more efficient.

✔ Administrative expenses are held to 90 per cent of the authorised budget.

✔ The organisation's mail is distributed in 1 hour instead of 1½ hours.

Book III

Getting the Staff

Some managers break incentives into two categories – 'results measures', where measures are linked to the bottom line, and 'process measures', where the link to the bottom line isn't as clear. You need to recognise achievement in both categories.

Starting with the Positive

You're more likely to lead your employees to great results by focusing on their positive accomplishments rather than by finding fault with and punishing their negative outcomes. Despite this fact, many managers' primary mode of operation is correcting their employees' mistakes instead of complimenting their successes.

In a recent study, 58 per cent of employees reported that they seldom received a personal 'thank you' from their manager for doing a good job even though they ranked such recognition as their most motivating incentive. They ranked a written thank you for doing a good job as motivating incentive No. 2, while 76 per cent said that they seldom received thanks from their managers. Perhaps these statistics show why a lack of praise and recognition is one of the leading reasons people leave their jobs.

Years of psychological research clearly show that positive reinforcement works better than negative reinforcement for several reasons. Without getting too technical, the reasons are that positive reinforcement:

- ✔ Increases the frequency of the desired behaviour
- ✔ Creates good feelings within employees

On the other hand, negative reinforcement may decrease the frequency of undesired behaviour, but doesn't necessarily result in the expression of desired behaviour. Instead of being motivated to do better, employees who receive only criticism from their managers eventually come to avoid their managers whenever possible. Furthermore, negative reinforcement (particularly when manifested in ways that degrade employees and their sense of self-worth) can create tremendously bad feelings in employees. And employees who are unhappy with their employers have a much more difficult time doing a good job than the employees who are happy with their employers.

The following ideas can help you seek out the positive in your employees and reinforce the behaviours you want:

- ✔ **Have high expectations for your employees' abilities.** If you believe that your employees can be outstanding, soon they believe it, too. When Peter was growing up, his parents rarely needed to punish him when he did something wrong. He needed only the words 'we know that you can do better' to get him back on course.

✔ **Recognise that your employees are doing their best.** If a shortfall in performance occurs, then support and encourage; punishing people for things that they cannot do in any case has little point.

✔ **Give your employees the benefit of the doubt.** Do you really think that your employees want to do a bad job? No one wants to do a bad job; so your job is to work out everything you can do to help employees do a good job. Additional training, encouragement, and support should be among your first choices – not reprimands and punishment

✔ **Catch your employees doing things right.** Most employees do a good job in most of their work, so instead of constantly catching your employees doing things wrong, catch them doing things right. Not only can you reinforce the behaviours that you want, but you can also make your employees feel good about working for you and for your organisation.

Making a Big Deal about Something Little

Okay, here's a question for you: Should you reward your employees for their little day-to-day successes, or should you save up rewards for when they accomplish something really major? The answer to this question lies in the way that most people get their work done on a daily basis.

The simple fact is that for most people in business, work is not a string of dazzling successes that come one after another without fail. Instead, the majority of work consists of routine, daily activities; employees perform most of these duties quietly and with little fanfare. A manager's typical workday, for example, may consist of an hour or two reading memos and e-mail messages, listening to voice-mail messages, and talking to other people on the phone. The manager spends another couple of hours in meetings and perhaps another hour in one-on-one discussions with staff members and colleagues, much of which involves dealing with problems as they occur. With additional time spent on preparing reports or filling out forms, the manager actually devotes precious little time to decision making – the activity that has the greatest impact on an organisation.

For a line worker, this dearth of opportunities for dazzling success is even more pronounced. If the employee's job is assembling lawnmower engines all day (and she does a good, steady job), when does she have an opportunity to be outstanding in the eyes of her supervisor?

We've taken the long way around to say that major accomplishments are usually few and far between, regardless of your place in the organisational chart. Work is a series of small accomplishments that eventually add up to big ones. If you wait to reward your employees for their big successes, you may be waiting a long time.

Therefore, reward your employees for their small successes as well as for their big successes. You may set a lofty goal for your employees to achieve – one that stretches their abilities and tests their resolve – but remember that praising your employees' progress towards the goal is perhaps even more important than praising them when they finally reach it.

Money and Motivation

You may think that money is the ultimate incentive for your employees. After all, who isn't excited when they receive a cash bonus or pay rise? *As visions of riches beyond her wildest dreams danced through her head, she pledged her eternal devotion to the firm.* The problem is that money really isn't the top motivator for employees – at least not in the way that most managers think. And it can be a huge demotivator if you manage it badly.

Compensating with wages and salaries

Money is clearly important to your employees. They need money to pay bills, buy food and clothes, put petrol in their cars, and afford the other necessities of life.

Most employees consider the money they receive to be a fair exchange for the work they put in. Payment for work carried out is a legal right. Recognition, on the other hand, is a gift. Using recognition, however, helps you get the best effort from each employee.

Realising when incentives become entitlements

In particular, employees who receive annual bonuses and other periodic, money-based rewards quickly come to consider them part of their basic pay.

The problem arises when achieving bonuses and incentives is easy or straightforward. Productivity and output begin to flatten out; and the incentive effect of the payments themselves begins to diminish. People work on the basis that the incentives and bonuses are forthcoming anyway.

Incentives work best when they're related to direct goals or targets and short-term performance. In particular, incentives do not make a bad or boring job more interesting – they make it more bearable, and that only in the short term.

So the issue becomes again: What are you rewarding? You need to work out what the goals and priorities are, what rewards people expect for achieving them, and the best way of delivering these rewards. Consolidating incentives into standard pay and reward packages simply puts up the payroll costs without any tangible returns.

The ineffectiveness of money as a motivator for employees is a good news/bad news kind of thing. We start with the bad news first. Many managers have thrown lots of money into cash-reward programmes, and for the most part these programmes really didn't have the positive effect on motivation that the managers expected. Although we don't want to say that you waste your money on these programmes, you can use it more effectively.

Now you get the good news: Because you know that money is not the most effective motivation tool, you can focus on using tools that are more effective – and the best forms of recognition cost little or no money!

Book III

Getting the Staff

Working out what motivates your staff

If you're a busy manager, cash rewards are convenient because you simply fill out a single request to take care of all your motivation for the year. By contrast, the manager-initiated, based-on-performance stuff seems like a lot of work. To be frank, running an effective rewards programme does take more work on your part than running a simple but ineffective one. But as we show you, the best rewards can be quite simple. After you get the hang of using them, you can easily integrate them into your daily routine. Doing so is part of managing today.

To achieve the best results:

- Concentrate on what the employees need, want, and expect. The only way to be absolutely sure is to ask them.
- Concentrate rewards on the things you really want done. And keep in mind that what gets rewarded gets done.

Don't save up recognition for special occasions only – and don't just use them with the top performers. You need to recognise every employee when they do good work in their job. Your employees are doing good things – things that you want them to do – every day. Catch them doing something right and recognise their successes regularly and often.

The following incentives are simple to execute, take little time, and are the most motivating for employees:

- ✔ Personal or written congratulations from you for a job well done
- ✔ Public recognition, given visibly by you for good job performance
- ✔ Morale-building meetings to celebrate successes
- ✔ Time off or flexibility in one's working hours
- ✔ Asking employees their opinions and involving them in decision making

---

Ten ways to motivate employees

Here are some easy, no-cost things you can do to create a motivating workplace:

1. Personally thank employees for doing a good job – one-on-one, in writing, or both. Do it timely, often, and sincerely.

2. Take the time to meet with and listen to employees – as much as they need or want.

3. Provide employees with specific and frequent feedback about their performance. Support them in improving performance.

4. Recognise, reward, and promote high performers; deal with low and marginal performers so that they improve.

5. Provide information on how the company makes and loses money, upcoming products, and services and strategies for competing. Explain the employee's role in the overall plan.

6. Involve employees in decisions, especially those decisions that affect them. Involvement equals commitment.

7. Give employees a chance to grow and develop new skills; encourage them to be their best. Show them how you can help them meet their goals while achieving the organisation's goals. Create a partnership with each employee.

8. Provide employees with a sense of ownership in their work and their work environment. This ownership can be symbolic, (for example business cards for all employees, whether they need them to do their jobs or not).

9. Strive to create a work environment that is open, trusting, and fun. Encourage new ideas, suggestions, and initiative. Learn from, rather than punish for, mistakes.

10. Celebrate successes – of the company, of the department, and of individuals. Take time for team- and morale-building meetings and activities. Be creative and fresh.

Realising that you hold the key to your employees' motivation

In our experience, most managers believe that their employees determine how motivated they choose to be. Managers tend to think that some employees naturally have good attitudes, that others naturally have bad attitudes, and that managers can't do much to change these attitudes. 'If only we could unleash the same passion and energy people have for their families and hobbies,' these managers think, 'then we could really get something done around here.'

As convenient as blaming your employees for their bad attitudes may be, looking in a mirror may be a more honest approach. Managers need to:

✔ Recognise their employees for doing a good job

✔ Provide a pleasant and supportive working environment

✔ Create a sense of joint mission and teamwork in the organisation

✔ Treat their employees as equals

✔ Avoid favouritism

✔ Make time to listen when employees need to talk

For the most part, you determine how motivated (and demotivated) your employees are. Managers create a motivating environment that makes it easier for employees to be motivated. When the time comes, recognise and reward them fairly and equitably for the work they do well.

When you give out rewards, keep in mind that employees don't want handouts, and they hate favouritism. Provide rewards for the performance that helps you be mutually successful. Don't give recognition when none is warranted. Don't give it just to be nice, or with the hope that people will like you better. Doing so not only cheapens the value of the incentive with the employee who received it, but makes you lose credibility in the eyes of your other employees. Trust and credibility are two of the most important qualities that you can build in your relationship with your employees; if you lose these qualities, you risk losing the employee.

Book III

Getting the Staff

Chapter 7

Coaching and Development

*T*he best managers are *coaches* – that is, individuals who guide, talk with, and encourage others on their journey. With the help of coaches, employees can achieve outstanding results, organisations can perform better than ever, and you can sleep well at night, knowing that everything is just fine.

Coaching plays a critical part in the learning process for employees who are developing their skills, knowledge, and self-confidence. Your employees don't learn effectively when you simply tell them what to do. In fact, they usually don't learn at all.

As the maxim goes:

> Tell me . . . I forget.
>
> Show me . . . I remember.
>
> Involve me . . . I learn.

Nor do your employees learn effectively when you throw a new task at them with no instruction or support whatsoever. Of course, good employees can, and do, eventually work things out for themselves, but they waste a lot of time and energy in the process. 'What on earth am I supposed to be doing? Let's have a go anyway and see what happens!'

Between these two extremes – being told what to do and being given no support whatsoever – is a happy medium where employees can thrive and the organisation can prosper. This is the happy land where everyone lives in peace, harmony, prosperity, and achievement – and this happy medium starts and finishes with coaching.

Playing a Coach's Role

Even if you have a pretty good sense of what it means to be a manager, do you really know what it means to be a coach? A coach is a colleague, counsellor, and cheerleader, all rolled into one. Based on that definition, are you a coach? How about your boss? Or your boss's boss? Why or why not?

We bet that you're familiar with the role of coaches in other non-business activities. A drama coach, for example, is almost always an accomplished actor. The drama coach's job is to conduct auditions for parts, assign roles, schedule rehearsals, train and direct cast members throughout rehearsals, and support and encourage the actors during the final stage production. These roles aren't all that different from the roles that managers perform in a business, are they?

Coaching a team of individuals isn't easy, and certain characteristics make some coaches better than others. Fortunately, as with most other business skills, you can discover, practise, and improve your grasp of the traits of good coaches. You can always find room for improvement, a fact that good coaches are the first to admit. The list that follows highlights some important characteristics of coaching:

- **Coaches set goals.** Whether an organisation's vision is to become the leading provider of wireless telephones in the world, to increase revenues by 20 per cent a year, or simply to get the break room walls painted this year, coaches work with their employees to set goals and deadlines for completion. Coaches then withdraw, to allow their employees time to work out how to achieve the goals.

- **Coaches support and encourage.** Employees – even the best and most experienced – can easily become discouraged from time to time. When employees are learning new tasks, when a long-term account is lost, or when business is down, coaches are there, ready to step in and help the team members through the worst of it. 'That's OK, Kim. You've learned from your mistake, and I know that you can get it right next time!'

- **Coaches emphasise both team success and individual success.** The team's overall performance, not the stellar abilities of a particular team member, is the most important concern. Of course, you need everyone's contribution; but coaches know that no one person can carry an entire team to success. Winning takes the combined efforts of everyone. The development of teamwork skills is a vital step in an employee's progress in an organisation.

- **Coaches can quickly assess the talents and shortfalls of team members.** The most successful coaches can quickly determine their team members' strengths and weaknesses and, as a result, tailor their approach accordingly. For example, if one team member has strong analytical skills but poor presentation skills, a coach can concentrate on providing support to help the employee develop better presentation skills. 'You know, Mark, I want to spend some time with you to work on making your sales' presentations more effective.'

- **Coaches inspire their team members.** Through their support and guidance, coaches are skilled at inspiring their team members to the highest levels of human performance. Teams of inspired individuals are willing to do whatever it takes to achieve their organisation's goals.

- **Coaches create environments that allow individuals to be successful.** Great coaches ensure that their workplaces are structured to let team members take risks and stretch their limits without fear of retribution if they fail.

- **Coaches provide feedback.** Communication and feedback between coach and employee form a critical element of the coaching process. Employees must know where they stand in the organisation – what they're doing right, and what they're doing wrong. Equally important, employees must let their coaches know when they need help or assistance. And this must be a continuous process for both parties. Otherwise problems get raised only at performance reviews and appraisals, or, worse still, get lost altogether.

Coaches are available to advise their employees or just to listen to their problems if need be, whether the issue is work related or personal.

Firing someone doesn't constitute effective feedback. Unless an employee has engaged in some sort of intolerable offence (such as physical violence, theft, or intoxication on the job), a manager needs to give the employee plenty of verbal and written feedback before even considering termination. With employees who simply cannot see what they are doing wrong, your coaching either makes or breaks. If you simply fire someone, you never know whether the problem was theirs – or yours.

Coaching: A Rough Guide

Besides the obvious coaching roles of supporting and encouraging employees in their quest to achieve an organisation's goals, coaches also teach their

Book III

Getting the Staff

employees *how* to achieve those goals. Drawing from their experience, coaches lead their workers step by step through work processes, or procedures. After the workers discover how to perform a task, the coach delegates full authority and responsibility for its performance to them.

For the transfer of specific skills, you can find no better way of teaching, and no better way of learning, than the *show-and-tell* method. If you need to get people up to speed on workplace skills, knowledge, and understanding, then do it on the job. There is simply no better place. And – if you need to – you can get people working fully productively very quickly.

Show-and-tell or on-the-job coaching has three steps:

1. *You do, you say.* **Sit down with your employees and explain the procedure in general terms while you perform the task.** Most businesses today use computers as a critical tool for getting work done. If you are coaching a new employee in the use of an obscure word processing or spreadsheet technique, the first thing you need to do is to explain the technique to the employee while you demonstrate it. 'I click my left mouse button on the Insert command on the toolbar and pull down the menu. Then I point the arrow to Symbol and click again. I choose the symbol I want from the menu, point my arrow to it, and click to select it. I then point my arrow to Insert and click to place the symbol in the document; then I point my arrow to Close and click again to finish the job.'

2. *They do, you say.* **Now, have the employee do the same procedure as you explain each step in the procedure.** 'Click your left mouse button on the Insert command on the toolbar and pull down the menu. OK, good. Now point your arrow to Symbol and click again. Excellent! Choose the symbol you want from the menu and point your arrow to it. Now click to select it. All right – point your arrow to Insert and click to place the symbol in the document. OK, you're almost done now. Point your arrow to Close and click again to finish the job. There you are!'

3. *They do, they say.* **Finally, as you observe, have your employees perform the task again as they explain to you what they are doing.** 'Okay, Miles, now it's your turn. I want you to insert a symbol in your document and tell me what you're doing.'

   'All right, Senti. First, I click my left mouse button on the Insert command on the toolbar and pull down the menu. Then I point the arrow to Symbol and click again. I decide the symbol I want from the menu, point my arrow to it, and click to select it. Next, I point the arrow to Insert and click to place the symbol in the document. Finally, I point my arrow to Close and click again to finish the job. I did it!'

It never hurts to have employees create a 'crib sheet' of the new steps to refer to until they become habit.

Coaching Metaphors for Success in Business

In business, we're constantly reminded that, when it comes to coaching and teamwork, the metaphor of a company as a winning sports team is strong. In many organisations, chief executives hire professional athletes and coaches to lecture their employees on the importance of team play and winning; managers are given the label of *coaches* or *team leaders;* and workers are given the labels of *players or team members.*

This being the case, ignoring the obvious parallels between coaching in sports and in business is difficult. So we're going to get this out of our system once and for all and refrain from linking coaching in sports and business anywhere else in this book after the following list of examples:

- Terry Venables, legendary football coach, on his appointment to Barcelona FC: 'The first thing that I had to do was to get this group of highly talented individuals playing as a team.'

- Clive Woodward, England world cup-winning rugby coach: 'To build a team, you have to coach people as a team. Of course, you work on individual strengths and weaknesses; in the end however, it is how they perform together, not how they perform individually, that determines your success.'

- Arsene Wenger, manager and head coach at Arsenal FC: 'One of the most important things that I have to do is to maintain the players' belief in themselves. This is easy when you are winning – sometimes you have to rein them in. But when you are losing – this is the most important part of the job. And if you simply shout at people or threaten them – you will always fail.'

- Duncan Fletcher, coach of the England Ashes winning cricket team in 2005: 'You have got to be consistent; and players have got to have confidence in you. If they think they are going to be left out of the team after one bad performance, they will be too worried to perform. So, once you pick someone – whoever it is – they need to know that they have your full confidence, backing and support.'

- Alf Ramsey, world cup-winning England football manager and coach: 'The best teams are not necessarily made up of the best individuals. The best teams are made up of talented individuals who can gel together for the good of each other and the team itself.'

One last point: In sports as in business, *everybody* needs a coach. Who's the greatest golfer of all time? Tiger Woods? Probably. But most people don't realise that even Tiger Woods has a coach to help him stay sharp and to improve.

Confronting Turning Points

Despite popular impressions to the contrary, 90 per cent of management isn't the big event – the blinding flash of brilliance that creates markets where none previously existed, the magnificent negotiation that results in unheard-of levels of union – management cooperation, or the masterful stroke that catapults the firm into the big league. No, 90 per cent of a manager's daily job consists of chipping away at problems and shaping talents.

The best coaches are constantly on the lookout for *turning points* – the daily opportunities to succeed that are available to all employees.

Making turning points into big successes

The big successes – the victories against competitors, the dramatic surges in revenues or profits, the astounding new products – are typically the result of building a foundation of countless small successes along the way. Making a voice-mail system more responsive to your customers' needs, sending an employee to a seminar on time management, writing a great sales agreement, conducting a meaningful performance appraisal with an employee, meeting a prospective client for lunch – all these are turning points in the average business day. Although each event may not be particularly spectacular on its own, when aggregated over time, they're what add up to the big things.

This is the job of a coach. Instead of using dynamite to transform the organisation in one fell swoop (and taking the chance of destroying the organisation, the employees, or themselves in the process), coaches are like the ancient stonemasons who built the great pyramids of Egypt. The movement and placement of each individual stone may not have seemed like a big deal when considered as separate activities. However, each was an important step in the achievement of the ultimate result – the construction of awe-inspiring structures that have withstood thousands of years of war, weather, and tourists.

Making coaching special

Coaches focus every day on spending time with employees to help them succeed – to assess employees' progress and to find out what they can do to help the employees capitalise on the turning points that present themselves every day. Coaches complement and supplement the abilities and experience of their employees by bringing their own abilities and experience to the table.

They reward positive performance and they help their employees learn important lessons from making mistakes – lessons that, in turn, help the employees to improve their future performance.

For example, suppose that you have a young and inexperienced, but bright and energetic, sales trainee on your staff. Your employee has done a great job contacting customers and making sales calls, but he has yet to close his first deal. When you talk to him about this, he confesses that he is very nervous about his own personal turning point: He's worried that he may become confused in front of the customer and blow the deal at the last minute. He needs your coaching.

The following guidelines can help you, the coach, handle any employee's concerns:

- ✔ **Meet with your employee.** Make an appointment with your employee as soon as possible for a relaxed discussion of the concerns. Find a place that is quiet and free of distractions and put your phone on hold or forward it to voice-mail.

- ✔ **Listen!** One of the most motivating things one person can do for another is to listen to them. Avoid instant solutions or lectures. Before you say a word, ask your employee to bring you up to date with the situation, his concerns, and any possible approaches or solutions that he's considered. Let him do the talking while you do the listening. If you don't listen, you may never know what the problem actually is! And that means you can't possibly help the employee to solve it.

- ✔ **Reinforce the positive.** Begin by pointing out the things that your employee did right in the particular situation. Let your employee know when he is on the right track. Give him positive feedback on his performance.

- ✔ **Highlight areas for improvement.** Point out the things that your employee needs to do to improve and tell him what you can do to help. Agree on the assistance that you can provide, whether your employee needs further training, an increased budget, more time, or whatever else is required. Be enthusiastic about your confidence in the employee's ability to do a great job.

- ✔ **Follow through.** After you determine what you can do to support your employee, do it! Notice when he improves! Periodically check up on the progress that your employee is making and offer your support as necessary.

Above all, be patient. Coaching is something that you can't accomplish on your terms alone. At the outset, understand that everyone is different. Some

Book III

Getting the Staff

employees catch on sooner than others, and some employees need more time to develop. Differences in ability don't make certain employees any better or worse than others – they just make them different. Just as you need time to build relationships and trust in business, your employees need time to develop skills and experience.

Tapping Into the Coach's Expertise

Coaching is not a one-dimensional activity. Because every person is different, the best coaches tailor their approach to their team members' specific, individualised needs. If one team member is independent and needs only occasional guidance, recognise where the employee stands and provide that level of support. This support may consist of an occasional, informal progress check while making the rounds of the office. If, on the other hand, another team member is insecure and needs more guidance, the coach recognises this employee's position and assists as required. In this case, support may consist of frequent, formal meetings with the employee to assess progress and to provide advice and direction as needed.

Although every coach has an individual style, the best coaches employ certain techniques to elicit the greatest performance from their team members:

- **Make time for team members.** Managing is primarily a people job. Part of being a good manager and coach is being available to your employees when they need your help. If you're not available, your employees may seek out other avenues to meet their needs – or simply stop trying to work with you. Always keep your door open to your employees and remember that they are your Number 1 priority. Manage by walking around. Regularly get out of your office and visit your employees at their workstations. 'Do I have a minute, Elaine? Of course, I always have time for you and the other members of my staff.'

- **Provide context and vision.** Instead of simply telling employees what to do, effective coaches explain *why*. Coaches provide their employees with context and a big-picture perspective. Instead of spouting long lists of do's and don'ts, they explain how a system or procedure works and then define their employees' parts in the scheme of things. 'Sanjeev, you have a very important part in the financial health and vitality of our company. By ensuring that our customers pay their invoices within 30 days after we ship their products, we're able to keep our cash flow on the plus side, and we can pay our obligations such as rent, electricity, and your salary on time.'

✔ **Transfer knowledge and perspective.** A great benefit of having a good coach is the opportunity to discover information and know-how from someone who has more experience than you do. In response to the unique needs of each team member, coaches transfer their personal knowledge and perspective. 'We faced the exact situation about five years ago, Hayden. I'm going to tell you what we did then, and I want you to tell me whether you think that it still makes sense today, or you may have a better idea that we could try.'

✔ **Be a sounding board.** Coaches talk through new ideas and approaches to solving problems with their employees. Coaches and employees can consider the implications of different approaches to solving a problem and role-play customer or client reactions before trying them out for real. By using active listening skills, coaches can often help their employees work through issues and come up with the best solutions themselves. 'Okay, David, you've told me that you don't think your customer will buy from us if we put the prices up by 20 per cent. What options do we have with price increases, and are some better than others?'

✔ **Obtain necessary resources.** Sometimes, coaches can help their employees make the jump from marginal to outstanding performance simply by providing the resources that their employees need. These resources can take many forms – money, time, staff, equipment, or other tangible assets. 'So, Kathleen, you're confident that we can improve our cash flow if we put two more staff on to invoicing? OK, let's give it a try.'

✔ **Offer a helping hand.** For an employee who is learning a new job and is still responsible for performing his current job, the total workload can be overwhelming. Coaches can help workers through this transitional phase by reassigning current duties to other employees, authorising overtime, or taking other measures to relieve the pressure. 'John, while you're learning how to de-bug the new software, I'm going to assign the rest of your workload to Rachel. We can get back together at the end of the week to see how you're doing.'

Book III

Getting the Staff

Chapter 8

Tackling Performance Appraisals

. . . .

. . . .

*T*imely and accurate performance appraisals are an extremely important tool for every business manager or supervisor. So, if performance appraisals are so important to the successful management of employees, why do most managers and supervisors dread doing them, and why do so many employees dread receiving them? According to studies on the topic, an estimated 40 per cent of all workers never receive performance appraisals. And for the 60 per cent of workers who do receive performance appraisals, most of the appraisals are conducted poorly. Very few employees actually receive regular, formal performance appraisals that are thoughtful, complete, and beneficial to the employee – or to the organisation.

Ask any human resources manager whether formal performance appraisals are really necessary and the answer, of course, is a resounding yes! However, if you look a little below the surface, the reality may be something quite different. Although most managers consider performance appraisals a necessary tool in developing their employees, reinforcing good performance, and correcting poor performance, these appraisals are often too little, too late. They often miss the mark as tools for developing employees. If performance appraisals are done poorly, managers are better off not doing them at all – especially if the alternative to appraisals is more frequent coaching.

In this chapter, we consider the benefits of performance appraisals and explore the right and wrong ways to do them.

Appraising Performance

You can find many good reasons for conducting regular formal performance appraisals with your employees. Formal performance appraisals are just one part of an organisation's system of delegation, goal setting, coaching, motivating, and ongoing informal and formal feedback on employee performance. If you don't believe us, try a few of these positive elements of performance appraisals on for size:

✔ **A chance to meet regularly:** In any case, you should be making sure that you know what your employees are doing and being available for support when needed. To do this, you need to meet regularly anyway; and so you have a much better basis for effective regular formal reviews when they happen.

✔ **A chance to summarise past performance and establish new performance goals:** All employees want to know whether they're doing a good job. Formal performance appraisals force managers to communicate performance results – both good and bad – to their employees and to set new goals. In many organisations, the annual performance appraisal is the only occasion when supervisors and managers speak to their employees about performance expectations and the results of employee efforts for the preceding appraisal period.

✔ **An opportunity for clarification and communication:** You need to continually compare expectations. Try this exercise with your manager. List your ten most important activities. Then ask your manager to list what she considers to be your ten most important activities. Surprise – the chances are that your lists are quite different. On average, business people who do this exercise find that their lists overlap only 40 per cent at best. Performance appraisals help the employer and employee to compare notes and make sure that assignments and priorities are in sync.

✔ **A forum for learning goals and career development:** In many organisations, career development takes place as a part of the formal performance appraisal process. Managers and employees are all very busy and often have difficulty setting aside the time to sit down and chart out the steps that they must take to progress in an organisation or career. Although career development discussions should generally take place in a forum separate from the performance appraisal process, combining the activities does afford the opportunity to kill both birds with the same stone . . . or something like that.

✔ **A formal documentation to promote advancement or dismissal:** Most employees get plenty of informal performance feedback – at least of the negative kind along the lines of: 'You did what? Are you nuts?' Most informal feedback is verbal and, as such, undocumented. If you're trying to build a case to give your employee a promotion, you can support your case much more easily if you have plenty of written documentation (including formal performance appraisals) to justify your decision. And, if you're coming to the conclusion that you need to dismiss someone for poor performance, then you must have written evidence, including performance appraisals, that you have tried to address this performance before.

So, the preceding list gives very important reasons for conducting regular formal performance appraisals. However, consider this statement: Many companies have paid a lot of money to employees and former employees who have successfully sued them for wrongful or unfair dismissal, or for other biased and prejudicial employment decisions. Imagine how lonely you'd feel on the witness stand in the following scene, a scene that's replayed for real in courts of law and employment tribunals the length and breadth of the country:

Lawyer: So, Manager-on-the-spot, would you please tell the court exactly why you terminated Employee X?

Manager-on-the-spot: Certainly, I'll be glad to. Employee X was a very poor performer – clearly the worst in my department.

Lawyer: During the five years that my client was with your firm, did you ever conduct formal performance appraisals with Employee X?

Manager-on-the-spot: Er . . . well, no. I meant to, but I'm a very busy person. I was never quite able to get around to it.

Lawyer: Manager-on-the-spot, do you mean to say that, in all the time with your firm, Employee X never received a formal performance appraisal? Exactly how was my client supposed to correct the alleged poor performance when you failed to provide Employee X with the feedback needed to do so?

Manager-on-the-spot: Hmmm . . .

Spelling Out the Performance Appraisal Process

Believe it or not, one of the very most important things you can do as a manager is to conduct accurate and timely performance appraisals of your employees.

Many managers, however, tend to see the performance appraisal process in very narrow terms: How can I get this thing done as quickly as possible so I can get back to my real job? (Whatever their 'real' job is as managers.) In their haste to get the appraisal done and behind them, many managers merely consider a few examples of recent performance and base their entire appraisal on them. And because few managers give their employees the kind of meaningful, ongoing performance feedback that they need to do their jobs better, the performance appraisal can become a dreaded event – full of surprises and dismay. Or it can be so sugar-coated that it becomes a meaningless exercise in management. Neither scenario is the right way to evaluate your employees.

Have separate discussions for each of the following:

- ✔ Pay rises and bonuses
- ✔ Promotions
- ✔ Career development
- ✔ Ways to improve present performance and develop future performance
- ✔ Poor performance

Of course, in practice you can't possibly keep each of the topics totally separate from the rest. But you can prioritise; and you must spell out to the employee the specific purpose of the present discussion.

The performance appraisal process begins on the day that your employees are hired, continues each and every day that they report to you, and doesn't end until, through transfer, promotion, dismissal, or resignation, they move out of your sphere of responsibility.

The performance appraisal process is much broader than just the formal, written part of it. The following five steps help you encompass the broader scope of the process. Follow them when you evaluate your employees' performance:

1. **Set goals, expectations, and standards – together.**

   Before your employees can achieve your goals, or perform to your expectations, you have to set goals and expectations with them and develop standards to measure their performance. And after you've done all this, you have to communicate the goals and expectations *before* you evaluate your employees – not after. In fact, the performance review really starts on the first day of work. Tell your employees immediately how you evaluate them, show them the forms to be used, and explain the process.

Make sure that job descriptions, tasks, and priorities are clear and unambiguous, and that you and your employees understand and agree to the standards set for them. This is a two-way process. Make sure that employees have a voice in setting their goals and standards and that you have their agreement.

2. **Give continuous and specific feedback.**

Catch your employees doing things right – every day of the week – and tell them about it then and there. And if you catch them doing wrong (nobody's perfect!), then let them know about that, too. Feedback is much more effective when you give it regularly and often than when you save it up for a special occasion (which can become victimisation if the feedback is constantly negative). The best formal performance appraisals contain the fewest surprises.

Constantly bombarding your employees with negative feedback has little to do with getting the performance that you want from them and costs you their respect.

3. **Prepare a formal, written performance appraisal with your employee.**

Every organisation has different requirements for the formal performance appraisal. Some appraisals are simple, one-page forms that require you to tick a few boxes; others are multi-page extravaganzas that require extensive narrative support. The form often varies by organisation, and by the level of the employee being evaluated (the ones you can buy at an office supply store are worthless). Regardless of the requirements of your particular organisation, the formal performance appraisal should be a summary of the goals and expectations for the appraisal period – events that you have discussed previously (and frequently) with your employees. Support your words with examples and make appraisals meaningful to your employees by keeping your discussion relevant to the goals, expectations, and standards that you developed in Step 1.

Book III

Getting the Staff

As a collaborative process, have the employee complete her own performance appraisal. Then compare your (the manager's) comments with the employee's comments; the differences that you find become topics of discussion and mutual goal setting.

4. **Meet personally with your employees to discuss the performance appraisal.**

Most employees appreciate the personal touch when you give the appraisal. Set aside some quality time to meet with them to discuss their performance appraisal. This doesn't mean five or ten minutes, but at least an hour or maybe more. When you plan performance appraisal meetings, less is definitely not more. Pick a place that's comfortable and free from distractions. Make the meeting positive and upbeat. Even when you have to discuss performance problems, centre your discussions on ways that you and your employees can work together to solve them.

The tone of performance appraisals and discussions can often become defensive as negative elements are raised and the employee starts to feel that she will get a small, or no pay rise. Start with letting the employee share how her job is going, what's working – and what's not – then share your assessment, starting with the positive.

5. **Set new goals, expectations, and standards.**

   The performance appraisal meeting gives you and your employee the opportunity to step back from the inevitable daily issues for a moment and take a look at the big picture. You both have an opportunity to review and discuss the things that worked well and the things that, perhaps, didn't work so well. Based on this assessment, you can then set new goals, expectations, and standards for the next review period. The last step of the performance appraisal process becomes the first step, and you start all over again.

The entire process consists of setting goals with your employees, monitoring their performance, coaching them, supporting them, counselling and guiding them, and providing continuous feedback on their performance – both good and bad. If you've been doing these things before you sit down for your annual or semi-annual performance appraisal sessions with your employees, you're going to find reviews a pleasant and positive experience, looking at the past accomplishments, instead of being a disappointment for both you and your employees.

When it comes to conducting performance appraisals, managers have plenty of things to remember. Here are a few more:

- ✔ Communication with employees should be frequent so no surprises occur (OK, *fewer* surprises). Give your employees informal feedback on their performance early and often.

- ✔ The primary focus of performance appraisals should be on going forward – setting new goals, improving future performance – rather than on looking back.

- ✔ Learning and development should always be included as a part of the performance appraisal process (although sometimes a discussion about pay rises can be separate).

- ✔ You need to make performance appraisal a priority yourself – a part of your 'real' job – you are, after all, dependent on the performance of your employees for your own success and effectiveness.

Avoiding Common Traps

Appraisers can easily fall into certain traps in the appraisal process. To avoid making a misstep that may result in getting your foot stuck in one of these traps, keep in mind these common mistakes that appraisers make:

- **The halo effect:** This happens when an employee is so good in a particular area of their performance that you ignore problems in other areas. For example, you may give your star salesperson (whom your firm desperately needs to ensure continued revenue growth) a high rating (a halo) despite the fact that she refuses to complete and submit paperwork within the required time limits.

- **The recency effect:** The opposite of the halo effect, the *recency* effect happens when you allow an instance of poor performance to adversely affect your assessment of an employee's overall performance. For example, your administrative assistant has done a very good job for you in the months preceding her appraisal, but last week she missed a customer's deadline for submission of a proposal to continue with their advertising account. Your firm lost the account and you gave your assistant a scathing performance appraisal as a result.

- **Stereotyping:** This occurs when you allow preconceived notions about your employees to dictate how you rate them. For example, you may be convinced that women make better electronic parts assemblers than men do. As a result, your stereotyping automatically gives female employees the benefit of the doubt and higher ratings, while men have to prove themselves before you take them seriously. In extreme cases, such an approach may land you in an employment tribunal or a court of law.

- **Comparing:** Often, when you rate two employees at the same time, you're tempted to compare their performances. If one of the employees is a particularly high performer, your other employee may look bad in comparison – despite her individual level of performance. Conversely, if one of the employees is a particularly low performer, the other employee may look really good in comparison. Make your assessment of an individual employee's performance and allow it to stand on its own two feet and not be subject to how good or bad your other employees are.

- **Mirroring:** Everyone naturally likes people who are most like themselves. That's why you can easily fall into the trap of rating highly those employees who are most like you (same likes, dislikes, interests, hobbies, and so forth) and rating lowly those employees who are least like you. Although this is great for the employees you favour, the employees you don't favour don't appreciate it. Take some advice: Don't do it.

Book III

Getting the Staff

✔ **Discomfort:** One reason that many managers dread doing performance appraisals is that it forces them to acknowledge the failings of their employees and then talk to their employees about them. Few managers enjoy giving their employees bad news, but employees need to receive the bad news as well as the good (just be ready to duck when you give them the bad news). Otherwise, they don't know where they need to improve. And if they don't know where they need to improve, you can bet they don't improve.

Sorting Out Why Appraisals Go Bad

Appraisals go bad for a variety of reason, including:

✔ They are not done regularly or frequently enough. The Chartered Institute of Personnel and Development recommends that appraisals are done every three months, or every six months as a minimum, if there is to be any effective or positive result.

✔ Appraisals are driven by bureaucratic processes, rather than employee development, career enhancement, or pay rises.

✔ They are imposed by the human resources department, rather than being driven by strategic and operational performance.

✔ Managers or employees lack genuine commitment to appraisals; and this invariably reflects the fact that a lack of genuine commitment exists throughout the organisation.

From our experience, few employee appraisals are done well. Not only do managers write appraisals that lack any meaningful examples and insights, but they also fail to give the main process of the performance appraisal – the discussion – the time and attention that it deserves. Performance appraisal meetings also often become one-way presentations from manager to employee, rather than two-way discussions or conversations. As a result, performance appraisals often fail to have the kind of impact that the managers and super-visors who gave them intended.

Real apprehension can surround the appraisal process from both sides of the equation. Often, managers don't feel adequate to the task, and workers don't get the kind of timely and quality feedback that they need to do the best job possible. In addition, an underlying tension often accompanies the perform-ance appraisal process and comes from the fact that most companies tie money and pay rises to performance appraisals. Appraisals that focus on the pay instead of on the performance, or lack of, are not uncommon.

Some managers practise bad appraisal methods that lead to negative consequences for all concerned – the manager, the employee, and the business:

- **Waiting to monitor and give feedback only at scheduled reviews:**
  Don't be among the many managers who fail to give their employees ongoing performance feedback, waiting for the scheduled review instead. Despite your best intentions and the best efforts of your employees, assignments can easily go astray. Schedules can stretch, roadblocks can stop progress, and confusion can wrap its ugly tentacles around a project. However, if you haven't set up systems to track the progress of your employees, you may not be aware of any of this until it is too late. So you end up angry and frustrated, and you shout at your employees because of mistakes you should have spotted.

- **Dropping bombshells:** A bombshell of negative feedback that comes out of the blue and blind-sides an employee leaves destruction in its wake. If instead of checking up on progress along the way, and coaching and supporting people's efforts, you choose to drop bombshells on people, you destroy the morale of the particular individual being ambushed as well as the morale of everyone else. Other employees quickly realise that, if this can happen to one person, it can happen to them also.

  Ambushes clearly take a lot less time to accomplish, and can get the bad manager through the discomfort of doing performance appraisals properly. However, they always store up trouble for the future.

Book III

Getting the Staff

Preparing for the No-Surprises Appraisal

If you're doing your job as a manager, the appraisal holds no surprises for your employees. Follow the lead of the best managers: Keep in touch with your employees and give them continuous feedback on their progress. Then, when you do sit down with them for their formal performance appraisal, the session is a recap of the things that you've already discussed during the appraisal period, instead of an ambush. Keeping up a continuous dialogue lets you use the formal appraisal to focus on the positive things that you and your employees can work on together to get the best possible performance.

Above all, be *prepared* for your appraisals!

Like interviews, many managers leave their preparation for performance appraisal meetings to the last possible minute – often just before the employee is scheduled to meet with them. 'Oh, no. Cathy is going to be here in five minutes. Now, what did I do with her file? I know it's here somewhere!' The average manager spends about one hour preparing for an employee review covering a whole year of performance.

To avoid this unprofessional and unproductive situation, follow these tips:

- Set time aside, make a proper appointment with the employee, and stick to it.
- Make a clear statement to the employee: 'The purpose of this perform-ance appraisal is as follows . . .' and stick to it.

Performance appraisal is a year-round job. Whenever you recognise a prob-lem with your employees' performance, mention it to them, make a note of it, and drop it in your employees' files. Similarly, whenever your employees do something great, mention it to them, make a note of it, and drop it in their files. Then, when you're ready to do your employees' periodic performance appraisals, you can pull out their files and have plenty of documentation available on which to base the appraisals. Not only does this practice make the process easier for you, but also it makes the appraisal a lot more mean-ingful and productive for your employees.

Book IV
How Not to Cook the Books

'The taxmen never give up, do they?'

In this book . . .

Smoothly negotiating your way through tax and bookkeeping helps keep your head above the financial high tide. You can, of course, employ specialists to do this work for you, but having a firm grasp of the basics means you can keep things in check through the financial year, or even manage your books yourself. We also look at keeping tabs on profit and loss.

Here are the contents of Book IV at a glance:

Chapter 1

Working for Yourself Can Be Less Taxing

● ●

In This Chapter

▶ Looking at what self-employment means

▶ Letting HMRC know what you're up to

▶ Ensuring accounts are to your best advantage

▶ Uncovering the classes of national insurance

▶ Putting employees to work for your and your tax bill

▶ Quitting your business

● ●

A ccording to the Federation of Small Businesses, around four million people in the UK work for themselves. But whatever the exact head-count, HMRC taxes all these business people. This chapter looks at dealing with the tax authorities as the owner of your own business instead of as an employee in someone else's.

Doing your taxes correctly can put your new firm on the road to success; messing them up is a sure-fire road to commercial oblivion or even bank-ruptcy. In this chapter we show you the tax advantages of self-employment and steer you away from some of the dangerous pitfalls.

Defining the Terms

Most people who strike out on their own, even if they go on to become multi-billionaires, often start as *sole traders* – the technical term for working for yourself, being a one-person band, or working as a freelancer.

For some, being self-employed means running a full-time business complete with commercial plans, business bank loans, staff, and public-liability insurance.

If that's you, then, one day, you may hope to be a really big company and even float the company on the stock market. Lots of quoted companies started off as ventures run from an entrepreneur's dining room table.

Some sole traders offer the skills they have, such as plumbing, management consultancy, car mechanics, or writing books about money, directly to the client or end-user. Most of these businesspeople will never be big firms but they enjoy the freedom (as well as the responsibilities) of self-employment.

And for a growing number, it's all about part-time boosts to their earnings from a paying job that can be anything from regular wheeling-and-dealing on online auction sites to being a buy-to-let landlord.

Whatever category you are in, you are in business. And that puts you firmly into the tax-paying net even if you already pay income tax because you work full-time for an employer.

Some small businesses decide to become companies rather than sole traders. The advantages, and tax implications, of limited company status are dealt with in *Paying Less Tax For Dummies* (Wiley).

Meeting HMRC's standards for self-employment

HMRC applies basic tests to determine whether you are really self-employed rather than working for someone else. Pass them and you can be on the way to tax savings! The standards are that:

- You work for more than one customer – and preferably several.

- You work from your own premises, or, if you don't, you work from several locations. If you're a writer, for example, you probably work from your home; however, if you're a plumber, you travel to your customers' premises.

- You're in control of what you do and the hours you work. You must be able to turn down work you do not fancy, and you should set your own prices.

- You have a business address – often your home – from which you carry out some business functions, if only message taking.

- You supply and maintain your own vehicles, tools, computers, and/or other items of equipment needed for your trade or profession.

  ✔ You correct bad work in your own time and at your own expense.

  ✔ You are legally liable for your mistakes.

Some businesses have acquired a reputation for turning people whose main function is selling their labour into self-employed workers when they should be employed under PAYE. Some examples are computer consultants who work for one company, sub-contract builders who work for others on sites, and hairdressers who rent the chair and basin space in the salon. HMRC makes big (and usually successful) efforts to deny such people self-employed status and the tax savings that can go with it.

Delving into the grey area: Sole trader or simple seller?

Most know when they start as a sole trader. They do work for customers in return for a commercial rate of reward. But there is a grey area where you may not know if you are trading or simply selling something.

One activity HMRC is targeting selling via online auction. Proceeds from these sales are not, as some believe, always outside the tax net. Nor are car boot sales. Tax inspectors look for evidence of trading.

If you buy goods, either from wholesalers, or from other auctions, or from junk or charity shops with the intention of selling these things on at a profit, you are *trading* and so face a potential tax bill.

If you're clearing out the loft or spare room and have a once-off sale as an alternative to carting the lot to the charity shop or dump, then you are not trading, so there are no tax hassles. Although, should you find a Picasso in your loft and sell it for wads of money, you can face a capital gains tax bill on the proceeds!

It is your responsibility to register so find out about your status if you are in doubt. You cannot argue against a fine or penalty by saying you did not know or that you were waiting for HMRC to contact you.

HMRC insists that the newly self-employed register within three months of starting up their activity. But in practice, someone on PAYE who earns a one-off payment, perhaps for contributing to a publication or a one-off consultancy payment, does not need to register as self-employed although the remuneration they receive for this must be declared for tax.

Book IV

How Not to Cook the Books

Formalising Your Status

Just as no job is complete until the paperwork is done, neither can you start a business without filing forms with HMRC and deciding when your tax year runs. The following sections tell you what you need to do.

Registering your new business

The self-employed have to register as such with HMRC. This procedure includes making arrangements to pay national insurance contributions which you will probably have to make. The upcoming 'Scanning National Insurance' section covers this issue.

You can register by:

- ✔ **Calling** a special helpline on 0845 915 4515. It's open between 8.00 a.m. and 8.00 p.m. seven days a week (except Christmas Day and one or two bank holidays).

- ✔ **Filing** form CWF1. Find it in Inland Revenue leaflet PSE1 *Thinking of working for yourself?* Or download it online at www.inlandrevenue. gov.uk/forms/cwf1.pdf or register online at www.inlandrevenue. gov.uk/startingup/register.htm.

Failing to register within three months of starting self-employment can bring a £100 penalty. In some cases, the business's exact start date may be debatable so it is best to register as soon as you can.

Larger penalties can be imposed if tax is paid late because an unincorporated business failed to register by October 5 of the following tax year in which it was set up.

Choosing your tax year carefully

Most businesses have an accounting year that runs alongside the tax year from 6 April to 5 April, though you may find it more convenient to use 31 March as the end date for your tax year. If you use 5 April or 31 March as the last day of your year, you're opting for *fiscal accounting,* so-called because your business year is the same as the tax, or fiscal, year. Fiscal year users account for tax by the 31 January following the end of their year.

You can use any other date for your year-end. Choosing a different date can give you longer to file and more time to keep the tax earning interest in the bank which sounds like a great tax saving idea. However, while many accountants still recommend choosing a different date, there are drawbacks.

Filing your first two returns

If you don't opt for a fiscal year-end, you have to meet extra requirements when filing tax returns for your first two years of operation. Your first year's tax bill is based on profits, if any, from the start of trading until the next 5 April – even though that's not the year-end date you chose. So, depending on when you start your business, your first tax bill may cover a matter of a few days or a whole year.

Taxes for the second year are based on either the 12 months trading that ends on the date you chose in that year or your first 12 months of trading. You have to use the second option if the selected year-end date is less than 12 months after the start of the business.

Lessening the effects of overlap

Having to pay tax on profits you haven't yet made is known in the tax trade as *overlap*. And you ignore it at your peril. For most small businesses, overlap is something to avoid. The answer is to align your business year with the tax year.

You can change your accounting year-end during the life of your business to lessen the effect of overlap if you need to. You can elect for a year-end change by notifying HMRC on a self assessment form or sending your tax inspector a letter.

If you don't cure your overlap while you are in self-employment, you only get your excess tax payment back when you cease trading. Such an event can be many years in the future, and the overpayments you made on starting will not be adjusted for inflation or changing tax rates.

If you have to borrow extra cash because paying overlap tax takes cash out of your business, you can claim the interest against a future tax bill.

Those setting up a business where the costs of the first year or so of trading are likely to be greater than their earnings obviously need have less fear of overlap as there will be no profits to tax.

Signing on for and paying VAT

Whether you are a self-employed sole trader, a partnership, or a limited company, you have to register for VAT once your annual sales top a threshold amount (£64,000 in 2007-08) determined by The Chancellor of the Exchequer. This threshold tends to rise each year roughly in line with inflation. (For the

Book IV

How Not to Cook the Books

current VAT threshold, go to HMRC Web site at `www.hmrc.gov.uk`.) You also need to register if your earnings in any one quarter are such that, multiplied by four, they would exceed the threshold.

The VAT threshold is determined by *total sales* – not total profits. You can make a loss and still need to be VAT registered.

Once you register for VAT, you have to charge VAT on all the work or goods you supply to customers (other than VAT-exempt goods and services) and account for these amounts. But then you can also deduct VAT on goods and services you have to buy in for your business.

Most goods and services are charged standard rate VAT, now 17.5 per cent. But some items are different. Supplying electricity to people's homes has a 5 per cent rate. More importantly, a number of everyday items largely fresh food, children's clothes, books, magazines, and newspapers have a special 0 per cent rate. This is called *zero-rating*. You must be VAT registered even if all the goods you supply are zero rated providing your sales top the VAT threshold.

Register with HMRC within 30 days of being aware that you will exceed the threshold. Failing to register on time brings a fine which is the greater of £50, or 5 per cent of the VAT owed, if registration is made within nine months of when registration should have taken place, 10 per cent where it is between nine and 18 months late and 15 per cent in all other cases. All these figures are on top of the VAT itself.

You can register for VAT even if your sales are below the threshold, and you may actually save tax by doing so. If you buy a £100 item for your business as a non-VAT trader and pay VAT on it, you have £117.50 (£100 plus 17.5 per cent VAT) to set against your profits for income tax. As a basic rate taxpayer with a 22 per cent rate (20 per cent from 2008), that cuts your bill by £25.85 as you can take off 22 per cent, so the asset costs £91.96. But if you were registered for VAT, you would reclaim the £17.50 *input* (the technical VAT term for anything you buy in for your business) and still have £100 to set against profits. Taking off 22 per cent gives a £22 tax reduction. In this case, the actual cost is £78. So, registering for VAT can be useful if your main clients are organisations that can reclaim VAT themselves.

VAT-registered businesses supplying goods and services to private individuals are at a disadvantage to their non-registered counterparts as they have to boost every bill by 17.5 per cent. If you supply goods or services, you may be able to keep below the annual VAT threshold by supplying labour only and getting your clients to buy the goods needed themselves. For instance, a decorator can ask a customer to buy the paint and wallpaper from the local DIY store. The customer still pays VAT on these items but not on the decorator's labour, which can be a substantial part of the total decoration cost.

Paying the VAT bill

The VAT return asks for two figures: your *output* – the amount you take in for selling goods or supplying services shown on your invoices to customers – and your *input* – the value of goods or services you buy in to help carry out your business shown on invoices you receive from suppliers.

In the past, you had to report your output and input on a quarterly basis. Accountants charged substantial sums for dealing with this work even for relatively small businesses. Some businesses, though, like the discipline of quarterly returns which make sure they get on top of their affairs and don't leave things to fester for up to a year.

But you can ease the VAT paperwork burden (and accountancy bills) through one of the following three options.

- **Cash accounting:** You pay tax according to what actually happens in your business. With this method there is no need to go through the complicated business of reclaiming VAT on a bad debt. You still pay quarterly.

- **Flat rate scheme:** This plan is aimed at businesses with taxable sales of up to £150,000 a year. In following this scheme, you bill customers in the normal way at 17.5 per cent. But instead of paying this amount, less your input, you agree a percentage of your turnover with HMRC and pay it. This percentage varies from 2 per cent for food and children's clothing retailers up to 13.5 per cent for builders and contractors who only supply their labour. You don't have to figure out your outputs and inputs, so it's a lot simpler, but you can end up paying more than you would have had you claimed for your inputs. However, you pay quarterly and can swap back at any time if your inputs rise (making the flat rate a bad deal). You can also claim VAT on any capital expenditure worth over £2000 excluding VAT. To join, submit form VAT 600 (FRS), which you can download from the HMRC Web site at www.hmrc.gov.uk.

- **Annual accounting:** This system is used for businesses with turnovers of up to £660,000 a year. You make one VAT return a year but make nine monthly interim estimated payments. The annual return allows you to balance your monthly payments either with another payment or asking for money back if you have over-estimated your sales. This is just like the way many pay for gas and electricity – 11 fixed amounts plus a balancing payment in the final month.

Book IV

How Not to Cook the Books

Deregistering for VAT

If your sales fall to below the VAT threshold (£62,000 in 2007-08) you can opt to deregister. This drop takes you out of the VAT net. But you don't have to deregister.

If you anticipate that your business downturn is temporary and if charging VAT does not harm your relationships with customers, stick with it if you can stand the paperwork as you'll only have to re-register when your sales go up again. And keeping a VAT number means you can continue to offset all the VAT on goods and services you buy in.

Keeping Accounts to Keep Everyone Happy

Here's a scary thought: The biggest single cheque you'll ever write out may well be to HMRC. In this section, we show you how to minimise your tax bite legally. And, in keeping with this book's theme of making sure that you don't give up all the tax you've saved by sending it all back, and, even worse, paying penalties, we focus on how to stick to the rules.

You need to keep records of transactions, not only to make your business run smoothly but in order to fill out your self assessment return. You can make use of a number of computer packages available for both record keeping and accounts.

You have to keep records of your business for five years following the final filing date for your trading year. Someone with a trading year ending on 31 March 2008 will file by 31 January 2009 and needs to keep the paperwork (or computer records) until 31 January 2014.

Filling out Schedule D can pay dividends

Self-employed people have to fill in the basic self assessment tax form and also the self-employment pages (downloadable from HMRC at `www.hmrc.gov.uk/sa/index.htm` or available via HMRC's helpline, telephone: 0845 9000444). (Chapter 2 offers help with the self assessment form.)

If you are self-employed, you will end up being taxed under what the taxman and accountants call Schedule D. Being on Schedule D can make your personal bank balance happier, most importantly because you can claim many expenses against what you earn. (See the following section.)

Those who work for someone else on PAYE can claim business expenses against tax only if those expenses are 'wholly, exclusively, and necessarily' incurred in carrying out their contract of employment. That definition is really tough to meet. But when you are on Schedule D, the 'necessarily' part of the PAYE definition goes. The reason? No outsider can define 'necessity'. Do you actually need to advertise your services in one particular way? Do you necessarily need a new vehicle when you can do the work using a clapped-out pushbike? Is your computer over-specified and do you need one at all?

All these choices are open to big companies and small companies alike and all the expenses can be set against the company's tax or your personal self assessment form.

Counting your credits

You have a lot of freedom as a self-employed person. You can choose how you'll carry out your business and money spent wholly and exclusively for your business can be set against your earnings.

The tax authorities are not idiots. Don't try putting the costs of a Rolls-Royce down against tax claiming it is a vehicle you use 'wholly and exclusively' for your business, unless, of course, you run a wedding limousine hire firm.

HMRC is always on the lookout for exaggerated expenses, but you don't have to exaggerate to minimise your tax bill. Just make sure you deduct everything you're legally allowed to, including:

- ✔ The administrative cost of running the business against your earnings from it. This sounds elementary, but many people with start-ups or those who have a small business on the side still have the mindset of working for an employer who picks up all the costs of running the business. All those little items such as postage stamps, fuel, mobile and fixed telephone charges, and even heating and lighting for your workplace add up over a year and are legally deductible.

- ✔ The cost of equipment including computers, machinery, and other big items. We explain how to deal with big items in the next section. Cars have rules of their own and are covered in the next section.

- ✔ Bank charges on business accounts and interest on loans for your business.

- ✔ A proportion of the costs of running your home if you use part of your property as a base. There are no specific rules for this. It's a question of common sense. If you have a house with six rooms and use one fairly regularly for your business, then look at your domestic bills and take a sixth-part.

Book IV

How Not to Cook the Books

Obviously, if you use other premises solely for business, then you can deduct all the costs.

Always make sure you say the rooms you use are 'non-exclusive' and don't claim mortgage interest or council tax for that portion of your property otherwise you could run into capital gains tax problems when you sell the home and incur a business rate from the local council.

✔ Accountancy and legal fees and the costs of debt collection.

✔ Pension contributions can count against self-employment earnings.

✔ Publications, stationery, postage, wages and other costs of employing people, insurance, travel, subsistence, gas, electricity, water – all the way down to the batteries in your calculator.

Accounting for big business items

Big expenditure items such as plant and machinery, cars, and computers are not counted against your profits in the same way as the goods and services you buy in to make your business work. With these big items, you can claim capital allowances against your profits. A *capital allowance* is a proportion of the purchase cost that you can set against profits each year as long as you own the item. The result is that tax relief against the expenditure made on these items can be spread out over several years.

The following list explains capital allowances for major items:

✔ On most **plant and machinery,** you can claim 40 per cent of the value in the first year, and then 25 per cent of the balance each following year. So something costing £1,000 has £400 (40 per cent) offset against tax in the first year, and 25 per cent of the £600 balance, or £150, offset in the second year. The starting figure is £450 for the next year, and goes down by a quarter each year.

✔ **Cars** qualify for a 25 per cent capital allowance each year with a limit of £12,000 on the value of the car. Using this ceiling, the maximum allowance in the first year is £3,000, then 25 per cent of the remaining £9,000 (£2,250) and so on.

Low-emission vehicles benefit from a 100% allowance for the first year. The vehicle manufacturer will tell you if your vehicle qualifies as less noxious – printing the rules in full would take up a large part of this book.

Capital allowances are available against the actual cost of the asset. You set the costs of any bank loan or other financing against business expenses.

You cannot claim capital allowances greater than your profits. But there is nothing to stop you claiming less than your maximum and then carrying the remaining amounts into a subsequent year.

Claiming extra help as you start up

Money you spend before you start can be counted against your profits once you set up. This expenditure may include the money you paid for a computer and other machinery you already possess and the cost of feasibility studies into your hoped for business. These sums will normally be counted against your first year's profits. But if you make a loss, you can count them against the next year (and so on for a total of four years if you fail to make a profit).

Accounting for loss making

With the best will in the world, your self-employment could result in a loss. In such a case, you have two tax options, which we explore in the next two sections.

Deducting the loss from other taxable sums

Provided you have earnings from a PAYE job, a pension, from dividends or interest, or from taxable capital gains, you could set your loss off against these amounts. This is a good route for a self-employed person whose business is part-time. Someone earning £20,000 from a PAYE post, and losing £2,000 on their business would end up with a tax bill based on £18,000.

If you make a loss in any of the first four years of a new business, you can offset this loss against tax on your salary in the three years preceding the establishment of your business. You may have to prove you intended to make profits during this period; Tax inspectors look out for loss-making 'hobbies' whose main function is to dodge tax.

You have to inform the tax inspector within 12 months following the 31 January after the end of your loss-making business year.

Subtracting the loss from future earnings

If your losses exceed your taxable sums, you can carry forward the loss against future profits. You can do this for as many years as you need – there is no limit. But you have to tell HMRC within five years of the 31 January following the end of the tax year in which your personal accounted year finished.

Book IV

How Not to Cook the Books

In most cases, it makes sense to offset your losses against earnings, dividends, interest, and capital gains from elsewhere. But if you expect your self-run business to be very remunerative in the future and take you into the top tax band, then consider subtracting early losses from future earnings.

Scanning National Insurance

As a self-employed person, profits you make from your business are added to other earnings, pensions, dividends, and interest for income tax. National insurance is different. There are special rules for the self-employed and two sets of payments you may have to make.

Complicating the classes

National insurance comes in four classes, numbered one through four. Class 1 is for employed persons. The self-employed have to look at Classes 2 and 4, which we do in the next sections. And in case you're wondering, Class 3 is voluntary – it's paid by people who do not work but who wish to keep up their record to qualify for the state retirement pension and other benefits.

Class 4 is collected through the annual self assessment return. It is the only national insurance to be collected in this way. Most people pay Class 1 via their salary packet while Class 2 and Class 3 are paid usually with a direct debit.

Paying Class 2

As a self-employed person you have to pay a fixed £2.20 a week (in 2007-08) in national insurance. This maintains your payment record for the state pension and health-related benefits – but not Jobseekers Allowance.

If your earnings from all self-employment is below the Class 2 threshold (£5,225 in 2005–06), you are exempt from Class 2.

Paying Class 4

Class 4 national insurance is effectively an additional tax on the self-employed. It does not provide any benefits, but that doesn't mean you don't have to pay it if your profits (what you take in less your costs) are at least £5,225 in a year. If your profits are below that figure, you don't have to worry about Class 4.

But if you do have to pay, it is currently (2007-08) charged at 8 per cent of your taxable profits from £5,225 a year to £34,840. The 8 per cent stops there. But there's a one per cent surcharge on all sums above that. So if your profits were £44,840, you would pay 1 per cent on the £10,000 above the upper profits level.

Putting a cap on national insurance

Someone with a mix of self-employment and employment could end up paying Class 1, Class 2, and Class 4. The bad news is that many pay more in national insurance for the same amount of income if it comes from a variety of sources, such as self-employment and employment, than they would if it all from one source. The good news is that there are ceilings on payments.

If all your income comes from being self-employed, then you cannot pay more than £2,483.60 (in tax year 2007-08) in Class 2 and Class 4 together. The HMRC Web site (www.hmrc.gov.uk) or your local tax office can give details of future rates. And if you have earnings from employment as well, there is a chance you have paid a lot more than you should when you add up all the sums from your job and your self-employment. Check with HMRC if you think you may have overpaid.

Hiring Helpers

Being a sole trader doesn't mean you have to work on your own. It's a tax definition, after all. You may need to pay for help on a part- or full-time basis or to hire someone to help out every now and again. If you have family, you may want to make the most of the tax advantages you can reap by employing them. The next sections tell you how to look at employees as tools to lower your tax.

Employing your family

You can employ your family in the business and thereby take advantage of the lower tax rates your spouse or children fall under to reduce your household's overall tax bill.

You do have to keep a few rules in mind, though:

- You have to hire your relative to do real work at commercial wage rates. You cannot get away with paying a small child £100 an hour for taking telephone messages!

- Local authorities have rules on children working. This will not apply to a few hours' working in the home. But if you want to employ a child under 16 in other circumstances, check out more details with your local authority.

 Family members who earn more than £100 (in 2007-08) in any week are liable for national insurance payments. As the employer, you also have to pay national insurance on their behalf. This is called the *national insurance lower earnings limit*. Accountants call it the LEL.

Book IV

How Not to Cook the Books

Your teenage children might have no income to offset against their personal allowance. Or you might be a top-rate tax payer and have a partner whose maximum is at the basic or lower rate.

You have to pay the money for real, of course. The taxman can ask for the audit trail to see how the payment goes from your business to the family member concerned.

Establishing a partnership with your partner

If you and your spouse or partner are both involved in running a business, it could be worth exploring a partnership structure. There are legal concerns such as each partner being liable for debts incurred by other partners. For tax reasons, it is best to have a partnership contract which sets out how profits will be shared.

HMRC is on the lookout for phoney partnerships, established solely with the aim of reducing a couple's overall tax bill. If you have a business partnership with your spouse, you may have to show that both work in the firm and both contribute work according to the proportion of the profits you each earn. This is a measure to prevent couples sharing profits on a 50-50 basis to use up tax allowances of the non-worker when only one works.

Paying employees

If you hire employees, you are in the same situation as any other employer. You have to sort out any PAYE tax and national insurance contributions they owe.

Giving Up Work

Stopping work is easier than starting. You should inform HMRC if you intend to stop working in your business. And if you were caught by overlap, now is the time to claim it back. Your final accounts can also take care of what happens when you sell plant, machinery, vehicles, or stock.

Chapter 2

Filling In and Filing Your Self Assessment Form

In This Chapter

▶ Looking at the form

▶ Completing the basic return

▶ Calculating the right amounts

▶ Sending in the paperwork

▶ Paying what you owe

*F*illing in your self assessment form (or, officially, your *tax return*) is an annual chore. And it could be followed by having to send a substantial cheque to HMRC. Painful.

This chapter doesn't give you hints on how to reduce your tax bill. Nor does it show you how to answer all the questions, most of which are self-explanatory anyway. Instead, it points out common errors that could derail your tax return, involve you in fines, interest and penalties, and possibly an investigation.

Managing the Mechanics of the Form

In these sections, we look at who gets the self assessment form, (or forms for a few), what they have to do with the form, and what happens if they don't fill it in.

Getting the forms

Around one in three taxpayers is sent a form automatically each year at, or just after, the start of the tax year on 6 April. These are people that HMRC believes should get a form because they:

- Have earnings from self-employment or are in partnerships
- Are top-rate taxpayers or are approaching the cut-off point for basic-level tax
- Are company directors
- Have more than one source of income
- Have earnings from overseas
- Are pensioners with a complex income mix
- Own substantial land or property
- Regularly have capital gains or losses from investments.

This is not an exhaustive list. And you may find the reason that you were sent a form no longer applies – perhaps you moved from self-employment to employment or spent all your savings. You do not have to send in a completed form if you do not owe tax.

HMRC is trying to cut down on the number of tax-payers who receive forms each year. It is experimenting with simple forms for those who only have the odd item to declare and taking around one million people out of the tax net altogether as it is more efficient to use PAYE to collect any extra tax an individual might owe.

If you go for the traditional paper-based method when you submit your tax forms, you are likely to receive three documents from HMRC. These are:

- **Tax Return:** Everyone has to complete this as it provides the basic information for your self assessment (around 10 pages).
- **Tax Return Guide:** This booklet offers substantial detail on how to fill in the return (around 36 pages).
- **Tax Calculation Guide:** This helpful guide enables you to work out the amount you owe (or are owed as a rebate) with no more technology than a pocket calculator (around 16 pages).

  HMRC does not send out the Tax Calculation Guide to everyone. You may not receive one if you have previously filed over the Internet or sent in forms based on a recognised computer program.

There are also supplementary pages that cover such areas as employment, share option schemes, self-employment, partnerships, owning land or property, receiving foreign income, receiving income from trusts or estates, capital gains and losses, and being not resident in the UK for tax purposes. HMRC normally sends supplementary pages you used previously. In many cases, these pages are bound together with your basic form. (The upcoming 'Seeing about supplementary pages' section talks about these pages in more detail.)

These supplementary pages are designed to cover some 99.9 per cent of needs. But if you're in doubt, or have a source of income that should be taxed that doesn't seem to fit any of the supplementary pages, you can make use of the additional information section on the form. You can always write a letter, as well, if you need to communicate with HMRC for any reason.

It is your legal duty to fill in a form if you have to. It is not an excuse to say you did not receive one. Or that you left it all up to your employer to sort out. Or that you thought an accountant would do it all for you. If you are in any doubt, apply for a form by telephoning the HMRC Order Line on 0845 9000 404. You can also fax your request to 0845 9000 604 or download the form from the Internet at www.hmrc.gov.uk. And don't forget to send it in. If you have not received a tax return and have further tax to pay, you must tell HMRC by the 5 October following the end of the tax year.

Your local tax office can provide you with the form and other material in Braille, large print, and audio format. You can also communicate with HMRC in Welsh. There is a Welsh language helpline on 0845 302 1489.

The standard forms are also available to print or use on screen in the many tax return computer program packages on sale.

Discovering you don't have to fill in a form

If your total earnings are from one employer under PAYE, you only have to fill in a form if you are a top-rate tax-payer. If you have an ordinary job and no extraordinary income, you pay tax through the PAYE system on a regular basis. So you don't have to fill in a self assessment form or pay anything extra at tax time.

If your total income, including investment income and savings interest and the value of any workplace perks such as a company car or company health scheme, leaves you firmly in the basic-tax rate zone (or lower), you do not have to fill in a form. The only exception is where you have other sources of taxable income from which tax was not deducted at source.

If you believe that your only need to contact HMRC is to ask for a rebate of previously paid tax, you can either fill in a self assessment form or, more simply, ask for form R40, which is a claim for repayment. R40 is also available as a download from www.hmrc.gov.uk/forms/r40.pdf.

Keeping records

Self assessment works on a file now, check later procedure. This means you file your self assessment return, then HMRC checks it. So saving the records of your finances is really vital. You have to keep paperwork for one year after the final filing date (31 January) after the end of the tax year (ending the previous 5 April). This is extended to five years if you are self-employed.

Filling In the Return

If you're like most taxpayers, you can ignore around four fifths of the form. If you do not tick the 'yes' box to any section, you can move on. You do not have to write in 'not applicable'. HMRC's gadgetry is trained to recognise blank pages.

Avoiding the most common self assessment errors

Don't fall into the trap of making any of the following common self assessment errors:

- ✔ Failing to sign the form – it's your responsibility.
- ✔ Failing to tick all the mandatory boxes.
- ✔ Failing to provide complete information about any repayment due you.
- ✔ Failing to tick your choice of repayment. You can opt to have repayments sent by cheque or repaid through PAYE (if you're an employee). And if you're feeling generous, see the next tip.
- ✔ Failing to tell HMRC where any repayment should go. You have to remember to put in details such as bank account numbers.
- ✔ Failing to tell HMRC to whom any repayment is to go.

- ✔ Failing to complete the correct supplementary pages (see the 'Seeing about supplementary pages' section) or to attach all the supplementary pages.

- ✔ Entering weekly or monthly amounts in an annual box – this applies especially to pension payments.

- ✔ Recording the capital in your savings account as well as the interest in the interest box on the form.

The Tax Return Guide is not the easiest document to use. Although not a legal document, it is written like one in many parts and is full of HMRC jargon. But you can call HMRC's helpline and get someone to translate it (and more) into everyday language. The telephone number is 0845 9000 444. With patience, you can make the Tax Return Guide, combined with the Tax Calculation Guide, work for you. You may still need a pocket calculator (or a good ability with long multiplication and division).

Listing income and credits

The basic tax return is designed to gather information about certain income including interest you earn from National Savings, bank, and building society accounts. You also need to provide information about interest from unit trusts and dividend income from trusts and investments.

If you draw a pension or receive Social Security benefits, HMRC wants to know about them. Remember state pensions and contribution-based job-seeker's allowance are taxable.

You also need to report any miscellaneous income, which can include small amounts of casual earnings, royalties, and commission you might get from selling for mail-order companies. In many cases, it's easier to record details by filling in a supplementary section. The basic form lists all the supplementary sections, which range from employment and self-employment to Lloyd's insurance names and foreign investment income.

The form also has space for you to list items you can claim as tax credits. These include:

- ✔ Personal and stakeholder pension contributions. Don't record these contributions if your only pension payments are through your employer as relief should occur automatically through PAYE.

- ✔ Venture capital trusts.

Book IV

How Not to Cook the Books

- Tax-deductible contributions to trade union and friendly society sickness and funeral plans. You cannot claim for standard trade union membership fees.

- Gifts to charities.

- The Blind Person's allowance.

- The Married Person's Allowance, which applies only if at least one partner was born before 6 April 1935.

You should not put pence into any box when you fill in the form. You can round down income and gains (items you owe tax on) to the nearest pound. Equally you can round up credits and deductions (items that HMRC owes you) to the nearest pound. This can sometimes lead to slight differences between boxes on the form. And it can save a few pounds!

Going into savings and investments

You should get an annual return for each UK savings account you have. This report shows the amount of interest, the amount taken off for taxation at source, and what you are left with. Investments such as shares, unit trusts, and investment trusts include similar information with each dividend payment. But if your investment does not pay dividends, you don't receive any such information.

Less than obvious areas to note include:

- **Purchased life annuities:** The annuity provider give you a certificate to show what proportion of each payment is tax-free.

- **Relevant discounted securities:** Items under this heading can include retail price index-linked UK government stocks, zero-dividend split capital investment trust shares, and some stock market index-tracking bonds which offer a minimum guaranteed return irrespective of the performance of the shares in the index.

- **Scrip dividends:** A scrip dividend is an offer of shares in place of cash. You should show the cash equivalent in the correct box. *Dividend reinvestment schemes,* in which you choose to have any dividends automatically go to buying new shares instead of getting cash, do not count as a scrip.

Don't forget to count investment trust shares under the 'dividends from companies' heading, but not dividend distributions from UK authorised unit trusts and UK authorised open-ended investment companies (OEICs).

Making friends with the blank page

You can use the blank box at the end of the form to tell the tax inspector about items you are not sure about. By showing your doubts at this stage, you can probably head off trouble later on.

You can also use this space to confess to any items you have estimated because, for one reason or another, you do not have the paperwork to hand.

Always over-estimate tax due if there is any doubt. You cannot be penalised if you overpay your tax and then receive a refund. Underpayment is a different matter entirely.

Seeing about supplementary pages

The basic form, with details such as your name and address and your national insurance number, is only the starting point. Most people have to fill in extra pages known as *supplementary pages*. These cover what makes you different as a tax-payer – you're employed or you're self-employed or you have overseas investments, for example. In fact, in many cases, the supplementary pages are the most important! They are part and parcel of the self assessment form so you can't avoid them.

The supplementary pages, in order of HMRC reference numbers, are:

- **Employment (SA101):** Fill this in if you have to file a self assessment return and were employed under PAYE on a full-time, part-time, or casual basis. This category also includes agency work and 'IR35' work where you provide your labour through a company. Ask HMRC for special pages if you are a paid minister of religion.

- **Share schemes (SA102):** On this page, you record the options granted and options exercised under a number of employee incentive schemes. You do not need to fill this in if you were in an HMRC approved scheme such as Save As You Earn and have met all the conditions.

- **Self Employment (SA103):** In addition to those who get some or all of their income from self-employment, you will need to fill this section in if you are a buy-to-let landlord or provide furnished accommodation in your home where you also offer meals, such as in a bed-and-breakfast. You need to complete a separate SA103 for each business you have. So if you work for yourself as a builder but also rent out properties, you have to complete two forms. If you invested your money into a Lloyd's of London insurance underwriting syndicate, there are special extra pages.

- ✔ **Partnership (SA104):** There are two versions of this form. The short version covers the standard situation in which you earn money from a partnership whose trading income is the only or main source of money coming in. The full version covers more complicated situations. Most partners can use the short version but if you are not sure, ask for the full version. All partners are jointly responsible for completing the partnership's returns.

- ✔ **Land and Property (SA105):** This section covers income from land and property in the UK, including furnished holiday lettings, but excluding buy-to-lets.

- ✔ **Foreign income (SA106):** This is a catch-all section for all sorts of income produced from sources outside the UK. It includes offshore bank accounts, investments, and insurance policies. It does not matter if the income has already been taxed at source by the overseas tax authority, you still have to fill in this section. There are a number of tax treaties between the UK and other countries that sort out what you pay in the source country and in the UK. Filling in this section enables HMRC to know whether you have more to pay or whether you qualify for a rebate.

- ✔ **Trusts (SA107):** If you are a beneficiary of trusts or settlements (but not the bare trusts used often by grandparents and others to give money to those under 18 who (or whose parents) have to account for any tax due themselves), you need to complete this page. You should also use this page to record regular income from a deceased person's estate, but not for one-off payments from a legacy (these are not taxed). If you receive an income from an income-producing asset such as shares you inherited, include the income in the standard return along with any other investment income.

- ✔ **Capital gains (SA108):** If you disposed of assets liable to capital gains tax worth at least four times the capital gains tax annual allowance, you have to fill this part in even if you don't have to pay any tax. In 2007-08, the allowance is £9,200 so the reporting level was £36,800. You also fill in these pages if you have a loss.

- ✔ **Non-residence (SA109):** This part is for people who earn income in the UK but are not regarded as UK 'tax citizens' (the proper phrases are 'not resident', 'not ordinarily resident' or 'not domiciled'). It can also apply if you are resident in the UK for tax purposes but also a tax resident of another country with which the UK has a 'double taxation' agreement.

Looking at the employment pages

You have to fill these in if you are a top-rate taxpayer or a director (even if you own the majority of the company's shares).

You do not necessarily have to enter any more than the name of your employer and the amount of pay you received (noted on your P60).

Considering the self-employment pages

You will need a separate set of forms for each form of self-employment. For instance, if you drive a cab as a self-employed driver by day, but earn a living as a freelance entertainer by night, you have two totally different forms of self-employment.

You also fill in these pages if you provided accommodation with a service attached such as regular meals or nursing. Buy-to-let is included under 'investments'.

You have to fill in the capital allowances section, where applicable, no matter what your turnover. This is where you can claim *depreciation* (the declining value of cars, plant and machinery, and some buildings) against your profits.

In general, you can write off 40 per cent of the value of most items in the first year, followed by 25 per cent of the balance in each successive year.

You need only show turnover (sales), expenses against turnover and the resulting profit or loss if your turnover is under £15,000. You still have to keep records and accounts, however, to show HMRC if your return is subject to additional checking. The £15,000 level has remained unchanged for many years. If your turnover exceeds £15,000 you have to show a more detailed breakdown of costs and tax adjustments as listed on the form.

If you received small or one-off earnings and you have no expenses to set against the sum, you might put these under 'other income' in the main pages. This might include a single payment for writing an article for a magazine or for selling a patented idea to a firm.

Counting the Ways of Doing the Sums

Even if you get professional help with your self assessment form, you still have to assemble all the paperwork needed. But you can find assistance at no cost. The following sections tell you how to figure out your bottom line as far as tax liability goes.

Book IV

How Not to Cook the Books

Finding out that the early form-filler works less

Filing a paper tax return before 30 September gives you the option of asking HMRC to calculate your tax. The calculations, of course, depend on you filling in the return correctly. You're told how much to pay or whether there is a repayment coming your way by the following January 31. You can, if you disagree with HMRC's figures, rework them yourself or hire an accountant. But the reality is that this 30 September option is generally only used by those with relatively simple tax affairs.

If, for some reason, your tax form was sent to you late, the window for asking HMRC to do the sums extends to two months after the return was sent to you.

Using purpose-built software

You can put all your details into a number of computer programs. These then lead you into the right additional sections and work out what you owe (or are owed).

Some programs don't support all the supplementary pages although most do. So check the 'Seeing about supplementary pages' section earlier in this chapter for the reference number of the pages you need before buying.

Filing Your Form

Self assessment depends on a strict annual timetable with deadlines reinforced by fines, interest and penalties. These dates can be stretched by a day or so year-by-year to avoid bank-holidays and weekends.

The four basic dates in each tax year are:

- ✔ **6 April:** New forms available.
- ✔ **30 September:** The final date to submit your form if you want HMRC to calculate your tax.
- ✔ **30 December:** The final date for internet filing if you owe less than £2,000 and want the payments taken out of your regular salary through PAYE.
- ✔ **31 January:** The deadline for returns to avoid automatic penalties and interest.

Paying a £100 penalty for filing a day late can easily undo all the tax-saving work you have done over the past year. Get your payments in on time!

From April 2008, the deadline for paper-based returns will be 30 September, rather than January 31 the following year. Online filing will still be accepted until the January 31 deadline.

Posting in your form

Around 90 per cent of self assessment taxpayers use some form of paper-based return. You can send it in through the post – you have to pay the postage – or you can hand deliver the forms to your local tax office (even if it is the office that handles your affairs.) If you post it, ask for proof of posting. If you hand it in, ask for a receipt. Many tax offices stay open from 8.30 a.m. to 8 p.m. on deadline day.

Submitting your form online

You can file electronically, and more and more people do so each year. HMRC is a big online filing enthusiast. Large companies and accountancy firms already do much of their communications online. You get automatic calculation without having to buy a software package that only lasts for one year. The system guides you through the questions and automatically steers you away from parts of the form that are not relevant to you.

Repayments are faster than with paper-based filing. And you have until 31 December (rather than 30 September) to file if you want any tax you have to pay to be collected through PAYE.

Print out a hard copy anyway, just to be sure. If you have some idea of your potential tax bill first, then you will see if you have done anything silly such as turning a £5,000 spare-time earning into £500,000 or £5!

Paying on Account

The self assessment tax system works with two formal payment dates a year. On 31 January you have to pay anything still outstanding from the tax year which ended on the previous 5 April, plus half your likely tax bill for the year which will end on the forthcoming 5 April. So on or before 31 January 2008 you should have paid any outstanding balances for 2006–07 plus half of what you are likely to owe in 2007–08.

You do not have to make payments on account if 80 per cent or more of your income tax bill (but not capital gains tax) is covered by tax deducted at source – PAYE and automatic deductions from savings interest are common deductions. It's up to you to work this out. It is best to ignore this concession if you are a 'borderline' 80 per cent case.

There is no interest benefit if your payment arrives early (but at least you know you've done it and won't get penalised!)

Asking for a reduction in payments

If your tax liability for this year is likely to be significantly lower than the previous year, you can ask for a reduction in your payments on account. Otherwise, you could end up paying more than you need until it is corrected in the following year's tax return.

You can claim a reduction on your payments on account on a tax return, or by writing to HMRC. You must give valid reasons to back your claim. HMRC adds interest to your repayment, but the rate is far lower than the interest they charge you if you owe them money.

Adding up the potential penalties

You face an automatic £100 penalty if you fail to get your return in by 31 January. And there is a further £100 if you have still not filed by the following 31 July. In addition, there is a 5 per cent surcharge on tax unpaid on 28 February, and a further 5 per cent if it is still unpaid (plus interest on the first surcharge). This is a painful sum!

Penalties cannot be greater than the tax owed. If you discover you owe nothing or are due a rebate, the 31 January deadline does not apply.

Some people who cannot fill in their form properly make an estimate and then pay over more tax than needed. If you pay more than you owe, you cannot be fined. You can claim any excess back later.

Chapter 3

Getting Down to Bookkeeping Basics

All businesses need to keep track of their financial transactions, which is why bookkeeping and bookkeepers are so important. Without accurate records, how can you tell whether your business is making a profit or taking a loss?

In this chapter, we cover the key aspects of bookkeeping: We introduce you to the language of bookkeeping, familiarise you with how bookkeepers manage the accounting cycle, and show you how to understand the more complex type of bookkeeping – double-entry bookkeeping.

Bookkeeping: The Record Keeping of the Business World

Bookkeeping, the methodical way in which businesses track their financial transactions, is rooted in accounting. *Accounting* is the total structure of records and procedures used to record, classify, and report information about a business's financial transactions. Bookkeeping involves the recording of that financial information into the accounting system while maintaining adherence to solid accounting principles.

The bookkeeper's job is to work day in and day out to ensure that transactions are accurately recorded. Bookkeepers need to be very detail-oriented and love working with numbers, because numbers and the accounts the numbers go into are what these people deal with all day long. Bookkeepers aren't required to belong to any recognised professional body, such as the Institute of Chartered Accountants of England and Wales. You can recognise a chartered accountant by the letters ACA after the name, which indicates that he or she is an Associate of the Institute of Chartered Accountants. If they've been qualified much longer, they may use the letters FCA, which indicate that the accountant is a Fellow of the Institute of Chartered Accountants.

Of course, both Scotland and Ireland have their own chartered accountant bodies with their own designations. Other accounting qualifications exist, offered by the Institute of Chartered Management Accountants (ACMA and FCMA), the Institute of Chartered Certified Accountants (ACCA and FCMA), and the Chartered Institute of Public Finance Accountants (CIPFA). The Association of Accounting Technicians offers a bookkeeping certificate (ABC) programme, which provides a good grounding in this subject. In reality, most bookkeepers tend to be qualified by experience.

If you're after an accountant to help your business, use the appropriate chartered accountants or a chartered certified accountant as they have the most relevant experience.

On starting up their businesses, many small businesspeople serve as their own bookkeepers until the business is large enough to hire a dedicated person to keep the books. Few small businesses have accountants on the payroll to check the books and prepare official financial reports; instead, they have bookkeepers (either on the payroll or hired on a self-employed basis) who serve as the outside accountants' eyes and ears. Most businesses do seek out an accountant, usually a chartered accountant (either ACA or FCA), but this is usually to submit annual accounts to HM Revenue & Customs.

In many small businesses today, a bookkeeper enters the business transactions on a daily basis while working inside the business. At the end of each month or quarter, the bookkeeper sends summary reports to the accountant who then checks the transactions for accuracy and prepares financial statements such as the profit and loss, and balance sheet statements.

In most cases, the accounting system is initially set up with the help of an accountant. The aim is to ensure that the system uses solid accounting principles and that the analysis it provides is in line with that required by the business, the accountant, and HM Revenue & Customs. That accountant periodically reviews the system's use to make sure that transactions are being handled properly.

Accurate financial reports are the only way to ensure that you know how your business is doing. These reports are developed using the information you, as the bookkeeper, enter into your accounting system. If that information isn't accurate, your financial reports are meaningless: As the old adage goes, 'Garbage in, garbage out'.

Wading through Basic Bookkeeping Lingo

Before you can take on bookkeeping and start keeping the books, you first need to get a handle on the key accounting terms. This section describes the main terms that all bookkeepers use on a daily basis.

Accounts for the balance sheet

Here are a few terms you need to know:

- **Balance sheet:** The financial statement that presents a snapshot of the business's financial position (assets, liabilities, and capital) as of a particular date in time. The balance sheet is so-called because the things owned by the business (assets) must equal the claims against those assets (liabilities and capital).

  On an ideal balance sheet, the total assets need to equal the total liabilities plus the total capital. If your numbers fit this formula, the business's books are in balance.

- **Assets:** All the items a business owns in order to run successfully, such as cash, stock, buildings, land, tools, equipment, vehicles, and furniture.

- **Liabilities:** All the debts the business owes, such as mortgages, loans, and unpaid bills.

- **Capital:** All the money the business owners invest in the business. When one person (sole trader) or a group of people (partnership) own a small business, the owner's capital is shown in a Capital account. In an incorporated business (limited company), the owner's capital is shown as shares.

  Another key Capital account is *Retained Earnings,* which shows all business profits that have been reinvested in the business rather than paid out to the owners by way of dividends. Unincorporated businesses show money paid out to the owners in a Drawings account (or individual drawings accounts in the case of a partnership), whereas incorporated businesses distribute money to the owners by paying *dividends* (a portion of the business's profits paid out to the ordinary shareholders, typically for the year).

Accounts for the profit and loss statement

Following are a few terms related to the profit and loss statement that you need to know:

- ✔ **Profit and loss statement:** The financial statement that presents a summary of the business's financial activity over a certain period of time, such as a month, quarter, or year. The statement starts with Sales made, subtracts out the Costs of Goods Sold and the Expenses, and ends with the bottom line – Net Profit or Loss.

- ✔ **Income:** All sales made in the process of selling the business's goods and services. Some businesses also generate income through other means, such as selling assets the business no longer needs or earning interest from investments.

- ✔ **Cost of Goods Sold:** All costs incurred in purchasing or making the products or services a business plans to sell to its customers.

- ✔ **Expenses:** All costs incurred to operate the business that aren't directly related to the sale of individual goods or services.

Other common terms

Some other common terms include the following:

- ✔ **Accounting period:** The time for which financial information is being prepared. Most businesses monitor their financial results on a monthly basis, so each accounting period equals one month. Some businesses choose to do financial reports on a quarterly basis, so the accounting period is three months. Other businesses only look at their results on a yearly basis, so their accounting period is 12 months. Businesses that track their financial activities monthly usually also create quarterly and *annual reports* (a year-end summary of the business's activities and financial results) based on the information they gather.

- ✔ **Accounting year-end:** In most cases a business accounting year is 12 months long and ends 12 months on from when the business started or at some traditional point in the trading cycle for that business. Many businesses have year-ends of 31st March (to tie in with the tax year) and 31st December (to tie in with the calendar year). You're allowed to change your business year-end to suit your business.

For example if you started your business on July 1, your year-end will be 31 June (12 months later). If, however, it is traditional for your industry to have 31 December as the year-end, it is quite in order to change to this date. For example, most retailers have 31 December as their year-end. You of course have to let HM Revenue & Customs know and get their formal acceptance.

- **Debtors (also known as Accounts Receivable):** The account used to track all customer sales made on credit. *Credit* refers not to credit card sales but to sales in which the business gives a customer credit directly, and which the business needs to collect from the customer at a later date.

- **Creditors (also known as Accounts Payable):** The account used to track all outstanding bills from suppliers, contractors, consultants, and any other businesses or individuals from whom the business buys goods or services.

- **Depreciation:** An accounting method used to account for the aging and use of assets. For example, if you own a car, you know that the value of the car decreases each year (unless you own one of those classic cars that goes up in value). Every major asset a business owns ages and eventually needs replacement, including buildings, factories, equipment, and other key assets.

- **Nominal (or General) Ledger:** Where all the business's accounts are summarised. The Nominal Ledger is the master summary of the bookkeeping system.

- **Interest:** The money a business needs to pay when it borrows money from anybody. For example, when you buy a car using a car loan, you must pay not only the amount you borrowed (capital or principal) but also additional money, or interest, based on a percentage of the amount you borrowed.

- **Stock (or Inventory):** The account that tracks all products sold to customers.

- **Journals:** Where bookkeepers keep records (in chronological order) of daily business transactions. Each of the most active accounts, including cash, Accounts Payable, and Accounts Receivable, has its own journal.

- **Payroll:** The way a business pays its employees. Managing payroll is a key function of the bookkeeper and involves reporting many aspects of payroll to HM Revenue & Customs, including Pay As You Earn (PAYE) taxes to be paid on behalf of the employee and employer, and National Insurance Contributions (NICs). In addition, a range of other payments such as Statutory Sick Pay (SSP) and maternity/paternity pay may be part of the payroll function.

- **Trial balance:** How you test to ensure that the books are in balance before pulling together information for the financial reports and closing the books for the accounting period.

Book IV

How Not to Cook the Books

Pedalling through the Accounting Cycle

As a bookkeeper, you complete your work by completing the tasks of the accounting cycle, so-called because the workflow is circular: Entering transactions, manipulating the transactions through the accounting cycle, closing the books at the end of the accounting period, and then starting the entire cycle again for the next accounting period.

The accounting cycle has eight basic steps, shown in Figure 3-1.

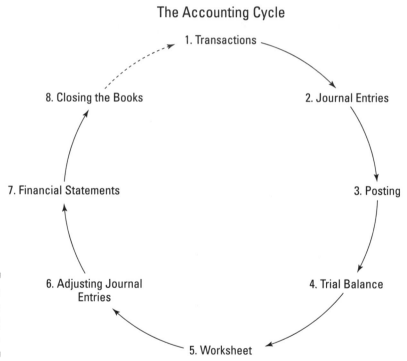

The Accounting Cycle

1. Transactions
2. Journal Entries
3. Posting
4. Trial Balance
5. Worksheet
6. Adjusting Journal Entries
7. Financial Statements
8. Closing the Books

Figure 3-1: The accounting cycle.

1. **Transactions:** Financial transactions start the process. Transactions can include the sale or return of a product, the purchase of supplies for business activities, or any other financial activity that involves the exchange of the business's assets, the establishment or payoff of a debt, or the deposit from or payout of money to the business's owners. All sales and expenses are transactions that must be recorded. We cover transactions in greater detail throughout the book as we discuss how to record the basics of business activities – recording sales, purchases, asset acquisition, or asset disposal, taking on new debt, or paying off debt.

2. **Journal entries:** The transaction is listed in the appropriate journal, maintaining the journal's chronological order of transactions. (The journal is

also known as the 'book of original entry' and is the first place a transaction is listed.)

3. **Posting:** The transactions are posted to the relevant account. These accounts are part of the Nominal Ledger, where you can find a summary of all the business's accounts.

4. **Trial balance:** At the end of the accounting period (which may be a month, quarter, or year depending on your business's practices), you prepare a trial balance.

5. **Worksheet:** Unfortunately, often your first trial balance shows that the books aren't in balance. In this case, you look for errors and make corrections called *adjustments,* which are tracked on a worksheet. Adjustments are also made to account for the depreciation of assets, and to adjust for one-time payments (such as insurance) that need to be allocated on a monthly basis to match monthly expenses with monthly revenues more accurately. After you make and record adjustments, you take another trial balance to be sure that the accounts are in balance.

6. **Adjusting journal entries:** You post any necessary corrections to the relevant accounts after your trial balance shows that the accounts balance (after the necessary adjustments are made to the accounts). You don't need to make adjusting entries until the trial balance process is completed and all needed corrections and adjustments have been identified.

7. **Financial statements:** You prepare the balance sheet and profit and loss statement using the corrected account balances.

8. **Closing the books:** You close the books for the Revenue and Expense accounts and begin the entire cycle again.

At the end of the accounting year (year-end) all the accounting ledgers are closed off. This situation means that Revenue and Expense accounts must start with a zero balance at the beginning of each new accounting year. In contrast, you carry over Asset, Liability, and Capital account balances from year to year, because the business doesn't start each cycle by getting rid of old assets and buying new assets, paying off and then taking on new debt, or paying out all claims to owners and then collecting the money again.

Understanding Accounting Methods

Many not-for-profit organisations, such as sports clubs, have very simple accounting needs. These organisations aren't responsible to shareholders to account for their financial performance, though they are responsible to their members for the safe custody of their subscriptions and other funds. Consequently, the accounting focus isn't on measuring profit but more on accounting for receipts and payments. For these cases, a simple cash-based accounting system may well suffice, which allows for only cash transactions – no provisions are made for giving or receiving credit.

However, complications may arise when members don't pay their subscriptions during the current accounting year and the organisation needs to reflect this situation in its accounts. In this case, the accrual accounting method is best.

A few businesses operate on a cash basis, and their owners can put forward a good case for using this method. However most accountants and HM Customs & Revenue don't accept this method as it doesn't give a very accurate measure of profit (or loss) for accounting periods.

In the next sections, we briefly explain how cash-based accounting works before dismissing it in favour of the more accepted and acceptable accrual method.

Realising the limitations of cash-based accounting

With *cash-based accounting*, you record all transactions in the books when cash actually changes hands, which means when the business receives cash payment from customers or pays out cash for purchases or other services. Cash receipt or payment can be in the form of cash, cheque, credit card, electronic transfer, or other means used to pay for an item.

Cash-based accounting can't be used when a business sells products on credit and collects the money from the customer at a later date. No provision exists in the cash-based accounting method to record and track money due from customers at some point in the future.

This situation also applies for purchases. With the cash-based accounting method, the business only records the purchase of supplies or goods that are to be sold later when it actually pays cash. When the business buys goods on credit to be paid later, it doesn't record the transaction until the cash is actually paid out.

Depending on the size of your business, you may want to start out with cash-based accounting. Many small businesses run by a sole proprietor or a small group of partners use the easier cash-based accounting system. When your business model is simple – you carry no stock, start and finish each job within a single accounting period, and pay and get paid within this period – the cash accounting method can work for you. But as your business grows, you may find it necessary to switch to accrual accounting in order to track revenues and expenses more accurately, and to satisfy the requirements of the external accountant and HM Revenue & Customs. The same basic argument also applies to not-for-profit organisations.

Cash-based accounting does a good job of tracking cash flow, but the system does a poor job of matching revenues earned with money laid out for expenses. This deficiency is a problem particularly when, as often happens, a business buys products in one month and sells those products in the next month. For example, you buy products in June paying £1,000 cash, with the intent to sell them that same month. You don't sell the products until July, which is when you receive cash for the sales. When you close the books at the end of June, you have to show the £1,000 expense with no revenue to offset it, meaning you have a loss that month. When you sell the products for £1,500 in July, you have a £1,500 profit. So, your monthly report for June shows a £1,000 loss, and your monthly report for July shows a £1,500 profit, when in reality you had revenues of £500 over the two months. Using cash-based accounting you can never be sure that you have an accurate measure of profit or loss – but as cash-based accounting is for not-for-profit organisations, this is not surprising.

Because accrual accounting is the only accounting method acceptable to accountants and HM Revenue & Customs, we concentrate on this method throughout the book. If you choose to use cash-based accounting because you have a cash only business and a simple trading model, don't panic: Most of the bookkeeping information here is still useful, but you don't need to maintain some of the accounts, such as Accounts Receivable and Accounts Payable, because you aren't recording transactions until cash actually changes hands. When you're using a cash-based accounting system and you start to sell things on credit, though, you better have a way to track what people owe you.

Our advice is to use the accrual accounting method right from the beginning. When your business grows and your business model changes, you need the more sophisticated and legally required accrual accounting.

Recording right away with accrual accounting

With *accrual accounting,* you record all transactions in the books when they occur, even when no cash changes hands. For example, when you sell on credit, you record the transaction immediately and enter it into a Debtors account until you receive payment. When you buy goods on credit, you immediately enter the transaction into a Creditors account until you pay out cash.

Like cash-based accounting, accrual accounting has drawbacks, doing a good job of matching revenues and expenses, but a poor job of tracking cash. Because you record income when the transaction occurs and not when you collect the cash, your profit and loss statement can look great even when you don't have cash in the bank. For example, suppose you're running a

Book IV

How Not to Cook the Books

contracting business and completing jobs on a daily basis. You can record the revenue upon completion of the job even when you haven't yet collected the cash. When your customers are slow to pay, you may end up with lots of income but little cash. Remember – *never* confuse profit and cash. In the short term cash flow is often more important than profit, but in the long term profit becomes more important.

Many businesses that use the accrual accounting method monitor cash flow on a weekly basis to be sure they have enough cash on hand to operate the business. If your business is seasonal, such as a landscaping business with little to do during the winter months, you can establish short-term lines of credit through your bank to maintain cash flow through the lean times.

Seeing Double with Double-Entry Bookkeeping

All businesses use *double-entry bookkeeping* to keep their books, whether they use the cash-based accounting method or the accrual accounting method. Double-entry bookkeeping – so-called because you enter all transactions twice – helps minimise errors and increase the chance that your books balance.

When it comes to double-entry bookkeeping, the key formula for the balance sheet (Assets = Liabilities + Capital) plays a major role.

In the bookkeeping world, you use a combination of debits and credits to adjust the balance of accounts. You may think of a debit as a subtraction, because debits usually mean a decrease in your bank balance. On the other hand, you probably like finding unexpected credits in your bank or credit card, because they mean more money has been added to the account in your favour. Now forget everything you know about debits or credits. In the world of bookkeeping, their meanings aren't so simple.

The only definite thing when it comes to debits and credits in the bookkeeping world is that a debit is on the left side of a transaction and a credit is on the right side of a transaction. Everything beyond that can get very muddled. We show you the basics of debits and credits in this chapter, but don't worry if you find these concepts difficult to grasp.

Before we get into all the technical mumbo jumbo of double-entry bookkeeping, here's an example of the practice in action. Suppose you purchase a new desk for your office that costs £1,500. This transaction actually has two parts: You spend an asset – cash – to buy another asset – furniture. So, you must adjust two accounts in your business's books: the Cash account and the Furniture account. The transaction in a bookkeeping entry is as follows:

Account	Debit	Credit
Furniture	£1,500	
Cash		£1,500

To purchase a new desk for the office.

In this transaction, you record the accounts impacted by the transaction. The debit increases the value of the Furniture account, and the credit decreases the value of the Cash account. For this transaction, both accounts impacted are Asset accounts so, looking at how the balance sheet is affected, you can see that the only changes are to the asset side of the balance sheet equation:

Assets = Liabilities + Capital

Furniture increase = No change to this side of the equation

Cash decrease

In this case, the books stay in balance because the exact pounds sterling amount that increases the value of your Furniture account decreases the value of your Cash account. At the bottom of any journal entry, include a brief explanation that explains the purpose for the entry. In the first example, we indicate this entry was 'To purchase a new desk for the office'.

To show you how you record a transaction that impacts both sides of the balance sheet equation, here's an example on recording the purchase of stock. Suppose that you purchase £5,000 worth of widgets on credit. (Have you always wondered what widgets were? Can't help you. They're just commonly used in accounting examples to represent something purchased where what is purchased is of no real significance.) These new widgets add value to your Stock Asset account and also add value to your Accounts Payable account. (Remember, the Accounts Payable account is a Liability account where you track bills that need to be paid at some point in the future.) The bookkeeping transaction for your widget purchase looks as follows:

Account	Debit	Credit
Stock	£5,000	
Accounts Payable		£5,000

To purchase widgets for sale to customers.

This transaction affects the balance sheet equation as follows:

Assets = Liabilities + Capital

Stock increases = Accounts Payable increases + No change

In this case, the books stay in balance because both sides of the equation increase by £5,000.

Book IV

How Not to Cook the Books

You can see from the two example transactions how double-entry bookkeeping helps to keep your books in balance – as long as you make sure that each entry into the books is balanced. Balancing your entries may look simple here, but sometimes bookkeeping entries can get very complex when the transaction impacts more than two accounts.

Differentiating Debits and Credits

Because bookkeeping's debits and credits are different from the ones you're used to encountering, you're probably wondering how you're supposed to know whether a debit or credit increases or decreases an account.

Believe it or not, identifying the difference becomes second nature as you start making regular entries in your bookkeeping system. But to make things easier for you, Table 3-1 is a chart that bookkeepers and accountants commonly use. Yep, everyone needs help sometimes.

Table 3-1	How Credits and Debits Impact Your Accounts	
Account Type	*Debits*	*Credits*
Assets	Increase	Decrease
Liabilities	Decrease	Increase
Income	Decrease	Increase
Expenses	Increase	Decrease

Copy Table 3-1 and post it at your desk when you start keeping your own books. We guarantee that the table helps to keep your debits and credits straight.

Chapter 4

Controlling Your Books, Your Records, and Your Money

In This Chapter

▶ Protecting your business's cash

▶ Maintaining proper paperwork

▶ Divvying up responsibilities

▶ Insuring your cash handlers

*E*very business takes in cash in some form or another: Notes and coins, cheques, and credit card and electronic payments are all eventually deposited as cash into the business's accounts. Before you take in that first penny, your initial concern must be controlling that cash and making sure that none of it walks out the door improperly.

Finding the right level of cash control, while at the same time allowing your employees the flexibility to sell your products or services and provide ongoing customer service, can be a monumental task. If you don't have enough controls, you risk theft or embezzlement. Yet if you have too many controls, employees may miss sales or anger customers.

In this chapter, we explain the basic protections you need to put in place to be sure that all cash coming into or going out of your business is clearly documented and controlled. We also review the type of paperwork you need to document the use of cash and other business assets. Finally, we tell you how to organise your staff to control the flow of your assets properly and insure yourself against possible misappropriation of those assets.

Putting Controls on Your Business's Cash

Think about how careful you are with your personal cash. You find various ways to protect the cash you carry around, you dole it out carefully to your family members, and you may even hide cash in a safe place in the house just in case you need it for unexpected purposes.

You're very protective of your cash when you're the only one who handles it, but consider the vulnerability of your business cash. After all, you aren't the only one handling that cash. You have some employees encountering incoming cash at cash registers, others opening the mail and finding cheques for orders to purchase products or pay bills, as well as cheques from other sources. And don't forget that employees may need petty cash to pay for mail sent COD (Cash on Delivery), or to pay for other unexpected, low-cost needs.

If you watch over every transaction in which cash enters your business, you have no time to do the things you need to do to grow your business. When the business is small, you can sign all cheques and maintain control of cash going out, but as soon as the business grows, you just may not have the time.

The good news is that just putting in place the proper controls for your cash can help protect it. Cash flows through your business in four key ways:

✔ Deposits and payments into and out of your current accounts

✔ Deposits and payments into and out of your savings accounts

✔ Petty cash funds in critical locations where quick access to cash may be needed

✔ Transactions made in your cash registers

The following sections cover some key controls for each of these cash flow points.

Current accounts

Almost every penny that comes into your business flows through your business's current account (at least that *should* happen). Whether the cash is collected at your cash registers, payments received in the mail, cash used to fill the cash registers or petty cash accounts, payments sent out to pay business obligations, or any other cash need, this cash enters and exits your current account. Thus, your current account is your main tool for protecting your cash flow.

Choosing the right bank

Finding the right bank to help you set up your current account and the controls that limit access to that account is crucial. When evaluating your banking options, ask yourself the following questions:

✔ Does this bank have a branch conveniently located for my business?

✔ Does this bank operate at times when I need it most?

✔ Does this bank offer secure ways to deposit cash even when the bank is closed?

Most banks have secure drop boxes for cash so you can deposit receipts as quickly as possible at the end of the business day rather than secure the cash overnight yourself.

Visit local bank branches yourself, and check out the type of business services each bank offers. Pay particular attention to

✔ The type of personal attention you receive

✔ How questions are handled

✔ What type of charges may be tacked on for personalised attention

Some banks require business account holders to call a centralised line for assistance rather than depend on local branches. Most banks charge if you use a cashier rather than an ATM (automatic teller machine). Other banks charge for every transaction, whether a deposit, withdrawal, or cheque. Many banks have charges that differ for business accounts. If you plan to accept credit cards, compare the services offered for that as well.

The general rule is that banks charge businesses for everything they do. However, they charge less for tasks that can be automated and thus involve less manual effort. So, you save money when you use electronic payment and receipt processes. In other words, pay your suppliers electronically and get your customers to pay you the same way, and you reduce your banking costs.

Deciding on types of cheques

After you choose your bank, you need to consider what type of cheques you want to use in your business. For example, you need different cheques depending upon whether you handwrite each cheque or print cheques from your computerised accounting system.

Writing cheques manually

If you plan to write your cheques, you're most likely to use a business cheque book, which in its simplest form is exactly the same as a personal cheque book, with a counter foil (or cheque stub) on the left and a cheque on the right. This arrangement provides the best control for manual cheques because each cheque and counter foil is numbered. When you write a cheque, you fill out the counter foil with details such as the date, the cheque's recipient, and the purpose of the cheque. The counter foil also has a space to keep a running total of your balance in the account.

Book IV

How Not to Cook the Books

Printing computer-generated cheques

If you plan to print cheques from your computerised accounting system, you need to order cheques that match that system's programming. Each computer software program has a unique template for printing cheques. Figure 4-1 shows a common layout for business cheques that a computerised accounting system prints out. The key information is exactly what you expect to see on any cheque – payee details, date, and amount in both words and numbers.

Figure 4-1:
Businesses that choose to print their cheques using their computerised accounting systems usually order them with their business name already printed on the cheque. This particular cheque is compatible with Sage Line 50.

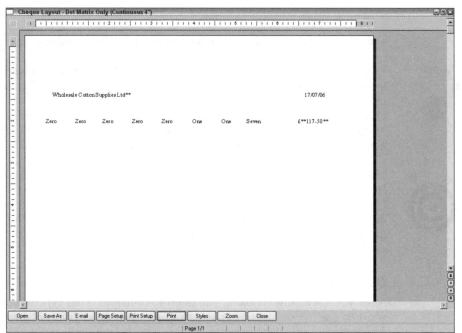

You can also set up your computer accounting system to print out the precise details you'd expect to find on a manual cheque – the current date, name of the recipient, and the value of the cheque. Unlike a manually-prepared cheque, you don't have a counter foil to fill in, which is not a problem because your computerised accounting system records this information for you: It keeps an internal record of all cheques issued. If you need to check that you issued a cheque correctly, you can always run a report or make an on-screen enquiry on your computerised accounting system.

Initially, when the business is small, you can sign each cheque and keep control of the outflow of money. But as the business grows, you may find that you need to delegate cheque-signing responsibilities to someone else, especially if you travel frequently. Many small business owners set up cheque-signing procedures that allow one or two of their staff to sign cheques up to a designated amount, such as £5,000. Any cheques above that designated amount require the owner's signature, or the signature of an employee and a second designated person, such as an officer of the business.

Making deposits in the current account

Of course, you aren't just withdrawing from your business's current account (that would be a big problem). You also need to deposit money into that account, and you want to be sure that your paying in slips contain all the necessary detail as well as documentation to back up the deposit information. Most banks provide printed paying in slips with all the necessary detail to be sure that the money is deposited into the appropriate account, together with who wrote each cheque, the value, and the date received.

A good practice is to record cheques immediately as part of a daily morning routine. Enter the details onto the paying in slip and update your computerised or manual accounting system at the same time. Make sure that you pay in any money received before 3:30 p.m. on the same day, to ensure that your bank account gets credit that day rather than the next. (We talk more about controls for incoming cash in the 'Dividing staff responsibilities' section, later in this chapter.) If you get both personal and business cheques sent to the same address, instruct the person opening the mail about how to differentiate the types of cheques and how each type of cheque needs to be handled to best protect your incoming cash, whether for business or personal purposes.

You may think that making bank deposits is as easy as 1-2-3, but when it comes to business deposits and multiple cheques, things get a bit more complicated. To make deposits to your business's current account properly, follow these steps:

1. **Record on the paying in slip the full details of all cheques being deposited as well as the total cash being deposited. Also make a note of how many cheques you're paying into the bank on that paying in slip.**

2. **Record the details regarding the source of the deposited cash before you make the deposit; file everything in your daily bank folder.**

   (We talk more about filing in the section 'Keeping the Right Paperwork', later in this chapter.)

3. **Make sure that the cashier at the bank stamps the paying in slip as confirmation that the bank has received all the cheques and cash.**

   If you're paying in cheques via the ATM then treat it exactly as if you were paying in via the cashier. Still prepare your own paying slip and make sure that you pick up the receipt that the ATM gives you. This does not ensure that things will not go wrong but it will ensure you have a paper trail if they do.

Savings accounts

Some businesses find that they have more cash than they need to meet their immediate plans. Rather than keep that extra cash in a non-interest bearing account, many businesses open a savings account to store the extra cash.

If you're a small business owner with few employees, you probably control the flow of money into and out of your savings account yourself. As you grow and find that you need to delegate the responsibility for the business's savings, ensure that you think carefully about who gets access and how you can document the flow of funds into and out of the savings account. Treat a savings account like a current account and use paying in slips to record deposits and cheque book stubs to record payments.

Petty cash accounts

Every business needs cash on almost a weekly basis. Businesses need to keep some cash on hand, called *petty cash,* for unexpected expenses such as money to pay for letters and packages delivered COD, money to buy a few emergency stamps to get the mail out, or money for some office supplies needed before the next delivery.

You certainly don't want to have a lot of cash sitting around in the office, but try to keep £50 to £100 in a petty cash box. If you subsequently find that you're faced with more or less cash expenses than you expected, you can always adjust the amount kept in petty cash accordingly.

No matter how much you keep in petty cash, make sure that you set up a good control system that requires anyone who uses the cash to write a petty cash voucher specifying how much was used and why. Also ask that a cash receipt, for example from the shop or post office, is attached to the voucher in order to justify the cash withdrawal whenever possible. In most cases, a member of staff buys something for the business and then gets reimbursed for that expense. If the expense is small enough, you can reimburse through the petty cash fund. If the expense is more than a few pounds, ask the person to fill out an expense account form and get reimbursed by cheque. Petty cash is usually used for minor expenses of £10 or less.

The best way to control petty cash is to pick one person in the office to manage the use of all petty cash. Before giving that person more cash, he or she should be able to prove the absence of cash used and why it was used.

Poor control of the petty cash box can lead to small but significant losses of cash. Quite often you can find it difficult or impossible to identify or prove who took the cash. The best solution is to make it slightly more difficult for employees to obtain petty cash, than having a free-for-all system. A locked box in cupboard works very well.

For the ultimate control of cash, use the imprest system in which a fixed amount is drawn from the bank and paid into petty cash (the float). After that, cash is issued only against a petty cash voucher. This system means that, at any point, cash, or cash plus vouchers, should be equal to the total of the petty cash float. At the end of the week (or month) the vouchers are removed and the cash made up to the original amount.

Cash registers

Have you ever gone into a business and tried to pay with a large note only to find out that the cashier has no change? This frustrating experience happens in many businesses, especially those that don't carefully monitor the money in their cash registers. Most businesses empty cash registers each night and put any cash not being deposited in the bank that night into a safe. However, many businesses instruct their cashiers to deposit their cash in a business safe periodically throughout the day and get a paper voucher to show the cash deposited. These daytime deposits minimise the cash held in case the store is the victim of a robbery.

All these types of controls are necessary parts of modern business operations, but they can have consequences that make customers angry. Most customers just walk out the door and don't come back when they can't buy what they want using the notes they have on hand.

At the beginning of the day, cashiers usually start out with a set amount of cash in the register. As they collect money and give out change, the register records the transactions. At the end of the day, the cashier must count out the amount of change left in the register, run a copy of all transactions that passed through that register, and total the cash collected. Then the cashier must prove that the amount of cash remaining in that register totals the amount of cash the register started with plus the amount of cash collected during the day. After the cashier balances the register, the person in charge of cash deposits (usually the shop manager or someone on the accounting or bookkeeping staff) takes all the cash out, except the amount needed for the next day, and deposits it in the bank. (We talk more about separation of staff duties in the section 'Dividing staff responsibilities', later in this chapter.)

In addition to having the proper amount of cash in the register necessary to give customers the change they need, you also must make sure that your cashiers are giving the right amount of change and actually recording all sales on their cash registers. Keeping an eye on cashier activities is good business practice in any case, but you can also protect against cash theft by your employees in this way. Three ways exist in which cashiers can pocket some extra cash:

✔ **They don't record the sale in the cash register and instead pocket the cash.** The best deterrent to this type of theft is supervision. You can decrease the likelihood of theft through unrecorded sales by printing up sales tickets that the cashier must use to enter a sale in the cash register and open the cash drawer. If cash register transactions don't match sales receipts, the cashier must show a voided transaction for the missing ticket, or explain why the cash drawer was opened without a ticket.

✔ **They don't provide a sales receipt and instead pocket the cash.** In this scenario the cashier neglects to give a sales receipt to one customer in the queue. The cashier gives the next customer the unused sales receipt but doesn't actually record the second transaction in the cash register. Instead, he or she just pockets the cash. In the business's books, the second sale never took place. The customer whose sale wasn't recorded has a valid receipt though it may not match exactly what was bought. Therefore, the customer is unlikely to notice any problem unless something needs to be returned later. Your best defence against this type of deception is to post a sign reminding all customers that they must get a receipt for all purchases and that the receipt is required to get a refund or exchange. Providing numbered sales receipts that include a duplicate copy can also help prevent this problem; cashiers need to produce the duplicates at the end of the day when proving the amount of cash flow that passed through their registers.

In addition to protection from theft by cashiers, the printed sales receipt system can be used to monitor shoplifters and prevent them from getting money for merchandise they never bought. For example, suppose a shoplifter takes a blouse out of a store, as well as some blank sales receipts. The next day the shoplifter comes back with the blouse and one of the stolen sales receipts filled out as though the blouse had actually been purchased the day before. You can spot the fraud because that sales receipt is part of a numbered batch of sales receipts that you've already identified as missing or stolen. You can quickly identify that the customer never paid for the merchandise and call the police.

✔ **They record a false credit voucher and keep the cash for themselves.** In this case the cashier writes up a credit voucher for a nonexistent customer and then pockets the cash refund. Most shops use a numbered credit voucher system to control this problem, so each credit can be carefully monitored with some detail that proves its connection to a previous customer purchase, such as a sales receipt. Customers are often asked to provide an address and telephone number before receiving a refund. Although this may not put off the determined fraudster, the opportunist thief is likely to be deterred. Also, shops usually require that a manager review the reason for the credit voucher, whether a return or exchange, and approve the transaction before cash or credit is given. When the bookkeeper records the sales return in the books, the number for the credit voucher is recorded with the transaction so that the detail about that credit voucher is easy to find if a question is raised later about the transaction.

Even if cashiers don't deliberately pocket cash, they can inadvertently give the wrong change. If you run a retail outlet, training and supervising your cashiers is a critical task that you must handle yourself or hand over to a trusted employee.

Keeping the Right Paperwork

When handling cash, you can see that a lot of paper changes hands, whether from the cash register, deposits into your current accounts, or petty cash withdrawals. Therefore, careful documentation is paramount to control the movement of cash into and out of your business properly. And don't forget about organisation; you need to be able to find that documentation if questions about cash flow arise later.

Monitoring cash flow isn't the only reason why you need to keep loads of paperwork. In order to do your taxes and write off business expenses, you need receipts for those expenses. You also need details about the money you pay to employees, and tax and National Insurance contributions collected for your employees, in order to file the proper reports with HM Revenue & Customs. Setting up a good filing system and knowing what to keep and for how long is very important for any small businessperson.

Creating a filing system

To get started setting up your filing system, you need the following supplies:

- **Filing cabinets:** Pretty self-explanatory – you can't have a filing system with nothing to keep the files in.

- **File folders:** Set up separate files for each of your suppliers, employees, and customers who buy on credit, as well as files for backup information on each of your transactions. Many bookkeepers file transaction information using the date the transaction was added to their journal. If the transaction relates to a customer, supplier, or employee, they add a duplicate copy of the transaction to the individual files as well.

    Even if you have a computerised accounting system, you need to file paperwork related to the transactions you enter into your computer system. You still need to maintain employee, supplier, and customer files in hard copy just in case something goes wrong – for example, if your computer system crashes, you need the originals to restore the data. Back up your computerised accounting system's data regularly to

Book IV

How Not to Cook the Books

minimise the effects of such a crisis. Daily backups are best; one week is the longest you should ever go without a backup.

✔ **Ring binders:** These binders are great for things like your Chart of Accounts, your Nominal Ledger and your system of journals because you add to these documents regularly and the binders make adding additional pages easy. Make sure that you number the pages as you add them to the binder, so you can quickly spot a missing page. How many binders you need depends on how many financial transactions you have each accounting period. You can keep everything in one binder, or you may want to set up a binder for the Chart of Accounts and Nominal Ledger and then a separate binder for each of your active journals. The decision is based on what makes your job easier.

✔ **Expandable files:** These files are the best way to keep track of current supplier activity and any bills that may be due. Make sure that you have

- **An alphabetical file:** Use this file to track all your outstanding purchase orders by supplier. After you fill the order, you can file all details about that order in the supplier's individual file in case questions about the order arise later.

- **A 12-month file:** Use this file to keep track of bills that you need to pay. Simply place the bill in the slot for the month payment is due. Many businesses also use a 30-day expandable file. At the beginning of the month, the bills are placed in the 30-day expandable file based on the dates that they need to be paid. This approach provides a quick and organised visual reminder for bills that are due.

If you're using a computerised accounting system, you don't need the expandable files because your accounting system can remind you when bills are due (as long as you add the information to the system when the bill arrives).

✔ **Blank computer disks or other storage media:** Use these to backup your computerised system on a weekly or, better yet, daily basis. Keep the backup discs in a fire safe or somewhere unaffected if a fire destroys the business. (A fire safe is the best way to keep critical financial data safe, and is therefore a must for any business.)

Working out what to keep and for how long

As you can probably imagine, the pile of paperwork you need to hold on to can get very large very quickly. As they see their files getting thicker and thicker, most businesspeople wonder what they can toss, what they really need to keep, and how long they need to keep it.

Generally, keep most transaction-related paperwork for as long as HM Revenue & Customs can come and audit your books. For most types of audits, that means six years. But if you fail to file your tax return or file it fraudulently (and we hope this doesn't apply to you), HM Revenue & Customs may question you at any time, because no time limitations exist in these cases.

HM Revenue & Customs isn't the only reason to keep records around for longer than one year. You may need proof-of-purchase information for your insurance company if an asset is lost, stolen, or destroyed by fire or other accident. Also, you need to hang on to information regarding any business loan until paid off, just in case the bank questions how much you paid. After the loan's paid off, ensure that you keep proof of payment indefinitely in case a question about the loan ever arises. Information about property and other asset holdings needs to be kept around for as long as you hold the asset and for at least six years after the asset is sold. You're legally required to keep information about employees for at least three years after the employee leaves.

Keep the current year's files easily accessible in a designated filing area and keep the most recent past year's files in accessible filing cabinets if you have room. Box up records when they hit the two-year-old mark, and put them in storage. Make sure that you date your boxed records with information about what they are, when they were put into storage, and when you can destroy them. Many people forget that last detail, and boxes pile up until total desperation sets in and no more room is left. Then someone must take the time to sort through the boxes and figure out what needs to be kept and what can be destroyed – not a fun job.

It is a legal requirement to keep information about all transactions for six years. After that, make a list of things you want to hold on to longer for other reasons, such as asset holdings and loan information. Check with your lawyer and accountant to get their recommendations on what to keep and for how long.

Protecting Your Business Against Internal Fraud

Many businesspeople start their operations by carefully hiring people they can trust, thinking: 'We're a family – they'd never steal from me.'

Often a business owner finds out too late that even the most loyal employee may steal from the business if the opportunity arises and the temptation becomes too great – or if the employee gets caught up in a serious personal financial dilemma and needs fast cash. In this section, we talk about the steps you can take to prevent people stealing from your business.

Facing the reality of financial fraud

The four basic types of financial fraud are

- **Embezzlement,** which is the illegal use of funds by a person who controls those funds. For example, a bookkeeper may use business money for his or her own personal needs. Many times, embezzlement stories don't appear in the newspapers because businesspeople are so embarrassed that they choose to keep the affair quiet. They usually settle privately with the embezzler rather than face public scrutiny.

- **Internal theft,** which is the stealing of business assets by employees, such as taking office supplies or products the business sells without paying for them. Internal theft is often the culprit behind stock shrinkage.

- **Payoffs and kickbacks,** which are situations in which employees accept cash or other benefits in exchange for access to the business, often creating a scenario where the business that the employee works for pays more for the goods or products than necessary. That extra money finds its way into the pocket of the employee who helped facilitate the access. For example, say Business A wants to sell its products to Business B. An employee in Business B helps Business A get in the door. Business A prices its product a bit higher and gives the employee of Business B the extra profit in the form of a kickback for helping it out. A payoff is paid before the sale is made, essentially saying 'please'. A kickback is paid after the sale is made, essentially saying 'thank you'. In reality, payoffs and kickbacks are a form of bribery, but few businesses report or litigate this problem (although employees are fired when deals are uncovered).

- **Skimming,** which occurs when employees take money from receipts and don't record the revenue on the books.

Although any of these financial crimes can happen in a small business, the one that hits small businesses the hardest is embezzlement. This crime happens most frequently when one person has access or control over most of the business's financial activities. For example, a single bookkeeper may write cheques, make deposits, and balance the monthly bank statement – talk about having your fingers in a very big till.

Dividing staff responsibilities

Your primary protection against financial crime is properly separating staff responsibilities when the flow of business cash is involved. Basically, never have one person handling more than one of the following tasks:

- **Bookkeeping:** Involves reviewing and entering all transactions into the business's books. The bookkeeper makes sure that transactions are accurate, valid, appropriate, and have the proper authorisation. For example, if a transaction requires paying a supplier, the bookkeeper makes sure that the charges are accurate and someone with proper authority has approved the payment. The bookkeeper can review documentation of cash receipts and the overnight deposits taken to the bank, but shouldn't actually make the deposit. Also, if the bookkeeper is responsible for handling payments from external parties, such as customers or suppliers, he or she shouldn't enter those transactions in the books.

✔ **Authorisation:** Involves being the manager or managers delegated to authorise expenditures for their departments. You may decide that transactions over a certain amount must have two or more authorisations before cheques can be sent to pay a bill. Spell out authorisation levels clearly and make sure that everyone follows them, even the owner or managing director of the business. (Remember, as owner, you set the tone for how the rest of the office operates; when you take shortcuts, you set a bad example and undermine the system you put in place.)

✔ **Money-handling:** Involves direct contact with incoming cash or revenue, whether cheque, credit card, or credit transactions, as well as outgoing cash flow. The person who handles money directly, such as a cashier, shouldn't also prepare and make bank deposits. Likewise, the person writing cheques to pay business bills shouldn't be authorised to sign those cheques; to be safe, have one person prepare the cheques based on authorised documentation, and a second person sign those cheques, after reviewing the authorised documentation.

When setting up your cash-handling systems, try to think like an embezzler to figure out how someone can take advantage of a system.

✔ **Financial report preparation and analysis:** Involves the actual preparation of the financial reports and any analysis of those reports. Someone who's not involved in the day-to-day entering of transactions in the books needs to prepare the financial reports. For most small businesses, the bookkeeper turns over the raw reports from the computerised accounting system to an outside accountant who reviews the materials and prepares the financial reports. In addition, the accountant does a financial analysis of the business activity results for the previous accounting period.

The high cost of employee versus customer theft

According to the British Retail Consortium internal theft by employees is the largest single component of white-collar crime. You don't hear much about it, though, because many businesses choose to keep quiet. The reality is that employee theft and embezzlement in UK are estimated to cost employers over £500 million per year. Over 50 per cent of all losses are the result of employee theft. Four key situations in the workplace provide opportunities for theft and embezzlement: poor internal controls, too much control given to certain individuals, lax management, and failure to prescreen employees adequately.

We realise that you may be just starting up a small business and therefore not have enough staff to separate all these duties. Until you do have that capability, make sure that you stay heavily involved in the inflow and outflow of cash in your business. The following tips tell you how:

- **Periodically (once a month) open your business's bank statements, and keep a close watch on the transactions.** Someone else can be given the responsibility of reconciling the statement, but you still need to keep an eye on the transactions listed.

- **Periodically look at your business cheque book counterfoils to ensure that no cheques are missing.** A bookkeeper who knows that you periodically check the books is less likely to find an opportunity for theft or embezzlement. If you find that a cheque or page of cheques is missing, act quickly to find out if the cheques were used legitimately. If you can't find the answer, call your bank and put a stop on the missing cheque numbers.

- **Periodically observe your cashiers and managers handling cash to make sure that they're following the rules you've established.** This practice is known as *management by walking around* – the more often you're out there, the less likely you are to be a victim of employee theft and fraud.

Balancing control costs

As a small businessperson, you're always trying to balance the cost of protecting your cash and assets with the cost of adequately separating those duties. Putting in place too many controls, which end up costing you money, can be a big mistake. For example, you may create stock controls that require salespeople to contact one particular person who has the key to your product warehouse. This kind of control may prevent employee theft, but can also result in lost sales, because salespeople can't find the key-holder while dealing with an interested customer. In the end, the customer gets mad, and you lose the sale.

When you put controls in place, talk to your staff both before and after instituting the controls to see how they're working and to check for any unforeseen problems. Be willing and able to adjust your controls to balance the business needs of selling your products, managing the cash flow, and keeping your eye on making a profit. Talk to other businesspeople to see what they do and pick up tips from established best practice. Your external accountant can be a good source of valuable information.

Generally, as you make rules for your internal controls, make sure that the cost of protecting an asset is no more than the asset you're trying to protect. For example, don't go overboard to protect office supplies by forcing your staff to wait around for hours to access needed supplies while you and a manager are at a meeting away from the office.

Ask yourself these four questions as you design your internal controls:

- ✔ What exactly do I want to prevent or detect – errors, sloppiness, theft, fraud, or embezzlement?
- ✔ Do I face the problem frequently?
- ✔ What do I estimate the loss to be?
- ✔ What is the cost to me of implementing the change in procedures to prevent or detect the problem?

You can't answer all these questions yourself, so consult with your managers and the staff the changes are likely to impact. Get their answers to these questions, and listen to their feedback.

When you finish putting together the new internal control rule, ensure that you document why you decided to implement the rule and the information you collected in developing it. After the rule's been in place for a while, test your assumptions. Make sure that you are in fact detecting the errors, theft, fraud, or embezzlement that you hoped and expected to detect. Check the costs of keeping the rule in place by looking at cash outlay, employee time and morale, and the impact on customer service. If you find any problems with your internal controls, take the time to fix them and change the rule, again documenting the process. Detailed documentation ensures that, if two or three years down the road someone questions why he or she is doing something, you have the answers and are able to determine whether the problem is still valid, as well as whether the rule is still necessary or needs to be changed.

Insuring Your Cash through Employee Bonding

If you have employees who handle a lot of cash, insuring your business against theft is an absolute must. This insurance, known as *employee bonding,* is often offered as an extension to an existing business insurance policy, and helps to protect you against theft and reduce your risk of loss.

If you carry a bond on your cash handlers, you're covered for losses sustained by any employee who's bonded. You also have coverage when an employee's act causes losses to a client of your business. For example, when you're a financial consultant and your bookkeeper embezzles a client's cash, you're protected for the loss.

A *fidelity bond* is a type of insurance that you can buy through the company that handles your business insurance policies. It is a stand alone policy, unlike employee bonding. The cost varies greatly depending on the type of business you operate and the amount of cash or other assets that are handled by the employees you want to bond. If an employee steals from you or one of your customers, the insurance covers the loss.

Employers also bond employees who may be in a position to steal something other than cash. For example, a cleaning service may bond its workers in case a worker steals something from one of its customers. If a customer reports something missing, the insurance company that bonded the employee covers the loss. Without a bond, an employer must pay back the customer for any loss.

Chapter 5

Producing a Profit and Loss Statement

. . . .

In This Chapter

▶ Sorting out the elements of a profit and loss statement

▶ Preparing the statement

▶ Analysing statement data

▶ Zeroing in on profitability

. . . .

*W*ithout one very important financial report tool, you can never know for sure whether or not your business is making a profit. This tool is called the *profit and loss statement,* and most businesses prepare this statement on a monthly basis, as well as quarterly and annually, in order to get periodic pictures of how well the business is doing financially.

Analysing the profit and loss statement and the details behind it can reveal lots of useful information to help you make decisions for improving your profits and business overall. This chapter covers the various parts of a profit and loss statement, how you develop one, and examples of how you can use it to make business decisions.

Lining Up the Profit and Loss Statement

Did your business make any profit? You can find the answer in your *profit and loss statement,* the financial report that summarises all the sales activities, costs of producing or buying the products or services sold, and expenses incurred in order to run the business.

Profit and loss statements summarise the financial activities of a business during a particular accounting period (which can be a month, quarter, year, or some other period of time that makes sense for a business's needs).

Normal practice is to include two accounting periods on a profit and loss statement: the current period plus the year to date. The five key lines that make up a profit and loss statement are

- ✔ **Sales or Revenue:** The total amount of invoiced sales taken in from selling the business's products or services. You calculate this amount by totalling all the sales or revenue accounts. The top line of the profit and loss statement is sales or revenues; either is okay.

- ✔ **Cost of Goods Sold:** How much was spent in order to buy or make the goods or services that were sold during the accounting period under review. The section 'Finding Cost of Goods Sold' below shows you how to calculate Cost of Goods Sold.

- ✔ **Gross Profit:** How much a business made before taking into account operations expenses; calculated by subtracting the Cost of Goods Sold from the Sales or Revenue.

- ✔ **Operating Expenses:** How much was spent on operating the business; these expenses include administrative fees, salaries, advertising, utilities, and other operations expenses. You add all your expenses accounts on your profit and loss statement to get this total.

- ✔ **Net Profit or Loss:** Whether or not the business made a profit or loss during the accounting period in review; calculated by subtracting total expenses from Gross Profit.

Formatting the Profit and Loss Statement

Before you actually create your business's profit and loss statement, you have to pick a format in which to organise your financial information. You have two options to choose from: the single-step format or the multi-step format. They contain the same information but present it in slightly different ways.

The *single-step format* groups all data into two categories: revenue and expenses. The *multi-step format* divides the profit and loss statement into several sections and offers some key subtotals to make analysing the data easier.

You can calculate the same subtotals from the single-step format in the multi-step format, although it means more work. Therefore, most businesses choose the multi-step format to simplify profit and loss statement analysis for those who read their external financial reports.

The following is an example of a basic profit and loss statement prepared in the single-step format:

Revenues	
Net Sales	£1,000
Interest Income	£100
Total Revenue	£1,100
Expenses	
Costs of Goods Sold	£500
Depreciation	£50
Advertising	£50
Salaries	£100
Supplies	£100
Interest Expenses	£50
Total Expenses	£850
Net Profit	£250

Using the same numbers, the following is an example of a basic profit and loss statement prepared in the multi-step format.

Revenues	
Sales	£1,000
Cost of Goods Sold	£500
Gross Profit	£500
Operating Expenses	
Depreciation	£50
Advertising	£50
Salaries	£100
Supplies	£100
Interest Expenses	£50
Total Operating Expenses	£350
Operating Profit	£150
Other Income	
Interest Income	£100
Total Profit	£250

Of course in both examples you end up with the same profit but the second profit and loss statement provides the reader with a better analysis of what happened in the business.

Preparing the Profit and Loss Statement

Before you can prepare your profit and loss statement, you have to calculate Net Sales and Cost of Goods Sold using information that appears on your worksheet.

Finding Net Sales

Net Sales is a total of all your sales minus any discounts. In order to calculate Net Sales, you look at the line items regarding sales, discounts, and any sales fees on your worksheet. For example, suppose that your worksheet lists Total Sales at £20,000 and discounts given to customers at £1,000. Also, according to your worksheet, your business paid £125 in credit card fees on sales. To find your Net Sales, you subtract the discounts and credit card fees from your Total Sales amount, leaving you with £18,875.

Finding Cost of Goods Sold

Cost of Goods Sold is the total amount your business spent to buy or make the goods or services that you sold. To calculate this amount for a business that buys its finished products from another business in order to sell them to customers, you start with the value of the business's Opening Stock (the amount in the stock account at the beginning of the accounting period), add all purchases of new stock, and then subtract any Closing Stock (stock that's still on the shelves or in the warehouse).

The following is a basic Cost of Goods Sold calculation:

Opening Stock + Purchases = Goods Available for Sale

£100 + £1,000 = £1,100

Goods Available for Sale – Closing Stock = Cost of Goods Sold

£1,100 – £200 = £900

To simplify the example for calculating Cost of Goods Sold, these numbers assume the Opening (the value of the stock at the beginning of the accounting period) and Closing Stock (the value of the stock at the end of the accounting period) values are the same. So to calculate Cost of Goods Sold you need just two key lines: the purchases made and the discounts received to lower the purchase cost, as in the following example.

Purchases – Purchases Discounts = Cost of Goods Sold

£8,000 – £1,500 = £6,500

Drawing remaining amounts from your worksheet

After you calculate Net Sales and Cost of Goods Sold (see the preceding sections), you can use the rest of the numbers from your worksheet to prepare your business's profit and loss statement. Figure 5-1 shows a sample profit and loss statement.

Profit and Loss Statement

May 2006

Month Ended	May
Revenues:	
Net Sales	£ 18,875
Cost of Goods Sold	(£ 6,500)
Gross Profit	£ 12,375
Operating Expenses:	
Advertising	£ 1,500
Bank Service Charges	£ 120
Insurance Expenses	£ 100
Interest Expenses	£ 125
Legal & Accounting Fees	£ 300
Office Expenses	£ 250
Payroll Taxes Expenses	£ 350
Postage Expenses	£ 75
Rent Expenses	£ 800
Salaries	£ 3,500
Supplies	£ 300
Telephone Expenses	£ 200
Utilities	£ 255
Total Operating Expenses	£ 7,875
Net Profit	£ 4,500

Figure 5-1: A sample profit and loss statement.

You and anyone else in-house are likely to want to see the type of detail shown in the example in Figure 5-1, but most business owners prefer not to show all their operating detail to outsiders: They prefer to keep the detail private. Fortunately, if you operate as a sole trader or partnership, only HM Revenue & Customs needs to see your detailed profit and loss figures. If your turnover is less than £15,000 per annum even HM Revenue & Customs only wants to see your profit figure. Also, if you are a small limited company, when you file your accounts at Companies House you can file abbreviated accounts, which means that you can keep your detailed profit and loss figures secret. Speak with your external accountant about whether you qualify as a small company because the exemption levels do change from time to time.

Gauging Your Cost of Goods Sold

Businesses that make their own products rather than buy them for future sale must record stock at three different levels:

- **Raw materials:** This line item includes purchases of all items used to make your business's products. For example, a fudge shop buys all the ingredients to make the fudge it sells, so the value of any stock on hand that hasn't been used to make fudge yet needs to appear in the raw materials line item.

- **Work-in-progress stock:** This line item shows the value of any products being made but that aren't yet ready for sale. A fudge shop is unlikely to have anything in this line item because fudge doesn't take more than a few hours to make. However, many manufacturing businesses take weeks or months to produce products and therefore usually have some portion of the stock value in this line item.

   Valuing work in progress can be very complex. As well as the raw material content, you need to add in direct wages and production overheads consumed to produce the products to the stage they're at. In reality most small businesses do not attempt to value work in progress.

- **Finished-goods stock:** This line item lists the value of stock that's ready for sale. (For a business that doesn't make its own products, finished-goods stock is the same as the stock line item.)

If you keep the books for a business that manufactures its own products, you can use a computerised accounting system to record the various stock accounts described here. However, your basic accounting system software won't cut it – you need a more advanced package in order to record multiple stock types.

Deciphering Gross Profit

Business owners must carefully watch their Gross Profit trends on monthly profit and loss statements. Gross Profit trends that appear lower from one month to the next can mean one of two things: Sales revenue is down, or Cost of Goods Sold is up.

If revenue is down month-to-month, you may need to find out quickly why, and fix the problem in order to meet your sales goals for the year. Or, by examining sales figures for the same month in previous years, you may determine that the drop is just a normal sales slowdown given the time of year and isn't cause to hit the panic button.

If the downward trend isn't normal, it may be a sign that a competitor's successfully drawing customers away from your business, or it may indicate that customers are dissatisfied with some aspect of the products or services you supply. Whatever the reason, preparing a monthly profit and loss statement gives you the ammunition you need to find and fix a problem quickly, thereby minimising any negative hit to your yearly profits.

The other key element of Gross Profit, Cost of Goods Sold, can also be a big factor in a downward profit trend. For example, if the amount you spend to purchase products that you sell goes up, your Gross Profit goes down. As a business owner, you need to do one of five things if the Cost of Goods Sold is reducing your Gross Profit:

- Find a new supplier who can provide the goods cheaper.
- Increase your prices, as long as you don't lose sales because of the increase.
- Find a way to increase your volume of sales so that you can sell more products and meet your annual profit goals.
- Find a way to reduce other expenses to offset the additional product costs.
- Accept the fact that your annual profit is going to be lower than expected.

The sooner you find out that you have a problem with costs, the faster you can find a solution and minimise any reduction in your annual profit goals.

Monitoring Expenses

The Expenses section of your profit and loss statement gives you a good summary of how much you spent to keep your business operating that wasn't directly related to the sale of an individual product or service. For example, businesses usually use advertising both to bring customers in and with the hopes of selling many different types of products. That's why you need to list advertising as an Expense rather than a Cost of Goods Sold. After all, rarely can you link an advertisement to the sale of an individual product. The same is true of all the administrative expenses that go into running a business, such as rent, wages and salaries, office costs, and so on.

Business owners watch their expense trends closely to be sure that they don't creep upwards and lower the business's bottom lines. Any cost-cutting you can do on the expense side is guaranteed to increase your bottom-line profit.

Using the Profit and Loss Statement to Make Business Decisions

Many business owners find it easier to compare their profit and loss statement trends using percentages rather than the actual numbers. Calculating these percentages is easy enough – you simply divide each line item by Net Sales. Figure 5-2 shows a business's percentage breakdown for one month.

Profit and Loss Statement

May 2006

Month Ended	May	
Net Sales	£ 18,875	100.0%
Cost of Goods Sold	(£ 6,500)	34.4%
Gross Profit	£ 12,375	65.6%
Operating Expenses:		
Advertising	£ 1,500	7.9%
Bank Service Charges	£ 120	0.6%
Insurance Expenses	£ 100	0.5%
Interest Expenses	£ 125	0.7%
Legal & Accounting Fees	£ 300	1.6%
Office Expenses	£ 250	1.3%
Payroll Taxes Expenses	£ 350	1.9%
Postage Expenses	£ 75	0.4%
Rent Expenses	£ 800	4.2%
Salaries	£ 3,500	18.5%
Supplies	£ 300	1.6%
Telephone Expenses	£ 200	1.1%
Utilities	£ 255	1.4%
Total Operating Expenses	£ 7,875	41.7%
Net Profit	£ 4,500	23.8%

Figure 5-2: Percentage breakdown of a profit and loss statement.

Looking at this percentage breakdown, you can see that the business had a gross profit of 65.6 per cent, and its Cost of Goods Sold, at 34.4 per cent, accounted for just over one-third of the revenue. If the prior month's Cost of Goods Sold was only 32 per cent, the business owner needs to find out why the cost of the goods used to make this product seems to have increased. If this trend of increased Cost of Goods Sold continues through the year without some kind of fix, the business makes at least 2.2 per cent less net profit.

You may find it helpful to see how your profit and loss statement results compare to industry trends for similar businesses with similar revenues, a process called *benchmarking*. By comparing results, you can find out if your costs and expenses are reasonable for the type of business you operate, and you can identify areas with room to improve your profitability. You also may spot some red flags for line items upon which you spend much more than the national average.

To find industry trends for businesses similar to yours with similar revenues, visit www.bvdcp.com/FAME.html. The FAME database contains full financial data on approximately two million limited companies that file their accounts at Companies House. A word of warning though: Small companies are required to file very little financial information – typically just a balance sheet. This means that if you want to see detailed profit and loss information you have to look at the big businesses with turnover above £22.8 million, more than 250 employees, and a balance sheet greater than £5.6 million.

However, the information available for all the companies on this database is useful and can be interrogated in a number of ways. For example, you can compile industry average statistics, which can be a useful way to see how your business compares with others in the same line of business. You can take this a stage farther and compare your business to other businesses that you already know or have found on this database.

You can also find out how your business looks to the outside world if you use FAME to dig out the financials for your business. A credit rating, details of any court judgements, and other interesting information are all included in the reports.

FAME is available by subscription, which may make it expensive for the occasional user. You may find that a regional library has FAME available to the public on a free basis or through a per session cost. Most of the UK universities have FAME, and so if you can access one of their library services you can also use this facility. This service may be available through an annual library subscription.

Another source of financial information is your local business link (www.businesslink.gov.uk). Business link acts as a signpost to help small and medium-sized businesses. They can help you access your trade association, and other business support agencies and consultancies that run benchmarking.

Book IV

How Not to Cook the Books

Testing Profits

With a completed profit and loss statement, you can do a number of quick ratio tests of your business's profitability. You certainly want to know how well your business did compared to other similar businesses. You also want to be able to measure your *return* (the percentage you made) on your business.

Three common tests are Return on Sales, Return on Assets, and Return on Shareholders' Capital. These ratios have much more meaning if you can find industry averages for your particular type of business, so you can compare your results. Check with your local Chamber of Commerce to see whether it has figures for local businesses, or order a report for your industry online from FAME.

Return on Sales

The Return on Sales (ROS) ratio tells you how efficiently your business runs its operations. Using the information on your profit and loss statement, you can measure how much profit your business produced per pound of sales and how much extra cash you brought in per sale.

You calculate ROS by dividing net profit before taxes by sales. For example, suppose your business had a net profit of £4,500 and sales of £18,875. The following shows your calculation of ROS.

Net profit before taxes ÷ Sales = Return on Sales

£4,500 ÷ £18,875 = 23.8%

As you can see, your business made 23.8 per cent on each pound of sales. To determine whether that amount calls for celebration, you need to find the ROS ratios for similar businesses. You may be able to get such information from your local Chamber of Commerce, or you can order an industry report online from FAME.

Return on Assets

The Return on Assets (ROA) ratio tests how well you're using your business's assets to generate profits. If your business's ROA is the same or higher than other similar companies, you're doing a good job of managing your assets.

To calculate ROA, you divide net profit by total assets. You find total assets on your balance sheet. Suppose that your business's net profit was £4,500 and total assets were £40,050. The following shows your calculation of ROA.

Net profit ÷ Total assets = Return on Assets

£4,500 ÷ £40,050 = 11.2%

Your calculation shows that your business made 11.2 per cent on each pound of assets it held.

ROA can vary significantly depending on the type of industry in which you operate. For example, if your business requires you to maintain lots of expensive equipment, such as a manufacturing firm, your ROA is much lower than a service business that doesn't need as many assets. ROA can range from below 5 per cent, for manufacturing businesses that require a large investment in machinery and factories, to as high as 20 per cent or even higher for service businesses with few assets.

Return on Shareholders' Capital

To measure how successfully your business earned money for the owners or investors, calculate the Return on Shareholders Capital (ROSC) ratio. This ratio often looks better than Return on Assets (see the preceding section) because ROSC doesn't take debt into consideration.

You calculate ROSC by dividing net profit by shareholders' or owners' capital. (You find capital amounts on your balance sheet.) Suppose your business's net profit was £4,500 and the owners' capital was £9,500. Here is the formula:

Net profit ÷ Shareholders' or owners' capital = Return on Shareholders' Capital

£4,500 ÷ £9,500 = 47.3%

Most business owners put in a lot of cash upfront to get a business started, so seeing a business whose liabilities and capital are split close to 50 per cent each is fairly common.

Book IV

How Not to Cook the Books

Branching Out with Profit and Loss Statement Data

The profit and loss statement you produce for external use – financial institutions and investors – may be very different from the one you produce for in-house use by your managers. Most business owners prefer to provide the minimum amount of detail necessary to satisfy external users of their financial statements, such as summaries of expenses instead of line-by-line expense details, a Net Sales figure without reporting all the detail about discounts and fees, and a cost of goods number without reporting all the detail about how that was calculated.

Internally, the contents of the profit and loss statement are a very different story. With more detail, your managers are better able to make accurate business decisions. Most businesses develop detailed reports based on the data collected to develop the profit and loss statement. Items such as discounts, returns, and allowances are commonly pulled out of profit and loss statements and broken down into more detail.

- **Discounts** are reductions on the selling price as part of a special sale. They may also be in the form of volume discounts provided to customers who buy large amounts of the business's products. For example, a business may offer a 10 per cent discount to customers who buy 20 or more of the same item at one time. In order to put their Net Sales numbers in perspective, business owners and managers must monitor how much they reduce their revenues to attract sales.

- **Returns** are transactions in which the buyer returns items for any reason – not the right size, damaged, defective, and so on. If a business's number of returns increases dramatically, a larger problem may be the cause; therefore business owners need to monitor these numbers carefully in order to identify and resolve any problems with the items they sell.

- **Allowances** cover gifts cards and other accounts that customers pay for upfront without taking any merchandise. Allowances are actually a liability for a business because the customer (or the person who was given the gift card) eventually comes back to get merchandise and doesn't have to pay any cash in return.

Another section of the profit and loss statement that you're likely to break down into more detail for internal use is the Cost of Goods Sold. Basically, you take the detail collected to calculate that line item, including Opening Stock, Closing Stock, purchases, and purchase discounts, and present it in a separate report. (We explain how to calculate Cost of Goods Sold in the section 'Finding Cost of Goods Sold', earlier in this chapter.)

No limit exists to the number of internal reports you can generate from the detail that goes into your profit and loss statement and other financial statements. For example, many businesses design a report that looks at month-to-month trends in revenue, Cost of Goods Sold, and profit. In fact, you can set up your computerised accounting system (if you use one) to generate this and other custom-designed reports automatically. Using your computerised system, you can produce these reports at any time during the month if you want to see how close you are to meeting your month-end, quarter-end, or year-end goal.

Many businesses also design a report that compares actual spending to the budget. On this report, each of the profit and loss statement line items appear with their accompanying planned budget figures and the actual figures. When reviewing this report, you flag any line item that's considerably higher or lower than expected and then research them to find a reason for the difference.

Chapter 6

Developing a Balance Sheet

*P*eriodically, you want to know how well your business is doing. Therefore, at the end of each accounting period, you draw up a balance sheet – a snapshot of your business's condition. This snapshot gives you a picture of where your business stands – its assets, its liabilities, and how much the owners have invested in the business at a particular point in time.

This chapter explains the key ingredients of a balance sheet and tells you how to pull them all together. You also find out how to use some analytical tools called ratios to see how well your business is doing.

Breaking Down the Balance Sheet

Basically, creating a balance sheet is like taking a picture of the financial aspects of your business.

The business name appears at the top of the balance sheet along with the ending date for the accounting period being reported. The rest of the report summarises

> ✔ **The business's assets,** which include everything the business owns in order to stay in operation
>
> ✔ **The business's debts,** which include any outstanding bills and loans that must be paid
>
> ✔ **The owners' capital,** which is basically how much the business owners have invested in the business

Assets, liabilities, and capital probably sound familiar – they're the key elements that show whether or not your books are in balance. If your liabilities plus capital equal assets, your books are in balance. All your bookkeeping efforts are an attempt to keep the books in balance based on this formula.

Gathering Balance Sheet Ingredients

You can find most of the information you need to prepare a balance sheet on your trial balance worksheet, the details of which are drawn from your final adjusted trial balance.

To keep this example simple, we assume that the fictitious business has no adjustments for the balance sheet as of 31 May 2008. In the real world, every business needs to adjust something (usually stock levels at the very least) every month.

To prepare the example trial balances in this chapter, we use the key accounts listed in Table 6-1; these accounts and numbers come from the fictitious business's trial balance worksheet.

Table 6-1	Balance Sheet Accounts
Account Name	*Balance in Account*
Cash	£2,500
Petty Cash	£500
Accounts Receivable	£1,000
Stock	£1,200
Equipment	£5,050
Vehicles	£25,000
Furniture	£5,600
Accounts Payable	£2,200
Loans Payable	£29,150
Capital	£5,000

Dividing and listing your assets

The first part of the balance sheet is the Assets section. The first step in developing this section is dividing your assets into two categories: current assets and long-term assets.

Current assets

Current assets are things your business owns that you can easily convert to cash and expect to use in the next 12 months to pay your bills and your employees. Current assets include cash, Accounts Receivable (money due from customers), marketable securities (including shares, bonds, and other types of securities), and stock.

When you see cash as the first line item on a balance sheet, that account includes what you have on hand in the tills and what you have in the bank, including current accounts, savings accounts, money market accounts, and certificates of deposit. In most cases, you simply list all these accounts as one item, Cash, on the balance sheet.

The current assets for the fictional business are

Cash	£2,500
Petty Cash	£500
Accounts Receivable	£1,000
Stock	£1,200

You total the Cash and Petty Cash accounts, giving you £3,000, and list that amount on the balance sheet as a line item called Cash.

Long-term assets

Long-term assets are things your business owns that you expect to have for more than 12 months. Long-term assets include land, buildings, equipment, furniture, vehicles, and anything else that you expect to have for longer than a year.

The long-term assets for the fictional business are

Equipment	£5,050
Vehicles	£25,000
Furniture	£5,600

Book IV

How Not to Cook the Books

Most businesses have more items in the long-term assets section of a balance sheet than the few long-term assets we show here for the fictional business. For example:

- ✔ A manufacturing business that has a lot of tools, dies, or moulds created specifically for its manufacturing processes needs to have a line item called Tools, Dies, and Moulds.

- ✔ A business that owns one or more buildings needs to have a line item labelled Land and Buildings.

- ✔ A business that leases a building with an option to purchase it at some later date considers that *capitalised lease* to be a long-term asset, and lists it on the balance sheet as Capitalised Lease. An example of a capitalised lease is where you pay a premium for a lease and regard that premium as a long-term asset rather than an expense. The premium becomes a capitalised lease and set against profits over the life of the lease.

- ✔ A business may lease its business space and then spend lots of money doing it up. For example, a restaurant may rent a large space and then furnish it according to a desired theme. Money spent on doing up the space becomes a long-term asset called Leasehold Improvements and is listed on the balance sheet in the long-term assets section.

Everything mentioned so far in this section – land, buildings, capitalised leases, leasehold improvements, and so on – is a *tangible asset*. These items are ones that you can actually touch or hold. Another type of long-term asset is the *intangible asset*. Intangible assets aren't physical objects; common examples are patents, copyrights, and trademarks.

- ✔ A **patent** gives a business the right to dominate the markets for the patented product. When a patent expires (usually after 20 years), competitors can enter the marketplace for the product that was patented, and the competition helps to lower the price to consumers. For example, pharmaceutical businesses patent all their new drugs and therefore are protected as the sole providers of those drugs. When your doctor prescribes a brand-name drug, you're getting a patented product. Generic drugs are products whose patents have run out, meaning that any pharmaceutical business can produce and sell its own version of the same product.

- ✔ A **copyright** protects original works, including books, magazines, articles, newspapers, television shows, movies, music, poetry, and plays, from being copied by anyone other than the creator(s). For example, this book is copyrighted, so no one can make a copy of any of its contents without the permission of the publisher, John Wiley & Sons, Ltd.

> ✓ A **trademark** gives a business ownership of distinguishing words, phrases, symbols, or designs. For example, check out this book's cover to see the registered trademark, *For Dummies,* for this brand. Trademarks can last forever, as long as a business continues to use the trademark and file the proper paperwork periodically.

In order to show in financial statements that their values are being used up, all long-term assets are depreciated or amortised. Tangible assets are depreciated. Intangible assets such as patents and copyrights are amortised (amortisation is very similar to depreciation). Each intangible asset has a lifespan based on the number of years for which the rights are granted. After setting an initial value for the intangible asset, a business then divides that value by the number of years it has protection, and the resulting amount is then written off each year as an Amortisation Expense, which is shown on the profit and loss statement. You can find the total amortisation or depreciation expenses that have been written off during the life of the asset on the balance sheet in a line item called Accumulated Depreciation or Accumulated Amortisation, whichever is appropriate for the type of asset.

Acknowledging your debts

The Liabilities section of the balance sheet comes after the Assets section and shows all the money that your business owes to others, including banks, vendors, contractors, financial institutions, and individuals. Like assets, you divide your liabilities into two categories on the balance sheet:

> ✓ **Current liabilities:** All bills and debts that you plan to pay within the next 12 months. Accounts appearing in this section include Accounts Payable (bills due to suppliers, contractors, and others), Credit Cards Payable, and the current portion of a long-term debt (for example, if you have a mortgage on your premises, the payments due in the next 12 months appear in the Current Liabilities section).

> ✓ **Long-term liabilities:** All debts you owe to lenders that are to be paid over a period longer than 12 months. Mortgages Payable and Loans Payable are common accounts in the long-term liabilities section of the balance sheet.

Most businesses try to minimise their current liabilities because the interest rates on short-term loans, such as credit cards, are usually much higher than those on loans with longer terms. As you manage your business's liabilities, always look for ways to minimise your interest payments by seeking longer-term loans with lower interest rates than you can get on a credit card or short-term loan.

Book IV

How Not to Cook the Books

The fictional business used for the example balance sheets in this chapter has only one account in each liabilities section:

Current liabilities:

Accounts Payable	£2,200

Long-term liabilities:

Loans Payable	£29,150

Naming your investments

Every business has investors. Even a small family business requires money upfront to get the business on its feet. Investments are reflected on the balance sheet as *capital.* The line items that appear in a balance sheet's Capital section vary depending upon whether or not the business is incorporated.

If you're preparing the books for a business that isn't incorporated, the Capital section of your balance sheet contains these accounts:

- **Capital:** All money invested by the owners to start up the business as well as any additional contributions made after the start-up phase. If the business has more than one owner, the balance sheet usually has a Capital account for each owner so that individual stakes in the business can be recorded.

- **Drawings:** All money taken out of the business by the business's owners. Balance sheets usually have a Drawing account for each owner in order to record individual withdrawal amounts.

- **Retained Earnings:** All profits left in the business.

For an incorporated business, the Capital section of the balance sheet contains the following accounts:

- **Shares:** Portions of ownership in the business, purchased as investments by business owners

- **Retained Earnings:** All profits that have been reinvested in the business

Because the fictional business isn't incorporated, the accounts appearing in the Capital Section of its balance sheet are

Capital	£5,000
Retained Earnings	£4,500

Pulling Together the Final Balance Sheet

After you group together all your accounts (see the preceding section 'Gathering Balance Sheet Ingredients'), you're ready to produce a balance sheet. Businesses in the United Kingdom usually choose between two common formats for their balance sheets: the Horizontal format or the Vertical format, with the Vertical format preferred. The actual line items appearing in both formats are the same; the only difference is the way in which you lay out the information on the page.

Horizontal format

The Horizontal format is a two-column layout with assets on one side and liabilities and capital on the other side.

Figure 6-1 shows the elements of a sample balance sheet in the Horizontal format.

Vertical format

The Vertical format is a one-column layout showing assets first, followed by liabilities, and then capital.

Balance Sheet
As of 31 May 2006

Fixed Assets			**Capital**	
Equipment	£ 5,050		Opening balance	£ 5,000
Furniture	£ 5,600		Net Profit for year	£ 14,500
Vehicles	£ 25,000			£ 19,500
		£ 35,650	Less Drawings	£ 10,000
				£ 9,500
			Long-term Liabilities	
			Loans Payable	£ 29,150
Current Assets			**Current Liabilities**	
Stock	£ 1,200		Accounts Payable	£ 2,200
Accounts Receivable	£ 1,000			
Cash	£ 3,000			
		£ 5,200		
		£ 40,850		£ 40,850

Figure 6-1: A sample balance sheet using the Horizontal format.

Book IV

How Not to Cook the Books

Using the Vertical Format, Figure 6-2 shows the balance sheet for a fictional business.

Whether you prepare your balance sheet as per Figure 6-1 or Figure 6-2, remember that Assets = Liabilities + Capital, so both sides of the balance sheet must balance to reflect this.

The Vertical format includes

- **Net current assets:** Calculated by subtracting current assets from current liabilities – a quick test to see whether or not a business has the money on hand to pay bills. Net current assets is sometimes referred to as *working capital*.

- **Total assets less current liabilities:** What's left over for a business's owners after all liabilities have been subtracted from total assets. Total assets less current liabilities is sometimes referred to as *net assets*.

Balance Sheet
As of 31 May 2006

Fixed Assets		
Equipment	£ 5,050	
Furniture	£ 5,600	
Vehicles	£ 25,000	
		£ 35,650
Current Assets		
Stock	£ 1,200	
Accounts Receivable	£ 1,000	
Cash	£ 3,000	
	£ 5,200	
Less: Current Liabilities		
Accounts Payable	£ 2,200	
Net Current Assets		£ 3,000
Total Assets Less Current Liabilities		£ 38,650
Long-term Liabilities		
Loans Payable		£ 29,150
		£ 9,500
Capital		
Opening Balance		£ 5,000
Net Profit for Year		£ 14,500
		£ 19,500
Less Drawings		£ 10,000
		£ 9,500

Figure 6-2:
A sample balance sheet using the Vertical format.

Putting Your Balance Sheet to Work

With a complete balance sheet in your hands, you can analyse the numbers through a series of ratio tests to check your cash status and monitor your debt. These tests are the type of tests that financial institutions and potential investors use to determine whether or not to lend money to or invest in your business. Therefore, a good idea is to run these tests yourself before seeking loans or investors. Ultimately, the ratio tests in this section can help you determine whether or not your business is in a strong cash position.

Testing your cash

When you approach a bank or other financial institution for a loan, you can expect the lender to use one of two ratios to test your cash flow: the *current ratio* and the *acid test ratio* (also known as the *quick ratio*).

Current ratio

This ratio compares your current assets to your current liabilities, and provides a quick glimpse of your business's ability to pay its bills in the short term.

The formula for calculating the current ratio is:

Current assets ÷ Current liabilities = Current ratio

The following is an example of a current ratio calculation:

£5,200 ÷ £2,200 = 2.36 (current ratio)

Lenders usually look for current ratios of 1.2 to 2, so any financial institution considers a current ratio of 2.36 a good sign. A current ratio under 1 is considered a danger sign because it indicates the business doesn't have enough cash to pay its current bills. This rule is only a rough guide and some business sectors may require a higher or lower current ratio figure. Get some advice to see what is the norm for your business sector.

A current ratio over 2.0 may indicate that your business isn't investing its assets well and may be able to make better use of its current assets. For example, if your business is holding a lot of cash, you may want to invest that money in some long-term assets, such as additional equipment, that you can use to help grow the business.

Acid test (quick) ratio

The acid test ratio uses only the financial figures in your business's Cash account, Accounts Receivable, and Marketable Securities – otherwise known as *liquid assets*. Although similar to the current ratio in that it examines current assets and liabilities, the acid test ratio is a stricter test of a business's ability to pay bills. The assets part of this calculation doesn't take stock into account because it can't always be converted to cash as quickly as other current assets and because, in a slow market, selling your stock may take a while.

Many lenders prefer the acid test ratio when determining whether or not to give a business a loan because of its strictness.

Calculating the acid test ratio is a two-step process:

1. **Determine your quick assets.**

   Cash + Accounts Receivable + Marketable securities = Quick assets

2. **Calculate your quick ratio.**

   Quick assets ÷ Current liabilities = Quick ratio

The following is an example of an acid test ratio calculation:

£2,000 + £1,000 + £1,000 = £4,000 (quick assets)

£4,000 ÷ £2,200 = 1.8 (acid test ratio)

Lenders consider that a business with an acid test ratio around 1 is in good condition. An acid test ratio less than 1 indicates that the business may have to sell some of its marketable securities or take on additional debt until it can sell more of its stock.

Assessing your debt

Before you even consider whether or not to take on additional debt, always check out your debt condition. One common ratio that you can use to assess your business's debt position is the *gearing ratio*. This ratio compares what your business owes – *external borrowing* – to what your business owners have invested in the business – *internal funds*.

Calculating your debt to capital ratio is a two-step process:

1. **Calculate your total debt.**

   Current liabilities + Long-term liabilities = Total debt

2. **Calculate your gearing ratio.**

Total debt ÷ Capital = Gearing ratio

The following is an example of a debt to capital ratio calculation:

£2,200 + £29,150 = £31,350 (total debt)

£31,350 ÷ £9,500 = 3.3 (gearing ratio)

Lenders like to see a gearing ratio close to 1 because it indicates that the amount of debt is equal to the amount of capital. Most banks probably wouldn't lend any more money to a business with a debt to capital ratio of 3.3 until its debt levels were lowered or the owners put more money into the business. The reason for this lack of confidence may be one of two:

- ✔ They don't want to have more money invested in the business than the owner.
- ✔ They are concerned about the business's ability to service the debt.

Generating Balance Sheets Electronically

If you use a computerised accounting system, you can take advantage of its report function to generate your balance sheets automatically. These balance sheets give you quick snapshots of the business's financial position but may require adjustments before you prepare your financial reports for external use.

One key adjustment you're likely to make involves the value of your stock. Most computerised accounting systems use the averaging method to value stock. This method totals all the stock purchased and then calculates an average price for the stock. However, your accountant may recommend a different valuation method that works better for your business. Therefore, if you use a method other than the default averaging method to value your stock, you need to adjust the stock value that appears on the balance sheet generated from your computerised accounting system.

Book IV

How Not to Cook the Books

Book V

Bigging Up
Your Business

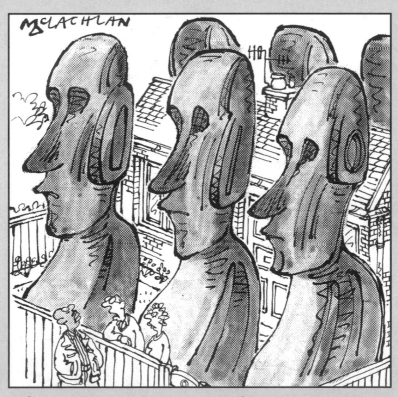

'When we bid for these half dozen garden
ornaments from an exotic island, they looked
a lot smaller on the screen.'

In this book . . .

You know what you want to be selling or what service you're providing . . . so let this book lead you through the best methods of getting your customers to buy from you. Covering a whole swathe of marketing styles and advertising ideas, we help you to work out who to sell to and how to do so.

Here are the contents of Book V at a glance:

Chapter 1

Taking a Closer Look at Customers

· ·

In This Chapter

▶ Checking out who your customers are

▶ Discovering why your customers buy

▶ Finding out how your customers make choices

▶ Remembering the big picture

▶ Dealing with business customers

· ·

The most crucial part of business planning involves taking a long, hard look at customers – those you enjoy having, those you would love to land, and those you would just as soon give away to some unsuspecting competitor. The stakes are high. How well you know your customers ultimately determines how successful you are.But figuring out what makes customers tick can be downright frustrating. If you've tried it before, you may be tempted to throw up your hands and leave the entire mess to the so-called experts – marketing gurus, consultants, or perhaps astrologers. Don't. This chapter shows you how to better acquaint yourself with your customers so that you can offer them more value and serve them more profitably than anyone else out there.

In this chapter, we take a closer look at why customers buy your products and services in the first place by exploring their needs and motives. And we investigate how they make choices in the marketplace by examining customer perceptions and their decision-making process. Finally, we take a quick look at your customers that are actually other businesses.

Checking Out Who Your Customers Are

A fresh look at customers starts with the ones you enjoy seeing – those who regularly purchase goods or services from you. But sometimes, knowing what something is *not* can be just as important as knowing what it *is*. You can learn as much about your own business and best customers by observing the other kinds of customers out there – the customers who are difficult, the customers who are gone, and the customers whom you never had.

The good customer

Good customers are the ones who bring a smile to your face, the ones you like serving, the ones who appreciate you, the ones who keep you in business. They are the customers you want to keep coming back time and again. To keep all those good customers happy, however, you may need to know more than the fact that Tom likes Chinese food, Mary has a weakness for chocolates, and Harry loves red ties.

Why? Isn't simply knowing individual customers on some personal basis enough? Well, not quite. What happens if you have hundreds or even thousands of small customers, such as a shop, or if your staff turnover is high as in most parts of the catering industry?

In such cases there is no substitute for a good database sytem for tracking your relationship with clients and then making appropriate product or sevice offers. For example supermarkets now analyse customer purchases and make targeted special offers based on their understanding of the customer profile. This all helps to make customers feel special and loved. Your business can measure and describe its customers in several ways:

- ✔ Track *where* your customers are, breaking them down by country, region, city, or postcode.

- ✔ Figure out *who* your customers are, including their age, gender, occupation, income, and ethnic origin.

- ✔ Learn more about *how* they live – their hobbies, favourite sports teams, restaurant choices, and holiday destinations, for example.

You're probably a step ahead of us here and have already noticed that many of these criteria result in groups of customers that look alike. When marketing gurus divide customers into specific groups, they call them *market segments*.

 When it comes to understanding customers, one good strategy is to find out what other businesses try to learn about their customers. Keep track of the questions that other companies ask you. Richer Sounds stores (a chain of hi-fi and home cinema retailers), for example, routinely ask for your postcode when you step up to the till. And you often find a list of personal questions on product registration forms, warranty cards, and customer service mailings.

Some companies even offer a small reward if you tell them something – anything – about yourself. But go easy here. Radio Shack, an American electronics retailer, began to lose a lot of goodwill when customers grew suspicious about – or just annoyed by – all the questions that their shop assistants were asking.

The bad customer

'A bad customer? Isn't that a contradiction in terms?' you ask. 'How can there be such a thing as a bad customer, especially for a customer-orientated company?' Keep in mind that your initial reaction doesn't always tell the whole story. Remember that *you* don't really define the business that you're in, your *customers* do. They place a series of demands on your company and then evaluate how well it performs against those demands.

Good customers do the following:

- ✔ Ask you to do things that you do well

- ✔ Place value on the things that you do and are willing to pay for them

- ✔ Challenge you to improve your skills, expand your knowledge, and focus your resources

- ✔ Take you in new directions that are consistent with your strategy and planning

Bad customers represent the flip side. They do the following:

- ✔ Ask you to do things that you aren't equipped to do well

- ✔ Distract you, causing you to veer away from your strategy and your business plan

- ✔ Purchase in such small quantities that the cost of doing business with them far outweighs any revenue that they generate

- ✔ Require so much service and attention that you can't focus your efforts on more valuable (and profitable) customers

- ✔ Remain dissatisfied with what you do, despite all your best efforts

- ✔ Fail to pay on time – or to pay at all!

The pundits have come up with a principle that we can apply here: the *80/20 principle*. In this case, the rule says that if you survey all your customers, 20 per cent of them account for about 80 per cent of your business. These 20 per cent are your good customers. You obviously want to keep them – and keep them happy! But look at the other 80 per cent of your customers, and you'll probably discover a few whom you'd rather hand over to the competition.

When you analyse what you do for that 80 per cent of customers and what they do for you, these customers are often more trouble than they're worth. Their shoe styles are never in stock, and their special orders are always returned. Maybe their finances are a mess, which makes them late in paying. Still, the lure of additional revenue and more customers – or the belief that you should never say no to any customer – often keeps you involved with this group. You would be better off without these customers, though, and leaving your competitors to handle such bad business impairs their ability to compete with you for good business.

To handle bad customers, follow these steps:

1. **Figure out who they are, by establishing if you can make a profit out of doing business with them.**

2. **Convert them into good customers, by exploring ways of turning loss-making customers into profitable ones. For example, by putting up prices, introducing minimum order sizes or minimum drop quantities or by encouraging them to order online.**

3. **Alternatively, hand them over to someone else. If they don't accept the changes to your service that you introduce to ensure they make you money, they will soon move on to other suppliers.**

A note of caution: some of this year's bad customers may become next year's good customers. Ensure you only divest yourself of *permanently* bad customers.

The other guy's customer

You may think that focusing on customers whom you've never had points to another sort of failure on your part, but actually, these people present an opportunity. The fact that you haven't been able to serve this group gives you a challenge: to find out what your market really thinks is important. Your competitors' customers are telling you what you are not. This information is extremely useful, especially when you are working on the big picture in the early stages of business planning, defining who you are and who you want to serve.

Unfortunately, getting information out of your competitors' customers is often an expensive proposition. You don't know them, and you don't have an ongoing relationship with them. Market research firms, of course, are always eager to work with you. These companies are willing to bring together focus groups and talk to consumers about all sorts of things that relate to your products in comparison to the competition. The catch, of course, is that their services don't come cheap.

Fortunately, you don't have to be quite this formal about the information-gathering process, at least in the initial stages. As long as you can get selected people to provide sincere answers, you probably can approximate the results of a focus-group study on your own.

Getting to know your competitors' customers is often difficult, but not impossible.

- ✔ Spend some time where customers gather. Use trade shows, user groups, and industry conferences to make informal contacts and begin a dialogue with your non-customers.

- ✔ Ask pointed questions of people who choose competing products. Did they take the time to see what was available on the market? Have they even heard of your product or service? If they have, did they actually take the time to look at it? If not, why not? If so, what were their impressions?

- ✔ Really listen to what they have to say, no matter how painful it is. Don't get defensive when people say negative things about your company or your products.

Information about your customers is valuable, if not priceless. A consultant will charge you thousands of pounds for the same information.

- ✔ To plan effectively, learn as much about your customers as you can.

- ✔ Of all your customers, 20 per cent are likely to account for 80 per cent of your business.

- ✔ Some of your customers may actually cost you money.

- ✔ Your competitors' customers can tip you off to new opportunities.

Discovering Why Your Customers Buy

Perhaps the most difficult – and useful – question that you can answer about your customers is why they buy what they buy. What actually compels them to seek out your products or services in the marketplace? What's important to them? What are they really looking for?

Understanding needs

Why do people buy things in the first place? Psychologist types tell us that *needs fulfilment* is really at the heart of all consumer behaviour (see Figure 1-1, based on the social psychologist Abraham Maslow's famous 'Hierarchy of Needs' model). Everybody has needs and wants. When a need is discovered, it creates the motivation that drives human activity.

- ✔ Survival, at the most basic level, results in the universal need for grocery shops, carpenters, and tailors.

- ✔ The urge for safety, security, and stability generates the need for bank accounts, disability health insurance, and home alarm systems.

- ✔ The desire for belonging and acceptance creates the need for designer-label polo shirts, members-only clubs, and participation in expensive diet programmes.

- ✔ The urge to be recognised and held in esteem establishes the need for company banquets, fast cars, and award plaques.

- ✔ The desire for self-achievement and fulfilment results in the need for adventure holidays, quiz shows, and correspondence courses.

Figure 1-1: A basic overview of people's needs.

Hierarchy of Needs

Highest Level

- Self-Achievement
- Recognition and Self-Esteem
- Belonging and Acceptance
- Safety, Security, and Stability
- Survival and Physiological Need

Basic

Highest Level

Basic

Determining motives

Motives are needs that have been awakened and activated, so to speak. Motives send people scurrying into the marketplace, searching for products or services that can fulfil a particular need. Motives aren't always what they seem to be.

- Greeting card companies, for example, don't just sell cute little jingles printed on glossy paper at exorbitant prices. The prices are justified because the companies are actually selling small insurance policies against their customers' fear of feeling guilty. Perhaps fear of guilt (over a missed birthday or a forgotten anniversary) is really what propels the buyer into the greeting card market.

- Recent MBA graduates have been asked to rank the things that are most important to them when they decide among various job offers. When asked point-blank, a substantial majority rank quality of life, community, and schools at the top of the list and place starting salary somewhere in the middle. A more careful survey and analysis of the MBA selection criteria, however, usually settles upon compensation as being the single most important variable in accepting a new position fresh out of university.

- Most of us have a need to be accepted and liked by other people. This powerful motivation creates great market opportunities for the likes of beauty salons, gyms, and breath-mint companies.

Although motives obviously apply to individual consumers, they work equally well in the context of business or corporate behaviour. When a particular manufacturing company contracts with a private health and medical insurance company, such as Bupa, for example, is the company motivated to improve the health of its employees? Or is it motivated to reduce the cost of its health insurance premiums so that it can better compete with foreign companies (fulfilling its own need to survive)? If you run Bupa, how you answer this question has a major impact on your internal management of costs versus the overall quality of the health care that you provide.

Your job, of course, is to dig beneath the obvious customer responses and consumption patterns to determine what the buyers' real motives are in purchasing goods and services in your own market. When you understand what's actually driving customer behaviour, you're in a much better position to talk about your own product in terms that customers will respond to.

Finding Out How Your Customers Make Choices

How do customers make choices in the marketplace? The most important thing to remember is that customers decide to buy things based on their own view of the world – their own perceptions of reality. Few customers buy without thinking. Instead, they bring their perceptions of the world into a decision-making process that (ideally) leads them to purchase your product or service instead of other options.

Perceptions are reality

Customer perceptions represent the market's world view and include not only what your customers think of your products and services, but also how they see your company and view your competitors.

As customers turn to the marketplace, they confront a mind-boggling array of competing products. Many variables influence your customers as they evaluate their choices: advertising, endorsements, reviews, and salesmanship, not to mention their own gut reactions. You need to know how customers respond to all these stimuli if you ultimately want to earn and keep their business.

Have you ever wondered, for example, why so few yellow jumpers are available in the men's departments of clothing shops? Market research consistently shows that a majority of men believe that the colour yellow suggests weakness. Subconsciously, men feel that they may be perceived as being wimps if they have anything to do with the colour. So the yellow-jumper option isn't too popular.

Or have you noticed that Madonna doesn't do many endorsements? Okay, it's not as though she needs the extra income. But companies may feel that her image is just too controversial, resulting in negative perceptions and the risk that potential buyers will be driven away.

Never lose sight of the marketer's motto:

Customer perceptions are the market reality.

People buy goods and services based on what they perceive to be true, not necessarily on what you know to be the facts. To be successful in the marketplace, you have to develop a clear insight into customers' perceptions, understanding how buyers react to products and services in your market before you complete your own business plans.

The five steps to adoption

Marketing gurus often refer to the customer's *decision-making process* as the *DMP* (the acronym makes the term sound more official). In many markets, the DMP involves a series of well-defined steps that are dubbed the *consumer adoption process.* (Okay, we'll call it the *CAP.*) In this case, of course, *adoption* refers to a newly formed relationship with a product, not a child.

By understanding the steps that consumers often go through, you are better able to take advantage of customers' behaviour and build strategies that help them complete the adoption process. The process involves five major steps, which are described in Table 1-1.

Table 1-1	The Consumer's Five-step Adoption Process	
Primary steps	*Description of consumer*	*Your task*
Awareness	Aware of a product or service, but lacking detailed knowledge	Develop a strategy that educates and excites potential customers
Interest	Curious because of publicity and seeking more information	Provide more detailed product information and continue to build momentum
Evaluation	Deciding whether to test the product or service	Make the product evaluation process as easy and rewarding as possible
Trial	Using the product or service on a test basis	Make the trial as simple and risk-free as you can
Adoption	Deciding to become a regular user	Develop strategies to retain good customers

Remembering the Big Picture

Remember that old saying about not seeing the forest for the trees? Well, when you first start to think about your customers, you don't want to fall into a similar trap. Seeing only the small number of individual customers whom you know, and focusing on their personal habits, likes, and dislikes, is tempting sometimes. Even when you begin to look at more general customer trends, including why your customers buy and how they make choices, getting buried in the details still is awfully easy.

Don't take the bait! Don't view your customers and your own business activities too narrowly. Look instead at the larger forest – those general customer behaviours and basic needs that define your market.

If you think about your business only in terms of your existing products, for example, you risk losing sight of customer needs that you've overlooked – needs that a competitor is no doubt going to satisfy at some point. You also create a short-sighted view of your own strategic choices that can result in missed market opportunities and woefully inadequate business plans.

The key point here is simple: If you don't know what your customers really want, you can't possibly fulfil their needs in an effective way.

Put yourself in your customer's shoes:

- ✔ Take a hard look at one of your own products or services, and honestly ask yourself, 'Why would *I* need this thing?'
- ✔ Ask the same question of several people who also use your product or service.
- ✔ Try to imagine a world without your product or service. What would you substitute for it?

Answering questions such as these goes a long way toward fostering creativity, generating new strategies, and providing expanded market opportunities.

Dealing with Business Customers

Although we've mentioned companies that sell principally to other companies (as opposed to those that sell primarily to individual consumers), some of you in this so-called *business-to-business market* may think that we're ignoring you. We aren't – honest! In this section, you find details on how companies, institutions, and government agencies act when they themselves are the customers. What makes the business buyer different? Many things.

Secondhand demand

Demand for goods and services in business-to-business markets is almost always *derived demand*. In other words, businesses purchase only those goods and services that they can use to better serve their own customers.

Steel, for example, is a product that no end-user buys. When was the last time you had the urge to go out and get your hands on some flat-rolled sheeting? Steel purchasers tend to be automobile manufacturers, construction firms, appliance companies, and the like. After these businesses use the steel to make their own products (cars, office blocks, and refrigerators), we come into the picture as potential customers.

What are the implications for the steel sellers? If a steelmaker cuts its prices across the board, for example, should it expect a huge increase in orders? Not necessarily. The steel buyers will increase their purchases only if they think that they can sell more of the things that *they* make, and their own sales may be affected by many factors beyond the underlying price of steel. How many of us dashed out to buy a new car the last time steel prices were reduced by 10 per cent?

Inelastic demand is a term that number crunchers use when they talk about demand for a particular product that doesn't stretch or change automatically when the price of the product changes.

If you offer products or services in the business-to-business market, make sure that you take the time to think through what your planning decisions mean to your business buyers. And that means thinking about your customers' customers as well:

- ✔ Will a price reduction on your part result in increased sales for your customers – and your company?
- ✔ Will your customers (and their customers) benefit if you offer them additional bells and whistles while raising their costs?
- ✔ Are your customers looking for continuity and price stability?

Decision making as a formal affair

Purchase decisions in the business-to-business marketplace tend to be more formal, rational, and professional than in most consumer markets. Many people from different parts of the target company are often involved in the decision-making process (DMP). One division in the company may recommend your product or service, another may acquire it, yet another may pay for it, and all of them do the work for a separate customer centre that actually uses that product. Taken together, these divisions form the *decision-making unit* (or DMU) – another marketing term foisted off on us nice folks by marketing gurus.

Table 1-2 describes three ways in which a business DMU may behave when it's thinking about buying a product or service.

Table 1-2	How Businesses Behave When They Buy
Buying behaviour	*Description of the customer's DMP*
Business as usual	Continues to order more of the product or service, perhaps even automating the process so that inventories don't fall below certain levels.
Yes, but . . .	Asks for changes in the existing sales arrangement, modifying one or more purchase terms (such as pricing, financing, quantities, and options) and including various people who are part of the DMU.
Opportunity knocks	Purchases a product or service for the first time, perhaps after putting out a request for proposal (RFP) to several possible suppliers and making a deliberate, complete decision involving all parties in the DMU.

Forces to be reckoned with

In working with business customers, you most likely have to deal with several powerful customer forces that you rarely encounter in consumer markets. If your business-to-business strategies are going to succeed over time, you must factor these forces into your business plans. Consider the following questions:

✔ What's the state of the customer's business?

- Is the customer's business booming, mature, or dying?

- Is it facing increased competition or enjoying record profits?

- Is it outsourcing business, creating new opportunities?

- Does it threaten to become a competitor?

✔ How does the customer's company operate?

- Does the customer purchase centrally, or does it have buyers scattered around the company?

- Does it require several levels of approval before a decision is made?

- Do senior executives (who may or may not know a lot about the product) make the ultimate purchase decisions?

✔ Who's important to whom?

- Do the customer's key decision-makers tend to be engineers or marketing people?
- Does the customer use both small and large suppliers?
- Does it have a policy of requiring more than one supplier in critical areas?

As you begin to develop strategies for your business customers, take the time to investigate the forces that are unique in business-to-business markets:

✔ Get out into the field and talk to potential business buyers.

✔ Read about customers' organisations and their industries.

✔ Attend the conferences and conventions that your customers attend, and learn about the critical events and forces that shape their thinking.

All these activities take time and resources, of course, but your investment will be rewarded many times over when you incorporate what you learn into your business-to-business planning.

Chapter 2

Marketing Your Wares

• •

In This Chapter:

▶ Understanding the marketing mix and how to use it

▶ Deciding the advertising message

▶ Choosing the media

▶ Reviewing selling options

▶ Appreciating the legal implications

• •

*E*ntering the market involves deciding on what mix of marketing ingredients to use. In cooking, the same ingredients used in different ways can result in very different products and the same is true in business. In business, the 'ingredients' are product (or service), price, place, and promotion. A change in the way these elements are put together can produce an offering tailored to meet the needs of a specific market. For example, a hardback book is barely more expensive to produce than a paperback. However with a bit of clever publicity, bringing them out a few weeks before the paperback edition and a hefty price hike, an air of exclusivity can be created which satisfies a particular group of customers.

Making Up the Marketing Mix

The key to successful promotion lies in knowing exactly what you want people to do. A few elements can make or break the successful marketing of your business. The elements you need to consider in the marketing mix are:

✔ The *product or service* is what people use, but what they buy are the underlying benefits it confers on them. For example, cameras, SLR or digital, lens, even film are not the end products that customers want; they are looking for good pictures.

✔ *Pricing* strategies can range from charging what the market will bear, right through to *marginal cost* (just enough to cover direct costs and a small contribution to overheads). While it is important to know your costs, this is only one element in the pricing decision. You also have to take account of the marketplace, your competition, and your product position (for example, if you offer a luxury item, your place in the market is different than someone who sells necessities).

✔ Place is a general title to cover everything from where you locate to how you get your product or service to market. Poor distribution often explains sluggish sales growth. If your type of product gets to market through several channels but you only use one of them, then no amount of price changes or extra promotion will make much difference.

Defining Your Product Parameters

To be successful in the marketplace, you need to have a clear picture of exactly what you want to do and for whom you're doing it. In other words, you need a vision and a mission. (*Starting a Business For Dummies* offers advice on developing your mission statement.)

To effectively market your product, you have to make decisions about factors such as product range and depth before you are ready to enter the market. Having decided to open a corner shop, for example, you still have to decide if you will focus on food only, or will you carry household items and perhaps newspapers and flowers too. You will also need to decide if you will carry more than one brand and size of each product.

If the key advantages of your corner shop are its location, opening hours, delivery service and friendly staff, all at competitive prices, then perhaps you don't need a wide or deep product range.

Using Advertising to Tell Your Story

The skill of advertising lies in reducing the global population to your target audience and reaching as many of them as you can at an economic cost. You first analyse the benefits or virtues of your product, isolate the features, and translate these into customer benefits. Who has a need for your product? Discover who your potential customers are.

Question all the time. Then set objectives for your campaign, decide on a budget, design the message, and pick the medium to reach your target audience, and determine how you're going to evaluate the success of your advertising.

When you understand the basics, which I go through in the following sections, you should be able to analyse advertisements better, to break them down, and avoid the all too common mistakes that are made every day.

Advertising by itself does not sell. It will not shift a bad product (more than once) or create new markets. Sales literature, order forms, a sales force, stocks, distributors, and a strategy must back it up.

Considering the customer's point of view

It is important to recognise that people buy a product or service for what it will do for them. Customers look for the benefits. As the seller, your mission is to answer the question 'What's in it for me?' from your potential customer's point of view.

Every time you compose a sales letter, write an advertisement, or plan a trade show, you must get to the heart of the matter. Why should customers purchase your wares? What benefit will it bring them?

All your marketing efforts need to be viewed from the prospect's point of view and not just your own. Once you know what you are selling and to whom, you can match the features of the product (or service) to the benefits the customer will get when they purchase. A *feature* is what a product has or is, and *benefits* are what the product does for the customer. Finally, include proof that these benefits can be delivered. Table 2-1 shows an analysis of features, benefits, and proofs.

Table 2-1	Listing Features and Benefits	
Feature	*Benefit*	*Proof*
We use a unique hardening process for our machine.	Our tools last longer and that saves you money.	We have a patent on the process; independent tests carried out by the Cambridge Institute of Technology show our product lasts longest.
Our shops stay open later than others in the area.	You get more choice when to shop.	Come and see.
Our computer system is fault tolerant using parallel processing.	You have no downtime for either defects or system expansion.	Our written specification guarantees this; come and talk to satisfied customers operating in your field.

You can use this format to examine the features, benefits, and proofs for your own products or services and use the information to devise your ads. Remember, the customer pays for the benefits and the seller for the features. So the benefit will provide the copy for most of your future advertising and promotional efforts.

Try this out for your business idea. Keep at it until you really have a good handle on what makes your customers tick. To make the process work you will need to talk to some real prospective customers in your target market.

Setting advertising objectives

There is no point in advertising your product or service unless it leads to the opportunity for a sale in a significant number of instances. Ask yourself what potential customers have to do to enable you to make these sales. Do you want them to visit your showroom, phone you, write to your office, return a card, or send an order in the post? Do you expect them to order now, or to remember you at some future date when they have a need for your services?

The more specifically you identify the response you want, the better you can tailor your promotional effort to achieve your objective, and the more clearly you can assess the effectiveness of your promotion.

The more general your advertising objective is – for example, to 'improve your image' or 'to keep your name in front of the public' – the more likely it is to be an ineffective way of spending your money.

Deciding the budget

Two methods are commonly used to calculate advertising budget numbers:

- **What can we afford?** This approach accepts that cash is usually a scarce commodity and advertising has to take its place alongside a range of competing demands.

- **Cost/benefit:** This approach comes into its own when you have clear and specific promotional goals. If you have spare capacity in your factory or want to sell more out of your shop, you can work out how much it will cost you to increase your production and sales, and how much you could benefit from those extra sales. You then figure out how much advertising money it takes to get you the extra business.

Suppose a £1,000 advertisement is expected to generate 100 enquiries for your product. If your experience tells you that on average 10 per cent of enquiries result in orders, and your profit margin is £200 per product, then you can expect an extra £2,000 profit. That benefit is much greater than the £1,000 cost of the advertisement, so it seems a worthwhile investment.

In practice, you should use all of these methods to decide how much to spend on promoting your products.

Defining the message

To define your message, you must look at your business and its products from the customer's standpoint and be able to answer the question, 'Why should I buy your product?' It is better to consider the answer in two stages:

1. **'Why should I buy your *product?*'**

   The answer is provided naturally by looking carefully at buying motives and the benefits customers get from the product.

2. **'Why should I buy *your* product?'**

   The only logical and satisfactory answer is: 'Because it is better and so it is different.'

   The difference can arise in two ways:

   1. You, the seller, are different. To achieve this, you establish a particular niche for your business.

   2. Your product is different. Each product should have a unique selling point, based on fact.

Your promotional message must be built around your product's strengths and must consist of facts about the company and about the product.

The stress here is on the word '*fact*' and although there may be many types of fact surrounding you and your products, your customers are only interested in two: the facts which influence their buying decisions, and the facts of how your business and its products stand out from the competition.

The assumption is that everyone buys for obvious, logical reasons only, but of course innumerable examples show that this is not so. Does a woman buy a new dress only when the old one is worn out? Do bosses have desks that are bigger than their subordinates' because they have more papers to put on them?

Choosing the media

Broadly, your advertising choices are media *above-the-line,* which is jargon for newspapers, TV, radio, and other broadcast media, and *below-the-line* activities such as distributing brochures, stationery letterhead, and the way you answer the phone. The printed word (newspapers and magazines) will probably take most of your above-the-line advertising budget. It is the accepted medium to reach the majority of customers. Most people read the newspaper, especially on Sunday, and there are magazines to cater for every imaginable interest from the parish magazine to the Sunday supplements.

You must advertise where your buyers and consumers are likely to see the message. Your market research tells you where your likely prospects lie. Before making your decision about which paper or journal to advertise in, you need to get readership and circulation numbers and the reader profile.

You can get this information directly from the journal or paper or from *BRAD* (British Rate and Data), www.brad.co.uk, which has a monthly classified directory of all UK and Republic of Ireland media. You should be able to access this through your local business library.

The approach to take when considering below-the-line advertising is to identify what business gurus call *moments of truth* – contact points between you, your product or service, and your customer. Those moments offer you a chance to shine and make a great impression. You can spot the difference at once when you get a really helpful person on the phone or serving you in a shop. The same is true of product literature that is actually helpful, a fairly rare event in itself.

Some of the most effective promotional ideas are the simplest, for example a business card with a map on the reverse side showing how to find you, or 'thank you cards', instead of letters, on which you can show your company's recently completed designs.

Choosing the frequency

The copy dates of some monthlies are two months before publication. This poses problems if you are waiting on a shipment or uncertain about a product change. Dailies or weeklies allow much prompter changes. The ultimate is probably radio, where messages can be slotted in on the same day. Yearbooks, diaries, and phone directories require long forward notice.

Providing opportunities to see

One claimed benefit of breakfast television is that it can get your message out before the shops open. Trade buyers are deluged with calendars, diaries, pen sets, and message pads in the hope that when the buyer is making a decision, the promotional materials are still close at hand and have an influence on the buyer's decision.

The more opportunities you give potential customers to see your name or your product, the greater the chance that they'll remember you. This is why direct mail letters usually involve more than one piece of literature. The theory is that each piece is looked at before being discarded. It may only be a brief scan but it gives the seller another chance to hook a customer. So rather than using different advertising messages, try getting the same or a similar message to one customer group several times.

Figuring your bang-for-the-buck ratio

Advertising should only be undertaken where the results can realistically be measured. Everything else is self-indulgent. The formula to keep in mind is:

Effectiveness = Total cost of the advertising activity concerned ÷ by the Results (in measurable units such as customers, new orders, or enquiries).

A glance at the advertising analysis below will show how one organisation tackled the problem.

Table 2-2 shows the advertising results for a small business course run in London. At first glance the Sunday paper produced the most enquiries. Although it cost the most, £340, the cost per enquiry was only slightly more than the other media used. But the objective of this advertising was not simply to create interest; it was intended to sell places on the course. In fact, only ten of the 75 enquiries were converted into orders – an advertising cost of £34 per head. On this basis the Sunday paper was between 2.5 and 3.5 times more expensive than any other medium.

Table 2-2		Measuring Advertising Effect			
Media used	*Enquiries*	*Cost of advertising*	*Cost per enquiry*	*No. of customers*	*Advertising cost per customer*
Sunday paper	75	£		£	£
		340	4.50	10	34
Daily paper	55	234	4.25	17	14
Posters	30	125	4.20	10	12
Local weekly paper	10	40	4.00	4	10
Personal rec-ommendation	20	N/A	N/A	19	N/A

Getting in the News

The surest way to get in the news is to write a press release. Better still write lots of them. To be successful, a press release needs to get attention immediately and be quick and easy to digest. Studying and copying the style of the particular journals (or other media) you want your press release to appear in can make publication more likely.

The introduction is the most vital part. You should ask yourself, 'Will it make the reader want to read on?' Avoid detail and sidetracks. The paragraphs should have bite and flow. Keep the sentences reasonably short. State the main point of the story early on. Follow these suggestions for a successful press release:

- ✔ Type the release on a sheet of A4 paper headed up 'Press Release' or 'Press Information'. Address it to the News Editor, News desk, or a named journalist.

- ✔ Use double spacing and wide margins to allow for editorial changes and printing instructions, respectively. Use one side of the paper only.

- ✔ Date the release and put a headline on to identify it.

- ✔ Tell your story in three paragraphs. The substance should come in the first one. The first paragraph must say who, what, why, when, and where, and succeeding paragraphs can fill in the detail. If space is short then the sub-editor will delete from the bottom and papers are always looking for fillers – short items that can be dropped into gaps. Even if the bulk of the story is cut, at least the main facts will get printed.

- ✔ Include at least one direct quotation or comment, always from a named individual and ideally from someone of standing or relevance.

- ✔ Keep it simple and write for the readership. The general public prefers images or descriptions to technical facts. For example a new car lock could be described as being able to keep out a professional thief for 30 minutes for a story in the general press. For the trade press the same story would be better supported by facts about the number of levers, codes, and so forth that are involved in beefing up the lock's security system.

- ✔ Finish with a contact for more information. Give phone numbers for work and home, as well as your e-mail and website addresses. This will help a journalist looking for more detail and by being available your story will be more attractive if a gap occurs suddenly.

- ✔ Submit the release before the paper or journal's deadline. All the media work to strict deadlines. Many local papers sold on a Friday are printed on a Tuesday or Wednesday morning. A release that fails to make it by then will probably be ignored. The national dailies, of course, have more flexibility and often have several editions. At the other end of the scale, many colour supplements and monthly journals have a cut-off date six weeks in advance.

- ✔ Steer away from selling your firm and product, and write news. Anything else is advertising and will be discarded. You are not writing an advertisement, you are telling a story to interest the readers.

- ✔ A good picture, they say, is worth a thousand words. Certainly from a journalist's point of view it's worth half a page of text they don't have to write themselves.

Deciding who to contact

Remember that the target audience for your press release is the professional editor; it is he or she who decides to print. With UK editors receiving an average of 80–90 press releases per week, make sure that you are making your latest newsworthy item public, but make sure it is free of puffery and jargon.

Do your research to find not only the right newspapers or journals, but also the right journalists. Read their columns, or listen to or watch their programmes and become familiar with their style and approach to news stories. Hollis (www.hollis-pr.com) publish the details of all news contacts, listed by business area. Your goal is to write a press release that is so close to their own style that they have almost no additional work to do to make your news usable.

Following through

You will get better results by following up your press release with a quick phone call. Journalists get bogged down and distracted like everyone else, so don't be too surprised if your masterpiece sinks to the bottom of a pile of prospective stories before the day is out. That phone call, or even an e-mail if you can't get through, is often enough to keep up interest and get your story through the first sifting.

Once you start getting results you will want to keep it going. But even if you are not successful at first, don't be disappointed or disheartened. Keep plugging away. Try to find a story regularly for the local press and get to know your local journalists and editors. Always be truthful, helpful, and available. If they ring you and you are at a meeting, make sure you always ring back.

Some companies always seem to get a piece in the paper every week. The stories published are not always earth-shattering news, but the continuous drip of press coverage eventually makes an impact. For example, Virgin Air has been virtually created by successful press coverage. Few of the millions of words of copy written about Branson or Virgin have been paid for.

Selling and Salesmanship

Selling is at the heart of every business. Whatever kind of selling your business involves, from moving goods over a counter to negotiating complex contracts, you need to understand the whole selling process and be involved with every aspect of it.

Telling the difference between selling and marketing

Marketing involves the whole process of deciding what to sell, who to sell it to, and how. The theory is that a brilliant marketing strategy should all but eliminate the need for selling. After all, selling is mostly concerned with shoe-horning customers into products that they don't really want, isn't it? Absolutely not! Whilst it is true that the more effort you put into targeting the right product or service to the right market, the less arduous the selling process is, you still have a selling job to do.

The primary job of the sales operation is to act as a bridge or conduit between the product and the customer. Across that gulf flows information as well as products and services. Customers need to be told about your great new ideas and how your product or service will perform better than anything they have seen to date.

Most businesses need selling and marketing activities in equal measure to get their message across effectively and get goods and services into their markets.

Selling yourself

One of the most important operational issues to address is your personal selling style. If you've sold products or services before, you may have developed a successful selling style already. If not, you need to develop one that is appropriate for your customers and comfortable for you. Regardless of your experience, assessing your selling style will help define and reinforce your business goals.

Check you and your salespeople always see things from the customer's point of view. Review the sales style of your salespeople to see how they can be improved.

Consider if your selling style is consultative, where you win the customer over to your point of view, or hard, where you try forcing them to take your product or service.

In assessing your selling style, consider the following:

- Always have a specific objective for any selling activity, together with a fall back position. For example your aim may be to get an order but you would settle for the chance to tender for their business. If you don't have objectives there is a danger that much of your sales activity will be wasted on courtesy calls that never reach the asking-for-an-order stage.

✔ The right person to sell to is the one who makes the buying decision. You may have to start further down the chain, but you should always know whom you finally have to convince.

✔ Set up the situation so you can listen to the customer. You can best do this by asking open questions. When they have revealed what their needs really are, confirm them back to them.

✔ Explain your product or service in terms of the customer's needs and requirements.

✔ Deal with objections without hostility or irritation. Objections are a sign that the customer is interested enough in what you have to say to at least discuss your proposition. Once you have overcome their objections and established a broad body of agreement you can try to close the deal.

✔ Your approach to closing can be one of a number of ways. The *assumptive close* takes the tack that as you and the customer are so much in agreement an order is the next logical step. If the position is less clear you can go for the *balance sheet close,* which involves going through the pros and cons, arriving at a larger number of pros. So once again the most logical way forward is for the customer to order. If circumstance allow, you can use the *special situation* closing technique. This might be appropriate if a product is in scarce supply or on special offer for a limited period.

✔ If you are unsuccessful, start the selling process again using your fall back objective as the goal.

Outsourcing selling

Few small start-up firms can afford to hire their own sales force at the outset as it costs over £40,000 a year to keep a good salesperson on the road, including commission and expenses. Inevitably there is a period where no sales are coming in yet salary and expenses are being paid out. Plus, you run the very real risk of employing the wrong person.

A lower-cost and perhaps less risky sales route is via agents. Good agents should have existing contacts in your field, know buyers personally, and have detailed knowledge of your product's market. Unlike someone you recruit, a hired agent should be off to a flying start from day one.

The big thing is that agents are paid purely on commission: if they don't sell they don't earn. The commission amount varies but is rarely less than 7 per cent and 25 per cent is not unknown.

You can find an agent by advertising in your specialist trade press or the *Daily Telegraph*, and *Exchange and Mart.* You can also find agents' associations listed in trade directories. However the most reliable method is to approach outlets where you wish to sell. They know the honest, competent, and regular agents who call on them. Draw up a shortlist and invite those agents to apply.

When interviewing a potential sales agent, you should find out:

- ✔ What other companies and products they already sell. You want them to sell related but not competing products.

- ✔ What is their knowledge of the trade and geographical area covered? Sound them out for specific knowledge of your target market.

- ✔ Who are their contacts?

- ✔ What is their proven selling record? Find out who their biggest customers are and talk to them directly.

- ✔ Do they appear honest, reliable, and a fit person to represent your business? Take up references and talk to their customers.

It is a challenge to find professional representation so your product has to be first-class, growth prospects good, with plenty of promotional material and back-up support.

When you do find a person to represent your product, draw up an agreement to cover the main points including geographic area, commission rates, when payable, customers you will continue dealing with yourself, training and support given, prohibiting competing agencies, and periods of notice required to terminate. Also build in an initial trial period after which both parties can agree to part amicably.

Measuring results

Sales results can take time to appear. In the meantime you need to make sure you're doing the things that will eventually lead to successful sales. You should measure the following:

Activities

- ✔ Sales appointments made

- ✔ Sales calls made per day, per week, per month. Monitor trends, as last quarter's sales calls will give you a good feel for this quarter's sales results

- ✔ Quotations given

Results

- ✔ New accounts opened
- ✔ Old accounts lost
- ✔ Average order size

Pricing for Profit

Pricing is the biggest decision you have to make about your business and the one that has the biggest impact on company profitability. You need to keep pricing constantly under review.

To get a better appreciation of the factors that could have an influence on what you should charge, every business should keep these factors in mind.

Caring about business conditions

Obviously, the overall condition in the marketplace has a bearing on your pricing policy. In boom conditions, where products are so popular that they're virtually being rationed, the overall level of prices for some products could be expected to rise disproportionately. Conditions can vary so much from place to place as to have a major impact on pricing. For example, one business starter produced her beauty treatment price list based on prices near to her home in Surrey. However she planned to move to Cornwall to start her business, where prices were 50 per cent lower, reflecting lower rates of pay in the county. So whilst she got a boost by selling her Surrey home for much more than she paid for a house in Cornwall, that gain was offset by having to charge much lower prices for her services.

Seasonal factors can also contribute to changes in the general level of prices. A turkey, for example, costs less on the afternoon of Christmas Eve than it does at the start of Christmas week.

Working to your capacity

Your capacity to produce your product or service, bearing in mind market conditions, influences the price you set. Typically, a new venture has limited capacity at the start. A valid entry could be to price so high as to just fill your capacity, rather than so low as to swamp you.

Understanding consumer perceptions

A major consideration when setting your prices is the perception of the value of your product or service to the customers. Their opinion of value may have little or no relation to the cost, and they may be ignorant of the price charged by the competition, especially if your product or service is a new one.

Skimming versus Penetrating

The overall image that you want to portray in the marketplace influences the prices you charge. A high-quality image calls for higher pricing, naturally. However, within that pricing policy is the option of either a high price which will just *skim* the market by only being attractive to the small population of wealthier customers; or to go for a low price to *penetrate* the market, appealing to the mass of customers.

Skim pricing is often adopted with new products with little or no competition that are aimed at affluent buyers who are willing to pay more to be the trend-setters for a new product. Once the innovators have been creamed off the market, the price can be dropped to penetrate to lower layers of demand.

The danger with this strategy is that high prices attract the interest of new competitors. If you have a product that's easy to copy and impossible to patent, you may be better off setting the price low to discourage competitors and to spread your product throughout the market quickly.

Avoiding setting prices too low

The most frequent mistake made when setting a selling price for the first time is to pitch it too low. Either through failing to understand all the costs associated with making and marketing your product, or through yielding to the temptation to undercut the competition at the outset, you set your price so low that you risk killing your company.

Pondering Place and Distribution

Place is the fourth 'p' in the marketing mix. Place makes you review exactly how you get your products or service to your customers.

If you are a retailer, restaurateur, or garage proprietor, for example, then your customers come to you. Your physical location probably is the key to success.

If your business is in the manufacturing field, you're more likely to go out and find customers. In this case, your channels of distribution are the vital link.

Even if you are already in business and plan to stay in the same location, it would do no harm to take this opportunity to review that decision. If you are looking for additional funds to expand your business, your location will undoubtedly be an area prospective financiers will want to explore.

Choosing a location

From your market research data you should be able to come up with a list of criteria that are important to your choice of location. Some of the factors you need to weigh up when deciding where to locate are:

- ✔ If you need skilled or specialist labour, is it readily available?

- ✔ Are the necessary back-up services, such as computer support, equipment repairs and maintenance, available?

- ✔ How readily available are raw materials, components, and other supplies?

- ✔ How does the cost of premises, rates, and utilities compare with other areas?

- ✔ How accessible is the site by road, rail, and air?

- ✔ Are there any changes in the pipeline, which might adversely affect trade? Examples include a new motorway by-passing the town, changes in transport services, and closure of a large factory.

- ✔ Are there competing businesses in the immediate neighbourhood? Will these have a beneficial or detrimental effect?

- ✔ Is the location conducive to the creation of a favourable market image? For instance, a high fashion designer may lack credibility trading from an area famous for its heavy industry and infamous for its dirt and pollution.

- ✔ Is the area generally regarded as low or high growth? Is the area pro-business?

- ✔ Can you and your key employees get to the area easily and quickly?

You may even have spotted a role model – a successful competitor, perhaps in another town, who appears to have got the location spot on. You can use their location criteria as a guide to developing your own.

Using these criteria you can quickly screen out most unsuitable areas. You may have to visit other locations several times, at different hours of the day and on different days of the week, before screening them out.

Selecting a distribution channel

Selecting a distribution channel involves researching methods and deciding on the best way to get your product to your customers. Distribution methods have their own language and customs. This section familiarises you with them.

Moving a product through a distribution channel calls for two sorts of selling activity. *Push* is the name given to selling your product in, for example, a shop. *Pull* is the effort that you carry out on the shop's behalf to help them sell your product out of that shop. Your advertising strategy or a merchandising activity may cause that pull. You need to know how much push and pull are needed for the channel you are considering. If you are not geared up to help the retailers to sell out your product, and they need that help, then this could be a poor channel.

The way in which you have to move your product to your end customers is an important factor to weigh up when choosing a channel. As well as such factors as the cost of carriage, you also have to decide about packaging materials. As a rough rule, the more stages in the distribution channel the more robust and expensive your packaging has to be.

Not all channels of distribution settle their bills promptly. Mail-order customers, for example, pay in advance, but retailers can take up to 90 days or more. You need to take account of this settlement period in your cash flow forecast.

If your customers don't come to you, then you have the following options in getting your product or service to them. Your business plan should explain which you have chosen and why.

- ✔ **Retail stores:** This general name covers the great range of outlets from the corner shop to Harrods. Some offer speciality goods such as hi-fi equipment, where the customer expects professional help from the staff. Others are mostly self-service, with customers making up their own minds on choice of product.

- ✔ **Wholesalers:** These organisations typically buy in bulk, store in warehouses and sell on in smaller quantities to retailers. The pattern of wholesalers' distribution has changed out of all recognition over the past two decades. It is still an extremely important channel where physical distribution, stock holding, finance, and breaking bulk are still profitable functions.

- ✔ **Cash & carry:** This slightly confusing route has replaced the traditional wholesaler as a source of supply for smaller retailers. In return for paying cash and picking up the goods yourself, the wholesaler shares part of their profit margin with you. The attraction for the wholesaler is improved cash flow and for the retailer a bigger margin and a wide product range.

Hypermarkets and discount stores also fit somewhere between the manufacturer and the marketplace.

- **Internet and mail order:** This specialised technique provides a direct channel to the customer, and is an increasingly popular route for new small businesses.

- **Door-to-door selling:** Traditionally used by vacuum cleaner distributors and encyclopaedia companies, this is now used by insurance companies, cavity wall insulation firms, double-glazing firms, and others. Many use hard-sell techniques, giving door-to-door selling a bad name. However, Avon Cosmetics have managed to sell successfully door-to-door without attracting the stigma of unethical selling practices.

- **Party plan selling:** A variation on door-to-door selling, which is on the increase with new party plan ideas arriving from the USA. Agents enrolled by the company invite their friends to a get-together where the products are demonstrated and orders are invited. The agent gets a commission. Party plan has worked very well for Tupperware and other firms who sell this way.

- **Telephone selling:** This too can be a way of moving goods in one single step from maker to consumer. Few products can be sold easily in this way; however, repeat business is often secured via the telephone.

Consider these factors when choosing channels of distribution for your particular business:

- *Does it meet your customers' needs?* You have to find out how your customers expect their product or service to be delivered to them and if they need that particular route.

- *Will the product itself survive?* Fresh vegetables, for example, need to be moved quickly from where they are grown to where they are consumed.

- *Can you sell enough this way?* 'Enough' is how much you want to sell.

- *Is it compatible with your image?* If you are selling a luxury product, then door-to-door selling may spoil the impression you are trying to create in the rest of your marketing effort.

- *How do your competitors distribute?* If they have been around for a while and are obviously successful it is well worth looking at how your competitors distribute and using that knowledge to your advantage.

- *Is the channel cost-effective?* A small manufacturer may not find it cost-effective to supply retailers in Bristol because the direct 'drop' size, that is the load per order, is too small to be worthwhile.

- *Is the mark-up enough?* If your product cannot bear at least a 100 per cent mark-up, then it is unlikely that you will be able to sell it through department stores. Your distribution channel has to be able to make a profit from selling your product too.

Working from home

If you plan to work from home, have you checked that you are not prohibited from doing so by the house deeds, or whether your type of activity is likely to irritate the neighbours? This route into business is much in favour with sources of debt finance as it is seen to lower the risks during the vulnerable start-up period. Venture capitalists, on the other hand, would probably see it as a sign of 'thinking too small' and steer clear of the proposition. Nevertheless, working from home can make sound sense.

You will also have to consider if working from home suits you and your partner's domestic arrangements. For instance, if you have young children it may be difficult to explain to them that you are really at work, when everything looks much the same all the time.

If you are the type of person who needs the physical separation of work and home to give a structure to their lives, then working from home may not be right for you.

Looking at Legal Issues in Marketing

Nothing in business escapes the legal eye of the law and marketing is no exception. If anything, marketing is likely to produce more grey areas from a legal point of view than most others. You have patent and copyright issues to consider.

There are a number of vitally important aspects of your business that distinguish it from other similar firms operating in or near to your area of operations. Having invested time, energy, and money in acquiring some distinction you need to take steps to preserve any benefits accruing from those distinctions. Intellectual property, often known as IP, is the generic title that covers the area of law that allows people to own their creativity and innovation in the same way that they can own physical property. The owner of IP can control and be rewarded for its use, and this encourages further innovation and creativity.

The following three organisations can help direct you to most sources of help and advice across the entire intellectual property field. They also have helpful literature and explanatory leaflets and guidance notes on applying for intellectual property protection:

- ✔ UK Patent Office (www.patent.gov.uk)
- ✔ European Patent Office (www.european-patent-office.org)
- ✔ US Patent and Trade Mark Office (www.uspto.gov)

We cover the most common types of intellectual property in the following sections.

Naming your business

You are reasonably free to use your last name for the name of your business. The main consideration in choosing a business name, however, is its commercial usefulness. You will want one that will let people know as much as possible about what you do. It is therefore important to choose a name that will convey the right image and message.

Whichever business name you choose, it will have to be legally acceptable and abide by the rules of the Business Names Act 1985. Detailed information on this subject is available from the Business Names section at the Companies House website. Go to `www.companieshouse.gov.uk` and click on 'Guidance Booklets & FAQ' and then 'Business Names'.

Looking at logos

It is not mandatory to have a logo for your business, but it can build greater customer awareness. A logo could be a word, typeface, colour, or a shape. The McDonald's name is a logo because of its distinct and stylistic writing. Choose your logo carefully. It should be one that is easily recognisable, fairly simple in design and one that can be reproduced on everything associated with your business. As far as the law is concerned a logo is a form of trademark.

Registering a domain name

A domain name is your own web address, which you register so that your business will have the exclusive right to use. It identifies your business or organisation on the Internet, and it enables people to find you by directly entering your name into their browser address box. You can check whether your choice of name is available by using a free domain search service available at Web sites that register domain names such as `www.yourname.com`.

If your company name is registered as a trademark, you may (as current case law develops) be able to prevent another business from using it as a domain name. Once you have decided on a selection of domain names, you can choose several different registration options:

- Use Nominet UK (`www.nic.uk`), which is the Registry for UK Internet domain names. Just as Companies House holds authoritative records for company names, Nominet maintains the database of UK registered Internet names. They charge £80 plus VAT for two years' registration.

- Most countries have a central registry to store these unique domain names. Two sites that maintain world directories of Internet domain registries are `www.internic.net` and `www.norid.no/domreg.html`, who between them cover pretty well every registration authority in the world.

In order to be eligible to register direct you must provide the Internet Protocol addresses of two named servers that are permanently connected to the Internet.

- ✔ Use Internet service providers (ISPs), which act as agents for their customers and will submit a domain name application for registration.

- ✔ Register online. Hundreds of websites now offer domain-name registration online; it's a good idea to search the Internet for these sites, as they often sell domain names as loss-leaders. Most of these providers also offer a search facility so you can see if your selected name has already been registered.

- ✔ Obtain free domain names along with free Web space by registering with an Internet community. These organisations offer you Web pages within their community space as well as a free domain name, but most communities only offer free domain names that have their own community domain tagged on the end – this can make your domain name rather long and hard to remember.

Once your domain name has been registered and paid for, you will receive a registration certificate, either directly or through your ISP. This is an important document as it confirms you as the legal registrant of a domain name. If any amendments need to be made at any point during the registration period, the registry and your ISP must be informed.

Protecting patents

The patent system in its current form was introduced over 100 years ago; although some type of protection has been around for about 350 years, as an incentive to get inventors to disclose their ideas to the general public and so promote technical advancement in general.

A patent can be regarded as a contract between an inventor and the state. The state agrees with the inventor that if she or he is prepared to publish details of their invention in a set form and if it appears that they have made a real advance, the state will then grant them a monopoly on their invention for 20 years: 'protection in return for disclosure'. The inventor uses the monopoly period to manufacture and sell the innovation; competitors can read the published specifications and glean ideas for their research, or they can approach the inventor and offer to help to develop the idea under licence.

The granting of a patent doesn't mean the proprietor is automatically free to make, use, or sell the invention themselves since to do so might involve infringing an earlier patent which has not yet expired. A patent really only allows the inventor to stop another person using the particular device which forms the subject of the patent. The state does not guarantee validity of a patent either, so it is not uncommon for patents to be challenged through the courts.

If you want to apply for a patent it is essential not to disclose your idea in non-confidential circumstances. If you do, your invention is already 'published' in the eyes of the law, and this could well invalidate your application. Ideally, the confidentiality of the disclosure you make should be written down in a confidentiality agreement and signed by the person to whom you are making the disclosure. This is particularly important if you are talking to a commercial contact or potential business colleague. The other way is to get your patent application on file before you start talking to anyone about your idea. You can talk to a Chartered Patent Agent in complete confidence as they work under strict rules of confidentiality.

There are two distinct stages in the patenting process:

- ✔ from filing an application up to publication of the patent
- ✔ from publication to grant of the patent

Two fees are payable for the first part of the process and a further fee for the second part. The UK Intellectual Property Office (IPO) Search and Advisory Service will give some estimate of the costs associated with a specific investigation. They suggest, for example, that 'patentability' searches will cost upwards of £750, and validity searches, and 'freedom to operate' searches from £1,500. And these are just the costs for the very start of the procedure.

The whole process takes two to three years. Relevant forms and details of how to patent are available free of charge from the IPO at www.ipo.gov.uk. You can also write to them: The UK Intellectual Property Office, Concept House, Cardiff Road, Newport, NP10 8QQ.

Registering a trademark

A *trademark* is the symbol by which the goods of a particular manufacturer or trader can be identified. It can be a word, a signature, a monogram, a picture, a logo, or a combination of these.

To qualify for registration the trademark must be distinctive, must not be deceptive and must not be capable of confusion with marks already registered. Excluded are national flags, royal crests, and insignia of the armed forces. A trademark can only apply to tangible goods, not services (although pressure is mounting for this to be changed).

The Trade Mark Act 1994 offers protection of great commercial value since, unlike other forms of protection, your sole rights to use the trademark continue indefinitely.

The IPO Search and Advisory Service can tell you if your trademark would be acceptable or is already in existence, before you commit time and money to making a formal application. You then apply by post on the official trademark from, or online via the IPO Web site; there is a £200 application fee. If the IPO finds no problems with the application, it is advertised in the weekly Trade Marks Journal to allow any objections to be raised, and if there are none, your registration certificate is issued.

Registration is initially for ten years. After this, it can be renewed for further periods of ten years at a time, with no upper time limit. It is not mandatory to register a trademark, but registration makes it easier to take legal action against any person who infringes the mark.

Unregistered trademarks rely on the common law of 'passing off'. If an unregistered trademark has been used for some time and could be construed as closely associated with the product by customers, it will have acquired a 'reputation' which will give it some protection legally; but it can be very difficult and expensive to prove a passing off action.

Detailing your design

You can register the shape, design, or decorative features of a commercial product if it is new, original, never published before or – if already known – never before applied to the product you have in mind. Protection is intended to apply to industrial articles to be produced in quantities of more than 50. The Design Registry can be accessed at the Patent Office website www.patent.gov.uk.

Design registration only applies to features that appeal to the eye – not to the way the article functions.

To register a design, you should apply to the IPO Design Registry and send a specimen or photograph of the design plus a registration fee (currently £60).

There is no such thing as an all-embracing international registration for designs. If you want protection of your design outside the UK, you generally have to make separate applications for registration in each country in which you want protection.

You can handle the design registration yourself but it might be preferable to let a specialist do it for you.

Controlling a copyright

Copyright gives protection against the unlicensed copying of original artistic and creative works – articles, books, paintings, films, plays, songs, music, engineering drawings. To claim copyright the item in question should carry this symbol (c) with the author's name and date.

No other action is required to take out copyright. The Copyright service is accessed through the IPO website (www.patent.gov.uk).

Copyright does not last forever. The duration is dependant on the type of copyright involved and can be anything from 25 to 70 years after the creator's death.

Setting terms of trade

All business is governed by terms of trade, which are in turn affected by *contractual* relationships. Almost everything done in business, whether it is the supply of raw materials, the sale of goods and services, or the hire of a fax machine is executed under contract law. This is true whether the contract is in writing or whether it is verbal – or even merely implied.

Only contracts for the sale of land, hire-purchase, and some insurance contracts have to be in writing to be enforceable.

To make life even more complicated, a contract can be part written and part oral. So statements made at the time of signing a written contract can legally form part of that contract. For a contract to exist three events must take place:

 ✔ There must be an offer.

 ✔ There must be an acceptance.

 ✔ There must be a consideration – some form of payment.

When selling via the Internet or mail order the contract starts when the supplier 'posts' an acceptance letter, a confirmation, or the goods themselves – whichever comes first.

Under the Distance Selling Regulations brought into effect in October 2001, customers have seven working days after they have received the goods to change their minds and return them. They do not need a reason and can get a full refund.

Consumers must also be given:

 ✔ Information about the company they are dealing with, such as the business name, registered and trading addresses and directors

 ✔ Written confirmation of the order – by fax, letter, or e-mail

 ✔ A full refund if their goods do not arrive by the date agreed in the original order; if no date was agreed they must be delivered within 30 days

- ✔ Information about cancellation rights
- ✔ Protection against credit card fraud

Certain standards have to be met by law for the supply of goods and services. Over and above these you need your own terms and conditions if you are not to enter into 'contracts' you did not intend. You will need help to devise these terms. The following four basic propositions will govern your conditions:

- ✔ The conditions must be brought to the other party's attention before he or she makes the contract.

- ✔ The last terms and conditions specified before acceptance of an offer apply.

- ✔ If there is any ambiguity or uncertainty in the contract terms they will be interpreted against the person who inserted them.

- ✔ The terms may be interpreted as unreasonably unenforceable being in breach of various Acts of Parliament.

The Office of Fair Trading (www.oft.gov.uk) and the Trading Standards Institute (www.tradingstandards.gov.uk) can provide useful information on most aspects of trading relationships.

Describing your goods

You can't make any claim you like for the performance of your goods or services. If you state or imply a certain standard of performance for what you are selling, your customers have a legally enforceable right to expect that to happen. So if you state your new slimming method will not only make people lose weight, but make them happier, richer, and more successful, then you had better deliver on all those promises.

The Trades Descriptions Acts and related legislation make it an offence for a trader to describe their goods falsely. The Acts cover everything from the declared mileage of second-hand cars to the country of manufacture of a pair of jeans.

The Trading Standards Institute is operated at county level throughout the country to ensure trading laws are met. Contact your council by phone or via their website (www.tradingstandards.gov.uk).

Abiding by fair business rules

The whole way in which businesses and markets operate is the subject of keen government interest. It is not a good idea, for example, to gang up with others in your market to create a *cartel,* in which you all agree not to lower your prices, or to compete with each other too vigorously.

Any such action may be brought to the attention of the Office of Fair Trading (OFT) (www.oft.gov.uk). The OFT's job is to make markets work well for consumers. Markets work well when businesses are in open, fair, and vigorous competition with each other for the consumer's custom. As an independent organisation, the OFT has three main operational areas which make up three divisions – Competition Enforcement, Consumer Regulation Enforcement, Markets and Policies Initiatives.

The OFT's Consumer Regulation Enforcement department

✔ ensures that consumer legislation and regulations are properly enforced

✔ takes action against unfair traders

✔ encourages codes of practice and standards

✔ offers a range of information to help consumers understand their rights and make good choices

✔ liaises closely with other regulatory bodies that also have enforcement powers

Dealing with payment problems

Getting paid is not always as simple a process as sending out a bill and waiting for the cheque. Customers may dispute the bill, fairly or unfairly.

A businessperson can use the Small Claims Court to collect bills, to obtain a judgement for breach of contract, or to seek money for minor property damage claims – for example, suing someone who broke a fence around your property or parking area. The Small Claims Court offers you an opportunity to collect money that would otherwise be lost as it would be too expensive to sue in regular court. True, for very small cases, it's not always cost-effective, and occasionally you'll have problems collecting your judgement. But the Small Claims Court should still be part of the collection strategies of your business.

The Small Claims Court aims to provide a speedy, inexpensive resolution of disputes that involve relatively small amounts of money. The advantage of the Small Claims Court is that if you cannot afford a solicitor and you are not entitled to Legal Aid you can still bring your case to the court yourself. Even if you can afford a solicitor, their fees may be more than the amount you are claiming. If you do not manage to get your opponent to pay your costs then you will not be any better off.

The *jurisdictional limits* (the amount for which you can sue) in these courts are rising fairly quickly. In the UK if the amount of money claimed is under £5,000, it is likely to come under the jurisdiction of the Small Claims Court. (If your claim is for personal injury it will only be heard in the Small Claims Court if the claim for the injury itself is not more than £1,000.) Claims of more than £5,000 are generally dealt with differently via the 'fast track' or the 'multi track'. www.hmcourts-service.gov.uk has information on how claims are allocated, and the different procedures.

Before you start legal proceedings, investigate alternatives. If your case involves a written contract, check to see if the contract requires mediation or arbitration of disputes. If so, this may limit or cut off your right to go to any court, including the Small Claims Court. Second, consider other cost-effective options, such as free or low-cost publicly operated mediation programmes. If you're in a dispute with a customer, or perhaps another business, and you still have hopes of preserving some aspect of the relationship, mediation – even if not provided for in a contract – is often a better alternative than going to court. Any litigation tends to sour people's feelings.

Anyone claiming up to £100,000 can sue through the Internet at any time, day or night. If the claim is undefended, the money can be recovered without anyone having to go to court. The service, called Money Claim Online, can be reached at www.courtservice.gov.uk.

Chapter 3

Writing a Marketing Plan

*Y*ou don't have to write a marketing plan to benefit from this chapter. But you may want to, because doing so is not as hard as you may think, and, most important, a good plan increases the odds of success. In fact, most of the really successful businesses we know – small or large, new or old – write a careful marketing plan at least once a year.

Marketing combines lots of activities and expenditures in the hope of generating or increasing sales and maintaining or increasing market share. You won't see those sales numbers rise without a coherent plan linking a strategy based on the strengths of your position to your sales and marketing activities that can convince targeted customers to purchase. Marketing can get out of control or confused in a hurry unless you have a plan. Every successful business needs a marketing plan. (Yes, even if you're in a small or start-up business. In fact, especially if you are. You don't have the resources to waste on unplanned or ineffective marketing.)

Identifying Some Planning Rules and Tips

Marketing plans vary significantly in format and outline from company to company, but all have core components covering

- ✓ **Your current position** in terms of your product, customers, competition, and broader trends in your market.

- ✓ **For established businesses, what results you achieved in the previous period** in terms of sales, market share, and possibly also in terms of profits, customer satisfaction, or other measures of customer attitude and perception. You may want to include measures of customer retention, size, and frequency of purchase, or other indicators of customer behaviour, if you think them important to your new plan.

- ✓ **Your strategy,** that is the big picture that will help you get improved results.

- ✓ **The details of your marketing activities,** including all your company's specific activities, grouped by area or type, with explanations of how these activities fit the company's strategy and reflect the current situation.

- ✓ **The numbers**, including sales projections and costs. Consider whether knowing these additional numbers would help your business: Market share projections, sales to your biggest customers or distributors, costs and returns from any special offers you plan to use, sales projections and commissions by territory, or whatever helps you quantify your specific marketing activities.

- ✓ **Your *learning plans*,** if you have a new business or new product, or if you're experimenting with a new or risky marketing activity, *and* want to set up a plan for how to test the waters or experiment on a small scale first. You need to determine what positive results you want to see before committing to a higher level. Wisdom is knowing what you don't know – and planning how to work it out.

The more unfamiliar the waters, the more flexibility and caution your plan needs. If you're a start-up, for example, consider a step-wise plan with a time-line and alternatives or options in case of problems. And if you're writing a marketing plan for the first time, make flexibility your first objective. Avoid large advance purchases of media space or time, use short runs of marketing materials at the copy shop over cheaper off-set printing of large inventories, and so on. Optimising your plan for flexibility means preserving your choice and avoiding commitments of resources. Spending in small increments allows you to change the plan as you go.

If your business has done this all before, however, and your plan builds on years of experience, you can more safely favour *economies of scale* over flexibility. (It is cheaper and more efficient to advertise, for example, if you do it on a large scale, because you get bigger discounts on design of ads and purchase of media space or airtime.) If you know a media investment is likely to produce leads or sales, go ahead and buy media in larger chunks to get good rates. And don't be as cautious about testing mailing lists with small-scale mailings of a few hundred pieces. A good in-house list supplemented by 20 per cent or fewer newly purchased names probably warrants a major mailing without as much emphasis on advance testing. Adjust your plan to favour economies of scale if you feel confident that you can make sound judgements in advance.

But always leave yourself at least a *little* wiggle room. Reality never reflects your plans and projections 100 per cent of the time. Aim for an 80 per cent match in marketing, and plan accordingly.

The following sections share a few other suggestions to follow if you want to increase your marketing plan's chances of success.

Avoiding common mistakes

Marketing campaigns end up like leaky boats very easily, so be sure to total up your costs fully and carefully. Each activity seems worthy at the time, but too many of them fail to produce a positive return – ending up like holes in the bottom of your boat: Too many of those holes, and the water starts rising. To avoid the costly but all-too-common mistakes that many marketers make, follow these suggestions:

✔ **Don't ignore the details.** You build good plans from details like customer-by-customer, item-by-item, or territory-by-territory sales projections. Generalising about an entire market is hard. Your sales and cost projections are easier to get right if you break them down to their smallest natural units (like individual territory sales or customer orders), do estimates for each of these small units, and then add those estimates up to get your totals.

✔ **Don't imitate the competitors.** Even though everyone seems to market their products in a certain way, you don't have to imitate them. High-performing plans clearly point out what aspects of the marketing are conventional and why – and these plans also include some original, innovative, or unique elements to help differentiate your company from and outperform the competition. Your business is unique, so make your plan reflect your special talents or advantages.

✔ **Don't feel confined by last period's budget and plan.** Repeat or improve the best-performing elements of the past plans, but cut back on any elements that didn't produce high returns. Every plan includes some activities and spending that aren't necessary and can be cut out (or reworked) when you do it all over again next year. Be ruthless with any underperforming elements of last year's plan! (If you're starting a new business, at least this is one problem you don't have to worry about. Yet.)

✔ **Don't engage in unnecessary spending.** Always think your plan through and run the numbers before signing a contract or writing a cheque. Many of the people and businesses you deal with to execute your marketing activities are salespeople themselves. These people's goal is to get *you* to buy their ad space or time, to use their design or printing services, or spend money on fancy Web sites. They want your marketing money and they don't care as much as you do whether you get a good return or not. You have to keep these salespeople on a tight financial rein.

Breaking down your plan into simple sub-plans

If all your marketing activities are consistent and clearly of one kind, a single plan is fine. But what if you sell services (like consulting or repair) and also products? You may find that you need to work up one plan for selling products (perhaps this plan aims at finding new customers) and another plan for convincing product buyers to also use your services. The general rule is that if the plan seems too complicated – divide and conquer! Then total everything up to get the big picture – overall projections and budgets.

If you have 50 products in five different product categories, writing your plan becomes much easier if you come up with 50 sales projections for each product and five separate promotional plans for each category of product. (Believe it or not, this method sounds harder but really is much simpler.) We've included some methods to break down your planning, making it easier and simpler to do:

✔ Analyse, plan, and budget sales activities by sales territory and region (or by major customer if you're a business-to-business marketer with a handful of dominant companies as your clients).

✔ Project revenues and promotions by individual product and by industry (if you sell into more than one).

✔ Plan your advertising and other promotions by product line or other broad product category, as promotions often have a generalised effect on the products within the category.

✔ Plan and budget publicity for your company as a whole. Only budget and plan publicity for an individual product if you introduce it or modify it in some way that may attract media attention.

✔ Plan and budget for brochures, Web sites, and other informational materials. Be sure to remain focused in your subject choices: One brochure per topic. Multipurpose brochures or sites never work well. If a Web site sells cleaning products to building maintenance professionals, don't also plan for it to broker gardening and lawn-mowing services to suburban homeowners. Different products and customers need separate plans.

Remember that every type of marketing activity in your plan has a natural and appropriate level of breakdown. Find the right level, and your planning will be simpler and easier to do.

Writing a Powerful Executive Summary

An executive summary is a one-page plan. This wonderful document conveys essential information about your company's planned year of activities in a couple of hundred well-chosen words or less. If you ever get confused or disorientated in the rough-and-tumble play of sales and marketing, this clear, one-page summary can guide you back to the correct strategic path. A good executive summary is a powerful advertisement for your marketing, communicating the purpose and essential activities of your plan in such a compelling manner that everyone who reads it eagerly leaps into action and does the right things to make your vision come true.

Draft the executive summary early in the year as a guide to your thinking and planning. But revise this summary often, and finish it after finishing all the other sections, because it needs to summarise them.

Help yourself (and your readers, if others in your company are going to be involved in approving or implementing the plan) by giving an overview of what's the same and what's different in this plan, compared with the previous period's plan. Draft a short paragraph covering these two topics.

Summarise the main points of your plan and make clear whether the plan is

✔ **Efficiency orientated:** Say that your plan introduces a large number of specific improvements in how you market your product.

✔ **Effectiveness orientated:** Say that your plan identifies a major opportunity or problem and adopts a new strategy to respond to it.

Make sure that you summarise the bottom-line results – what your projected revenues will be (by product or product line, unless you have too many to list on one page) and what the costs are. Also show how these figures differ from last year's figures. Keep the whole summary under one page in length if you possibly can.

If you have too many products to keep the summary under one page in length, you can list them by product line. But a better option is to do more than one plan. You probably haven't clearly thought out any plan that can't be summarised in a page. We've worked with many businesses in which marketing prepares a separate plan for each product. Divide and conquer.

Clarifying and Quantifying Your Objectives

Objectives are the quantified, measurable versions of your strategies. For example, if your strategy involves raising the quality of service and opening a new territory in order to grow your sales and market share, you need to think through how you'll do all that and set a percentage increase goal for sales and a new, higher goal for market share. These numbers become your objectives. The objectives flow from your thinking about strategies and tactics, but put them up near the front of your plan to help others quickly understand what you're saying.

What objectives do you want your plan to help you accomplish? Will the plan increase sales by 25 per cent, reposition a product to make it more appealing to upmarket buyers, introduce a direct marketing function via the Internet, or launch a new product? Maybe the plan will combine several products into a single family brand and build awareness of this brand through print and radio advertising, which will gain market share from several competitors and cut the costs of marketing by eliminating inefficiencies in coupon processing, media buying, and sales force management. Address these sorts of topics in the objectives section of the plan. These points give the plan its focus.

If you write clear, compelling objectives, you'll never get too confused about what to write in other sections – when in doubt, you can always look back at these objectives and remind yourself what you're trying to accomplish and why.

Try to write this part of the plan early, but keep in mind that you'll rewrite it often as you gather more information and do more thinking. Objectives are such a key foundation for the rest of the plan that you can't ever stop thinking about them. However, for all their importance, objectives don't need a lot of words – half a page to two pages, at most. (Paradoxically, we have to tell you more about these short upfront sections than about the longer, detail-orientated sections in the back because planners find the short sections more conceptually challenging.)

Preparing a Situation Analysis

The context is different for every marketing plan. A *situation analysis* examines the context, looking at trends, customer preferences, competitor strengths and weaknesses, and anything else that may impact sales. The question your situation analysis must answer is, 'What's happening?' The answer to this question can take many forms, so we can't give you an easy formula for preparing the situation analysis. You should analyse the most important market changes to your company – these changes can be the sources of problems or opportunities.

But what most important changes have occurred since you last examined the situation? The answer depends on the situation. See the difficulty? Yet somehow you have to gain enough insight into what's happening to see the problems and opportunities clearly.

Seeing trends more clearly than others do

Your goal is to see the changes more clearly than the competition. Why? Because if your situation analysis isn't as accurate as the competition's, you'll lose market share to them. If your analysis is about the same as your competition's, then you may hold even. Only if your situation analysis is better than your rivals' can you gain market share on the competition.

What you want from your situation analysis is

- ✔ **Information parity:** When you know as much as your leading competitors know. If you don't do enough research and analysis, your competitors will have an information advantage. Therefore, you need to gain enough insight to put you on a level playing field with your competitors. (That includes knowing about any major plans they may have. Collect rumours about new products, new people, and so on. At a minimum, do a weekly search on a Web-based search engine for any news about them.)

- ✔ **Information advantage in specific areas:** Insight into the market that your competitors don't have. Information advantage puts you on the uphill side of an uneven playing field and that's an awfully good place from which to design and launch a marketing campaign. Look for new fashions, new technologies, new ways to segment the market – anything that you can use to change the rules of the game even slightly in your favour.

Most marketing plans and planners don't think about their situation analysis in this way. We're telling you one of our best-kept secrets because we don't want you to waste time on the typical *pro forma* situation analysis, in which the marketer rounds up the usual suspects and parades dull information in front of them without gaining an advantage from it. That approach, although common, does nothing to make the plan a winner.

Using a structured approach to competitor analysis

What kinds of information can you collect about your competitors? You can gather and analyse examples of competitors' marketing communications. You may have (or be able to gather) some customer opinions from surveys or informal chats. You can group the information you get from customers into useful lists, like discovering the three most appealing and least appealing things about each competitor. You can also probably get some information about how your competitors distribute and sell, where they are (and aren't) located or distributed, who their key decision-makers are, who their biggest and/or most loyal customers are, and even (perhaps) how much they sell. Gather any available data on all-important competitors and organise the information into a table for easy analysis.

Building a competitor analysis table

Here's an example of a format for a generic Competitor Analysis Table. Make entries on the following rows in columns labelled for Competitor #1, Competitor #2, Competitor #3, and so on:

- **Company.** Describe how the market perceives it and its key product.

- **Key personnel.** Who are the managers, and how many employees do they have in total?

- **Financial.** Who owns it, how strong is its *cash position* (does it have spending power or is it struggling to pay its bills), what were its sales in the last two years?

- **Sales, distribution, and pricing.** Describe its primary sales channel, discount/pricing structure, and market share estimate.

- **Product/service analysis.** What are the strengths and weaknesses of its product or service?

- **Scaled assessment of product/service.** Explore relevant subjects like market acceptance, quality of packaging, ads, and so on. Assign a score of between 1 and 5 (with 5 being the strongest) for each characteristic you evaluate. Then add the scores for each competitor's row to see which seems strongest, overall.

✔ **Comparing yourself to competitor ratings.** If you rate yourself on these attributes, too, how do you compare? Are you stronger? If not, you can include increasing your competitive strength as one of your plan's strategic objectives.

Explaining Your Marketing Strategy

Many plans use this section to get specific about the objectives by explaining how your company will accomplish them. Some writers find this task easy, but others keep getting confused about the distinction between an objective and a strategy. The objective simply states something your business hopes to accomplish in the next year. The strategy emphasises the big-picture approach to accomplishing that objective, giving some good pointers as to what road you'll take.

A strategy sounds like this: Introduce hot new products and promote our brand name with an emphasis on high quality components, in order to increase our market share by 2 points.

Combining strategies and objectives

Some people view the difference between objectives and strategies as a pretty fine line. If you're comfortable with the distinction, write a separate *Strategy* section. If you're not sure about the difference, combine this section with the objectives section and title it *Objectives and Strategies*; what you call the points doesn't matter, as long as they're good.

Your strategies accomplish your objectives through the tactics of your marketing plan. The plan explains how your tactics use your strategies to accomplish your objectives.

Giving your strategy common sense

This advice is tough to realise. Unlike a mathematical formula or a spreadsheet column, you don't have a simple method to check a marketing strategy to make sure that it really adds up. But you can subject a marketing strategy to common sense and make sure that it has no obvious flaws – as outlined in the following sections.

Strategy fails to reflect limitations in your resources

Don't pull a Napoleon. If you're currently the tenth-largest competitor, don't write a plan to become the number one largest by the end of the year simply based on designing all your ads and mailings to claim you're the best. Make sure that your strategy is achievable. Would the average person agree that your strategy sounds attainable with a little hard work? (If you're not sure, find some average people and ask them.) And do you have enough resources to execute the strategy in the available time?

Strategy demands huge changes in customer behaviour

You can move people and businesses only so far with marketing. If you plan to get employers to give their employees every other Friday off so those employees can attend special workshops your firm sponsors, well, we hope you have a back-up plan. Employers don't give employees a lot of extra time off, no matter how compelling your sales pitch or brochure may be. The same is true of consumer marketing. You simply cannot change strongly held public attitudes without awfully good new evidence.

A competitor is already doing the strategy

This assumption is a surprisingly common error. To avoid this mistake, include a summary of each competitor's strategy in the *Strategy* section of your plan. Add a note explaining how your strategy differs from each of them. If you're marketing a computer installation and repair service in the Liverpool area, you really need to know how your strategy differs from the multiple competitors also trying to secure big corporate contracts in that area. Do you specialise in certain types of equipment that others don't? Do you emphasise speed of repair service? Are you the only vendor who distributes and supports CAD/CAM equipment from a leading maker? You need a distinctive strategy to power your plan. You don't want to be a me-too competitor.

Strategy requires you to know too much that you don't already know

You can't use some brilliant strategies for your business because they would require you to do too many things you don't know anything about. For example, there is a growing need for computer skills training, but if your business is in selling and servicing computer equipment, that doesn't automatically give you experience in developing, selling, or delivering computer courses. Strategies that involve doing a lot of things you have little or no expertise in are really start-up strategies, not marketing strategies. If you want to put a minority of your resources into trying to start a new business unit, go ahead. But don't put your entire marketing plan at risk by basing it on a strategy that takes you into unfamiliar waters.

Summarising Your Marketing Mix

Your *marketing mix* is the combination of marketing activities you use to influence a targeted group of customers to purchase a specific product or line of products. Creating an integrated and coherent marketing mix starts, in our view, with an analysis of your *touchpoints* – in other words, how your organisation can influence customer purchases. And the creative process ends with some decisions about how to use these touchpoints. Usually you can come up with tactics in all seven of the marketing Ps: Product, price, place (or distribution), promotions, people, process, and physical presence.

Prioritising your touchpoints and determining cost

Prioritise by picking a few primary touchpoints – ones that will dominate your marketing for the coming planning period. This approach concentrates your resources, giving you more leverage with certain components of the mix. Make the choice carefully; try to pick no more than three main activities to take the lead. Use the (usually many) other touchpoints in secondary roles to support your primary points. Now you begin to develop specific plans for each, consulting later chapters in this book as needed to clarify how to use your various marketing components.

Say that you're considering using print ads in trade magazines to let retail store buyers know about your hot new line of products and the in-store display options you have for them. That's great, but now you need to get specific. You need to pick some magazines. (Call their ad departments for details on their demographics and their prices.) You also need to decide how many of what sort of ads you'll run, and then price out this advertising campaign.

Do the same analysis for each of the items on your list of marketing components. Work your way through the details until you have an initial cost figure for what you want to do with each component. Total these costs and see if the end result seems realistic. Is the total cost too big a share of your projected sales? Or (if you're in a larger business), is your estimate higher than the boss says the budget can go? If so, adjust and try again. After a while, you get a budget that looks acceptable on the bottom line and also makes sense from a practical perspective.

A spreadsheet greatly helps this process. Just build formulas that add the costs to reach subtotals and a grand total, and then subtract the grand total from the projected sales figure to get a bottom line for your campaign. Figure 3-1 shows the format for a very simple spreadsheet that gives a quick and accurate marketing campaign overview for a small business. In this figure, you can see what a campaign looks like for a company that wholesales products to gift shops around the UK. This company uses personal selling, telemarketing, and print advertising as its primary marketing components. The company also budgets some money in this period to finish developing and begin introducing a new line of products.

This company's secondary influence points don't use much of the marketing budget when compared with the primary influence points. But the secondary influence points are important, too. A new Web page is expected to handle a majority of customer enquiries and act as a virtual catalogue, permitting the company to cut back on its catalogue printing and postage costs. Also, the company plans to introduce a new line of floor displays for use at point of purchase by selected retailers. Marketers expect this display unit, combined with improved see-through packaging, to increase turnover of the company's products in retail stores.

Overview of Campaign to Target Retail Store Buyers	
Components	**Direct Marketing Costs (£)**
Primary influence points:	
– Sales calls	£265,100
– Telemarketing	162,300
– Ads in trade magazines	650,000
– New product line development	100,000
	Subtotal: £1,177,400
Secondary influence points:	
– Quantity discounts	£45,000
– Point-of-purchase displays	73,500
– New Web page with online catalogue	15,000
– Printed catalogue	30,500
– PR	22,000
– Packaging redesign	9,200
	Subtotal: £195,200
Projected Sales from This Programme	£13,676,470
Minus Campaign Costs	– 1,372,600
Net Sales from This Marketing Campaign	**£12,303,870**

Figure 3-1:
A campaign budget, prepared on a spreadsheet.

Marketing plans for multiple groups

If your marketing plan covers multiple groups of customers, you need to include multiple spreadsheets (such as the one in Figure 3-1) because each group of customers will need a different marketing mix.

For example, the company whose wholesale marketing campaign you see in Figure 3-1 sells to gift shops. But the company also does some business with stationery shops. And even though the same salespeople call on both, each of these customers has different products and promotions. They buy from different catalogues. They don't use the same kinds of displays. They read different trade magazines. Consequently, the company has to develop a separate marketing campaign for each customer, allocating any overlapping expenses appropriately. (For example, if you make two-thirds of your sales calls to gift shops, then the sales calls expense for the gift shop campaign should be two-thirds of the total sales budget.)

Exploring Your Marketing Components

In this part of your plan, you need to explain the details of how you plan to use each component of your marketing mix. Devote a section to each component, which means that this part of your plan may be quite lengthy (give it as many pages as you need to lay out the necessary facts). The more of your thinking you get on paper, the easier implementing the plan will be later – as will rewriting the plan next year.

At a minimum, this part of the plan should have sections covering the *seven Ps* – the product, pricing, place (or distribution), promotion, people, process, and physical presence. But more likely, you'll want to break these categories down into more specific areas.

Don't bother going into detail in your marketing plan on components that you cannot alter. Sometimes, the person writing the marketing plan can't change pricing policy, order up a new product line, or dictate a shift in distribution strategy. Explore your boundaries and even try to stretch them, but you need to admit they exist or your plan can't be practical. If you can only control promotion, then this section of the plan should concentrate on the ways that you'll promote the product – in which case, never mind the other Ps. Acknowledge in writing any issues or challenges you have to cope with, given that you can't change other factors. Now write a plan that does everything you can reasonably do given your constraints. (A section called *Constraints* ought to go into the *Situation analysis* if your company has such constraints.)

Managing Your Marketing

The main purpose of the management section of the plan is simply to make sure that enough warm bodies are in the right places at the right times to get the work done. The management section summarises the main activities that you, your employees, or your employer must perform in order to implement the components of your marketing mix. The section then assigns these activities to individuals, justifying the assignments by considering issues such as an individual's capabilities, capacities, and how the company will supervise and control that individual.

Sometimes this section gets more sophisticated by addressing management issues, like how to make the sales force more productive or whether to decentralise the marketing function. If you have salespeople or distributors, develop plans for organising, motivating, tracking, and controlling them. Also develop a plan for them to use in generating, allocating, and tracking sales leads. Start these subsections by describing the current approach, and do a strengths/weaknesses analysis of that approach, using input from the salespeople, reps, or distributors in question. End by describing any incremental changes/improvements you can think to make.

Make sure that you've run your ideas by the people in question *first* and received their input. Don't surprise your salespeople, sales reps, or distributors with new systems or methods. If you do, these people will probably resist the changes, and sales will slow down. So schmooze and share, persuade and propose, and enable them to feel involved in the planning process. People execute sales plans well only if they understand and believe in those plans.

Projecting Expenses and Revenues

Now you need to put on your accounting and project management hats. (Neither hat fits very well, perhaps, but try to bear them for a day or two.) You need these hats to

- ✔ Estimate future sales, in units and by value, for each product in your plan.

- ✔ Justify these estimates and, if they're hard to justify, create worst-case versions, too.

- ✔ Draw a timeline showing when your marketing incurs costs and when each component begins and ends. (Doing so helps with the preceding section and also prepares you for the unpleasant task of designing a monthly marketing budget.)

✔ Write a monthly marketing budget that lists all the estimated costs of your activity for each month of the coming year and breaks down sales by product or territory and by month.

If you're a start-up or small business, we highly recommend doing all your projections on a *cash basis*. In other words, put the payment for your year's supply of brochures in the month in which the printer wants the money, instead of allocating that cost across 12 months. Also factor in the wait time for collecting your sales revenues. If collections take 30 days, show money coming in during December from November's sales, and don't count any December sales for this year's plan. A cash basis may upset accountants, who like to do things on an accrual basis but cash-based accounting keeps small businesses alive. You want a positive cash balance (or at least to break even) on the bottom line during every month of your plan.

If your cash-based projection shows a loss some months, fiddle with the plan to eliminate that loss (or arrange to borrow money to cover the gap). Sometimes a careful cash-flow analysis of a plan leads to changes in underlying strategy. One business-to-business company adopted as its primary marketing objective the goal of getting more customers to pay with credit cards instead of on invoices. The company's business customers co-operated, and average collection time shortened from 45 days to under 10, greatly improving the cash flow and thus the spending power and profitability of the business.

Several helpful techniques are available for projecting sales, such as build-up forecasts, indicator forecasts, and time-period forecasts. Choose the most appropriate technique for your business based on the reviews in this section. If you're feeling nervous, just use the technique that gives you the most conservative projection. Here's a common way to play it safe: Use several of the techniques and average their results.

Build-up forecasts

These predictions go from the specific to the general, or from the bottom up. If you have sales reps or salespeople, ask each one to project the next period's sales for their territories and justify their projections based on what changes in the situation they anticipate. Then aggregate all the sales force's forecasts to obtain an overall figure.

If you have few enough customers that you can project per-customer purchases, build up your forecast this way. You may want to work from reasonable estimates of the amount of sales you can expect from each shop carrying your products or from each thousand catalogues sent out. Whatever the basic building blocks of your marketing, start with an estimate for each element and then add these estimates up.

Indicator forecasts

This method links your forecast to economic indicators that ought to vary with sales. For example, if you're in the construction business, you find that past sales for your industry correlate with *GDP* (gross domestic product, or national output) growth. So you can adjust your sales forecast up or down depending upon whether experts expect the economy to grow rapidly or slowly in the next year.

Multiple scenario forecasts

You base these forecasts on what-if stories. They start with a straight-line forecast in which you assume that your sales will grow by the same percentage next year as they did last year. Then you make up what-if stories and project their impact on your plan to create a variety of alternative projections.

You may try the following scenarios if they're relevant to your situation:

- What if a competitor introduces a technological breakthrough?
- What if your company acquires a competitor?
- What if the government deregulates/regulates your industry?
- What if a leading competitor fails?
- What if your company has financial problems and has to lay off some of your sales and marketing people?
- What if your company doubles its ad spending?

For each scenario, think about how customer demand may change. Also consider how your marketing would need to change in order to best suit the situation. Then make an appropriate sales projection. For example, if a competitor introduced a technological breakthrough, you may guess that your sales would fall 25 per cent short of your straight-line projection.

The trouble with multiple scenario analysis is that . . . well, it gives you multiple scenarios. Your boss (if you have one) wants a single sales projection, a one-liner at the top of your marketing budget. One way to turn all those options into one number or series of numbers is to just pick the option that seems most likely to you. That's not a very satisfying method if you aren't at all sure which option, if any, will come true. So another method involves taking all the options that seem even remotely possible, assigning each a probability of occurring in the next year, multiplying each by its probability, and then averaging them all to get a single number.

For example, the Cautious Scenario projection estimates £5 million, and the Optimistic Scenario projection estimates £10 million. The probability of Cautious Scenario occurring is 15 per cent, and the probability of Optimistic Scenario occurring is 85 per cent. So you find the sales projection with this formula: $[(£5,000,000 \times 0.15) + (£10,000,000 \times 0.85)] \div 2 = £4,630,000$.

Time-period projections

To use this method, work by week or month, estimating the size of sales in each time period, and then add these estimates for the entire year. This approach helps you when your marketing activity or the market isn't constant across the entire year. Ski resorts use this method because they get certain types of revenues only at certain times of the year. And marketers who plan to introduce new products during the year or to use heavy advertising in one or two *pulses* (concentrated time periods) also use this method because their sales go up significantly during those periods. Entrepreneurs, small businesses, and any others on a tight cash-flow lead need to use this method because you get a good idea of what cash will be flowing in by week or month. An annual sales figure doesn't tell you enough about when the money comes in to know whether you'll be short of cash in specific periods during the year.

Creating Your Controls

This section is the last and shortest of your plan – but in many ways, it's the most important. This section allows you and others to track performance.

Identify some performance benchmarks and state them clearly in the plan. For example:

- ✔ All sales territories should be using the new catalogues and sales scripts by 1 June.

- ✔ Revenues should grow to £75,000 per month by the end of the first quarter if the promotional campaign works according to plan.

These statements give you (and, unfortunately, your employers or investors) easy ways to monitor performance as you implement the marketing plan. Without these targets, nobody has control over the plan; nobody can tell whether or how well the plan is working. With these statements, you can identify unexpected results or delays quickly – in time for appropriate responses if you have designed these controls properly.

A good marketing plan gives you focus, a sense of direction and increases your likelihood to succeed, but writing a good one takes time and many businesses don't have a lot of that to spare. A sensible rule is to spend time on your marketing plan, but not so much that you don't have a chance to look up and see whether the market has changed since you started writing it. If the plan you wrote at the start of the year is no longer relevant because business conditions have changed quickly then tear it up and start again – don't stick rigidly to it.

Chapter 4

Brochures, Press Ads, and Print

· ·

In This Chapter

▶ Recognising the elements of printed advertising

▶ Understanding design and layout issues

▶ Designing with type

▶ Designing the simplest print product of all – brochures

▶ Placing and testing your print ad

· ·

*M*ost marketers budget more for print advertising than any other type – the exception being the major national or multinational brands that market largely on television. But for most local and regional advertising, print probably provides the most flexible and effective all-around advertising medium.

Print advertising also integrates well with many other marketing media. You can use written brochures and other sales support materials (which have many design elements in common with print advertising) to support personal selling or telemarketing. Similarly, a print ad in a magazine can generate leads for direct marketing. Print ads also work well to announce sales promotions or distribute coupons.

And anyone with a basic computer and inkjet printer can now set up shop and create his or her own fliers, brochures, business cards, and ad layouts. In fact, Microsoft Word includes a number of excellent templates that simplify layout and allow you to bang out a new brochure or other printed marketing piece in as little as an hour. Print advertising and print-based marketing are the backbone of most marketing campaigns, even today in this high-tech world.

Designing Printed Marketing Materials

Many marketers start with their printed marketing materials (such as ads, brochures, or downloadable PDF-format product literature on their Web sites), and then work outward from there to incorporate the appeal and design concepts from their printed materials or ads into other forms of marketing. (A common look and feel should unite your print ads, brochures, and Web site, for example.)

Brochures, *tear sheets* (one-page, catalogue-style descriptions of products), posters for outdoor advertising, direct mail letters, and catalogues all share the basic elements of good print advertising: Good copy and visuals, plus eye-catching headlines. Therefore, all good marketers need mastery of print advertising as an essential part of their knowledge base. This section covers the essentials.

When designing anything in print, remember this: Your ad's purpose is to stimulate a sale. Think ahead to that goal. What will people see when they make that purchase? If your product sells in shops, create signs, packaging, displays, or coupons that echo the ad's theme and remind the buyer of that theme. If the sale occurs on your Web site, adjust the appearance of the site to be consistent with the ad. And if you make the sale in person, supply the salespeople or distributors with catalogues, order forms, PowerPoint presentations, or brochures (see the 'Producing Brochures, Fliers, and More' section later in this chapter) that are consistent with your design, to remind them of the ad that began the sales process. Roll the ad's design forward to the point of purchase and beyond if you plan follow-up mailings, a reply-paid warranty card, or other post-purchase contacts.

Dissecting the anatomy of printed materials

Before you can create great printed marketing materials, you need to dissect an ad, brochure, tear sheet, or similar printed marketing matter and identify its parts. Inside most printed marketing materials you'll find parts and each part has a special name:

- **Headline:** The large-print words that first attract the eye, usually at the top of the page.
- **Subhead:** The optional addition to the headline to provide more detail, also in large (but not quite as large) print.

✔ **Copy or body copy:** The main text, set in a readable size.

✔ **Visual:** An illustration that makes a visual statement. This image may be the main focus of the ad or other printed material (especially when you've designed an ad to show readers your product), or it may be secondary to the copy. Such an image is also optional. After all, most classified ads use no visuals at all, yet classifieds are generally more effective than display ads for the simple reason that people make a point to look for classified ads (instead of making a point to avoid them, as many people do with displays!).

✔ **Caption:** Copy attached to the visual to explain or discuss that visual. You usually place a caption beneath the visual, but you can put it on any side or even within or on the visual.

✔ **Logo:** A unique design that represents the brand or company (like Nike's swoosh). Register logos as trademarks.

✔ **Signature:** The company's trademarked version of its name. Often, advertisers use a logo design that features a brand name in a distinctive font and style. The signature is a written equivalent to the logo's visual identity. Here's how a furniture maker called Heritage Colonial Furniture may do it:

HERITAGE
Colonial Furniture®

✔ **Slogan:** An optional element consisting of a (hopefully) short phrase evoking the spirit or personality of the brand. In all its print ads, Renault uses the slogan 'Createur D'Automobiles'. Of course, everyone knows that Renault creates automobiles, but this slogan, which emphasises the company's Frenchness, works in tandem with the advertising theme for all its cars and is as much a part of Renault's identity as the diamond logo and the signature. As another example, a furniture maker called Heritage Colonial may use as its slogan, 'Bringing the elegance and quality of early antiques to the modern home.'

Figure 4-1 shows each of these elements in a rough design for a print ad (a brochure's layout is a bit more complicated and is covered at the end of this chapter). We use generic terms in place of actual parts of an ad ('headline' for the headline, for example) so that you can easily see all the elements in action. This fairly simple palette for a print ad design allows you endless variation and creativity. You can say or show anything, and you can do so in many different ways. (And you can use this layout for a one-page marketing sheet to include in folders or as handouts at trade shows even if you aren't buying space to run the ad in a magazine or newspaper.)

HEADLINE!
SUBHEADS

VIS-UAL

copy copy
copy copy
copy copy
copy copy
copy copy

CAPTION ...

Trade Mark

Signature ™
our slogan is
a slogan!

Figure 4-1:
The
elements of
a print ad.

Putting the parts together:
Design and layout

Design refers to the look, feel, and style of your ad or other printed marketing
materials. Design is an aesthetic concept and, thus, hard to put into precise

terms. But design is vitally important: It has to take the basic appeal of your product and make that appeal work visually on paper. Specifically, the design needs to overcome the marketer's constant problem: Nobody cares about your advertising. So the design must somehow reach out to readers, grab their attention, and hold it long enough to communicate the appeal of the product you're advertising and attach that appeal to the brand name in the readers' memories.

A memorable photograph is often the easiest way to grab the reader. And if you don't have a better idea, use a photo of an interesting face or of a child, as long as you can make the image relevant in some way to your product. Beautiful nature scenes are also good eye-catchers.

Great advertising has to rise off the page, reach out, and grab you by the eye-balls. In the cluttered world of modern print-based marketing, this design goal is the only one that really works. So we want you to tape up a selection of ads from the same publication(s) yours will go in (or use samples of competitor brochures or catalogue sheets or whatever exactly it is you will be designing in print). Put a draft of your design up along with these benchmarks. Step back – a long way back. Now, does your ad grab the eye more than all the others? If not . . . back to the drawing board!

Understanding the stages in design

Designers often experiment with numerous layouts for their print ads or other printed materials before selecting one for formal development. We strongly recommend that you do the same – or insist that your designer or agency do the same. The more layouts you look at, the more likely you are to get an original idea that has eye-grabbing power. But whether you design your own print materials or have experts do the work for you, you want to be familiar with the design stages:

- ✔ **Step 1. Thumbnails:** The rough sketches designers use to describe layout concepts are called *thumbnails.* They're usually small, quick sketches in pen or pencil. You can also use professional design and layout packages like Quark XPress or InDesign to create thumbnails.

- ✔ **Step 2. Roughs:** Designers then develop thumbnails with promise into *roughs,* full-size sketches with headlines and subheads drawn carefully enough to give the feel of a particular font and *style* (the appearance of the printed letters). Roughs also have sketches for the illustrations. The designers suggest body copy using lines (or nonsense characters, if the designer does the rough using a computer).

Are you using an ad agency or design firm to develop your print ads or other printed marketing materials? Sometimes clients of ad agencies insist on seeing designs in the rough stage, to avoid the expense of having those designs developed more fully before presentation. We recommend that you ask to see rough versions of your designs, too, even if your agency hesitates to show you its work in unfinished form. After the agency realises that you appreciate the design process and don't criticise the roughs simply because they're rough, you can give the agency more guidance and help during the design process.

✔ **Step 3. Comprehensive layout:** After a rough passes muster, designers develop that rough into a *comp* (short for *comprehensive layout*). A comp should look pretty much like a final version of the design, although designers produce a comp on a one-time basis, so the comp may use paste-ups in place of the intended photos, colour photocopies, typeset copy, and headlines. Designers used to assemble comps by hand, but now many designers and agencies do their comps on computer. A high-end PC and colour printer can produce something that looks almost like the final printed version of a four-colour ad or other printed marketing material. Designers refer to a computer-made comp as a *full-colour proof*.

✔ **Step 4. Dummy:** A *dummy* is a form of comp that simulates the feel – as well as the look – of the final design. (Every design should have a feel or personality of its own, just as products should have a personality. Often you can create the best personality by simply carrying over the personality you've created for the product. Consistency helps.) Dummies are especially important for brochures or special inserts to magazines, where the designer often specifies special paper and folds. By doing a dummy comp, you can evaluate the feel of the design while you're evaluating its appearance.

Designing and submitting your ads the old-fashioned way

The traditional way to submit a design to a printing firm is to generate what printers call *camera-ready artwork*, a version of the design suitable for the printer to photograph with a large-scale production camera in order to generate *colour keys* (to convert colours to specific inks) and *films*, clear sheets for each layer of colour to be printed. You (or the designer) produce this camera-ready art by making a *mechanical* or *paste-up*, in which you paste typeset copy, visuals, and all the other elements of the design onto a foam-core board, using a hot wax machine.

A hot wax machine heats wax and spreads it on a roller so that you can roll a thin layer of warm wax onto the back of each element. The wax sticks each piece neatly to the board, allowing those pieces to be peeled off easily, in case you want to reposition anything. When you have everything the way you want it, you send the artwork off to your printer.

Designing and submitting your ads on a computer

You can still work with a glue stick or hot wax and scissors to do rough layouts if you want to, but the modern, and more popular, way to design and submit your ad to a printer is to do so electronically. If you're quick and able on a computer and like to work in design and layout programs (such as Adobe InDesign or Quark XPress), you can do the same kind of creative rough designing simply by searching for images on the Web. (To find an image, try specifying an image search in Google, but remember not to use copyrighted images in your final design without permission or payment.) Copy the images onto your computer, and you can click and drag them into different programs and pages.

We recommend that you invest a bit of time and effort in honing these computer-based design techniques. Look up the latest *For Dummies* books on how to use Quark XPress, Microsoft Publisher, or any other design and layout program of your choice, or just work in Word, which is pretty impressive in its latest incarnations as a basic design program itself. Also take a look at the growing number of great-looking ad templates you can purchase on CD or via e-mail, and then adapt them in any of the common graphic design programs. As an example, see many options at www.stocklayouts.com.

When your preliminary design is ready for the printer, you (or the ad agency) can send the design over the Web using desktop publishing software that the printing firm accepts. You can even do the colour separations for four-colour work on your PC and send those colour separations, too. (Ask the printer for instructions to make sure that you submit the design in a format that the printer's system can use.) The printer then makes plates for printing the design straight from the file that you've e-mailed to them. *(Plates* are metal or plastic sheets with your design on them – the printer applies the ink to the plates when the printing press does its thing.)

Until recently, electronic submission to printing firms generally had to be done from a professional software package like Quark XPress, but increasingly, printers are accepting Word files or PDF files generated by Acrobat (we prefer this route, because it reduces the chances of incompatibility problems). And if you're designing in a recent version of Word, you'll find that creating a PDF file can be done right out of your program, because Acrobat is now built in.

Finding your font

A *font* is a particular design's attributes for the *characters* (letters, numbers, and symbols) used in printing your design. *Typeface* refers only to the distinctive design of the letters (Times New Roman, for example). Font, on the other hand, actually refers to one particular size and style of a typeface design (such as 10-point, bold, Times New Roman).

The right font for any job is the one that makes your text easily readable and that harmonises with the overall design most effectively. For a headline, the font also needs to grab the reader's attention. The body copy doesn't have to grab attention in the same way – in fact, if it does, the copy often loses readability. For example, a *reverse font* (light or white on dark) may be just the thing for a bold headline, but if you use it in the body copy, too, nobody reads your copy because it's just too hard on the eye to read.

Choosing a typeface

What sort of typeface do you want? You have an amazing number of choices because designers have been developing typefaces for as long as printing presses have existed. (Just click Format⇨Font in Microsoft Word to see an assortment of the more popular typefaces.)

A clean, sparse design, with a lot of white space on the page and stark contrasts in the artwork, deserves the clean lines of a *sans serif typeface* – meaning one that doesn't have any decorative *serifs* (those little bars or flourishes at the ends of the main lines in a character). The most popular body-copy fonts without serifs are Helvetica, Arial, Univers, and Avant Garde. Figure 4-2 shows some fonts with and without serifs.

Figure 4-2:
Fonts with and without serifs.

But a richly decorative, old-fashioned sort of design needs a more decorative and traditional serif typeface, like Century or Times New Roman. The most popular body-copy fonts with serifs include Garamond, Melior, Century, Times New Roman, and Caledonia.

Table 4-1 shows an assortment of typeface choices, in which you can compare the clean lines of Helvetica, Avant Garde, and Arial with the more decorative designs of Century, Garamond, and Times New Roman.

Table 4-1	Popular Fonts for Ads
Sans Serif	*Serif*
Helvetica	Century
Arial	Garamond
Univers	Melior
Avant Garde	Times New Roman

In tests, Helvetica and Century generally top the lists as most readable, so start with one of these typefaces for your body copy; only change the font if it doesn't seem to work. Also, research shows that people read lowercase letters about 13 per cent faster than uppercase letters, so avoid long stretches of copy set in all capital letters. People also read most easily when letters are dark and contrast strongly with their background. Thus, black 14-point Helvetica on white is probably the most readable font specification for the body copy of an ad (or other printed marketing materials), even if the combination does seem dull to a sophisticated designer.

Generalising about the best kind of headline typeface is no easy task because designers play around with headlines to a greater extent than they do with body copy. But as a general rule, you can use Helvetica for the headline when you use Century for the body, and vice versa. Or you can just use a bolder, larger version of the body copy font for your headline. You can also reverse a larger, bold version of your type onto a black background for the headline. Use anything to make the headline grab the reader's attention, stand out from the body copy, and ultimately lead vision and curiosity into the body copy's text. (Remember to keep the headline readable. Nothing too fancy, please.)

Sometimes the designer combines body copy of a decorative typeface, one with serifs, like Times New Roman, with headers of a sans serif typeface, like Helvetica. The contrast between the clean lines of the large-sized header and the more decorative characters of the smaller body copy pleases the eye and tends to draw the reader from header to body copy. This book uses that technique. Compare the sans serif bold characters of this chapter's title with the more delicate and decorative characters in which the publishers set the text for a good example of this design concept in action.

Making style choices within the typeface

Any typeface gives the user many choices, and so selecting the typeface is just the beginning of the project when you design your print. How big should the characters be? Do you want to use the standard version of the typeface, a lighter version, a **bold** (or darker) version, or an *italic* version (one that leans to the right, like the letters spelling *italic*)? The process is easier than it sounds. Really! Just look at samples of some standard point sizes (12- and 14-point text for the body copy, for example, and 24-, 36-, and 48-point for the headlines). Many designers make their choice by eye, looking for an easy-to-read size that isn't so large that it causes the words or sentences to break up into too many fragments across the page – but not so small that it gives the reader too many words per line. Keep readability in mind as the goal.

Figure 4-3 shows a variety of size and style choices for the Helvetica typeface. As you can see, you have access to a wonderful range of options, even within this one popular design.

Keep in mind that you can change just about any aspect of type. You can alter the distance between lines – called the *leading* – or you can squeeze characters together or stretch them apart to make a word fit a space. Assume that anything is possible, and ask your printer, or consult the manual of your desktop publishing or word-processing software, to find out how to make a change.

Figure 4-3: Some of the many choices that the Helvetica typeface offers designers.

Helvetica Light 14 point

Helvetica Italic 14 point

Helvetica Bold 14 point

Helvetica Regular 14 point

Helvetica Regular 24 point

Helvetica Regular Condensed 14 point

Helvetica Bold Outline 24 point

While anything is possible, be warned that your customers' eyes read type quite conservatively. Although most of us know little about the design of typefaces, we find traditional designs instinctively appealing. The spacing of characters and lines, the balance and flow of individual characters – all these familiar typeface considerations please the eye and make reading easy and pleasurable. So, although you should know that you can change anything and everything, you must also know that too many changes may reduce your design's readability. Figure 4-4 shows the same ad laid out twice – once in an eye-pleasing way and once in a disastrous way.

Don't just play with type for the sake of playing (as the designer did in the left-hand version of the classified ad in Figure 4-4). Stick with popular fonts, in popular sizes, except where you have to solve a problem or you want to make a special point. The advent of desktop publishing has led to a horrifying generation of advertisements in which dozens of fonts dance across the page, bolds and italics fight each other for attention, and the design of the words becomes a barrier to reading, rather than an aid.

Book V

Bigging
Up Your
Business

Figure 4-4: Which copy would you rather read?

WHEN LIFE GIVES YOU LEMONS...

What should you do? Juggle them? Make lemonade? Open a farm stand? Or give up and go home to Momma?

WHO KNOWS? It's often hard to come to grips with pressing personal or career problems. Sometimes it's hardest to see your **own** problems clearly. Fortunately, JEN KNOWS. Jen Fredrics has twenty years of counseling experience, a master's in social work, and a busy practice in personal problem solving. Call her today to find out how to turn your problems into opportunities.

And next time, when life gives you lemons, you'll know just what to make. An appointment.

WHEN LIFE GIVES YOU LEMONS...

What should you do? Juggle them? Make lemonade? Open a farm stand? Or give up and go home to Momma?

WHO KNOWS? It's often hard to come to grips with pressing personal or career problems. Sometimes it's hardest to see your own problems clearly. Fortunately, JEN KNOWS. Jen Fredrics has twenty years of counseling experience, a master's in social work, and a busy practice in personal problem solving. Call her today to find out how to turn your problems into opportunities.

And next time, when life gives you lemons, you'll know just what to make. An appointment.

Choosing a point size

When designers and printers talk about *point sizes*, they're referring to a traditional measure of the height of the letters (based on the highest and lowest parts of the biggest letters). One *point* equals about ½₂ of an inch, so a 10-point type is ¹⁰⁄₇₂ of an inch high, at the most.

Personally, we don't really care – we've never measured a character with a ruler. We just know that if the letters seem too small for easy reading, then we need to bump the typeface up a couple of points. Ten-point type is too small for most body copy, but you may want to use that size if you have to squeeze several words into a small space. (But why do that? You're usually better off editing your body copy and then bumping up the font size to make it more readable!) Your eye can't distinguish easily between fonts that are only one or two sizes apart, so specify a larger jump than that to distinguish between body copy and subhead, or subhead and headline.

Producing Brochures, Fliers, and More

You can get your print design out to the public in an easy and inexpensive way, using brochures, fliers, posters, and many other forms – your imagination is the only limit to what you can do with a good design for all your printed materials. Your word-processing or graphics software, a good inkjet or laser printer, and the help of your local photocopy or print shop (which also has folding machines) allows you to design and produce brochures quite easily, and also come up with many other forms of printed marketing materials. In this section, however, we focus largely on a basic brochure, because it's easy, a business staple, and effective at marketing your company.

You can also do small runs (100 or less) straight from a colour printer. Buy matte or glossy brochure paper designed for your brand of printer, and simply select the appropriate paper type in the print dialog box. Today's inexpensive inkjet printers can produce stunning brochures. But you have to fold these brochures yourself, and the ink cartridges aren't cheap. So print as needed rather than inventory a large number of brochures. Or try contacting your local copy shop. Kall Kwik and many other copy shops now accept e-mailed copies of files, and can produce short runs of your brochures, pamphlets, catalogue sheets, or other printed materials on their colour copiers directly from your file.

Many brochures foolishly waste money because they don't accomplish any specific marketing goals; they just look pretty, at best. To avoid a pretty, but pointless, brochure that doesn't achieve a sales goal, make sure that you know:

✔ Who will read the brochure

✔ How they will get the brochure

✔ What they should discover and do from reading the brochure

These three questions focus your brochure design and make it useful to your marketing.

Marketers often order a brochure without a clear idea of what purpose the brochure should serve. They just think a brochure is a good idea: 'Oh, we need them to, you know, put in the envelope along with a letter, or, um, for our salespeople to keep in the boots of their cars, or maybe we'll send some out to our mailing list, or give them away at the next trade show.'

With this many possibilities, the brochure can't be properly suited to any single use. The brochure becomes a dull, vague scrap of paper that just talks about the company or product but doesn't hit readers over the head with any particular appeal and call to action.

Listing your top three uses

Define up to three specific uses for the brochure. No more than three, though, because your design can't accomplish more than three purposes effectively. The most common and appropriate uses for a brochure are:

✔ To act as a reference on the product, or technical details of the product, for prospects

✔ To support a personal selling effort by lending credibility and helping overcome objections

✔ To generate leads through a direct-mail campaign

Say you want to design a brochure that does all three of these tasks well. Start by designing the contents. What product and technical information must be included? Write the information down, or collect necessary illustrations, so that you have the *fact base* (the essential information to communicate) in front of you. You will include in your brochure copy (and perhaps illustrations) designed specifically for each of these three purposes.

Writing about strengths and weaknesses

After you create your fact base (see the preceding section), organise these points in such a way that they highlight your product's (or service's) greatest strengths and overcome its biggest challenges. Don't know what your product's strengths and weaknesses are? List the following, as they relate to sales:

✔ The common sales objections or reasons prospects give for why they don't want to buy your product

✔ Customers' favourite reasons for buying, or aspects of your product or business that customers like most

With your fact base organised accordingly, you're ready to begin writing. Your copy should read as if you're listening to customers' concerns and answering each concern with an appropriate response. You can write subheads like 'Our Product Doesn't Need Service' so that salespeople or prospects can easily see how your facts (in copy and/or illustrations) overcome each specific objection and highlight all the major benefits.

Incorporating a clear, compelling appeal

Add some basic appeal, communicated in a punchy headline and a few dozen words of copy, along with an appropriate and eye-catching illustration. You need to include this appeal to help the brochure stand on its own as a marketing tool when the brochure is sent out to leads by post or passed on from a prospect or customer to one of his or her professional contacts.

The appeal needs to project a winning personality. Your brochure can be fun or serious, emotional or factual – but it must be appealing. The appeal is the bait that draws the prospect to your hook. Make sure your hook is well baited!

Putting it all together

When you have all the parts – the appeal, the fact base, and so on – you're ready to put your brochure together. The appeal, with its enticing headline and compelling copy and visual, goes on the front of the brochure – or the outside when you fold it for mailing, or the central panel out of three if you fold a sheet twice. The subheads that structure the main copy respond to objections and highlight strengths on the inside pages. And you organise the fact base, needed for reference use, in the copy and illustrations beneath these subheads.

Although you can design a brochure in many ways, we often prefer the format (along with dimensions for text blocks or illustrations) in Figure 4-5. This format is simple and inexpensive because you print the brochure on a single sheet of 490mm x 210mm paper that you then fold three times. The brochure fits in a standard DL (110mm x 220mm) envelope, or you can tape it together along the open fold and mail it on its own. This layout allows for some detail, but not enough to get you into any real trouble. (Larger formats and multi-page pieces tend to fill up with the worst, wordiest copy, and nobody ever reads those pieces.)

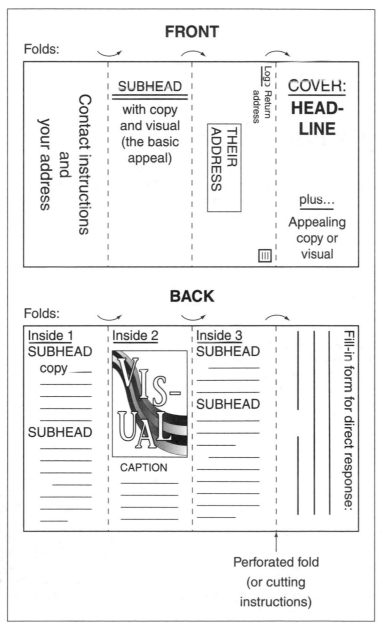

Figure 4-5:
A simple, multi-purpose brochure layout.

FRONT

Folds:

Contact instructions and your address

SUBHEAD
with copy and visual (the basic appeal)

Logo Return address

THEIR ADDRESS

COVER:
HEAD-LINE

plus...
Appealing copy or visual

BACK

Folds:

Inside 1
SUBHEAD
copy

SUBHEAD

VISUAL
CAPTION

Inside 3
SUBHEAD

SUBHEAD

Fill-in form for direct response:

Perforated fold
(or cutting instructions)

You can use the design shown in Figure 4-5 for direct mailings to generate sales leads, and you can also hand the brochure out or use it for reference in direct-selling situations. You can produce this brochure, using any popular desktop publishing software, and you can even print and fold it at the local photocopy shop (if you don't need the thousands of copies that make off-set printing cost-effective). To convert this design to an even simpler, cheaper format, use A4 paper and eliminate the *return mailer* (the left-hand page on the front, the right-hand on the back, which can be returned with the blanks filled in to request information or accept a special offer). If you do remove the return mailer, however, be sure to include follow-up instructions and contact information on one of the inside pages!

Placing a Print Ad

This section covers a marketing speciality called *media buying*, with an emphasis on buying print ad space. Media agencies and the marketing departments of big companies have specialists who do nothing but buy media, and some brokers specialise in it for mid-sized or smaller marketers. But if you're a smaller-scale marketer, you can easily work out how to buy media space on your own.

Can you afford to advertise?

If you're marketing a small business, start by buying magazines or newspapers that you're sure your prospective customers read. Then look for the information in them that identifies the publisher and gives a phone number for advertisers to call. Call and request a *rate card* (a table listing the prices of ads by size of ad and also showing the discount rate per ad if you buy multiple ads instead of just a single one). With a magazine, also ask for the *schedule,* which tells you when ads for each issue need to be placed and what the topics of future issues will be. Alternatively, you can get information for advertisers on the Web sites of many publications.

After you've collected a selection of rate cards from magazines or newspapers, take a hard look at the pricing. How expensive is the average ad (in the middle of the size range for each publication)? This may be a broad number.

If a single ad costs 5 per cent or more of your marketing budget for the entire year, throw the rate sheets away and forget about advertising in those publications. Your business is not currently operating on a large enough scale to be able to do this kind of advertising. You need dozens of ad placements at a minimum to make a good print ad campaign, so don't begin unless you can easily afford to keep going.

Instead of blowing that much money on a single ad, spread it over more economical forms of advertising and marketing, like brochures, mailings, and e-mails. If you operate on too small a scale or budget to afford advertising, try turning that ad design into a good flier and mailing it, instead. You can send the flier to 200 names and see what happens – that's a lot less risky and expensive than buying space in a magazine that goes to 200,000 names. Or you can search for smaller-circulation publications with a more local or specialist readership, where the rates may be much cheaper.

Finding inexpensive places to advertise

Many local businesses buy ad space in theatre programmes. What does this cost? Less than £70 for many programmes. Compare that price to an ad in a major magazine, which can cost £15,000. That's a big difference! If buying ads in the best publications to reach your market is too expensive, you can always find smaller-circulation publications that charge less.

One great way to advertise for less is to take advantage of the tens of thousands of newsletters published by professional groups and interest groups. You can buy ad space in 10 or 20 such newsletters for far less money than buying one ad insertion in a national daily newspaper. But you may have to be creative and persistent, because opportunities to advertise in newsletters aren't as obvious as with larger and more professional publications.

Professional associations' monthly newsletters provide an excellent opportunity for small-budget advertising. Professionals are people who have buying power, so even if you don't sell a product aimed at the people the newsletter is written for, they may still respond to your ad. Some insurance agents have advertised successfully in newsletters that go to doctors, for example. And increasingly, such newsletters are published in Web versions in addition to – or even instead of – print versions. With a Web publication, you can take advantage of the larger reach of the Web with the lower price of a small publication.

Also explore local newspapers. You can find hundreds of newspapers and weeklies with *circulation* (readership) only in the tens of thousands, which means their rates for ads are one-fifth to one-tenth the price of a national newspaper. Of course, you don't reach as many people, either – advertising tends to be priced on a *cost per thousand readers* basis (the cost of buying that ad divided by the number of readers who read the publication, then multiplied by 1,000), so you generally get as much exposure as you're willing to pay for. But by buying ads in small-circulation publications, you avoid taking huge risks, and you minimise your investment. If an ad pays off, you can try running it in additional publications. But if the ad doesn't produce the results you want, you can afford to write off the cost without feeling too much pain.

Keep the scale of your print advertising (and indeed any advertising) at a level such that you can afford to run an ad that may produce zero sales. Although that's certainly not your goal, zero sales are always a possibility, and you want to base your buying decision on that possibility.

Selecting the ad size

What size ad should you buy? The answer depends in part on the design of your ad. Does the ad have a strong, simple visual or headline that catches the eye, even if it's only a third of a page in size? Or does the ad need to be displayed in a larger format to work well?

In addition to your (or your designer's) judgement about the specifics of your ad, also take into account some general statistics on what percentage of readers *notice* an ad based on its size. As you may expect, the rate goes up with size – bigger ads get more notice (all other things being equal), according to a study by Media Dynamics (see Table 4-2).

Table 4-2	Selecting the Right Size
Size of Ad	*Index (recall scores)*
Page, colour	100
2-page spread, colour	130
2/3-page vertical, colour	81
1/2-page horizontal, colour	72

The bigger the ad, the bigger the impact. But also consider the fact that the percentage of readers noticing your ad doesn't go up *in proportion* to the increase in size. Doubling the size of your ad gives you something like a quarter more viewers, not twice as many – that's partly why the cost of a full-page ad isn't twice the cost of a half-page ad.

If you're watching your pennies, a full-page ad is often your best choice. Even though a large ad costs more, it is sufficiently more noticeable than smaller sizes, which means you'll reach more readers and, thus, bring the cost per exposure down a bit. However, remember that while a full-page ad is more economical, it's also more risky, because you will have blown more money if the ad doesn't work. You may want to try testing a new design with a quarter-page, inexpensive ad, and if that pays off, buy a full-page ad the next time.

Testing and improving your print ad

Is anybody actually reading your ad? A *direct-response* ad, one that asks readers to take a measurable action like call, fax, or go to a shop, gives you a clear indication of that ad's effectiveness within days of its first appearance. Say you expect to receive a lot of enquiries and orders over the telephone during the week the issue with your ad goes on sale. If you don't receive those calls, you know you have a problem. Now what?

Troubleshooting your ad

What if you want to know more about why that direct-response ad didn't get the desired level of response? Or what if you want to study an *indirect-response ad* – one that creates or strengthens an image or position in order to encourage sales? Much brand advertising is indirect, leaving it to the retailer or local office to close the sale. No phones ring, whether consumers liked the ad or not, so how do you know whether the ad worked?

To get this sort of information, you can go to a market research firm and have your ad tested for effectiveness. In fact, if you plan to spend more than £100,000 on print ads, you can probably consider the £12,000 or so needed to hire a research firm to pretest the ad money well spent. *Pretesting* means exposing people to the ad in a controlled setting and measuring their reactions to it.

To test an ad and see whether it's effective, assemble your own panel of customers and ask them to rate your ad and give you feedback about why they do or don't find that ad appealing. This feedback can give you good ideas for a new, improved version next time. You can also tap into the large-scale studies of ad readership done routinely by some research firms. Just subscribe to the study, and the firm feeds you detailed data about how well each ad you publish works.

A number of commercial media research services can give you additional information about how and to what extent people read your ad, as well as telling you what your competitors are up to and how much they're spending. Roper Starch Worldwide (www.roper.com) may be the best known of these services. If you sign up for its Starch Ad Readership service, you can find out how your ad performs compared with the industry norm. Starch surveys 75,000 consumers each year, asking them about specific ads to find out to what extent consumers notice and read an ad, and to measure the level of interest the ad generated.

Say that the Starch data shows that readership of your ad falls a little lower than average and that, although many people note the ad, few read enough to get the point or even the brand name. Should you kill this ad and start over?

The answer depends on what's wrong with the ad. Starch data (or data from similar services or even a volunteer consumer panel) can help you find out because the Starch survey looks at individual elements of the ad, as well as the overall ad. You can find out how many people read the headline (or even the first versus second line of a two-line headline). Then you can see how many continued on to the first paragraph of the body copy, the photograph, or the logo and signature.

Sometimes you find a problem that can be fixed without starting from scratch. Maybe your headline and photo get high Starch scores, but the body copy flunks. You can try rewriting and shortening the copy, and you may also try changing the layout or your choice of fonts. Perhaps the body copy is in reverse font, which consumers find hard to read. Often, switching the text to dark letters on a white or light background raises the Starch score, without any other changes!

Or maybe you need to switch from a black-and-white or two-colour visual to a four-colour one. Sure, you have to pay more, but if the Starch scores go up enough, the resulting ad may yield a better return, despite its higher price. Studies show that full-colour ads are recalled better than two-colour ads, which in turn outperform mono ads. So, as with size, more is better when it comes to colours. However, you need to run the numbers to see how the extra costs and extra readers affect your cost per thousand figure. As with all print ad decisions, you should be able to reduce the options to reasonable estimates of costs and returns and then pick the highest-yielding option.

Ad analysis for free?

Maybe you don't really need to spend good money on a research service to find out if your ads are working. Here are some alternatives:

- ✔ Run three variations on the ad and see which one generates the most calls or Web site visits (offering a discount based on a code number tells you which responses come from which ad).

- ✔ Do your own ad tests. Ask people to look at your ads for 20 seconds, and then quiz them about what they remember. If they missed much of the ad, you probably need to rewrite it.

- ✔ Run the same ad (or very similar ones) in large and small formats and see which pulls in the largest number of consumers.

Any experiments you can run as you do your marketing give you useful feedback about what's working and what isn't. Always think of ways to compare different options and see how those options perform when you advertise, giving you useful insight into ad effectiveness.

Chapter 5

Signs, Posters, and More

. . . .

In This Chapter

▶ Finding successful signs for your business

▶ Using flags, banners, and awnings

▶ Designing billboards and other large signs

▶ Utilising transport advertising

▶ Opting for bumper stickers, umbrellas, and shopping bags

. . . .

*O*utdoor advertising refers to a wide variety of advertising. The most obvious (but not necessarily most important for you) are large (to very large!) signs and posters, including roadside billboards, but we also include signs, flags, and banners in this medium. *Outdoor advertising* also includes what the experts call *ambient advertising*, which means putting an ad in any unexpected place to catch people by surprise.

All these methods try to communicate your message through public display of a poster, sign, or something of similar design requirements. That's why we incorporate signs, flags, banners, bumper stickers, transit advertising, and even T-shirts in this chapter, along with the traditional poster formats. These media are more powerful than many marketers realise – some businesses succeed by using no other advertising, in fact. In this chapter, you find out how to design for and use *outdoor advertising* (the term we use to indicate outdoor signs and banners, plus related displays like posters and signs, which, just to keep you on your toes, can be displayed indoors as well as out).

Whenever you review your marketing, do an audit of your signs, posters, T-shirts, and other outdoor ads. How many do you have displayed? Are they visible? Clear and appealing? Clean and in good repair? And then ask if you can find an easy way to increase the number and impact of these signs. When you need to make your brand identity and marketing messages visible, you can never do too much. The more the merrier!

The Essential Sign

Signs (small, informational outdoor ads or notices) don't show up in the index or table of contents of most books on marketing. *Signs* are displays with brand or company names on them and sometimes a short marketing message or useful information for the customer, too. In my experience, every marketer needs to make good use of signs.

Signs are all over – if you're in an office right now, look out of the nearest window and you can probably see a handful with ease. And signs are undeniably important. Even if signs serve only to locate a shop or office, they do a job that marketers need done. If your customers can't find you, you're out of business. So why do marketers – or at least those marketing experts who write the books – tend to ignore signs so completely?

You can't find a national or international set of standards for signs. You also can't find a major association to promote standards and champion best practices. When evaluating signs, we can't send you to the experts easily as we can with radio, TV, print, or other outdoor media. You'll probably end up working with a local sign manufacturer, and you and your designer have to specify size, materials, copy, and art. Fortunately, you're not all on your own; you can find some guidance and help. Following are a few things to remember:

✔ There is some information on the use of signs in the UK, but it's more about what you are allowed and not allowed to display. The Communities and Local Government Web site (www.communities.gov.uk) has a document called 'Outdoor advertisements and signs: A guide for advertisers' under its 'Planning, Guidance and Advice' section. Many basic signs will normally be permitted, while others will require planning application consent from your local authority.

✔ If you rent retail or office space, your landlord may have put some restrictions regarding signs into your lease. Research these possible constraints and talk to those who feel they have authority over your sign and seek their approval based on a sketch and plan before you spend any money having signs made or installed.

✔ Consult your local or regional business telephone listings when you need to have a sign made. You should find several options. You may want to talk to a good design firm or experienced designer for a personal reference, too. And modern high street copy shops now provide cheap high-tech solutions for smaller or temporary signs.

✔ To stand out next to those shiny, high-tech signs and project a quality image, have your sign designed and painted by an artist or consider hiring a cabinet-maker, stained glass artist, oil painter, or other arts and crafts professional. Most signs have little real art about them. Unusual and beautiful signs tell the world that your company is special. In fact, a really special sign, well displayed in a high-traffic area, has more power to build an image or pull in prospects than any other form of local advertising.

What your sign can do

Signs have limited ability to accomplish marketing goals – but perhaps not as limited as you think. As well as displaying the name of your business, you can include a phone number or email address so that even when your premises are closed, potential customers know how to get in touch with you. And you can say what your business does – a butcher doesn't have to be just a 'butcher', he can be a 'family-owned free range butcher'. With signs, as with all marketing communications, it's the way that you say it that counts!

Aside from their practical value (letting people know where you are), signs can and should promote your image and brand name. An attractive sign on your building or vehicle can spread the good word about your business or brand to all who pass by. Don't miss this brilliant opportunity to put your best foot forward in public.

You will see many commercial signs that are in poor condition. Signs sit out in the weather, and when they fade, peel, or fall over, they give negative advertising for your business. Don't let your sign give the public the impression that you don't care enough to maintain your signs (they may even think you're going out of business!). Renew and religiously maintain your signs to get the maximum benefit from them.

Writing good signs

As a marketer, you need to master the strange art of writing for signs. Too often, the language marketers use on signs is ambiguous. The sign just doesn't say anything with enough precision to make its point clear. Keep in mind the suggestions outlined in the following sections.

Make sure your sign says what you want it to

One of my favourite stories about how to easily turn a bad sign into a good sign comes from the marketing consultant Doug Hall. A friend of his put up a sign that read 'Seasons in Thyme – EPICUREAN FOOD & WINE'. Do you have any idea what that company does? Doug changed his friend's sign to 'Seasons in Thyme RESTAURANT. Casual, Elegant, Island Dining'. For the first time in all his years in business the owner received some customers who said they came in because they had seen the sign.

Before you approve any design, review the copy to make sure that the writing provides a model of clarity! Try misinterpreting the wording. Can you read the sign in a way that makes it seem to mean something you don't intend to say? And try thinking of questions the sign doesn't answer that seem obvious to you – remember that the consumer may not know the answers. For example, some people have a terrible sense of direction, so a sign on the side of a shop leaves them confused about how to enter that shop. Solution? Put an arrow and the instructions 'Enter from Front' on the sign.

Use a header to catch your customer's eye

Marketers design some signs to convey substantial information – directions, for example, or details of a shop's merchandise mix. Informational signs are often too brief or too lengthy. Divide the copy and design into two sections, each with a separate purpose, as follows:

- **Have a header.** The first section is like the header in a print ad (see Chapter 4), and you design it to catch attention from afar and draw people to the sign. Given this purpose, brevity is key – and don't forget the essential large, catchy type and/or visuals.

- **Communicate essential information.** The second section of the sign needs to communicate the essential information accurately and in full. If the first section does its job, viewers walk right up to the sign to read the informational part, so you don't need to make that type as large and catchy. The consumer should be able to easily read and interpret the wording and type of the information, and this section needs to answer all likely viewer questions.

Most signs don't have these two distinct sections, and so they fail to accomplish either purpose very well – they neither draw people very strongly nor inform them fully. Unfortunately, most sign makers have a strong urge to make all the copy the same size. When pressed, the sign makers sometimes make the header twice as big as the rest of the copy; but going further than that seems to upset them. Well, to get a good sign, you may have to upset some people. As in many aspects of marketing, if you want above-average performance, you have to swim against the current.

You may have to make your sign bigger to fit the necessary words on it in a readable font. So be it. The form of the sign must follow its function.

Be creative!

Speaking of being unconventional, what about adding a beautiful photograph to your sign to give it more of the eye-catching appeal of a good print ad? Most sign printers/makers can include photographs now, but few marketers take advantage of this option.

Another problem – marketers write the copy on most signs in the most tired and obvious manner. Tradition says that a sign, unlike any other marketing communication, must simply state the facts in a direct, unimaginative way. One reason you don't see much creativity in signs? Most marketers assume people *read* signs. That's the conventional wisdom – that your customers and prospects automatically find and read your signs.

Try walking down an average high street and then listing all the signs you remember seeing. Some stand out, but most go unseen. And we bet you can't re-create the text of very many of those signs your eye bothered to linger on long enough to read. To avoid having your sign being lost in this sea of similar signs, you have to make yours stand out!

 Whenever you find other marketers making silly mistakes, you can turn their errors into your opportunities. And signs permit innovation in two interesting areas. You can innovate in the copy and artwork, just as you can in any print medium – from a magazine ad to a roadside billboard. But you can also innovate in the form of the sign itself. Experiment with materials, shapes, lighting, location, and ways of displaying signs to come up with some novel ideas that give your sign drawing power. Signs should be creative and fun. (So should all marketing, for that matter.)

Here are some of the many variations in form that you can take advantage of when designing a creative sign:

- Vinyl graphics and lettering (quick and inexpensive but accurate to your design)
- Hand-painted (personal look and feel)
- Wood (traditional look; routing or hand carving enhances the appeal)
- Metal (durable and accurate screening of art and copy, but not very pretty)
- Window lettering (hand-painted or with vinyl letters/graphics)
- Lighted boxes (in which lettering is back-lit; highly visible at night)
- Neon signs (high impact)
- Magnetic signs (for your vehicles)
- Signs printed from an inkjet printer output, sent out from a local frame shop to be laminated on a display board with a plastic coating (this new form of framing is intended for indoor use, but I've seen some companies use it out of doors and it holds up surprisingly well. With it, you can make your own signs on your own printer)

✔ Electronic displays (also known as *electronic message repeaters*; movement and longer messages, plus a high-tech feel, make these displays appropriate in some situations)

✔ Flat-panel TV screens (with shifting sign content and images or video; the price of these TVs has been coming down)

✔ Pavement projection (a unit in the shop window moves and spins a logo or message at the feet of passers-by at night)

Discovering Flags, Banners, and Awnings

Movement is eye-catching, so think of flags as more dynamic kinds of sign, and try to find ways to use them to build brand awareness, to make your location(s) more visible, or to get a marketing message displayed in more forms and places than you could otherwise. Also note that the costs of cloth-based forms of advertising can be surprisingly reasonable – that's why outdoor messages on canvas or synthetic cloth make up an important part of many marketing campaigns.

Flagging down your customers

Theatres, galleries, and museums are some of the biggest users of flags and banners because they can adorn their buildings with colourful banners that promote forthcoming performances – the temporary nature of the medium suits the rotation of the plays and exhibitions. Do you have a similar short-term message that you could get across on a flag or banner?

A number of companies specialise in making custom-designed flags and banners. Of course, you see tacky paper banners – often produced by the local copy shop – hanging in the windows of retail shops on occasion. But we're not talking about those banners (because they probably don't help your image). I mean a huge, beautiful cloth flag flapping in the breeze. Or a bold 3-x-5-foot screen-printed flag suspended like a banner on an office or trade-show wall. Or a nylon table banner that turns the front and sides of a table into space for your marketing message.

Consider using a flag or banner as a sign for your shop or business. So few marketers take advantage of this way to use a banner that it can help you stand out. A flag or banner is less static and dull than the typical metal or wood sign. Cloth moves, and even when it isn't moving, you know it has the potential for movement – giving the banner a bit of excitement. Also, flags or banners often seem decorative and festive. People associate flags and banners with special events because these decorations are traditionally used in that context, instead of for permanent display.

Flag companies give you all these options and more. These businesses regularly sew and screen large pieces of fabric, and they can also supply you with cables, poles, and other fittings you need to display flags and banners. In recent years, silk-screening technology and strong synthetic fibres have made flags and banners brighter and more permanent, expanding their uses in marketing.

You can find suppliers of a full line of stock and custom products by searching online, looking in your local Yellow Pages or in the services section directories of trade magazines such as *Marketing*. Whoever you contact, ask to see their custom flag and banner price list, which includes a lot of design ideas and specs, and also ask to see photos of effective banners from previous clients.

Canopies and awnings

If appropriate for your business, consider using an awning and canopy. For retailers, awnings and canopies often provide the boldest and most attractive form of roadside sign. Office sites may also find awnings and canopies valuable.

Awnings combine structural value with marketing value by shading the interior and can even extend the floor space of your store by capturing some of the sidewalk as transition space. An awning can perform all the functions a sign can, and more, and it can do so in a way that's highly visible but not intrusive. Even a row of awnings does not look as crass and commercial as huge signs because your eye accepts them as a structural part of the building. So you get the same amount of advertising as with a big sign without looking pushy.

Posters: Why Size Matters

If you are planning to use posters to advertise, one of the first things to think about is how long customers will have to read your ad and from how far away. This will help you decide how much you can say in your ad, and how to say it.

Here's a simple exercise to help you understand the design requirements for a large-format poster. Draw a rectangular box on a sheet of blank paper, using a ruler as your guide. Make the box 12 cm wide and 6 cm high. That's the proportion of a standard *48-sheet* poster (we talk more about poster formats later in this chapter). Although a poster is large (over 6 metres wide in this instance), from a distance it will look as small as that box on your sheet. (See Figure 5-1.) Now hold your paper (or Figure 5-1) at arm's length and think about what copy and artwork can fit in this space, while remaining readable to passers-by at this distance. Not much, right? Now imagine they are driving past it in a car. Next imagine them staring at it for minutes while waiting for the 8.30am train from Dorking to Waterloo. Sometimes you have to take care to limit your message to a few, bold words and images, or your poster becomes a mess that no one can read. At other times you can afford to include more detail – the people waiting for that train may even be grateful for the distraction!

Figure 5-1:
From a distance, a large roadside poster looks no bigger than this image.

CAN YOU READ THIS
CAN YOU READ THIS
CAN YOU READ THIS
CAN YOU READ THIS
CAN YOU READ THIS
CAN YOU READ THIS

That's the problem with outdoor advertising, in general – viewers have to read the ad in a hurry, and often from a considerable distance. So the ad has to be simple. Yet people who walk or drive the same route view the same ad daily. So that ad has to combine lasting interest with great simplicity.

With all these constraints, you see the difficulty of designing effective outdoor ads. Make your message fun, beautiful, or at least important and clear, so that people don't resent having to see it often.

Deciding on outdoor ad formats

The Outdoor Advertising Association (www.oaa.org.uk) describes four different sectors in the outdoor market: Roadside, transport, retail, and non-traditional & ambient:

✔ **Roadside.** You can choose anything from phone kiosks to 96-sheet ads, which at 40-feet wide by 10-feet high are the largest of the standard poster formats. Special builds, such as a real car stuck to a billboard, and banners count as roadside ads, too.

✔ **Transport.** While it includes standard poster sites in stations, airports, and on trains and tubes, transport is a wide-ranging outdoor sector that covers (literally) bus-sides, taxis, and trucks. For that reason, it has its own lexicon of jargon – from *L-Sides* to *T-Sides* and the enticingly named *Super Rears*. All that really matters is that they're ways of advertising on the outside of buses, which we cover later in this chapter.

✔ **Retail.** If you have a product that is sold through retailers then outdoor ads near those outlets can make a lot of sense. As well as poster sites at supermarkets, the retail sector includes shopping centres, cinemas, gyms, and petrol stations – and can include ads on trolleys and screens.

✔ **Non-traditional formats & ambient.** They couldn't even come up with a straightforward name for this sector, which just proves how diverse it is. Think petrol pump nozzles, takeaway lids, ticket backs, beermats, floor stickers – in fact, think anything at all. We talk about some of the more popular ambient formats, as well as the truly outlandish, later in the chapter.

Figure 5-2 shows the proportions and relative sizes of the standard *roadside* outdoor formats.

You can also explore the growing number of variations on these standards. Want your message displayed on the floor of a building lobby, on a shopping trolley, or alongside the notice boards at leisure centres? Or how about on signs surrounding the arenas and courts of athletic events? You can use all these options and more, by directly contacting the businesses that control such spaces or using one of a host of ad agencies and poster contractors that can give you larger-scale access.

Maximising your returns

The costs of outdoor advertising vary widely. But to give you some idea of what's involved, a 48-sheet poster at a roadside in the North West region (Manchester and Liverpool) will cost you around £300 for a two-week period – the standard time for an outdoor campaign. You are unlikely to buy just one poster site, and even more unlikely to find an outdoor advertising company that will sell you one. The typical way poster space is sold is by a predetermined group of panels in one area, or a national campaign. So, if you wanted to advertise on 25 of the best 48-sheet sites in Manchester and Liverpool for two weeks it would cost you approximately £7,500. Or 70 sites giving coverage across the North West region would cost £19,250.

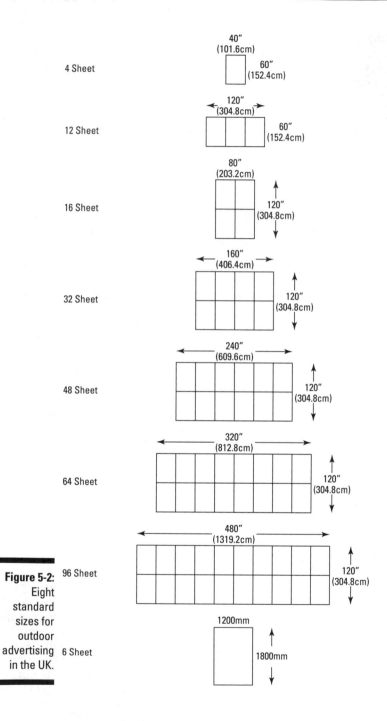

The money is one thing, but who is seeing your posters is quite another. The audience for poster campaigns is measured in several ways, broadly how many of the local or national population will see it, how often, and how clearly. For example, you can buy 100 48-sheet posters in London for £42,000, which will be seen by 2 million Londoners over a two-week period. That's around 26 per cent of the area's population, so you achieve a *cover* of 26 per cent. Your *frequency* is the number of times a person sees your ad over the period, in this case 8.1 times. And your *Visibility Adjusted Impacts (VAIs)* for each panel is a score telling you who actually looks at each panel. VAI is a measure of the quality or location of your panels – basically the higher the score, the more effective the campaign (but also the higher the cost). Your 100 48-sheets in London have a VAI of 100, but if you were to splash out £105,000 on the 50 best 96-sheets in the capital you would get a VAI of 205.

You can get measurements on outdoor advertising effectiveness from Postar (www.postar.co.uk), but as you have to pay a subscription fee we suggest that you go direct to the outdoor advertising companies for ratecards and data. You can find the main poster companies through the Outdoor Advertising Association Web site (www.oaa.org.uk).

Messages on the Move: Transport Advertising

Transport advertising is any advertising in or on railway or underground systems, airports, buses, taxis, on the sides of vans or lorries, and more. Although transport advertising is a form of outdoor advertising, this is misleading because you set up some transit ads indoors: Ads at airport terminals, ads displayed within tube carriages, and so on.

Transport ads work well if you get the people in transit to take an interest in your product, from consumer products to business services. We've seen transit ads generate sales leads for local estate agents and for international consulting firms. Yet few marketers make use of them. Consider being an innovator and trying transit ads, even if your competitors don't.

Standard options – the ones most easily available through media buying firms and ad agencies – include bus shelter panels, and bus and taxi exterior signs, and posters and back-lit signs in airports.

You find one definite advantage in transport advertising – it typically delivers high frequency of viewer impacts in a short period of time. Public transport vehicles generally travel the same routes over and over, and so almost everyone along the route sees an ad multiple times.

Bus shelter panels

Shelter panels are 6-sheet (120 cm x 180 cm) posters. These ads appear at bus-stop shelters. You can mount them behind a Lucite sheet to minimise the graffiti problem. In many cities, the site owners have back-lit some of the shelter panels for night-time display. A two-week showing typically costs anywhere from £120 to £280, depending upon the area, or up to £550 per panel for the busiest London sites.

Bus advertising comes with well-accepted standards in the UK, largely due to the fixed available space on any single- or double-decker bus – although some companies now offer the option of full-bus branding, as well. Figure 5-3 shows the standard bus ad sizes, but you should contact a poster contractor who specialises in this kind of advertising (such as Viacom Outdoor www. viacom-outdoor.co.uk) before producing any posters.

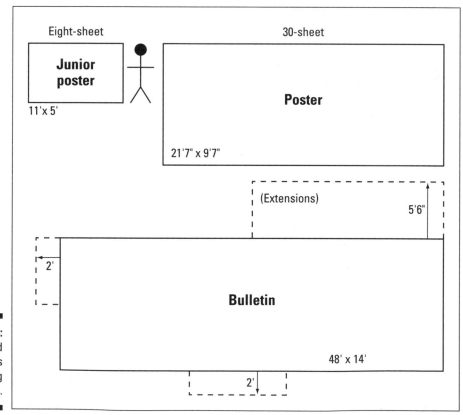

Figure 5-3: Standard sizes for bus advertising in the UK.

Sometimes advertisers combine an L-Side with a Superside and rear panels to maximise impact on pedestrians and drivers as they watch the bus go by. Add a shelter poster to the mix, and you have incredibly good coverage! Such combinations can be effective, especially if you think your ad may be challenging to read or you want to display two or three complementary ads to the same viewer.

Taxi advertising

Taxi advertising provides you with a route to target local customers and high-value businesspeople. You can advertise on the outside, inside, cover the whole cab, or on the back of receipts – there's even a company called Cabvision that sells ads on its in-taxi TV channel! Again, contact a company that specialises in this form of advertising, such as Taxi Media (`www.clearchannel.co.uk/taximedia`).

Airport advertising

Airport advertising is a comparatively new option but is taking off fast. If you want a relatively well-to-do audience with a rich mix of tourists and professional travellers, enquire about airport advertising options with international site owners and domestic specialists such as JCDecaux (`www.jcdecaux airport.co.uk`) or Airport Advertising (`www.airport-advertising.co.uk`).

A note about your own vehicles

Does your company have its own vehicles on the road? If so, are you using them for outdoor advertising? Most marketers say either 'no' or 'sort of' when we ask them this question. Small, cheap, magnetic signs on the doors don't count. Nor does just a painted name on the door or side panel of a van or lorry. If you pay for as much display space as even a standard-sized van offers, you would probably hire a designer or agency and put great care into your message. And, in fact, you are paying for the exterior space on your vehicles; the cost just doesn't show up in the marketing budget. So why not cash in on this investment more fully by treating that lorry or van as a serious advertising medium? Mount frames for bus-sized posters and display a professionally designed ad that you change monthly or weekly. Or hire a competent airbrush painter to do a more permanent, custom job on each vehicle.

Ambient Media — Your Ad in Unusual Places

Ambient or *non-traditional advertising* does exactly what it says on the tin – or takeaway lid, or egg, or petrol pump nozzle. In fact, we can't really tell you what ambient media is, as it covers so much and changes so rapidly. We can tell you what it isn't, which is any of the traditional outdoor advertising opportunities. Ambient is one of the fastest-growing sectors within outdoor advertising, because you can create a lot of impact for relatively little outlay. The nature of ambient advertising also means it can offer you precise targeting by area or by audience type.

We like to divide ambient advertising into two parts: The *uncontroversial* and the *unconventional*. *Uncontroversial* includes all forms of outdoor advertising that are really just poster ads in disguise, and which are in almost constant use by some fairly major advertisers. These ads appear on petrol pump nozzles, floor stickers in supermarkets and train stations, and posters in public conveniences. *Unconventional* includes everything else. We've heard about ads that appear on pretty much everything you can imagine – and a lot of what you probably wouldn't. These unconventional places include tube maps and tickets, urinal stickers, and even on cows standing by the side of major roads.

Just because it's different doesn't mean ambient advertising is a great idea for your product or service. You should only use ambient advertising when you know that the idea is a good fit for your brand or you're prepared to take a gamble with the investment (most of the wilder ideas have pretty poor audience measurement, so it's more about whether it feels right to you).

Here are some of the most interesting ambient media ideas we've heard of – and some of the companies that have used them effectively:

- **Rubbish skips.** Directory enquiries service 118 118 used skips to communicate the idea of people throwing away their old telephone directories.

- **Petrol pump nozzles.** Good for targeting drivers with impulse buys, and used by food and drink brands such as Polo and Red Bull.

- **Takeaway lids.** Full-colour Adlids have been used by a host of organisations, from Blockbuster Video ('Here's just four of our new takeaways', plus a money-off coupon) to HMRC.

- **Chalk ads.** Sometimes known as vandaltising, chalk-drawn ads on pavements have been used by companies such as Gossard to advertise a new range of underwear. Be careful, though, this idea is less popular with local councils, despite the fact that the ads eventually wash away.

- ✔ **Car park tickets.** A great way to reach people just before they go shopping. This method has been used by retailers such as Sainsbury's and Specsavers.

- ✔ **Shopping trolleys and floor posters.** We group these together as they offer the same great benefits to you if your products are found on supermarket shelves. Did you know that 75 per cent of purchasing decisions are made in-store and over 90 per cent of advertising budget is spent out of store? Trolleys and floor posters act as reminders to shoppers that your product exists, and can even direct them to the right shelf.

- ✔ **ForeheADS.** Why use your head when you can use someone else's? This is a wacky idea, which involves renting out the foreheads of cash-strapped students, who must be seen out in public for at least three hours a day to earn their fee. Companies including *FHM* magazine and CNX have used ForeheADS to carry their logos as a temporary tattoo.

Small but Effective – From T-shirts to Shopping Bags

A broad definition of a sign may include any public display of your brand or marketing message. To me, a message on a T-shirt is just as legitimate as a message on a poster. And it is often a lot easier and cheaper to make. The following sections share simple, small-scale ways to get your message across.

T-shirts, umbrellas, and bumper stickers, anyone?

Don't forget that you can sometimes get people to advertise your company on their vehicles or bodies for free. Your customers may think of a nice T-shirt as a premium item or gift for them, but you can see that T-shirt as a body billboard! It's nice that people are willing to go around with your advertising messages on their clothes (or even on their bodies – temporary tattoos are also a marketing option). Don't overlook this concept as a form of outdoor advertising. In fact, use it as much as you can. People happily display marketing messages if they like them.

Similarly, umbrellas can broadcast your logo and name and a short slogan or headline – although only in especially wet or overly sunny weather.

Don't overlook bumper stickers and car-window stickers. If you make them clever or unique enough, people eagerly seek those stickers out. Don't ask me why. But because people do, and because the cost of producing bumper stickers is cheap, why not come up with an appealing design and make stickers available in target markets as giveaways on shop counters or at outdoor events?

Commercial or brand-orientated bumper stickers are used by people who think the brand is so cool that it enhances the car – and this is a hard thing to achieve for some marketers. An alternative is to keep your brand identity small, and star an appealing message, instead. A clever joke, an inspiring quote, or something similar is appealing enough to get your message displayed. And for mugs, window stickers, and other premium items, the secret is to have a great visual design or other picture that people enjoy, or to offer a humorous cartoon.

You can even include a nice sticker in a direct-mail piece, where that sticker can do double duty – acting as an incentive to get people to retain and read the mailing and giving you cheap outdoor advertising when they display the sticker on their vehicles. (Contact local print shops, sign makers, or T-shirt silk-screeners; any of these businesses sometimes produce bumper stickers, too.)

It's in the bag

The big department stores believe in the importance of shopping bags as an advertising medium. But many other businesses fail to take advantage of the fact that shoppers carry bags around busy shopping centres and high streets, and also on trains and buses, giving any messages on the bags high exposure.

To use bags effectively, you need to make them far easier to read and far more interesting than the average brown paper or white plastic shopping bag. Remember, you're not just designing a bag – you're designing a form of outdoor advertising. So apply the same design principles. Come up with a *hook* – a striking image or attention-getting word or phrase that gets everyone looking at that bag. And try alternative colours or shapes. (By the way, most bag suppliers can customise their bags – check with suppliers in your local area. If no suppliers around you can customise bags, contact printers and silk-screeners, they can always handle bag orders for you, too.)

If you offer the biggest, strongest bag in a shopping area, you can be sure that shoppers stuff everyone else's bags into yours, giving your advertising message the maximum exposure. Of course, bigger, stronger bags cost more, which is why most shops offer wimpy bags that hurt your hands or rip open and spill their contents in the mud. But if you have an ad message you can get across with a bag, compare the cost of a better bag to other media. Pretty cheap, right? So why not go for it?

If you aren't in the retail business, you may think that this idea doesn't apply to you. Wrong! Plenty of store managers view bags as an irritating expense, rather than a marketing medium. Offer to supply them with better bags for free, in exchange for the right to print your message on the bags. Voilà! A new marketing medium for your campaign. A specialist such as Bag Media (www.bagmedia.co.uk) can design and distribute bags for you to pre-selected groups of retailers, from veterinary practices to garden centres and sandwich bags to pizza boxes.

A Few Commonsense Rules for Outdoor Advertising

Depending on whether you're advertising on roadside or transport sites, follow these commonsense rules when designing your poster to make sure that it catches and holds customers' attention:

- ✓ If your poster site is by the side of a main road, people will have just a few seconds to see and understand your ad. Keep the image simple and use as few, large words as possible. Make sure that you use colours that contrast, so they can be seen from a good distance.

- ✓ Think like a bored passenger. When you advertise on interior tube panels, inside taxis or on train platform posters you can afford to use more complex visuals and a greater number of words.

- ✓ Can you layer the message, so that you provide a clear, large-scale, simple message for first-time viewers, but also a more detailed design and message for repeat viewers to find within the poster?

- ✓ Humour and wordplay work well for posters. Try to use them in your ad to build involvement from the viewer.

- ✓ Show your logo. Whether you're just using posters or are including other media in your marketing campaign, don't forget the logo! You will get improved recognition for your business, and better results from your advertising, if you use your logo consistently across everything you do.

Chapter 6

Public Relations and Word of Mouth

*W*hen people bump into reminders of your company name, brand name, product, or service, they are more likely to buy. And if those exposures to your identity create a strongly positive impression, they can have a big impact on sales. So far, so simple.

But while advertising does work, most people who are affected by it don't like to admit to it. There are plenty of people who will deny ever having bought anything as a result of seeing an ad for it, but we'll bet you've never come across anyone who says the same about a magazine article, or who is so resistant to something a relative or friend recommends to them.

Independent endorsements for your product or service can be so much more powerful than 'pure' advertising, for the simple reason that consumers are more sceptical about a message that has been paid for and is self-serving.

In this chapter, we discuss the two key ways of gaining independent endorsement for your business: *Public relations* (when exposure to or mention of your company, service, or product becomes part of the news or an editorial feature) and *word of mouth* (what people say about you to others). Each endorsement can make a positive impression in a low-key, polite manner, and can do so (if managed well) for surprisingly low cost.

Public relations and word of mouth are both vastly underrated techniques for communicating with your customers. These endorsements are ignored or given only minor attention by marketers, but they belong in the front lines of your marketing plan because of their ease of use, simplicity, low cost, and potential.

Using Publicity to Your Advantage

Publicity is coverage of your product or business in the editorial portion of any news medium. Why would journalists cover a product as a story? Because the product is better or worse than expected. If, for example, *Which?* magazine runs an article praising your product as best in a category, that's publicity. Good publicity. If, in contrast, the evening television news programmes run a story saying that experts suspect your product caused numerous accidents, that's publicity, too. Bad publicity. But bad publicity can be turned to an organisation's advantage – Johnson and Johnsons baby powder was found to contain traces of ground glass but they responded so promptly and responsibly that their image improved! Perrier on the other hand denied all suggestions that traces of benzene existed in their water and suffered the consequences.

In both cases, product quality is the key to the publicity. Keep this fact in mind.

When you use publicity, remember the all-important factor – the quality of your product development and production/delivery. You can gain positive publicity simply by designing and making a truly superior product. If you want to generate negative publicity, just make your product shoddy or do your service poorly. *Good publicity starts with a pursuit of quality in your own business!*

The following sections list ways that you can take advantage of good publicity (and, if the need arises, neutralise bad publicity) in your marketing materials.

Tackling public relations

Public relations (PR) is the active pursuit of publicity for marketing purposes. You use PR to generate good publicity and try to minimise bad publicity. Generally, marketers have the responsibility of generating good publicity. If marketers create good stories and communicate them to the media effectively (see the following two sections), the media pick them up and turn them into news or entertainment content. Good publicity.

Although marketers or general managers wear the PR hat in smaller organisations, large companies generally have a PR person or department whose sole job is to manage its reputation – generating good publicity but also reacting promptly and effectively to publicity crises. Also, many businesses hire *PR consultancies*— agencies that can work for a number of clients, planning and delivering messages to the press or reacting to incoming enquiries.

If you need help writing a good press release and placing the story then it is worth enlisting this professional help – you may not get any coverage without it.

PR consultancies vary in size from international groups employing thousands to single owner-operator PR professionals. You can also find specialists, who have expertise in industry sectors such as IT or healthcare. There are around 3,000 PR consultancies operating in the UK, so you'll need help narrowing down your search. If you're serious about hiring one, the Public Relations Consultants Association offers a free online service called PReview (www.prca.org.uk), which matches your needs with the member consultancies that most closely match them.

Creating a good story

To a journalist, a *good story* is anything that has enough public interest to attract readers, viewers, or listeners and hold their attention. A good story for a journalist covering the plastics industry must hold the attention of people in that industry.

We're sorry to say that most of what you want to communicate to your market doesn't fall into the category of a good story. For that reason, you need to develop your story (by collecting the right facts and quotes and writing them down clearly and well) to a level that may qualify as good editorial content. And when you think of good editorial content, think like a journalist would.

Finding the hook

The *hook* is what it sounds like: The compelling bit of information that snags your reader's interest and draws him or her to the story.

Here's a simple exercise to help you understand how hooks work. Scan today's newspaper (whichever one you like to read) and rank the top five stories based on your interest in them. Now analyse each one in turn to identify the one thing that made that story interesting enough to hold your attention. The *hooks,* the things that made each story interesting to you, differ. But every story has a hook, and all hooks have certain elements in common:

- ✔ Hooks often give you new information (information you didn't know or weren't sure of).
- ✔ Hooks make that new information relevant to your activities or interests.

✔ Hooks catch your attention, often by surprising you with something you hadn't expected.

✔ Hooks promise some benefit to you – although the benefit may be indirect – by helping you understand your world better, avoid something undesirable, or simply enjoy yourself as you read the paper.

Combining the hook with your marketing message

You need to design hooks to make your marketing message into stories that appeal to journalists. And your hooks need to be just like the ones that attracted your attention to those newspaper stories, with one exception: *You need to somehow tie them to your marketing information.* You have to make sure that at least a thin line exists connecting the hook to your brand identity, the news that you've just introduced a new product, or whatever else you want the public to know. That way, when journalists use your hook in their own work, they end up including some of your marketing information in their stories as an almost accidental side effect.

Journalists don't want to help you communicate with your target market – but they'll happily use any good stories that you're willing to write for them, and if your product gets mentioned or you get quoted as a result, they don't have a problem giving you the reference. So the secret, the key, the essence of good publicity? Develop stories with effective hooks and give those stories to overworked journalists with empty pages to fill.

Communicating your story to the media: Press releases

The most basic format for communicating a news story is the press release. The trouble is that journalists don't like press releases. I (Craig) know this because I am one (a journalist, that is, not a press release). As editor of *Marketing* magazine I get hundreds of press releases e-mailed and posted to me every day. Most of them are rubbish, which is exactly where they end up. At the head of every magazine, covering every imaginable professional or consumer interest there is the equivalent of me – a stressed-out editor with the next deadline looming. So you should look on your challenge as getting past me, or at least the equivalent of me.

When I say that journalists don't like press releases, what I mean is that we don't like admitting to being influenced by them – a bit like consumers with advertising, really. Now I'm not going to single-handedly attempt to hold back the tide of press releases, but I am going to give you some insider advice about how to get on the right side of journalists by giving them what they need and not troubling them with what they do not.

A list of do's

Here is a list of ways that you can get a positive response from the journalists you call.

- Do offer exclusives
- Do make it relevant and timely
- Do build up a list of media contacts
- Do think creatively
- Do offer yourself as an expert commentator on industry-related matters in case they need a quote for another article
- Do keep it brief
- Do post your press releases on your Web site
- Do send releases to every local editor in your area no matter how small their publication or station

And a few don'ts

These do's must be balanced by a few helpful don'ts that will help your information stand out from the junk that flies into every journalist's inbox:

- Don't make a nuisance of yourself
- Don't ask for clippings
- Don't make any errors
- Don't give incomplete contact information
- Don't ignore the journalists' research needs
- Don't forget that journalists work on a faster clock than you do

Considering video and electronic releases

You can get a story out to the media in ways other than press releases. You can generate a video release, with useful footage that a television producer may decide to run as part of a news story. You can also put a written press release on the PR Newswire or any other such service that distributes hard copy or electronic releases to its media clients – for a fee to the source of the release, of course. You can also pitch your stories to the Associated Press and other newswires (but we recommend hiring a major PR firm before trying to contact a newswire).

prnewswire.co.uk and businesswire.co.uk

For easy access to a cheap way to distribute releases, check out `www.prnewswire.co.uk`, where you can click on `Small Business Toolkit` and see what it currently charges for a 400-word press release. At time of writing, the site offers to create and send a release to all the media in the UK, plus consumer and trade publications, thousands of news-orientated Web sites, and online services and databases for prices from £205. Not bad, but we recommend using it as well as making key journalistic contacts – there's nothing like the personal touch. A similar service is offered at `www.businesswire.co.uk`.

Being interviewed for TV and radio

So now you've got a hook or a reputation for expertise within your sector, the requests for interviews will come flooding in. Okay, it's not usually that simple, you need to be prepared for when a broadcast interview does come your way. There are a few people who are naturally confident and gifted when speaking publicly or on radio or TV – these people are not normal! You're going to feel nervous the first time you're in an unusual interview situation – that's only natural. You can prepare yourself by getting professional media training, where you will be put into mock interviews in front of real cameras and microphones and put through your paces by professional journalists. Or you could simply follow these basic (and much cheaper) tips:

- Give no more than three key messages
- Know your audience
- Be positive
- Speak like a normal human being

Making the Most of Word of Mouth

Word of mouth (WOM) gives a consumer (or a marketer) the most credible source of information about products, aside from actual personal experience with those products. What consumers tell each other about your products has a huge impact on your efforts to recruit new customers. Word of mouth also has a secondary, but still significant, impact on your efforts to retain old customers.

If you survey customers to identify the source of positive attitudes toward new products, you generally find that answers like 'my friend told me about it' outnumber answers like 'I saw an ad' by ten to one. Word-of-mouth communications about your product don't actually outnumber advertising messages; but when customers talk, other customers listen.

How can you control what people say about your product? You can't very effectively encourage customers to say nice things about and prevent them from criticising your product – many marketers assume that no one can do it. But you can influence word of mouth, and you have to try. The most obvious way to influence word of mouth is to make your product special. A product that surprises people because of its unexpectedly good quality or service is special enough to talk about. A good product or a well-delivered service wins fans and turns your customers into your sales force. Other tactics for managing WOM about your business or product may not be so obvious. Fortunately, we discuss them in the following sections.

Do good deeds

If no aspect of your product itself is particularly wonderful or surprising, do some attention-grabbing activity and associate that with your product. Here are some strategies that have worked well in the past to generate positive publicity and word of mouth:

- Get involved with a charity or not-for-profit organisation that operates in your area.
- Stage a fun event for kids.
- Let your employees take short sabbaticals to volunteer in community services.

Get creative. You can think of something worthwhile, some way of helping improve your world that surprises people and makes them take notice of the good you're doing in the name of your product.

Spice up your sales promotions

A 20p-off coupon isn't worth talking about. But a competition in which the winners get to spend a day with the celebrity of their choice can get consumers excited – and can be cheaper, too. A premium like this generates positive PR and a lot of WOM. We cover this area more in the next chapter.

Identify and cultivate decision influencers

In many markets, some people's opinions matter a lot more than others. These people are *decision influencers,* and if you (hypothetically) trace back the flow of opinions in your industry, you may find that many of them originate with these people. In business-to-business marketing, the decision influencers are often obvious. A handful of prominent executives, a few editors working for trade magazines, and some of the staff at trade associations probably exert a strong influence over everybody else's opinions. You can find identifiable decision influencers in consumer markets, as well. In the market for football equipment, youth-team coaches, league managers, and the owners of independent sporting goods shops are important decision influencers.

Seize control of the Internet

Okay, you can't actually take over the Internet, but you should be aware of what people are saying about your product or service on the Web. Weblogs, or blogs as they are commonly known, are one of the latest phenomena of the Internet age. What are blogs? The term *blogs* refers to personal Web publishing based on a topic or topics that attract a like-minded community of online participants. In other words, blogging is word of mouth on the Web. There are blogs dedicated to pretty much every subject you can imagine, from cars to politics to chocolate bars. You need to know this because there are two key ways you can use blogs to your advantage:

- ✔ **Get in on the discussion.** If there is a Web site dedicated to your market, then try to get your product mentioned or even establish a link between your site and the Weblog (blogs make extensive use of links to other sites). A recent survey among more than 600 blog publishers found that two-thirds would be happy to consider a direct public relations approach.

- ✔ **Create your own Weblog.** Blogs are cheap and easy to set up, which is why they are blossoming on the Web. You can download blog software for free from many sites such as www.myblogsite.com, and start publishing within the day. You can use this to promote your products and services and elicit feedback (bad as well as good) from potential customers.

Not all blogs or their users are business friendly, and you should remember this when making approaches or setting up you own blog. Blogs are run by enthusiasts and are usually independent of any corporate ties: That's the point, as well as the appeal of them. Many businesses have been hit by Web users criticising their products and services. That's the kind of word of mouth you don't want. Legally speaking, the Weblog publisher can be held responsible for libellous information but in reality there isn't much you can do about it – except improve your product!

Chapter 7

Planning Your Business Web Site

· ·

· ·

A marketing-orientated business Web site is the meat and drink of the online marketing world: not too exciting, but satisfying and extremely sustaining. By creating and maintaining a straightforward business Web site, you can easily provide customers, press, and analysts with vital information about your company and products. If the initial effort is successful, your site can lay the groundwork for a larger online marketing effort, possibly including your first move into online sales.

You've probably seen a lot of advanced Web technology used in high-profile Web sites – technologies such as Flash and Dynamic HTML. These innovations are all good, if used properly, but they have little place in a marketing-orientated business Web site. You can create a basic business Web site without too much planning. You can even begin to construct the site while you're in the midst of the planning process. The idea here is to jump-start your online presence by getting a competent representation of your company up and running – fast.

In this chapter, we describe how to create the initial site yourself or by working with a few colleagues or consultants.

Although some companies and consultants advertise that they'll create a basic business Web site for you for as little as £200, many of these ads are teasers designed to get you to pick up the phone and begin a process that can lead to you spending big money. Although you can and should use consultants or specialist suppliers for larger Web efforts, developing and publishing the initial site yourself is sensible. After you get some hands-on experience, you can know what you're paying for when you hire a Web-design agency to expand your Web site later. If you do hire help for the initial Web site effort, use this chapter to do as much of the work as you can on your own, and to double-check the outsiders' advice so that you can make sure that you're getting your money's worth.

Guiding Principles for Business Sites

A basic business Web site is like a simple, glossy brochure that briefly describes your company and is a showcase for your products. It reassures people that you're a competent player who'll be around for a while and from whom they can buy with confidence. Your Web site also lets users move easily from picking up basic information to more active steps such as contacting you by writing to you, or sending you an e-mail. But watch this last option, because it can backfire on you; you can receive so many e-mails that you have trouble responding to all of them.

These underlying principles should guide your effort to create a basic business Web site:

- **Harmlessness:** The first words of the doctors' Hippocratic Oath are 'First, do no harm', and this dictum should be honoured by people doing marketing as well. Misspellings, poor grammar, and basic errors in your site's text harm your company's image of competence. Web pages with large graphics that download slowly, or that have been developed using advanced technologies that not everyone can use, irritate potential customers. Allowing people to send you e-mail that goes unanswered can cause lost sales. Be cautious and avoid problems.

- **Fast build:** Your initial Web site effort should develop quickly from the initial idea to a live site. If you can do all the work yourself and don't need anyone's approval, you may get the site up and running in two weeks. If you need to discuss certain aspects of your site in advance and you need approval of the final product at the end, you may need a month or two to complete the site. Keep the project time as short as possible. However, make sure that you have a long-term plan in mind of what the site will look like once launched and evolved. Think about content and other sections you may want to add so that when you do, you don't have to completely rebuild your Web site!

- **Cheap:** A basic Web site can be created in-house, with perhaps some outside help on the look and feel, and published on a Web server by your Internet Service Provider (ISP) or Web-hosting service for very little cost. Expect to spend a few weeks on creating the site, possibly

£1,000 on a consultant for graphics and navigation help, and around £20 a month for an ISP to host the site on its server.

✔ **Effective:** Any marketing effort needs to support moving a prospective customer along the sales cycle. A basic Web site helps potential customers consider you as a possible supplier and encourages them to contact you in order to go further. (A Web site gets press, analysts, and investors to take you seriously, as well.)

✔ **Widely usable:** A basic Web site needs to be usable by anyone with an Internet connection and a Web browser; it should not contain any advanced Web technology that isn't supported by almost every available browser. That means no frames, no Flash, no Dynamic HTML – so no complicated animations or clever graphics. Keeping it simple makes your Web site easier to design and use.

✔ **Fits in on the Net:** Because of its origins among academics and scientists, the Internet has certain standards and practices that you ignore at your peril. (Until early in the 1990s, any commercial use of the Internet was forbidden, and even now, although it's dying out, some resistance to online commerce remains.) Respect the history of the medium by avoiding hype, overstatement, alarming layouts and graphics, and so on. A conservative or formulaic approach will serve you well until you develop a good feel for where you can have some fun.

Specifying Your Site Content

A basic business Web site is not something you should advertise or market heavily. The site is there for people to find when they're looking for information on the Web. Therefore the site's contents should be simple and easy to access, attractive but not exuberant. In footballing terms, the idea is that the position's early in the match, and you want to start things on a positive note by not being too gung ho in attack for the first quarter of the game.

A basic Web site will help you fulfil the first marketing-related function that any Web site must fulfil, that of a validator. 'Valid' means 'worthy', and a Web site functions as a validator by showing that you're worthy of doing business with. Validators do much of their work on a subconscious level, so the absence of key validators makes people feel uncomfortable, in ways that they find difficult to define but that operate very effectively in steering them clear of you. The powerful role of validators is why, as we mention in the 'Guiding Principles for Business Sites' section earlier in this chapter, ensuring your Web site is free of errors, technical barriers, and other irritants is important. (Would you send out salespeople who were poorly trained, ignorant of your products, and unable to speak the same language as your customers? Apply similar considerations to your Web site.)

A basic Web site has to meet fundamental information needs, but not much more than that. In fact, putting more information on it than is absolutely necessary is more likely to make your site difficult to navigate than to make it more useful. Avoid piling on a lot of content until you can also devote some time and energy to making your Web site easy to navigate.

If some of your planned material seems like a good idea but not strictly necessary, drop it (or, better still, put it on a list for later). Your final list of contents will vary depending on your company, your industry, and the available information resources you have at hand that can readily be repurposed for the Web. But most sites include the following:

- ✔ **About Us and Contact information:** This information is vital, and many sites – even big ones that cost a lot to create and maintain – either don't include it at all or bury it. Remember your customers may well be looking on your Web site to find out what your company does/how it does it. Also make sure that you provide your company, address, main phone number, and fax number. Make your contact information easily accessible, one link away from your homepage.

- ✔ **Where you do business:** If your geographic range is limited, make this fact clear up front. Be subtle and positive. On your homepage or contact information page, include a phrase like 'London's leading supplier of electrical services to business' or 'Western Europe's most innovative maker of widgets'. Help people who don't need to spend time on your Web site find that fact out quickly and in a positive context so that they leave happy, rather than annoyed.

- ✔ **Key people:** A brief list of key people, with a paragraph or so of descriptive information about each, can go far to make people comfortable with your company. (Some companies are reluctant to include this kind of information because they're afraid of attracting executive recruiters, but the benefits to your site's visitors outweigh this risk.) Don't include spouse-hobbies-and-kids stuff – just name, title, and a brief biography.

- ✔ **Key clients:** Though some companies are reluctant to include it for fear of attracting competitors, a list of key clients is a very strong validator of your success. List their names and a sentence or two about how they use your product or what you did for them. (Make sure that you ask your customers whether they mind this inclusion and whether they want you to include a link to their Web sites.) But don't include this kind of list until your customer list is at least a little bit impressive.

- ✔ **Products and services:** Include simple, brief descriptions of your products and services. You can also link to more detailed information, but put the simple descriptions in one place and make them easy to access; that way, prospects can scan descriptions quickly to decide whether to explore your site further.

✔ **Price:** Include specific price information if you can. Price can vary by
sales channel, by location, by options, or by many other factors, so
including specific prices can be difficult, but at least find some way to
communicate the rough price range of your product. Describing the price
paid in a few specific instances does nicely. People hate to 'turn off' customers, which may happen when you indicate your pricing structure,
but encouraging people who can't afford your product to contact you
(by not letting them know your price range) is not in anyone's interest.

✔ **Where and how to buy:** Tell people who visit your Web site where and
how to buy your products and services. This kind of information is
hidden or absent on all too many Web sites. If you have several sales
channels, list each of them, along with a brief description of each channel that highlights its unique advantages. One excellent method is to set
up an interactive area of a Web page that lets people enter their locations and then receive information about nearby sales outlets. If this feature involves too much work to handle right now, consider getting and
publicising an 0800 number as a stand-by until you can design and
implement an interactive Web capability.

✔ **Company, product, and service validators:** You put information that
validates specific products and services, employees, or the company as
a whole here. List positive descriptions of your company, people, products, and services from any reputable source, including analyst reports,
the general press, the trade press, and individual customers from well-
known companies or other organisations. Include any awards you've
won. Like your company Web site itself, these validators let people know
that your company is worth doing business with.

✔ **Company news:** People visit your Web site when they hear about your
company in connection with offline events such as trade shows, product
launches, and even that bit of legal action which seems to be never
ending. You look clueless if you don't list a few basics: trade-show
appearances, product launches, press releases, article mentions of your
company, and so on. Figure 7-1 shows the news section of a well-
designed Web site. Construct this section after you've cut your teeth on
the others and then put some real time and energy into getting it right.

✔ **Industry news:** This detail is optional, but important. A great way to
position your company as an industry leader is to put industry news on
your site. The goals of such an area include educating your customers
about your industry, validating your place in the industry, and getting
repeat visitors by creating a 'must-read' news area for customers, analysts, and press. (You think your competitors won't be annoyed when
everyone in your industry goes to your site for news? Especially when
they find themselves doing it too!) Don't hold up your site launch in
order to get this detail in, but seriously consider creating such an area
as soon as you can.

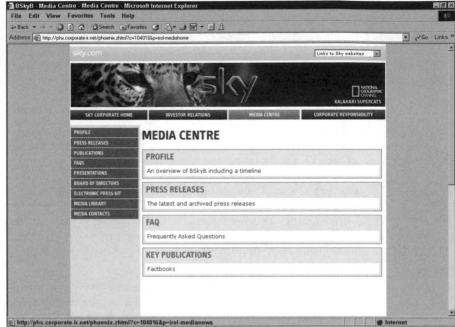

Figure 7-1:
Sky gets the
message
across
through
Sky.com.

If you don't want to develop your own news area, you can even link to a blog through one of the mainstream blogging tools like `www.blogger.com`. These self-publishing sites can be updated as regularly as you want and can be easily linked to your business Web site.

Creating a Look and Feel for Your Site

Most marketers that we know are very good with words – either in writing, public speaking, or both – and can create vivid pictures in listeners' minds. However, like many other people, most of them lack graphic-design skills.

Graphic design is the art of using visual elements to create a pleasing impression in the viewer's mind, and is a very important element in Web site design – to some of your Web site visitors, the most important element of all. Having a good design, or look and feel as it's called within the industry, is crucial to getting the right message across. Making a snap decision on the design of your site is wrong as it's probably one of the most vital decisions you may make when building your Web site.

Graphic design for the Web is a specialised art. Users view a company Web page in different-sized windows, using different-sized screens, with different colour capabilities, in all sorts of lighting conditions. Some users have custom settings to override the designer's choice of font, size, and text colours. Large graphics may make a page look strikingly attractive, yet take such a long time to download that they annoy and drive away users.

Using colour correctly on the Web is an art in and of itself. Colours and colour combinations that look attractive on one computer can look awful on another. In fact, out of the millions of shades of colour that a higher-end computer system can display, only 216 'browser-safe' colours exist that work well across most people's Web setups. If you use other colours, your site is likely to look awful to at least some of your visitors.

All these complexities and opportunities for error add up to a simple rule: Unless you have graphic-design experience and know, or are willing to learn, the details of Web-specific design, you need specialist help in designing the look and feel of your site. Here are a few possible sources of help:

- **Existing resources:** Your company may already have brand guidelines or a style guide based on its logo and marketing collateral, such as annual reports. Consider adapting this look for the Web, giving people who are familiar with your company in an offline context a comfortable feeling when they encounter your firm online.

- **Other well-designed sites:** Stealing the designs of other sites just isn't on. Looking at other sites, finding ones you like, and using the same *principles* as they do, however, is fine. (You're also free to avoid the practices of the sites that irritate you!)

- **Online advice:** Many sources of online advice on all aspects of Web page creation, including graphics, are available. Two good places to start are the World Wide Web Consortium at www.w3.org and www.webreview.com.

- **CD-ROM resources:** CD-ROMs with 'clip art' – professionally designed, non-copyrighted graphics optimised for online use – are available. You can pick up a few thousand buttons, backgrounds, icons, and other graphical elements for under £50 in many cases. An average person can achieve amazing effects with a little time and a good CD-ROM art collection.

- **Printed advice:** Many good books and articles describe how to create and deploy online graphics.

Outside help is an always available resource, and an especially good idea when creating your first site. Consider hiring a graphic designer to assist with the look of your Web site. Graphic designers who advertise on the Web are likely to have designed several sites they can refer you to as examples of their work. An example of one designer's Web presence is shown in Figure 7-2. If you need help finding a designer consider using a graphic design student; increasing numbers are available as the number of courses offering Web design grows. One of the best known is the University of Brighton (`www.brighton.ac.uk`).

Hiring a graphic designer is different from hiring a Web-design company. A Web-design company will construct your entire site for you; a graphic designer will just work on the look. For a basic site, which you want to do quickly and cheaply while learning as much as possible yourself, a graphic designer is preferable. You can get him or her involved early in the process, late, or even after your initial site is live.

Tell the designer who your expected visitors are, share any existing design elements that you have, and then let the designer work. Unlike a Web-design company, a graphic designer will need clear instructions on everything else about the site, including content and navigation. Expect to get a couple of alternatives and a quote for updating your site to include the design. (The designer may even offer to update your printed materials as well, improving consistency.)

Figure 7-2: Design8 has a simple but effective Web site.

At the end of the job, you should own the designer's work. This arrangement is called *work for hire* and is looked down upon by top professionals doing large jobs but is a fact of life for smaller jobs and for designers who haven't yet made a name for themselves. Avoid complicated intellectual property arrangements in which the designer retains rights to the design.

Having Your Site Done for You

Although creating your initial site yourself is a good idea, you may simply feel that you don't have the time or the expertise to do so. If you feel that way, get outside help.

The good news is that many individual consultants and Web-design agencies have sprung up to help companies create and maintain their Web sites. The bad news is that many, many ways exist to go wrong in hiring a digital agency.

But wait, we have more bad news! Having an external supplier or an individual do your Web site will probably save only a small amount of your time. A Web site is such an important reflection of your business that you should expect to be heavily involved with the project from start to finish.

The important steps in working with an outside supplier are setting up the engagement, managing the work, and following through when the work is done. Although these steps are the same for any general project, some specifics exist for a Web project that may surprise you.

Many of these steps apply to managing an internal Web project as well. Check these steps out even if you're doing the work yourself.

Getting engaged

Hiring an agency is often referred to as an 'engagement', and starting one may require more forethought than some marriages! Here are some simple rules that will help you get good results from a Web agency:

   ✔ **Find a site that has the elements you need.** Spend some time surfing Web sites, both inside and outside your own industry, to find a site that has most of the pieces you need. A clean and attractive front page, easy-to-find contact info, simple navigation, and brief, clear product descriptions are some of the elements you may be looking for. Figure 7-3, which incidentally is one of the authors' business Web sites, is a good example of a site with these elements.

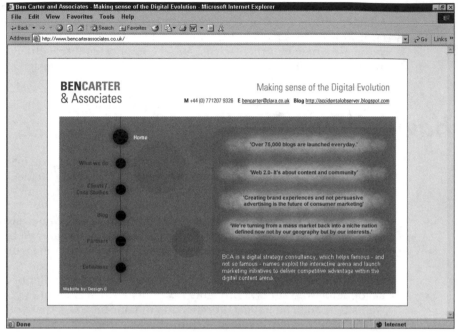

Figure 7-3:
BCA is an
uncompli-
cated Web
site with
clear aims.

✔ **Decide how many pages you want in your site.** Remember those sites you surfed in the previous step? See what the major areas are in some sites you like and count how many pages are in each area. Come up with a rough estimate of the number of pages in your site. *Hint:* The lower the number, the lower the cost and the greater the odds that your project will be a success.

✔ **Find several local agencies or consultants.** Even in this wired age, being able to meet with someone in person is a real benefit – especially for your initial project. Look at local business sites that you like and find out who created them. Talk to friends and colleagues to find specialists in your local area who have done good work. Check the *Yellow Pages* or the trade press for any local suppliers.

✔ **Set a budget.** Now that you have some idea of what you want and what other sites have cost in your local area, set an upper limit for your budget. Make sure that the figure you come up with is in line with the benefits you expect to get from your site. As a test, consider the impact that spending the same amount of money on radio advertising may have for you.

✔ **Hold a pitch.** Talk to the agencies you identified earlier. (Talking to more than one really helps, so don't rush this stage.) Get their ideas of what they think you need. Tell them what you're looking for and get a ballpark estimate as to timeframe and budget. *Hint:* Consider going to a marketing services intermediary like the AAR (`www.aargroup.co.uk`) or Haystack (`www.thehaystackgroup.com`) to help you find your digital agency.

✔ **Choose an agency.** Make an initial choice. Don't throw away the others' business cards until your first choice has shown you some good initial results!

Picking someone you believe you can trust is the most important part of engaging a specialist. You can always have your Web site made larger or flashier later, but the initial site simply needs to look good, be complete within a limited initial scope, and be delivered on time and on budget.

Make sure that you understand before engaging a firm whether it considers itself primarily a Web-programming company, a Web-design company, or a balance of both. Some agencies are excellent at creating the technical infrastructure of a site and making it work well but aren't adept at doing the graphics and copywriting. Others are excellent at look-and-feel but have little understanding of good Web site navigation or making things work 'under the hood'. The ideal firm is one with a good grasp of both aspects – or one that admits what its expertise isn't, allowing you to hire a freelancer to fill the gap.

As the focus moves away from building Web sites to what customers expect from Web sites, a need exists for more strategic thinking. Agencies often can't provide this strategy overview, so working with digital consultants (such as the authors of this book, say) to get the bigger picture of where your Web site will fit, what it will do, and how it will develop is useful.

Projecting your management style

Project management for Web sites has a lot in common with other projects, but a few Web-specific techniques exist that you should be aware of in addition to your usual tactics. The main problem with a Web project is that people react strongly to the look of a Web site – and if you wait until the end, an influential person could send the whole project back to the beginning. So clear up process hurdles early on to avoid hassle later.

✔ **Identify approvers.** Before you start, identify everyone who'll need to approve the site before it can go live and be publicised. This list should be short – and the people on it given status reports and updates at every major step.

✔ **Image is everything!** People are likely to react first and foremost to the look and feel of your Web site – the way background colours, images, navigation elements, and layout work together. Get a mock-up early on, and have all your approvers look at it and, when they find it acceptable, initial it. Better still, get two or three mock-ups that you can live with, and let the approvers make their choice on which should go forward to the next step.

✔ **Make a first impression.** Have your agency create a working version of the first page of your Web site hosted on a development site. At this point, get everyone's final okay on the basic look of the site. Figure 7-4 shows the first page of a Web site we like.

The first page of a Web site commonly gets 20–25 per cent of all the page views for the site, so getting it right is important. Also, if the first page meets with everyone's approval, the rest of the site is likely to receive only minor comments.

✔ **Get skeleton text ready.** Next, fill out the site by creating a dummy page for each and every page on the site. Each dummy page should have the agreed-upon look and feel for the site plus a one-paragraph description of what will be on that specific page. You can use the skeleton to test overall navigation. Have people review the dummy pages too – providing a last chance for 'shouldn't we have a page about our company history?' type comments.

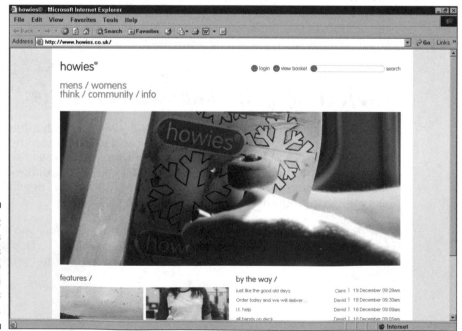

Figure 7-4:
Howies uses its Web site to get its green credentials across.

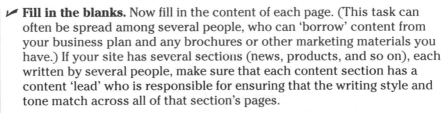

A caution about copyright

Getting wrapped up in the gorgeous graphics and clean navigation that a Web-site consultant develops for you is easy. But take a deep breath and – before making the new site live – ask the agency the difficult question, 'You do have the right to use all those design elements, don't you?'

A few inexperienced, rushed, or simply unscrupulous Web agencies have been known to copy graphic elements they like from existing Web sites and reuse them in sites they're creating, without permission. Doing so can violate the copyright of whoever created or owns the original site – and cause legal problems for you later.

In one case, a pioneering car Web site found that another car site was eerily similar – largely because most of the other site's design, graphics, and even text was identical to the pioneer's own. Lawyers quickly got involved.

Play it safe. Make sure that you get assurance from your agency, in writing, that all its design elements and text are either original or properly licensed.

✔ **Fill in the blanks.** Now fill in the content of each page. (This task can often be spread among several people, who can 'borrow' content from your business plan and any brochures or other marketing materials you have.) If your site has several sections (news, products, and so on), each written by several people, make sure that each content section has a content 'lead' who is responsible for ensuring that the writing style and tone match across all of that section's pages.

If you don't already have an in-house copywriter then you need to consider hiring one who can rewrite your draft copy. Again, choosing the right copywriter is vital as the content of your site is imperative to getting the right message across to your customers!

✔ **Time for the testing.** After the site's dummy pages are filled in, set aside some time to test it. Have one person read through all the pages to make sure that they're consistent in how they present your company and its products. If there's a danger that your customers may stumble across it then consider hosting it on a development or a test server to iron out the tweaks. Also make sure that the Web site works with all the different browsers like Internet Explorer, Mozilla Firefox, and Safari. When you are happy, then do a 'soft launch' – put the site up on the Web, but don't publicise its existence until everyone who needs to approve of the site has had a chance to do so.

✔ **Go, go, go!** After the site's up and you're happy with it, get the word out. Put the URL on business cards, stationery, advertisements, and more. Ask for feedback from people you know and from site visitors as well.

This process crucially has many checkpoints, making it difficult for the project to get too far off-track without your knowing about it – and having a chance to fix the problem.

Beating the wrap-up

Plan now for future updating of your Web site. The basic structure you've created should last for a long time. Work with your agency now to identify procedures for the following important tasks:

- **Updating content:** You should be able to update the site's content without the agency's help and to do this you will need to have access to a content management system, unless you want them involved as a checkpoint. Specify how content within a page will be updated.

  Content Management Systems (CMS) are important if you want to be able to update your Web site regularly and they should be considered if you are going to have a lot of text that will need changing regularly. Having CMS built in from the start will save you a lot of hassle and will mean that you can access/change your site very easily. There are lots of different CMS options but if you are a complete Web novice then you will need the simplest one. Known as *WYSIWYG* CMS (standing for 'What you see is what you get'), such a system will enable you to cut and paste copy into text boxes via a simple Web interface. You don't need to understand HTML to operate this, which is why it appeals to those who aren't Web wizards.

- **Adding pages:** Identify likely areas in which you may want to add a new page; the product area will need to be extended, for instance, if you launch a new product. Work out how long it should take to add a page from initial idea to launch, and who needs to be involved.

- **Revising the whole site:** At some point, you'll want to revise the whole site. Work out what might trigger that revision, and set up regular meetings with your agency – say, quarterly – to identify needed changes and to start the next major overhaul.

Don't be afraid to tell your agency that you may get other people involved for some or all of the work ahead; for your first agency to play a lesser role as the project develops, or even to have no role at all, is very common. Do let your consultants know about any expectations that weren't met, as well as the things you were happy about, and whether they can expect a good reference from you for future clients.

Making your site accessible

Make your site as accessible to as many people as possible. Avoid being in a situation where some of your customers can't use your site when they find it – you'll commit corporate suicide.

Lots of agencies will offer you an *analytics* service as part of the Web build project, in which they monitor how a test-base of users use and navigate the site. These 'test sessions' are crucial for you to identify any problems or pitfalls in the way the site has been designed and built. Better to spot flaws now rather than when the site goes live: Bad Web sites result in lost custom.

Also make sure that your site can be accessed and used by disabled people. Since 1999, the Disability Discrimination Act has put the onus on Web publishers to ensure that their sites have a basic level of accessibility. Ignore this advice at your peril: You could be breaking the law!

More information on accessibility guidelines and standards, which are endorsed by the UK government, can be found at the World Wide Web Consortium: www.w3.org.

Chapter 8

Choosing and Equipping Your New E-Business

Starting your online business is like refurbishing an old house. Both projects involve a series of recognisable phases:

- **The idea phase:** First, you tell people about your great idea. They hear the enthusiasm in your voice, nod their heads, and say something like, 'Good luck.' They've seen you in this condition before and know how it usually turns out.

- **The decision phase:** Undaunted, you begin honing your plan. You read books (like this one), ask questions, and shop around until you find just the right tools and materials to get you on your way. Of course, when you're up to your neck in work, you may start to panic, asking yourself whether you're really up for the task.

- **The assembly phase:** Undeterred, you forge ahead. You plug in your tools and go to work. Drills spin, and sparks fly, as your idea becomes reality.

- **The test-drive phase:** One fine day, out of the dust and fumes, your masterpiece emerges. You invite everyone over to enjoy the fruits of your labour. All those who were sceptical before are now awe-struck and full of admiration. Satisfied with the result, you enjoy your project for years to come.

If refurbishing a house doesn't work for you, think about restoring an antique car, planning an anniversary party, or devising a mountain-climbing excursion in Tibet. The point is that starting an online business is a project like any other – one that you can construct and accomplish in stages. Right now, you're at the first stage of launching your new business. Your creativity is working overtime. You may even have some rough sketches that only a mother could love.

This chapter helps you get from concept to reality. Your first step is to imagine how you want your business to look and feel. Then you can begin to develop and implement strategies for achieving your dream. You've got a big advantage over those who started new businesses a few years ago: You've got thousands of predecessors to show you what works and what doesn't.

Starting Off on the Right Foot

As you travel along the path from idea to reality, you must also consider equipping your online business properly – just like you would have to equip a traditional, bricks-and-mortar business. One of the many exciting aspects of launching a business online, however, is the absence of many *overheads* (that is, operating expenses). Many real world businesses resort to taking out loans to pay the rent and design their shop fronts, pay fees, and purchase shop furniture. In contrast, the primary overhead for an online business is computer gadgetry. It's great if you can afford top-of-the-line equipment, but you'll be happy to know that the latest bells and whistles aren't absolutely necessary in order to build a business online and maintain it effectively. But in order to streamline the technical aspects of connecting to the Internet and creating a business Web site, some investment is always necessary.

Mapping Out Your Online Business

How do you get off square one? Start by imagining the kind of business that is your ultimate goal. This step is the time to indulge in some brainstorming. Envisioning your business is a creative way of asking yourself the all-important questions: Why do I want to go into business online? What are my goals? Table 8-1 illustrates possible objectives and suggests how to achieve them. By envisioning the final result you want to achieve, you can determine the steps you need to take to get there.

Table 8-1	Online Business Models	
Goal	**Type of Web Site**	**What to Do**
Make big bucks	Sales	Sell items or get lots of paying advertisers
Gain credibility and attention	Marketing	Put your CV and samples of your work online
Turn an interest into a source of income	Hobby/special interest	Invite like-minded people to share your passion, participate in your site, and generate traffic so that you can gain advertisers or customers.

Looking around

You don't need to feel like you have to reinvent the wheel. A great idea doesn't necessarily mean something completely fresh that has never been done before (although if you have a great, new idea, then good for you!). Sometimes, spending just half an hour surfing the Net can stimulate your mental network. Find sites with qualities you want to emulate.

Many people start up online selling to people just like themselves. For example, a motorbike enthusiast may start up a parts business or an informative site about the best bikes and where to buy them. If you're a hobby geek, then your own likes and dislikes have a lot of value. As you search the Web for inspiration, make a list as you go of what you find appealing and jot down notes on logos, designs, text, and *functionality* (how the site lets you access its features). That way, you'll have plenty of data to draw upon as you begin to refine what you yourself want to do.

Making your mark

The online world has undergone a population explosion. According to Internet Systems Consortium's Domain Survey (www.isc.org), in 2007, 433.2 million computers that hosted Web sites were connected to the Internet, compared with 171.6 million in 2002. As an *ontrepreneur* (online entrepreneur), your goal is to stand out from the crowd – or to 'position yourself in the marketplace', as business consultants like to say. Consider the following tried-and-tested suggestions if you want your Web site to be a popular corner of the Internet:

- Do something you know all about.
- Make a statement.
- Include contact details.
- Give something away for free.
- Be obvious.
- Find your niche.
- Do something you love.

Evaluating commercial Web sites

Is your Web site similar to others? How does it differ? (Or to put it another way: How is it better?) Your customers will be asking these questions, so you may as well start out by asking them as well.

Commercial Web sites – those whose Internet addresses usually end with `.co.uk`, `.com`, or `.biz` – are the fastest-growing segment of the Net and is the area you'll be entering. The trick is to be comfortable with the size and level of complexity of a business that's right for you. In general, your options are

- **A big commercial Web site:** The Web means big business, and plenty of big companies create Web sites with the primary goal of supplementing a product or service that's already well known and well established. Just a few examples are the Ribena Web site (`www.ribena.co.uk`), the Pepsi World Web site (`www.pepsiworld.com`), and the Toyota Web site (`www.toyota.com`). True, these commercial Web sites were created by corporations with many millions of pounds to throw around, but you can still look at them to get ideas for your own site.

- **A mid-size site:** You can look at mid-sized companies, too, who use the Web as an extension of their brand. Brilliant examples of mid-sized companies are Ben & Jerry's ice cream (`www.benjerry.co.uk`) and Innocent Smoothies (`www.innocentsmoothies.co.uk`). John Cleese has a simply awesome Web site (`www.thejohncleese.com` – note that `www.johncleese.com` was pinched by a look-alike before the real one could get in there, which businesses can learn a lot from). Sites such as CD Wow (`www.cdwow.co.uk`) and Play.com (`www.play.com`) are mid-sized companies, but their Web sites are as good as any blue chip you're likely to come across.

- **A site that's just right:** No prerequisites for prior business experience guarantee success on the Web. It's also fine to start out as a single person, couple, or family. In fact, the rest of this book is devoted to helping you produce a top-notch, home-grown entrepreneurial business with the minimum of assistance. This chapter gets you off to a good start by examining the different kinds of business you can launch online and some business goals you should be setting yourself.

Flavours of Online Businesses You Can Taste Test

If you're an excitable character, you may have to curb your enthusiasm as you comb the Internet for ideas. Use the following examples to create a picture of your business and then zero in on the kind of sites that can help you formulate its look and feel.

Selling consumer products

The Web has always attracted those looking for unique items or something customised just for them. Consider taking your wares online if one or both of the following applies to you:

- ✔ You're a creative person who creates as a hobby the type of stuff people may want to buy (think artists, designers, model makers, and so on). For example, Dan's mum is great at calligraphy, and he thinks she'd make a packet by selling her writing online.

- ✔ You have access to the sort of products or services that big companies simply can't replicate. Those items may mean regional foods, hand-made souvenirs, or items for car enthusiasts; the list is truly endless – you just have to find your niche.

Sorry to bang on about Ben & Jerry's (we're all big fans), but we sometimes go to their Web site (www.benjerry.com or www.benjerrys.co.uk) just to drool. These guys should be your role models. The motivation for starting their business was that they just couldn't get enough of ice cream and loved creating bizarre flavours. They're entrepreneurs just like you, and we think their Web site is nearly as tasty as their products. It focuses on the unique flavours and high quality of their ice cream, as well as their personalities and business standards.

Innocent Smoothies (www.innocentdrinks.co.uk) are the same. They build on that 'community' feel by offering you fun things to do when you're bored. They even suggest popping over to Fruit Towers (their headquarters) for a visit. Their branding is brilliant and rare – try to match it (without copying), but remember that you must reflect your own business-style and the people you want to sell to.

Punting what you're good at

Either through a Web site or through listings in indexes and directories, offering your professional services online can expand your client base dramatically. It also gives existing clients a new way to contact you or just see what's new with your business. Here are just a few examples of professionals who are offering their services online:

- **Solicitors:** John Pickering and Partners are personal injury solicitors (aren't they all nowadays) who specialise in severe diseases and critical injuries sustained at work. The firm is based in Manchester, but its Web site gives it a national and even global reach (www.johnpickering.co.uk). To give it a professional feel, something which is vital in this profession, the Web site features relevant news updates, information about claims, and even information on how to choose a solicitor.

- **Psychotherapists:** Dr. Thomas Kraft, a Harley Street practitioner, has a nice, easy-to-understand Web site at www.londonpsychotherapy.co.uk see Figure 8-1). The format is simple, yet a good amount of important information appears on the home page. Without clicking, we know his name, fields of expertise, and phone number. On top of this easy navigation there are chunky buttons providing a visible route to other facts you may need to know.

- **Architects:** At the time of writing, the Web site of Robertson Francis Partnership, a chartered architect based in Cardiff, was under construction (www.rfparchitects.co.uk). Plenty of professional Web sites take an age to get up and running because people are too busy running their businesses. If this sounds like you, do what these guys did and at least get something up there – even if it's just your name and contact details.

- **Music teachers:** Do a search on Gumtree (www.gumtree.com) or Google local (local.google.co.uk) and you'll see just how many music teachers are plying their wares online. Many don't have a Web site themselves, but are savvy enough to know that people will be searching for their services online.

We're busy people who don't always have the time to pore over the small print. Short and snappy nuggets of information draw customers to your site and make them feel as though they're getting 'something for free'. One way you can put forth this professional expertise is by starting your own online newsletter. You get to be editor, writer, and mailing-list manager. Plus, you get to talk as much as you want, network with tons of people who subscribe to your publication, and put your name and your business before lots of people.

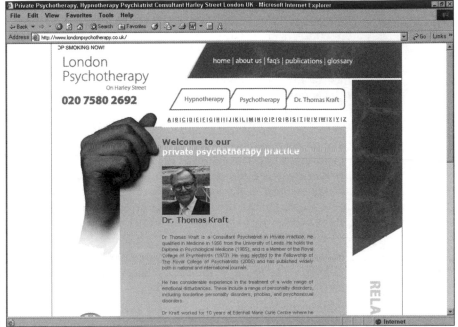

Figure 8-1:
A London psycho-therapist provides his contact information and fields of expertise on this simple, yet informative, Web page.

Making money from your expertise

The original purpose of the Internet was to share knowledge via computers, and information is the commodity that has fuelled cyberspace's rapid growth. As the Internet and commercial online networks continue to expand, information remains key.

Collecting and disseminating data can be a profitable pastime. Think of all the Web sites where information is the chief commodity rather than clothes or music. The fact is, people love to get knowledge they trust from the comfort of their own homes.

Here are just a few examples of the types of business that feed on our love of knowledge:

- ✔ **Search engines:** Some businesses succeed by connecting Web surfers with companies, organisations, and individuals that specialise in a given area. Yahoo! (www.yahoo.co.uk) is the most obvious example. Originally started by two college students, Yahoo! has become an Internet behemoth by gathering information in one index so that people can easily find things online.

✔ **Links pages:** On her 'Grandma Jam's I Love to Win' sweepstakes site (www.grandmajam.com), Janet Marchbanks-Aulenta gathers links to current contests along with short descriptions of each one. Janet says her site receives as many as 22,000 visits per month and generates income through advertising and affiliate links to other contest Web sites. She says she loves running her own business despite the hard work involved with keeping it updated. 'The key to succeeding at this type of site is to build up a regular base of users that return each day to find new contests – the daily upkeep is very important,' she says.

✔ **Personal recommendations:** The personal touch sells. Just look at Web 2.0 site Digg.com. This guide to the online world provides Web surfers with a central location where they can track down popular news stories. It works because real people submit the stories, and only the most popular stories make it to the top of page one. The users themselves are who 'digg' stories – the most popular ones rise up the rankings. Just listen to Digg's description of itself:

> *'Digg is all about user powered content. Every article on digg is submitted and voted on by the digg community. Share, discover, bookmark, and promote the news that's important to you!'*

Note that the emphasis is on *the user* and that it's written for *you*. Describing your services in this way makes people feel at home.

Resource sites can transform information into money in several ways. In some cases, individuals pay to become members. Sometimes, businesses pay to be listed on a site. Other times, a site attracts so many visitors on a regular basis that other companies pay to post advertising on the site. Big successes – such as MySpace (www.myspace.com) and Digg (www.digg.com) – carry a healthy share of ads and strike lucrative partnerships with big companies as well.

Creating opportunities with technology

What could be more natural than using the Web to sell what you need to get and stay online? The online world itself, by the very fact that it exists, has spawned all kinds of business opportunities for entrepreneurs:

✔ **Computers:** Some discount computer houses have made a killing by going online and offering equipment for less than conventional high street shops. Being on the Internet means that they save on overheads and then pass on those savings to their customers.

✔ **Internet Service Providers:** These businesses connect you to the Internet. Many ISPs, such as AOL or BT Retail, are big concerns. But smaller companies, such as Eclipse Internet, offer home-based broadband, similar levels of service, and sometimes discounts, too.

✔ **Software:** Matt Wright is well known on the Web for providing free computer scripts that add important functionality to Web sites, such as processing information that visitors submit via online forms. Matt's Script Archive site (www.worldwidemart.com/scripts) now includes an ad for a book on scripting that he co-authored, as well as an invitation to businesses to take out advertisements on his site.

Being a starving artist without starving

Being creative no longer means you have to live out of your flower-covered VW van, driving from art fairs to craft shows (unless you want to, of course). If you're simply looking for exposure and feedback on your creations, you can put samples of your work online. Consider the following suggestions for virtual creative venues (and revenues):

✔ **Host art galleries.** Thanks to online galleries, artists whose sales were previously limited to one region can get enquiries from all over the world. Artists Online (www.artistsonline.org.uk) is a new Web site dedicated to promoting artists who are not yet well known. It showcases and sells artwork and lets users know about upcoming events and exhibitions. The personal Web site (see Figure 8-2) created by artist Marques Vickers (www.marquesv.com) has received worldwide attention.

Figure 8-2:
A California artist created this Web site to gain recognition and sell his creative work. It's very basic — but seems all the more artistic for that fact.

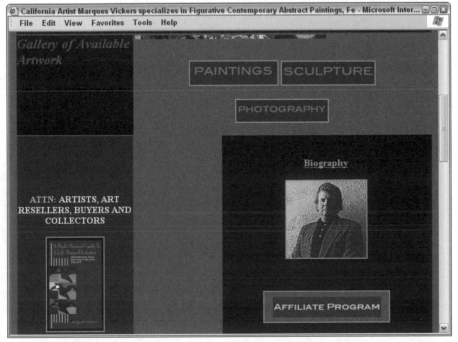

- ✔ **Publish your writing.** *Blogs* (Web logs, or online diaries) are all the rage these days. The problem is that absolutely millions exist, and most aren't worth your time. However, the most successful are generating ad revenue. To find out how to create one yourself, check out Blogger (`www.blogger.com`). For inspiration, check out a successful independent blog, such as Seth Godin's (`sethgodin.typepad.com`) or a blog attached to an online newspaper. *The Times*'s Web site has a whole host of them.

- ✔ **Sell your music.** Singer-songwriter Sam Roberts sells his own CDs, videos, and posters through his online shop (`www.samrobertsband.com`).

You can, of course, also sell all that junk that's been accumulating in your loft, as well as anything else you no longer want, on eBay.co.uk.

Marketing One-to-One with Your Customers

After you've reviewed Web sites that conduct the sorts of business ventures that interest you, you can put your goals into action. First you develop a marketing strategy that expresses your unique talents and services. People need encouragement if they're going to flock to your Web site, so try to come up with a cunning plan. One marketing ploy may be enough; we suggest coming up with five individual means to bring the customers in. For example, you can blog about your Web site, answer questions in forums, do a competition, go to networking events, and so on.

The fact is that online communities are often close-knit, long-standing groups of people who are good friends. The Web, newsgroups, and e-mail allow you to communicate with these communities in ways that other media can't match.

Focus on a customer segment

Old-fashioned business practices, such as getting to know your customers as individuals and providing personal service, are alive and well in cyberspace. Your No. 1 business strategy when it comes to starting your business online sounds simple: Know your market.

What's not so simple about this little maxim is that, in cyberspace, it takes some work to get to know exactly who your customers are. Web surfers don't leave their names, addresses, or even e-mail addresses when they visit your site. Instead, when you check the raw, unformatted records (or *logs*) of the visitors who have connected to you, you see pages and pages of what appears to be computer gobbledygook. You need special software, such as the program WebTrends, to interpret the information.

How do you develop relationships with your customers?

✔ **Get your visitors to identify themselves.** Encourage them to send you e-mail messages, place orders, enter contests, or provide you with feedback.

✔ **Become an online researcher.** Find existing users who already purchase goods and services online that are similar to what you offer. Visit newsgroups that are relevant to what you sell, search for mailing lists, and participate in discussions so that people can find out more about you.

✔ **Keep track of your visitors.** Count the visitors who come to your site and, more importantly, the ones who make purchases or seek out your services. Manage your customer profiles so that you can sell your existing clientele the items they're likely to buy.

✔ **Help your visitors get to know you.** Web space is virtually unlimited. Feel free to tell people about aspects of your life that don't relate directly to your business or to how you plan to make money. Consider Judy Vorfeld, who does Internet research, Web design, and office support. Her Web site (www.ossweb.com), shown in Figure 8-3, includes the usual lists of clients and services; however, it also includes a link to her personal home page and a page that describes her community service work.

Book V

Bigging Up Your Business

Figure 8-3:
Telling potential customers about yourself makes them more comfortable telling you about themselves.

After you get to know your audience, job No. 2 in your marketing strategy is to catch their attention. You have two ways to do this:

- **Make yourself visible.** In Web-space, your primary task is simply making people aware that your site exists at all. You do so by getting yourself included in as many indexes, search sites, and business listings as possible. You can also do a bit of self-promotion in your own online communications.

- **Make your site an eye-catcher.** Getting people to come to you is only half the battle. The other half is getting them to shop when they get there. Combine striking images with promotions, offering useful information, and providing ways for customers to interact with you.

Boost your credibility

Marketing task No. 3 is to transfer your confidence and sense of authority about what you do to anyone who visits you online. Convince people that you're an expert and a trustworthy person with whom they can do business.

Customers may have fewer reasons to be wary about using the Internet nowadays. But remember that the Web as we know it has been around only a short time, and a large minority of people are still wary of surfing online, let alone shopping. Here, too, you can do a quick two-step in order to market your expertise.

Document your credentials

Feature any honours, awards, or professional affiliations you have that relate to your online work. If you're providing professional or consulting services online, you may even make a link to your online CV. If you feel it's relevant, give details about how long you've been in your field and how you got to know what you know about your business.

If these forms of verification don't apply to you, all is not lost. Just move to the all-important technique that we describe in the next section.

Convince with must-have information

Providing useful, practical information about a topic is one of the best ways to market yourself online. One of the great things about starting an online business is that you don't have to incur the design and printing charges to get a brochure or flyer printed. You have plenty of space on your online business site to talk about your sales items or services in as much detail as you want. Try not to bore people though, will you!

Most Internet Service Providers (ISPs) give you 20MB (megabytes, that is) or more of space for your Web pages and associated files. Because the average Web page occupies only 5 to 10K (that's kilobytes) of space not counting the space taken up by images and multimedia files, it'll take a long time before you begin to run out of room.

What, exactly, can you talk about on your site? Here are some ideas:

- ✓ Provide detailed descriptions and photos of your sale items.

- ✓ Include a full list of clients you have worked for previously.

- ✓ Publish a page of testimonials from satisfied customers.

- ✓ Give your visitors a list of links to Web pages and other sites where people can find out more about your area of business.

- ✓ Toot your own horn: Explain why you love what you do and why you're so good at it.

Ask satisfied customers to give you a good testimonial. All you need is a sentence or two that you can use on your Web site.

A site that contains compelling, entertaining content will become a resource that online visitors bookmark and return to on a regular basis. Be sure to update it regularly, and you'll have fulfilled the dream of any online business owner.

Create customer-to-customer contact: Everybody wins

People regularly take advantage of freebies online by, for example, downloading *shareware* or *freeware* programs (programs that are developed and distributed for free). They get free advice from newsgroups, and they find free companionship from chat rooms and online forums. Having already paid for network access and computer equipment, they actually *expect* to get something for free.

Your customers will keep coming back if you devise as many promotions, giveaways, or sales as possible. You can also get people to interact through online forums or other tools.

In online business terms, anything that gets your visitors to click links and enter your site is good. Provide as many links to the rest of your site as you can on your home page. Many interactions that don't seem like sales do lead

to sales, and it's always your goal to keep people on your site as long
as possible.

For more about creating Web sites, check out *Creating Web Pages For Dummies,*
7th Edition, by Bud E. Smith and Arthur Bebak (Wiley).

Be a player in online communities

You may wait until the kids go off to school to tap away at your keyboard in
your home office, but that doesn't mean that you're alone. Thousands of
home-office workers and entrepreneurs just like you connect to the Net
every day and share many of the same concerns, challenges, and ups and
downs as you.

Starting an online business isn't only a matter of creating Web pages, scanning photos, and taking orders. Marketing and networking are essential to
making sure that you meet your goals. Participate in groups that are related
either to your particular business or to online business in general. Here are
some ways that you can make the right connections and get support and
encouragement at the same time.

Be a newsgroupie

Businesspeople tend to overlook newsgroups or forums because of admoni-
tions about *spam* (pesky e-mails sent without permission by people trying to
make money dishonestly) and other violations of *Netiquette* (the set of rules
that govern newsgroup communications). However, when you approach
newsgroup participants on their own terms (not by spamming them but by
answering questions and participating in discussions), newsgroups can be a
wonderful resource for businesspeople. They attract knowledgeable consumers who are strongly interested in a topic – just the sort of people who
make great customers.

A few newsgroups (in particular, the ones with `biz` at the beginning of their
names) are especially intended to discuss small business issues and sales.
Here are a few suggestions:

- ✔ www.realbusiness.co.uk/Forums.aspx
- ✔ www.startups.co.uk/Forums/ShowForum.aspx?ForumID=223
- ✔ www.ukbusinessforums.co.uk/forums

The easiest way to access newsgroups is to use Google's Web-based directory (www.google.co.uk/grphp?hl=en). You can also use the newsgroup
software that comes built into the most popular Web browser packages. Each

browser or newsgroup program has its own set of steps for enabling you to access Usenet. *Usenet* is an Internet discussion system that has existed since the earliest days of the Web; users post messages to distributed newsgroups in a kind of bulletin board system. Use your browser's online help system to find out how you can access newsgroups in this way.

Be sure to read the group's FAQ (frequently asked questions) page before you start posting. It's a good idea to *lurk before you post* – that is, simply read messages being posted to the group in order to find out about members' concerns. Stay away from groups that seem to consist only of get-rich-quick schemes or other scams. When you do post a message, be sure to keep your comments relevant to the conversation and give as much helpful advice as you can.

The most important business technique in communicating by either e-mail or newsgroup postings is to include a signature file at the end of your message. A *signature file* is a simple message that newsgroup and mail software programs automatically add to your messages (just like corporate e-mails). A typical one includes your name, title, and the name of your company. You can also include a link to your business's home page. A good example is Judy Vorfeld's signature file, shown in Figure 8-4.

Figure 8-4:
A descriptive signature file on your messages serves as an instant business advertise-ment.

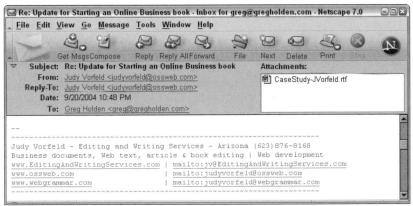

Be a mailing list-ener

A *mailing list* is a discussion group that communicates by exchanging e-mail messages between members who share a common interest. Each e-mail message sent to the list is distributed to all the list's members. Any of those members can, in turn, respond by sending e-mail replies. The series of back-and-forth messages develops into discussions.

The nice thing about a mailing list is that it consists only of people who have subscribed to the list, which means that they really want to be involved and participate.

An excellent mailing list to check out is the Small and Home-Based Business Discussion List (`www.talkbiz.com/bizlist/index.html`). This list is *moderated,* meaning that someone reads through all postings before they go online and filters out any comments that are inappropriate or off-topic. Also, try searching the Topica directory of discussion groups (`lists.topica.com`). Click Small Business (under Choose From Thousands Of Newsletters And Discussions) to view a page full of discussion groups and other resources for entrepreneurs.

The number of groups you join and how often you participate in them is up to you. The important thing is to regard every one-to-one-personal contact as a seed that may sprout into a sale, a referral, an order, a contract, a bit of useful advice, or another profitable business blossom.

It's not a newsgroup or a mailing list, but a Web site called iVillage.com (`www.ivillage.com`) brings women together by providing chat rooms where they can type messages to one another in real time, as well as message boards where they can post messages. (Men, of course, can participate, too.) Experts (and some who just claim to be experts) often participate in these forums.

Add ways to sell and multiply your profits

Many successful online businesses combine more than one concept of what constitutes electronic commerce. You can sell your goods and services on your Web site, but the Internet offers other venues for promoting and selling your wares.

Selling through online classifieds

If you're looking for a quick and simple way to sell products or promote your services online without having to pay high overhead costs, consider taking out a classified ad in an online publication or a popular site like Craigslist (`www.craigslist.org`) or InfoZoo (`www.infozoo.co.uk`).

The classifieds work the same way online as they do in print publications: You pay a fee and write a short description along with contact information, and the publisher makes the ad available to potential customers. However, online classifieds have a number of big advantages over their print equivalents:

✔ **Audience:** Rather than hundreds or thousands who may view your ad in print, tens of thousands, or perhaps even millions, can see it online.

✔ **Searchability:** Online classifieds are often indexed so that customers can search for particular items with their Web browser. This index makes it easier for shoppers to find exactly what they want, whether it's a Precious Moment figurine or a Martin guitar.

✔ **Time:** On the Net, ads are often online for a month or more.

✔ **Cost:** Some sites, such as Commerce Corner (www.comcorner.com), let you post classified ads for free.

On the downside, classifieds are often buried at the back of online magazines or Web sites, just as they are in print, so they're hardly well-travelled areas. Also, most classifieds don't make use of the graphics that help sell and promote goods and services so effectively throughout the Web.

Dan's site InfoZoo.co.uk gets around this obstacle by letting customers upload their own logo and by including a search mechanism that prevents adverts from becoming buried. It's aimed at small UK-based businesses, too – so you're in good company.

Classifieds are an option if you're short on time or money. But don't forget that on your own online business site you can provide more details and not have to spend a penny.

Selling via online auctions

Many small businesses, such as antique dealerships or jewellery shops, sell individual merchandise through online auctions. eBay.co.uk and other popular auction sites provide effective ways to target sales items at collectors who are likely to pay top dollar for desirable goodies. If you come up with a system for finding things to sell and for turning around a large number of transactions on a regular basis, you can even turn selling on eBay into a full-time source of income.

Software Solutions for Online Business

One of the great things about starting an Internet business is that you get to use Internet software. As you probably know, the programs you use online are inexpensive (sometimes free), easy to use and install, and continually updated.

Although you probably already have a basic selection of software to help you find information and communicate with others in cyberspace, the following sections describe some programs you may not have as yet and that will come in handy when you create your online business.

Don't forget to update your insurance by sending your insurer a list of new software (and hardware) or even by purchasing insurance specifically for your computer-related items.

Anyone who uses firewall or antivirus software will tell you how essential these pieces of software are, for home or business use. Find out more about such software in Greg's book *Norton Internet Security For Dummies* (Wiley).

Web browser

A *Web browser* is software that serves as a visual interface to the images, colours, links, and other content contained on the Web. The most popular such program is Microsoft Internet Explorer, which powers 90 per cent of UK Web browsers (that's why Bill Gates has so much dosh). However, new and increasingly popular browsers such as Mozilla Firefox and Opera are gaining new fans every day. See which one you like the best.

Your Web browser is your primary tool for conducting business online, just as it is for everyday personal use. When it comes to running a virtual shop or consulting business, though, you have to run your software through a few more paces than usual. You need your browser to

- Preview the Web pages you create
- Display frames, animations, movie clips, and other goodies you plan to add online
- Support some level of Internet security, such as Secure Sockets Layer (SSL), if you plan to conduct secure transactions on your site

In addition to having an up-to-date browser with the latest features, installing more than one kind of browser on your computer is a good idea. For example, if you use Microsoft Internet Explorer because that's what came with your operating system, be sure to download the latest copy of Firefox as well. That way, you can test your site to make sure that it looks good to all your visitors. Remember, too, that people use Apple Macs as well as PCs, laptops, palmtops, and, increasingly, 4G mobile phones. Your Web site has to look good on all of them.

Web page editor

HyperText Markup Language (HTML) is a set of instructions used to format text, images, and other Web page elements so that Web browsers can correctly display them. But you don't have to master HTML in order to create your own Web pages. Plenty of programs, called *Web page editors,* are available to help you format text, add images, make hyperlinks, and do all the fun assembly steps necessary to make your Web site a winner.

In many cases, Web page editors come with electronic shop front packages. QuickSite comes with Microsoft FrontPage Express. Sometimes, programs that you use for one purpose can also help you create Web documents: Microsoft Word has an add-on called Internet Assistant that enables you to save text documents as HTML Web pages, and Microsoft Office 98 and later (for the Mac) or Office 2000 or later (for Windows) enable you to export files in Web page format automatically.

Taking e-mail a step higher

You're probably very familiar with sending and receiving e-mail messages. But when you start an online business, you should make sure that e-mail software has some advanced features:

- ✔ **Autoresponders:** Some programs automatically respond to e-mail requests with a form letter or document of your choice.

- ✔ **Mailing lists:** With a well-organised address book (a feature that comes with some e-mail programs), you can collect the e-mail addresses of visitors or subscribers and send them a regular update of your business activities or, better yet, an e-mail newsletter.

- ✔ **Quoting:** Almost all e-mail programs let you quote from a message to which you're replying, so you can respond easily to a series of questions.

- ✔ **Attaching:** Attaching a file to an e-mail message is a quick and convenient way to transmit information from one person to another.

- ✔ **Signature files:** Make sure that your e-mail software automatically includes a simple electronic signature at the end. Use this space to list your company name, your title, and your Web site URL.

Both Outlook Express, the e-mail component of Microsoft Internet Explorer, and Netscape Messenger, which is part of the Netscape Communicator suite of programs, include most or all these features.

Discussion group software

When your business site is up and running, consider taking it a step farther by creating your own discussion area right on your Web site. This sort of discussion area isn't a newsgroup as such; it doesn't exist in Usenet, and you don't need newsgroup software to read and post messages. Rather, it's a Web-based discussion area where your visitors can compare notes and share their passion for the products you sell or the area of service you provide.

Programs such as Microsoft FrontPage enable you to set up a discussion area on your Web site.

FTP software

FTP (File Transfer Protocol) is one of those acronyms you see time and time again as you move around the Internet. You may even have an FTP program that your ISP gave you when you obtained your Internet account. But chances are you don't use it that often.

In case you haven't used FTP yet, start dusting it off. When you create your own Web pages, a simple, no-nonsense FTP program is the easiest way to transfer them from your computer at home to your Web host. If you need to correct and update your Web pages quickly (and you will), you'll benefit by having your FTP software ready and set up with your Web site address, username, and password so that you can transfer files right away.

Image editors

You need a graphics-editing program either to create original artwork for your Web pages or to crop and adjust your scanned images and digital photographs. In the case of adjusting or cropping photographic image files, the software you need almost always comes bundled with the scanner or digital camera, so you don't need to buy separate software for that.

In the case of graphic images, the first question to ask yourself is, 'Am I really qualified to draw and make my own graphics?' If the answer is yes, think shareware first. Two programs we like are Adobe Photoshop Elements (www.adobe.co.uk) and Paint Shop Pro by Jasc, Inc. You can download both these programs from the Web to use on a trial basis. After the trial period is over, you'll need to pay a small fee to the developer in order to register and keep the program.

The ability to download and use free (and almost free) software from shareware archives and many other sites is one of the nicest things about the Internet. Keep the system working by remembering to pay the shareware fees to the nice folks who make their software available to individuals like you and me.

Instant messaging

You may think that MSN Messenger, AOL Instant Messenger, Google Talk, and Yahoo Messenger are just for chatting online, but instant messaging has its business applications, too. Here are a few suggestions:

- ✔ If individuals you work with all the time are hard to reach, you can use a messaging program to tell you whether those people are logged on to their computers. The program allows you to contact them the moment they sit down to work (provided they don't mind your greeting them so quickly, of course).

- ✔ You can cut down on long-distance phone charges by exchanging instant messages with far-flung colleagues.

- ✔ With a microphone, sound card, and speakers, you can carry on voice conversations through your messaging software.

MSN Messenger enables users to do file transfers without having to use FTP software or attaching files to e-mail messages.

Backup software

Losing copies of your personal documents is one thing, but losing files related to your business can hit you hard in the pocket. That makes it even more important to make backups of your online business computer files. Iomega Zip or Jaz drives (www.iomega.com) come with software that lets you automatically make backups of your files. If you don't own one of these programs, we recommend you get really familiar with the backup program included with Windows XP, or you can check out backup software on the Review Centre Web site (www.reviewcentre.co.uk).

Chapter 9

E-Marketing

*W*hat does e-marketing make you think of? Web sites, yes. But e-marketing includes online advertising and e-mail as well as using text, pictures, or even video to reach customers through their mobile phones. These digital tools have opened up lots of new ways to help you sell your products or services. Even better, a lot of these tools are cheaper and certainly more cost effective than traditional advertising using press or TV.

It seems that nearly every month there is a new way to communicate with customers using digital media. The principle of rapid evolution is a good one, but in practice it can be safe to wait a while before jumping in to the newest techniques, as they can be costly, untried and worse, aggravating to the very people you were trying to win over. We encourage our readers to watch and wait before trying out techniques such as *blogging* (personal diary-type Web sites by an independent author, which some companies have tried to mimic for commercial gain and been damagingly exposed for it) or *blue-jacking* (sending unsolicited messages to Bluetooth-enabled portable devices and mobile phones). There are plenty of more traditional techniques that work and which have sufficient numbers of the public using them to make them an essential part of any company's marketing activity.

Over half the UK population is now online, and mobile phone usage is above 80 per cent – meaning that however much or little you spend on e-marketing, you should definitely find a line for it in your marketing budget. For that reason, this chapter covers just what you need to know to begin your foray into e-marketing.

Reaching Out with a Web Site

E-marketing changes fast and changes often, and the best way to use it is to change with it. And that means creating a Web site for your business.

Consider this: People spend more time using the Internet than they do with any other media apart from TV. We bet you're surprised by that fact, but it's true. A Europe-wide survey of Web users by Forrester Research found that people spent eight hours and 20 minutes a week online compared with 11 hours watching TV and just under seven hours listening to the radio. You would advertise on TV if your budget stretched to it (and few people use the TV to do their shopping), so you should have a presence on the second-most used medium because you can afford to. In fact, you can't afford not to!

Getting a Web presence is relatively easy. Sometimes this can be as simple as getting a listing on an online business directory covering your area, so that when consumers key in your business name or search for the type of services you offer using a search engine such as Google or MSN they can find your address and phone number. We strongly believe that every business – including yours – should have a Web site, even if all it does is provide your contact details and opening hours. You can think of your Web site as a shop window, where potential customers from all over the world can look at the products or services you offer. You can even turn this site into an actual shop. Having a transactional Web site can be one of the lowest cost ways to expand geographically without having to move out of your neighbourhood (it's not called the World Wide Web for nothing, you know!).

A good Web site can bring in customers who would never have found your product or service were it not for the Internet. So it's worth spending some time and money creating a decent Web site to attract them.

You need a unique and memorable Web site address, and an easy to use and appealing design (doubly so, if it's going to be a *transactional site* where customers can buy using a credit or debit card). The following sections tell you what you need to know. Of course, you also need to think about how customers will find your site out of the millions out there. Head to the section 'Getting Your Site Noticed' later in this chapter for that info.

Choosing a Web address

First you must find and register a Web address (also known as a *domain name* or *URL*). Unless you are starting a business from scratch, you probably already have a Web address in mind that you would like to use. Your Web address should be as close as you can possibly get to the name of your business, or, if you need a site for each of your products and services, then it should relate closely to them. You may think this sounds obvious, but we see too many Web addresses that fall into the trap of having little to do with the parent business (usually because the most obvious name is being used by someone else, which we cover later in this chapter).

As you search for potential Web addresses, keep the following points in mind to make sure you end up with the best name for your site:

- ✔ **A good address relates to your business or product.** The Web address `www.streetspavedwithgold.com` is available to register, along with all of the other main name extensions. It's catchy. It's amusing. Should you rush off and register it? Not if it fails this first test: Does the name relate to your product or service? Remember, it's better to be relevant than to be clever.

- ✔ **A good name is memorable.** Customers should be able to remember your Web address easily. That doesn't mean you have to register anything stunningly cool or clever – and besides, if the Web address is obscure people are less likely to remember it. Using your company name makes the site memorable to anyone who knows the name of your business. You can easily remember that IKEA's global Web address is `www.ikea.com` and it's `www.ikea.co.uk` in the UK. But you can just as easily combine two or three easy words and make a string into a memorable address. An online competitor to IKEA in the UK is the very simply named `www.thisisfurniture.com`.

- ✔ **A good name is not easily confused with other addresses.** If consumers can easily mix up your site with similar addresses, some will go to the wrong site by accident. If your company name is a common word or is similar to others, add an extra term or word to your Web address to distinguish it. For example, Triumph is a brand name that both the lingerie maker and the motorcycle manufacturer have equal claim to. Although customers are unlikely to mistake one brand for the other, they could easily find themselves on the wrong Web site. As a result, the motorbike brand trades from `www.triumphmotorcycles.com` while Triumph International uses `www.triumph.com`.

- ✔ **A good name doesn't violate trademarks.** You don't want to bump into someone's trademark by accident. Legal rights now favour the trademark holder rather than the domain name holder – putting an end to the ugly practice of 'cyber-squatting' that existed a few years ago. To be sure that you don't inadvertently step on someone else's toes, check any Web address against a database of trademarks. The Patent Office provides a searchable database at `www.patent.gov.uk` but if you think you may run into an issue you should ask a lawyer to do a more detailed analysis.

Checking your name's availability

Picking a name is the easy part. The trickier part is finding out whether that name is available, and getting creative if you find out it's not.

Any good provider of Web services will have its own site that allows you to check on the availability of a Web address. Just go to a search engine like Google, type in 'domain names' and use one of the many registrant sites that come up. At this stage, it doesn't matter which site you choose as you're not committing any money. Just be sure that your Internet service provider (ISP) checks your name against all of the main *extensions* – `.com`, `.co.uk`, `.net`, or `.org` are among the most desirable, as people remember them first.

In the best of all possible worlds, your Web name search will reveal that your name is free and clear. If that's the case, thank your lucky stars, jump up and down, and make a few happy noises. Then register your name. The section 'Registering your site name' tells you how. But, as few of us live in the best of all possible worlds, you're more likely to find that your name is already taken. In that case, don't despair. You still have options and, depending on which avenue you take, you may still get to use your name.

If someone has registered the name you want with one or most of the main extensions, but left the more obscure `.biz`, `.org.uk`, or even `.me.uk` extensions, you're wisest seeking another name because customers could forget your extension and go to someone else's site instead.

When the Web is an important sales route for your business, a simple rule to follow is that it is best to own most or all of the possible extensions and versions of your Web address.

If the person who owns the rights to your Web address isn't willing to sell it to you, you may want to go back to the drawing board and find another name that isn't being held hostage. Many online operators are looking to make easy money by buying up Web addresses for the purpose of selling them at a profit.

Other routes can help you secure the name you want. Many sites that were registered in the frenzy of the dotcom boom eventually come back on to the open market because they were never used or because the original registrar forgot to re-register. When this happens the Web address becomes *detagged*. Alternatively, if you believe you have a stronger or more legitimate claim to a Web address than someone else, you can use a disputes resolution service, or even legal action, to make them give the name up. For information on detagging and disputes, visit Nominet at `www.nominet.org.uk`, which is officially recognised as the `.uk` name registry by the industry and government.

Registering your site name

After you ensure that your Web address is available, you're ready to register your name. Doing so is inexpensive, and the process is simple. The example we give here is based on the provider `easily.co.uk`, which charges £35 to register a `.com`, `.org`, or `.net` address for two years, or £9.99 to register a `.uk` address. All you need to do is type in the domain name you want, and the easily site will tell you which extensions are available (if any are not available you can also see who owns them). Highlight all the extensions you want and then get out your credit card. The process is as easy as that – and easily will even e-mail you a reminder when the address needs to be renewed.

You can use any provider to register your Web address, and some are half as cheap as the example we give here. The only thing to stop you going for the cheapest price is to consider whether you also want the provider to *host* the site (meaning to provide the server space where your site resides on the Web). You can transfer Web addresses to another provider after the event, but it is simpler (and sometimes cheaper) to find the right provider for your needs in the first place.

If consumers may get confused by alternate spellings or mis-spellings of your domain name, register them, too. Registering a name is cheap, so you shouldn't lose a prospective customer just because they can't spell your name.

Creating a Compelling Web Site

Designing good Web pages is a key marketing skill, because your Web site is at the centre of all you do to market on the Web. Also, increasingly, Web sites are at the heart of companies' marketing – businesses put their Web addresses on every marketing communication, from premium items (like company pens) to letterheads and business cards, and also in ads, brochures, and catalogues. Serious shoppers will visit your Web site to find out more about what you offer, so make sure your site is ready to close the sale. Include excellent, clear design, along with plenty of information to answer likely questions and move visitors toward a purchase. Web sites have earned their place in the core of any marketing activity. If you're a consumer-orientated marketer, you want your Web site to be friendly and easily navigated as well as to do the following:

✔ Engage existing customers, giving them reasons to feel good about their past purchases and connect with your company and other consumers (at least to connect emotionally, if not in actual fact).

✔ Share interesting and frequently updated information about your products or services and organisation on the site, so the consumer can gain useful knowledge by visiting it.

✔ Maintain a section of the site or a dedicated site for business-to-business (BtoB) relationships that matter to your marketing (such as distributors, stores, and sales reps). Almost all consumer marketers also work as business-to-business marketers, and the same advice we gave on BtoB at the beginning of this section should apply to this aspect of consumer marketing, too.

Finding resources to help with design

You can easily create a basic Web site – one that includes your contact details plus a few pages showing what your business does – on your own. This is the simplest and cheapest route to create a web presence, if all you need is to let customers know where to find you and why they should get in touch. If your needs are more advanced – you want customers to be able to buy direct from your site, for example, you should skip down to the section on 'Hiring a professional designer'. This section doesn't tell you how to use authoring languages or how to do any of the programming. That would fill an entire book, not a chapter, let alone a section. If you decide to do it yourself, you can find excellent books that do go into all the details.

If you want to create your own Web pages, we recommend, in particular, *Creating Web Pages All-in-One Desk Reference For Dummies* by Emily A. Vander Veer (Wiley). It goes a bit deeper than the also good *Creating Web Pages For Dummies* by Bud E. Smith (also by Wiley). Or, if you really want the light version, check out *Cliffs Notes' Creating Your First Web Page* by Alan Simpson (Wiley). These three titles cover the range in both price and detail, so take your pick. If you like tinkering, you can certainly build your own Web pages using Web authoring software like FrontPage or Dreamweaver and contract with a Web provider to put them up on the Web.

You can find a provider to host your site quite easily – and searching the Web is the best place to start. Just pick one that offers the fee structure, services, and flexibility you want at the right price – and change providers if they don't satisfy.

Hiring a professional designer

If you aren't a do-it-yourselfer, you have a very easy way to create good Web pages: Find an expert who can do it for you under contract.

Good Web site design is harder than it looks and you should probably go to a reputable design firm and ask them to do it for you. We recommend a business relationship (spelled out on paper in advance) that specifies that you, not they, own all content at the end (so that you can switch to another vendor if it doesn't work out) and also specifies an hourly bill rate and an estimate of the site's size and complexity with a cap on the number of billable hours needed to design it.

You can expect to pay anything from £750 for a basic brochure-style Web site of ten pages to upwards of £10,000 for a Flash-animated fully transactional (or e-commerce) Web site.

Beyond the cost of the site, you also need to be aware of additional costs that you may incur – or that you should budget for – in order to enhance the professional appearance and functionality of your Web site:

- Consider an online shopping trolley, for an extra £300 to £500 on top of your bespoke site design. Many basic hosting plans include a shopping trolley, so you can implement this feature fairly easily by using theirs (but you lose out on the custom-look Web site). Assume that you will be adding products over time, so select a shopping trolley that gives you room to grow.

- Consider streaming video, animation, and database management. You can use these technologies as important delivery methods, like showing a speaker in action, demonstrating a new product or providing services, and supporting the consumer online.

- Build some room for stock photography into your budget because sites with relevant images – especially of real people – are graphically more appealing and hold the visitor's attention longer. We highly recommend using photographs in most sites. If you use high-resolution files of the photos, they may be slow to load, which means you could lose some impatient viewers or the few who are still on low-speed phone lines. But stock photography houses sell (at a lower price) low-resolution images that are optimal for the Web and load quickly. These won't slow your site down.

- You should also have your contractor update your site monthly (Web designers will charge around £70 per hour) because these updates give customers good reasons to keep coming back to the site. Special promotions or some other monthly feature will add to this evolving appeal.

- Plan to spend more for search engine submission, a service which automatically submits your Web site to all the major search engines so that traffic goes up. This will cost around £100 per year for monthly submissions. We cover the details of how to do this in the 'Getting Your Site Noticed' section later in this chapter because, even if you hire someone to do it, you ought to be involved in the strategising.

Developing a registration-based site

If you visit the Interactive Investor Web site at www.iii.co.uk you can get access to a host of financial news and share price information. When you try to access the interactive information, however, you get redirected to the registration page, where you can create your own share portfolio to track the performance of your investments, and can contribute to the discussion boards.

Registering costs you nothing, and you have much to gain, because of the many extra options and prize competitions that Interactive Investor offers. Why do they give extra content to registered users, and why give away this valuable content? They want to find out who their customers are. The registered users stay in touch and may choose to trade shares directly over the site. Interactive Investor uses its Web site to develop direct marketing relationships with registered users and it's a very savvy way to use the Web site as a major marketing tool. You may want to consider this option, too.

Getting Your Site Noticed

Search engines *locate* (or index) billions of sites from user queries each day. Google alone indexes more than 3.3 billion Web site pages. A lot of prospective customers are in that statistic somewhere. Research shows that 70 per cent of all Internet users go to one of the main search engines to research the options before making an online purchase. In other words, if your site isn't at or near the top of the list of relevant sites, you lose customers to the sites that are. So how can relevant queries find their way to your pages rather than to all the others? You're a needle in an immense haystack.

Search engine marketing can be a financial black hole. Search engines have become so sophisticated and complex in such a short space of time that the rules have changed fundamentally in the space of just a few years, and the techniques needed to get to the top of search pages have become more complex, too. Some Web providers and consultants will try to convince you that search engines can be fooled into giving your site an artificially high ranking. Others will make out that it's rocket science and can be done at the right price. The truth lies somewhere in between. We can tell you that you do need help in getting to the top or close to the top of any list. Trust us, paying for good advice is well worth it. You may have the ability, but certainly don't have the time to spend trying to beat highly complex search systems. In the following sections we explain some of the basics so you know what a good search marketing company can do for you.

Buying visibility on search engines

Because the search engines look at traffic when ranking pages, anything you do through direct communication with your customers to build traffic can help. Also, you should use a link to related sites to improve your ranking. You can use the simple but powerful strategy of doing a search, like one your customers may do, and see what sites appear in the top ten listings. Then visit each of these sites and see if you can find appropriate places and ways to link from your site to theirs (and vice versa, if possible). For example, a company that distributes products for you or vice versa is a natural to link to your site. Also, a professional association in your industry may be a good fit for you to link to, although it may be harder to talk into linking back to your site. Build such links and the higher-ranked sites tend to draw yours up toward them. But make sure that you have great, useful content to justify those links.

Next, to make your site visible to anyone searching for it, optimise your listing by spending some money on it. Sorry, but there's no such thing as a free lunch on the Internet any more!

We advise you to forget anything you might have heard about *meta tags*. Things have changed so quickly in search marketing that these tags, which used to influence where and how your Web site appeared in search engines, are now largely ignored by the major search engines. They can have an effect on how your Web site is described on a search engine, but these days the *title tag* is the only tag worth worrying about. Title tags determine what words appear in the little blue bar at the top of a user's Web browser (and the same words would appear if they chose to save the Web site in their 'Favourites' file). We consider this a technicality best left to your Web site designer. The Internet Web world has moved on, and so should you.

DIY search marketing with Google

If you do want to have a go at search marketing yourself, then here's an example of how to begin with *pay-per-click* advertising. But bear in mind that a good search marketing consultant can work with you to identify the key words that will generate the best returns for your business, not just for Google but for all the top search engines.

Go to www.google.com and click the 'Advertising Programmes' link. They lay out the most recent offerings for us marketers here. We specifically recommend that you look (by clicking on another link) at Google AdWords, a facility allowing you to pay per click when people click through to your site. To use this option, do the following:

1. **Designate a short list of highly specific and appropriate key terms that customers may use to search for you.**

2. **Bid by saying how much you'd pay for a click. You can get in to the game for just a few pence per click. Web advertisers call this offer your *per-click bid*.**

   Google allows you to track your results day by day, see your ranking, and see what results (clicks and costs) you get.

3. **If you want more clicks, raise your bid for a higher listing or improve your use of terms or descriptive sentences, and watch to see if your results improve. Google will also recommend a maximum cost per click (CPC), based on estimated clicks per day – matching the amount will give you the highest exposure and number of clicks.**

We're not going to tell you more about it because Google presents your advertising options well and simply. Just go and have a look at the options – and pick any that seem to fit your site and budget. You don't need to make a long-term commitment; you can experiment at low cost until you find a mix that works.

Yahoo! advertising

Yahoo! (as well as MSN, Wanadoo, AltaVista, and Lycos) uses Overture as its service for buying search engine visibility. Overture uses a bidding system based on the number of clicks your site gets, much like Google's AdWords (see the preceding section for more on Google). You can find Overture by going to `www.content.overture.com`. This link takes you to areas where you can research the Overture options we describe in this book and, if you want, actually make purchases and begin to do your marketing on Yahoo! A Nielsen audit found that Yahoo! search engine listings reached more than 80 per cent of active Internet users. We don't know if that percentage is really true, but Yahoo! certainly has an extensive reach. You may want to buy some visibility in Yahoo! searches, as well as Google. Often, you can use the same key terms in both, which simplifies your work as a marketer. However, you may need to adjust your per-click bids (see the preceding section) differently to get good visibility on Yahoo! Depending on your industry, one or the other search engine may tend to be more expensive. You just have to see and make appropriate adjustments as you go.

Content as a traffic driver

Most Web sites are really just huge, interactive advertisements or sales pro-motions. After a while, even the most cleverly designed ad gets boring. To increase the length of time users spend with your materials, and to ensure high involvement and return visits, you need to think like a publisher, not just an advertiser. For this reason, we consider Web content to be the hidden factor for increasing site traffic. Unless you have valuable and appealing content, you may have difficulty building up traffic on your site.

Tracking Your Site's Traffic

The Web offers an unmatched ability to evaluate how effectively your online marketing is working and to capture information on the people who are visiting your site. Compared with other media, digital marketing is entirely transparent – meaning you can see how many visitors you get and, if they register on your site, who they are. You should make the most of this rare opportunity to measure the impact of your expenditure.

Interpreting click statistics

You may find click-through statistics a useful and easy-to-get indicator of how well an ad or search-engine placement is performing. If you get a lot of people clicking through to your site from an ad or placement, that ad is clearly doing its job of attracting traffic for you. So, all else being equal, more clicks are better. However, all else isn't equal all the time. Here are a few wrinkles to keep in mind when interpreting click rates:

✔ When a pop-up ad pops up, the companies you buy the ad space through usually report it as a click. But don't believe the numbers because you have no indication that someone actually read or acted on that pop-up – they may have just closed it without looking. Dig deeper into the statistics from whoever sold you that pop-up ad to find out how it actually performed. You can probably get some more detailed data if you ask, but you need more than the simple click count.

✔ Some ads have multiple elements that load in sequence, creating a countable click with each loading so that one ad may generate several click-through counts. This counting method may lead you to think that the more complex ad is better, but the higher number can be an artifact of the way those who sell ad space on the Web count the clicks. (Ask your provider if it can sell Web ad space to you, or visit any really popular site and look for the section in it that's for advertisers if you want to buy ad space.)

✔ Quality is more important than quantity. Who are these people who clicked to your site? That information is harder to know but more important. If you get ten thousand clicks in a week, that's nice – but do they include relevant and active prospects or not? Only by digging into detailed reports on who goes where and looks at what on your Web site, plus information on what types of e-mailed questions you get and the average order size in that week, can you really begin to evaluate the quality of those clicks. See the following section 'Paying attention to your site's visitors' for details on how to find out who's visiting your site.

If you're getting poor quality of traffic clicking through, experiment with putting ads in other places or redesign your ads to specifically focus on your desired target. Keep working on it until you have not the most click-throughs, but the best.

You can evaluate performance of Web advertising every day or week, and you can get statistics on each and every ad that you run. So use this data intelligently to experiment and adjust your approach. Aim to increase both the quantity and the quality of clicks week by week throughout your marketing campaign and track the impact on enquiries and sales.

Paying attention to your site's visitors

Each time someone visits your Web site, they are exhibiting interest in you and your products (or they're lost – which is less likely if your site is aptly named and clearly designed so that no one can confuse it with unrelated types of businesses). And when someone exhibits interest, that makes them interesting to you. So whatever you do, however you go about setting up a site, make sure that you capture information about your visitors in a useful form that gets sent to you regularly.

Ask your Web provider what kinds of reports they can offer you – probably more than you imagined possible. With these reports in hand, you can track traffic to your site. You probably notice that you, unlike the giants of the Web, don't have as much traffic as you may want. Sure, millions of people use Google to do searches or go to eBay to bid on auctioned products. But the average Web site only has a few dozen visitors a day. For an effective site, you need to build up this traffic at least into the thousands of visitors per day. How? By making sure it gets noticed in search engines.

Designing and Placing a Banner Ad

A lot has changed in just a few years in Internet advertising. You can see how quickly things have moved on just by looking at what has happened to the most common form of online advertising – the *banner ad*. A banner used to be the only format for online advertising. That traditional format still exists, but for many marketers 'banner' has become a generic term for a whole host of different online ad formats.

We've jumped from one-size-fits-all banners, through as many different types of ad formats as you could wish for, and have come out at the other end with a selection of standard sizes that fit the needs of most advertisers (see Figure 9-1). The *Universal Advertising Package* (UAP), as its creators at the Internet Advertising Bureau (IAB) call it, comprises a superbanner (running across the top of a Web page), skyscraper, large rectangle, and a regular rectangle. The UAP formats are much larger than existing online formats, meaning your ad will stand out better. You can find out all about the technical specifications for UAP formats at the IAB's Web site (www.IABuk.net).

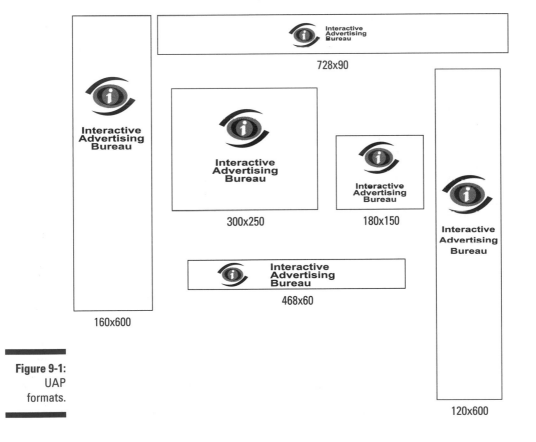

Figure 9-1:
UAP
formats.

The most important advantage of the UAP formats is that they can make the whole process of buying online advertising much more cost-effective. You should pay less for the production of an online campaign if you're not having to re-create your ad for each Web site you advertise on, and you can compare costs of online ad space more easily if you're comparing like with like – rather than apples with oranges, as was the case before.

Hiring a Web media service

Companies that provide *Web media services* (meaning Web page design) can also design and place banner ads and pop-up ads for you. The search for agencies or individuals to do this work for you can be a long and random one. If you're lucky enough to know a competent Web designer or programmer, seriously consider using their services – they can create custom banners to your specification quite easily because it's such a small ad format.

If you have more ambitious plans for rich media online ads, however, you will need to study the extensive field. To make it easier, we recommend you go straight to the Internet Advertising Bureau Web site at `www.iabuk.net` and visit the membership directory section. In this section, you will find companies offering every kind of Web media service, from ad server and counting providers (online campaign analysis) to Web site design. In the 'creative agencies' list alone there are 50 suppliers, from Advertising.com to Zenith Optimedia.

We have to point out that the larger (and more expensive) agencies are well represented in the IAB membership, so you can find cheaper, local assistance if you're prepared to put in the leg work.

Creating your own banner ad

Creating your own banner ads is a relatively easy process, particularly if you have designed your own Web site and are familiar with HTML coding. Basic banner ads can be created using off-the-shelf design software such as Photoshop or Paint Shop Pro. Not surprisingly, the Web is a good starting point for finding templates for banner ads. Because the format is now so common, a lot of sites allow you to use their standard designs for free. One of the best known is AdDesigner.com (you can guess the Web address), which makes it easy to design a professional looking animated banner ad within minutes. We can't seen why any marketer planning a small-scale online campaign would take anything other than the DIY route, given the high standards of these templates, but if you're really not keen on having a go, it is just as simple to search for one of the many factory-orientated banner ad designers that can make you an ad quickly and for less than £50.

Focusing on a simple design

We think the best design for starters is a banner that flashes a simple one-line offer or headline statement, shows an image of your logo or product, and then switches to a couple more lines of text explaining what to do and why to do it ('Click here to take advantage of our introductory offer for small business owners and get 20 per cent off your first order of . . . ').

You want your ad to be simple and bold – able to attract the viewer's attention from desired information elsewhere on the screen for long enough to make a simple point.

This ad style delivers a clear marketing message using both print and illustration. Make sure that if prospects click on the banner, they go directly to a page on your Web site that supports the product or service with more information and with several easy purchase options.

Being positively creative with your ad

Online advertising that's well done can do many more tasks for you than a TV ad, press ad, or poster. For a start, users who click on your ad can be delivered directly to your transactional Web site. Job done (well, almost – see 'Creating a Compelling Web Site' earlier in this chapter). An online ad can be tactical, by alerting customers to a special offer for instance, or brand-building, by raising awareness of your product or service without a clear call to action. And unlike TV or press ads, you (or the size of your budget) control how intrusive your ad becomes.

Why would you want any Web user to miss an ad you're paying good money for? Obviously, you wouldn't. So be careful about the gimmicks your ad uses. Case in point: Bells-and-whistles online advertising gimmickry (or *rich media*, as the experts call it). With this type of media, you can buy an ad that totally obscures a page someone is trying to view, that chases their cursor around the screen, and basically forces them either to pay attention or close it. That technology runs contrary to every other trend in the advertiser–customer relationship, which is why we don't believe it will be around for long. In the meantime, you can create some eye-catching online ad designs that integrate with the Web page they appear on – and don't irritate potential customers.

Placing your banner ads

Designing the banner is just the beginning because you have to buy space to display it from publishers. If you poke around on large sites like www.yahoo.com, you can find sections devoted to advertisers like you, where you can explore ad buying options and rates and ask for help from a salesperson. Alternatively, you can go to an online media-buying agency and hire them to do the placement. These agencies take a small commission but probably more than make up for this loss by knowing where to place the ads to target your core customer base, negotiating better rates and avoiding some of the inflation of exposure numbers that can happen when you have to rely on the publisher's accounting.

What can it cost you to place a banner ad? Typically between £5 and £10 per thousand viewers – not bad if you have an ad that actually generates some responses. But watch the banner ad closely and pull or modify it, or try running it elsewhere, if the click rate is too low to justify the cost. You may have to make a few tries to get it right, but with the rapid feedback possible on the Web, this experimentation can take place fairly quickly and inexpensively.

Using E-Mail for Marketing

You can create, or hire your Web site designer to create, an e-mail that looks like a well-designed Web page, with animation and clickable buttons linking to your site. Now, all you have to do is blast it out to millions of e-mail addresses and surely you can make millions overnight.

Not so fast! Okay, so you have this great marketing message or sales pitch, and you want to send it to everyone in the world who has an e-mail address. You can actually do that, but we don't advise it. The more specific and narrow your use of e-mail for marketing, the better. And since the introduction of legislation in the UK, Europe, and the US, marketers must be careful to avoid violating all sorts of restrictions on *spam*, or junk e-mails. We help you stay on the sunny side of the law in this section.

The only e-mail to send: Good e-mail

The best e-mail is a personal communication with a customer you know (and who wants to hear from you), sent individually from you with an accurate e-mail return address as well as your name, title, company name, full mailing address, and phone number. The e-mail may read as follows:

> Dear so-and-so
>
> I wanted to follow up after your purchase of (your product) on (date) to see how it's working out for you and to thank you for your continuing business. If you have any concerns or questions, please let me know by return e-mail, or feel free to call me directly on 0123 123 1234.
>
> Best wishes
>
> Your Name

Your customer is going to receive, open, read, and appreciate an e-mail like this one. She may even respond to it, especially if the customer has any current concerns or questions or has another order on its way. Even if she doesn't reply to it, however, she appreciates that e-mail. And that message doesn't irritate anyone or look like spam.

Use e-mail as much as you can for legitimate, helpful one-to-one contact and support of customers or prospects.

Sometimes, you can also send out an e-mail to a list rather than an individual, but please make sure that you have a clear purpose that benefits those people on the list. And ensure that your list only includes people who have indicated they are happy to be communicated with – to stay within the law and, more importantly, to avoid angering people.

Understanding e-mail etiquette

Good will is a valuable asset, and you don't want to destroy it with your e-mail! The following list has some additional rules of good mass e-mailing that marketers should all follow. Our inspiration for these rules comes from the Direct Marketing Association, where they have guidelines for responsible use of e-mail. We've also kept the legal restrictions in mind.

> ✔ **Send e-mails only to those people who ask for them.** Your bulk e-mails should go only to those people who have given you permission. The law (The Privacy and Electronic Communications Regulations 2003) now requires that no e-mails are sent without prior consent. What does that mean? It means that everyone you send an e-mail to should have 'opted in' to receive e-mails from you, and each time you contact them you must give them an option to reply and be taken off the list.

If you have a 'prior relationship' with that contact (such as their being a previous customer or them requesting information from you) the rules are slightly softer. You can get these requests by creating a useful e-newsletter and advertising it on the Web as a free subscription. Those people who sign up really want it, and they're happy to see the next issue arrive.

✔ **Remove addresses from your list immediately when people ask for them to be removed.** Remember that refusing to allow people to opt out is illegal. Also, people have such widespread distrust of Web marketers that you may consider writing the person a brief, individual e-mail from you (identify yourself and your title for credibility), letting them know that you have eliminated them from the list and are sorry if you've inconvenienced them. You shouldn't say any more in the e-mail. Don't try to make a sale – you just irritate the person even more. You generally make a positive impression by being so responsive to the person's complaint, so don't be surprised if your special attention to their request leads them to initiate a sale later on.

✔ **If you insist on buying e-mail lists, test them before using them.** We're assuming that the list you buy in is legal (check first that the people on it have agreed to being contacted by third-party advertisers, like yourself). Then try sending a very simple, short, non-irritating message to people on the list, like an offer to send them a catalogue or free sample, and ask for a few pieces of qualifying information in return. See what happens. Cull all the many bounce-backs and irritated people from the list. Now your list is a bit better in quality than the raw list was. Save those replies in a separate list – they're significantly better and more qualified and deserve a more elaborate e-mail, mailing, or (if the numbers aren't too high) a personal contact.

✔ **Respect privacy.** People don't want to feel like someone's spying on them. Never send to a list if you'd be embarrassed to admit where you got the names. You can develop an e-mail list in plenty of legitimate ways (from customer data, from Web ads, from enquiries at trade shows, from return postcards included in mailings, and so on), so don't do anything that your neighbours would consider irritating or sleazy.

✔ **Send out your bulk e-mails just like you send an individual one.** Use a real, live, reply-able e-mail address. We hate it when we can't reply to an e-mail – it makes us angry! And – a good rule of marketing – try not to anger customers and prospects.

✔ **Make sure that the subject line isn't deceptive.** Good practice and good sense dictate that you make the subject line straightforward. In marketing, you want to get to know straight away if someone isn't a good prospect, instead of wasting your time or theirs when they have no interest in your offer.

✔ **Keep your e-mail address lists up to date.** When you get a *hard bounce-back* (notice that a message was undeliverable) from an address, remove it immediately and update your e-mail list for the next mailing.

A *soft bounce-back* is an undeliverable message resulting from some kind of temporary problem. Track it to see if the e-mail eventually goes through. If not, eliminate this address from your list, too.

People change their e-mail addresses and switch servers. You can have bounce-backs on your list who may still be good customers or prospects. At least once a year, check these inactive names and try to contact them by phone or mail to update their e-mail addresses. Some of these people are still interested and don't need to be cut from your list; they just need their e-mail addresses updated.

If you're e-mailing to an in-house list of people who have bought from you, gone to your seminar, or asked for information in the past, remind them of your relationship in the e-mail – they may have forgotten.

We hate *spam* – junk e-mails that clog up our mailboxes. In fact, we change our e-mail addresses whenever the spam begins to find us. We bet you feel the same way. So don't let your Web marketing make you part of this problem. Use good quality lists, be polite and respectful, and integrate e-mail into your broader Web strategy so that you don't have to rely too heavily on e-mail. Real people live at the end of those e-mail addresses. Treat them as such!

Spreading your message virally

There is one way to bypass the tight restrictions on sending out e-mail messages to people you don't know – and that's getting the people you do know to do it for you. *Viral marketing*, as it's known, doesn't require any great technical know-how. All you need is such a good idea, or compelling offer, that your customers are going to spread the word without you even asking! Viral marketing quite simply means an idea or an ad that is so good it spreads from one person to many more – like a virus, but in a good way!

Getting Mobile with Your Marketing

Seven out of ten people in the UK use a mobile phone and 75 per cent of them send and receive text messages. *Mobile marketing* is held up as being one of the most important methods of the future, while the possibilities for now aren't half bad either. We emphasise that things are changing in mobile marketing constantly, so the technologies of today will certainly have been superceded by tomorrow.

The most basic, and therefore most developed, method of mobile marketing is by Short Message Service, or SMS – which most people simply call texting. You can send a personal, targeted message by text in the same way as you would send an e-mail (and subject to the same laws on privacy; see 'Understanding e-mail etiquette' earlier in this section) – and you can reach your customers 24 hours a day.

Of course, you can also use a mobile phone as the launch pad for a whole host of marketing wonderment. MMS, EMS, WAP, GPRS, Bluetooth, 3G – the terminology is almost as impenetrable as the average marketer's ability to take advantage of it. These technologies will become commonplace, but for the time being, if you're interested in trying out mobile marketing you should stick to the tried and tested methods (or at least as tried and tested as a four-year-old method can be). The following list gives some pointers and ideas on how to use mobile marketing:

- ✔ Keep it short and to the point.
- ✔ Be prepared for a good response.
- ✔ Respect privacy at all times.
- ✔ Get help (you'll need it).

Knowing How Much to Budget for the Web

If you're in a business-to-business marketing situation, we strongly urge you to put at least 10 per cent of your marketing budget into the Web, both for maintaining a strong Web site and for doing some Web advertising and search-engine placement purchases. If you add an e-newsletter, Web distribution of press releases, and occasional announcements to your e-mail list, you may need to make the percentage as high as 20 per cent.

The Internet Advertising Bureau has recorded massive growth in online advertising over the last year or two: online market share rose to 11.4 per cent of total advertising spend by the end of 2006, up from 7.8 per cent in 2005. As a result, the IAB recommends marketers spend 10–20 per cent of their total budget on online advertising. Our own recommendations are more modest because you must find the budget to allocate to the full range of e-marketing activities, and online advertising is just a part of that. Unless you're an online-only trader, the 10–20 per cent range for e-marketing will bring you the benefits of these new media without blowing the budget for traditional forms of promotion.

But you can find exceptions to every rule, and being the exception often gives you the most profitable and powerful strategy in marketing. If you find that your Web ads, search engine listings, or e-mails are pulling well for you and making a profit, try doubling your effort and spending on them for a month and see what happens. Still working well? Double again. You may find that the Web can do a lot more of your basic marketing work than you think. Many marketers hold Web spending down to a small minority of their budget for no good reason other than tradition and fear of all things new.

One Final – But Important! – Thought

The single most important point to remember about Web sites and e-marketing in general is that you must invest routinely so that you're always changing and improving your presence. Whether you're a do-it-yourself online marketer or are willing to hire a professional online agency, your e-marketing needs to be a living thing. Don't let parts of your site get old and stale. Don't continue to run a *banner ad* (an ad that appears on a major Web site or service) or bid on a *key term* (a word people use in searching for Web sites, which you can pay to have your message linked to) if you aren't getting results in clicks and sales. Do adapt and change every month. The Web is a dynamic marketing medium. Be dynamic!

Book VI
Getting Bigger

'I like a young man who knows where he's going.
If you'll just go through that door while
my directors & I discuss your promotion
application . . .'

In this book . . .

*I*f all goes according to plan, or your business is already booming, we take this opportunity to suggest ways to grow your business. From expanding your own skills as a manager to improving your company's overall performance, this book contains some great ideas for helping your business to grow and grow and grow.

Here are the contents of Book VI at a glance:

Chapter 1: Thinking Strategically

Chapter 2: Managing More Than One Product

Chapter 3: Improving Performance

Chapter 4: Franchising for Growth

Chapter 5: TV and Radio Ads (or Your Own Show!)

Chapter 6: Becoming a Great Manager

Chapter 1

Thinking Strategically

*I*n this chapter, we help you formulate a strategy for your company that's in keeping with its basic mission. First, we explore why strategy is so important to the business-planning process. We examine what it means to have a strategy and when that strategy works best, and introduce several basic strategies that you can apply across many industries. These off-the-shelf strategies include efforts

✔ To be the low-cost provider

✔ To differentiate your products

✔ To focus on specific market and product areas

We talk about several other general strategic alternatives as well, answering questions such as 'What does it mean to become more vertically integrated as a company?' and 'How should you act when you're the market leader or a market follower?' We also give you some pointers about creating a strategic blueprint for your own company.

Making Strategy Make a Difference

Some companies think that *strategy* and *planning* are four-letter words. Those companies would never think of using either term in the context of their own organisations. It isn't that these companies don't move forward; it's just that they don't talk much about it ahead of time. So why do the two terms have such bad reputations in certain quarters? More than likely, it's because they've been misunderstood or applied incorrectly. *Strategy* and *planning* have become such buzzwords in today's business world that their real meanings are easily lost in all the muddle surrounding them.

We know that strategic planning works, because we've seen it with our own eyes. We've also seen where a lack of strategic planning can lead. A 2000 survey of close to 500 small companies backs us up; it found that companies that have strategic plans have 50 per cent more revenue and profit growth than companies that fail to plan. It's that simple.

What strategy means

The word *strategy* comes to us from the ancient Greeks and translates literally as *the art of generalship*. When you compete, you probably feel that you're suiting up for battle, jousting with your competitors for the hearts and minds of customers.

Modern definitions of the word are even less precise, so we're proposing our own standard definition of *strategy* in the business arena. A strategy does the following things:

- Describes how to reach the goals and objectives that you set for the company
- Takes into account the personal and social values that surround your company
- Guides the way that you allocate and deploy your human and financial resources
- Creates an advantage in the marketplace that you can sustain, despite intense and determined competition

Putting together a strategic business plan requires you to gather data, analyse the information, and then do something with it – something more than just reformatting it, printing it, and packaging it in a tidy report titled 'The Five-Year Plan'. In most cases, that kind of report begins and ends with numbers – revenue projections, cash flows, expense allocations, and the like, which are things that don't help you figure out what to do next. Reports like this are sure to fall victim to the dreaded SPOTS (Strategic Plans on Top Shelves) syndrome: they gather dust and little else. These reports don't represent strategy or planning; they represent a waste of time.

What can you do to make sure that this doesn't happen to your business plan? For one thing, a healthy dose of plain old common sense works wonders as you pull all the pieces together to create your strategy. Experience in your industry and some nous are advantages, too. Unfortunately, we can't give you any of these gifts. But we can offer you some solid advice about laying out your strategy, including some hints that make you look like a planning pro.

Keep the following questions in mind as you begin to formulate your strategic plan:

- ✔ What markets and segments does your company plan to compete in?
- ✔ Which products and services will your company develop and support?
- ✔ Where is your company's competitive advantage in these markets and products?
- ✔ How will your company sustain that competitive advantage over time?

The answers that you come up with go a long way toward keeping your strategy focused and on target, so you want to return to them from time to time at each phase of the planning process.

When strategy works

Strategy works when you have a process to ensure that planning is consistently tied to the ongoing operations of your business. If strategic plans fail, it's usually because they don't seem to be relevant to the issues and problems at hand. Strategy and planning get linked with committee meetings, bureaucracy, overheads, and all those other barriers that are thrown up to ensure that results aren't achieved. As a result, strategy and planning are seen by some companies as a part of the problem, not a solution.

Strategy works best when strategic planning is integrated into every aspect of your business, every day of the week and every week of the year. An ongoing strategic-planning process means that you do the following things:

- ✔ Always question what makes your company successful.
- ✔ Continually observe customers and markets, tracking their wants and needs.
- ✔ Relentlessly examine the competition and what it's up to.
- ✔ Steadily work at maintaining your competitive advantage.
- ✔ Continually search for ways to leverage your core competence.

Some managers may do all these things automatically and intuitively. But if you want to make sure that strategy and planning are carried out in all parts of your company, you have to create a framework to ensure that it happens. When you make strategic planning a basic responsibility, you get the added benefit of including all levels of employees in the planning process. Employees often have different and equally valuable viewpoints about shaping strategy, and a strategic-planning framework ensures that their voices are heard.

To start the ball rolling in your own company, pull together a group of employees who represent different functions and various levels in your organisation. Meet on a regular basis to talk about strategy and planning. Concentrate on how to set up a framework to promote strategic thinking, and focus on problems associated with the strategic-planning process itself. Then group members can take what they learn back to their own areas and begin to integrate strategic planning into the way that they do business.

Applying Off-the-Shelf Strategies

Maybe you think your company's situation is absolutely unique and the issues you face are one-of-a-kind. Does this mean that your strategy and business plan have to be unique as well? Not entirely. If you look through a microscope, every snowflake is different. But snowflakes have a great deal in common when you stand back and watch them pile up outside. Companies are like snowflakes. Although all the details give companies their individual profiles, companies and industries in general display remarkable similarities when you step back and concentrate on their basic shapes.

Master business strategist and Harvard University professor Michael Porter was one of the first to recognise, and take an inventory of, standard business profiles. Based on what he saw, he came up with three generic approaches to strategy and business planning. These *generic strategies* are important because they offer off-the-shelf answers to a basic question: What does it take to be successful in a business over the long haul? And the answers work across all markets and industries.

Generic strategies boil down to the following standard approaches (highlighted in Figure 1-1):

- ✔ **Cut costs to the bone.** Become the low-cost leader in your industry. Do everything that you can to reduce your own costs while delivering a product or service that measures up well against the competition.

- ✔ **Offer something unique.** Figure out how to provide customers with something that's both unique and of real value, and deliver your product or service at a price that customers are willing to pay.

- ✔ **Focus on one customer group.** Decide to focus on the precise needs and requirements of a narrow market, using either low cost or a unique product to woo your target customers away from the general competition.

It's not surprising that cutting costs and offering something unique represent two generic strategies that work almost universally. After all, business, industry, and competition are all driven by customers who base their purchase decisions on the value equation – an equation that weighs the benefits of any product or service against its price tag. Generic strategies merely concentrate your efforts on influencing one side of the value equation or the other.

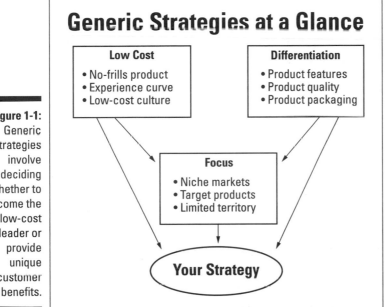

Figure 1-1: Generic strategies involve deciding whether to become the low-cost leader or provide unique customer benefits.

Low-cost leadership

Becoming the low-cost leader in your industry requires the commitment and coordination of every aspect of your company, from product development to marketing, from manufacturing to distribution, from raw materials to wages and benefits. Every day and in every way, you track down and exterminate unnecessary costs. Find a new technology that simplifies manufacturing? Install it. Find a region or country that has a more productive labour force? Move there. Find suppliers to provide cheaper raw materials? Sign 'em up.

A cost-leadership strategy is often worth the effort because it gives you a powerful competitive position. When you're the low-cost leader, you call the shots and challenge every one of your competitors to find other ways to compete. Although the strategy is universal, it works best in markets and industries in which price tends to drive customer behaviour – the bulk- or commodity-products business, for example, or low-end, price-sensitive market segments.

The following sections describe the ways in which you can carry out a cost-leadership strategy.

No-frills product

The most obvious and straightforward way to keep costs down is to invoke the well-known KISS (Keep It Simple, Stupid!) principle. When you cut out all the extras and eliminate the options, your product is bound to be cheaper to put together. A no-frills product can be particularly successful if you're able to match it with a market that doesn't see any benefit in (or is even annoyed by) other products' bells and whistles – the couch potatoes whose video recorders sport a flashing 12:00, for example, or famous-writers-to-be who are baffled by their word processors.

In addition to removing all the extras, you can sometimes take advantage of a simple product redesign to gain an even greater cost advantage. Home developers have replaced plywood with pressed board, for example, to lower the costs of construction. Camera makers have replaced metal components with plastic. And, of course, there's always the Pizza Express solution; the company reduced costs at one point simply by making its pizzas a wee bit smaller.

Stripped-down products and services eventually appear in almost every industry. The most obvious examples today are:

- No-frills airlines such as easyJet and Ryanair
- Warehouse stores such as Aldi, Costco, and Lidl, which offer a wide selection, low prices, and no help
- Bare-bones brokerage houses such as Hargraves Lansdown and TD Waterhouseand Quick & Reilly, which charge low commissions on trades without any hand-holding or personal investment advice

Experience curve

Cost leadership is often won or lost based on the power of the *experience curve,* which traces the declining unit costs of putting together and selling a product or service over time (see Figure 1-2).

The curve measures the real cost per unit of various general business expenses: plant construction, machinery, labour, office space, administration, advertising, distribution, sales – everything but the raw materials that make up the product in the first place. All these costs combined tend to go down over time when they're averaged out over all the products that you make or services that you provide.

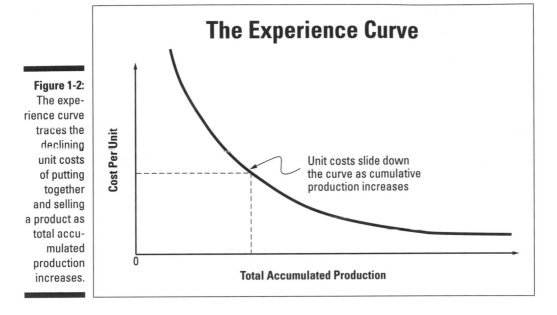

Book VI

**Getting
Bigger**

Figure 1-2:
The expe-
rience curve
traces the
declining
unit costs
of putting
together
and selling
a product as
total accu-
mulated
production
increases.

The underlying causes of the experience curve include the following:

- **Scale.** *Scale* refers to the fact that you have fixed business costs, which are fixed in the sense that they're not affected by how much of your product you make and sell. (Fixed costs usually include such things as your rent, the equipment that you buy, and some of your utility bills.) The more products you produce, the more you gain an immediate scale advantage, because the fixed costs associated with each unit go down automatically.

- **Scope.** *Scope* works a little like the scale effect, but scope refers to the underlying cost benefit that you get by serving larger markets or by offering multiple products that share overhead expenses associated with such things as advertising, product service, and distribution. These expenses aren't exactly fixed, but you do gain an automatic scope advantage if the ad that you decide to run reaches a larger market or if your delivery trucks deliver two or three products to each of your sales outlets instead of one.

- **Learning.** Remember the first time you tried to tie your shoelaces? Big job. A lot of work. Now you can do it in your sleep. What happened? The more you tied your shoes, the better you got at it. The same is true whether you're on a factory floor, at a computer workstation, or in a conference room. You (and your employees) get better at something the more you do it. As you learn, the overall cost of doing business goes down.

A general rule suggests that all these underlying causes result in what's known as an 80 per cent experience curve. Every time you double the total number of products produced, unit costs go down by about 20 per cent – to 80 per cent of what they were before.

The cost benefit that you actually get out of your own company's experience is bound to vary and depends partly on your industry. A few industries don't benefit from experience effects at all. In industries in which the basic costs of raw materials are high, for example, there's not much room for gaining a big advantage through experience. Many service industries may not get much of an advantage from experience, either. It doesn't matter how good hairstylists become at what they do; it still takes them about an hour to wash and style each customer's hair, so the company's costs don't change.

Low-cost culture

You can sustain low-cost leadership only if every part of your company is committed to keeping costs under control, reducing or eliminating expenses and unnecessary spending. This kind of commitment doesn't occur without leadership and the example set by the owners themselves.

Perhaps more than any other strategy and business plan that you can pursue, the push to be the low-cost leader in your industry succeeds or fails based on how well you actually carry it out. Knowing where and when to bring in cost-saving technology may be one important aspect of your drive, for example. But at the heart of your plan, it's absolutely critical that you figure out how to structure the company, reward your employees, and create the spirit of a 'lean, mean fighting machine'. In the end, your employees determine just how efficient your company really is. This may mean that you don't drive a company car or that you never, ever make personal long-distance calls from work. You can bet that your employees will follow your lead.

Low-cost leadership means exactly what it says. It's just not good enough to be first, second or third runner-up; it's not even all right to be first among equals. If you can't assume the cost-leadership position, you run the risk of playing a part in your own worst nightmare: a high-stakes, cut-throat industry in which price-war shoot-'em-outs threaten to destroy all the players. After all, if no one's a clear leader, everyone's a challenger, and when low-cost challengers decide to battle for market-share advantage, they use price as their favourite weapon. If you happen to find yourself in such a Wild West industry, take action. Look for new and different ways to compete – alternative strategies that are more likely to reward you in the end.

Standing out in a crowd

Not every company can be the low-cost leader in an industry, and many companies don't even want to be. Instead, they prefer to compete in the marketplace by creating products and services that are unique, offering customers things that they just have to have – things that they're willing to pay a little extra for. The strategy is known as *differentiation*.

Differentiation has a great deal going for it, because companies can be different in many ways, which means that there are many ways to be successful. Although the low-cost strategy that we talked about in the preceding sections can easily produce a win-lose situation for many companies, differentiation often creates room for more players, each of which competes successfully in its own special ways. That's not to say that competition isn't fierce, even when companies offer distinctly different products or services.

Companies that can make themselves distinct from their competitors often enjoy enviable profits, and they frequently use those extra pounds to reinforce their unique positions in the marketplace. A premium winery, for example, earns its reputation based on the quality of grapes and expertise of the winemaker, but it goes on to polish that reputation through expensive packaging and promotional campaigns. All these added investments make it more difficult for competitors to join in, but they also raise the cost of doing business. Although a maker of house wine has trouble competing in premium markets, a premium winery really can't afford to compete on price alone. No company can ignore cost, of course, even if it offers something that no one else does. Wine-lovers may be willing to spend £15 for a special bottle of chardonnay but may baulk at a £30 price tag.

Chances are that you can make your company unique in a number of ways. You can set your product or service apart based on what it can do, how well it works, or the way that it is packaged and distributed. Then you can go on to develop any of these aspects into a successful differentiation strategy, creating a loyal set of customers along the way.

Because a differentiation strategy hinges completely on your relationship with customers, however, stop and ask yourself several questions before you move ahead:

- ✔ Who are your customers?
- ✔ How would you best describe them?

✔ What are their basic wants and needs?

✔ How do they make choices?

✔ What motivates them to buy things?

Check out Book V for an insight on customers. The following sections describe ways that you can set yourself apart from the competition.

Product features

You can often find the basic outlines of a successful differentiation strategy in what your product can and can't do for customers. After all, a product's features are frequently among the first things that a potential buyer considers. How do your products stack up? Are you particularly strong in product design and development? If so, you probably want to consider how to leverage your strength in developing new features to make your company's product stand out.

Unfortunately, product features represent a big target for your competitors to aim at, and trying to be different based on major product attributes alone is sometimes hard to sustain over the long haul. Technology-driven companies such as Sony, 3M, and Intel have managed to stay one step ahead of the competition for many years by always offering the latest and greatest products. But it's not easy (or inexpensive) to be chased all the time.

Rather than always take the lead in product development, you can make your company stand out by enhancing a product in more subtle ways, offering customers unique and tailored options that are appreciated all the more because they're often unexpected. Examples include a camera that senses when you've forgotten to put the film in, an insurance policy that makes it easy to keep track of what you own and then automatically updates your coverage, and software that actually helps you remove every bit of itself from your hard drive when you want to get rid of it.

Product quality

When you offer a product or service that's known for its quality, you take a big step toward standing out in the marketplace. In some sense, quality captures what differentiation is all about. Quality of one sort or another is what everybody seems to be looking for, and it's often in the eyes of the beholder. Although customers can't always tell you exactly what quality is, they know it when they see it, and when they see it, they like it – and may even pay a little extra for it.

Customers are likely to perceive quality in your product a bit differently than they do quality in a service that you may offer. The differences between product and service quality are big enough, in fact, that we treat the two separately in Table 1-1.

Table 1-1	Product and Service Quality Examples
Product quality	*Example*
Performance	Do pots and pans get clean in the dishwasher?
Consistency	Is the restaurant's pasta special always tasty?
Durability	How long will the hiking boots last?
Reliability	Will the answering machine save all the messages?
Appearance	Does the watch have that special look and feel?
Brand name	Which stereo system is known for its quality?
Service quality	*Example*
Capability	Does the brain surgeon know what she's doing?
Dependability	Will the newspaper be delivered in the morning?
Responsiveness	Can the 999 emergency team arrive in time?
Integrity	How much should the lawyer be trusted?
Attentiveness	Does the bank clerk smile and say hello?
Tangibles	Which airline has the cleanest onboard toilets?

Book VI

Getting Bigger

The different quality dimensions depend on the industry that you're in and on the customers you're serving. Even in a particular industry, companies create successful differentiation strategies for distinct dimensions. The car industry is a prime example. When you think of Porsche, for example, you think of performance; Volvo means safety; and Toyota and Honda are reliable choices. These differences allow competitors to prosper in the same industry, each in its own way.

Things are a bit different in service industries. For one thing, you can't help but face the importance of customers' impressions when you're dealing with services. By definition, a service is something that can't be held; you can't really touch it, feel it, or kick its tyres. So customers are in a bit of a quandary when it comes to making well-informed decisions. Figuring out what is and isn't a quality service is harder. How do you really know whether your doctor's a genius or a quack, for example? Is the pilot of today's flight an ace or just so-so? Is your dentist a saint or a sadist?

That's why perceptions come into play. When customers don't have all the data, they go with what they see. No matter what other dimensions are important, the tangibles – equipment, facilities, and personnel – play a significant part in customers' perceptions of service quality. As an airline executive said:

> *Filthy toilets and dirty trays are bound to lead to engine failure.*

Because customers have no way of evaluating the quality of an airline's engine-maintenance programme, they look at the things that they *can* judge, and they form their opinions accordingly.

Product packaging

Customers often look beyond the basics in making the final decision on what to buy. In fact, your customers may be influenced as much by the packaging as by the standard set of features that your product or service has to offer. Accordingly, you can develop an effective differentiation strategy based on product packaging – how it's advertised, when it's serviced, and where it's sold.

Given creative advertising, attentive service, and sophisticated distribution, almost anything can be made unique in one way or another. If you don't believe us, check out the produce section in a classy supermarket. Fruit and vegetables are routinely identified by country, state, or even farm of origin. Signs tell customers whether the produce was grown with or without chemicals and even specify the harvest date. Each combination represents a differentiated product to be advertised, displayed, and priced based on the unique benefits that it offers.

A focus on focus

The two generic strategies that we've talked about so far concentrate on one side of the customer value equation or the other. A cost-leadership strategy points out the price tag, whereas differentiation emphasises the unique benefits that a product or service has to offer. The final generic strategy plays off the first two strategies. A *focus strategy* still aims at either price or uniqueness, but it concentrates on a smaller piece of the action.

A focus strategy works because you concentrate on a specific customer group. As a result, you do a better job of meeting those customers' particular needs than do any of your competition, many of whom are trying to serve larger markets. The following sections discuss several ways to concentrate your efforts.

Niche markets

Small, well-defined market segments provide an opportunity not only to meet customers' needs, but also to exceed their expectations. If these market segments happen to be at the high end, you're likely to be well rewarded for your attentions as the money keeps rolling in. Small, upmarket hotels, for example, pamper their well-heeled customers with valets, butlers, and even a chauffeured service to restaurants and the airport. A new breed of takeaway food services treats customers to mix-and-match offerings from the best restaurants in town, well-dressed delivery people, and even sit-down catering complete with china, crystal, and kitchen staff.

Customers are willing to pay a premium for this kind of service, and that means big profits. Niche markets don't have to be upmarket, of course; factory outlet stores are thriving by serving cost-conscious customers who have high-end tastes.

Book VI

Getting Bigger

Targeted products

Companies that are driven by volume sales in large markets often ignore so-called speciality products and services – all those non-standard items and services that have limited appeal and not much market potential. If these companies do get into a speciality business, they're usually fairly inefficient at it; size and overhead costs simply work against them. Speciality products and services spell potential opportunity for a focused strategy to be successful.

Limited territory

Sometimes, a focus on geography results in cost advantages, better-served markets, or both. Where local tastes are strong, for example, or service and distribution costs are particularly high, a regional business can flourish. Independent restaurants and grocery shops, TV stations, and newspapers all attract a community of customers who want local news, buy regional products, and like to patronise neighbourhood shops. Commuter airlines focus on regional service, offering frequent flights and the best schedules to out-of-the-way destinations, and they keep costs down by flying smaller planes, limiting facilities, and running bare-bones operations.

A focus strategy works especially well if you're the new kid on the block, trying to establish a foothold in an industry in which the big guys have already staked out their claims. Rather than go after those fat, juicy markets (and get beaten up right away), you can sometimes avoid head-on competition by focusing on smaller markets, which may be less attractive to existing players. Once you're established in a niche market, you may decide that it's time to challenge the market leaders on their own turf. Morrisons, the supermarket chain, for example, started out as a small local chain offering bargain prices and a limited range. The company became a major regional player, and with its acquisition of Safeways, is now the third most successful supermarket nationally.

For small established companies in a market, a focus strategy may be the only ticket to survival when the big guys decide to come to town. If your company has few assets and limited options, concentration on a specific customer segment at least gives you a fighting chance to leverage the capabilities and resources that you do have.

Unfortunately, a focus strategy is one of the most difficult to defend over time. Dangers lurk both inside and outside the company. If the market segment that you're in suddenly takes off, you can pretty much count on intense competition down the road from much bigger players with much deeper pockets.

If your market niche stays small, you face a powerful urge to spread your wings and expand into new and different markets, knowing full well that you may lose many of your original strengths and advantages. Your best bet is to stay focused. Small companies have the best chance of sticking around over the long haul if they stick to a strategy and business plan that concentrate their resources and capabilities, focusing their energies on serving a specific market segment better than anyone else out there.

Checking Out Strategic Alternatives

A successful strategy and plan depend on your business circumstances – what's happening in the industry and marketplace, and what your competitors are up to. In particular, consider a couple of common business situations that you may find yourself in.

Up, down, or sideways

The range of activities that define your industry – called *vertical integration* – measures how many phases of the business you and your competitors are involved in. Vertically integrated companies are involved in many parts of an industry, from supplying raw materials to selling products and services to customers. Companies that are not vertically integrated tend to focus on one or two major aspects of the business. Some breweries, for example, concentrate on one central activity: the brewing of beer. Other breweries also get involved in growing the barley and hops; in making the beer bottles, labels, and cans; in trucking the beer around; and even in running the pubs that sell the beer to all those loyal customers.

Exactly where does your company stand in terms of vertical integration in your own industry? The question's important, because it affects your decision about whether to become more or less vertically integrated over time. Several terms have been coined by business gurus to describe the strategic moves that you may decide to make:

- ✔ **Backward integration.** *Backward integration* means extending your business activities in a direction that gets you closer to the raw materials, resources, and expertise that go into creating and producing your company's products.

- ✔ **Forward integration.** *Forward integration* means extending your business activities in a direction that gets you closer to the marketplace by involving the company in packaging, marketing, distribution, and customer sales.

- ✔ **Outsourcing.** *Outsourcing* means concentrating on your core business activities by farming out other parts of your company's operations to outside contractors and vendors that specialise in those particular areas.

- ✔ **Divesting.** *Divesting* means reducing your company's activities to focus on specific aspects of your business by spinning off or selling other pieces of the company.

Book VI

Getting
Bigger

Tables 1-2 and 1-3 describe some of the pros and cons of vertical integration.

Table 1-2	Pros of Vertical Integration
Pro	*Reason*
Efficiencies	If you're in charge, it's sometimes easier to coordinate activities at the various business stages along the way, combining related functions or getting rid of overlapping areas to streamline your overall operations.
Resources	If you have a hand in the upstream (early-stage) activities of a business, you can guarantee that your company has access to the raw materials and resources that it needs to stay in business.
Customers	If your company is involved in downstream (late-stage) activities, you not only get to know a great deal about customers, but also create lasting relationships and secure your own long-term access to the market.

Table 1-3	Cons of Vertical Integration
Con	**Reason**
Overhead	If your company tries to control all stages of its industry, it can run into all sorts of extra expenses because of mismatched operations, idle resources, and added coordination costs.
Mediocrity	If your company is involved in a wide range of activities, it's much tougher to be the best at any of them, and the company risks becoming average in everything that it does.
Size and slowness	If your company is vertically integrated, its size often makes it difficult to quickly respond to change, and commitments to various parts of the industry leave it little room to be flexible.

There's both good news and bad news in terms of deciding just how much vertical integration is best. Over the years, there have been swings in the popularity of vertically integrated companies: A rush toward control of all aspects of an industry is followed by the race to break up companies and concentrate on specific business activities. Then the cycle repeats itself.

Today's wisdom seems to come down on the side of breaking companies apart. Worldwide competition in all industries over the past decade has made it more cost-effective to go out and buy what you need rather than to try to build up resources and expertise inside the company. That practice has resulted in a wave of downsizing and restructuring as companies struggle to remain competitive at what they do best.

And the future? One thing seems to hold true across the swings and cycles: The most successful and profitable businesses most often do business at one of the two extremes of integration. Companies that are heavily integrated reap all the real benefits of vertical integration; those that concentrate on a single activity eliminate all the costs and inefficiencies. Whatever you do, try not to get stuck in the middle, with few of the benefits and too many of the costs.

Leading and following

No matter what industry you're in, you can divide your competition into two major groups: the market leaders and all the market followers nipping at their heels. *Market leaders* are those top-tier companies that set the agenda for the industry and make things happen; they're the ones in the driver's seat. The *market followers,* well, they follow along. But in this second group, you find the companies that work hard, think big, and keep the market leaders on their toes.

Depending on the market situation, companies in both groups behave very differently. Whether you're already a part of an industry or are thinking of joining it as a new business owner, it's important that you understand what motivates both the market leaders and the rest of the pack. The following sections explore some market strategies.

Market-leader strategies

Market leadership comes in various forms, from the absolute dominance of one company to shared control of the industry by several leading players. If you're a market leader, here are some possible strategic approaches for you:

- ✔ **Full speed ahead.** In this situation, your company is the clear market leader. Even so, you always try to break further away from the pack. You're always the first to make a move, whether in implementing new technology and introducing innovative products or in promoting new uses and setting aggressively low prices. You not only intend to stay on top, but also want to expand your lead.

- ✔ **Hold the line.** Your company's certainly in the top tier in the market, but it doesn't have a commanding position of strength in the industry, so your goals centre on hanging on to what you've already got. Those goals may involve locking distributors into long-term contracts, making it more difficult for customers to switch to competing brands or going after new market segments and product areas to block competitors from doing the same thing.

- ✔ **Steady as she goes.** In this case, your company is one of several powerful companies in the market. As one among equals, your company takes on part of the responsibility of policing the industry to see that nothing upsets the boat. If an upstart challenger tries to cut prices, for example, you're there to quickly match those lower prices. You're always scanning the horizon for new competitors, and you work hard to discourage distributors, vendors, and retailers from adding new companies and brands to their lists.

Market-follower strategies

Market followers are often forced to take their cues and develop strategies based on the strength and behaviour of the market leaders. An aggressive challenger, for example, may not do well in an industry that has a powerful, assertive company on top. Fortunately, you can choose among several strategic alternatives if you find yourself in a market-follower position:

- ✔ **Make some waves.** In this case, your company has every intention of growing bigger by increasing its presence in the industry, and you're quite willing to challenge the market leadership head-on to do it. Perhaps your strategy includes an aggressive price-cutting campaign to gain as much market share as you can. Maybe you back up this campaign with a rapid expansion of distribution outlets and a forceful marketing effort. The strategy requires deep pockets, will, and the skill to force a market leader to blink, but in the end, it could make you the leader of the pack.

- ✔ **Turn a few heads.** In this situation, your company is certainly not one of the market leaders, but it's successful in its own market niche, and you want it to stay that way. So although you're careful not to challenge the market leadership directly, you're fierce about defending your turf. You have strengths and advantages in your own market segment because of the uniqueness of your product and customer loyalty. To maintain this position, you focus on customer benefits and the value that you bring to the market.

- ✔ **Just tag along.** It's easy to point out companies that have settled into complacency. Frankly, they're usually in rather boring industries in which not much ever happens. These companies are quite happy to remain toward the end of the pack, tagging along without a worry. Don't count on them to do anything new or different in the marketplace. (If you find yourself in a company like this, you may want to think about making a change while you're still awake.)

Remember the following when checking out strategic alternatives:

- ✔ A successful strategy must take into account what your competitors are up to.

- ✔ Vertically-integrated companies control many aspects of their business and can streamline their operations.

- ✔ Companies that concentrate on one or two activities are more flexible and can focus on what they do best.

- ✔ Market leaders set the agenda for the industry and shape the competitive landscape.

- ✔ Market followers aren't in the driver's seat, but they work hard, think big, and sometimes become leaders of the pack.

Coming Up with Your Own Strategy

If you feel a bit overwhelmed by all the possibilities for devising a strategy for your own company, stop and take a deep breath. Remember one important thing: Strategy isn't a test that you take once and have to get a perfect score on the first time. Instead, it's the way that you decide to do business over the long haul. Strategy is an ongoing process, so don't be alarmed if you can't see how all the pieces fit together all at once.

Coming up with the right strategy is something that you have the chance to work on over and over again – rethinking, revising, reformulating. If you approach strategy in the right way, you probably won't ever finish the task.

Book VI

Getting Bigger

As you begin to shape your own strategy, the following pointers can guide you:

- ✔ Never develop a strategy without first doing your homework.
- ✔ Always have a clear set of goals and objectives in front of you.
- ✔ Remember what assumptions you make, and make sure that they hold up.
- ✔ Build in flexibility, and always have an alternative.
- ✔ Understand the needs, desires, and nature of your customers.
- ✔ Know your competitors, and don't underestimate them.
- ✔ Leverage your strengths and minimise your weaknesses.
- ✔ Emphasise core competence to sustain a competitive advantage.
- ✔ Make your strategy clear, concise, consistent, and attainable.
- ✔ Trumpet the strategy so that you don't leave the organisation guessing.

These guidelines are not only helpful for creating a strategy, but also useful for reviewing and revising one as well. Make sure that you return to them on a regular basis as part of your ongoing commitment to the strategy and planning process.

Companies that take strategy and business planning seriously know that to reach a target, it's 'ready, aim, fire' – not 'ready, fire, aim'. It's that simple. In other words, almost any strategy is better than no strategy at all. Companies that have clear strategies don't hit the bull's-eye every time; no strategy can promise that. But these companies succeed in the end because they sub-scribe to a strategic process that forces them to ask the right questions and come up with good answers – answers that are often better than their com-petitors' answers.

Chapter 2

Managing More Than One Product

• •

In This Chapter

▶ Working with the product life cycle

▶ Expanding your market

▶ Extending your product line

▶ Diversifying into new businesses

▶ Identifying strategic business units

▶ Managing your product portfolio

• •

*I*n this chapter, we explain the product life cycle and what it means for your company. We talk about ways to keep your company growing. We show you how to expand into new markets with existing products, as well as how to extend your product line to better serve current customers. We explore the opportunities and pitfalls of trying to diversify. We talk about strategic business units (SBUs) and introduce several portfolio tools to help you plan and manage a family of products.

Facing the Product Life Cycle

If you could use only one word to describe what it feels like to be in business and to compete in a marketplace, that word probably would be *change*. The forces of change are everywhere, ranging from major trends in your business environment to the shifting tastes and demands of your customers and the unpredictable behaviour of your competitors.

You may think that all these factors, stirred together, create a world filled with chaos and uncertainty. Not so. The experts have stumbled onto some basic patterns, and the cycles that they've created do a good job of describing what happens in the face of all the market turmoil and confusion.

One of these patterns – the *product life cycle* – illustrates what happens to a new kind of product or service after you launch it in the market. The product life cycle describes four major stages that your product is likely to go through:

✔ An introduction period

✔ A growth period

✔ Maturity

✔ A period of decline

Most product life cycles look something like Figure 2-1.

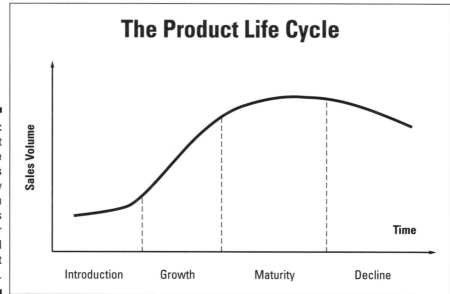

Figure 2-1:
The product life cycle represents what's likely to happen to sales volume for a typical product over time.

The curve traces your product sales volume over time. You can think about the sales volume in terms of the revenue that you take in or the number of units that you sell, and you may end up measuring the time scale in weeks, months, years, or even decades.

Every stage of your product's life cycle presents a unique set of market conditions and a series of planning challenges. The different stages require different management objectives, strategies, and skills. The following sections discuss what you should think about at each stage.

Starting out

You introduce a new kind of product or service in the market, and it begins to generate revenue. Because costs are relatively high at this stage, you usually don't find too many competitors around. Growth is limited instead by your company's ability to make the product, generate market awareness, and get customers to accept and adopt the new product.

At this stage in the product life cycle, efforts focus on getting your product out the door or on rolling out the new service and ensuring that everything works the way that it's supposed to. At the same time, you have to drum up lots of interest and struggle to create a brand-new market. Table 2-1 points out many characteristics of the introduction stage.

Table 2-1	Major Characteristics of the Introduction Stage
Component	*Characteristics*
Industry	One or two companies
Competition	Little or none
Key function	Research and development
Customers	Innovators and risk-takers
Finances	High prices and expenses
Profits	Non-existent to negative
Objectives	Product adoption
Strategy	Expanding the total market

Growing up

Your new product or service gains a reputation during the growth stage. Demand rises rapidly, and sales increase. Competition increases as well, as competing products jump into the fray to take advantage of an expanding market. Customers begin to develop brand loyalties, and companies tweak their product features to better serve customer needs – needs that are now easier to recognise.

As the growth stage kicks in, your priorities turn toward meeting growing product demand, improving your product or service, and targeting specific groups of customers. Along the way, you have to fend off a growing crop of competitors. Table 2-2 highlights characteristics of the growth stage.

Table 2-2	Major Characteristics of the Growth Stage
Component	*Characteristics*
Industry	Many companies
Competition	Growing strength and numbers
Key function	Marketing
Customers	Eager to try products
Finances	Variable prices and costs
Profits	Growing rapidly
Objectives	Sales growth and market share
Strategy	Establishing and defending position

Middle age

The growth of your product or service begins to slow in the maturity stage, as market demand levels off and new customers become harder to find. New competitors are also harder to find, and the competition stabilises. Profits keep on growing, however, as costs continue to fall. Changes in market share reflect changes in product value and often come at the expense of competing products.

As maturity sets in, your attention turns toward reducing costs and finally reaping the benefits of stable profits. Although it's easy to feel comfortable at this stage, you need to think about what's going to happen next. Table 2-3 identifies the characteristics of the maturity stage.

Table 2-3	Major Characteristics of the Maturity Stage
Component	*Characteristics*
Industry	Not as many companies
Competition	Stronger, but stable
Key function	Operations

Component	Characteristics
Customers	The majority of buyers
Finances	Competitive prices and lower costs
Profits	At or near peak
Objectives	Cash flow and profit
Strategy	Maintaining competitive position

Senior stretch

At some point in your product's life cycle, sales start to fall off, and revenue begins to decline. Competitors drop out of the market as profits all but disappear. The decline stage may be triggered by large-scale changes in the economy or technology, or it may simply reflect changing customer needs and behaviour. Products still on the market in this stage are either redesigned, repositioned, or replaced.

As the decline stage looms, you have to get back into the business trenches. Your work shifts to redesigning your product or redefining its market, or maybe coming up with new uses or different kinds of customers. If all these attempts fail, you have to concentrate on ways to get out of the market and not lose too much money. Table 2-4 shows various characteristics of the decline stage.

Table 2-4	Major Characteristics of the Decline Stage
Component	Characteristics
Industry	Few companies
Competition	Declining in number
Key function	Finance and planning
Customers	Loyal, conservative buyers
Finances	Falling prices and low costs
Profits	Much reduced
Objectives	Residual profits
Strategy	Getting out alive

Where you are now

Take your own product or service and see whether you can come up with its estimated position on the product life cycle curve (refer to Figure 2-1 earlier in this chapter). If you're stumped, ask yourself the following kinds of questions:

- ✔ How long has the product been on the market?
- ✔ How rapidly is the market growing?
- ✔ Is the growth rate increasing, decreasing, or flat?
- ✔ Is the product profitable?
- ✔ Are profits heading up or down?
- ✔ How many competitors does the product have?
- ✔ How fast are product features changing?
- ✔ Are there more or fewer competing products than there were a year ago?

Perhaps you feel confident about where your product is in its life cycle. That's good. Just make sure, though, that you take the time to confirm your analysis. Chances are that you're going to get mixed signals from the marketplace, and the clues may even contradict one another. No two products ever behave the same way when it comes to the product life cycle. Unfortunately, acting prematurely on the evidence at hand can lead to hasty planning and a self-fulfilling prophecy.

What good is a business concept if you can't really count on it? Well, don't get us wrong here. The product life cycle is a powerful planning tool if you use it to support – not replace – your own solid skills. When it's deployed as an early warning system, the product life cycle alerts you to potential changes, allowing you time to plan for a different business environment and to respond quickly when your product finally enters a new stage in its life cycle.

Finding Ways to Grow

Let's face it – your product simply isn't going to be the same tomorrow as it is today. You may not plan to do anything to it at all, but everything around your product is going to change. The world will take another step ahead. The economy, technology, your industry, and the competition will all change a bit. As a result, your customers will think about your company and your product a bit differently, even if you see yourself as being exactly the same.

How does your company find ways to grow and prosper in the face of almost-certain product mortality? You probably have every intention of creating a new business plan (beyond turning off the lights and locking all the doors) as your product begins to age. But which way do you turn? Mark Twain had a bit of tongue-in-cheek advice for people who prefer to keep things just as they are:

> *Put all your eggs in one basket . . . and watch that basket!*

Trouble is, the eggs are going to hatch, and the chicks will probably run away. So doing nothing except watching and waiting is not really an option. But what are your alternatives?

Fortunately, you don't have to invent the alternatives yourself, planning for long-term growth has been a philosophical favourite of management gurus for decades. One of the pioneers of business-growth techniques was a man named Igor Ansoff, who came up with a simple matrix to represent the possible directions of growth (see Figure 2-2).

Book VI

Getting
Bigger

Figure 2-2:
The Growth
Directions
Matrix
describes
different
ways in
which your
company
can grow,
based on a
combination
of products
and markets.

The Growth Directions Matrix really captures nothing more than basic common sense: it says that if you want to make your business grow, you have to start somewhere. The logical place to begin is to take advantage of where you are today and what you have to work with. How fast you grow in any of these directions has everything to do with your own capabilities and resources, as well as the rate of change in your industry. Consider the following ways in which you can move your company ahead:

> ✔ **You are here (existing product and market).** Continue to grow by doing what you're already doing, but do it a little bit better, so that customers use more of your product or service more often and in more ways than before. Encourage people to use more toothpaste, for example, by brushing their teeth (or even their dog's teeth) more often.

✔ **New market, existing product.** Grow in the near term by finding a fresh market for your existing product, either by expanding geographically or by reaching out to completely different kinds of customers. If you make baking soda, for example, get people to put baking soda in their refrigerators to keep them odour-free.

✔ **New product, existing market.** Grow by developing additional product features, options, or even a related product family with the intention of enticing your existing customers. Think of the array of apple drinks that are available these days – everything from Appletize to apple-flavoured water.

✔ **New market, new product.** Grow over the long term by going after new and unfamiliar markets with new and different products. Ford Motor Company, for example, used to make and sell prefabricated homes.

Without getting bogged down in a lot of details, try to come up with a dozen different ways to grow your company. Get yourself into the right frame of mind by first reviewing your company's mission and vision statements. (Don't have 'em? Check out *Business Plans For Dummies* for everything that you need to know.) Then complete the following steps:

1. **Identify three things that you can do right away to stimulate demand for your existing product in your current markets.**

   These things may include cutting costs, offering rebates, or maybe coming up with some new product uses.

2. **List three steps that you can take in the next six months to capture new markets for your existing product.**

   Some ideas include radio or television ads that target new customers, direct-mail campaigns, and stepped-up appearances at trade shows.

3. **Specify three development efforts that you can launch over the coming year to extend your current product line.**

   These efforts may include enhancing product features or adding options.

4. **Describe three directions that you can take over the next three to five years that will move you into new products and markets.**

More than one or two experts believe that any talk about brand-new products for completely new markets is really none of your business as a manager. These financial gurus think that managers are simply too biased to be objective when it comes to assessing totally new opportunities. They argue that you should return all your extra profits to investors and let them decide where to place their bets on the future. You probably don't agree with them; after all, investors have made monumental mistakes in the past. But they do have a good point. It's probably worth remembering that growth in new directions is a tricky business, no matter how it's done or who ends up doing it.

Same product, same market

Many successful big-name companies have become as big and successful as they are by relentlessly pursing a single business, a single market, or even an individual product decade after decade. When you hear the name BT, for example, you think of picking up a telephone. When you see a Coca-Cola sign, you imagine drinking a Coke. And when you pass a McDonald's, you probably picture a Big Mac. But these companies haven't turned into billion-pound corporations simply by launching their flagship products and letting the marketplace take care of the rest. Companies that largely depend on a single product spend enormous amounts of time and effort to continually rejuvenate and revitalise their core markets.

If you glance back at the Growth Directions Matrix shown in Figure 2-2 earlier in this chapter, you notice that these companies invest heavily in the top-left box. How do they manage to do that successfully? They use the four main strategies described in the following sections.

Encourage greater product use. A company increases demand by encouraging its customers to consume more of a product or service every time they use it. Maybe that means getting customers to feel good about buying more or giving them a better deal when they do. Customers may do the following things:

- Buy larger bottles of cola because they can save some money
- Apply for more insurance coverage because you carefully show them that it's the prudent thing to do
- Stay on the phone longer because the rates are lower
- Opt for a packaged computer or stereo system with all the components because it's simpler to assemble

Generate more-frequent product use. A company stimulates sales by getting customers to use its product or service more often. That may mean making the product more convenient, introducing it as part of customers' regular routine, or offering incentives to frequent customers. Customers may do the following things:

- Use toothpaste after every meal because they think it's hygienic
- Regularly drink wine at dinner because they think it's healthy
- Join a frequent-flyer programme and take an extra trip just to build more miles

Devise new uses. A company expands its market by coming up with new ways for customers to use its product or service. That may include getting customers to use the product at different times, in different places, on novel occasions, or in unconventional ways. All of a sudden, customers may do the following things:

✔ Snack on breakfast cereal during the day because it's handy and tastes good

✔ Put a radio in the shower and a TV in the car because they're convenient

✔ Make videos of every imaginable event from childbirth to pet funerals

Woo customers away from competitors. A company can also increase demand for its product or service the old-fashioned way: by taking customers away from the competition. Although the result is sometimes a fierce and unwanted response from competitors, companies can do the following things:

✔ Create incentives to switch from competing products and give rewards for staying put

✔ Concentrate on becoming a low-cost provider with the best prices around

✔ Package a product so that it's distinctive and stands out in the marketplace

✔ Focus on meeting or exceeding the needs of specific customer groups

Companies that manage to grow in the same old market with the same old product do so by continually generating new demand as well as maintaining or even increasing their market share. Often, these companies succeed in slowing the product life cycle, extending its maturity stage almost indefinitely. In some cases, they even manage to reset the life cycle, pulling the product back into the growth stage by inventing new and creative product uses. But steady and sustained market penetration based on a single product doesn't always work forever, and companies sometimes have to look in new directions for growth.

New market or new product

At some point in the life of your company, a single product or service may not be enough to sustain an attractive level of growth in your business. Where do you turn? The Growth Directions Matrix (refer to Figure 2-2, earlier in this chapter) suggests that the most reliable and productive paths point to market expansion in the near term, as well as to extending your product line. These two directions for growth have the distinct advantage of building on capabilities and resources that you already have. Market expansion leverages your current product expertise, and product extension builds on your experience and knowledge of current customers and the marketplace.

New market

Expanding into a new market is something that your company can do rather quickly, because it can take advantage of its current business model, copying many of the activities that it's already engaged in – producing, assembling, and distributing products, for example.

You can expand your market in two basic ways: move into new geographical areas or go after new market segments.

- ✔ **Geography.** The most obvious way to grow beyond your core product and market is to expand geographically, picking up new customers based solely on where they live and work. This kind of expansion has many advantages. You not only do business in the same way as before, but you also have a head start in understanding many of your new customers, even with their regional differences. Because geographic expansion may require you to do business in unfamiliar areas or even new countries, however, you have to pay special attention to how your company must change to accommodate the specific demands of your expanded market.

- ✔ **New market segments.** Sometimes you can expand the market for your product or service by finding new kinds of customers. If you're creative, maybe you can identify a group of customers that you've neglected in the past. Look carefully at your product's features and packaging, how it's priced and delivered, who's buying, and why they buy. Also, reassess the customer benefits that you provide. Then ask yourself how attractive a new market segment is in terms of its size and potential to grow. What strengths do you bring to the market? What competitors are already there? How do you plan to gain an advantage over the long haul?

New product

Extending the number of products or types of services that you offer is something that you should plan for well ahead of time. All too often, companies develop new product features, options, and major product enhancements without giving much thought to the implications for the company's future direction and growth. Instead, a customer asks for this or that special feature, or a distributor requests a particular option or accessory, and before you know it, you have additional products to support.

The good news, of course, is that you already have customers. But you also have to be sure that those customers represent a larger market that benefits from your product extension and that the additional products make sense in terms of your own business strategy and plan.

You can extend your product or service in two basic ways: offer new features and options or create related families of products.

- ✔ **New features and options.** The most common way to extend a product line involves adding bells and whistles to your product and giving customers the chance to choose which bells and whistles they want. The advantages are easy to tick off: You work from your existing strengths in product design and development, and you use real live customers to help you decide which incremental changes to make. It sounds like the perfect game plan.

   The danger comes from losing track of the bigger picture – where you want your company to end up. Individual customers, no matter how good they are, don't always reflect the direction of larger markets. So avoid creating a bunch of marginal products that you can't really sell or support. Instead, plan to develop a smaller number of products with features and options that are designed to meet the needs of specific market segments.

- ✔ **Related product groups.** You may create a group of products based on a common element of some sort. You can develop a product family to use the same core technology, to meet a series of related customer needs, or to serve as accessories for your primary product.

   You want the product group to look stronger in the market than the individual products do separately. That way, the risks inherent in product development are reduced, and the rewards are potentially greater. Take time to understand just how products in the group actually work together. Also, make sure that you address the separate challenges that each product poses in terms of customers, the competition, and your own company's assets and capabilities.

Before you put your plans for growth into action, make sure that they draw on your company's strengths, reflect the capabilities and resources that you have available, and help maintain your competitive advantage. Ask yourself the following questions:

- ✔ How well are you doing in the markets that you're already in?
- ✔ In what ways is the expanded market different from your current market?
- ✔ What parts of your business can you leverage in the expanded market?
- ✔ What functions and activities have to change to accommodate more products?
- ✔ How well will your extended product line meet specific customer needs?

✔ Is your extended product family stronger than each product by itself?

✔ How easy is it to scale up your business to meet the expected growth?

✔ How will your competitive environment change?

New product and new market

Has your company hit a midlife crisis? Do you find yourself searching for attractive new customers, sexy technologies, and aggressive competition? Well, it's not unusual for a company to think about rejuvenating itself from time to time. A plan to move in new directions often involves diversifying the company, moving down into the bottom-right corner of the Growth Directions Matrix (refer to Figure 2-2 earlier in this chapter). That corner, after all, is where the grass always looks much greener – and the profits look greener, too.

But you have to balance the potential rewards against the challenges and risks that go along with diversification. Too many companies end up looking foolish as they try to learn new tricks in unfamiliar businesses without much time to practise – and they often face the financial consequences.

To better your odds of success, start by doing your homework, which means researching all the new issues and new players. If this task sounds daunting, it's meant to. The stakes couldn't be much higher.

Your chances of success improve substantially when you identify the ways that a potential new business is related to what your company already does. But even without the benefit of any existing product or market expertise, you can often discover aspects of a new business opportunity that play right into your company's core competence. Here's what to look for:

✔ **Name recognition.** If your company has worked hard to create a name for itself, you can sometimes make use of its brand identity in a new business situation. Name recognition is particularly powerful when the associations are positive, clearly defined, and can be carried over to the new product and market. Luxury-car companies such as BMW, for example, now give their names to expensive, upmarket lines of touring and mountain bikes.

✔ **Technical operations.** The resources and skills required to design, develop, or manufacture products in your own industry – or perhaps the technical services that you offer – may be extended to support additional product areas. Japanese electronics giants such as Sony and Mitsubishi, for example, are experts in miniaturisation, automation, and quality control. Given those skills, they can acquire original technology or experimental products and then go on to create product lines based on their expertise.

✔ **Marketing experience.** If your company has a great deal of marketing expertise available, you can often put that expertise to good use to expand the awareness and strengthen the positioning of a new product. Examples include the creative software products that small, independent developers produce and then sell to larger companies such as Symantec or Netscape – companies that have the marketing muscle to successfully advertise, promote, and distribute those products.

✔ **Capacity and scale.** Sometimes you can take the excess capacity that your company has in production, sales, or distribution and apply that capacity directly to a new business area. That way, you reap the benefits of a larger scale of operations and use your resources more efficiently. Many car dealerships around the UK, for example, reached out in the 1980s to show, sell, and service Toyotas and Hondas, permanently adding them to their British car lines. Now, of course, that's all that UK motor dealerships have to offer, so their new products eventually became their main and only products.

✔ **Financial considerations.** Persistent demands on your company's revenue, cash flow, or profits may inevitably point you in a new business direction. Although a financial opportunity by itself offers a fairly flimsy link to your existing products and markets, a new business may – just may – be justified on the basis of financial considerations alone. Large tobacco companies, for example, use their huge cash reserves to diversify into unrelated business areas that have brighter, smoke-free futures.

The temptation to set off in new directions and diversify into new businesses, creating brand-new products for brand-new markets, has bewitched and bothered business planners for decades. Unfortunately, the failure rate for new products can be as high as 75 per cent. And the most perplexing part of the puzzle is the fact that in the beginning, everything looks so good on paper. Here are some examples:

✔ Campbell Soup Company thought that it had a winner when it decided to launch a family of juice drinks for kids. But its Juice Works brand had trouble, in part because so many competitors had better brand-name recognition in the juice business.

✔ Federal Express set out to create the future of immediate document delivery by introducing a new computer network-based product. But customers turned to FedEx to send hard copy, not e-mail, and the company got zapped by its Zap Mail service.

✔ Laura Ashley, co-founder with her husband Bernard of the firm of the same name, never liked the concept of fashion, insisting instead that her clothes and furnishings were designed to endure. In the 1960s, the company's fresh cotton print dresses offered a clear alternative to the miniskirts of Mary Quant. In the late 1980s, following Laura Ashley's tragic death, the company made the mistake of trying too hard to get with it, downplaying its heritage, neglecting its long print tea-dresses and Viyella checks. The flirtation with fashion was a disaster, heralding a decade or so of revolving doors at management level, and strategic twists and turns that make fascinating, if depressing, case study material for MBA classes the world over.

A few companies, however, manage to succeed with new products and markets time and time again. Think Tesco, and you could be forgiven for thinking of value food in the UK. But the company has successfully introduced thousands of non-food products in the past decade-everything from fashion clothing, to microwaves; they even have a substantial personal finance business, and perhaps the world's only profitable Internet home delivery service. Tesco's stated goal is to bring value, choice and convenience to customers, notice that there is no mention of food here. It is a goal it pursues with vigour in Asia, Central and Eastern Europe, and the US.

Book VI

Getting Bigger

Managing Your Product Portfolio

When you decide that it's time to branch out into new products and markets or to diversify into new businesses, you're going to have to learn how to juggle. You no longer have the luxury of doting on a single product or service; now you have more than one product and market to deal with. You have to figure out how to keep every one of your products in the air, providing each one with the special attention and resources that it needs, depending on which part of the product life cycle it's in.

Strategic business units

Juggling usually requires a bit of preparation, of course, and the first thing that you want to find out is how many oranges and clubs – or products and services, in this case – you have to keep in the air at one time. It's easy to count oranges, and counting clubs isn't tough, either. For products and services, though, the following questions tend to pop up. Often, these questions have no right answer, but just taking time to think through the issues helps you better understand what you offer.

✔ Just how many products or services does your company have?

✔ When you add another feature or an option to your product, does the addition essentially create a new product that requires a separate business plan?

✔ When you have two separate sets of customers using your service in different ways, do you really have two services, each with its own business plan?

✔ When you offer two different products to the same set of customers, each of which is manufactured, marketed, and distributed in much the same way, are you really dealing with one larger product area and a single business plan?

 A *strategic business unit* (SBU) is a piece of your company that's big enough to have its own well-defined markets, attract its own set of competitors, and demand tangible resources and capabilities from you. Yet a SBU is small enough that you can craft a strategy with goals and objectives designed to reflect its special business environment. Consider ways to reorganise your own company around strategic business units. Each time you outline a separate business plan, you identify a potential SBU. How do you get started? Because strategic business units often refer to particular product and market areas taken together, begin with the following steps:

1. **Break your company into as many separate product and market combinations as you can think of.**

2. **Fit these building blocks back together in various ways, trying all sorts of creative associations of products and markets on different levels and scales.**

   Think about how each combination may work in terms of creating a viable business unit.

3. **Keep only those combinations of products and markets that make sense in terms of strategy, business planning, customers, the competition, and your company's structure.**

4. **Step back to determine how well these new SBUs mesh together and account for your overall business.**

   If you don't like what you see, try the process again. Don't make the changes for real until you're satisfied with your new organisation.

Aiming for the stars

Rather than juggle a set of who knows how many ill-defined products, practise your juggling technique on the Strategic Business Units (SBUs) that you identify instead.

Start by dividing your SBUs into two basic groups, depending on the direction of their cash flow: put the ones that bring money into your company on one side and the ones that take money out on the other side. Maybe you're surprised that you have two sides here. Because every product goes through a life cycle that's likely to include an introduction stage, growth, maturity, and then decline, different SBUs naturally have different cash-flow requirements. You must invest in products during their introduction and growth phases, and your mature products end up paying all the bills. So as a successful juggler, you always need at least one mature SBU aloft to support the SBUs that are coming along behind.

Some of this juggling stuff may sound familiar if you've ever tried to manage your own personal savings or retirement accounts. Every financial adviser tells you the same thing: spread your investments out to create a more stable and predictable set of holdings. Ideally, financial advisers want to help you balance your portfolio based on how much money you need to earn right away and what sort of nest egg you expect to have in the future. Given your financial needs and goals, planners may suggest buying blue-chip stocks and bonds that generate dividends right away, and also investing in more speculative companies that pay off well down the road.

Your company's strategic business units have a great deal in common with a portfolio of stocks and bonds – so much, in fact, that the SBU juggling that we're talking about is called *portfolio management*. To manage your own SBU portfolio as professionally as financial experts track stocks and bonds, you need some guidance, which is where portfolio analysis comes in. *Portfolio analysis* helps you look at the roles of the SBUs in your company and determine how well the SBUs balance one another so that the company grows and remains profitable. In addition, portfolio analysis offers a new way to think about strategy and business planning when you have more than one strategic business unit to worry about.

You could make your first attempt at simple portfolio analysis with two SBU categories: those that make money and those that take money. Then all you have to do is make sure that the first category is always bigger than the second. But the two categories don't give you much help in figuring out what's going to happen next. Fortunately, the people at the Boston Consulting Group came up with an easy-to-use portfolio-analysis tool that provides some useful planning direction.

The Boston Consulting Group's Growth-Share Grid (see Figure 2-3) directs you to divide your SBUs into four groups.

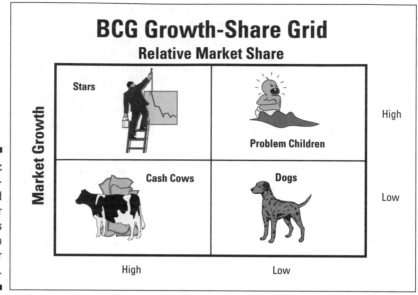

Figure 2-3:
The Growth-
Share Grid
divides your
company's
SBUs into
four major
groups.

You base your portfolio analysis on two major factors: market growth and market share.

✔ **Market growth.** Is the SBU part of a rapidly expanding market, or does it fall somewhere in a slow- or no-growth area? You use market growth to define your portfolio because it forces you to think about just how attractive the SBU may be over the long haul. The exact point that separates high-growth and low-growth markets is rather arbitrary; start by using a 10 per cent annual growth rate as the midpoint.

✔ **Relative market share.** Does your SBU command a market-share advantage over its nearest competitors, or does its market share place it down the list relative to the competition? You use relative market share as a major characteristic to define your SBU portfolio because all sorts of evidence suggests that a strong market-share position is closely tied to the profitability of the SBU. Separate your SBUs into those where you have the highest market share and those where you don't.

Here's a review of the types of SBUs:

Problem children. *Problem children* are SBUs that have relatively low market share in high-growth markets. Problem children often represent newer businesses and are sometimes referred to as *question marks*, because you aren't quite sure which path these SBUs may take. Because problem children are in expanding markets, these SBUs require lots of cash just to tread water, maintaining what market share they already have, but their relatively low sales tend to generate little or no revenue in return. If you can substantially increase their market share over time – and that means shelling out even more cash – problem children can blossom into stars. If not, you may have to give them up.

Stars. *Stars* are SBUs that have a dominant market-share position in high-growth markets. Every SBU wants to be a star. Stars usually have an expensive appetite for the cash to fund continual expansion and to fend off competitors that are eager to get a piece of the turf. But their market-share advantage gives these SBUs an edge in generating revenue, high margins, and profits. On balance, stars usually support themselves, both producing and consuming large amounts of money. You shouldn't hesitate to step in and support a star SBU, however, if additional resources are required to maintain its market-share lead.

Cash cows. The name *cash cows* says it all – these SBUs have a major market-share position in low-growth markets. Because of their market-share advantage, these SBUs generate a great deal of cash, and the best part is the fact that they don't require much in return. Their low-growth markets usually are mature, and the products are already well-established. The bottom line: You can milk cash cows to produce a cash surplus and then redirect that cash to fund promising SBUs in other quadrants.

Dogs. *Dogs* are SBUs that deliver low market share in low-growth markets – and little else. Although many of us are dog lovers, it's hard to love this particular breed. Revenue and profits usually are small or non-existent, and the SBUs are often net users of cash. Although they require periodic investments, these marginal businesses usually never amount to much, so it may be best to turn your attention to more-promising SBU candidates.

It's time to put all the pieces together so that you can construct a Growth-Share Grid to represent your own portfolio of strategic business units. Ideally, of course, you see mostly stars and cash cows, with enough problem children (the question marks) to ensure your company's future. Ideally, you have few dogs to contend with.

But the world isn't always ideal. Fortunately, you can also use the Growth-Share Grid as a tablet to sketch out what you plan to do with your SBUs to balance them in the future. Here's what you do:

1. **Sort through your company's SBUs, and get ready to put them in a blank Growth-Share Grid.**

   To see the grid format, refer to Figure 2-3 earlier in this chapter.

2. **Place each SBU in its proper quadrant, given what you know about market growth and the SBUs relative market share.**

3. **Draw a circle around each SBU to represent how big it is in relation to your other SBUs.**

   Base the size of your SBUs on revenue, profits, sales, or whatever measure is most convenient.

4. **For each SBU in the grid, forecast its movement in terms of overall market growth and market-share position.**

   Use a time frame that's appropriate for your industry and its rate of change.

5. **To capture this forecast, draw arrows indicating the direction of movement and where you plan to have each SBU end up in the future.**

   Arrows that point outside the grid indicate that you plan to get rid of the SBUs in question.

The BCG Growth-Share Grid, with its quirky cast of characters and its black-and-white view of the world, is hard to resist, because it makes the complex, difficult job of juggling several businesses seem to be almost effortless. After it first caught on around 30 years ago, however, the model became so widely overused and misapplied that the entire business of understanding business portfolios went out of fashion. Today, of course, we understand that portfolio-analysis tools have their place, but they have to be used sensibly. As the saying goes, if something looks too easy to be true, it probably is.

Before you start moving your SBUs around the Growth-Share Grid like pieces on a chessboard, remind yourself that the following strings are attached:

- ✔ Market growth is singled out as the only way to measure how attractive a market is and to determine whether or not you'd like to be in business there. But growth isn't the only interesting variable. Markets may turn out to be attractive because of advances in technology, changes in regulation, profits – you name it.

- ✔ Relative market share alone is used to describe how competitive you are and how profitable your company is likely to be. But market share is really relevant only when you're competing on the basis of size and sales volume. There are other ways to compete, including making your product unique in some way, focusing on a particular group of customers, or concentrating on service.

- ✔ The SBUs in the Growth-Share Grid are linked only by the flow of cash in and out of the different businesses. But there are many other ways to think about how strategic business units may relate to one another and function together, including views that stress the competition or focus on market risk factors.

- ✔ The differences between a star and a cash cow (or a problem child and a dog) are arbitrary and subject to all sorts of definition and measurement problems, so without careful analysis and a dose of good judgement, it's easy to cast your SBUs in the wrong roles. You may end up abandoning a problem child too soon, for example, because you think that the SBU is a dog, or you may neglect and hurt a star SBU by assuming that it's a cash cow that you can milk for money.

Looking strong and attractive

If you feel that the Growth-Share Grid doesn't represent your own business situation (if you'd like something in Technicolor, maybe with a few more bells and whistles), dozens of other models, methods, and tools are available, all of which promise to guide you to the right answers with little fuss. Many of the other models claim to work particularly well for certain industries or in specific business conditions, and one of them may be just right for your company. But before you turn to the pros for guidance, however, you may want to take one more step in analysing your SBU portfolio on your own.

Book VI

Getting Bigger

During the 1960s, General Electric (with the help of the consulting gurus at McKinsey and Company) came up with a portfolio-analysis framework that's a little more complicated than the Growth-Share Grid. But the GE Framework is richer and can be applied successfully in a wider range of business situations.

To make use of the GE Framework, start by examining the complicated-looking box shown in Figure 2-4.

Figure 2-4:
The GE framework arranges your company's SBUs into three bands and nine boxes, based on the strength of each SBU and its industry's attractiveness.

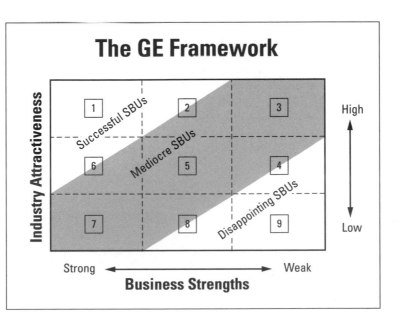

Don't worry; we'll help. The GE Framework creates two primary categories that shape your SBU portfolio analysis: industry attractiveness and your business strengths. Unlike the Growth-Share Grid, the GE Framework requires you to go on and define exactly what you mean by *industry attractiveness* and *business strengths*.

Coming up with what's attractive and what's a strength can be more ambiguous and less obvious than dealing with market-growth figures and relative market-share numbers. These definitions should help you get started:

Industry attractiveness. This category may include any number of components, depending on your industry. In most situations, however, you want to emphasise the factors that are likely to lead to fatter returns on your own SBU investments. Some of the things that you should look at (in addition to the overall market growth rate) are:

- Industry size
- Industry ups and downs
- Intensity of competition
- Customer and supplier relationships
- Average revenue and profits
- Rate of innovation
- Entry and exit barriers
- Government regulations

Business strengths. This category should be based on your specific business situation relative to your industry. Instead of relying on relative market share as the only indication of your company's capability to compete, you should include other factors that reflect your company's particular strengths and advantages, such as the following:

- Product uniqueness
- Service quality
- Customer loyalty
- Brand recognition
- Costs and profitability
- Manufacturing capacity
- Research and development
- Patents
- Organisational skills

Rearrange your SBU portfolio so that every strategic business unit falls somewhere in one of the nine newly-minted boxes. Depending on the location of each box, the GE Framework presents a set of planning guidelines. Here are the options that the numbered boxes suggest:

1. Protect position. Concentrate your resources and efforts on maintaining your strengths. Invest to grow at a fast but manageable pace.

2. Try harder. Challenge the market leaders. Build up the aspects of your company that are strong and reinforce areas in which the company is vulnerable.

3. Be choosy. Seek ways to overcome your business weaknesses. Keep an eye open for new opportunities if the risks are low.

4. Harvest. Limit your investments, and try to reduce costs to maximise your profits. Back away if you begin to lose ground.

5. Manage carefully. Maintain your existing programmes. Concentrate any new investments in promising areas in which the risks are manageable.

6. Grow wisely. Build on your competitive position. Invest in attractive areas in which you can gain or need to maintain an advantage.

7. Regroup. Try to preserve your current cash flow. Defend your strengths, and focus on areas that remain attractive.

8. Coast along. Keep any further investment to the bare minimum. Protect the position that you have, and try to sustain revenue.

9. Get out. Cut your costs to the bare bones, and avoid making any new investments. Bide your time until you can sell to the highest bidder.

Chapter 3

Improving Performance

. . . .

In This Chapter

▶ Seeing why retaining customers matters

▶ Measuring customer satisfaction

▶ Discovering ways to cut costs and work smarter

▶ Evaluating market growth strategies

▶ Looking at new product opportunities

. . . .

An unpleasant truism in business, and in much else, is that once resources are allocated they become misallocated over time. Another way of looking at this problem is to say that just because something 'ain't broke' it doesn't mean it can't be made to perform better still. To get your business to grow and keep growing needs a continuous effort to improve every aspect of your business.

In this chapter, we tell you how to keep your business going strong by keeping your customers happy, improving your efficiency and effectiveness, and increasing and expanding your business.

Checking Your Internal Systems

In order to improve performance you have to have systems in operation that help you measure performance in the first place. The two sub-sections following give you tips for evaluating how you spend your time and how to keep on top of your markets.

Keeping track of your routine

A good test of whether you are allocating enough time to the task of improving performance is to keep a track of how you spend your time, say, over a month. As well as recording the work you do and the time you spend on each major task, put the letter R, for routine, S for strategic, or I for improving performance next to the task.

A routine task is something like meeting a customer or the bank manager, delivering a product or service, or taking on a new employee. Strategic tasks would include considering a major shift of activities, say from making a product to just marketing it, forming a joint venture, or buying out a competitor. Improvement activities include all the elements we talk about in this chapter – activities focused on getting more mileage, lower costs, or higher yields out of the existing business.

Most owner managers spend 95 per cent of their day on routine tasks and only tackle improvement and strategic issues when they hit the buffers. For example most entrepreneurs don't worry too much about cash until it runs out. Then they pick up the phone and press customers into paying up. What they should have done, however, is introduce new procedures for collecting cash *before* the crunch.

If you are not spending at least 30 per cent of your time on improving your business and strategic issues, then you're probably heading for the buffers.

Analysing market position

A *SWOT analysis* is a way of consolidating everything you know about your competitive market position. SWOT stands for Strengths, Weaknesses, Opportunities, and Threats. Many businesses use SWOT analysis regularly, and very few people try it once and never again. For our money, SWOT is the way to go.

A SWOT analysis can't be carried out on the business as a whole. You have to analyse each important market segment separately. Because customer needs in each segment are different, it follows that you have to do different things in each segment to satisfy those needs. You may be up against different competitors in each segment so your strengths and weaknesses will be particular to that competitive environment. For example, look at travel methods: for families, car, coach, and to a lesser extent, train compete with each other; for business people, car, plane, and first-class rail travel are the biggest competitors.

Discovering strengths and weaknesses

A strength or weakness is an element that matters to the customers concerned. In fact it has to be such an important factor in the customer's mind that they would not buy without it. These are known as Critical Success Factors and it is your performance against these that confirm you strengths and weaknesses.

Find out the five or so things you have to get right to succeed in your market. For retail booksellers, location, range of books, hours of operation, knowledgeable staff, and ambiance may be the top five elements. Rank how well you think your competitors perform in these critical areas, or better still ask their existing, soon to be your, customers. If they score badly, you may have a strength.

Keeping an eye on opportunities and threats

It is important to recognise that an idea, invention or innovation is not necessarily an opportunity to grow your business. An opportunity has to be attractive, durable and timely. It is centred on a product or service that creates or adds value for its buyer or end user.

Working out what is attractive to you is fairly straightforward. Estimating the likely life of an opportunity or whether the time is right for its launch is not so easy. In a way that is the essence of an entrepreneur's skill. With opportunities you are looking for those that will bring the maximum benefit to the business whilst at the same time having a high probability of success. The benefits you are looking for may vary over time. In the early years cash flow may feature high on the list. Later fast growth and high margins may be more important.

Threats can come from all directions. Changes in the political or economic climate, new legislation or hackers and computer viruses can all have an impact on your business. For example, one business founder found to his dismay that his new Web site linked into dozens of pornography sites – the work of professional hackers. This set his operation back two months.

Changes in the demographic profile of populations (more older people and fewer of working age) or changing fashions, hit all businesses, old and new economy alike.

There are always too many potential threats for you to consider so you need to focus on those with the greatest possible impact that seem most likely to occur.

Doing the actual analysis

The actual SWOT process is asking various groups to share their thoughts on your company's greatest strength, its most glaring weakness, the area of greatest opportunity, and the direction of greatest threat.

Book VI

Getting Bigger

To carry out a SWOT analysis, you need to consider each element separately for each major market segment.

Use the following steps to find out your SWOT quotient in each SWOT area:

1. **Determine your own view.**

   Decide what you think your business's best feature is, what the greatest weakness is, where your opportunities to gain more customers lie, and what the biggest threat facing your business is.

2. **Find out what other entrepreneurs and your management team think about these issues.**

3. **Ask your newest front-line staff the same questions.**

4. **Form a customer focus group to consider the same questions.**

5. **Analyse how far apart the views of each group are.**

   If you are close to your customers and to your market, there should be little difference among the various groups. If there is a large difference, figure out what you can do to make sure the gap is narrowed and stays that way.

The question 'so what?' is a good one to apply to all aspects of your SWOT analysis. That will help you concentrate only on the important issues. Once completed the SWOT will provide the ingredients and framework for developing your marketing strategy, which we look at in Book V.

Retaining Customers

Businesses spend an awful lot of time and money winning customers and nothing like enough time and money on keeping them. This behaviour is as pointless as pouring water, or perhaps molten gold might be a better material to keep in mind, into a bucket with a big hole in the bottom. Most if not all of the flow is required to keep the bucket partially full. However fast the flow in, the flow out is just as fast.

Virtually all managers agree that customer care is important. A recent survey of major UK companies showed that 75 per cent had recently instituted customer care quality schemes. Sadly another survey, conducted by Bain and Company, the American consultants, also revealed that less than a third of those companies saw any payback for their efforts in terms of improved market share or profitability.

Bain suggests that the reason companies are disappointed with their attempts to improve customer care is that they don't have anything tangible to measure. To help overcome that problem Bain suggests that managers focus on the Customer Retention Ratio, a Bain invention. For example, if you have 100 customers in January and 110 in December, but only 85 of the original customers are still with you, then your retention rate is 85 per cent. Bain's study demonstrated that a 5 per cent improvement in retention had a fairly dramatic effect on clients. For a credit card client it boosted profits by 125 per cent; for an insurance broker there was a 5 per cent increase in profits; and for a software house a 35 per cent improvement in profits. Bain claims that the longer customers stay with you the more profitable they become. The next section explains why.

Realising why retaining customers matters

Studies and common sense indicate several principal reasons why retaining customers is so vitally important:

- ✔ It costs more to acquire new customers than to retain the ones you have. What with market research, prospecting, selling time, and so on, it costs between three and seven times as much to acquire a new customer as to retain an old one.

    This is nothing more than the old military maxim applied by Montgomery, that attacking forces need several times the strength of the defenders to guarantee success.

- ✔ The longer you retain a customer, the more years you have to allocate the costs of acquiring that customer. By spreading the costs of acquiring new customers over ten years, instead of one or two, the annual profit per customer will be higher. Suppose it costs you £500 to get a new customer, and that customer makes you £1,000 profit each year you keep them. If you keep the customer one year, your annual profit is £500 (£1,000 minus £500). However, if you keep the customer ten years, your annual profit is £950 (£1,000 minus £500/10). Customers who stay tend, over time, to spend more.

- ✔ Regular customers cost less to serve than new customers. Insurance and underwriting costs as a percentage of sales fall by 40 per cent for renewal policies. You don't incur up-front costs again.

- ✔ Long-term customers are often willing to pay a premium for service. Long-term customers also are less prone to check your competitors because they know and like you.

Avoiding the consequences of losing customers is a powerful motivator for keeping in your customers' good graces. Some of those consequences are:

- ✔ Dissatisfied customers tell between eight and 15 others about their experience. Just avoiding this negative publicity has a value.

- ✔ Your former customers are fertile ground for your competitors. If you keep your customers, your competitors have to offer inducements to dislodge your customers and this is expensive and time-consuming for them.

Working to retain customers

Use these five rules to make sure you retain customers and so improve your profit growth:

- ✔ Make customer care and retention a specific goal, and reward people for keeping customers not just for getting them.

- ✔ Find out why you lose customers. Don't just let them go – have either a follow-up questionnaire or get someone other than the salesperson concerned to visit former customers to find out why they changed supplier. You'd be surprised how pleased people are to tell you why they didn't stay with you, if you explain that it may help you serve them better the next time.

- ✔ Research your competitors' service levels as well as their products. If it's practical, buy from them on a regular basis. If you can't buy from competitors, keep close to people that do.

- ✔ If one part of your organisation is good at caring for customers, get them to teach everyone else what they do.

- ✔ Recognise that the best people to provide customer care are those staff who work directly with customers. But this means you have to train them and give them the authority to make decisions on the spot. Ciphers don't convince customers that you really want to keep their business.

Retaining customers is not the passive activity it sounds. The next sections offer concrete ways to keep your customers happy.

Monitoring complaints

One terrifying statistic is that 98 per cent of complaints never happen. People just don't get round to making the complaint, or worse still, they can find no one to complain to. You would have to be a hermit never to have experienced something to complain about, but just try finding someone to complain to at 8 p.m. on a Sunday at Paddington Station and you will get a fair impression of how the Gobi Desert feels.

You can never be confident that just because you're not hearing complaints your customers and clients aren't dissatisfied and about to defect. It also doesn't mean that they won't run around bad mouthing you and your business. It's as well to remember that on average people share their complaint with a score of others, who in turn are equally eager to share the tidings with others. The viral effect of e-mail has the potential to make any particularly juicy story run around the world in days if not hours.

Set up a system that will ensure your customers have ample opportunity to let you know what they think about your product or service. This could involve a short questionnaire, a follow up phone call or an area on your Web site devoted to customer feedback. As a bonus you will probably get some great ideas on how to improve your business.

Ninety-eight per cent of customers who have a complaint will buy from you again if you handle their complaint effectively and promptly. Not only will they buy from you again, but also they will spread the gospel about how clever they were in getting you to respond to their complaint. Nothing makes people happier than having something to complain about that ends up costing them next to nothing.

Setting customer service standards

Customer service is all those activities that support a customer's purchase, from the time they become aware that you could supply them with a particular product or service, to the point at which they own that product or service and are able to enjoy all the benefits they were led to believe were on offer.

The largest part of the value of many products and services lies in how customer service is delivered. It is also the area most likely to influence whether customers come back again or recommend you to others. Customer service works best when:

- Customers are encouraged to tell you about any problems.
- Customers know their rights and responsibilities from the beginning.
- Customers know the circumstances under which they are entitled to get their money back and how to take advantage of other rights.
- Customers feel in control. It's far better to provide a full refund if the customer is dissatisfied than to demand that the customer come up with a good reason for the refund. A refund, or any other recourse you offer, should be prompt.

Repeat business is another key profit-maker. Repeat business comes from ensuring customers are genuinely completely satisfied with – and preferably pleasantly surprised by – the quality of your product. Repeat sales save unnecessary expenditure on advertising and promotion to attract new customers.

It is certain that as standards of living rise, the more that quality, convenience, and service will become important relative to price. An investment in a strategy of quality customer service now is an investment in greater future profitability.

You need to have a model to follow for effective customer service and you should consider using mystery shopping as a way to keep tabs on your customer service standards – both issues are covered in the next sections.

Customer service is often the difference between keeping customers for life and losing customers in droves. You and your staff have to deliver outstanding customer service at all times.

In order to do this everyone has to know what the important elements of good customer service are and everyone needs to incorporate those elements into their everyday customer interactions.

The key elements of your customer service plan should include:

- **Initial contact:** The customer's first contact with staff creates a lasting impression and can win and sustain customers. All your staff need to be aware of how to handle enquiries quickly and competently. They should know how to leave potential customers feeling confident that their requirements will be met.

- **Information flow:** Keeping customers informed of where their orders are in the process influences their feelings about the way you do business. Your action plan needs to specify each step of your process: quotation; order confirmation; delivery notification; installation instructions. A regular flow of information throughout this period makes your customers feel that they matter to you.

- **Delivery:** Delivering the goods or service is a key part of customer service. Your product needs to be available in a timely manner, delivery lead times must be reasonable, and the delivery itself must be in a way that meets the customer's requirements.

- **After-sales support:** Good coverage in areas such as maintenance, repairs, help-lines, upgrade notification, instruction manuals, returns policy, and fault tracing help customers feel that you care about their total experience with your products and business.

> ✔ **Problem solving:** Often the acid test of customer service; your staff need to be able to recognise when a customer has a real crisis and what your procedure is for helping them.

High customer service standards enable many firms to charge a premium for their products. Yet in many ways, good customer service can be a nil-cost item. After all it takes as much effort to answer the phone politely as it does with a surly and off-putting tone. So improved customer service is one route to increased profitability.

Carrying out mystery shopping

No, mystery shopping is not the feeling of surprise that comes over you when you unpack the result of your weekly family shop at the supermarket. Mystery shopping is the process that investigates your staff's service, friendliness, speed, and product knowledge to ensure that your customers are being well cared for.

Mystery shopping is the evaluation, measurement, and reporting of customer service standards by use of agents acting as if they were customers. It is arguably the fastest and most effective method of obtaining hard objective management data about customer service levels. Your employees have to be on their toes for every customer, since any of them could be a mystery shopper.

Companies such as the aptly named Mystery Shoppers (www.mystery-shoppers.co.uk) or National Opinion Polls (www.nop.co.uk/mystery) employ thousands of people around the country who routinely visit thousands of locations, make tens of thousands of phone calls, and ask for millions of quotations or pieces of advice, none of which will result in an order for the business concerned.

Key aspects that mystery shopping can measure:

> ✔ Are the staff knowledgeable, helpful and polite?
>
> ✔ Are the staff competent at selling your products and services?
>
> ✔ Do the staff try to sell products or services that are related to the one(s) they are enquiring about?
>
> ✔ How are customers treated when they are complaining or returning products?
>
> ✔ Do the staff comply with all the regulations governing your industry?
>
> ✔ How competitive are your prices and other terms?
>
> ✔ Is your product being properly displayed with the right literature and any other point-of-sale materials?

- ✔ Are the premises in a clean workmanlike condition?
- ✔ How do your staff perform on the telephone?
- ✔ How effective is your website?

Rewarding loyalty

The reasons that loyalty improves profitability are: retaining customers costs less than finding and capturing new ones; loyal customers tend to place larger orders; and loyal customers don't always place price first, whilst new ones do. So what works and what doesn't when it comes to keeping customers loyal?

One of the things that hasn't lived up to its promise is customer loyalty cards. When they were launched, retailers made big claims of how they would be gathering tons of invaluable data about customers. But mostly they have been left with huge virtual warehouses of information that hasn't been used.

Analysing the buying habits of millions of shoppers as their cards are swiped at the till can be prohibitively expensive and few companies have used much of the data gathered to make their customers feel special and hence want to stay loyal.

Asked to give reasons for their loyalty, the top five elements consumers list are:

- ✔ Convenience
- ✔ Price
- ✔ Range
- ✔ Customer service
- ✔ Quality

What this means is that you have to get your basic marketing strategy right and understand what your customer wants and how much they are prepared to pay. If that is wrong no loyalty scheme will keep them on board. Customer service and quality are about getting it right first time, every time. This can usually be helped if you always under promise and over deliver.

The way you handle a customer's complaint can make all the difference between whether a customer comes back or not. Most people who complain will buy from you again if their complaint is handled well.

Care and help-lines, where customers are encouraged to call for advice, information or help with problems, will keep customers loyal and make them more likely to buy from you in the future. If the line is a free phone service it will be even more effective.

Keeping in touch with customers can also bind them more securely. Questionnaires, newsletters, magazines, letters about incentive, customer service calls, invitations to sales events, and 'member get member' schemes are all ways of achieving this result.

Improving Productivity

Improving productivity is a constant requirement for a growth-minded business, not simply an activity during periods of economic recession (when it is still, nonetheless, important – much better than adopting the 'turtle position', pulling in your head and your hands and getting off the road!). Productivity needs to be improved by acting on both your costs and your margins.

Increasing margins can be achieved by changing the mix of products and services you sell to focus on those yielding the best return, or by raising your selling price. Cutting cost has the merit of showing quick and certain returns.

Cutting costs

Costs need to be constantly controlled and balanced against the need for good quality and good service. In particular you need to separate and act on your variable and your fixed costs (see *Starting A Business For Dummies* for more on fixed and variable costs).

Variable cost cutting is always in evidence in recession; witness the automotive and banking staff cuts in the early 1990s and in 2002–3. Cutting variable costs include such things as wages and materials that are directly related to the volume of sales.

Cutting fixed cost such as cars, computers and equipment that do not change directly with the volume of sales should not include scrapping investments in technology that could bring economies and extra nimbleness in the future (like flexible-manufacturing facilities, where, for example, Peugeot has invested in product lines that can turn out two models at once). Many firms, following Japanese practice, increase their use of subcontractors to help offset increased risk.

Equally, alliances between firms, aiming to reduce fixed cost investments, can be advantageous. In the soft drinks industry, Perrier provide distribution for Pepsi in France, while Bulmers reciprocated for Perrier in England, avoiding the need for extra investment in warehousing and transport.

Focusing attention on the 20 per cent of items that make up 80 per cent of your costs will probably yield your biggest savings. The 80/20 rule is helpful in getting costs back into line, but what if the line was completely wrong in the first place?

Budgeting from zero

When you sit down with your team and discuss budgets, the arguments always revolve around how much more each section will need next year. The starting point is usually this year's costs, which are taken as the only facts upon which to build. So, for example, if you spent £25,000 on advertising last year and achieved sales of £1 million, your advertising expense was 2.5 per cent of sales. If the sales budget for next year is £1.5 million, then it seems logical to spend £37,500 next year on advertising. That, however, presupposes last year's sum was wisely and effectively spent in the first place, which it almost certainly was not.

Zero-based budgeting turns the cost argument on its head. It assumes that each year every cost centre starts from zero spending and, based on the goals of the business and the resources available, arguments are presented for every pound spent, *not just for the increase*.

Increasing margins

To achieve increased *profit margins*, which is the difference between the costs associated with the product or service you sell and the price you get in the market, you need first to review your sales. This requires accurate costs and gross margins for each of your products or services. Armed with that information you can select particular product groups or market segments that are less price sensitive and potentially more profitable.

 No-one rushes out to buy expensive overpriced products when cheaper ones that are just as good are readily available. The chances are that your most profitable products are also the ones that your customers value the most. You should start your efforts to increase margins by concentrating on trying to sell the products and services that make you the most money.

Pricing is the biggest decision your business has to make, one it needs to keep constantly under review. Your decision on pricing is the one that has the biggest impact on company profitability. Try the consultants' favourite exercise of computing and comparing the impact on profits of a 5 per cent:

- ✔ Cut in your overheads
- ✔ Increase in volume sales
- ✔ Cut in materials purchased
- ✔ Price increase

All these actions are usually considered to be within an owner-manager's normal reach. Almost invariably, the 5 per cent price increase scores the highest, as it passes straight to the net profit, bottom line. Even if volume falls, because of the effect price has on growth margin, it is usually more profitable to sell fewer items at a higher price. For example, at a constant gross margin of 30 per cent with a 5 per cent price increase, profits would be unchanged even if sales declined 14 per cent. Yet if prices were cut 5 per cent, an extra 21 per cent increase in sales would be needed to make the same amount of profit.

Frequently, resistance to increasing prices, even in the face of inflationary cost rises, can come from your own team members, eager to apportion blame for performance lapses. In these instances it is important to make detailed price comparisons with competitors.

Working smarter

Making more money doesn't always have to mean working longer hours. You could just work smarter and who knows you may even end up working fewer hours than you do now and still make more money.

One way to get everyone's grey matter working overtime is to create smart circles, comprising of people working in different areas of your business who are challenged to come up with ideas to make the business better (and smart rewards, which include extra resources, holidays and recognition for their achievements, rather than cash). You could formalise the process of encouraging employees to rethink the way they work and reward them in such a way as to make their working environment better still.

Rewarding excellent results

Nick White's Ecotravel company sends people to off-the-beaten-track exotic locations and to conservation areas where money goes into research projects. Ecotourists who book with Ecotravel pay to see animals in conservation areas and a proportion of the money they spend on the holiday goes directly to conservation projects.

White expanded slowly until two years ago when he introduced a 'rewarding excellence' initiative and sales shot up by 40 per cent in just six months. The basis of the reward is an accelerating bonus. If the company hits its sales targets staff share in a 5 per cent bonus. If it exceeds targets the bonus rates rise too. For every 20 per cent of achievement above target the bonus rate goes up 1 per cent. Targets are reset each year using a similar formula but starting from a new and higher base level.

Rewarding results

If you can get the people who work for you to increase their output, you can improve productivity. The maxim 'What get measured gets done and what gets rewarded gets done again' is the guiding principle behind rewards, and setting objectives is the starting point in the process.

The objectives you want people to achieve in order to be rewarded beyond their basic pay need to be challenging but achievable too, which is something of a contradiction in terms. Problems start to arise as soon as professional managers and supervisors come on board with experience of working in big companies. They, and probably you yourself, tend to take objectives and the ensuing budgets very seriously. They have to be hit, so it makes sense to pitch on the conservative side.

But in a small business growth and improvement percentages have the potential to be much greater than in larger firms. A big business with a third of its market can only grow very quickly by acquisition or if the market itself is growing very fast. A small firm, on the other hand, can grow by very large amounts very quickly. Moving from 0.01 per cent of a market to 0.02 per cent is hardly likely to upset many other players, but it represents a doubling in size for the small firm. However exceptional performance, even in a small firm, will only be attainable with breakthrough thinking and performance. The question may not be how can we grow the business by 20 per cent a year, but how can we grow it by 20 per cent a month.

But if goals are set too aggressively people may leave. Even, perhaps especially, great performers will balk if the hurdle is put too high.

A way to get the best of both worlds is to have a performance band rather than just one number. The reward for achieving a really great result should be massive, but if this high goal is missed slightly, the employee is rewarded as if the goal had been set at the level reached. The reward is proportionately smaller, so your rewards budget still balances. This technique can get an 'inspiration dividend'. Teams can be persuaded to set higher goals than they might otherwise have set, and even when they miss them, the year-on-year improvements can be stunning.

Increasing Sales

The most obvious way to grow a business is to get more sales. This is often easier said than done, but there are some tried and proven techniques that usually deliver the goods. A helpful framework to keep in mind is the one developed by the business guru, Igor Ansoff, and named after him as Ansoff's Growth Matrix.

Ansoff's model has four major elements:

- ✔ Business development, which is about getting more customers like the ones you already have and getting them to buy more from you.

- ✔ Market development, which involves entering new markets in your home country or overseas.

- ✔ Product or service development, which involves launching new products or extensions to existing products or services. A courier service adding an overnight delivery service to its existing 48-hour service is an example of this activity.

- ✔ Diversification, which means, in a nutshell, launching off into the unknown.

Getting customers to buy more

This is a no-brainer starting point for achieving profitable growth. Winning a new customer can be an expensive and time-consuming activity, so once you have them the more you can get them to spend with you rather than a competitor, the better your bottom line will be.

You can avoid this experience if you use this framework to categorise your customers:

- **Courtship:** This is the stage before a customer has bought anything from you. At this stage the customer is suspicious and your objective is to get your first order. Any order will do just to get the relationship underway.

- **Engagement:** Having got your first order in the bag, your customer may still be moderately suspicious of you and is still not sure if your intentions are wholly honourable. Your goal is to get your first repeat order and cement the relationship. Getting to this stage means that your first order must go well and your customer must be at least satisfied, or delighted if you want to get to the honeymoon stage in your relationship. To make that happen you need to stand out from the crowd and go the extra mile to make that customer feel special by meeting their particular needs.

- **Honeymoon:** With several repeat orders successfully fulfilled, your customer now trusts you and is susceptible to new ideas. Here you should be looking to increase sales volume. It is almost certain that as a new supplier your customer has not put all their eggs in your basket. Now your task is to get as many eggs as you can and build up to being the preferred and perhaps only supplier.

- **Wedlock:** When you first started talking to your customer you were the new kid on the block, to them at least. Your ideas and products or services were refreshingly new and their existing suppliers had had ample opportunity to disappoint them and let them down. Now you have become, or are fast becoming, that old boring supplier. You need to think of ways to keep your relationship exciting and fresh.

- **Deadlock:** Your customer has become disenchanted and is considering divorce. The time has come to bring on new products and services to whet their appetite and make them see you as the exciting vigorous supplier you appeared when your relationship started.

Encouraging referrals

Referrals are the most valuable marketing asset any business can have. Whether you are selling direct to an end consumer or user, or operate in the business-to-business arena your goal is the same – to get those using your product or service to talk in glowing terms about their experience with your business.

Passive word of mouth is rarely as effective as encouraging satisfied customers to pass on the glad tidings. Happy customers tell an average of 0.7 other people if they have had a positive experience with you. Unhappy customers tell 11 to 20 other people.

You can make word-of-mouth advertising work, however. It just requires discipline and a programmed effort to ask your customers for referrals. Make it easy for them – give them brochures, flyers, samples, or whatever it takes to make your case. Then follow up.

Discounts for introductions come out of your advertising budget. So you need to work out how much an introduction to a prospect is worth before you can decide on the discount. The rules to follow are:

- Be specific in the type of introductions you want. In particular make the sales volume and product specifications clear. There is no point in giving a discount for products on which your margins are already tight.

- Have a sliding scale of discount. The more introductions you get the more you give.

- Make it easy for people to give you introductions. Send them fax back forms or have a place on your Web site for them to tap in minimum details. A name and company should be enough for you to find the other details you need.

- Follow up and let people know that their introduction paid off. People are usually interested in more than just the discount when they give introductions.

- Have a specific programme such as member-gets-member and run it as a campaign for a set period of time. Then change the programme and the discounts. That keeps people interested.

- Give the discount promptly, but not until the new introduction has bought and paid their bill.

- Give extra discount for introductions to loyal customers. Perhaps when the new customer has placed their third or fourth order you can give the extra discount.

- Research the market and find out what introductory schemes are on offer in your sector.

- Set up a database to monitor the effectiveness of your introductory discount scheme.

Entering new markets at home

Generally the most rewarding market growth for small businesses comes in the first few months and years when the whole of what is known as the home market is up for grabs. New markets can take a number of shapes. The two most common of these are:

 ✔ Geographic. Once you are confident that you have extracted as much business as you can get from your immediate business area, be that a town, city, or region, move onto another one. You need to make sure that the new geographic area is broadly similar to the one you have been successful in already. For example Bristol and Bath, are broadly similar to Bradford and Sheffield, as cities, but if your business has tourists as customers, the last two cities will be less appealing as a new market than the first two.

 ✔ Demographic. This covers factors particular to customer groups. If you make clothes for women in Bristol, you could consider making clothes for children, men or teenagers also sticking to the Bristol area.

You can get help and advice from Business Link (www.businesslink.org) who can provide practical support in this area and in most other areas of marketing your business.

Selling overseas

Motley Fool's entry into the German market involved a modest change in a well-proven product, as for its entry to the British, French, and Italian markets between 1998 and 2001. But expanding overseas is not quite as easy as it looks.

Marks and Spencer made a mess of its foray into America and retired in some ignominy from the French market, closing 38 stores virtually overnight and exciting the wrath of the French trade unions on the way. The Body Shop, a world business if ever there was one, found it hard going in the French market, where people take beauty, as they do wine, rather more seriously than most.

Don't let these stories of failure discourage you. After all, millions of businesses export successfully and you can always get some help in getting started.

A good place to start is UK Trade and Investment (UKIT), the government's export advisory organisation (www.uktradeinvest.gov.uk). UKIT offers a range of market research and support services for both experienced exporters and companies new to the international marketplace.

For newcomers, UKIT's Passport to Export programme provides a package of skills and guidance tailored to the specific requirements of the company. These include:

- ✔ A free export capability health check.

- ✔ Free export mentoring from a locally based expert in international trade.

- ✔ Flexible, subsidised training in specific skills needed to win and deliver business.

- ✔ The resources of UKIT, including a wealth of information, market research and sales leads.

- ✔ A subsidised visit to an overseas market identified in your export plan.

- ✔ Ongoing support once you're up and running.

The Passport to Export scheme is run by UKIT's regional network of offices. There is no registration fee, but places are limited and companies are selected on the basis of their export potential. Contact your local UKIT office for more details.

Adding new products or services

At one end of a spectrum are truly new and innovative products; at the other are relatively modest product or service line extensions. For example, Amazon's Music and Video/DVD business could be seen as product line extensions of their book trade. Their Tools and Hardware operation looks more like a new product. New to them, of course, not to the thousands of other businesses in that sector.

Most new products are unsuccessful. A new product has to be two or three times better in some respect – price, performance, convenience, availability – to dislodge a well-entrenched rival.

They don't necessarily have to be your new products and services, of course. Alliances, affiliations, joint ventures, and the like abound.

The sources of successful new products include:

- ✔ Listening to customers, who can tell you their needs and dissatisfactions with current products and services.

- ✔ Your sales team, who are also close to the market and so can form a view as to what might sell well.

- ✔ Competitors who are first to market usually make lots of mistakes on the way. Following in their wake you can avoid the worst of their errors and succeed where they have not.

- ✔ Exhibitions and trade fairs are where other firms, not necessarily competitors, but those on the margins of your sector meet and exchange ideas. Products and services that work well in one environment may be adapted for use in your market with little cost.

- ✔ Markets that are known to be in advance of your own. Many new ideas start their lives in the US and only arrive in Europe 18 months to five years later. Following trends there will give you useful pointers for successful new products in your own market.

- ✔ Research and development departments often throw up innovative ideas for which there are no obvious market need. You may know of profitable ways to exploit those technologies.

Diversifying as a last resort

Diversification involves moving away from the products, service and markets that you currently operate in, to completely new areas of business. This is the riskiest strategy of all – selling things you know little about to people you know even less about. Sure you can do market research and buy in industry expertise but there is still a risk.

Companies that succeed in diversifying do so by hastening slowly, sometimes by acquisition, and above all by listening to customers and front-line staff.

Unless you can quantify the value added in an acquisition or diversification, for example in better buying with quantity discounts or by being able to spread your costs over a bigger sales volume, don't bother.

However, if you can get acquisitions right, the growth through diversification can be phenomenal.

Chapter 4

Franchising for Growth

. . . .

. . . .

*F*ranchising is a great way into business; it's a great way to grow a business too. Over 652 different types of franchise are on offer somewhere in the world so it's hard to see how you can't find one that suits your needs and aspirations.

Franchising is a marketing technique used to improve and expand the distribution of a product or service. The franchiser supplies the product or teaches the service to the franchisee, who in his turn sells it to the public. In return for this, the franchisee pays a fee and a continuing royalty based usually on turnover. They may also be required to buy materials or ingredients from the franchiser, giving them an additional income stream.

You have two possible strategies for harnessing the power of franchising to your business. You could consider taking on a franchise that is complementary to your existing business or you could franchise your own business concept, taking on self-employed franchisees instead of hired-in managers to run your new branches or outlets.

Finding the right franchise

Over 750 different types of franchise are currently on offer in the UK, and there are now more than 30,000 franchisee businesses up and running. This pool of franchise opportunities is being added to each year with the steady influx of new franchise chains, particularly from the US and Canada.

Adding a franchise

In August 2003, Harrods, London's up-market department store, opened the first UK outlet of Krispy Kreme Doughnuts. For Harrods the sales of doughnuts are complementary to their other food and beverage sales, so it represents pure extra revenue. For Krispy Kreme, it's a chance to enter the UK market that they believe is ripe for development as there is no dominant doughnut brand in the market.

The aim in adding a franchise to your existing business is to *leverage*, as the business gurus would say, your customer or resource base, in order to get more sales per customer or square metre of space.

So if your customers are buying chocolate, sweets, and stationery from you, adding a freezer with ice cream is no big deal. Chances are the ice cream supplier will be so keen to extend their distribution that they will throw in the freezer cabinet for free. You are taking someone else's business model, product, and support systems and bolting them on to your business to add turnover and profits.

Knowing what to look for

So how should you go about looking for a franchise? Well, for a start it should meet all the criteria you can identify in Book I that lead you to start up your main business.

The franchise you are considering may be new or it may be already established. There is nothing wrong with a product or service being new, provided it has been tested and found to work, preferably for at least a couple of years in a location or community similar to that for which it is now being offered (as is a condition for membership of the British Franchise Association) and provided also that the franchisee is satisfied that it enjoys a good reputation among users and customers. Equally, there is no automatic guarantee of success in dealing with an established product or service. You must check whether the market is growing, static, or declining. Where the franchise relates to a new or established product or service, you need to be satisfied that it has staying power, to what extent the demand is seasonal (people in the UK are less addicted to ice cream in winter than in some other countries) and whether its appeal is to any extent confined to a specific age group or sector of the community.

Check whether the franchise product has some unique feature protected by a patent or trademark. If its success is tied to a celebrity name, you will have to find out how active the celebrity is in promoting it and judge how durable his or her fame is likely to be.

Judge how competitive the product or service is in price and quality with similar ones on the market and, in particular, available in your vicinity.

These points are all brought painfully home each year by the well-publicised failures of one or two franchisers that were thought, even by the banks, to be soundly based. In each case, though, questions addressed to the actual franchisees would have shown that all was far from well. In other words, there is no substitute for first-hand investigation and research – not even expert hearsay.

Searching for a business

There are literally dozens of ways of finding out more about franchise opportunities. The best starting point is a discussion with your bank manager. This may seem a bit far-fetched – after all you may not necessarily be looking for money. But the chances are that the franchiser who runs the chain will have run their plans past one of the major clearing banks to ensure that they will view with favour any business plans put forward by their potential franchisees. The big five banks have lent over £150 million to franchisees and even have special departments to oversee their franchise business. They track the performance of major franchise chains and can offer advice and assistance in evaluating them. The Royal Bank of Scotland (www.rbs.co.uk/franchise) and Barclays (www.barclays.co.uk/business.html) are particularly strong in the franchise area, but the others are well represented too.

If you are taking up a franchise you may find that some banks offer a special franchise funding facility, which has been put together with the help of the franchiser. This will make getting that loan much easier than going to the bank with your own business idea and plan.

After the banks come a number of consultancy businesses specialising in the sector. Big accountancy practices such as BDO Stoy Hayward (www.bdo.co.uk) and legal firms such as Brodies (www.brodies.co.uk) and Mundays (www.mundays.co.uk) all offer high quality advice and contacts in the field.

The sector has a sprinkling of magazines describing franchises in detail, giving case histories and listing current franchise opportunities. *Franchise World* (www.franchiseworld.co.uk) and *The Franchise Magazine* (www.franchise-magazine.co.uk) are amongst the leaders in the sector. Newspapers such as *The Daily Telegraph*, *Daily Mail*, and *The Sunday Times* all have franchise sections each week and sponsor exhibitions in London and Birmingham where you can meet both franchisers and franchisees. Don't forget that great book, *Franchising For Dummies*, by Dave Thomas, that covers pretty well everything you could possibly need to know.

There are dozens of websites that offer franchises for sale. These include: *Daltons Weekly* (`www.daltons.co.uk`), *Grant Thornton* (`www.companies forsale.uk.com`) and *Which Franchise?* (`www.whichfranchise.com`).

Investigating and appraising

Most franchisers have discovered that the hard sell is neither in their own interest nor that of the franchisee. Successful franchising is a question of mutual dependence and a franchisee who finds or feels that they has been sold a pup is not likely to be a co-operative member of the franchise family.

The 1973 Fair Trading Act offers very little specific legal protection to the franchisee. Basically, what protection there is, is embodied in the franchise agreement but that document is subject to omissions and commissions of wording which can make a great deal of difference to the deal that is being offered to the franchisee. The franchise agreement can also throw much light on the good intent or experience of the franchiser. You should ask a great many questions about the agreement in order to put the provisions of the contract into context. Three areas, aside from the product or service, which may not be fully covered in the contract but which require close investigation and scrutiny are covered in the following sections.

Checking out the territory

Though the franchiser should provide a map showing the exact extent of the territory, this is not in itself a guarantee of absolute protection. Under EC competition laws the franchiser cannot prevent one franchisee trading in another's exclusive territory, though he may decline to license a competitor within it. You can do very little about this except to check for the location or planned location of the next nearest operator of the same franchise.

You should also check whether the agreement specifies any circumstances under which your territory could be reduced.

Examine the rationale behind the territory assignment. Has the franchiser picked it out arbitrarily or has he conducted – as he should have done – market surveys to indicate that the franchise is likely to be viable in that territory? Market research should cover aspects like traffic flows, access, population mix by age and class, and so forth, and the information should be made available to the franchisee.

Checking out the franchiser

The most important questions to put to the franchiser are:

- How long have you been in the UK?
- How many outlets have you established?
- How successful are your franchises?
- How many franchises have been shut down and why?

Failing a track record in the UK, you need to find out how well they have performed elsewhere and to what extent they have been successful in those markets. You need to make sure those markets are similar to the one you will be operating in, as success in one market is no guarantee of success in other markets.

Investigating the franchise package

Franchisers make their money in a variety of ways. Every franchiser charges an initial fee, a royalty on turnover, and/or a mark-up on goods supplied for resale. However, there can be considerable – and significant – differences in the amounts and the way they are collected.

My advice is to be very careful about franchises with a high initial fee and a low royalty (unless, of course, the franchiser receives part of his income in the form of a mark-up on goods supplied): the franchiser may be of the take-your-money-and-run variety. Equally, low royalties may reflect a high mark-up on the goods and services you're required to buy from the home company. The question then is whether the product being offered is competitive in price.

A low initial fee is not necessarily favourable either – it may mask high royalties or hidden charges. Another point to watch out for is whether the franchiser sets a minimum figure the franchisee must pay, irrespective of income from the franchise. If so, is the amount reasonable? The advice of an accountant would be invaluable.

Related to the question of fees is that of advertising. Typically, an advertising fee is collected from all the franchisees, held on account by the franchiser and then spent in line with the terms of the franchise agreement. It may be included as part of the management fee or levied separately. As the franchisee, you need to be satisfied that the advertising is good and relevant, both as regards content and medium. Local press, radio, TV, and cinema advertising can be helpful to the franchisee. National campaigns are costly and the purpose behind them may be to sell franchises rather than to further the franchisee's particular business. Nevertheless, some national advertising may be essential if a nationwide franchise chain is to be developed, with its knock-on benefits to individual franchisees.

Franchising your Business Idea

If your business concept looks as though it could be replicated in several other places, you have a number of choices. The most obvious is to open up more branches. But you could consider a faster, and in some ways safer route, by franchising your business for others to roll out and share the risk.

Weighing the advantages and disadvantages

From the franchiser's point of view, one huge financial advantage is that you don't have any direct investment in any of your franchises. The inventory and equipment are owned by the franchisee.

Because of the shortage of prime sites, there is a growing trend for franchisers to acquire leases on behalf of franchisees or at any rate to stand as guarantors. Nevertheless, the effect on the liquidity of the franchiser, in contrast to expansion by opening branches, is enormous.

However, you do face heavy start-up costs in piloting the franchise and in setting up and maintaining training if you do the job properly. Thereafter there are further costs in providing a continuing service to franchisees in such matters as research and development, promotion, administrative back up, and feedback and communication within the network. The expectation is that these costs are offset because:

- ✔ The franchisee, as the owner of the business, is more likely to be highly motivated than an employee and more responsive to local market needs and conditions.
- ✔ As the franchiser, you receive an income from the franchises.
- ✔ As the franchiser, you can save on personnel and administrative costs by running your operation from a central location. You can negotiate quantity discounts from your suppliers by ordering for all your franchises at the same time.
- ✔ As the franchiser, you realise some of the benefits of expanding your business without direct financial involvement.

On the other hand, the failure of an individual franchise may reflect badly on your entire business, even though you have no direct control. In extreme cases, you may terminate or not renew a franchisee's agreement, but you cannot fire the franchisee as you could an employee.

As a franchiser, you are dependent on the willingness of the franchisee to observe the rules and play the game, and any failure of the franchisee to do so is equally and perhaps more damaging to you and to other franchisees than it is to the wayward franchisee.

Sometimes the mixture of dependence and independence of franchising produces a curious problem. The franchisee is encouraged to think of him or herself as an independent business entity and to a large extent this is indeed the situation. Nevertheless, he or she is operating your business concept under a licence and pays a fee to do so. The franchisee may identify so closely with the business that he or she resents having to pay a fee, feeling that the franchise's success is due to his or her own efforts, not to the franchise concept or to you, the franchiser. This is apt to be particularly so if the franchiser adopts a low profile, either in terms of direct help or in matters such as national advertising. Clearly, of course, the franchisee is obliged to pay under the terms of the agreement, but a sour relationship is not good for either party, so it is up to you to maintain your part of the bargain both in letter and in spirit. Franchises are a matter of mutual interest and obligation.

Doing the pilot

After a franchise concept has been developed, a pilot operation should be run for a period of at least a year. The pilot should be run by someone as similar to the intended typical franchisee for the chain as is practicable. The aim is to test not just the business concept, but to see if the operating systems have been described well enough for people outside the founding business organisation to run.

Let's use as an example a fast food outlet offering slimmers' lunches. You already own a couple of outlets for which you have found a catchy name, Calorie Counter. You have established a standard image in terms of décor, layout, tableware, menus, and graphics and your staff have a stylish uniform. Your gimmick is that every dish has a calorie rating and a breakdown of the fibre and salt content on the menu, and along with their bill customers get a calorie and fibre count for what they have bought. You also have some recipes that you have pioneered.

In the year since you opened you have ironed out most of the start-up bugs and learned a lot about the catering, accounting, and staffing problems in running a business of this kind.

The indication is that there is demand for more restaurants like yours, but you have neither the capital nor the inclination to take on restaurant managers. Being a thorough sort of person you have documented every aspect of running your restaurant, covering everything from recipes, ingredients, and cooking times, to opening hours, wages, incentives, and dress code. You have also standardised your accounting system and linked the electronic till to your raw material and stock systems, so that key ingredients can be re-ordered automatically. From your experience in opening two of your own restaurants you know how and where to advertise, how much to spend, and how sales demand is likely to grow in the early weeks and months. You have captured all this knowledge in a sort of manual, which you propose to use as a guide for whosoever you select to open your next outlet.

You are now ready to run your first pilot franchise. This involves using your manual and procedures with a real live franchisee. True, you may have to give them some incentive to join you in the risk. But whatever you end up negotiating, as long as it gives you the benefits of franchising listed above, you are ahead of the game.

Once your pilot franchisee gets under way you will have the opportunity to test your manual in action. You, after all, invented the business, so you should know what to do in every situation, but seeing if a green franchisee straight off the street can follow your map and get a result is the acid test.

Put what you learn from the pilot into a revised franchise manual, sort out your charging and support systems, and you are ready to start to roll the franchise out.

Finding franchisees

Sorry, but that last sentence in the previous section was a bit misleading. Despite having a great business, a robust and proven business manual, and a couple of pilot runs under your belt, you are not quite ready to roll the franchise out around the world, or even around your neighbourhood. The most recent NatWest/British Franchise Association survey (they do one every year and have done for the last 20) asked franchisers what they consider to be the biggest barrier to the growth of the number of franchises they operate. By far the greatest number of respondents – 41 per cent – said it was the lack of suitable franchisees.

Visit any franchise exhibition, and you visit many if you are serious about growing in this way, and the thousands of people milling around the stands and in the seminar rooms will convince you that there is no lack of interest amongst the general public to taking up a franchise.

Finding potential franchisees is not a problem. Use the contact details earlier in the chapter to advertise for applicants and attend as many exhibitions as you can and you will have applicants coming out of your ears. Yet turning that latent demand into done deals is not so easy. One international franchise chain only offer franchises to 30 per cent of the people they interview, and they only interview a small fraction of the number of people they see at exhibitions.

This begs the obvious question. What sort of person makes the ideal franchisee? Well, looking at past career patterns may not be much help. Les Gray, chairperson of Chemical Express, the 104-outlet cleaning products franchise chain, lists a postman, a sales manager, a buyer, a farmer, and a shipping agent as the occupations of their most successful franchisees.

Franchisers say they have the most success with franchisees that are motivated, able to work hard, have some management aptitude, good communication and people skills and are *not* too entrepreneurial. They are not looking for people with relevant industry skills and experience, as they want to inculcate candidates into their formula.

Rolling out the franchise

So now you have a proven formula and a steady stream of candidates you are ready for the big roll out. But you still have some choices to make about the best way to expand.

Starting with strategy-led expansion

Taking the strategy-led approach means you carefully select locations and areas that most closely fit your business model. For example, the Hard Rock Café model is what is known as a capital city business. In other words there is room for one only in each major international city. ProntaPrint, on the other hand, can accommodate an outlet in each major business area within a city, or a single outlet in any major town with a population over around 30,000 people.

Your equation depends on your customer profile. A fast print outlet might find the going tough in a seaside town with 20,000 pensioners and 10,000 holidaymakers.

Opting for opportunity-led expansion

Using the opportunity model you build the business around the key resources you find. So if great premises comes on the market 100 miles from your headquarters, it may make good business sense to go for it. Premises only come on the market every seven to ten years, so waiting around can be an impractical option if you are impatient for growth.

The same goes with franchisees. You may want to launch in Brighton, but if you find a great franchisee in Scarborough then maybe that's the place to go for.

Investing in international expansion

Only about 400 of the US's 3,500 franchisers are doing business abroad, but that 11 per cent are doing good business. Chico's Tacos, based in Temulco, Southern California, launched their first overseas franchise in Cairo, the Egyptian capital, only three years after starting up in the US.

The factors that drive franchisers to look at overseas markets are:

- ✔ Saturation of the existing domestic market
- ✔ Relaxation of trade barriers
- ✔ Heightened awareness of global markets and brands
- ✔ Improved transportation and communication systems, which make doing business internationally easier

In addition franchisers are benefiting from the growing awareness of franchising as a concept in countries where it was virtually unknown only a few years ago.

Perhaps the best way into international markets is to sell a master franchise for a particular country or region – the master franchise owner in that region can then develop and sell units there, following your model. You can advertise your master franchise via any of the magazines or networks listed earlier in the chapter. But don't expect a rush until you can prove the concept in your home market.

Chapter 5

TV and Radio Ads (or Your Own Show!)

● ●

In This Chapter

▶ Designing ads for radio

▶ Creating great video ads for little cash

▶ Using the emotional power of television

● ●

*R*adio and television are well-established, extremely powerful marketing media, while video (especially if shot in digital format) is a hot new item for streaming-video messages on your Web site. Video also offers marketing messages on television screens and computers on your stand at a trade show.

The problem, traditionally, with radio and TV is that the costs associated with producing and broadcasting ads have been quite high, making these media too expensive for smaller marketers. We want to encourage you to be open-minded about radio, video, and TV, because new and easier ways to produce in these media are emerging all the time, along with a growing number of low-cost ways to broadcast your ads. Every year brings more radio and television stations, including cable and satellite TV channels, and digital radio that you can 'listen' to through a digital set, digital TV, or through your PC.

And even if you don't use these commercial media, you can quite possibly find more limited ways to share your ads with prospects. In fact, more and more marketers use CDs or Web sites that communicate in digital video, or with PowerPoint-type slides and radio-style voice-overs. Modern technology is making these media more flexible and affordable for all marketers.

Creating Ads for Radio

Conventional wisdom says you have only three elements to work with when you design for radio: Words, sound effects, and music. In a literal sense that's true, but you can't create a great radio ad unless you remember that you want to use those elements to generate *mental images* for the listener. And that means you can often perform the same basic plot on radio as on TV. Radio isn't really as limited as people think – it's just rarely used to full advantage anymore. Society's love affair with radio has been eclipsed by its love of TV and films.

Favour direct over indirect action goals for radio ads. Sometimes you want to use radio just to create brand awareness *(indirect-action advertising)*. But in general, the most effective radio ads call for direct action. Give out a Web address (if the listener can remember that address easily) or a freefone number in the ad.

Put your brand name into your radio ad early and often, regardless of the story line. If you fail to generate the desired direct action, at least you build awareness and interest for the brand, which supports other points of contact in your marketing campaign. Radio is a great support medium, and not enough marketers use it that way. You may as well fill the vacuum with *your* marketing message!

Here's a simple rule that can help you avoid confusion in your radio ad: Ensure that your script identifies all sound effects. Sound effects are wonderful and evocative, but in truth, many sound very similar. Without context, rain on the roof can sound like bacon sizzling in a pan, a blowtorch cutting through the metal door of a bank vault, or even an alien spaceship starting up. So the script must identify that sound, either through direct reference or through context. You can provide context with the script, the plot, or simply by other sound effects. The sounds of eggs cracking and hitting a hot pan, coffee percolating, and someone yawning all help to identify that sizzle as the breakfast bacon, rather than rain on the roof or that blowtorch.

Buying airtime on radio

We often find ourselves urging marketers to try radio in place of their standard media choices. Why? Because, although local retailers frequently use radio for pull-orientated advertising, many other marketers overlook radio as a viable medium. Those advertisers don't realise how powerful radio can be – and they may not be aware of its incredible reach. In the UK, around 66 per cent of the adult population tune into radio every week and over 80 per cent each month, and from early morning until mid-afternoon there are more people listening to radio than are watching TV (according to RAJAR). We bet your target audience is in there somewhere! (Also consider radio for all your publicity needs. You can find a lot of radio talk shows willing to invite you on as a guest if you pitch your expertise well and have a unique angle to discuss.)

RAJAR (or Radio Joint Audience Research, as it's less commonly called) is the UK's single audience measurement system for commercial radio stations and the BBC. Every quarter RAJAR releases detailed listening figures for all the UK's national and local radio stations, which you can access for free at www.rajar.co.uk. You can also get in touch with the Radio Advertising Bureau (or RAB), which does a good job of promoting radio as an advertising medium and is a great source of advertiser data and ideas for creative radio advertising (www.rab.co.uk).

Radio is one of the biggest media in terms of time spent with it (see Figure 5-1). And while people are spending less time watching TV and DVDs, radio is growing owing to the fact that people can listen to it while doing other things – like cleaning, driving, or more likely being stuck in a traffic jam! Those people can only welcome the distraction of your well-crafted radio ad.

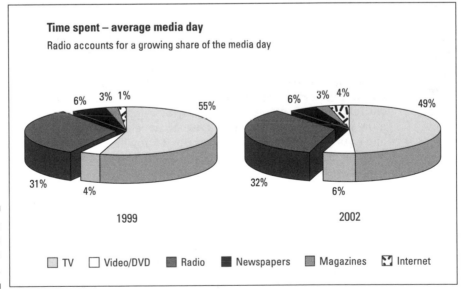

Figure 5-1: Radio's share of the media day.

You can also target radio advertising quite narrowly – both by type of audience and by geographic area. This fact helps make radio a very good buy. The general lack of appreciation for this medium also helps by keeping ad prices artificially low.

Radio airtime is cheaper and more cost-effective than TV airtime, but you need to use the figure we're about to give you with caution – the price of both media can vary widely by region and audience, and, for the biggest advertisers, you can reach a larger total audience by using TV than by using radio. So here goes. Studies have shown that radio airtime is a seventh of the price of TV and that radio offers three-fifths of the advertising awareness effect of TV. If you divide effectiveness by cost, you can see that radio is around four times as cost-effective as TV.

Targeted advertising via radio

We like the fact that radio stations make a real effort to target specific audiences – after all, most advertisers try to do the same thing. You can get good data, both demographic and lifestyle- or attitude-orientated information, on radio audiences. And you can often find radio stations (or specific programmes on those stations) that reach a well-defined audience, rich in those people you want to target, making radio an even better buy.

You can get details of radio station formats and audience characteristics for all UK commercial radio stations from the communications regulator Ofcom, just by looking at the UK Radio Licensees section of its Web site, at www. ofcom.org.uk.

And here's another option for radio advertising that you may not have considered. How about running ads over the internal broadcasting systems used in many shops? This opportunity gives you another great way to target a particular audience going about a particular task – for instance, you could advertise your brand of tiles to DIY shoppers using Tiles FM. *In-store radio* is an entirely different medium from a buying perspective because the shop, or more usually a specialist media owner, develops and controls the programming. As a result, most marketers don't know how to use in-store radio. But an ad agency may be able to help you gain access, and some media-buying firms handle this kind of advertising, too.

So remember: Don't overlook radio! It can give you better reach, better focus on your target market, and greater cost-effectiveness than other media. Like TV, radio can *show* as well as tell – you just have to use the listener's imagination to create visual images. And if you manage to create a really good script, we guarantee you can catch and hold audience attention.

If you're planning to make radio a big part of your marketing plan, then we can recommend a book dedicated to telling you how to do it better – *An Advertiser's Guide to Better Radio Advertising*, by Andrew Ingram and Mark Barber from the RAB, also published by Wiley.

Cheaper Ways to Use the Power of Video

If you're thinking of skipping this section, consider this: Video can cost £1,000 per minute to produce – or even £10,000 if you're making a sophisticated national TV ad. But video can also cost £50 a minute or less.

Do you have access to a high-quality hand-held digital video camera? Well, that camera (when combined with a good microphone) is actually capable of producing effective video for your marketing, especially for use on the Web, where low-resolution video files are usually used, making camera quality less important. Many marketers don't realise that the limiting factor in inexpensive or homemade video is usually the sound quality, not the picture quality. So as long as you plug in a remote microphone and put it near anyone who is speaking, you can probably make usable video yourself.

Here are some tips if you decide to shoot video yourself:

- ✔ Write a simple, clear script, and time it before you bother to shoot any video.

- ✔ Clean up the background. Most amateur efforts to shoot video presentations or ads for marketing are plagued by stuff that shows up in the background. Eliminate rubbish bins, competitors' signs, and anything else unsightly.

- ✔ Use enough light, and try to have multiple light sources. A digital video camera is just a fancy camera, and it needs light to work. Normal indoor lighting is too dim for quality video. Instead, add more lights, including bright floodlights and open windows. And make sure light shines from both sides so that you fill the shadows. (Shadowed areas get darker in the video.)

- ✔ Shoot everything more than once. Editing is easy (well, easier) as a result of the many software programs you can use on your own PC to edit video. But editing is much easier if you have lots of footage to select from. Always repeat each short section several times, then, in editing, choose the version that came out best. That's how they make films stars look good, and it can work well for you, too!

- ✔ You can produce radio ads or sound-only messages for your Web site using the same digital recording and editing capabilities as you use to do home-made digital video. The key is a quiet environment and a good microphone for recording. Or you can go into a production studio's sound booth and let the technicians there worry about the technical aspects.

✔ If you want actors, consider recruiting them locally and even asking people to volunteer. We hate to promote this idea, but if you can avoid paying Equity rates for your actors, you're better off. Paying union rates and residuals is appropriate for major or national campaigns but can be prohibitive for small marketers.

For information on editing and production, check out the many *For Dummies* books that help you better understand what's involved. Or hire a media production firm that can do high-quality work at moderate rates. With plenty of smaller production firms around, try interviewing some in your area and getting samples of their work plus price quotes – you may find that by the time you master the software and come up to speed, you're spending as much doing your own work!

Designing Ads for TV

Television is much like theatre. TV combines visual and verbal channels in real-time action, making it a remarkably rich medium. Yes, you have to make the writing as tight and compelling as good print copy, but the words must also sound good and must flow with the visuals to create drama or comedy.

TV ads must use great drama (whether funny or serious), condensed to a few seconds of memorable action. These few seconds of drama must etch themselves into the memory of anyone who watches your ad. In terms of a great film, you can't reduce it to a formula. A good script with just the right touch of just the right emotion. Great acting. Good camera work and a good set. The suspense of a developing relationship between two interesting characters. You don't need to achieve this level of artistry to make a good TV ad, but you certainly need to achieve a higher-than-average level to stand out. And if you can create truly great TV, your ad pays off in gold.

TV looks simple when you see it, but don't be fooled – it's not simple at all. Hire an experienced production company to help you do the ad, or do what many marketers do and hire a big ad agency (at big ad agency prices) to design and supervise the production of it. This choice costs you, but at least you get quality work. Just remember that *you* ultimately decide whether the script has that star potential or is just another forgettable ad. Don't let the production company shoot until they have something as memorable as a classic film (or at least close).

If you work for a smaller business and are used to shoestring marketing budgets, you may be shaking your head at my advice. You think you can do it yourself. But why waste even a little money on ads that don't work? If you're going to do TV, do it right. Either become expert yourself or hire an expert. Without high-quality production, even the best design doesn't work. Why?

Because people watch so much TV that they know the difference between good and bad ads – and they don't bother to watch anything but the best.

If you're on a shoestring budget and can't afford to hire an expert or don't have the time to become one yourself, consider the following bits of advice:

- **Forgo TV ads and put your video to work in more forgiving venues.** Simple video can look great in other contexts, like your Web site or a stand at a trade show, even if it would look out of place on television. (See the 'Cheaper Ways to Use the Power of Video' section earlier in this chapter.)

- **Consider doing a self-made *spoof ad*.** Make fun of one of the silly TV ad genres, like the one where a man dressed in black scales mountain peaks and jumps over waterfalls to deliver a box of chocolates to a beautiful woman. Because the whole point is to make a campy spoof, you don't want high production value. You can do this strategy on your own pretty easily, but you still need help from someone with experience in setting up shots and handling camera and lights.

- **Find a film student at a nearby college who is eager to help you produce your ad.** To budding film-makers, your video is an opportunity to show they can do professional work. For you, using a student may be an opportunity to get near-professional work at a very low price. But make sure the terms are clear upfront. Both the student and their tutor need to clarify (in writing) that you will own the resulting work and can use it in your marketing.

Book VI

Getting Bigger

Getting emotional

TV differs from other media in the obvious way – by combining action, audio, and video – but these features make TV different in less obvious ways, as well. It is especially easy to evoke emotions in TV and video, just like traditional theatre. When you plan to use TV as your marketing tool, always think about what emotion you want your audience to feel.

Select an emotional state that fits best with your appeal and the creative concept behind your ad. Then use the power of imagery to evoke that emotion. This strategy works whether your appeal is emotional or rational. Always use the emotional power of TV to prepare your audience to receive that appeal. Surprise. Excitement. Empathy. Anxiety. Scepticism. Thirst. Hunger. Protective instincts of the parent. You can create all these emotional states and more in your audience with a few seconds of TV. A good ad generates the right emotion to prime viewers for your appeal. The classic Hamlet cigar ad is a strictly emotional appeal ('Happiness is a cigar called Hamlet' – we bet you can even hear the music as you read that line).

Some marketers measure their TV ads based on warmth. Research firms generally define warmth as the good feelings generated from thinking about love, family, or friendship. Although you may not need to go into the details of how researchers measure warmth, noting *why* people measure warmth can help you. Emotions, especially positive ones, make TV ad messages far more memorable. Many marketers don't realise the strength of this emotional effect because you can't pick the effect up in the standard measures of ad recall. In day-after recall tests, viewers recall emotional-appeal TV ads about as easily as rational-appeal ads. But in-depth studies of the effectiveness of each kind of ad tend to show that the more emotionally charged ads do a better job of etching the message and branding identity in viewers' minds.

So when you think TV advertising, think emotion. Evoking emotion is what TV can do – often better than any other media, because it can showcase the expressiveness of actors and faces – and emotion makes for highly effective advertising.

Look, Mum . . .

Be sure to take full advantage of TV's other great strength: Its ability to show. You can demonstrate a product feature, show a product in use, and do a thousand other things just with your visuals.

Actually, in any ad medium, you want to show as well as tell. (Even in radio, you can create mental images to show the audience what you want them to see, see 'Creating Ads for Radio' earlier in this chapter.) The visual and verbal modes reinforce each other. And some people in your audience think visually, although others favour a verbal message, so you have to cover both bases by using words and images in your advertising. But in TV, you have to adapt this rule: The TV ad should *show* and tell (note the emphasis on showing). Compare this scenario with radio, where you show by telling; or print, where the two modes balance each other out, so the rule becomes simply to show and tell.

Because of this emphasis on showing, TV ad designers rough out their ideas in a visually-orientated script, using quick sketches to indicate how the ad will look. You – or preferably the competent agency or scriptwriter you hire – need to prepare rough storyboards as you think through and discuss various ad concepts. A *storyboard* is an easy way to show the key visual images of film, using pictures in sequence. The sketches run down the centre of a sheet of paper or poster board in most standard storyboard layouts. On the left, you write notes about how to shoot each image, how to use music and sound effects, and whether to superimpose text on the screen. On the right, you include a rough version of the *script* (the words actors in the scenes or in a voice-over say). See Figure 5-2 for an example storyboard.

VIDEO		AUDIO
Lightning and thunder. Rabbit pops out of top hat. Zoom in.		Surprise!
Cut to dark room. Lights come up on birthday party. Zoom in on cake.		Many voices: Surprise!
Cut to dark; sudden flash of lightning illuminates new product. Zoom in.		Even more voices: SURPRISE!
Inset product in slide.	(SLIDE) Company name and logo	ANNCR: Until you try the new *** from ***, you don't know what a surprise is!

Figure 5-2: Roughing out a TV ad on a storyboard.

A question of style

You can use a great variety of styles in TV advertising. A celebrity can endorse the product. Fruit modelled from clay (claymation) can sing and dance about it. Animated animals can chase a user through the jungle in a fanciful exaggeration of a real-life situation. Imagination and videotape know no limits, especially with the recent growing availability of high-quality computerised animation and special effects at a reasonable cost. But some of the common styles work better – on average – than others in tests of ad effectiveness. Table 5-1 shows styles that are more and less effective.

Table 5-1	It Don't Mean a Thing If It Ain't Got That Swing
More Effective Styles	**Less Effective Styles**
Humorous commercials	Candid-camera style testimonials
Celebrity spokespeople	Expert endorsements
Commercials with children	Song/dance and musical themes
Real-life scenarios	Product demonstrations
Brand comparisons	

Most studies show that the humour and celebrity endorsement styles work best. So try to find ways to use these styles to communicate your message. On the other hand, making ads that are the exception to the rule may give you an edge, so don't give up hope on other styles. Just make sure that your ad lands well above average if you don't want the rule of averages to apply to it.

Buying airtime on TV

Which television stations work best for your ad? Should you advertise on a national (*terrestrial*) channel or on a digital channel? Should the ad run in prime time, evening, or late night-time slots? What programmes provide the best audience for your ad?

The UK's main provider of TV audience measurement is BARB (Broadcasters' Audience Research Board), at www.barb.co.uk. BARB is a not-for-profit organisation owned jointly by the BBC, ITV, Channel 4, Five, BSkyB, and the Institute of Practitioners in Advertising (IPA). You can get television audience data minute by minute through BARB, which keeps track of how many people are watching which channel (and TV programme) by installing homes around the country with a little black box that sits on top of the TV set. Although BARB is not for profit, you can't get this data for free. An annual subscription will cost you upwards of £3,850, so it's worth considering whether you really need that depth of data. For instance, if you're trying to selling gardening products to amateur gardeners and know that you're only interested in home-improvement TV programmes, the channels themselves can give you the viewing figures you need.

Some of BARB's biggest customers are research firms such as AC Nielsen (www.nielsenmedia.co.uk), Thomson Intermedia (www.thomson-intermedia.com), TNS (www.tns-global.com), and Mediatel (www.mediatel.co.uk), through which you can get comparative media data, including TV coverage. These companies are also able to overlay the BARB data with more comprehensive demographic and lifestyle data. In turn, these companies' customers include the ad agencies and media-buying agencies, so if you're using an agency to buy your airtime or create your ad, it's worth asking them for media data before getting out your own credit card.

Working out the cost of a TV ad

There are several different factors that affect how much you will pay for a TV advertising campaign.

The first, and most important, bit of jargon you need to know is *TVRs*, which means television ratings. Audience delivery is measured in TVRs, which can be confusing but has the merit of giving you an idea of how many people in a particular target audience will see your ad – and target audiences are important because it means you're not wasting money advertising to people who are unlikely to buy your product. A TVR is defined as the percentage of a particular audience that has seen an advertising break (it's worth remembering that they may have spent the ad break talking to their partner or making the tea, so it's always an approximation). So, 10 adult TVRs = 10 per cent of all adults saw the ad break.

You can actually get a TVR that is higher than 100 per cent, which means that a viewer may see your ad more than once, and is counted separately each time. The actual number of times viewers are exposed to a commercial break is called *impacts*. If you think that repeat viewing is important to your campaign, these can be useful programmes or times of the day to target.

The target audience

You can choose to target any of the 13 target audiences, shown in the following list, that are commonly sold by broadcasters. Heavy TV viewers such as housewives or general audiences are usually cheaper to buy because they are easier to reach than audiences such as upmarket men.

Adults

16- to 34-year-old adults

ABC1 (upmarket) adults

Men

16- to 34-year-old men

ABC1 Men

Women

16- to 34-year-old women

ABC1 women

Housewives

Housewives & children

ABC1 Housewives

Children

Time of the broadcast

The size and type of audience likely to see your ad is governed by the time of day it appears – so that's another factor that will affect how much you pay. Broadcasters call these *dayparts*, and they're timed as follows:

Daytime 6am–5.29pm

Early peak 5.30pm–7.29pm

Late peak 7.30pm–11pm

Night-time 11.01pm–5.59am

The highest price you will usually pay is for the highest audience – in peak time, between 5.30pm and 11pm.

Other factors

You also need to factor in a few other variables to the cost of your ad:

- ✔ **The length of your commercial.** Airtime is sold in multiples of 10 seconds, with the most common ad length at 30 seconds.

- ✔ **What time of year you need to advertise.** If you're in the business of selling Christmas gifts, you will pay considerably more for airtime than if you can advertise in the cheaper months of January, February, March, and August.

- ✔ **Size of the region you advertise in.** Prices also vary by *macro region*, which reflects the size of the local population and relative demand. The highest advertiser demand is for London, which is why it is the most expensive to buy. If you operate in the Border region, Tyne Tees, or

Yorkshire, however, you can expect to pay the lowest prices for TV airtime. Some TV macro regions can even be split into *micro regions*. So if your business is in the East Anglia area, for instance, you can buy just that part of the larger Anglia macro region, giving you tighter targeting and better value for money.

Because of the complexity of some of these calculations, think hard about using a media agency to plan and buy the airtime. You can let a media agency know what you're trying to achieve with your ad, and what type of people you need to target and let their experts do the rest. Many of these agencies buy up chunks of airtime in advance, so you benefit from an agency-wide deal and don't have to negotiate individually with the TV sales houses. Media agencies can also advise you on TV opportunities you may not have previously considered.

Making your own TV (or radio) programme

There are a lot of TV and radio ads out there, and there is a constant danger of your ad becoming just one of the many that people are exposed to, and increasingly, trying to avoid. You don't want your ad to be the one that makes the viewer leave the room to make the tea. The following sections give you a few alternative strategies to consider.

Advertiser-funded programming (AFP)

The experts have come up with a new term, *branded content*, to describe something that is not quite an ad, but which can be used to communicate a commercial message. In TV and radio, that means creating your own show (or at least, segment of a show) – the official term for this is *advertiser-funded programming* or *AFP*. This type of communication is still in its early days, and there are a lot of restrictions in place about what you can or cannot say about your product. But it's worth asking your agency, or the radio stations and channels themselves, about these opportunities, because they allow your message to stand out from the clutter of all the other ads.

Sponsoring a TV or radio programme

If AFP is still waiting in the wings, then sponsorship must be centre stage. Alright, you don't quite get your own TV or radio programme, but if you find a show that is a good fit with your product, then it's almost as good (and with a lot of the risk taken out).

TV and radio sponsorship is growing fast in the UK as advertisers try to avoid the dual issues of ad clutter and digital personal video recorders (PVRs) such as Sky+ and TiVo, which allow viewers to skip through the ad break. You don't need us to tell you that TV and radio sponsorship (together worth nearly £215 million, and representing a quarter of all sponsorship spend) is growing – you'll have seen it for yourself. Ford and Sky's football coverage, Talk Talk and *Big Brother*, Pizza Hut and *The Simpsons* are all good examples of current sponsorship deals because you can see the relevance between the brand and the programme.

You don't need to pay anything like the £10 million for three years that Cadbury pays to sponsor *Coronation Street*. You can find relevant programmes at less popular times of the day, or on digital channels, for a sponsorship price of around £150,000.

Interactive TV advertising

Interactive TV advertising has more in common with traditional spot TV advertising, but we include it here because, if you can get viewers to press the red button, you can take them away from the mainstream TV environment and into your own dedicated space. Interactive TV advertising gives you a lot of opportunities to do things a traditional 30-second spot would not. You can give additional product information, issue a call to action (such as requesting a brochure), and you can capture your prospective customers' data. It is even possible to fulfil a transaction entirely using interactive TV ads. There is an additional cost for constructing the microsite and capturing the data (upward of £100,000), on top of the cost of the airtime for the ad itself. The benefit of interactive TV ads is that you get real, measurable customer transactions from your investment – and that's something traditional TV advertising can't always deliver.

Chapter 6

Becoming a Great Manager

. . . .

. . . .

*I*n business, one of the simplest profit calculations is profit per employee. Until you become a massive company with more than 500 employees, each employee you add increases your profit. Still we need not worry too much about what happens when you have 500 employees on your hands. Well, not in this book, anyway.

But employees are not a trouble-free resource. To maximise the employee-profit ratio, you have to manage your employees so that they produce quality work for you. You have to build them into teams, and lead and manage them to prepare them for the roller-coaster life of change that is the inevitable lot of a small growing business.

In this chapter, we give you the tools you need to become a successful and effective manager.

Building a Team

Teams are a powerful way to get superb results out of even the most average individual employees. With effective team-work, a small firm can raise its efficiency levels to world-class standards. Some small firms have built their entire success around teams.

A group of people working together is not necessarily a team. A successful sports team will have the right number of players for the game, each with a clearly defined role. There will be a coach, to train and improve players' performances, and there will be measurable goals to achieve in the shape of obvious competitors to beat. Contrast that with the situation that usually prevails in a typical small firm. The number of players is the number who turn up on a particular day, and few have specific roles to play. Some are trained and properly equipped and some are not. For the most part the business's objectives are not clearly explained to employees, nor are any performance measuring tools disclosed. It is highly likely that most of the players in the home team do not even know the name or characteristics of the enemy against whom they are competing.

Clearly a successful sports team and an unorganised group of co-workers have little in common, but what needs to be done to weld people at work into a team is also clearly visible.

Successful teams have certain features in common. They all have strong and effective leadership; have clear objectives; appropriate resources; the ability to communicate freely throughout the organisation; the authority to act quickly on decisions; a good balance of team members, with complementary skills and talents; the ability to work collectively; and a size appropriate to the task.

However talented the soloists are in a small business, in the end it's orchestras that make enough noise to wake up a slumbering customer and make them aware of your virtues as a supplier. But teams don't just happen. However neat the CVs and convincing the organisational chart, you can't just turn out a team-in-a-box. The presumption that people are naturally going to work together is usually a mistake. Chaos is more likely than teamwork.

Looking at types of teams

Just like employees themselves, teams come in all shapes and sizes – or at least a few different types, explained in the following list:

- **Management teams:** These are groups of people tasked with managing functions and achieving specific results over the long term. You may have, for example, three teams to cover sales, support, and warehousing. The sales team is expected to meet sales targets and the warehouse team to get goods to customers on time. In practice every firm will have its own definition of business functions.

✔ **Project teams:** Often cross-functional, made up of people from different areas, project teams can be assembled for any period of time to look at a particular project. That project may be improving customer service, or increasing overall efficiency, or cutting costs. The value of having someone from other functions in these teams is to ensure that too parochial a view is not taken.

✔ **Taskforces:** A taskforce is a team put together for a short period of time to look at one narrow issue or specific problem of immediate concern. For example if you propose changing your working hours, you may put together a taskforce to report on the implications for everyone inside and outside the firm. Then a decision based on the best information provided by people most affected by the change can be made.

Small company teams can be made up of anything from two to six people. Anything above six is frankly too unwieldy and will take up more resources than a small firm can afford to devote to one aspect of the business. Even quite small businesses can find they have several teams running at the same time.

Founding principles

Successful teams share common principles, outlined in the following list:

✔ **Balanced team roles:** Every team member must have a valuable team role. Experts in team behaviour such as R Merideth Belbin have identified the key team profiles that are essential if a team is to function well (full details on Belbin can be found at www.belbin.com). Any one person may perform more than one of these roles. But if too many people are competing to perform one of the roles, or one or more of these roles are neglected, the team will be unbalanced. They will perform in much the same way as a car does when a cylinder misfires. The key roles as described by Belbin, who developed the team role evaluation system used my many organisations, are:

• **Chairperson/team leader:** Stable, dominant, extrovert. Concentrates on objectives. Does not originate ideas. Focuses people on what they do best.

• **Plant:** Dominant, high IQ, introvert. A 'scatterer of seeds' who originates ideas. Misses out on detail. Thrustful but easily offended.

• **Resource investigator:** Stable, dominant, extrovert, and sociable. Lots of contacts with the outside world. Strong on networks. Salesperson/diplomat/liaison officer. Not an original thinker.

- **Shaper:** Anxious, dominant, extrovert. Emotional and impulsive. Quick to challenge and to respond to a challenge. Unites ideas, objectives, and possibilities. Competitive. Intolerant of woollyness and vagueness.

- **Company worker:** Stable, controlled. A practical organiser. Can be inflexible but likely to adapt to established systems. Not an innovator.

- **Monitor evaluator:** High IQ, stable, introvert. Goes in for measured analysis not innovation. Unambiguous and often lacking enthusiasm, but solid and dependable.

- **Team worker:** Stable, extrovert, but not really dominant. Much concerned with individuals' needs. Builds on others' ideas. Cools things down when tempers fray.

- **Finisher:** Anxious introvert. Worries over what could go wrong. Permanent sense of urgency. Preoccupied with order. Concerned with 'following through'.

✔ **Shared vision and goal:** It is essential that the team has ownership of its own measurable and clearly defined goals. This means involving the team in business planning. It also means keeping the communication channels open as the business grows. The founding team knew clearly what they were trying to achieve and as they probably shared an office they shared information as they worked. But as the group gets larger and new people join, it becomes necessary to help the informal communication systems work better. Briefing meetings, social events, and bulletin boards are all ways to get teams together and keep them facing the right way.

✔ **A shared language:** To be a member of a business team people have to have a reasonable grasp of the language of business. It's not much use extolling people to improve return on capital employed or reduce debtor days if they have only the haziest notion of what those terms mean, why they matter, or how they can influence the results. So you need to develop rounded business skills across all the core team members through continuous training, development, and coaching.

✔ **Compatible personalities:** Whilst having different team profiles are important, it is equally vital to have a team who can get on with one another. They have to be able to listen to and respect each other's ideas and views. They need to support and trust one another. They need to be able to accept conflict as a healthy reality and work through it to a successful outcome.

✔ **Good leadership:** First-class leadership is perhaps the most important characteristic that distinguishes winning teams from the also-rans. However good the constituent parts, without leadership a team rapidly disintegrates into a rabble bound by little but a pay cheque.

People cannot just be picked and put into teams because of their particular professional or job skills. If the team is to function effectively the balance of behavioural styles has to mesh too.

Coaching and Training

Coaching and *Training* are two ways to help individuals and teams improve their performance. Coaching is carried out by a skilled and experienced person watching an individual or small group performing a task. The coach shows them individually how they can improve their performance. The emphasis is on personalised instruction. Training is usually a more formal process where the trainer has a set agenda for the event based on the knowledge required by the trainees. Everyone being trained goes through much the same process, at the same time.

Small firms are notoriously bad at recognising the need for training of any type. Over 40 per cent of small firms devote only one day or less to staff training each year. Only 13 per cent invest five days or more in training. Amateur football teams spend more time in training than the average small firm, so it is hardly surprising that few teams in that firm ever realise their true potential, or come anywhere near becoming professionals.

And yet all the evidence is that training pays a handsome and quick return.

The choices a small firm has for training are:

- ✔ **On-the-job coaching:** This is where people learn from someone more experienced about how a job should be done. The advantages are that it is free and involves no time away from work. It should also be directly related to an individual's training needs. However it is only as good as the coach and if they are untrained you could end up simply replicating poor working standards.

- ✔ **In-house classroom training:** This is the most traditional and familiar form of training. Some, or all, of your employees gather in a 'classroom' either on your premises or in a local hotel. You hire in a trainer or use one of your own experienced staff. This method provides plenty of opportunity for group interaction and the instructor can motivate the class and pay some attention to individual needs. The disadvantages, particularly if it is help away from your premises, are that you incur large costs that are more to do with hospitality than training and it is time-consuming and difficult for a small firm to release a number of its employees at the same time.

✔ **Public courses:** These are less expensive than running a training programme in a hotel. You can also select different courses for different employees and so tailor the training more precisely to their needs. Most public courses are generic and the other attendees are more likely to come from big business or even the public sector so much of what is covered may be of little direct relevance to your business. Quality can be patchy.

✔ **Interactive distance learning:** This kind of training can be delivered by a combination of traditional training materials, teleconferencing, and the Internet and e-mail discussions. You miss out on the personal contact, but the costs are much lower than traditional training. Most of the learning programmes are aimed at larger firms, so some material may not be so relevant.

✔ **Off-the-shelf training programmes:** These come in packaged kits, which may consist of a training manual, video, and/or a CD-Rom. Once again the cost is lower than for face-to-face training, but you miss out on a professional trainer's input.

✔ **College courses:** Many universities and business schools now offer programmes tailored for the needs of small firms. Professional instructors who understand the needs of small firms deliver these. They are relatively expensive but can often be very effective.

✔ **Government initiatives:** Governments have an interest in encouraging training in small firms. As well as providing information on where their training schemes are being run, governments often provide training grants to help with the costs.

To make sure you get the best out of your training, follow these guidelines:

✔ Introduce a routine that ensures all employees attending training are briefed at least a week beforehand on what to expect and what is expected of them.

✔ Ensure that all employees discuss with you or their manager or supervisor what they got out of the training programme – in particular did it meet both their expectations? This should take place no later than a week after the programme.

✔ You or their manager need to check within a month, and then again at regular intervals, to see whether skills have been improved, and that those skills are being put into practice.

Evaluate the costs and financial benefits of your training and development plans, and use this information to help set next year's training budget.

Appraising Performance

Appraising performance of both teams and individuals is not primarily concerned with blame, reward, or praise. Its purpose is to develop people and help them perform better and be able to achieve career goals. The end result of an appraisal is a personal development plan.

Appraisal lies at the heart of assessing, improving, and developing people's performance for the future of the business. However, to be an effective tool, appraisal needs to be approached seriously and professionally by all involved. The appraisal has to be a discussion between people who work together rather than simply a boss dictating to a subordinate. It should be an open two-way discussion for which both the appraiser and appraisee prepare in advance.

Book VI

Getting Bigger

The ground rules for successful appraisals are:

- ✔ It should be results orientated. The appraisal interview starts with a review against objectives and finishes by setting objectives for the year to come.

  Set intermediate goals and objectives for new staff even if final goals can't be realistically set. For example, challenge new salespeople to acquire product knowledge and visit all the key customers, leaving actual sales achievement objectives until later in the year.

- ✔ The appraisal discussion should be separate from salary review. A discussion about salary is unlikely to encourage people to be open and frank, but an appraisal must be both those things. The salary review and the appraisal must be seen as different events and if possible carried out at different times of the year.

- ✔ The appraisal format is a narrative rather than tick boxes and ratings schedules. It covers a discussion of achievements, areas for improvement, overall performance, training and development, and career expectations.

Allow plenty of time for each appraisal interview (one and a half hours on average). The setting should be free from interruptions and unthreatening.

Carry out appraisals at least once a year, with more regular quarterly reviews – new staff should be reviewed after three months. Some owner-managers question the necessity of a formal annual appraisal when they feel that they are already appraising their team informally on a day-to-day basis. This approach would be rather like trying to assess a business by its daily trading figures rather than its annual profit and loss account. The changes in behaviour and performance you're trying to assess happen over a longer time-span and may not be easy to see on a day-to-day basis. Also your assessments on a day-to-day basis are likely to be influenced by pressures and feelings on the day and may not reflect the true longer-term picture.

Use appraisals to identify training needs and incorporate any deficiencies into a personal or company-wide training plan.

Developing a Leadership Style

Most large organisations today have grown up according to basic management principles. If you started your business career working for a bigger firm, or your present managers worked in such enterprises, you know the scenario. Managers in these organisations plan, organise, and control in a way that produces consistent, if unexciting results. It's a formula that worked remarkably well for much of the 20th century when all a successful company had to do to prosper was more of the same. But management which is all about maintaining order and predictability is ill-equipped to deal with change, which is the order of the day for the 21st century. To cope with it effectively you need to be a leader as well as a competent manager and young businesses are in greater need of leaders than they are of managers, at the outset at least.

Understanding leadership

Leadership and management are not the same thing, although many business people fail to make the distinction.

In a world where product life cycles are shrinking, new technologies have an ever-shorter shelf life, and customers demand faster delivery and higher quality, the leader's job increasingly means defining and inspiring change within a company. By setting a company's direction, communicating this to its workforce, motivating employees and taking a long-range perspective, a leader adapts the firm to whatever volatile environment it does business in. In short, the leader becomes the change master in their own firm.

Delegating

Overwork is a common complaint of those running their own business. There is never enough time to think or plan. But if you don't make time to plan you will never move forward. Delegating some tasks would ease the stress.

Delegation is the art of getting things done your way by other people. Or as one entrepreneur succinctly put it, 'making other people happy to make you rich'.

Many owner-managers are unable to delegate either because they draw comfort from sticking to routine tasks such as sending out invoices, rather than tackling new and unfamiliar ones such as keeping up on developments in the industry, or because they just don't know how to delegate. Either way, neither the business nor those in it can grow until delegation becomes the normal way to operate.

Delegating brings benefits to everyone involved in the process.

Benefits for the boss include:

- ✔ **More time** to both achieve more today and to plan for the future. In this way time can be freed up to tackle high value-added tasks such as recruitment and selection, or motivation.

- ✔ **Back up** for emergencies and day-to-day tasks. By delegating, you have a reserve of skilled people who can keep the business running profitably if you're not there. This can also give customers and financial backers the comfort of knowing that they are not dealing with a one-man-band whose operation would fall apart without him or her.

Benefits for employees include:

- ✔ **The opportunity to develop new skills:** Failing to delegate deprives employees of the opportunity to learn new skills and to grow themselves, and drives good employees, just the ones a growing organisation desperately needs, away for greater challenges. Employees who have assumed the responsibility for new tasks train their staff in the same way. Then the organisation can grow and have management in depth.

- ✔ **Greater involvement:** Research consistently shows that employees rank job satisfaction to be of equal or greater value than pay in their working life. Delegation encourages people to take ownership of their decisions and will increase their enthusiasm and initiative for their work, and so get more satisfaction from their work.

Benefits for the business are:

- ✔ **Efficiency improves** by allowing those closest to the problems and issues being faced to take the decisions in a timely manner.

- ✔ **Flexibility of operations increases** because several people are able to perform key tasks. In this way teams and tasks can be rotated and expanded or contracted to meet changing circumstances. Delegation also results in more people being prepared for promotion.

Delegating successfully

Delegation is a management process not to be confused with 'dumping', in which unpopular, difficult, or tedious tasks are unceremoniously shoved onto the shoulders of the first person who comes to hand. To make it work successfully you should adopt the following five-point plan for delegating.

1. **Decide what and what not to delegate.**

   The general questions for deciding what should be delegated are:

   - Can anyone else do or be trained to do the work to a satisfactory standard?

   - Is all the information necessary to carry out the task available to the person(s) to whom the task could be delegated?

   - Is the task largely operational rather than strategic?

   - Would delegating the task save you a reasonable amount of time?

   - Would some initial teething problems whilst the new person settles into the task cause undue problems? Delegation itself is a form of risk-taking, so if you can't deal with a few mistakes delegation will prove difficult.

   - Can someone other than you properly exercise direct control over the task?

   Any routine jobs, or information gathering, or assignments involving extensive detail or calculations, can usually be readily delegated. Tasks that are less easy to delegate include all confidential work, discipline, staff evaluation, and complex or sensitive issues.

2. **Decide whom to delegate to.**

   The factors to consider here are:

   - Who has the necessary skills?

   - Who could or should be groomed for future promotion?

   - Who is most likely to respond well to the challenge?

   - Who is most likely to be or continue to be a loyal employee?

   - Whose workload will allow them to take on the task(s)?

3. **Communicate your decision.**

   Factors to consider here are:

   - Discuss the task you propose to delegate one to one with the individual concerned.

   - Confirm that they feel up to the task or agree any necessary training, back-up, or extra resources.

- Set out clearly in writing the task broken down into its main components, the measurable outcomes, the timescales, and any other important factors.

- Allow time for the implications to sink in and then discuss with the person concerned how they propose going about the task.

- Let others in the business know of your decision.

4. **Manage and evaluate.**

   From the beginning clearly establish set times to meet with the person delegated to and review their performance. Make the time intervals between these reviews short at first, lengthening the period when their performance is satisfactory. The secret of successful delegation is to follow up.

5. **Reward results.**

   Things that get measured get done and those that are rewarded get done over again. The reward need not be financial. Recognition or praise for a job well done are often more valuable to an ambitious person than money.

Barriers to delegation

Delegation is difficult and most people experience a loss of control or a fear that the people they are delegating to are not really capable of doing the task well. You have to understand and manage these natural fears and concerns if you're to succeed at delegating.

These problems are further compounded by the fact that the manager of a small firm is usually the owner or at least part-owner too. As the business owner that means that the ultimate penalty if the person delegated to fails falls back onto you with potentially serious consequences. After all the responsibility for all borrowings rests with the owner and if poor delegation leads to poor business results then the owner will be the one to suffer the most. Also if the business is a limited company, you will be a director. Directors have particular legal obligations that they are not absolved from simply because they delegated responsibility.

The main reasons owner-managers give for being unable to delegate are:

- ✔ I can do it better and quicker myself. This may well be true when you start up, but will inevitably lead to being overworked and overburdened. Some key tasks will just not get done or will wait until they become a crisis. Employees will never develop the skills to help you if you don't delegate to them, so working long and often unproductive hours will become the norm for you.

✔ I don't want to lose control. This is natural and also a major problem for small firms with unsophisticated information systems. It's something of a chicken-and-egg type problem. Without good control systems you will never be able to delegate and still feel in control. But if you do everything yourself, why would you need systems to show others what is going on. For example until you have an accounting system that shows how much money you are owed, by whom, and for how long, it's impossible to effectively delegate the task of collecting money owed to the firm. Without such a system there is no way to define or investigate the task, nor are there the tools to allow the person who has been delegated, to do a good job.

✔ I'm too busy to delegate. This is a variation of the first barrier. Overworked owner-managers are often disorganised, and have no personal plan. They deal with things as they occur. Without a way to categorise tasks they misallocate their time and so leave insufficient time for key tasks. This creates more problems, taking up more time, and so a vicious spiral begins. Every day starts behind schedule. Until the boss organises their own schedule, building in enough time to plan and delegate properly, the process can't start.

✔ I've tried delegating, but it doesn't save me any time. Delegation probably won't save the boss any time. All it will do is let them spend the time they want to dedicate to work more productively, profitably, and enjoyably.

✔ I've tried delegating, but they made a mess of it and I had to do it myself anyway. Like anything else in management things will fail. Learning to how to delegate effectively takes time and practice. It won't happen overnight, but if it doesn't happen the business will never realise its potential.

Evolving leadership styles for growth

Whilst all businesses require leadership, they don't require the same type or amount of leadership all the time. As with children, businesses do not grow seamlessly from being babies to adulthood. They pass through phases: infancy, adolescence, teenage, and so on. Businesses also move through phases if they are to grow successfully. Each of these phases is punctuated by a crisis, a word which derives from the Chinese and translates loosely as dangerous opportunity.

Researchers have identified several distinctive phases in a firm's growth pattern, and provided an insight into the changes in organisational structure, strategy, and behaviour that are needed to move successfully on to the next phase of growth. This inability to recognise the phases of growth and to manage the transition through them is probably the single most important reason why most owner-managed firms fail to achieve their true potential, let alone their founder's dreams.

Typically a business starts out taking on any customers it can get, operating informally, with little management and few controls. The founder, who usually provides all the ideas, all the drive, makes all the decisions, and signs the cheques, becomes overloaded with administrative detail and operational problems. Unless the founder can change the organisational structure, any further growth will leave the business more vulnerable. The crises of leadership, autonomy, and control loom large.

Over time, the successful owner-manager tackles these crises and finds a clear focus, builds a first-class team, delegates key tasks, appraises performance, institutes control and reporting systems, and ensures that progress towards objectives is monitored and rewarded. The firm itself consistently delivers good results. There is no set time that each of these phases should last. An old economy firm may take anything from three to ten years to reach the third phase of growth.

Each phase of growth calls for a different approach to leading the business. Sometimes strong leadership is required; at others a more consultative approach is appropriate. Some phases call for more systems and procedures, some for more co-operation between staff. Unfortunately, as the business gets bigger most founders try to run their business in much the same way as they did when it was small. They end up with a big small company, rather than the small big company that is required if successful growth is to be achieved. They believe taking on another salesperson, a few hundred square metres' of space, or another bank loan can solve the problems of growth. This approach is rather like suggesting that the transition from infancy to adulthood could be accomplished by nothing more significant than providing larger clothes.

Managing change

Peter Drucker, the management guru, claims that the first task of a leader is to define the company's mission. In a world in which product and service life-cycles are shrinking, new technologies have an ever-shorter shelf life and customers demand ever higher levels of both quality and innovation. Entrepreneurial leadership means inspiring change.

Book VI

Getting Bigger

Being flexible enough to change

In adapting the business to an increasingly volatile and competitive environment, the boss must become the change master in the firm. Small firms are usually better at handling change than big firms. A speedboat can always alter course faster than a supertanker. However small firms often have to adapt to much more change than big established firms. Big firms usually define the standards in an industry and it's the small firms who have to scramble to keep up.

Also the turbulence created by changes in the economy can create a wash that can sink small firms unless they can adapt and change quickly. Those small firms most able to adapt and change, and of course those who are most prepared are most likely to survive and prosper during turbulent times.

But recognising the need for change falls a long way short of being able to implement it successfully. Few people like change and even fewer can adapt to new circumstances quickly and without missing a heartbeat.

By definition a small business seeking growth must be able to manage a fast rate of change. Entrepreneurs must see change as the norm and not as a temporary and unexpected disruption, which will go away when things improve.

Planning for change

Change management is a business process, like any other business process. Following a tried and proven procedure can improve your chances of getting it right more often.

These four steps show how you can break down change management into its elements.

1. **Tell staff why change is necessary (or better still help them to find out for themselves).**

   The benefits of change are not always obvious. So spell them out in much the same way as you would explain the benefits of your product or service to a prospective customer.

   Explaining the background to the changes you want to make will help people see the changes as an opportunity to be competitive rather than a threat to existing work practices.

   Better than just explaining is to encourage staff to look outside the business for themselves and identify potential problems and suggest their own solutions. Not only might they have great ideas for change – perhaps better than yours – they will be more willing to accept them and take responsibility for making the changes succeed.

2. **Make the change manageable.**

   Even when people are dissatisfied with the present position and know exactly what needs to be done to improve things, the change may still not happen. The change may be just too big for anyone to handle. But if you break it down into manageable bits it can be made to happen.

3. **Take a shared approach.**

   Involve people early on. Asking them to join you in managing change only at the implementation stage is too late to get their full co-operation. Give your key participants some say in shaping the change right from the start. This will mean that nobody feels the change is being imposed and more brains will be brought to bear on the problem.

   Individual resistance to change is a normal reaction. By understanding why people are resisting you can help them overcome their doubts and embrace the change. Try to anticipate the impact of the change on the people involved:

   - Get an overview of the forces at work both in favour of and against the change.

   - Make a list of those most affected by the change. Put each person into one of four categories: no commitment; will let it happen if others want it; will help it happen; will make it happen.

     Examine how each person will be affected by the change. Look at career prospects, working hours and conditions, team membership, and so forth.

   - Anticipate retraining. Often a fear of failing is the principal reason people won't try something new.

   Open, face-to-face communication is the backbone of successful change. It gets across the 'why' of change and allows people to face up to problems openly. It also builds confidence and clears up misunderstandings.

   Whilst open communication is vital, it is risky to announce intended changes until you have some committed participants alongside you.

4. **Reinforce individual and team identity.**

   People are more willing to accept change and to move from the known to the unknown if they have confidence in themselves and their boss. Confidence is most likely to exist where people have a high degree of self-esteem. Building up self-esteem involves laying stress on the positive rather than the negative aspects of each person's contribution. Exhortations such as 'you guys have had it too easy for too long' are unlikely to do much for people when you are faced with major competitive pressure.

The importance to the change project of each person, both as an individual and where appropriate as a team member, needs to be emphasised. To survive a positive, confident climate for change needs lots of reinforcement, such as:

- Reward achievement of new goals and achieving them quickly

- Highlight success stories and create as many winners as possible

- Have social events to celebrate milestones

- Pay personal attention to those most affected by the change

Change takes longer than you think. Most major changes make things worse before they make them better. More often than not the immediate impact of change is a decrease in productivity as people struggle to cope with new ways of working, whilst they move up their own learning curve.

The doubters will gloat and even the change champions may waver. But the greatest danger now is pulling the plug on the plan and either adopting a new plan or reverting to the status quo.

To prevent this 'disappointment' it is vital to both set realistic goals for the change period and to anticipate the time lag between change and results.

Measuring Morale

How your employees feel about their jobs, their co-workers, the company, and you and other bosses has a direct effect on how well or poorly they do their jobs. You need to stay on top of morale issues to keep your business running smoothly.

The most reliable way to measure morale at work is to carry out an attitude survey. In a big company, such surveys may be accompanied by one-to-one interviews and focus groups. But in a small firm that is not really an option.

In much the same way as you might survey customers to find out how happy they are with your products and services, survey your employees to find out what they feel about their employment conditions. Attitude surveys provide an objective measure to counterbalance the more descriptive view obtained from discussions and gossip. They also provide a useful way to see if morale is getting better or worse over time.

You may decide to introduce attitude surveys because of a particular event, such as a number of key staff leaving at the same time, or some other obvious problem. Change can upset morale and that can have a knock-on effect on business performance. But once started it makes sense to keep the practice up. At the very least, surveying your employees demonstrates your concern, and at the best it gives you valuable pointers to raising morale, output, and profits.

A word of warning: your attitude survey will reveal two basic facts that every attitude survey reveals. The first is that everyone believes himself or herself to be underpaid. The second is that everyone believes that communication is awful. Both these feelings are fairly normal and you can at least draw comfort from that.

Most people believe they are underpaid both by market standards and in relation to the effort they put in. They also believe that the gap between levels is too great. This belief that they are poorly rewarded exists irrespective of how much people are actually paid, or indeed how hard they work. If you ask them why they don't leave, they will tell you about loyalty to a small firm or perhaps, more flatteringly, loyalty to you.

Nearly all employees also believe their boss knows a secret that directly affects them that he or she is not willing to divulge. It may be about restructuring, moving, merging, or outsourcing. This phenomenon happens at all levels. The shop floor believes supervisors have secrets; supervisors believe managers withhold crucial information on plans that involve them; while those remaining managers know the directors are planning their future in secret. So they become convinced there is a communication problem in the organisation because no one will tell them what is *really* going on.

You have to take all the information from your employees into consideration when sizing up the situation, and not just the results of one attitude survey.

Index

• *D* •

• E •

• *G* •

• *H* •

• P •

• *T* •

Notes

Notes

FOR DUMMIES

Do Anything. Just Add Dummies

PROPERTY

978-0-7645-7027-8

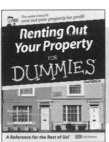

978-0-470-02921-3

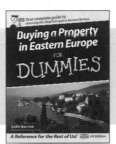

978-0-7645-7047-6

PERSONAL FINANCE

978-0-7645-7023-0

978-0-470-51510-5

978-0-470-05815-2

BUSINESS

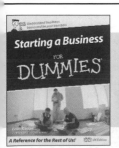

978-0-7645-7018-6

978-0-7645-7056-8

978-0-7645-7026-1

Answering Tough Interview
Questions For Dummies
(978-0-470-01903-0)

Arthritis For Dummies
(978-0-470-02582-6)

Being the Best Man
For Dummies
(978-0-470-02657-1)

British History
For Dummies
(978-0-470-03536-8)

Building Self-Confidence
For Dummies
(978-0-470-01669-5)

Buying a Home on a Budget
For Dummies
(978-0-7645-7035-3)

Children's Health
For Dummies
(978-0-470-02735-6)

Cognitive Behavioural Therapy
For Dummies
(978-0-470-01838-5)

Cricket For Dummies
(978-0-470-03454-5)

CVs For Dummies
(978-0-7645-7017-9)

Detox For Dummies
(978-0-470-01908-5)

Diabetes For Dummies
(978-0-470-05810-7)

Divorce For Dummies
(978-0-7645-7030-8)

DJing For Dummies
(978-0-470-03275-6)

eBay.co.uk For Dummies
(978-0-7645-7059-9)

English Grammar For Dummies
(978-0-470-05752-0)

Gardening For Dummies
(978-0-470-01843-9)

Genealogy Online
For Dummies
(978-0-7645-7061-2)

Green Living For Dummies
(978-0-470-06038-4)

Hypnotherapy For Dummies
(978-0-470-01930-6)

Life Coaching For Dummies
(978-0-470-03135-3)

Neuro-linguistic Programming
For Dummies
(978-0-7645-7028-5)

Nutrition For Dummies
(978-0-7645-7058-2)

Parenting For Dummies
(978-0-470-02714-1)

Pregnancy For Dummies
(978-0-7645-7042-1)

Rugby Union For Dummies
(978-0-470-03537-5)

Self Build and Renovation For
Dummies
(978-0-470-02586-4)

Starting a Business on
eBay.co.uk For Dummies
(978-0-470-02666-3)

Starting and Running an Online
Business For Dummies
(978-0-470-05768-1)

The GL Diet For Dummies
(978-0-470-02753-0)

The Romans For Dummies
(978-0-470-03077-6)

Thyroid For Dummies
(978-0-470-03172-8)

UK Law and Your Rights
For Dummies
(978-0-470-02796-7)

Writing a Novel and Getting
Published For Dummies
(978-0-470-05910-4)

FOR DUMMIES®

Do Anything. Just Add Dummies

HOBBIES

978-0-7645-5232-8

978-0-7645-6847-3

978-0-7645-5476-6

Also available:

Art For Dummies
(978-0-7645-5104-8)

Aromatherapy For Dummies
(978-0-7645-5171-0)

Bridge For Dummies
(978-0-471-92426-5)

Card Games For Dummies
(978-0-7645-9910-1)

Chess For Dummies
(978-0-7645-8404-6)

Improving Your Memory
For Dummies
(978-0-7645-5435-3)

Massage For Dummies
(978-0-7645-5172-7)

Meditation For Dummies
(978-0-471-77774-8)

Photography For Dummies
(978-0-7645-4116-2)

Quilting For Dummies
(978-0-7645-9799-2)

EDUCATION

978-0-7645-7206-7

978-0-7645-5581-7

978-0-7645-5422-3

Also available:

Algebra For Dummies
(978-0-7645-5325-7)

Algebra II For Dummies
(978-0-471-77581-2)

Astronomy For Dummies
(978-0-7645-8465-7)

Buddhism For Dummies
(978-0-7645-5359-2)

Calculus For Dummies
(978-0-7645-2498-1)

Forensics For Dummies
(978-0-7645-5580-0)

Islam For Dummies
(978-0-7645-5503-9)

Philosophy For Dummies
(978-0-7645-5153-6)

Religion For Dummies
(978-0-7645-5264-9)

Trigonometry For Dummies
(978-0-7645-6903-6)

PETS

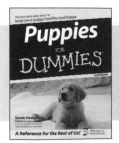

978-0-470-03717-1

978-0-7645-8418-3

978-0-7645-5275-5

Also available:

Aquariums For Dummies
(978-0-7645-5156-7)

Birds For Dummies
(978-0-7645-5139-0)

Dogs For Dummies
(978-0-7645-5274-8)

Ferrets For Dummies
(978-0-7645-5259-5)

Golden Retrievers
For Dummies
(978-0-7645-5267-0)

Horses For Dummies
(978-0-7645-9797-8)

Jack Russell Terriers
For Dummies
(978-0-7645-5268-7)

Labrador Retrievers
For Dummies
(978-0-7645-5281-6)

Puppies Raising & Training
Diary For Dummies
(978-0-7645-0876-9)

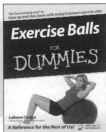
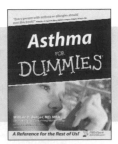

FOR DUMMIES®

Helping you expand your horizons and achieve your potenti[al]

INTERNET

The Internet FOR DUMMIES
A Reference for the Rest of Us!
John R. Levine, Margaret Levine Young, Carol Baroudi
978-0-470-12174-0

Search Engine Optimization FOR DUMMIES
A Reference for the Rest of Us!
Peter Kent
978-0-471-97998-2

Creating Web Pages FOR DUMMIES
A Reference for the Rest of Us!
Bud E. Smith, Arthur Bebak
978-0-470-08030-6

Also available:

Building a Web Site For Dummies, 2nd Edition
(978-0-7645-7144-2)

Blogging For Dummies
(978-0-471-77084-8)

Creating Web Pages All-in-One Desk Reference For Dummies, 3rd Edition
(978-0-470-09629-1)

eBay.co.uk For Dummies
(978-0-7645-7059-9)

Web Analysis For Dummi[es]
(978-0-470-09824-0)

Web Design For Dummie[s], 2nd Edition
(978-0-471-78117-2)

DIGITAL MEDIA

Digital Photography FOR DUMMIES
Julie Adair King
978-0-7645-9802-9

iPod & iTunes FOR DUMMIES
A Reference for the Rest of Us!
Tony Bove, Cheryl Rhodes
978-0-470-04894-8

Digital SLR Cameras & Photography FOR DUMMIES
David D. Busch
978-0-7645-9803-6

Also available:

BlackBerry For Dummies
(978-0-471-75741-2)

Digital Photo Projects For Dummies
(978-0-470-12101-6)

Digital Photography All-In-One Desk Reference For Dummies
(978-0-470-03743-0)

Photoshop CS3 For Dummies
(978-0-470-11193-2)

Podcasting For Dummies
(978-0-471-74898-4)

Zune For Dummies
(978-0-470-12045-3)

COMPUTER BASICS

PCs FOR DUMMIES
A Reference for the Rest of Us!
Dan Gookin
978-0-7645-8958-4

Laptops FOR DUMMIES
A Reference for the Rest of Us!
Dan Gookin
978-0-470-05432-1

Windows Vista FOR DUMMIES
A Reference for the Rest of Us!
Andy Rathbone
978-0-471-75421-3

Also available:

Macs For Dummies, 9th Edition
(978-0-470-04849-8)

Office 2007 All-in-one Desk Reference For Dummies
(978-0-471-78279-7)

PCs All-in-One Desk Reference For Dummies, 3rd Edition
(978-0-471-77082-4)

Upgrading & Fixing PCs Fo[r] Dummies, 7th Edition
(978-0-470-12102-3)

Windows Vista All-in-One Desk Reference For Dumm[ies]
(978-0-471-74941-7)

Windows XP For Dummies, 2nd Edition
(978-0-7645-7326-2)